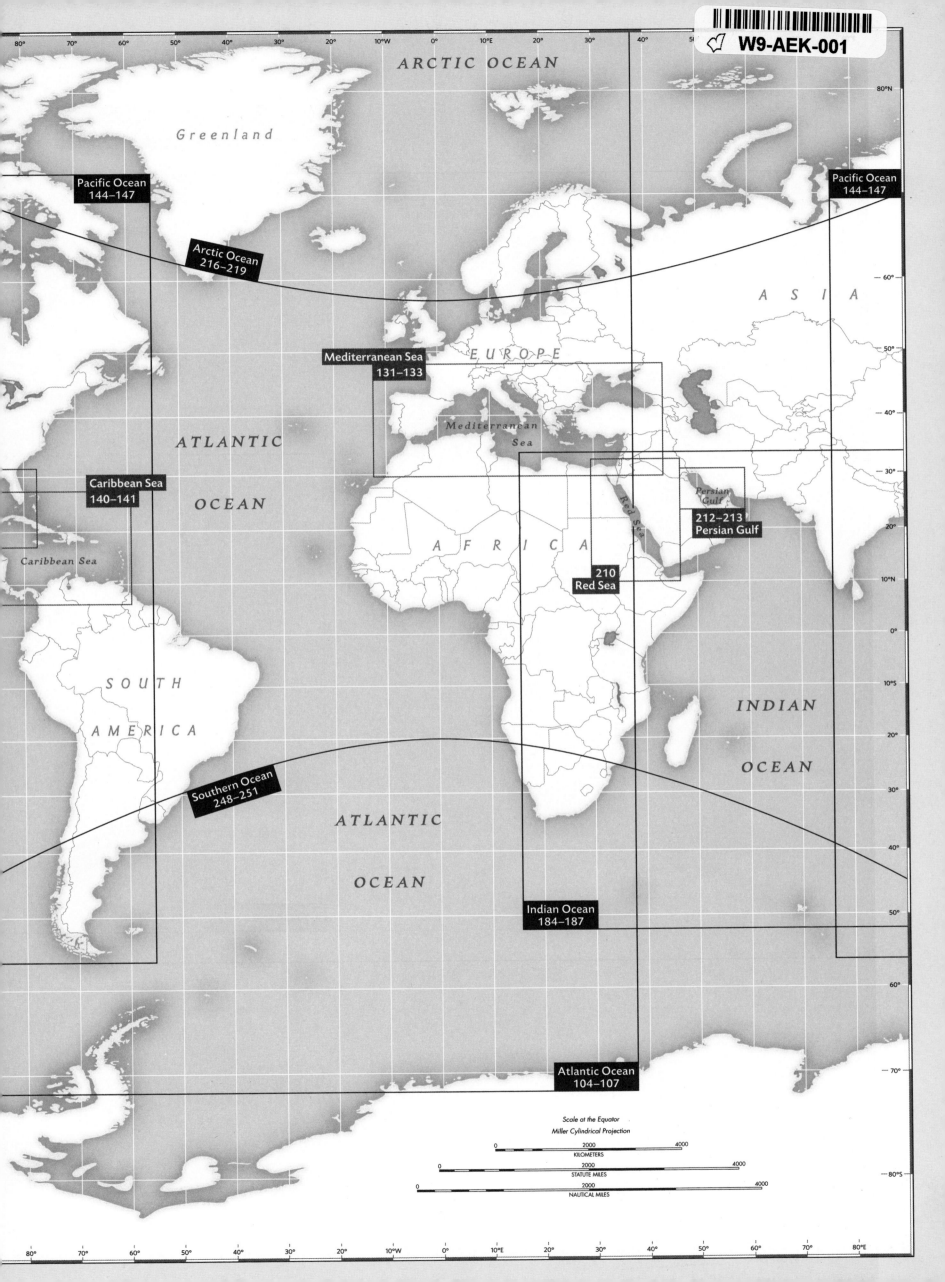

ARCTIC OCEAN

Greenland

ASIA

EUROPE

Pacific Ocean
144–147

Pacific Ocean
144–147

Arctic Ocean
216–219

Mediterranean Sea
131–133

Mediterranean
Sea

Persian
Gulf

212–213
Persian Gulf

ATLANTIC

OCEAN

Caribbean Sea
140–141

Caribbean Sea

AFRICA

Red Sea

210
Red Sea

SOUTH

AMERICA

INDIAN

OCEAN

Southern Ocean
248–251

ATLANTIC

OCEAN

Indian Ocean
184–187

Atlantic Ocean
104–107

Scale at the Equator
Miller Cylindrical Projection

| 0 | 2000 | 4000 |
KILOMETERS

| 0 | 2000 | 4000 |
STATUTE MILES

| 0 | 2000 | 4000 |
NAUTICAL MILES

OCEAN

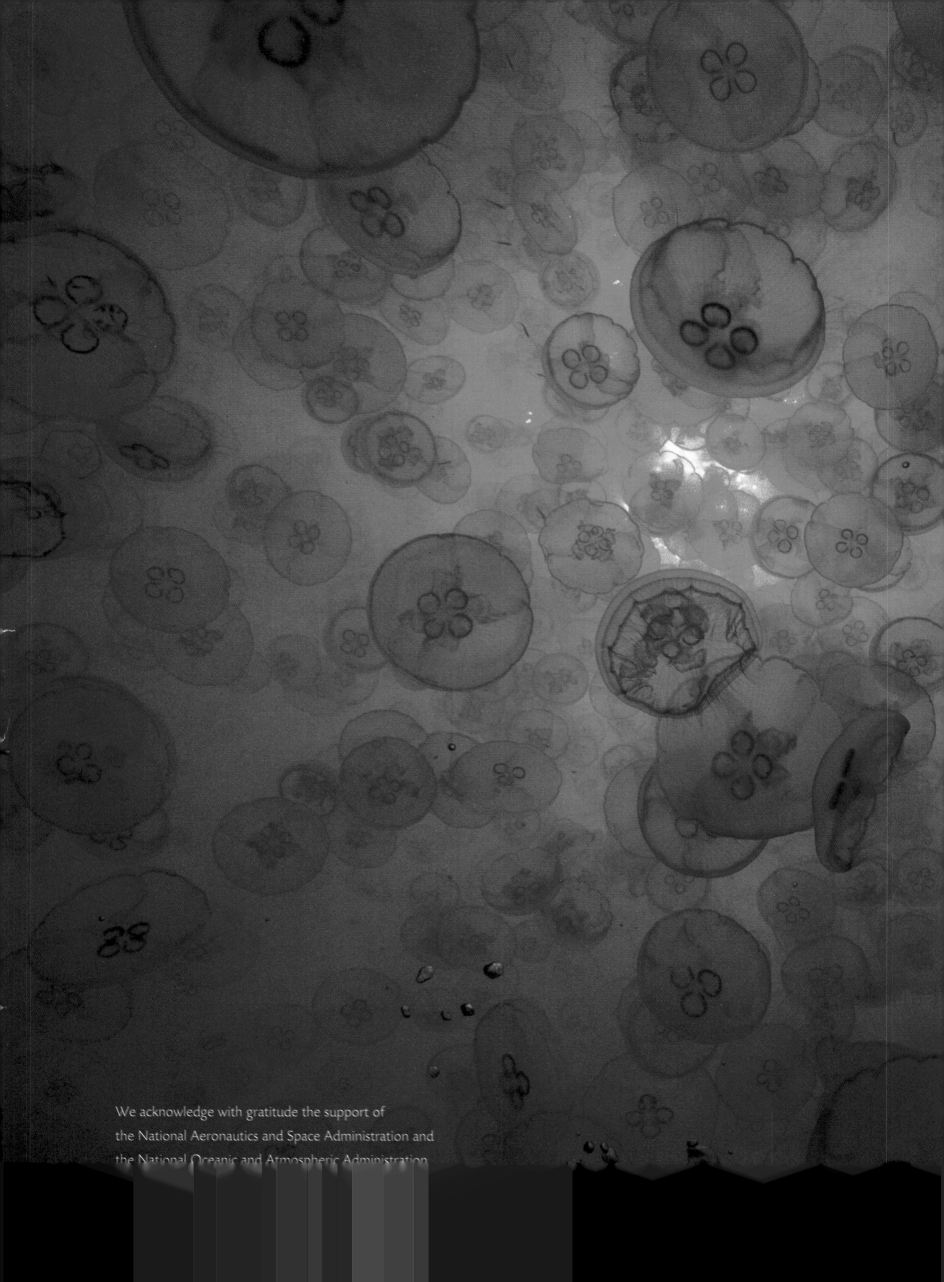

We acknowledge with gratitude the support of
the National Aeronautics and Space Administration and
the National Oceanic and Atmospheric Administration.

OCEAN

An Illustrated Atlas

SYLVIA A. EARLE AND LINDA K. GLOVER

NATIONAL GEOGRAPHIC

Washington, D.C.

With every gulp, this whale shark,
Rhincodon typus, *engulfs thousands of*
the minute animals that live in Australia's
plankton-rich waters.

Pages 2–3: *The blue waters of Ningaloo*
Reef in western Australia pulse with
thousands of diaphanous carnivores:
moon jellies, Aurelia aurita.

CONTENTS

Contributors

PRINCE ALBERT OF MONACO was an early leading light in the campaign to raise awareness of global warming and protect the environment. One of his first acts as sovereign was to sign the Kyoto Protocol. He has been involved in the United Nation's "plant a billion trees" campaign, has visited the Arctic to publicize the melting glaciers, and takes a lead role in demonstrating that a wealthy country can also be an environmentally sound one. • *Oceanographic Museum of Monaco, page 129.*

DALE ANDERSEN is a scientist with the Carl Sagan Center for the Study of Life in the Universe at the SETI Institute. His current research focuses on studies of life in extreme environments on Earth, the evolution of Earth's earliest biosphere, and the origin evolution and distribution of life beyond Earth. • *Ice and Life, page 237.*

DIEGO ARCAS is a research scientist at the Joint Institute for the Study of the Atmosphere and Ocean, a collaboration between the National Oceanographic and Atmospheric Administration and the University of Washington. His research specializes in tsunamis and computational fluid dynamics. • *Tsunamis, pages 202-203.*

EDWARD VANDEN BERGHE is a data and information management specialist in marine ecology and biological oceanography. He is currently leading the Ocean Biogeographic Information System, hosted by the Rutgers University Institute of Marine and Coastal Sciences. • *Census of Marine Life 2010, pages 62-63.*

ANTONIO J. BUSALACCHI, JR., is director of the Earth System Science Interdisciplinary Center at the University of Maryland, College Park, and chairman of the joint scientific committee for the World Climate Research Program. His research interests include tropical ocean circulation and its role in the coupled climate system. • *El Niño, pages 172-173.*

EDWARD CASSANO is a 23-year veteran of marine resource management, marine education, and at-sea research expeditions within the maritime industry. For 14 years he was a commissioned officer with the National Oceanic and Atmospheric Administration, participating in many multi-disciplinary scientific missions. • *Northwest Passage, pages 242-243.*

RITA COLWELL is a professor at both the University of Maryland at College Park and The Johns Hopkins University Bloomberg School of Public Health. She is also the chair of Canon U.S. Life Sciences, Inc. Her professional interests are focused on global infectious diseases, water, and health. • *Climate, Ocean, and Cholera, page 307.*

JEAN-MICHEL COUSTEAU, the son of Jacques Cousteau, continues his father's legendary work with the TV series *Jean-Michel Cousteau: Ocean Adventures* on PBS and through his Ocean Futures Society, which educates people about the ocean's vital importance to the survival of life on our planet. • *The Recovery of Coral Reefs, page 168.*

SCOTT DONEY is a senior scientist at the Woods Hole Oceanographic Institution. He is the chair of the Ocean Carbon and Biogeochemistry group and has published more than 100 research papers on oceanography, climate, and biogeochemistry. • *Ocean Acidification, page 39.*

DANIEL J. FORNARI is a senior scientist in the geology and geophysics department at the Woods Hole Oceanographic Institution and the director of its Deep Ocean Exploration Institute. He is internationally recognized for his research on volcanic and hydrothermal processes. • *The Birth of an Ocean: The Red Sea, pages 208-209.*

J. FREDERICK GRASSLE is a professor of marine and coastal sciences and the director of the Institute of Marine and Coastal Sciences at Rutgers University. He founded the Institute in 1989 to consolidate university programs in marine and coastal sciences and develop an internationally known program of education and research in marine and coastal sciences. • *Census of Marine Life 2010, pages 62-63.*

BRIAN HUBER is a curator of foraminifera at the Smithsonian National Museum of Natural History. He has published more than 80 peer-reviewed research papers, co-edited five books, and done geology fieldwork worldwide on land and from the Integrated Ocean Drilling Program's deep-sea vessel JOIDES Resolution. • *The Supergreenhouse Ocean, page 97.*

ANTHONY KNAP is the president and senior scientist at the Bermuda Institute of Ocean Sciences. He has been the principal investigator of the Bermuda time-series programs at the institute since 1980. • *The Bermuda Atlantic Time-Series, page 121.*

DAN LAFFOLEY is marine vice chair of International Union for Conservation of Nature's World Commission on Protected Areas. He is also the principal specialist for the marine environment for Natural England, the U.K. governmental body that advises on the conservation of the environment. • *Marine Protected Areas, pages 320-321.*

LARRY P. MADIN is executive vice president and director of research at the Woods Hole Oceanographic Institution. His research interests include the biology of oceanic and deep-sea zooplankton, particularly medusae, siphonophores, ctenophores, and pelagic tunicates. • *Water Column Life, page 65.*

GUILLAUME CONSTANTIN DE MAGNY is a member of the faculty at the University of Maryland's Institute for Advanced Computer Studies, where his research focuses on the ecology of cholera in Asia in relation to environmental and climate variability. • *Climate, Ocean, and Cholera, page 307.*

LYNN MARGULIS is a distinguished professor in the geosciences department at the University of Massachusetts, Amherst. A recipient of the Presidential Medal of Science in 1999, she has published numerous scholarly articles on evolution (by symbiogenesis) and the Gaia hypothesis (of J. E. Lovelock). • *Marine Microbes Move Mountains, page 58.*

REAR ADMIRAL TIMOTHY McGEE, a graduate of the U.S. Naval Academy, served as Commander of the Naval Meteorology and Oceanography Command and was Hydrographer of the U.S. Navy from 2004 to 2007. He retired from the Navy in 2008. • *Mapping the Ocean, page 289.*

CHRIS McKAY is a planetary scientist with the space science division at NASA Ames. His current research focuses on the evolution of the solar system and the origin of life. He was a co-investigator on the Titan Huygen's probe in 2005, the Mars Phoenix lander mission in 2008, and the Mars Science Lander mission for 2009. • *Space Studies of Antarctica, pages 268-269.*

R. STEVEN NEREM is a professor in the department of aerospace engineering sciences at the University of Colorado. He is currently associate director of the Colorado Center for Astrodynamics Research and a fellow at the Cooperative Institute for Research in Environmental Sciences, both at the University of Colorado. • *Global Sea-Level Rise, page 318.*

TONY RIBBINK is the CEO of Sustainable Seas Trust, the first multinational marine trust in Africa. He has led coelacanth studies since 2001 for six countries with a view to conservation of coelacanths and their ecosystems. • *Windows to the Past, page 206.*

BRUCE ROBISON is a senior scientist at the Monterey Bay Aquarium Research Institute. He is a deep-sea ecologist and is also a certified submersible pilot. He has used several different HOVs in his work, and he developed the first mid-water research program utilizing deep-diving ROVs. • *Using Submersibles to Find Life, page 287.*

PETER RONA is a professor of marine geology and geophysics at Rutgers University. He is a pioneer in exploration of the deep ocean, credited with many discoveries including hot springs and associated life in the Atlantic Ocean. • *Life at Deep-Sea Hot Springs, page 159.*

WILLIAM B. F. RYAN is a Doherty Senior Scholar at the Lamont-Doherty Earth Observatory of Columbia University. In 1970, he led the first deep-sea drilling campaign in the Mediterranean that discovered the isolation and drying out of this seaway five and a half million years ago. • *The Disappearing Tethys, page 98.*

DORION SAGAN is the co-director of Sciencewriters Books, the author of *Notes from the Holocene: A Brief History of the Future* and the co-author of *Into the Cool, Dazzle Gradually, Microcosmos,* and seventeen other books. • *Marine Microbes Move Mountains, page 58.*

TIMOTHY M. SHANK is an associate scientist in the biology department at the Woods Hole Oceanographic Institution. He is one of the few researchers whose work combines multiple molecular genetic approaches and ecological field studies to understand the conditions that allow various species to migrate, evolve, and thrive in deep-sea habitats. • *The Birth of an Ocean: The Red Sea, pages 208-209.*

KATHRYN SULLIVAN, the first American woman to walk in space, is a veteran of three space shuttle missions, and a former Navy Reserve oceanographer. She is director of the Battelle Center for Math and Science Education Policy at Ohio State University's John Glenn School of Public Affairs and a member of the National Science Board. • *Observing the Ocean from Space, page 291.*

MARIE THARP was a cartographer and researcher at the Lamont-Doherty Earth Observatory at Columbia University. She and her colleague Bruce C. Heezen were the first to map details of the ocean floor on a global scale. Their map, first published in 1977, provided evidence for the then-controversial theory of continental drift. • *Ocean Cartography, pages 32-33.*

JOHN W. TUNNELL, JR., is a broadly trained marine biologist who specializes in coral reef and coastal ecology at Texas A&M University, Corpus Christi. He has studied the Gulf of Mexico for more than 40 years, publishing numerous papers and reports as well as three books on Gulf of Mexico topics. • *Gulf of Mexico, pages 136-137.*

PETER TYACK is a senior scientist in biology at the Woods Hole Oceanographic Institution. He specializes in acoustic communication and social behavior in marine mammals. He has developed new methods to observe the behavior of marine mammals and has applied them in his research on communication and echolocation. • *Effects of Sound in the Ocean, page 311.*

PETER VOGT is affiliated with the Marine Science Institute at the University of California, Santa Barbara. He was a marine geophysicist for the U.S. Navy from 1968 to 2004 and has published more than 150 academic articles on topics as varied as plate tectonics, methane hydrates, and mud volcanoes. • *Geology of the Arctic Ocean, page 228.*

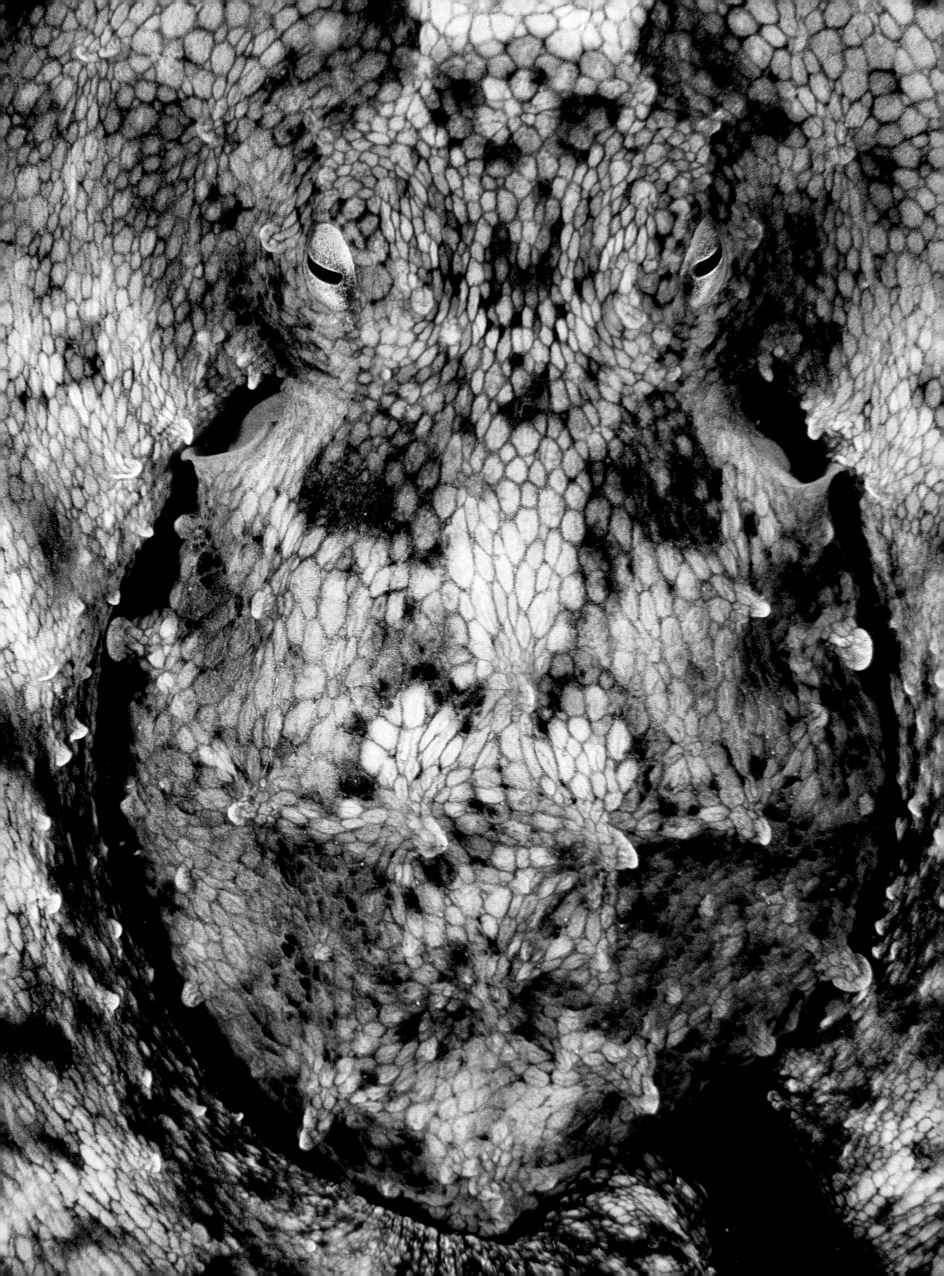

Preface

"Global warming may seem gradual in the context of a single lifetime, but in the context of the Earth's history, it is actually happening with lightning speed."

—Al Gore, *An Inconvenient Truth*

Perhaps the greatest challenge in gathering all the elements of this atlas has been to keep up with the stream of new discoveries and the swift changes affecting the ocean, which, in turn, influence matters of great concern to humankind. Change in the ocean is natural, continuous, inevitable, expected; but the electrifying speed of change in recent years is not. This is especially true of the far-reaching impact of global warming, a gradual phenomenon that has been underway for thousands of years, but has recently been given a significant boost by human actions. Since the ocean drives climate and weather, regulates temperature, governs planetary chemistry, and is otherwise the backbone of Earth's life support system, any serious disruption of ocean systems should command our rapt attention. Curiously, while climate change has inspired global attention recently, the role of the ocean and the serious decline of ocean health has been notably neglected. One reason may be the widely held but erroneous view that the ocean is so big, so vast, that nothing people do could possibly alter its nature.

Underlying the crafting of this book is a sense of urgency to convey what is known about the ocean and to unravel its major mysteries. Framing each chapter are extraordinary new maps of the five major ocean basins, the first major revision undertaken by the National Geographic Society in three decades. They are based on the most scientifically accurate unclassified information currently available, developed by veteran cartographer Carl Mehler and exquisitely rendered by master cartographic artist Tibor Tóth. Various scientific experts were enlisted to share their insights on topics of current concern and help convey awareness of the profoundly important issues facing the ocean and people everywhere. Throughout, the theme reflects an understanding that the ocean is undergoing unprecedented change, including the following:

- In 2003, a report in *Nature* documented a 90-percent decline in the populations of many of the fish commonly offered in markets and on restaurant menus, owing to expanding global markets, decades of overfishing, and the loss of habitat by destructive trawling and long-lining gear. Three years later, Stanford biologist Stephen Palumbi predicted a total collapse of all world fisheries by 2048.

- In 2004, a report on the status of coral reefs showed that 20 percent had been destroyed in half a century, and 60 percent were degraded and at risk of loss from human actions. In the Caribbean, decline as great as 80 percent had occurred in many areas, and in Jamaica, 95 percent of reefs were already gone. Coastal "dead zones" had essentially doubled in a decade.

- In 2005, the hottest year since 1860, an unprecedented series of 27 hurricanes formed in the Caribbean Sea with consequences measured in thousands of lives, billions of dollars, and for many the end of their complacency. The same year, a report in *Nature* warned of the corrosive effects of ocean acidification on various marine organisms.

- In 2006, Al Gore challenged the world to consider global warming a planetary emergency, not just for the obvious consequences of sea-level rise but also for the profound changes in agriculture and other fundamental underpinnings of human society.

- In 2007, the United Nations' Intergovernmental Panel on Climate Change (IPCC) issued its sobering report on global trends. As if underscoring the findings, the amount of summer ice cover in the Arctic precipitously plummeted.

In this atlas, these troubling issues are taken into account, but so are the many positive actions that are aimed at stabilizing our relationship with the ocean and the natural systems that underlie the planetary processes that keep us alive. A review of the geological forces that have shaped the ocean basins and the history of life in the sea provides perspective on the past—and insight into the pivotal role of humankind in shaping the future. Most of all, the ocean is celebrated here as the blue heart of the planet, the aquatic realm that makes possible the existence of life on Earth.

—Sylvia Earle, July 2008

Editor's Note

Throughout this atlas, there are three different kinds of margin elements: cross-references for help in finding other places in the book where particular topics are discussed or illustrated; useful web links (listed on pages 330-331); and fact boxes, developed by author Linda Glover, that summarize and explain key aspects of ocean lore.

Newly commissioned maps of the seafloor, followed in each case by same-scale geopolitical and sea-surface-temperature maps, appear in each of the five regional ocean chapters. Several depth maps of principal seas were also commissioned for these chapters. The place names on these maps have all been indexed; see pages 338-349. There are also 145 thematic maps or diagrams of other key aspects of the ocean spread throughout the book. A complete list of maps can be found on page 335.

Opposite: *Like humans, this octopus is versatile, successful, and intelligent, but has no power and, therefore, no choice and no voice in shaping the overall future of the planet. We do.*

The View From...

NASA

NASA OCEANOGRAPHY
HTTP://NASASCIENCE.NASA.GOV

FOR CENTURIES, EXPLORERS HAVE BEEN DRAWN to the mysteries of the ocean, but until recently, most knowledge of its nature has come from data gathered by ships and a few observations made by those who descend directly into the deep. In recent decades, however, revolutionary discoveries have been made by scientists using satellites, aircraft, remotely operated vehicles, instrumented buoys, and other new technologies. Powerful new computers use mathematical models to simulate the ocean environment and forecast ocean conditions. The science of oceanography depends on such quantitative descriptions and analyses to understand how the ocean works. But we cannot model what we have yet to discover—and vast areas of the ocean remain unexplored and uncharacterized.

In *Ocean: An Illustrated Atlas*, Sylvia Earle, Linda Glover, and their colleagues expose you to the ocean they know—and seek to know—both as oceanographers and as individuals who sense the remarkable time of discovery and unprecedented change. In their words you will discover the beauty, wonder, and importance of the seas. And, through carefully plotted maps and diagrams, you will see the workings of the ocean—its physics, chemistry, biology, and geology. NASA has contributed images of the ocean from the unique vantage point of space, giving the atlas a truly global view. Maps based on satellite sensor data illustrate how surface temperature and winds, sea level, and ocean color all help determine the character and circulation of the sea. Data from satellites vastly expand the perspective and context that oceanographers obtain from the detailed but sparse in situ measurements made from ships. As remote-sensing satellites orbit Earth, they measure ocean properties and provide data to initialize and verify model simulations of ocean circulation and biological productivity. The global perspective now provided by satellites is as essential to the development of 21st-century oceanography as ships were to the founding of modern oceanography in the 20th century.

Particularly relevant to understanding how the ocean functions are the maps that begin each chapter on the Atlantic, Pacific, Indian, Arctic, and Southern Oceans showing winter surface temperatures. Every "parcel" of ocean water gains its temperature and salinity properties at the surface, where water meets air. Cold deep waters gain their chilly character when exposed to polar latitudes in winter, especially in the North Atlantic and in the region around Antarctica. If air-sea interaction makes surface water colder and saltier, it will sink; if warmer and fresher, it will remain at the surface. Once submerged, a cold watermass tends to keep its temperature and salinity characteristics and the relationship between the two stays strong. Observing ocean surface temperature (and salinity) helps us understand how the deep ocean gains its characteristic vertical temperature and salinity structure. We "expose" to your view the deep ocean by showing you the winter sea-surface temperature patterns. This atlas clearly illustrates this fundamental but "deep" lesson in oceanography.

Every astronaut is touched by the view of the fragile blue Earth hanging in the vast emptiness of space. Many return to Earth with more profound feelings about global environmental issues. Appreciate the unique vantage point of space as you open each ocean basin chapter in this atlas. This global view, of an ocean planet, where humankind does have measurable impact, has become critical for ocean science and conservation in this century.

Glancing through this book, with the magnitude of new discoveries reported in it, one might be led to believe that the ocean has yielded its major secrets, but an underlying message resounds: Most of the subsurface ocean remains a mystery. We have learned enough to know that the sea is vital to all of us and that we must continue to explore its nature. This book is a good place to begin.

—Eric Lindstrom, Earth Science Division, NASA

NOAA

NOAA OCEAN PORTAL
HTTP://WWW.NOAA.GOV/OCEAN.HTML

EVERYTHING WE DO—ALL THAT WE NEED, our daily safety, and our very quality of life—depends on the ocean. We rely on the seas to provide life support: food, air, and water. We seek the ocean for entertainment and pleasure. We study the life systems of the ocean to yield lifesaving medicines and materials. We scour the ocean for the materials needed to build cities. We analyze the ocean's physical state to improve our prediction of weather. We ride the ocean to move the precious commodities of life from one point on our globe to another. We exploit the complex structure of the ocean to ensure the security of our nations. And, increasingly, we comprehend that a fuller understanding of the ocean is the seminal element in assuring our continued ability to rely upon it sustainably as we have for centuries.

The fascinating aspect of our dependence on the ocean is that no part of it—no specific geographic area nor any particular life system—can be treated as a disconnected and unique component. The ocean is a complex system of systems. The more we learn about the ocean the more we appreciate its interconnectedness.

Consider three examples of this. First, the bloom of algae at the surface of the coastal ocean—a fundamental *biological* phenomenon—cannot be fully described without invoking the *physical* process of wind-driven circulation that causes the upwelling of waters with unique *chemical* makeup over a continental shelf formed by *geological* processes. Second, the most complete prediction of where and when cyclones will form over the tropical ocean requires what mathematicians call a "fully coupled ocean-atmosphere model"—a set of equations that describes how the sea and the air above it exchange heat, mass, and momentum. And perhaps the best example is the extraordinarily complex ecosystem evident around deep-sea hydrothermal vents, where we have an amazing balance of heavy metals, extreme temperatures, swirling currents, and primordial geological processes, yielding a matrix of life forms and physical structures that astound even the most jaded observer.

The Earth's ocean serves as the central operating system for our whole planet. As we rely increasingly on the ocean, it is critical that we learn as much as we can about its component elements and the nature of their interactions. We do so by observing, understanding, and applying knowledge. We build wonderful systems to take measurements and monitor the diverse parameters that characterize the ocean's state and variability. We do this from under, within, and above the seas. We use sensors on human-occupied vehicles, remotely operated vehicles, autonomous vehicles, buoys, floats, drifters, gliders, ships, aircraft, satellites, and even land-based observing systems.

Then we feed all the data from these observing systems into the most powerful computers and run the complex set of equations and algorithms that define our models in order to predict, forecast, hindcast, nowcast, and project the behavior of the seas. In so doing, we invariably learn there are yet other observations to be made, and more processes at work that must be described by new equations.

The challenges are daunting and at the same time exquisite, yet the satisfaction comes from the successes we have in characterizing ever more accurately the behavior of the ocean's systems. At the National Oceanic and Atmospheric Administration (NOAA), for example, we predict how and when El Niño will form; we forecast when increased sea temperature may threaten corals; we protect coastal populations with accurate predictions of tsunami arrival times and hurricane-induced flooding; and over longer time scales we project how climate change will affect ocean acidity, temperatures, general circulation, and sea level.

This atlas is a unique portrayal of the nature of the world's ocean and its systems. Our understanding of the ocean is dynamic, and is a consequence of a diverse breadth of studies, involving an impressive range of expertise, skills, tools, and perspectives. Each reader's experience will likely be different and personal . . . as is each individual's reaction to the seas themselves.

—Richard W. Spinrad, Office of Oceanic and Atmospheric Research, NOAA

The rounded tentacles and pursed mouth
of Discosoma, a corallimorph anemone,
are poised to snare passing prey 20
meters under the clear waters around
the Solomon Islands.

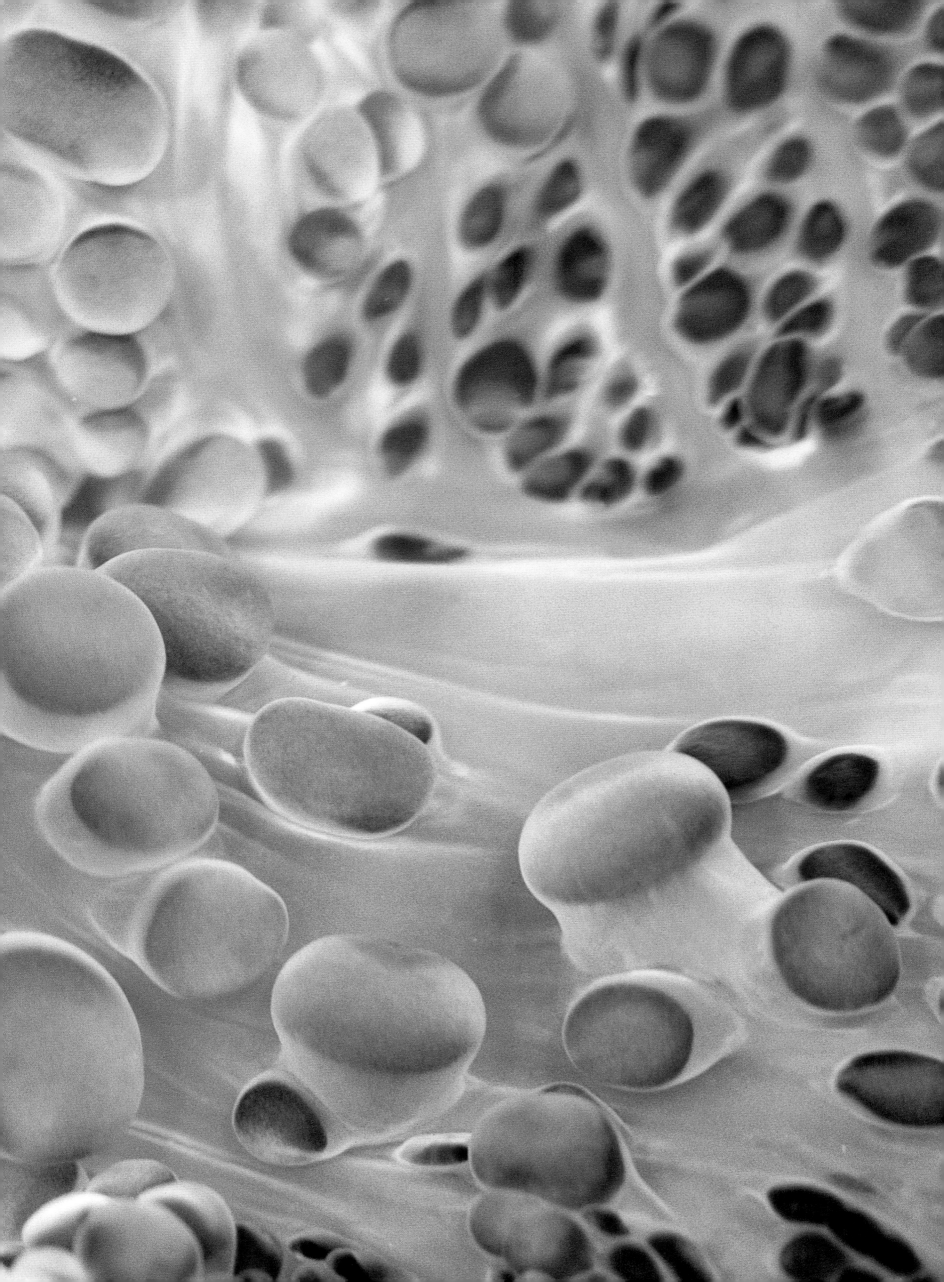

Three for dinner in the Bahamas: Atlantic spotted dolphins, Stenella frontalis, gather above a school of snapper, one of many reef fish species on the dolphins' menu.

Described by Apollo astronauts
as a "beautiful blue marble," Earth
appears here as a composite true-color
image, the most detailed ever produced,
based on months of observations.
Largely derived from NASA's Moderate
Resolution Spectroradiometer, or MODIS,
aboard the Terra satellite, flying more
than 700 kilometers high, scientists and
visualizers stitched together data into
a seamless mosaic of land, oceans,
sea ice, and clouds.

Chapter 1

OCEAN BASICS

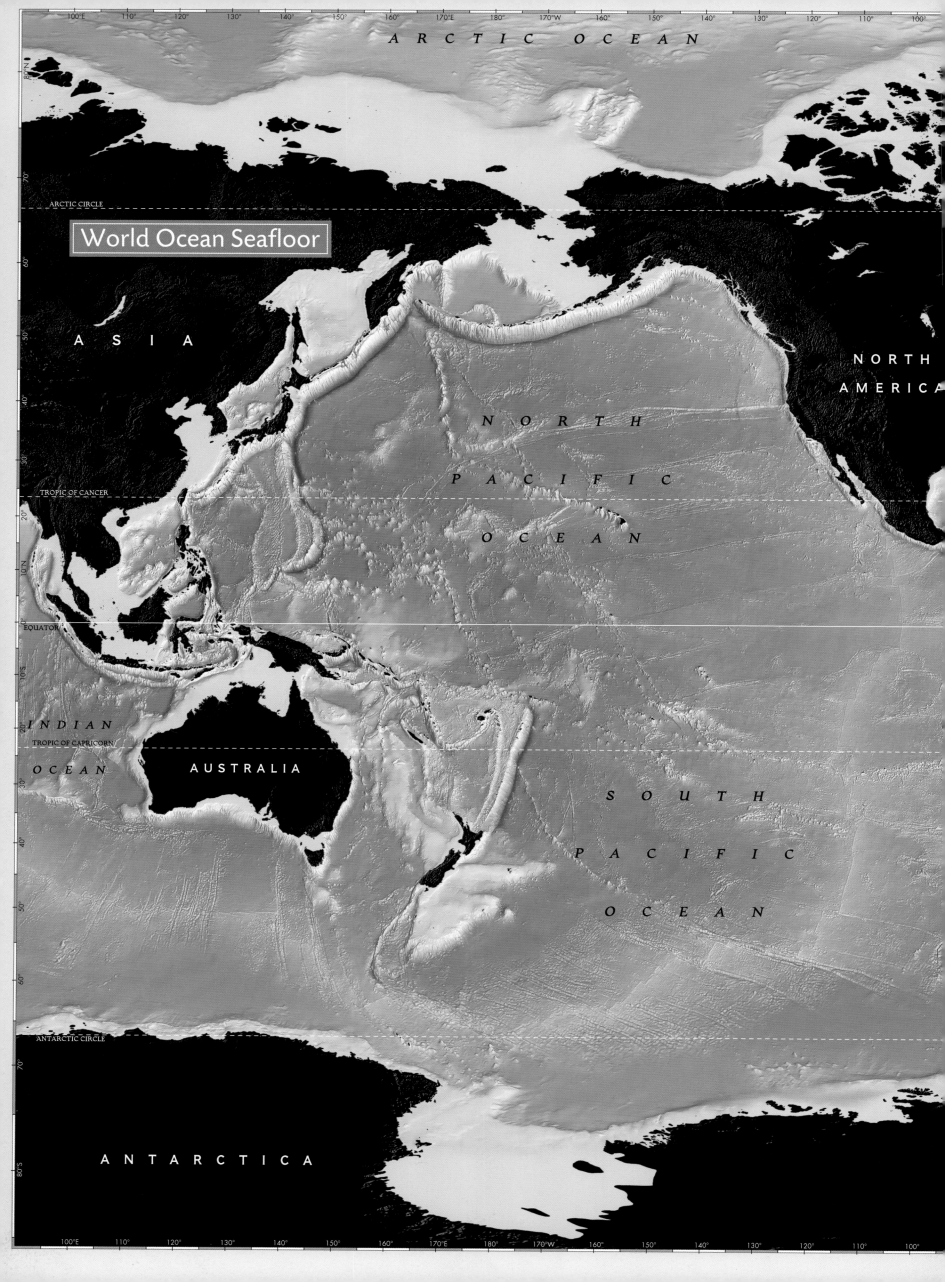

World Ocean Seafloor

ARCTIC OCEAN

ARCTIC CIRCLE

ASIA

NORTH
AMERICA

TROPIC OF CANCER

N O R T H

P A C I F I C

O C E A N

EQUATOR

INDIAN

TROPIC OF CAPRICORN

OCEAN

AUSTRALIA

S O U T H

P A C I F I C

O C E A N

ANTARCTIC CIRCLE

A N T A R C T I C A

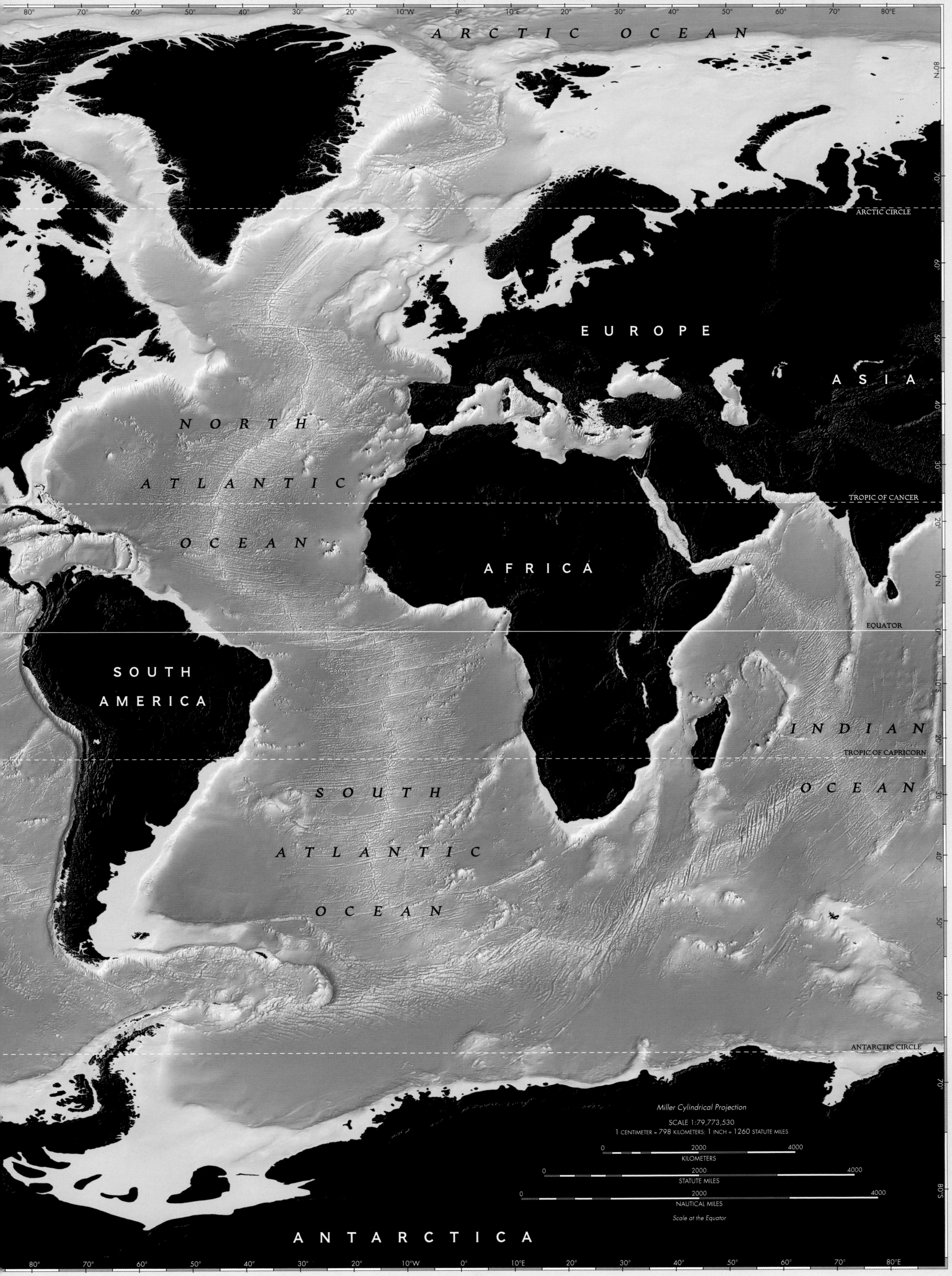

ARCTIC OCEAN

80°N

70°N

ARCTIC CIRCLE

60°

EUROPE

ASIA

50°

NORTH

40°

ATLANTIC

TROPIC OF CANCER

20°

OCEAN

AFRICA

10°N

EQUATOR

SOUTH
AMERICA

10°S

INDIAN

20°

TROPIC OF CAPRICORN

SOUTH

30°

ATLANTIC

OCEAN

40°

OCEAN

50°

60°

ANTARCTIC CIRCLE

70°

Miller Cylindrical Projection

SCALE 1:79,773,530
1 CENTIMETER = 798 KILOMETERS; 1 INCH = 1260 STATUTE MILES

0   2000   4000
KILOMETERS

0   2000   4000
STATUTE MILES

0   2000   4000
NAUTICAL MILES

Scale at the Equator

80°S

ANTARCTICA

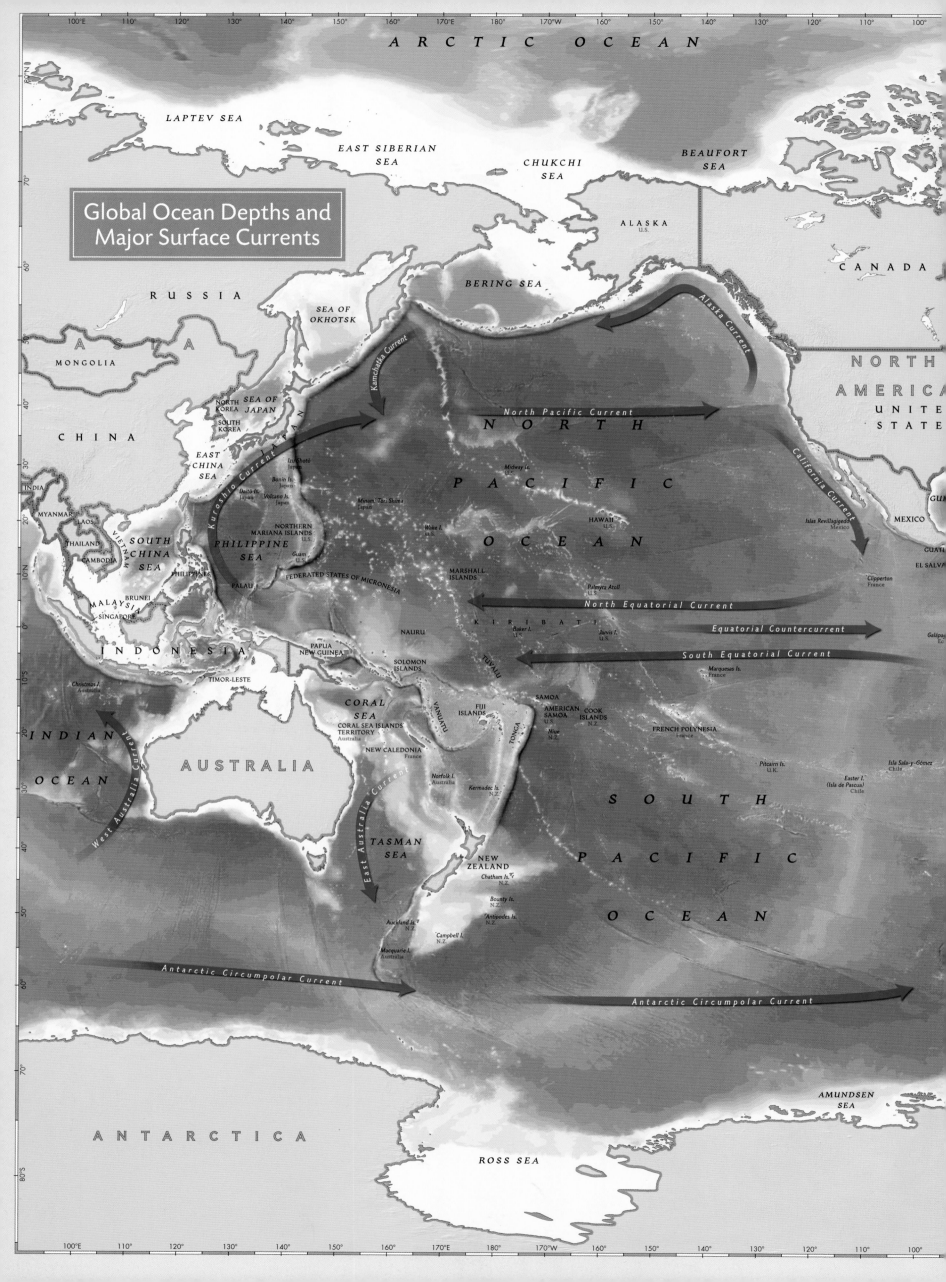

Plate Tectonics and Volcanic Activity

Kodiak-Bowie

Cobb

JUAN DE FUCA PLATE

Yellowstone

ROCKY MOUNTAINS

NORTH AMERICAN PLATE

Iceland

Mid-Atlantic Ridge

Azores

Raton

Guadalupe-Baja

New England

Hawaiian Islands

Cape Verde

Hawaiian

CARIBBEAN PLATE

PACIFIC PLATE

COCOS PLATE

Galápagos

ANDES

SOUTH AMERICAN PLATE

Samoa

NAZCA PLATE

St. Helena

Tahiti-Society

Trindade

Mid-Atlantic Ridge

Gambier

Easter

Austral-Cooks

Juan Fernández

Walvis Ridge

Louisville

SCOTIA PLATE

Bou

ANTARCTIC

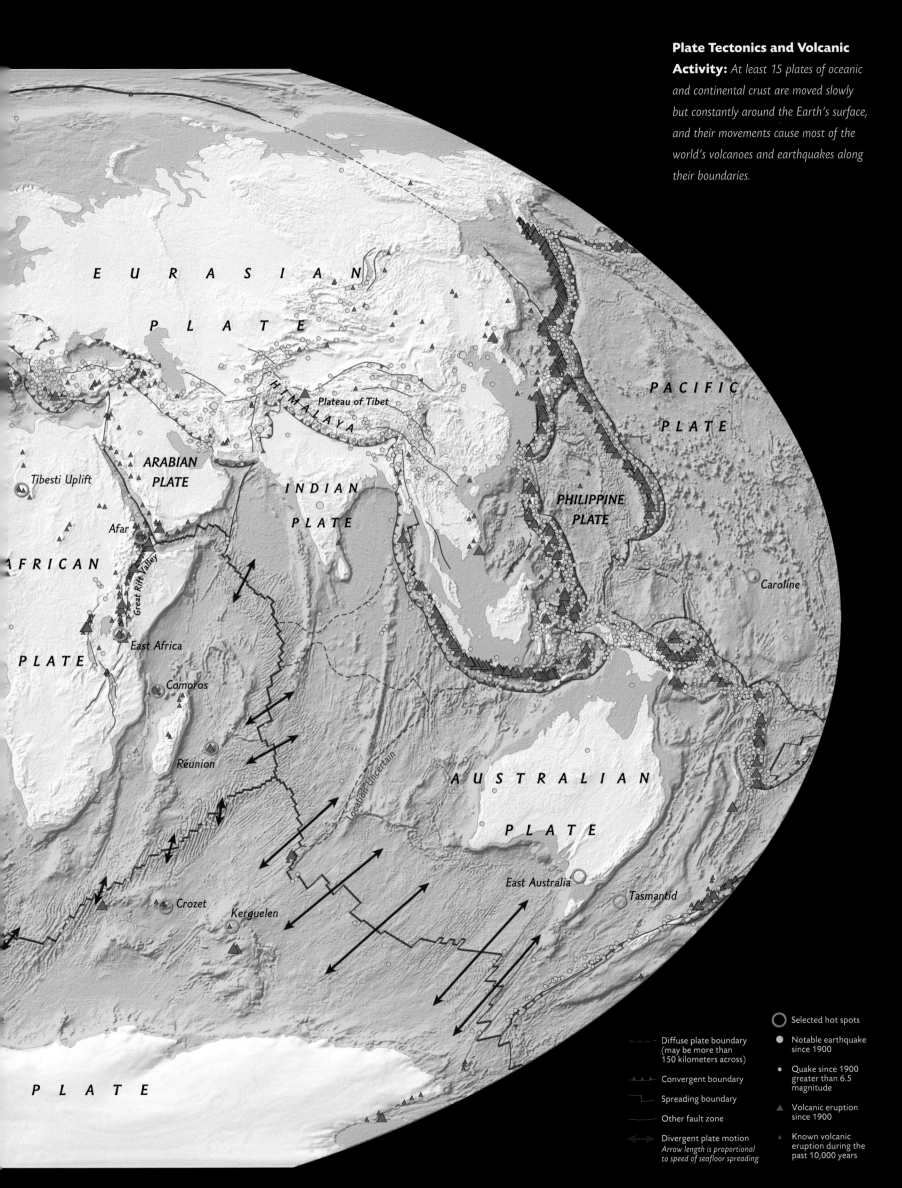

**Plate Tectonics and Volcanic
Activity:** *At least 15 plates of oceanic
and continental crust are moved slowly
but constantly around the Earth's surface,
and their movements cause most of the
world's volcanoes and earthquakes along
their boundaries.*

E U R A S I A N

P L A T E

PACIFIC

PLATE

HIMALAYA

Plateau of Tibet

ARABIAN
PLATE

INDIAN

PLATE

PHILIPPINE

PLATE

Tibesti Uplift

Afar

AFRICAN

Great Rift Valley

East Africa

PLATE

Comoros

Caroline

Réunion

Location Uncertain

AUSTRALIAN

P L A T E

East Australia

Tasmantid

Crozet

Kerguelen

P L A T E

○ Selected hot spots

◦ Notable earthquake
since 1900

- - - - Diffuse plate boundary
(may be more than
150 kilometers across)

• Quake since 1900
greater than 6.5
magnitude

▲▲▲ Convergent boundary

▲ Volcanic eruption
since 1900

⌐_ Spreading boundary

Other fault zone

⟷ Divergent plate motion
*Arrow length is proportional
to speed of seafloor spreading*

▲ Known volcanic
eruption during the
past 10,000 years

23

Surf's up! This is a call to ride great waves such as the one shown here at Waimea shorebreak in Oahu, Hawaii. After traveling unimpeded for hundreds of kilometers, such waves peak and crash magnificently as they come in contact with the shallowing rim of special coastal areas around the world.

World Ocean by the Numbers

Total area: 331,441,932 square kilometers

Total volume: 1,303,155,354 cubic kilometers

Average depth: approximately 4 kilometers

Greatest depth: 10,920 meters (Challenger Deep, in the Mariana Trench, North Pacific)

Mean ocean crust thickness: approximately 6.5 kilometers

Longest mountain range: 16,000 kilometers (the Mid-Atlantic Ridge)

Length of global mid-ocean ridge: 64,370 kilometers

REGIONAL AREAS

Atlantic: 81,705,396 square kilometers

Pacific: 152,617,159 square kilometers

Indian: 67,469,539 square kilometers

Arctic: 8,676,520 square kilometers

Southern: 20,973,318 square kilometers

REGIONAL VOLUMES

Atlantic: 307,923,430 cubic kilometers

Pacific: 645,369,567 cubic kilometers

Indian: 261,519,545 cubic kilometers

Arctic: 16,787,461 cubic kilometers

Southern: 71,515,351 cubic kilometers

"Standing on the shore and looking out to sea,

the boy said, 'There's a lot of water out there.'

And the wise old oceanographer responded,

'And that's only the top of it.'"

—Richard Ellis, *Singing Whales and Flying Squid*

C old, bleak, barren, inhospitable to life—that is what Earth would be without the flowing blue mantle that engulfs the planet's highest mountains, rolls over the deepest valleys, sweeps across the broadest plains, and covers most of the planet's surface, with the only substance that living creatures absolutely require—water. Astronauts looking at the blue Earth from afar readily see what most terrestrial primates do not: This planet is dominated by water. Sunlight sparkles from the faces of lakes; rivers curl across continents like silver ribbons; water-laden clouds wreathe the entire planet; frozen water frosts mountaintops and gleams starkly white at the Poles. But mostly, from afar, Earth is an ocean where even the largest landmasses are islands surrounded by a single, interconnected body of water—1.3 billion cubic kilometers of it, averaging 4 kilometers deep, with a maximum depth of 10.4 kilometers, covering 331 million square kilometers, more than two-thirds of Earth's surface.

Since the 1950s more has been learned about the nature of the ocean than during all preceding history—and the pace is picking up. New technologies and new awareness of the ocean's critical role in governing global temperature, climate, weather, chemistry—and its significance as the place that harbors 97 percent of Earth's water and 97 percent of the biosphere, including the greatest diversity and greatest amount of life on the planet—have inspired increased exploration and research. New discoveries are bringing into focus the importance of the sea to all that humankind holds near and dear—wealth, health, security, and most fundamentally the existence of life itself.

There are three sections to this atlas with new data and insights throughout about the physical and chemical nature of the sea, the ocean's role in climate change, the rocks and sand that hold the ocean, the fundamental Earth processes that have shaped and continue to change the ocean, the life that thrives there, and the impacts that the ocean has had on humankind and vice versa. Part 1 provides an overarching view of the nature of the ocean as a whole, and Part 2 covers the five major ocean basins:

- the Atlantic, notable for its prominent mid-ocean ridge and a history of forming, being destroyed, and re-forming several times;
- the Pacific, the largest, oldest, and widest ocean basin, with the greatest number of active volcanoes around its rim;
- the Indian, dominated by a distinctive Y-shaped mid-ocean ridge, located almost entirely in the Southern Hemisphere;
- the Arctic, a mostly ice-covered ocean centered at the North Pole and surrounded by continental and island landmasses;
- and the Southern Ocean, where waters flow uninterrupted around the Antarctic continent, regarded by some as a southern extension of the Atlantic, Pacific, and Indian Oceans.

Part 3 focuses on the exploration of the technologies used to understand the ocean, the change brought about by human actions, and finally consideration of the future ocean.

WEB LINK: Earth's water

Using senses humans can only imagine, each of these striped grunts keeps pace— and a place—among fellow swimmers near North Pier, Bonaire Island, West Indies.

The Ocean Floor

STRUCTURE OF THE EARTH AND ITS CRUST

No one has yet seen, or even sent a probe into, the molten heart of the Earth, but from measurements and models, it appears that there is an inner iron core surrounded by a liquid metallic layer that releases enormous amounts of heat and provides the basis for Earth's magnetic field. Surrounding the innermost part of the sphere is the mantle. The Earth's rocky crust, or lithosphere, is lighter than the mantle material and floats above the soft, hot interior.

The Earth's crust is made up of 15 or so great slabs, called tectonic plates. Some are continental crust averaging about 50 kilometers thick; some are thinner oceanic crust usually about 10 kilometers thick; and some plates are a combination of the two. These plates move around—ever so slowly but continuously—on the Earth's surface, and their movements over the ages result in the formation of mountain ranges, the building of island chains, and in the forces that trigger volcanoes and generate earthquakes.

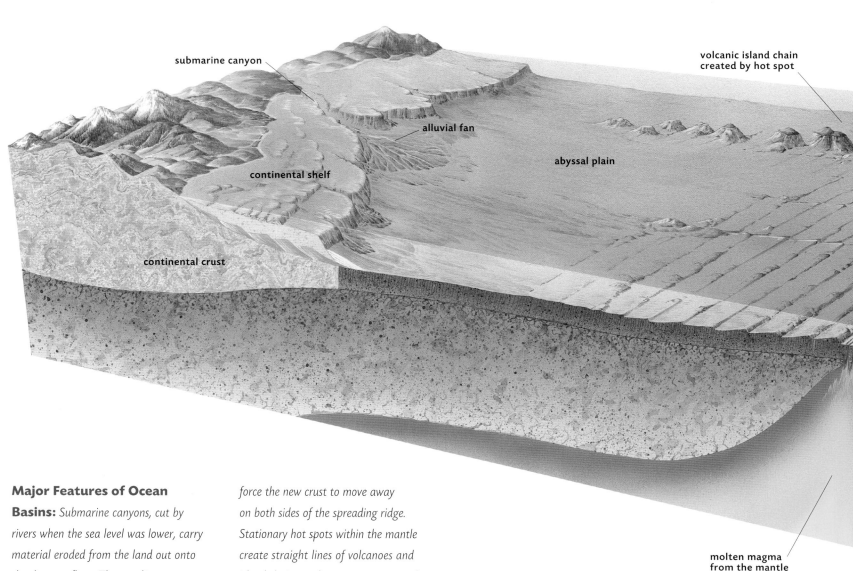

submarine canyon

volcanic island chain
created by hot spot

alluvial fan

continental shelf

abyssal plain

continental crust

molten magma
from the mantle

Major Features of Ocean Basins: *Submarine canyons, cut by rivers when the sea level was lower, carry material eroded from the land out onto the deep seafloor. These sediments, plus the shells of trillions of microscopic creatures from the surface waters, cover the rough seafloor terrain with immense, flat abyssal plains.*

Seafloor spreading ridges create new oceanic crust from molten mantle material that emerges through the central rift valley of the ridge and cools into new rock. Convection cells deep in the mantle then force the new crust to move away on both sides of the spreading ridge. Stationary hot spots within the mantle create straight lines of volcanoes and island chains as the crust moves over them.

Oceanic crust is destroyed when it is subducted, or pushed down under another plate and melted back into the mantle. As the oceanic crust is forced down, it creates deep-sea trenches, the deepest places in the ocean. The melted material escapes back to the surface in volcanic island arcs formed on the other side of the trenches.

THE MID-OCEAN RIDGES

The centuries-old method for measuring water depth involved dropping a lead weight on the end of a line until the weight struck the bottom, then measuring the line's length. In deeper water, a hollow lead cylinder was lowered on a line, a crude but ingenious way to determine depth: The greater the crushing of the cylinder, the greater the pressure from the weight of the water, and thus the greater the depth. In the 1950s, sonar used to find submarines in World War II was adapted to ping all the way to the seafloor, and timing the return gave a good measure of water depth.

The efforts of a trio of scientists—Maurice Ewing, Bruce Heezen, and Heezen's student, Marie Tharp, all at Columbia University's Lamont Geological Observatory—laid the foundation for one of those scientific revolutions that come along every century or so. First, Heezen and Tharp painstakingly assembled information gathered during cruises of diverse ships using the sonar "echo sounders." Results were compiled into charts to develop data-rich images of the ocean floor, with a vertical exaggeration to highlight its submerged features. Based on their work, the National Geographic Society and the Geological Society of America began issuing a

WEB LINK: plate tectonics

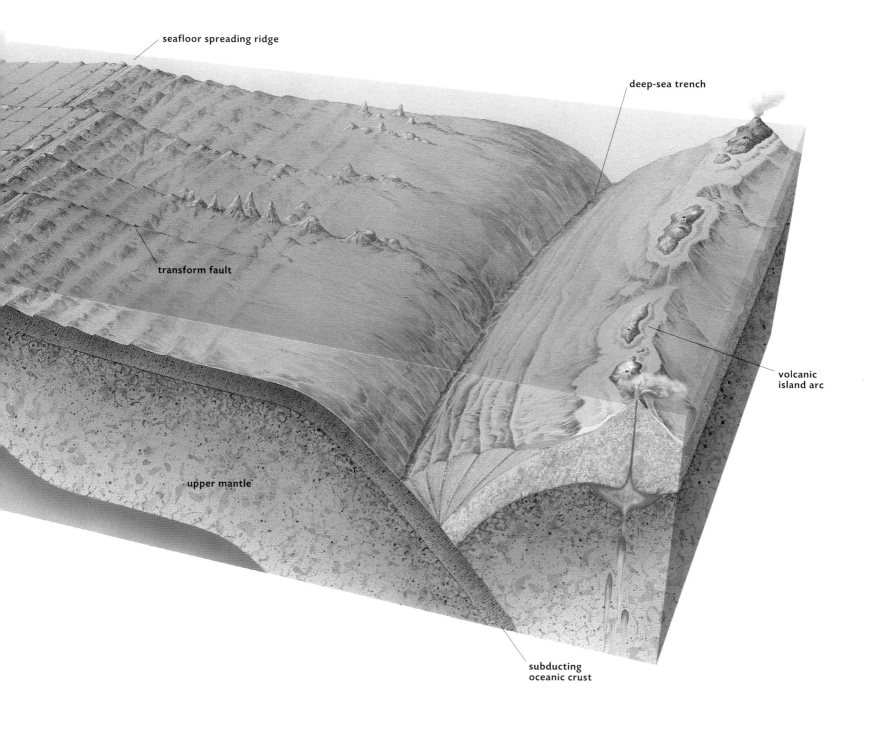

seafloor spreading ridge

deep-sea trench

transform fault

volcanic island arc

upper mantle

subducting oceanic crust

series of maps late in the 1950s that for the first time showed the seafloor features that would appear if the water were drained away.

When Tharp began plotting the data, the magnitude and meaning of the Atlantic's underwater mountain range began to come into focus. There, running down the middle of the ocean like a huge backbone, was a continuous ridge with hundreds of peaks, some more than 6,100 meters high. Heezen and Ewing found there was a correlation between the location of this Mid-Atlantic Ridge and the pattern of earthquakes in the Atlantic. Studying underwater earthquake patterns worldwide, they ventured an educated guess in 1956 that ranges of mountains must extend throughout all of the oceans, literally, a mid-ocean ridge. Data gathered by research vessels operating worldwide during the International Geophysical Year, 1957–58, proved their prediction. Finally, the existence of the largest feature on the surface of the Earth—more than 64,000 kilometers of almost continuous mountain ranges in the depths of the Atlantic, Pacific, Indian, Arctic, and Southern Oceans—was at last made known.

Observations from space have greatly enhanced understanding of ocean and Earth dynamics as illustrated in these images from NASA's Gravity Recovery and Climate Experiment (GRACE) satellite mission and the University of Texas, depicting gravity fields. Bigger lumps and warmer colors represent areas of greater gravitational attraction, while depressions and cooler colors show lower attraction.

WEB LINK: GRACE Mission

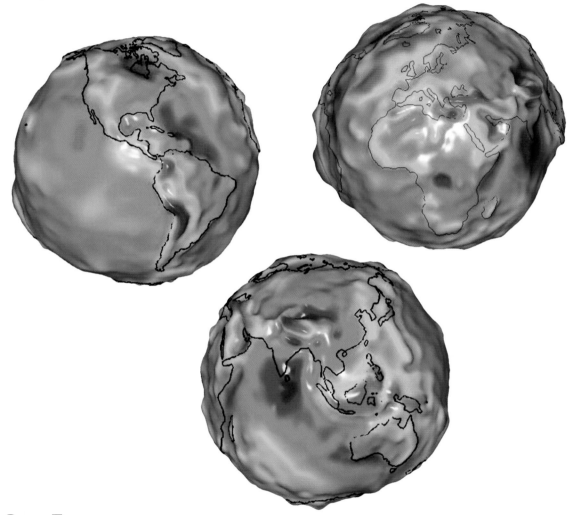

PLATE TECTONICS

Marie Tharp was the first to point out a puzzling recurrent pattern that appeared in the Mid-Atlantic Ridge: a cleft a kilometer or so deep—deeper and much wider than the Grand Canyon—running down the center of the entire underwater range. In the early 1960s, Harry Hess and Robert Dietz independently proposed an explanation for this and other mysterious features of the ocean floor, and thereby launched a new field of science, and a whole new understanding of the Earth's crust and its ocean basins. The clues were diverse: the continuous crack down the middle of the mid-ocean ridges; the deep trenches around the rim of the Pacific and elsewhere; the preponderance of volcanoes and earthquakes on one side of these deep trenches; the fact that sediments in the deep sea appear to be younger close to the center than along the edges of the continents; and the way the configuration of continents on one side of the Atlantic seemed to fit nicely against continents on the other, like pieces of a giant puzzle.

The explanation that fit the evidence is that the seafloor is spreading—with molten material rising from the mantle into the middle of the mid-ocean ridges, cooling, forming new seafloor,

SEE ALSO: movement of the plates, pages 92-93

then moving away from both sides of the ridge, driven by currents of heat deep within the Earth. The continents are drifting in response, riding along on the moving tectonic plates as the seafloor spreads apart. Where a moving oceanic plate butts into a thicker continental plate, the thinner ocean crust is subducted, or thrust down under the continent, pulling the seafloor down into deep ocean trenches. The subducted plate heats and melts as it is pushed deeper and reabsorbs into the mantle, some of it returning explosively to the surface through volcanoes that form over the subducting plate. Many of these volcanic island arcs near deep trenches can be seen in the western Pacific. Where two continental plates are rammed together by the spreading plates carrying them, high plateaus and huge mountain chains are thrust up. Other curious features such as the Red Sea, the Gulf of California, and the great East African Rift Valleys are now identified as new spreading centers, where briny lakes will grow to salty seas, and eventually to new ocean basins and the land on either side will be pushed far apart.

For reasons that are not well understood, the Earth's magnetic field periodically reverses itself, the North Pole becoming the South Pole and vice versa. When this happens bits of iron embedded in cooling lava solidify into tiny magnets permanently aligned with the north magnetic pole at the time they become rock. This leaves a record of reversals of the magnetic poles. First in the Indian Ocean and then in the northern Atlantic, bands of magnetized rock perfectly matching in their widths, rock ages, and magnetic signature were discovered aligned on either side of seafloor spreading ridges.

Enthusiasm grew for the idea of actually diving to where the action was—right to the heart of a seafloor spreading ridge. A project called FAMOUS (French-American Mid-Ocean Undersea Study) involved scientists and several submersibles from both countries in a collaboration geophysicist Robert Ballard called "a combination of basic science and adventurous exploration." Ballard, one of the expedition's leaders, had a front-row seat 2,700 meters down for the visual confirmation of seafloor spreading. He expressed amazement at the narrowness of the zone where fresh volcanic intrusion flowed up between the two plates, each one "thousands of miles across, slowly

The Abyss

New ocean crust is formed along the ridges, which are raised up by heat from the mantle beneath them. As older seafloor is pushed away from the ridge, it cools and sinks. These broad, deep areas—between the spreading ridges and the continental margins—are the abyssal plains. They are very flat over huge expanses because the rough terrain is covered over by thick layers of sediments, tiny shells from animals drifting near the sea surface and dirt washed down rivers and through underwater canyons to fill the deep ocean. Sediment layers in the abyssal plains can be many kilometers thick.

SEE ALSO: magnetic pole reversals, pages 91, 98, 114

Curtains of gas emitted from volcanic action deep within the Earth emerge like blue champagne among corals at Great Abaco, Bahamas.

Marie Tharp
OCEAN CARTOGRAPHY

From time immemorial, the standard way of measuring water depth was with a rope tied to a rock. H.M.S. *Challenger* opened up the sea in the 1870s on a world-encircling cruise, taking one sounding every hundred miles with a 91-kilogram weight on a hemp line attached to a hand-operated winch.

Reginald Fessenden in 1917, aware that light does not penetrate far into seawater, chose to use sound as an energy source. During World War II the use of sound was developed into the continuous echo sounder by the team of Maurice Ewing and J. L. Worzel of the Woods Hole Oceanographic Institution for the U.S. Navy.

With data from the basic instruments of sounder, corer, and ocean-bottom camera, I began mapping the deep-ocean floor with Bruce Heezen in 1952. As soundings were classified by the U.S. Navy, we decided to use the physiographic diagram style of A. K. Lobeck, professor of geomorphology at Columbia University. Even after soundings were declassified in 1961, I still used the diagrams for sketching seafloor topography because they were more effective visually, showing slope variants and bottom textures. Gradually the echo sounder grew into the precision depth recorder—accurate to 1 meter in 3,000; the coring rig took cores in hours, not days; throwing dynamite charges overboard from a fast-moving ship was replaced by shooting an air gun as a sound source to measure the depth to the top of the Earth's crust under seafloor mud; and the one-shot ocean bottom camera became the multiple-shot, computerized camera—today's floating jewel.

In 1952 I discovered at the crest of the Mid-Ocean Ridge a seismically active rift valley. The correlation of earthquakes and depths in the Mid-Atlantic Rift Valley enabled Bruce and me to estimate the location of a similar rift valley—on the basis of earthquakes alone—for 64,370 kilometers around the world. All the data for these physiographic diagrams were reduced by hand in the precomputer era. With contributions from Britain, Germany, and Japan, we published "North Atlantic Physiographic Diagram" (1956); "South Atlantic" (1961); and "Indian Ocean" (1964).

Later, Bruce and I worked with National Geographic and Heinrich Berann, a superb painter in the style of Leonardo da Vinci, to produce a more colorful panoramic map of the Indian Ocean. Then, over the next ten years, we made maps of the Pacific, Antarctic, and Arctic Oceans; with new data from ships of Lamont, Scripps, and the U.S. Navy, Bruce updated the "World Ocean Floor" map. The following decades found us discovering and publishing new finds: Our many crossings by ship over the equatorial fracture zones revealed the trend of the fracture zones in

the North and South Atlantic. Using the deep-sea drilling vessel *Glomar Challenger*, Bruce surmised that Pacific seamounts are Cretaceous in age and rest on a Jurassic basement, while the Atlantic and Indian Oceans have fewer seamounts that are younger. By studying the 1929 Grand Banks earthquake, Bruce documented the speed of turbidity currents—underwater avalanches—that deposit sediments far out to sea, forming abyssal plains. We determined that the Atlantic has more abyssal plains than the Pacific; and in 1978, in "World Ocean Floor

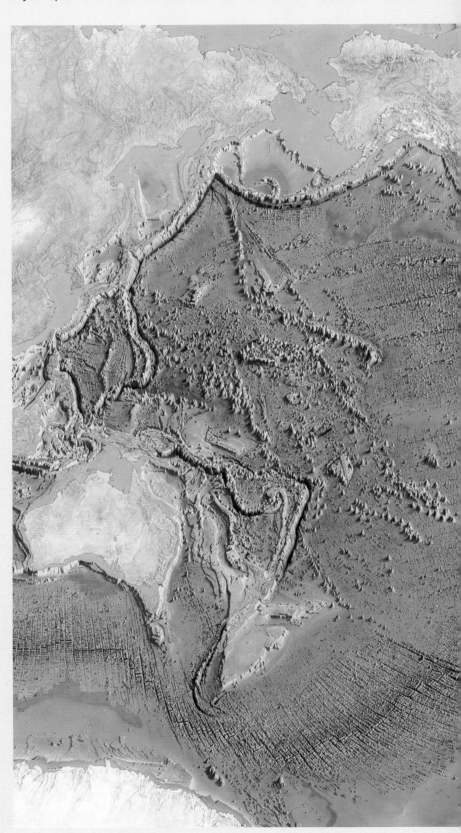

In what has been called "one of the most quixotic quests in cartographic history," student Marie Tharp, with oceanographer Bruce Heezen, made this first detailed map of the Mid-Ocean Rift Valley, which paved the way for acceptance of the theory of seafloor spreading and continental drift.

Panorama," we showed that plate tectonics is the result of the crust's horizontal movement only.

Mapping the continental shorelines has taken about 300 years, whereas mapping the ocean floor has taken 30. But the final map of Earth is yet to come. Recent discoveries reveal that vertical movements of the crust create the relief on the ocean floor and the continents. In less than 30 years this, and the remaining puzzle pieces, will be mapped.

In Memoriam
Marie Tharp died August 23, 2006. Her prediction that all the world's seafloor would be mapped in 30 years has been realized, but vast areas have still not been surveyed in detail. Tharp will forever be celebrated by the marine geology community as a consummate cartographer with an uncanny ability to discover important trends in mounds of data before the help of computer GIS (geographic information system) programs.

As a cartographer and researcher from 1949 to 1982 at the Lamont-Doherty Geological Observatory, she called attention to the consistent "gap" along the top of the Mid-Atlantic Ridge that offered strong support to the then-controversial theory of seafloor spreading. She turned her Nyack home on the Hudson River into a strange and wonderful cartographic laboratory, full of inspired students laboring late into the night with piles of ship survey data in different rooms of the house that were dedicated to different parts of the world ocean.

drifting apart, yet the actual zone into which the fresh lava flowed, creating the earth's outer skin, was only a mile or so wide."

SEE ALSO: map of seafloor spreading, pages 84-85

Later, it was shown that the Atlantic Ocean is growing larger at a rate of about 2.5 centimeters a year, not a great amount until multiplied by almost 200 million (the number of years estimated to be the age of the Atlantic), and the multiple, not coincidentally, is close to the number of centimeters between North America and Europe. Spreading rates of all mid-ocean ridges have since been measured. The patterns of newly formed seafloor would be straight and neat if the Earth were flat, but with all the spreading and subducting moving across the Earth's spherical surface, the spreading ridges are deeply scored by offsets along prominent fracture zones, giving the ridges their characteristic sawtooth appearance. Another prominent result of the roundness of the globe and the complex movements of the tectonic plates is the formation of numerous triple junctions, where three spreading ridges intersect.

THE SEAFLOOR

The major provinces of the seafloor across most ocean basins include the continental margins, sometimes bordered by deep-ocean trenches; the abyssal plains; usually narrow regions of abyssal hills; and the broad mid-ocean ridges that occupy about a third of the area of most oceans. Basically, the mid-ocean ridge forms rough, new crust that cools and sinks deeper as it spreads away from the ridge, forming abyssal hills. Much of this terrain is covered by sediments derived from the shells of billions of planktonic organisms deposited over millions of years, combined with silt, sand, and mud eroded from the land into the sea. These sediments form broad, flat abyssal plains, masking the underlying roughness.

Vast areas of the seafloor are paved with potato-size lumps of manganese, iron, copper, and other minerals generally referred to as manganese nodules. First discovered during the H.M.S. *Challenger* expedition of 1872-76, they were regarded mostly as a curiosity until the magnitude of their abundance and potential value of their strategically important metals became known. Iron typically accounts for most of a nodule's composition. As much as 25 percent may be manganese, with cobalt and copper about 2 percent each and nickel 1.6 percent. Despite considerable investments in exploring how to retrieve them, the cost of mining these nodules presently outweighs the economic benefits, and there are significant concerns about environment issues.

Another important feature of the seafloor is the widespread occurrence of clathrates, called gas hydrates by oil field geologists. For years, fishermen trawling in deep water occasionally brought to the surface chunks of icy white material that fizzled and popped, eventually dissolving into a pool of gas and water. The glistening masses typically consist of methane frozen within a latticelike structure of water molecules. Formed at depths greater than 300 meters and in near-freezing temperatures, gas hydrates are common in the deep sea along continental margins, and in latitudes near the Poles. Gas hydrate layers mixed with sediment may exceed a thickness of 1,000 meters directly beneath the seafloor, and the icy deposits apparently cement and help hold soft sediments in place, with breakdowns triggering massive underwater landslides. They sequester enormous amounts of carbon, and thus affect the amount of carbon dioxide (CO_2) in the atmosphere, which in turn influences global climate.

Among the most celebrated discoveries in the ocean in the past century is the existence of hydrothermal vents. Lava erupting into near-freezing seawater at seafloor spreading ridges swiftly hardens and cracks. Cold seawater flows into deep crevices, where it comes in contact with molten

A tapestry of life cloaks a six-meter mineral tower nicknamed "the flying buttress." Fueled by bacteria that draw nutrients from the mineral-laden water, communities of life such as this one have prospered in the deep sea in the absence of sunlight for hundreds of millions of years.

rock hot enough to dissolve iron, manganese, silicon, and other minerals. This heated, mineral-laden water then rises out of the seafloor, sometimes as gentle warm-water flows, but sometimes as hot, gushing, towering underwater geysers. Water from the vents can be hot enough to melt temperature-measuring probes on research subs, which happened on an early dive near the Galá-pagos Islands. As superheated water from under the seafloor pours back into the near-freezing, deep seawater, minerals melted in it solidify into metallic crusts, or sometimes into tall columns known as chimneys, rising in fantastic shapes from the seafloor as high as multistoried buildings. Geologist John Edmond has calculated that all the water in the ocean circulates through deep hydrothermal vents about every ten million years, and in so doing gives the saltiness of the ocean its amazingly uniform state.

Since the first discovery in 1977, hydrothermal vents have been found off the northwestern coast of the United States at the Gorda and Juan de Fuca Ridges, at sites near Baja California, and in various parts of the Atlantic, Indian, and Arctic Oceans. In December 2000, oceanographers encountered something totally unexpected while exploring a seamount in the North Atlantic—an underwater mountain 3,700 meters high, with its peak rising to within 914 meters of the sea surface. Through the viewing port of the submersible *Alvin*, they saw amazing white structures, oddly sculpted towers as much as 18 stories high, larger than any previously seen near hydrothermal vents. Their composition appears to be carbonate minerals and hard, glassy silica, not the iron- and sulfur-rich materials around vents previously encountered.

SEAMOUNTS AND ISLANDS

Seamounts are mostly volcanic mountains that are entirely underwater and rise above the seafloor 1,000 meters or more. Lesser peaks, between 500 and 1,000 meters, are termed knolls, and bumps in the seafloor 500 meters or less are referred to as hills. The existence of seamounts has long been known, but only about 1,000 have been surveyed well enough with sonar mapping efforts to be named and featured on charts.

A new data source—satellites kilometers overhead—provides evidence that there are many more seamounts yet to be found. Satellite sensors over the past two decades have collected precise measurements of the height of the sea surface, altimetry, and measurements of the gravitational field across the oceans. Variations in the gravitational pull of rock masses at the bottom of the ocean are reflected on the sea surface—submerged mountains appear as very slight bulges at the surface and trenches at the bottom. Various ways of interpreting these data have led to estimates of 15,000 to as many as 100,000 seamounts worldwide.

If every emergent chunk of rock and reef is included, many thousands of islands occur in every major ocean basin. Some—like Madagascar, Sri Lanka, Cuba, and the British Isles—sit on pieces of continental crust pulled away from their parent continent through the never-ending dance of sea-floor spreading, or by being separated from their parent landmass through sea level rise or erosion of the rocks connecting them.

Most oceanic islands are formed by volcanoes, though, in three areas: at seafloor spreading ridges, above subduction zones in volcanic island arcs, and above stationary hot spots in the Earth's mantle.

SEE ALSO: Atlantic island formation, page 116

Sea Level Isn't Level

Water normally seeks its own level, but measurements of sea-surface height from satellite sensors called altimeters show that the average sea level varies considerably across the world ocean. Warmer waters are less dense than colder and tend to stand up higher. Water temperature and currents create sea-height differences of about 3 meters worldwide. Gravity forces from rock masses far beneath the ocean can be seen at the surface as permanent mounds over seamounts and depressions over trenches. These gravity-induced changes in sea level can be as much as 100 meters.

Evolution of a Volcanic Island:

Many volcanic islands are formed as molten material erupts from a hot spot deep in the mantle below. As the islands are moved away from the heat source through seafloor spreading, they often sink below the sea surface over time, leaving barrier reefs, atolls, seamounts, and flat-topped seamounts called guyots.

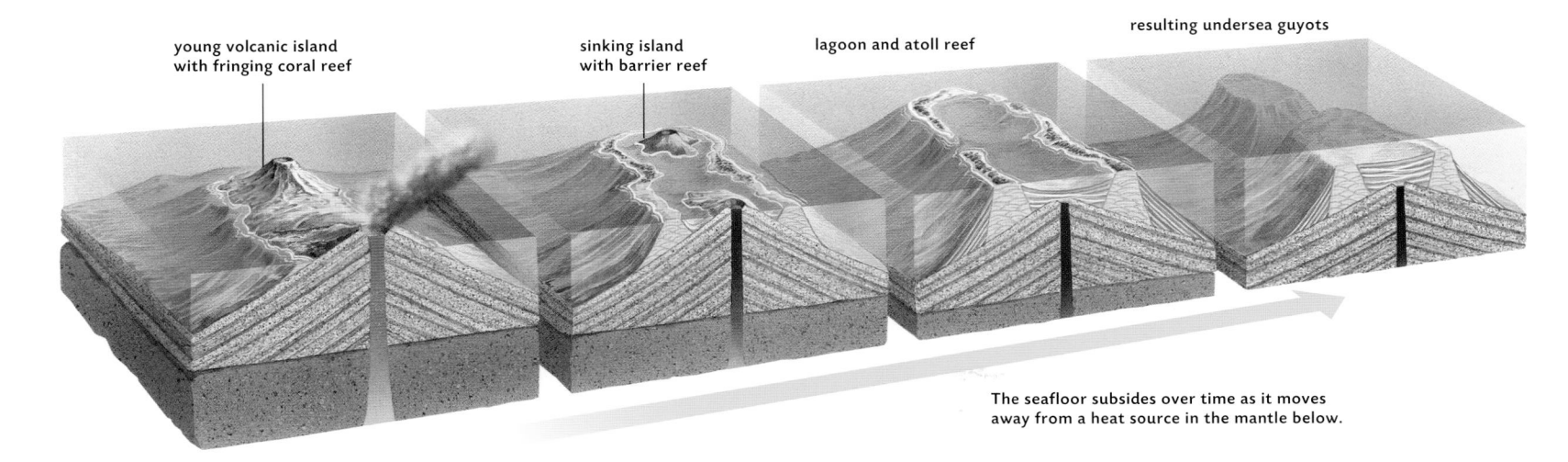

young volcanic island with fringing coral reef

sinking island with barrier reef

lagoon and atoll reef

resulting undersea guyots

The seafloor subsides over time as it moves away from a heat source in the mantle below.

SEE ALSO: Northwest Hawaiian Islands National Monument, pages 166-167

Many islands formed by hot spots can be seen on maps of the ocean, arrayed in long, linear chains created one by one as the ocean crust was pushed by seafloor spreading over the mantle's hot spot. In these island chains, the lineage of the hot spot is even more pronounced if their associated submerged seamounts are included—former islands that have slipped beneath the sea surface as the buoyant heat of the hot spot passed them by. In the same ocean basin, these island chains will line up in the direction of seafloor spreading over millions of years. In the Pacific, the Hawaiian and the Galápagos Islands are clear examples of this process.

Other islands are formed independently as undersea volcanoes that eventually break through the water's surface. In the tropics, fringing reefs may evolve into atolls as the above-water peaks erode away, leaving a living circle of coral around a volcanic husk. Whatever the cause of formation, over the millennia many volcanoes have grown into islands, and many islands have eroded or sunk to become submerged seamounts, a process that continues.

CONTINENTAL MARGINS

Fringing Earth's large landmasses are continental shelves, underwater extensions of the land that average about 70 kilometers wide, deepening gradually to a shelf break at about 200 meters, then dropping off more sharply down the continental slope to greater depths below. The width of continental shelves varies greatly, from broad expanses—along Florida's west coast, the eastern edge of Australia, the southeastern edge of South America, and the Arctic coast of Russia—to narrow shelves such as those of the western United States and Chile, where deep water comes close to shore.

The nature of continental shelves usually reflect the coasts they border, including enormous underwater submarine canyons—some wider and deeper than the Grand Canyon—off the mouths of most major rivers. Nearly all continental shelves were above sea level during the maximum extent of ice cover in the Pleistocene era 18,000 years ago, and many rivers cut deep canyons across the

A jungle of red mangrove roots shelters a school of carnivorous silversides from larger fish-eaters while they seek sustenance for themselves: smaller fish, tiny crustaceans, and the larvae of hundreds of other kinds of marine life.

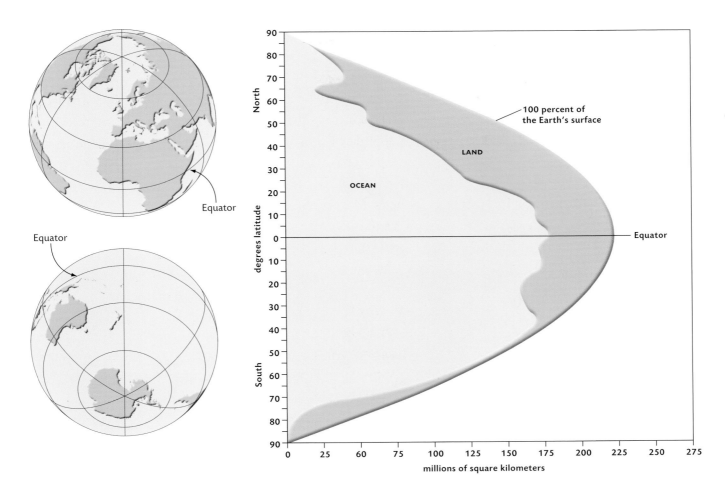

100 percent of the Earth's surface

LAND

OCEAN

Equator

degrees latitude

North

South

millions of square kilometers

exposed land on their way to the sea. Submarine canyons are preserved by the flow of turbidity currents—slurries of water and suspended material from the land—that periodically flow through them in underwater landslides, eventually depositing their sediments on the deep seafloor.

Ice ages have come and gone many times in the past, with sea level rising and falling by as much as 200 meters, coincident with cycles of freezing and melting. When ice cover is extensive, the shelves are largely above water, but during the warm phases, the sea may totally inundate the shelf and can extend far inland. In Florida, Mexico, the Persian Gulf, and elsewhere, springs of fresh water bubble up in the ocean several kilometers from the nearest dry land. Ancient shorelines are evident today well offshore, while beaches that were formed long ago underlie places many miles from the sea. People living along the margins of the continents occupy some of the planet's most dynamic real estate.

Ocean vs. Land: *As shown in these diagrams, ocean and landmasses are asymmetrically distributed over Earth's surface. Land is more than 50 percent of the Earth's surface area only between latitudes 45° N and 70° N and, to the south, from latitude 70° S to the South Pole. Water with an average depth of about 4 kilometers covers the rest.*

Ocean Water

ORIGIN OF THE OCEAN'S WATER

Mystery still surrounds the formation of Earth's ocean and, with it, the origins of life. But the discovery of water in other parts of the universe and new knowledge about early development of the solar system indicate that much of the ocean may have come from collisions with water-rich comets and meteorites in the early stages of planetary development. Some suggest that a planetoid as large as Mars may have struck the Earth with an impact that gave birth to the moon and, in the process, vaporized whatever water was then on Earth. Later collisions with water-rich meteorites could account for much of the ocean's water, together with water vapor erupted through volcanoes from rocks deep beneath the Earth's surface.

Over millennia, all the water in the world repeatedly cycles in a vast system linking the atmosphere above to the ocean and the seafloor below. Surface waters evaporate into clouds and return as rain, sleet, and snow. Deep-ocean water sinks through cracks in the seafloor, becomes superheated, and gushes or flows back up into the sea through hydrothermal vents laden with minerals and fostering wondrous forms of life hidden to humankind until the last quarter of the

Where in the World Is the Water?

Almost all of the water on Earth is in the ocean—97 percent of it. Most of the remaining 3 percent is ice, frozen in mountain glaciers or polar ice caps. Only 3 percent of this 3 percent—less than one-tenth of 1 percent of all water on the planet—makes up all of the lakes, ponds, rivers, streams, groundwater, clouds, rain, and puddles in the world.

20th century. Oceanic crust pushed down into the mantle and melted through the collision of tectonic plates releases water vapor back into the atmosphere through the volcanoes that form above subduction zones.

THE NATURE OF WATER

Despite its apparent simplicity, water's molecular anatomy, bound together in ways unlike any other substance, accounts for some of its most amazing characteristics. So unusual and mysterious is water that the poet D. H. Lawrence felt compelled to write: "Water is H_2O, hydrogen two parts, oxygen one part, but there is a third thing that makes it water and nobody knows what that is."

Hydrogen and oxygen have a tremendous affinity for each other, a fact graphically illustrated in 1937 when the great hydrogen-filled dirigible *Hindenburg* exploded in flight over New Jersey. A spark ignited the hydrogen, which fused violently with oxygen in the atmosphere, producing water—and an enduring, catastrophic lesson in chemistry. Once fused, it takes an enormous amount of energy to break the bonds that hold water molecules together. Whether frozen, liquid, or heated to the point where water turns to vapor, the atoms of water molecules remain intact. A few potent chemicals, or electrical energy, can split water into its basic elements, but stability is the rule. On one side of each molecule are two atoms of negatively charged hydrogen; on the other side is a large, positively charged atom of oxygen. In water molecules, each hydrogen atom can be shared between two molecules, forming a hydrogen bond and creating a kind of liquid latticework.

Like miniature magnets, in a mass of water molecules at the right temperature—not too hot, not too cold—the opposite charges attract and form bonds that readily part, then attach to another, then another, in a moving flow. Science writer Robert Kunzig likens the phenomenon to "the passing touch exchanged by dancers in a quadrille, as they constantly change partners. Water molecules change partners billions of times a second." When water is heated, the pace of the dance picks up until the bonds break apart, and individual molecules fly off as a gas. Because of water's electrically polarized design, molecules of water readily attract not just one another, but also other substances, giving rise to its wondrous nature as a near-universal solvent.

So readily do materials dissolve in water that pure water rarely occurs in nature. Snow, sleet, and rain fall to Earth together with hitchhikers picked up along the way, from soot and dust to extra atoms of oxygen and molecules of carbon dioxide. Rivers gradually dissolve the very rocks over which they flow, and carry downstream millions of tons of suspended minerals, sand, sediment, and organic matter.

Water has other amazing properties. When heated, water expands and the molecules move apart, ultimately vaporizing into a gas. When cooled, water, like most substances, contracts, becoming heavier and denser. But near freezing, hydrogen atoms in molecules of water attach to each other in a six-sided ring that creates a solid—ice—that occupies more space and is lighter than the liquid from which it came. Fortunately for life, frozen water floats, a phenomenon that shields liquid water in ponds, lakes, and most of the Arctic Ocean, allowing life to prosper in the frigid waters below.

THE NATURE OF SEAWATER

Chemically, seawater is only about 96.5 percent water; the remaining ingredients are mostly salts, largely sodium chloride, although 11 constituents account for the ocean's overall mineral content. Every cubic mile of ocean water holds nearly 90 million tons of chlorine, close to 50 million tons of sodium, more than 6 million tons of magnesium, 4 million tons of sulfur, and about 1.8 million tons each of calcium and potassium. Dozens of other elements are present as well, from carbon and nitrogen to lead and even gold.

Formation of Water: *Water is known as H_2O, each molecule consisting of two atoms of hydrogen and one atom of oxygen. The bond between the oxygen and hydrogen atoms are at angles that yield a slightly positive charge on one side, negative on the other, causing molecules to attract one another and line up according to their charges. This structure underlies some of water's unique characteristics as a flowing liquid, crystalline solid, and gaseous vapor.*

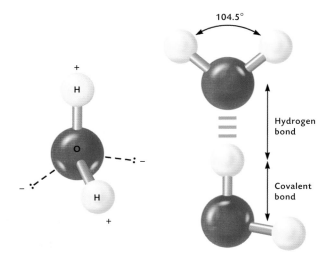

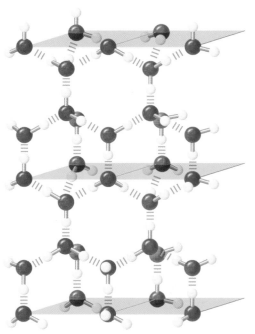

Scott Doney
OCEAN ACIDIFICATION

The current rapid rise in atmospheric carbon dioxide levels, caused by the intensive burning of fossil fuels for energy, is fundamentally changing the chemistry of the sea, pushing surface waters toward conditions that are more acidic. Greater acidity slows the growth of, or even dissolves, ocean plant and animal shells built from calcium carbonate, the mineral found in chalk and limestone. Acidification thus threatens a wide range of marine organisms, from microscopic plankton and shellfish to massive coral reefs, as well as the food webs that depend upon these shell-forming species.

Burning gasoline in cars or using electricity from a natural gas or coal-fired power plant releases carbon dioxide gas into the air, some of which eventually dissolves in the ocean, where it forms carbonic acid and a series of dissociation products. The release of hydrogen ions from the breakdown of carbonic acid lowers the pH of seawater, causing the normally somewhat alkaline water (surface pH about 8.2) to become more acidic. Based on an extensive global ocean survey conducted in the 1990s, scientists estimate that ocean surface pH has already dropped by 0.1 pH unit relative to preindustrial conditions, equivalent to a 25 percent increase in acidity.

Atmospheric carbon dioxide levels are already more than one-third greater than preindustrial concentrations, and if fossil fuel consumption continues unabated, it could double or triple before the end of this century. The resulting surface ocean acidification would represent an additional 0.3 to 0.4 pH drop, larger and more rapid than anything experienced by sea life for tens of millions of years. The most sensitive areas may be the surface subpolar North Pacific, the Southern Ocean, and at mid-depth along the Pacific continental shelf and margin, where waters are already closer to being corrosive for carbonate shells. And the problem will be with us for a long time, because it takes centuries to thousands of years for natural processes to remove excess carbon dioxide from the air.

Laboratory experiments have shown that acidification directly harms many marine species by reducing shell formation, slowing growth rates and hindering reproduction. Tropical corals are the backdrop for rich and diverse reef environments, and many fish species would disappear along with the corals. Clams and oysters, sea urchins, shrimp, and lobsters are

Skies darken over Washington, D.C., with plumes of CO_2-laden emissions from several factories.

important sources of seafood. About half of the dollar value for marine fisheries in the United States comes from these acidification-sensitive species. Less familiar are the many shell-forming planktonic organisms, including plants like coccolithophores and marine snails called pteropods, which are an important food source for salmon and whales. Recent discoveries have indicated extensive deep-water coral reefs around the edges of continents and on seamounts, which may decline before we really begin to understand their contribution as a habitat for fish. Some preliminary experiments suggest that larval and juvenile fish may also be at risk.

Future ocean acidification will occur in conjunction with other human-driven stresses like global warming, pollution, overfishing, and nutrient inputs. The biological consequences of ocean acidification and these other factors will ripple through marine food webs in ways that are difficult to predict. But it is likely that the ocean of the future under high carbon dioxide will look quite different within the lifetimes of today's children if we continue on our current course.

So what can be done about ocean acidification? The most obvious answer is to slow and eventually eliminate fossil fuel carbon emissions and to develop approaches for removing carbon dioxide from the atmosphere. Although there is no single panacea, a suite of promising technologies is emerging, involving increased energy efficiency; renewable energy like wind, solar, and biofuels; and carbon capture and sequestration, in which carbon dioxide produced by power plants is pumped deep into the Earth rather than being released into the atmosphere. We need to take action soon, however, to ensure the long-term health of the ocean and, therefore, ourselves.

....

CO$_2$ and Acidification Facts

• Since the early 1800s, atmospheric CO_2 concentrations have increased from approximately 280 to 385 parts per million (ppm). • The pH of ocean surface waters has already decreased by 0.1 units, from an average of about 8.2 to 8.1. • An increase to more than 800 ppm would result in an additional surface water pH decrease of about 0.3 pH units by 2100.

Average Concentrations of Elements in the Ocean

ATOMIC NUMBER	ELEMENT	CHEMICAL SPECIES	CONCENTRATION	UNIT
1	Hydrogen	H_2O	–	–
17	Chlorine	Cl^-	19.35	g/kg
11	Sodium	Na^+	10.78	g/kg
12	Magnesium	Mg_2^+	1.28	g/kg
16	Sulfur	SO_4^{2-}	898.00	mg/kg
20	Calcium	Ca_2^+	412.00	mg/kg
19	Potassium	K^+	399.00	mg/kg
35	Bromine	Br^-	67.00	mg/kg
6	Carbon	Inorganic CO_2	27.00	mg/kg
7	Nitrogen	Dissolved N_2	8.30	mg/kg
38	Strontium	Sr_2^+	7.80	mg/kg
5	Boron	Borate	4.50	mg/kg
8	Oxygen	Dissolved O_2	2.80	mg/kg
14	Silicon	Reactive SiO_2	2.80	mg/kg
9	Fluorine	F^-	1.30	mg/kg
18	Argon	Dissolved gas	620.00	µg/kg
7	Nitrogen	NO_3^-	420.00	µg/kg
3	Lithium	Li^+	180.00	µg/kg
37	Rubidium	Rb^+	120.00	µg/kg
15	Phosphorus	Reactive PO_4	62.00	µg/kg
53	Iodine	I(V)	58.00	µg/kg
56	Barium	Ba_2^+	15.00	µg/kg
42	Molybdenum	–	10.00	µg/kg
92	Uranium	–	3.20	µg/kg
23	Vanadium	–	2.00	µg/kg
33	Arsenic	As(V)	1.20	µg/kg
28	Nickel	–	480.00	ng/kg
30	Zinc	–	350.00	ng/kg
36	Krypton	Dissolved gas	310.00	ng/kg
55	Cesium	Cs^+	306.00	ng/kg
24	Chromium	Cr(VI)	210.00	ng/kg

Based on research analysis by Yoshiyuki Nozaki, Ocean Research Institute, University of Tokyo, Japan

Salinity, the concentration of salt in ocean water is often expressed in parts per thousand (ppt), with a lower level characteristic of coastal areas near river mouths but 35 ppt overall for most of the ocean. In some shallow semi-enclosed areas such as Laguna Madre, the 402-kilometer-long "Mother Lagoon" bordering south Texas and northern Mexico, where evaporation exceeds the freshwater input from rain, salinity may exceed 50 ppt. The amount of salt in seawater affects the temperature at which it freezes: minus 2°C for salinity of 35 ppt, minus 1°C at 17 ppt, and so on, in a linear progression.

Sunlight striking the ocean is partly reflected—3 to 30 percent of it, depending on the angle of the beams and the smoothness of the water's surface. Sunlight appears white but is made up of all the colors in a rainbow. The characteristic blue of the open sea is caused by the absorption and scattering of other wavelengths of light, with red the first to disappear. Suspended material in coastal areas often gives the ocean a murky green or brown appearance. Even in the clearest ocean water, 90 percent of red light striking the surface of the ocean is absorbed 9 meters down; by 152 meters, only blue light penetrates—barely one percent of what is available in the uppermost inches. Zoologist William Beebe describes the phenomenon in *Half Mile Down:* "As we descend, there vanish in turn the red, orange, yellow, green, and blue, leaving only the faintest tinge of violet. . . . The eye sees only a blackish-blueness, which darkens until, at 2000 feet, every trace of light disappears."

TIDES AND CURRENTS

WEB LINK: tides and tidal predictions

In response to the tug of the sun and the moon, tides rock most of the ocean twice a day, creating rhythmic cycles of shoreline ebb and flow and generating forces that gnaw away and replenish the coastline within an intertidal area that may span a few centimeters or many meters. The tug of gravity on the ocean from the sun is much greater, but the impact far less because the sun is 400 times as far away as the moon. Tidal heights therefore follow the phases of the moon. When the sun and moon are in a line with the Earth—either in a full moon, when they are on opposite sides of the Earth, or a new moon, when they are on the same side—the combined gravitational pulls yield spring tides, creating the highest high tides and the lowest lows. During the first and third quarters of the moon, when it is at a right angle to the line between the Earth and sun, the gravitational pulls of the sun and moon work in different directions, causing neap tides, when tidal range is the most moderate.

Many other factors influence the tides: the tilt of the Earth on its axis relative to the sun; the changing distance from other planets in their orbits, with their gravitational effects on the ocean; the shape of the shoreline; the topography of the seafloor; and the direction and strength of the winds, locally and globally. Semidiurnal tides—with two high and two low tides each day—are most common around the global ocean, with diurnal tides (only one high and one low each day) occurring in some places.

Opposite, below: *Swirled by the spin of the globe, shaped by landmasses and driven by winds and differences in temperature and salinity, ocean currents constantly move in three dimensions like an enormous conveyor belt.*

Ocean water is in constant motion, driven by winds at the surface and by differences in density in layers below the surface. Water warmed at the Equator moves north and south toward the Poles, deflected by the Earth rotating beneath it, and complicated by contact with landmasses. The density, and thus weight, of seawater increases when cooled or when salt is added; and it decreases when warmed or when salinity is reduced. These properties of seawater are critical in determining the flow of great ocean currents. Lighter than the cold water below, warm currents sweep around the surface of the ocean basins, generally in great circular gyres—clockwise in the Northern Hemisphere, and counterclockwise in the Southern—that influence temperature, weather, and climate. Light winds at the Equator enable a generally westward flow of surface waters, but underneath the surface currents a countercurrent moves in the opposite direction.

Gradually, an understanding has emerged that broad patterns of ocean circulation can be likened to a giant three-dimensional "conveyor belt." Along North America's east coast, water flows north from the Equator through the Gulf of Mexico to the North Atlantic, carried by the powerful Gulf Stream current. The Gulf Stream is one of the world's two primary western boundary currents (the other is the Kuroshio off Japan) that are concentrated against the western shore of their respective oceans by the Earth rotating eastward under them. Most of the Gulf Stream water continues across the Atlantic to warm the British Isles' west coast. But some of it merges with cold outflows from the Arctic. It is further chilled by huge storms in the North Atlantic, where it becomes more dense and sinks to the seafloor. It then flows southward toward Antarctica, where it meets more sinking, frigid water. The dense, cold waters move back north deep within the Atlantic, Pacific, and Indian Oceans, warming and rising to join warmer waters of the Pacific and Atlantic, flowing west along the Equator, and eventually rejoining the Gulf Stream. The journey of a single parcel of water around the globe may take more than a thousand years.

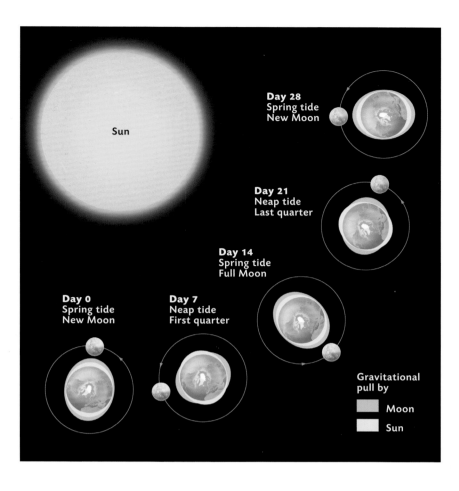

Effects of Gravity: *Tides are caused by gravitational forces from the sun and moon. The highest high (spring) tides occur when the sun and moon are in a line with the Earth and their gravitational pulls are combined. When they are at right angles to Earth, partially cancelling out their gravitational pulls, the lowest high (neap) tides occur.*

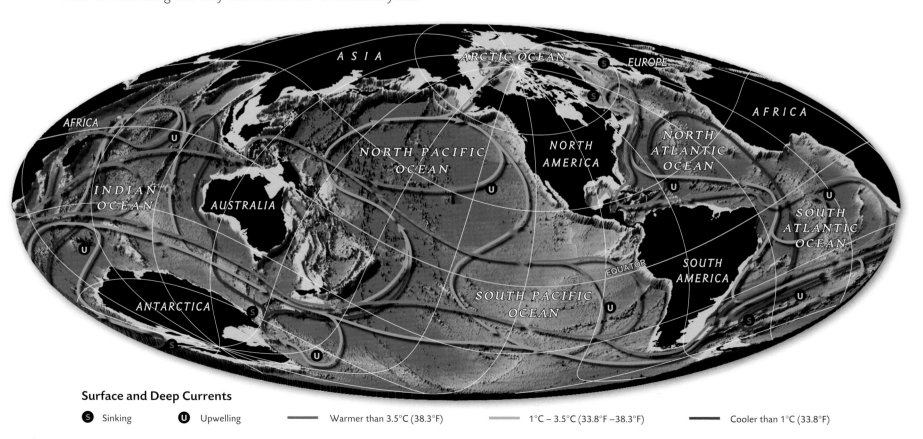

Surface and Deep Currents

S Sinking **U** Upwelling — Warmer than 3.5°C (38.3°F) — 1°C – 3.5°C (33.8°F –38.3°F) — Cooler than 1°C (33.8°F)

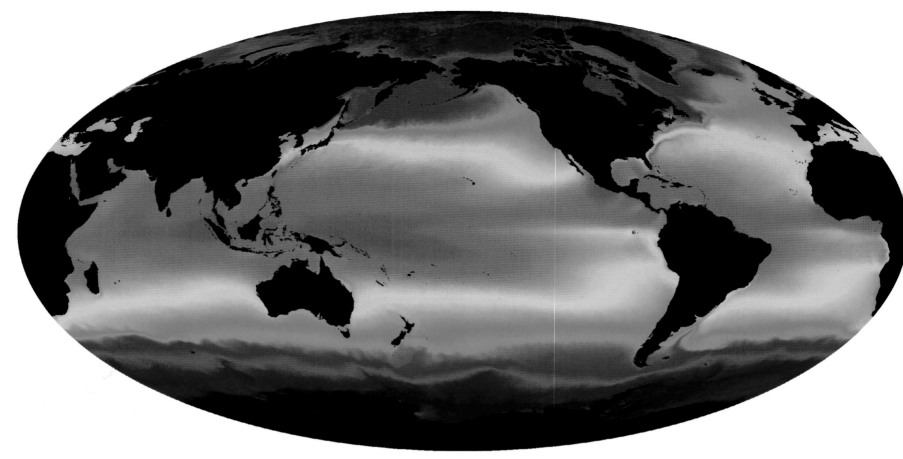

Average Sea-surface Temperature

Above: *Warmest surface waters occur in the tropics, which receive the most sun. Near the Poles, sunlight hits the Earth less directly, so surface waters are cooler. Stretched and pulled by ocean currents, temperature patterns reflect more than just warming from the sun. For instance, two of the great gyres of the Pacific Ocean can be seen bringing cooler waters toward the Equator along the west coast of the Americas. The Gulf Stream is also visible as an orange jet north of Florida carrying warm waters eastward across the Atlantic.*

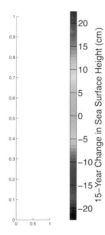

Change in Sea-surface Height

Below: *Since the early 1990s, satellites have monitored the ever-changing height of the ocean surface. Areas of the ocean highlighted in red have risen by as much as 20 centimeters during the satellite record. In the blue regions, such as the eastern Pacific, sea levels have dropped, despite the addition of water from melting land-ice and a global rise in sea level. These patterns are caused by decade-long changes in ocean currents.*

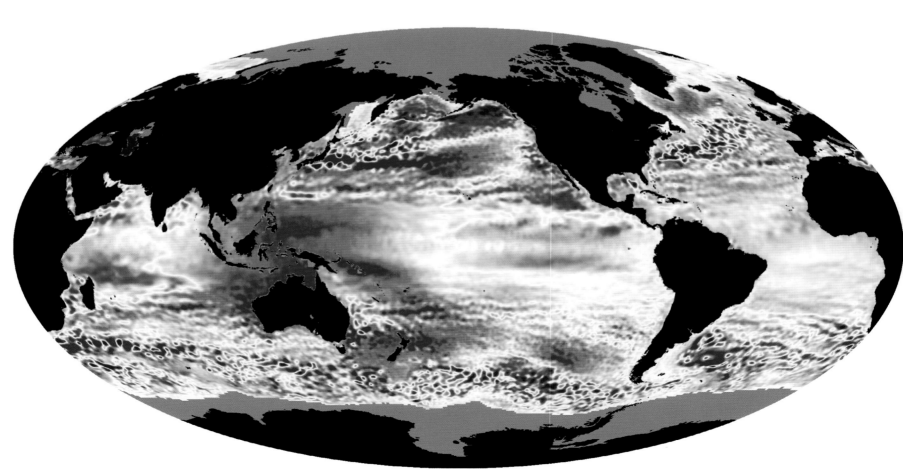

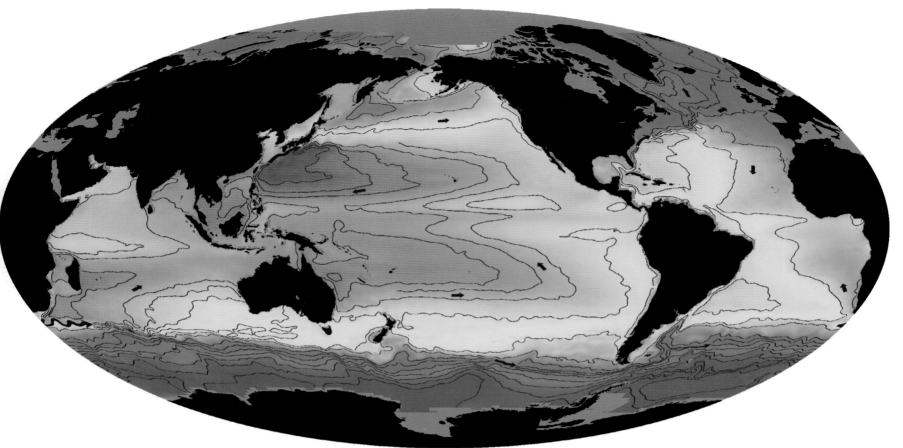

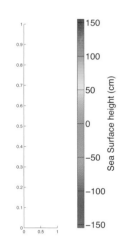

Average Sea-surface Height

Above: The height of the sea surface shows the ocean's major current systems. Water flows along the lines of constant sea-surface height (drawn in gray) and in the direction of the arrows. The red patches show the great subtropical gyres of the Pacific Ocean, spinning counter-clockwise in the Northern Hemisphere and clockwise in the Southern. Tightly bunched lines show fast-moving currents such as the Gulf Stream, along the east coast of the United States, and the Antarctic Circumpolar Current, which circles the world around Antarctica.

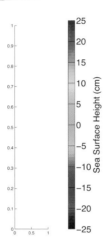

Ocean Eddies

Below: Swirling currents called eddies fill the ocean. Shown here in a map of sea-surface height with other effects filtered out, eddies help to stir and mix the ocean, bringing nutrients to the surface and allowing phytoplankton to bloom. The fastest-spinning eddies, in red or purple, are associated with the fastest-flowing ocean currents such as the Gulf Stream, the Kuroshio (off the coast of Japan), and the Antarctic Circumpolar Current.

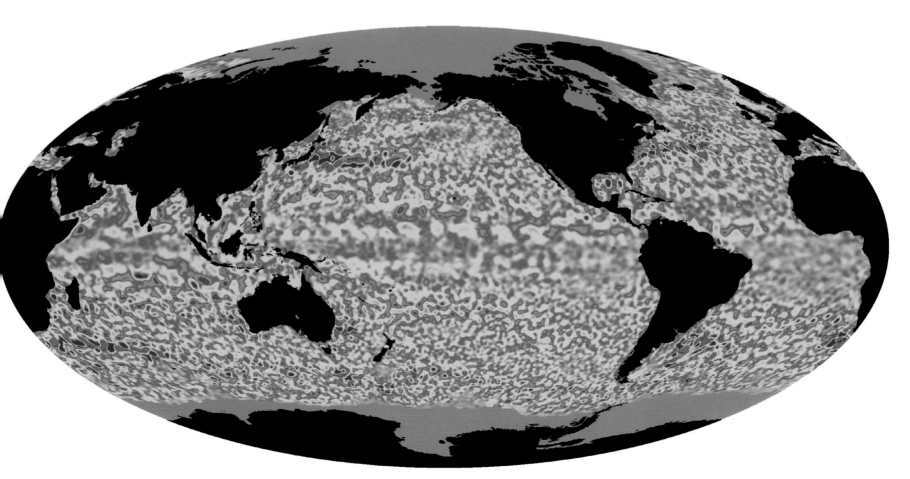

Atlantic Ocean Temperature Transect

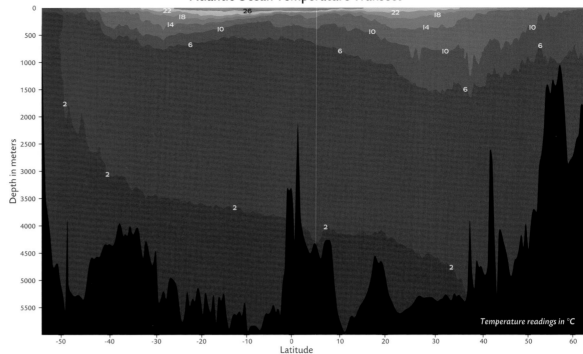

Temperature readings in °C

Pacific Ocean Temperature Transect

Temperature vs. Depth: *These three north-south slices of temperature from the Pacific, Atlantic, and Indian Oceans show the sharp change in temperature vertically, which is known as the thermocline. The thermocline is strongest near the Equator and weakest in the high latitudes. Lines of constant temperature, or isotherms, reach the surface at various latitudes, indicating where each isotherm is exposed to the atmosphere. The deepest, coldest waters of the ocean are largely formed in the far North Atlantic in the Norwegian-Greenland Sea, and at the southern end of the slices around the Antarctic continent in the Southern Ocean.*

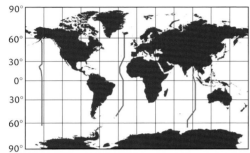

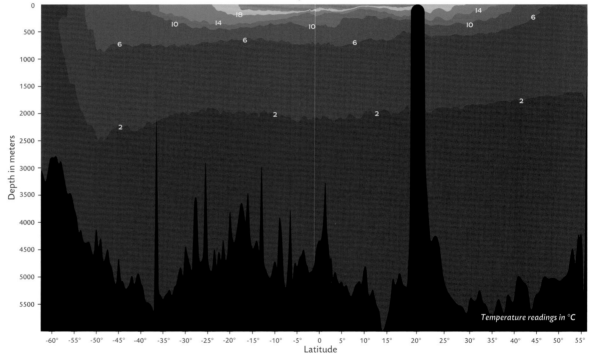

Temperature readings in °C

Indian Ocean Temperature Transect

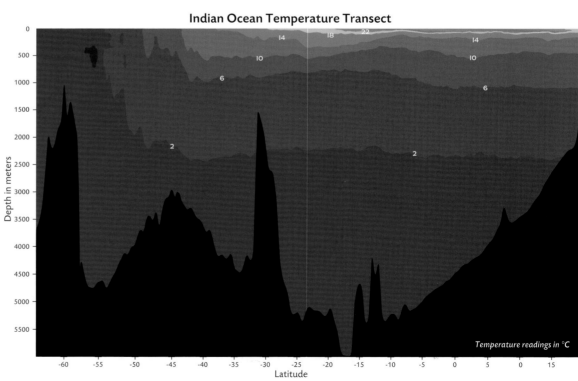

Temperature readings in °C

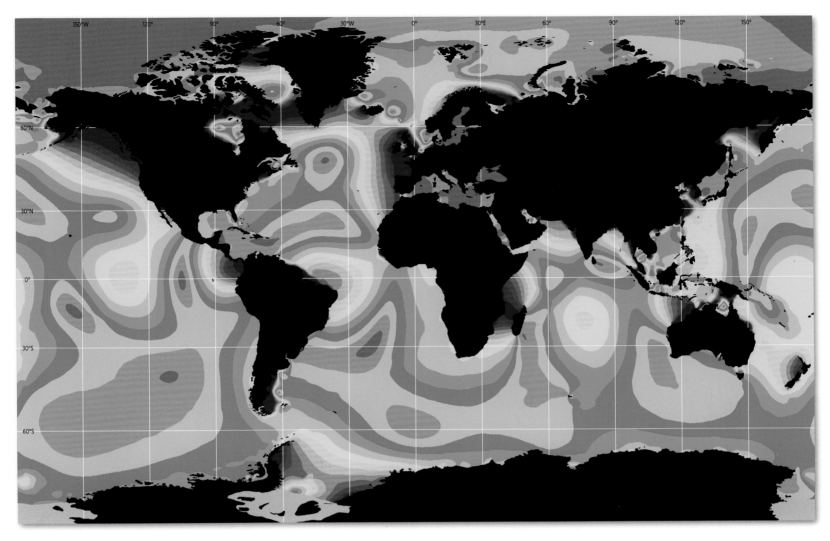

The global system of currents is still not fully understood. The existence of a previously unknown large, deep current was discovered in 2007. It flows south down the eastern coast of Australia, around the island of Tasmania, and moves west past Australia's southern coast, at a depth of about 800 to 1,000 meters, into the Indian Ocean. K. R. Ridgway and J. R. Dunn from Australia's Commonwealth Scientific and Industrial Research Organization (CSIRO) identified the current—which they named the Tasman Outflow—based on an analysis of data collected over 50 years from satellites, ships, and ocean monitoring stations. This flow connects the mid-depth waters of the Pacific, Indian, and Atlantic Oceans and provides a critical missing link in understanding the global conveyor belt that carries ocean currents—and heat—around the world ocean. On a grand scale, the ocean has a tremendous capacity to gather, hold, and move heat from the sun as well as heat generated from volcanic action deep within the sea. The ocean, therefore, serves as a built-in temperature regulator, stabilizing and maintaining temperature within a range congenial to life on Earth.

WINDS AND WAVES

The Earth's basic wind patterns develop primarily because of the powerful but uneven heating by the sun, which strikes more directly at the Equator than along the curved surfaces to the north and south. Nearly 65 percent of the sunlight that hits the surface of the ocean is absorbed in the first meter, resulting in warming of only the topmost waters. Much of the heat is retained in the water, but some is transferred to the air; then it does what warm air always does—it rises. The heated, rising air moves toward the Poles, where it cools, sinks, and returns to the Equator. This global convection would occur in fairly simple circular patterns if it weren't for the rotation of the Earth beneath the winds and the effect of mountain ranges and other features on the land.

Winds blowing across the ocean are the primary source of energy powering waves. Generally speaking, the stronger the winds, the higher the waves. Another factor is the fetch, or the distance the winds and waves travel unimpeded by land. Between about 60° S and 69° S latitude, "the screaming sixties," infamous high winds swoop around the globe unimpeded by continents and give rise to equally notorious wave action. High winds are also characteristic of comparable latitudes in northern

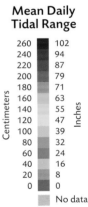

Mean Daily Tidal Range

Centimeters	Inches
260	102
240	94
220	87
200	79
180	71
160	63
140	55
120	47
100	39
80	32
60	24
40	16
20	8
0	0

No data

Tides are largely governed by the combined tug of gravity from the sun and the moon, but are influenced by winds and geography, as shown on this map based on TOPEX/POSEIDON satellite data. The arrangement of landmasses in the northern hemisphere yields more areas of greater tidal range and variability.

seas, but are more complex because of interactions with landmasses. A single wave can travel thousands of kilometers, with individual particles of water moving in a gentle, circular pattern at each site as the wave of energy passes through. Giant waves, known as rogue waves, form from the convergence of several smaller ones, yielding a colossal open-ocean wave sometimes more than 50 meters tall.

Winds are not the cause, however, of tsunamis, the so-called tidal waves notorious for surprising coastal inhabitants with sudden, huge walls of water that sometimes cause incredible damage and loss of life. An underwater earthquake, landslide, or volcanic eruption that creates a vertical movement in the seafloor—or a meteorite or other large object striking the ocean surface—causes a vertical disturbance at the ocean surface. As the raised water drops back again, the energy moves away from the source in all directions as a tsunami, a series of low, very long, fast-moving waves that are virtually imperceptible at sea as they pass by. But after traveling hundreds, even thousands of kilometers from the source, the waves can swiftly achieve frightening size and power upon contact with a shallow slope.

WEB LINK: tsunami research

storm

wind

wash zone

water particle circulation

breaking wave

Winds Make Waves: *The stronger the winds, the higher the waves. But fetch, the distance waves travel unimpeded, is also a factor. As the bottom becomes shallow near a land mass, individual waves grow steeper until they peak, break, and wash back under oncoming waves. A long fetch backed by strong winds coupled with a steep slope yield the enormous waves beloved by surfers.*

Opposite: *Sky, sea, and earth converge on a living reef at Indonesia's Bunaken Island, Mana Tua Marine National Park, a place that retains the distillation of billions of years of history within an ocean from which much has been lost in the past century.*

The Ocean and Life

Nutrients are transported within living cells by water, and water transports wastes away. All biochemical reactions—the chemistry of life—take place in water. Other characteristics of water critical for life relate to temperature. Water has a high boiling point—100°C—and a low freezing point—0°C. Maintaining water in its liquid state is vital for living cells, given that most creatures—large and small, land or ocean—are composed of 60 percent to more than 90 percent water.

A professor of botany at Duke University sometimes began lectures by asking, "Have you thanked a green plant today?"—his way of reminding students that green plants are Earth's primary energy engine, generating life-sustaining food and oxygen. Within living cells, energy from the sun is transformed by photosynthesis—a process of combining water and carbon dioxide in the presence of chlorophyll into oxygen and simple sugar. Some might ask: "Have you thanked the plankton today?" since most of the photosynthesis on Earth actually occurs through tiny organisms drifting in the surface waters of the ocean.

The basic constituents that make up seawater do not, by themselves, account for the ocean's chemistry—or even for its physical nature. The sea, after all, is a living "minestrone," home to small, medium, and sometimes very large creatures, each one a microcosm of chemicals acting on the surrounding sea. In short, the ocean is not only filled *with* life; its very nature is shaped *by* life. □

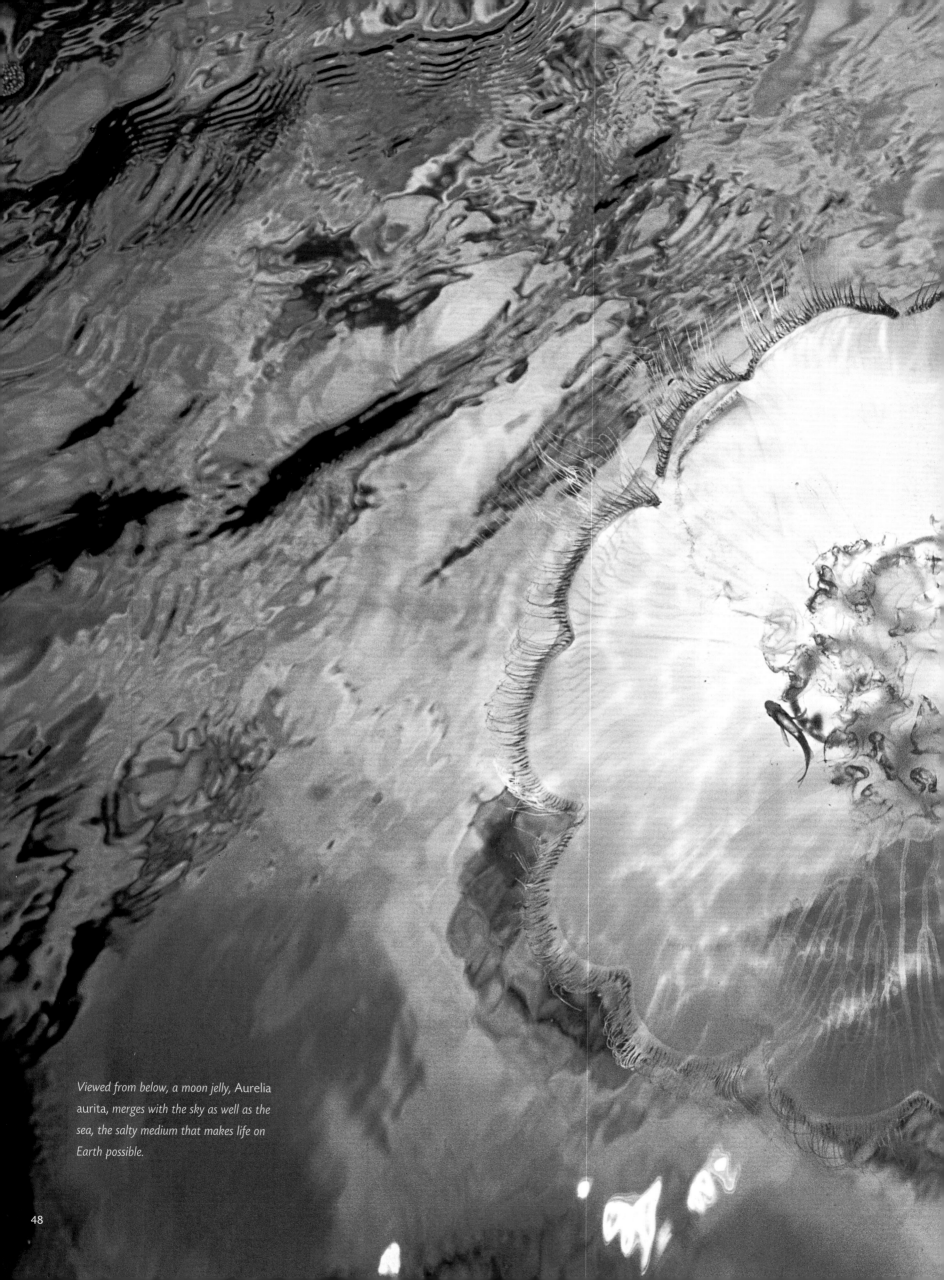

Viewed from below, a moon jelly, Aurelia
aurita, merges with the sky as well as the
sea, the salty medium that makes life on
Earth possible.

Chapter 2

OCEAN LIFE

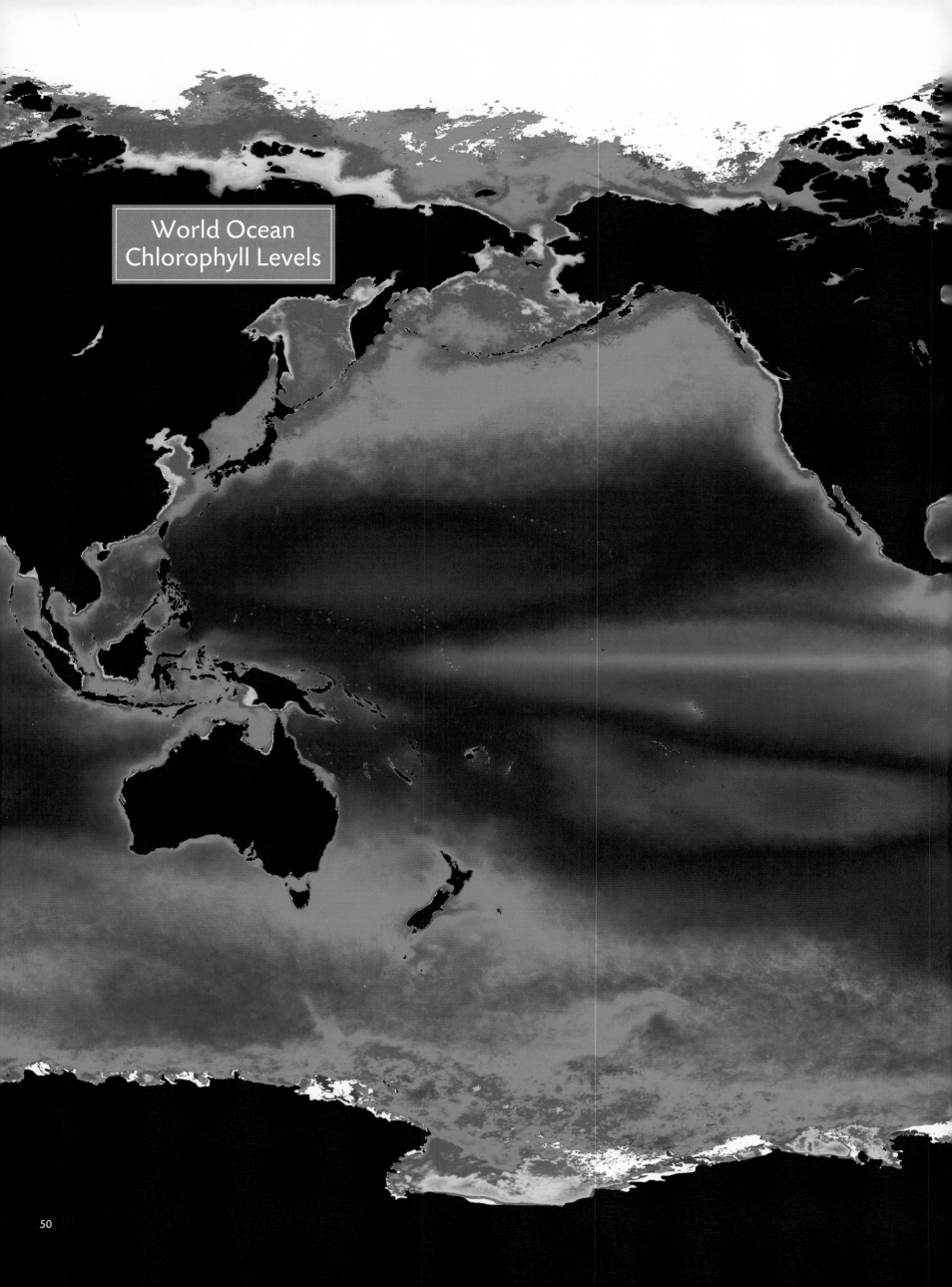

World Ocean
Chlorophyll Levels

Chlorophyll

0.01 0.03 0.1 0.3 1 3 10 30 60
(milligrams per cubic meter)

51

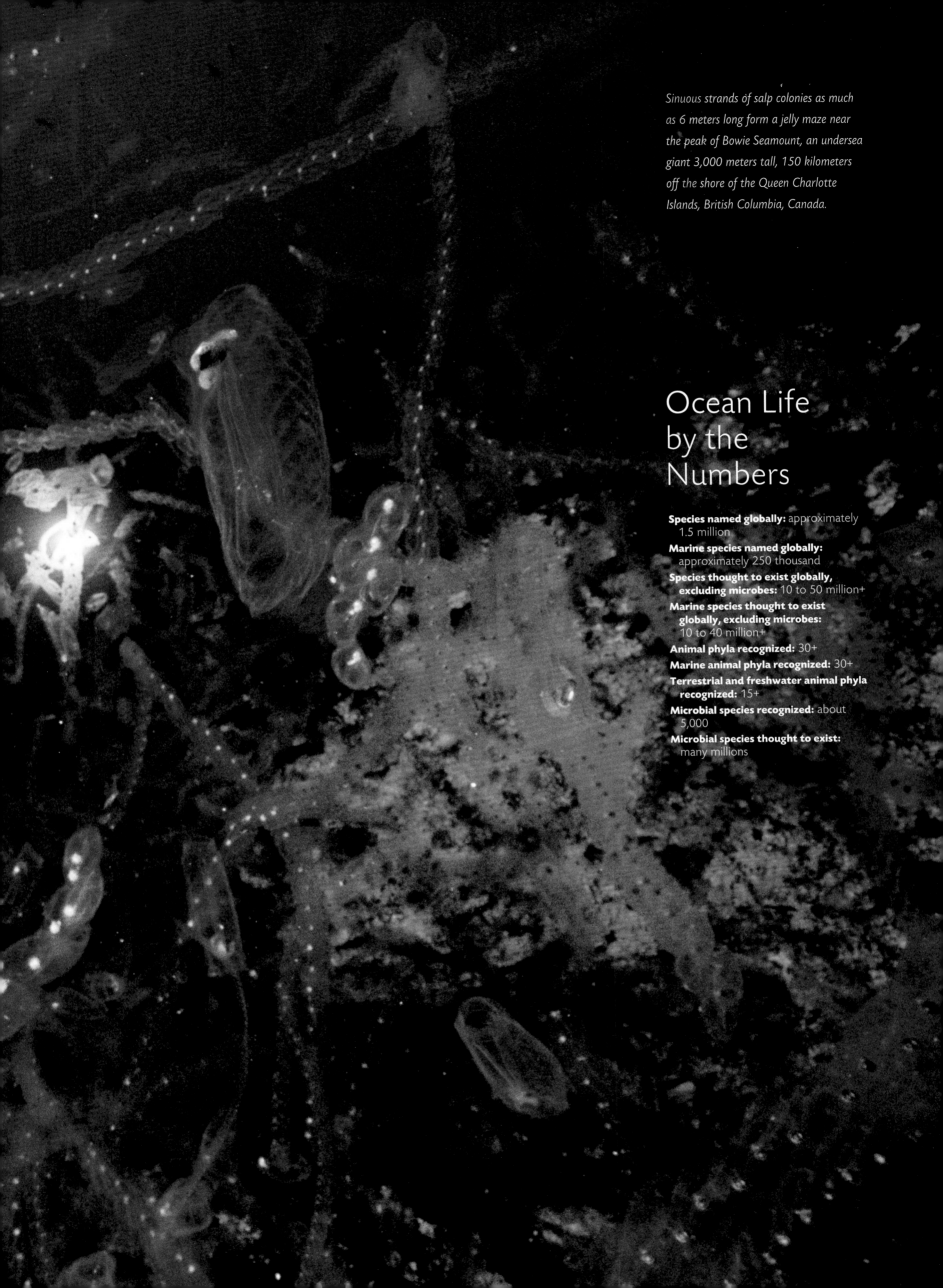

Ocean Life
by the
Numbers

Species named globally: approximately
1.5 million

Marine species named globally:
approximately 250 thousand

**Species thought to exist globally,
excluding microbes:** 10 to 50 million+

**Marine species thought to exist
globally, excluding microbes:**
10 to 40 million+

Animal phyla recognized: 30+

Marine animal phyla recognized: 30+

**Terrestrial and freshwater animal phyla
recognized:** 15+

Microbial species recognized: about
5,000

Microbial species thought to exist:
many millions

"In 2001 . . . I took my first dive into the deep. . . . Fabulous creatures . . . undulated with infinite grace, producing iridescent sparkles. Strange animals without head or tail twisted and unwound, like fluid ribbons in some sensuous sort of dance. . . . How is it possible that the Earth bears such marvels and that people don't even know about them?"

—Claire Nouvian, *The Deep*

W

hen Jacques Piccard and Don Walsh peered out of the tiny porthole of the bathyscaphe *Trieste* in the deepest part of the ocean, nearly 11 kilometers down, they saw something totally unexpected—eyes looking back. As they descended, Walsh noted flashes of bioluminescent light from thousands of small creatures, and as the submersible neared the seafloor, a red shrimp came into view. Piccard wrote in *Seven Miles Down* that, once settled at the deepest point in the sea, "I saw a wonderful thing. Lying on the bottom just beneath us was some type of flatfish, resembling a sole, about 1 foot long and 6 inches across. Even as I saw him, his two round eyes on top of his head spied us. . . . Here, in an instant, was the answer [to the question] that biologists had asked for decades. Could life exist in the greatest depths of the ocean? It could!"

C. Wyville Thomson wrote in 1874 in *The Depths of the Sea* of the popular notion that beyond a certain depth there was "a waste of utter darkness, subjected to such stupendous pressure as to make life of any kind impossible." Thomson personally helped dispel this idea during various expeditions throughout the world, but it has taken more than a century of exploration to set the record straight: The ocean is alive, harboring the greatest abundance and diversity of life in the world—or in the universe, as far as anyone knows.

No terrestrial or freshwater system compares with the magnitude and complexity of the communities of life that are embraced by the ocean, especially the vast realm of plankton, mostly small creatures living their entire life cycles suspended mid-water while being moved by waves, tides, and currents. Airborne pollen, seeds, and many insects and spiders can be regarded as the "plankton of the skies," but the majority of life on the land is more two-dimensional, adhering to or flying from point to point over the land—not thriving midair. Large animals such as the great whales, leatherback sea turtles, and giant jellies are buoyed by the liquid surrounding them, as are even the smallest microbes, the sleekest eels, the fastest tunas. The existence of abundant drifting life in the sea has allowed organisms that, as adults, do not move around much—corals, clams, oysters, sponges, barnacles, brachiopods, bryozoans, crinoids, basket starfish, and many more—to prosper as filter feeders. There is no real counterpart on the land for this widespread means of making a living in the ocean, except, perhaps, spiders snaring windborne insects.

The structure, lifestyles, life histories, even the size and shape of organisms that live in the sea, are influenced by the fundamental characteristics of ocean water, a substance that is 830 times as dense as air and 60 times more viscous. Sound travels 4 times faster than in air, the electrical resistivity is 10 ohms greater underwater than above, and light is much more strongly absorbed by water than by air—all features that affect the nature and distribution of life in the sea.

Pages 50-51: This global ocean image was created from data collected between July 2002 and February 2008 by the Moderate Resolution Imaging Spectroradiometer (MODIS) sensor on NASA's Aqua satellite that is focused on Earth's water. It shows the average chlorophyll concentrations in ocean surface waters over that time period. The chlorophyll reflects the distribution of biomass from phytoplankton. Each regional ocean chapter opens with an Aqua-MODIS image, reflecting the distribution of life in the surface waters of each ocean basin.

Opposite: A young swell shark begins life within its translucent leathery case. The attached yolk sac will shrink as the shark grows.

Zonation of Life in the Sea

Since the ocean is a three-dimensional realm, zonation can be viewed both laterally and vertically. Broad zones based on surface temperature are familiar as polar, cold temperate, temperate,

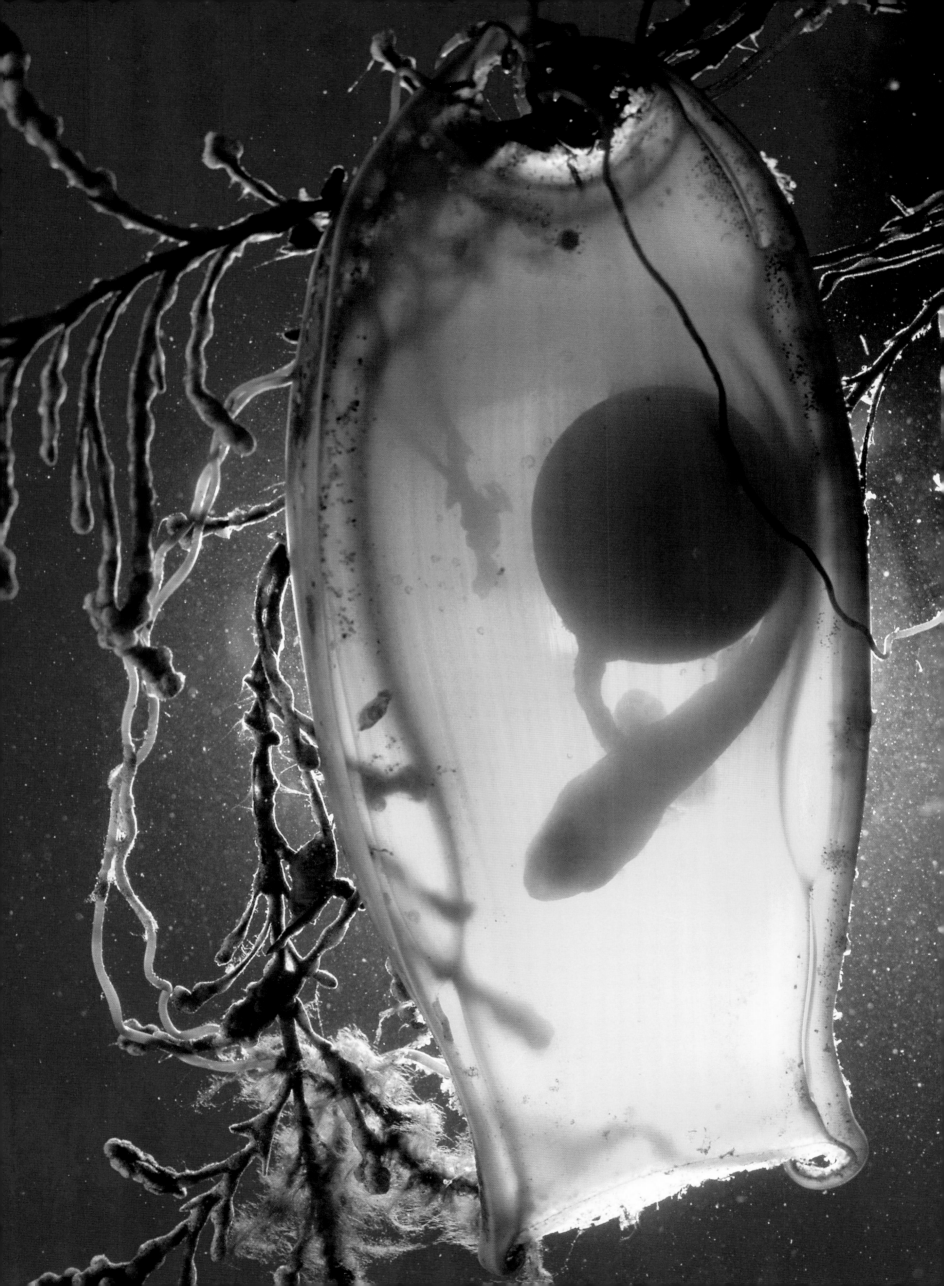

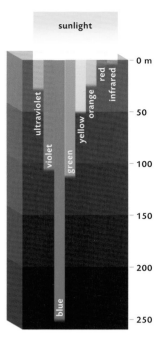

sunlight

Light Penetration: *In clear ocean water, the quality as well as the quantity of sunlight penetration diminishes with depth, with red, orange and yellow absorbed in the upper few meters and blue reaching beyond 250 meters.*

tropical, subtropical, warm temperate, and so on. In coastal and surface waters, these terms are appropriate, but below 300 meters or so, most of the ocean is cold and dark. Creatures living in near-freezing deep water in equatorial seas have more in common with animals living thousands of kilometers away in darkness under polar ice than they do with those living in warm, sunlit coral reefs a few thousand meters above.

Waters overlying continental shelves are known as neritic, while the open sea beyond generally is regarded as the pelagic realm, a habitat for creatures such as tunas, oceanic white-tipped sharks, and sea turtles. Those living on or in substrates—whether along coasts, at the sides of seamounts, or across the bottom of the ocean—are benthic organisms, at least as adults. Corals, sponges, clams, burrowing worms, encrusting algae, starfish, and many others are bottom dwellers as adults, but as larvae may spend days, weeks, or months as pelagic plankton. A few, such as certain jellyfish, are benthic in their early stages of development but launch into the open sea as adults.

The benthic zone in the region underlying the neritic area of the continental shelf is the sublittoral or shelf area, a generally sunlit region populated by diverse communities of sea grass meadows, kelp forests, and coral reefs systems dependent on light and an appropriate substrate to grow on. The region from the edge of the shelf and shelf slope to 4,000 meters is the bathyal zone, leading to the broad abyssal zone, or abyssal plains, the enormous portion of the seafloor at a depth of between 4,000 and 6,000 meters. The bottoms of deep trenches beyond are in the hadal zone.

Light penetration provides a way to view zonation vertically. The photic or euphotic zone is defined by the part of the water column that is illuminated by sunlight. The full spectrum of light strikes the ocean's atmospheric cocoon, each photon having traveled 150 million kilometers from the sun, with a much smaller amount arriving from distant stars. Some is reflected back into space or absorbed by various gases, water vapor, clouds, dust, pollen, soot, and other ingredients that make up air. Whatever actually reaches the sea surface is then so effectively absorbed that barely one percent penetrates to a depth of 100 meters, even in the clearest, calmest ocean. At 600 meters, illumination is equivalent to faint starlight; at 693 meters, the

Zones in the Ocean: *This stylized vertical perspective of the ocean indicates the major depth zones.*

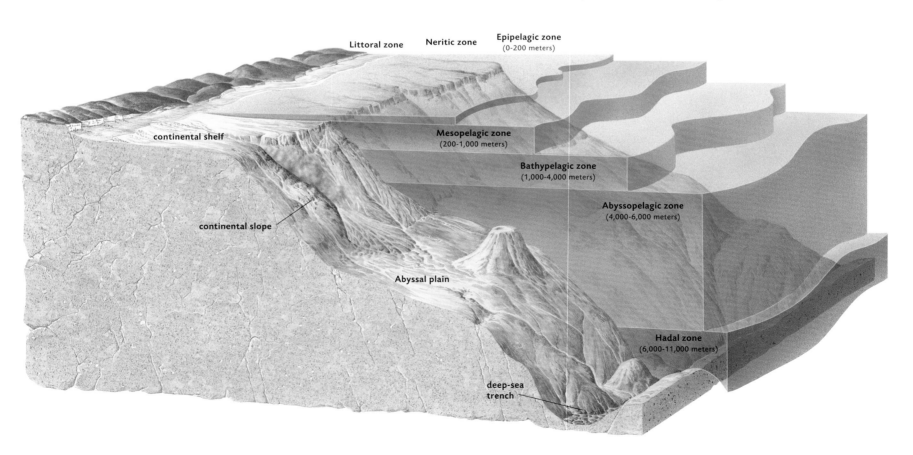

intensity is approximately one ten-billionth of that at the surface; and below 1,000 meters, there is darkness, the aphotic zone, illuminated only by bioluminescence and, around hydrothermal vents, the faint glow of thermolumination.

Aptly named, jewel fairy basslets, Pseudanthius, brighten a Red Sea reef.

The exact place in the ocean where sunlight fades and darkness begins depends on the time of day, the season, the weather, surface roughness, and water clarity. In some murky coastal waters, light barely penetrates more than a meter or so, but in the open sea, the area of almost-light almost-dark, the twilight zone, starts about 200 meters down. Another term applied to this region is mesopelagic. In the tropics, the lower boundary is regarded as the 10°C isotherm, extending down to about 1,000 meters. In this region the largest migrations of animals on the planet take place at dusk every night as billions of deep-dwelling fish (such as lantern fish, hatchet fish, and cyclothones), squids, small crustacea, swimming mollusks, jellies, arrow worms, and many more travel from the edge of darkness to feed in the nutrient-rich waters hundreds of meters above; at dawn, they return to the depths.

Below the mesopelagic zone is the bathypelagic, roughly 1,000 meters to 4,000 meters, within a temperature range of 10°C and 4°C. A vast portion of the seafloor below the open ocean encompasses depths between 4,000 and 6,000 meters, the abyssopelagic zone. Deeper still, between 6,000 meters and the ocean's maximum depth in deep trenches to more than 10,000 meters, is the hadal zone.

PHOTOSYNTHESIS

The great ocean food webs begin with photosynthesis, a process involving chlorophyll-bearing bacteria, protists, and plants that use the sun's energy through conversion of carbon dioxide and water into simple sugar and oxygen. Estimates vary, but well over half—perhaps as much as 70 percent—of the oxygen in the atmosphere is generated by photosynthetic organisms that mostly occupy the relatively well-illuminated upper 10 to 30 meters or so of the ocean. Two decades ago, a previously unknown

It's Nearly Freezing in the Tropics

Tropical areas are known for warm waters that support beautiful, abundant coral reefs. But tropical waters are warm only in their shallow surface layers. Most tropical islands are volcanic in origin, and drop off sharply into very deep water a short distance from shore. Below about 1,000 meters seawater is less than 10°C, and below 4,000 meters it is less than 4°C, nearly freezing, everywhere in the world ocean.

SEE ALSO: photosynthesis, page 160

Lynn Margulis and Dorion Sagan
MARINE MICROBES MOVE MOUNTAINS

As the Dutch microscopist Antoni van Leeuwenhoek, the German naturalist Christian Ehrenberg, and the French chemist Louis Pasteur proved, life is almost everywhere on the surface of the Earth. This is nowhere more the case than in the world's ocean, where bacteria and more complex cells (those with nuclei and mitochondria in them, such as ours) derive food from the sun, grow, and are essential to the biosphere's great biogeochemical cycles: the necessary flow of carbon, nitrogen, and sulfur through the water and atmosphere.

Emblematic of the contribution of microbial life to the oceans is the role of one of these sorts of ocean-going nucleated cells, *Emiliana huxleyi*, a microscopic species of hard-shelled algae coated in elaborate button-shaped scales known as coccoliths. Although individual *E. huxleyi* are invisible to the naked eye, they grow in blooms so vast that they are clearly visible from space by satellite. Moreover, en masse, they fall to the sea bottom and contribute to rich calcium deposits such as the famous ones on the coast of Britain known as the White Cliffs of Dover. A gaseous compound normally emitted by these prevalent plankton (they are also a kind of plankton, which refers to any tiny floating sea creatures), dimethyl sulfide, is commercially added to orange juice for flavor and is even considered to be (along with algae pheromones) what makes the sea smell like the sea.

But the importance of this algae—it is also a form of algae, because it grows photosynthetically, despite its tiny skeletons (theorized to behave as tiny venetian blinds that adjust levels of sunlight reaching the organism's chloroplasts)—does not end here. The same dimethyl sulfide wafting over the ocean where *E. huxleyi* grows serves, after some chemical reactions, as cloud condensation nuclei for raindrops forming in the atmosphere. Many marine clouds, in other words, which have a global effect on cooling because their white surface reflects light back to space, owe their existence to the microbial life growing beneath them. This may, therefore, have a regulatory function, since their growth leads to more clouds, which can lead to cooling of the ocean to temperatures that then curtail that growth. Moreover, because sulfur is part of the essential chemical matrix—in terms of percentage mostly carbon, hydrogen, nitrogen, oxygen, phosphorus, and sulfur—of all life on the planet, the marine machinations

Communities of bacteria laced with oxidized iron drip like icicles from the metal framework of the sunken German ship Herman Kunne *off the coast of Norway.*

of *E. huxleyi* are implicated in the global availability and circulation of this life-sustaining element.

The space limits of this atlas preclude an exhaustive survey of the contribution of microbes in the ocean to the diversity and activities of global life, but recall that *E. huxleyi* is only one of an estimated 30 million species on this planet, the surface of which is mostly ocean. Marine microbes include single-celled *Prochloron* bacteria whose ancestor cousins became symbiotically involved with other cells to form eukaryotes that evolved into the vast forests of plant life on the land. They extend to archaean extremophiles (bacteria with distinct RNA, many of which are able to grow at extreme temperatures and under intense pressures) and chemolithotrophs (microorganisms that do not require food or light, but grow directly on chemical reactions such as found when hydrogen-rich gases bubbling from the dark abyss interact with oxygen from the sunlit surface). Deep-sea bacteria form the basis of subsea "octopus garden" ecosystems around heat vents. Discovered only in 1977, they are now investigated in part for their role as a possible model for life's marine origins. Archaean extremophiles and chemolithotrophs have also taken over the famous *Titanic* shipwreck, upon whose hull they grow by tapping into the electron flow between adjacent metals, which they have transformed into slow-growing iron-containing "rusticles."

The importance of microbial ocean life to life on Earth as a whole can hardly be overestimated. Stromatolites—strange, domed rocks that inhabit remote seaside regions in various places around the world, and that have been left as remains by many species of cyanobacteria growing on top of each other—are among the world's oldest fossils. Not observed elsewhere in our solar system, the process of tectonism, by which the great continental plates slowly move and occasionally crash into each other, leading to outbursts such as the Himalayan mountain range, may be due to marine microbes. This is because the continental plates float on calcium carbonate, much of it from vast collections of subocean microbial skeletons, the carbon of which would originally have been in the atmosphere as carbon dioxide (which still forms more than 90 percent of the atmospheres of Mars and Venus). Ocean microbes may thus literally be able to move mountains.

kind of extremely small cyanobacteria, prochlorococcus, was found to be one of the most abundant forms of life in the sea. Prochlorococcus provides food for minute grazers and is thought to generate the oxygen of one in five breaths taken by people globally. Assemblages of macroscopic algae armed with special light absorbing pigments occur in depths of greater than 100 meters, and crustose red algae prosper at 268 meters, where light is about 0.0005 percent of full-surface sunlight.

The quantity of light penetrating the sea is a major factor in determining ocean productivity, but so is the quality. The amount of light filtering through a dense forest on land may be low, but the full spectrum of colors are present. Light shining through ocean water quickly changes, with the long red and yellow wavelengths absorbed in the first meter or so; the shorter wavelengths of green, blue, and violet travel the deepest, yielding an overall atmosphere of blue. It is a sapphire world, where bright red looks gray, yellow appears drab, and silver-blue creatures seem to disappear, blue against blue. The maximum depth where photosynthesis can occur is not yet resolved, but new insight came as a result of a recent discovery made more than 2,000 meters deep at a

SEE ALSO: light penetration in the ocean, pages 56 and 66

hydrothermal vent on the East Pacific Rise more than 2,000 kilometers west of Costa Rica. There, in 350°C water, faint geothermal light appears to trigger a previously unknown kind of photosynthesis involving green sulfur bacteria. While this process contributes little to food production in the sea, it provides clues to the origin of photosynthesis and other aspects of the chemistry of life.

In the year 2000, a discovery near the surface of the sea, right under the noses of generations of seagoing scientists, rocked conventional thinking about how carbon is translated into carbohydrates. A team of biologists from Rutgers University discovered that some bacteria prospering in the upper meter or so of ocean water contain a pigment similar to chlorophyll that makes possible the conversion of light energy to biochemical energy. Another group, led by Ed DeLong of the Monterey Bay Aquarium Research Institute in California, found that some common oceanic bacteria translate light energy to food using pigments called rhodopsins,

A fine carpet of seaweed on the back of a green sea turtle attracts grazing surgeonfish on a Hawaiian reef. Once venturing throughout tropical and warm temperate seas globally, all sea turtle species are presently endangered.

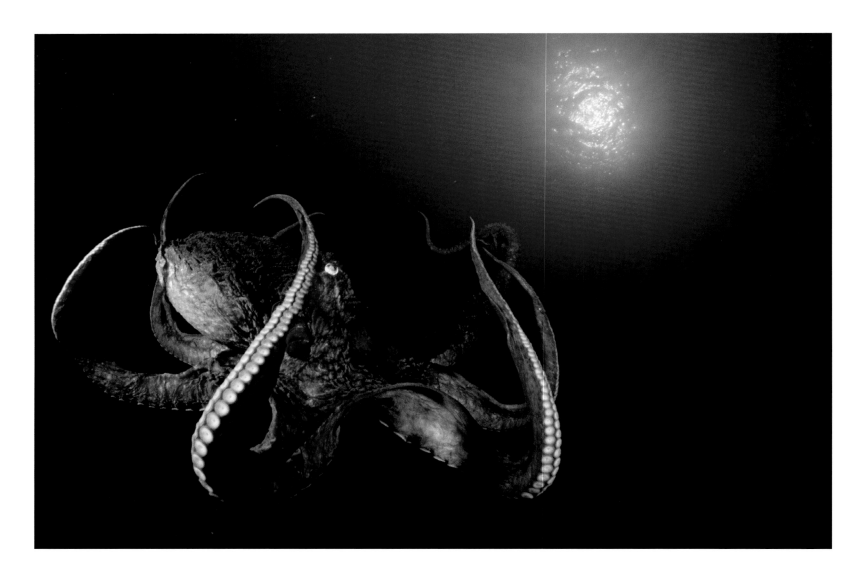

With sweeping grace, a Pacific giant octopus, Octopus dofleini, *lands on the sea floor near Quadra Island, British Columbia, Canada. Known for their engaging curiosity and intelligence, octopuses have been effective ocean predators for hundreds of millions of years.*

SEE ALSO: food chain, pages 240-241

What Life Requires

For centuries, scientists believed ocean life absolutely required sunlight, directly or indirectly. Minute photosynthetic organisms drifting near the surface use sunlight to create simple sugars for food, and life in the deep was assumed sparse because so little of the food settled down into the depths. In 1977, scientists discovered an entirely different basis for ocean life, with microbes making food from chemicals bubbling up through the seafloor. Life does not require sunlight, but it does require water.

a type of photosynthesis that had not been previously detected in the ocean. More than half of Earth's photosynthesis and most of what occurs in the sea is accomplished by very small organisms that live very short lives. The entire mass of floating, photosynthesizing, carbon-grabbing, and oxygen-producing phytoplankton turns over every few days, its biomass transformed into millions of small, medium, and very large animals, then renewed. Legions of minute grazers—copepods, krill, planktonic larvae of crabs, clams, and many others—convert food produced by phytoplankton into animal biomass. As herbivores, they are to the sea what rabbits, mice, deer, antelope, and other grazers are to the land.

Jellyfish, whales, whale sharks, sponges, corals, fish, and numerous other zooplankton consumers are the ocean equivalent of terrestrial animals that feed upon grazers: They are the lions, tigers, and wolves of the sea. Most fish, marine mammals, and seabirds are carnivores that, in turn, have eaten other carnivores and, therefore, are higher in the food chain than most land predators. In the fish-eat-fish ocean realm, there may be dozens of steps between photosynthesis and the mackerel that is eaten by an orca, tuna, shark, or human. It may take thousands of kilograms of plankton and small fish invested over a period of five or six years to make a single kilogram of swordfish, halibut, or cod. The older the animal, the greater the investment. Many top predators mature slowly and live for decades.

Phytoplankton that escapes being eaten in surface waters gradually sinks, much of it becoming tangled in skeletons shed by small crustaceans, fragments of jellyfish, fecal pellets, bacteria, mucus, dust, and other debris and forming an organic blizzard of marine "snow," each flake measured in millimeters. Individual cells sink slowly but descend faster when clinging together or snared in the gelatinous webs of larvaceans, globally abundant planktonic relatives of sea squirts. Clusters of sinking organic material are significant food sources for creatures living in the water column, as well as for those that occupy the deep seafloor far below.

CHEMOSYNTHESIS

Like photosynthesis, chemosynthesis is a process whereby organic carbon compounds—carbohydrates—are generated from simple chemical ingredients. Photosynthesis requires light, whereas

chemosynthesis most often takes place in the dark—in forest soils, in salt marsh mud, and in the deep sea. Scientists diving on the Galápagos Rift in 1977 were perplexed about the source of sustenance for richly populated communities of previously unknown creatures thriving around hydrothermal vents 2,000 meters deep. Chemosynthesis proved to be the key. Sulfur-consuming bacteria utilize hydrogen sulfide, a substance common around hydrothermal vents and, in so doing, produce carbohydrates sufficient for their growth, with enough spin-off to power huge, complex ecosystems. Many of the bacteria live within the tissues of host organisms such as clams and tube worms, which in turn are consumed by carnivorous fish and crabs.

Heat was thought to be essential for supporting the abundant life associated with hydrothermal vents until similar forms were found around cold seeps of methane gas bubbling up from the seafloor in the Gulf of Mexico. Energy-rich fluids and gas flow into the ocean there and are acted on by microbes that in turn power fields of slender, long-lived tube worms, masses of mussels and clams, pale white crabs, brilliant red starfish, and numerous other species. Methane-consuming bacteria perform comparable chemosynthetic action in the vast areas of the ocean harboring gas hydrates—masses of ice and methane that form in the sea at low temperature and high pressure.

Another recent discovery made by geophysicists is that about 20 percent of the top 600 meters of rock may have spaces filled with water. Marine scientist Paul Johnson suggests that "every single place where there's water, space, and temperature below 100°C, you've got life." Johnson is among those who believe that more life—all of it microbial—is sustained within the fractured rock beneath the seafloor than in the enormous volume of water above—jellyfish, whales, and all. Such organisms

Unmindful of its family ties with snails, slugs, clams, and squid, this minute nudibranch glides over an Indonesian reef in the western Pacific.

SEE ALSO: Gulf of Mexico, pages 136-139

Sunlight in the sea drives food webs that begin with microscopic phytoplankton. They are consumed by minute zooplankton that in turn are consumed by small fish and other organisms. It takes tons of fast-growing phytoplankton to eventually make a pound of a top ocean predator such as this Galápagos shark, Carcharhinus galapagensis, *eyeing lunch.*

J. Frederick Grassle and Edward Vanden Berghe
CENSUS OF MARINE LIFE 2010

Scientists all over the world are busy working to produce a census of marine life by 2010 to assess and explain the diversity, distribution, and abundance of marine life in the oceans past, present, and future. In more than 80 nations, they are discovering information on organisms of all sizes and shapes, living in all environments, from the tropics to the Poles, and from the coasts to the deepest parts of the ocean. Most of the effort defines the present. Teams of scientists worldwide are measuring the diversity and abundance of life from six ocean realms: human edges (near-shore and coastal areas most accessible to humans), hidden boundaries (deep continental margins and abyssal plains), central waters (the realm of whales and the top oceanic predators, divided on the bottom by 64,000 kilometers of deep-ocean ridges), geologically active regions (hydrothermal vents and cold seeps, where life is fueled by chemicals generated by the internal heat of the planet), ice oceans (ice-covered polar regions), and the microscopic ocean (where the viscous properties of seawater are important).

In describing past oceans, historians, biologists, and anthropologists have tracked the long-term records of fishermen and their catches from national fishery records since 1900, and port and customs archives back to about 1850 in several regions. Early fishing activities were gleaned from bones, shells, and scales in sediments and soils. Sources of information range from menu offerings showing cultural preferences for seafood over time and geographical area, to meticulous records of fishing activity kept by coastal monasteries. The future of fish populations is being predicted from statistical analysis of population trends and interactions of species from the best data sets available.

An electronic atlas, the Ocean Biogeographic Information System (OBIS), is keeping track of historical observations and new discoveries. OBIS makes it possible to draw distribution maps for tens of thousands of species, based on information from hundreds of different sources, making the conclusions less dependent on the idiosyncrasies of single species or small data sets. This large database is expected to contain upwards of 20 million records by 2010. Along with the *World Register of Marine Species*, the official globally accepted list of all marine species, and the *Encyclopedia of Life*, an online reference source and database of

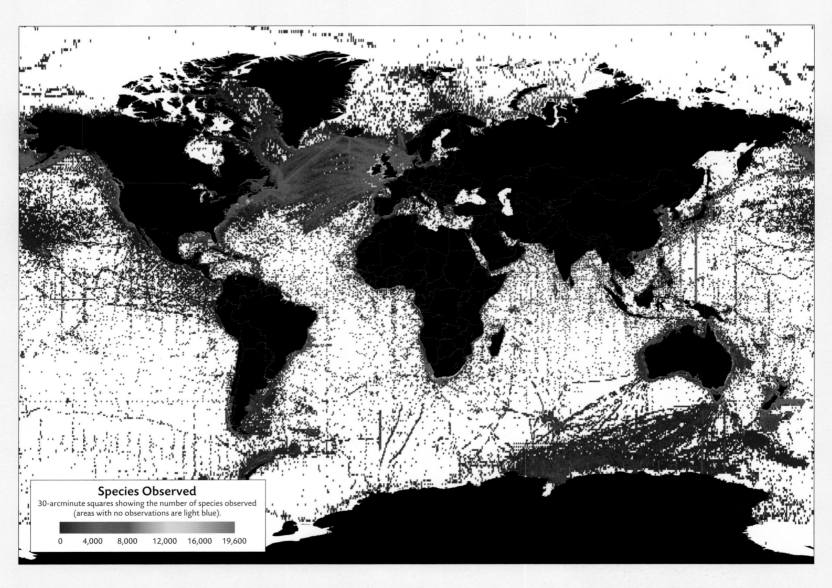

Species Observed
30-arcminute squares showing the number of species observed (areas with no observations are light blue).

0   4,000   8,000   12,000   16,000   19,600

This map of the number of species recorded in the Census of Marine Life database OBIS shows how uneven our knowledge of the oceans is, with vast areas of the ocean without a single record. The 30-minute squares are color-coded, with red indicating the highest number of species and blue the lowest. Background color indicates no data.

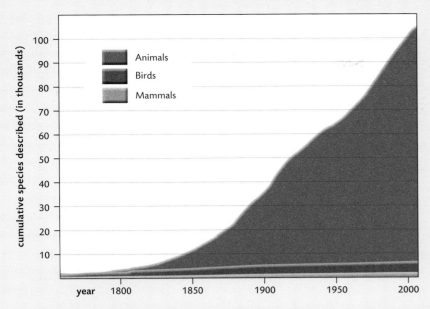

Number of marine species discovered from 1758 to the present. Only for reptiles, birds, and mammals do the curves level off, allowing an estimate of the total number of species. The number of species described in all other groups increases steadily.

OBIS gives these data a second life, by making them useful for global analysis. By 2010, enough information will have been accumulated to estimate marine species diversity within every five-degree square of latitude and longitude.

Describing distribution patterns of a species requires several records for that species, but too often none exist. OBIS currently has observations of about 80,000 species out of an estimated 240,000 named marine species, and scientists are working with marine taxonomists to uncover the rich information sources that are buried in their collections. Data from the census projects are beginning to pour in and are expected to provide information about each of the known marine species. The progress being made in the number of species documented in OBIS, however, is not the end of the story. Many marine species are not yet known to science, are discovered on each new expedition. Census of Marine Life scientists are actively involved in this process.

The many discoveries the census has made are fascinating, but also a bit disconcerting—fascinating because of the beauty of ocean life and the unexpected forms that it can take, disconcerting because there is still so much that we don't know about the ocean, the largest ecosystem on Earth. The Census of Marine Life will be the first catalog of marine life from which future changes can be assessed and measured.

all of the estimated 240,000 marine species, OBIS will enable analysis of biodiversity patterns on an unprecedented scale. Scientists have lots of data in notebooks, on shelves, and in preserved specimens in bottles.

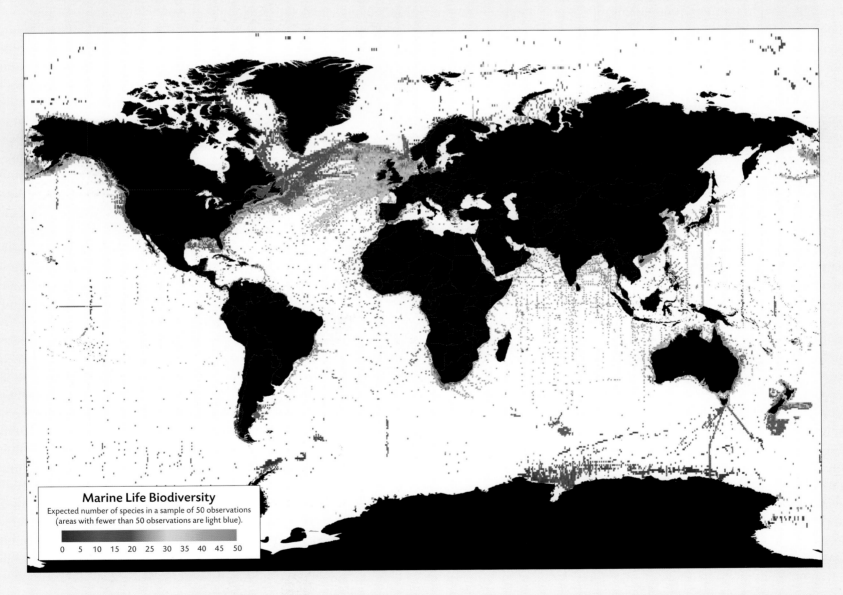

Marine Life Biodiversity
Expected number of species in a sample of 50 observations (areas with fewer than 50 observations are light blue).

0 5 10 15 20 25 30 35 40 45 50

Here, the estimated number of species, calculated as the number of species in a random sample of 50 observations, is shown, again with red indicating the higher number and blue the lower. This estimate removes the bias caused by uneven effort as seen in the map on the opposite page and reflects better the known patterns of biodiversity.

WEB LINK: marine microbes

are referred to as SLIME (subsurface lithoautotrophic microbial ecosystems), assemblages of bacteria and fungi living within the grains of rock below the bottom of the sea. A 2008 report in *Science* magazine indicates that microbes are present in marine sediments as old as 111 million years and at depths greater than a kilometer beneath the seafloor.

Until recently, bacteria and other microbes in the ocean have not been on the balance sheet of most of those assessing the planet's overall "productivity," or other basic planet-shaping processes, but new thinking suggests that when it comes right down to it, the world may well function as it does largely because of the actions that occur in the hidden realms of the very deep—and the very small.

BIOLUMINESCENCE

About 90 percent of the creatures in the deep ocean have survival strategies involving bioluminescence—the ability to generate light. Many fish cultivate bioluminescent bacteria in their tissues, a symbiotic relationship that provides a home for the microbes and light for the host.

A predator becomes prey, as a goby is engulfed by a lizardfish on a reef near the Lembeh Strait Suluwesi, Indonesia.

Certain crustacea have their own light-producing chemicals useful for finding food, flashing signals, and frightening would-be predators. Some squid not only flash when touched but also emit puffs of bioluminescent ink that confuse pursuers.

Marine biologists Bruce Robison and Larry Madin have pioneered the use of small submersibles to witness the behavior of glow-in-the-dark mid-water and deep-sea creatures by becoming part of the plankton themselves. Both specialize in "jellies," a term used to refer collectively to deep-sea animals that share a notably squishy nature: certain free-swimming mollusks and sea cucumbers, various gelatinous open-ocean relatives of sea squirts, jellyfish, siphonophores, and comb jellies. Madin says, "By drifting along as a part of the action in the deep sea, you

Larry P. Madin
WATER COLUMN LIFE

The world ocean is the largest living space in the solar system, more than 1.3 billion cubic kilometers, with an average depth of about 4 kilometers, and holding 97 percent of all the water on Earth. Organisms that occupy this vast space are among the most numerous of Earth's creatures, but they are also some of the most unfamiliar to us.

The water column is essentially without boundaries, and everything living in it swims or drifts continuously. Sunlight fuels the initial production of food through photosynthetic phytoplankton, single-celled algae and bacteria that

on each other. Extending to 1,000 meters is the mesopelagic region, with only enough sunlight to signal whether it is day or night. With this information, many animals of the mesopelagic migrate up to the surface to feed at night, and then retreat into darker water during the day to hide from visual predators. In this "twilight zone" of the ocean, most of the animals, whether invertebrates or fish, produce light of their own by bioluminescence. Nowhere on Earth is there a greater abundance and variety of living light displays, some for attracting prey, some for repelling predators, some

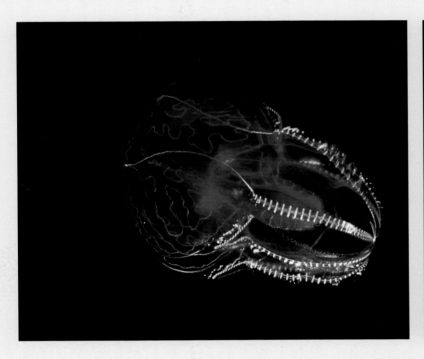

Above left: *Scarlet in artificial light but glowing blue-green in the dark, the comb jelly,* Lampocteis, *prospers in the Monterey Canyon.* Above right: *Bioluminescent photophores cover the body of this deep-dwelling squid,* Histioteuthis. Below: *The dragonfish,* Idiacanthus, *attracts small prey with a glow-in-the-dark lure swinging from its chin.*

live in the upper layers of the water column. The greatest abundance and variety of zooplankton—copepods and other crustaceans; tiny worms, mollusks, and tunicates; and larval stages of many invertebrates and fish—live here, too. Many of them graze directly on the phytoplankton, with elaborate appendages or fine-mesh sieves made of mucus. These grazers fall prey to predators, other types of zooplankton or fishes or marine mammals.

Some of the most abundant and beautiful creatures in the water column are little more than seawater themselves. These "jellies" include medusae and siphonophores, ctenophores and tunicates, as well as jelly-like members of other groups. Though fragile and transparent, without bones, teeth, or claws, some gelatinous animals are among the most voracious predators in the sea.

Sunlight sufficient for photosynthesis penetrates only about 200 meters, so below this depth live only animals subsisting on detritus drifting down from the surface or

for signaling mates, and some for blending in to the dim background.

Once below 1,000 meters in the bathypelagic zone, it is always dark. Sunlight disappears and fewer animals are luminous. This is the largest and least known part of the ocean, sparsely inhabited by slow-moving fish, fragile squids, strange-looking crustaceans, and worms. There are likely to be many undiscovered species in this environment, which will remain hidden from human eyes for millions of years.

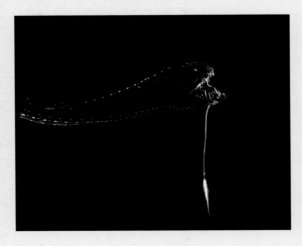

Living in the huge and seemingly featureless environment of the meso- and bathypelagic must be challenging. The water is cold, food is scarce, predators lurk in the dark, potential mates are scattered over great distances, and there are few cues that animals can use to find their way around. Yet more than 15,000 species of invertebrates and fishes live here, all having evolved successful ways to eat, grow, escape, reproduce, and populate Earth's largest habitat.

Strange Life on Seamounts

Tens of thousands of underwater mountains called seamounts are scattered around the seafloor worldwide, but only about 300 have been sampled to find what type of life exists in these deep, dark, cold, remote environments. Newly discovered deep-water corals are thousands of years old, and every seamount surveyed so far has revealed many previously unknown species. Seamounts are only one of the deep-sea habitats revealing unimagined new forms of life on Earth.

get a feel for what it is like to live in the dark and how important bioluminescence is to life in the ocean."

Edith Widder, a bioluminescence specialist and director of the Ocean Research and Conservation Association, has spent hundreds of hours quietly observing how creatures use light to signal one another, lure prey, and avoid becoming prey. Considering that more than 95 percent of the biosphere is ocean, that all of it is dark some of the time and most of it is dark all of the time, and that 90 percent of the animals of the deep sea are bioluminescent, it is no wonder that Widder concludes, "Bioluminescence may be the most common form of communication on Earth."

HABITAT DIVERSITY

Superficially, the ocean appears to be relatively consistent over large regions, giving the impression that sea creatures do not face the same level of environmental inhibitions and barriers as their counterparts on land, especially in the open sea and the deep sea. Ocean species have been regarded as largely widespread creatures, carried unconstrained over long distances by currents in a flowing, liquid medium. That view has changed.

Although some large, migratory animals (notably sea turtles, many tunas, jellyfish, and some whales) do range widely, most ocean-dwelling organisms are "homebodies," held to a specific area owing to boundaries or enticements as varied as temperature, salinity, acidity or alkalinity, oxygen level, the amount of light or darkness, turbidity, pressure, substrate, chemical constituents in the water, food availability, predators, currents, tides, and other factors. "Home" may be a moving mass

Light Gradation: *Most photosynthesis in the sea occurs in the upper 100 meters or so, with some bacteria and protists equipped with special light-gathering pigments that enable them to photosynthesize and thrive in depths greater than 200 meters where a small fraction of sunlight penetrates. Since the average depth of the sea is more than 4,000 meters, most of the ocean is without sunlight all of the time, and all of it is dark some of the time. The image here artistically portrays the transition from sunlight to twilight to the eternal blackness of the deep sea.*

of water, the back of a turtle, the gills of a sardine, the surface of a rock, or a patch of soft mud. Many forms of ocean life produce drifting eggs, larvae, seeds, or spores, but these, too, face all of the factors that influence the range of adults, restricting or enhancing their ultimate range.

The World Conservation Union, NOAA, and other organizations have characterized the biology and physical nature of more than 60 Large Marine Ecosystems (LMEs), regions of ocean space encompassing coastal areas from river basins and estuaries to the seaward edge of continental shelves and the outer margins of major currents. Primarily aimed at fisheries, the data acquired for the LMEs, published in ten volumes, provide a wealth of information concerning habitats within the waters bordering major landmasses of the world.

Scientists developing an inventory of life in the sea through the Census of Marine Life recognize six major ocean realms: near-shore and coastal areas; deep continental margins and abyssal plains; the central waters of the open sea, including the deep-ocean ridges extending more than 64,000 kilometers under the giant watermasses; geologically active regions, including hydrothermal vents and cold seeps; the ice-covered polar seas; and microscopic life in the ocean. Within these broad areas, countless habitats exist—large to small, some highly specialized. Some, such as coral reefs, kelp forests, and sea grass meadows, superficially have a similar appearance wherever in the world they occur, but the number and kind of species found in these habitats vary widely, and within each are unique microhabitats, such as the communities of life that form only on the shells of certain kinds of abalone, the unique assemblages of organisms living within the hollows and crevices of large Caribbean sponges, or the bioluminescent microbes that prosper in the intestinal tracts of certain cardinal fish.

Numerous new habitats and their associated ecosystems have been discovered in recent years in places ranging from hydrothermal vents and the deep cracks in rocks underlying the seabed to complex assemblages of organisms living on the underside of polar ice. Increasingly, it is obvious that the ocean cannot be neatly parceled into a definitive number of habitats and ecosystems. Rather, the ocean is a continuous, interconnected habitat, supporting ever-changing assemblages of life, all responding to the nature of their surroundings, moment by moment.

Off the coast of Massachusetts in the Stellwagen Bank National Marine Sanctuary, a humpback whale dines on small fish and thousands of minute planktonic organisms. Enterprising gulls snag the scraps.

WEB LINK: **Large Marine Ecosystems**

The Diversity of Life in the Sea

WEB LINK: Tree of Life Web Project

SPECIES ARE THE BASIC UNITS OF BIODIVERSITY, but recognition of what that means goes far beyond just giving something a name. Biologist E. O. Wilson gives a biological definition of a species in *The Diversity of Life:* a population whose members are able to interbreed freely under natural conditions. Individuals of a single species may vary considerably in their appearance, but as long as they can successfully interbreed under natural circumstances, they are considered to be the same species biologically. New techniques for sorting out species using "genetic fingerprints" are helping not only to distinguish one species from another but also to establish relationships that may be obscured by outward appearances.

Among the basic wonders of life is not just the enormous diversity of species, but of every individual within a species. Superficially, all of the fish in a school of tunas, mackerels, or sardines may appear identical, as might a mass of blue crabs, shrimp, or moon jellies. But upon close examination, small differences can be found in the number and arrangement of spots, lines, or pigments; subtle variations in angles and curves; as well as differences in behavior. Physician and essayist Lewis Thomas observed in *The Medusa and the Snail* that even individual, free-swimming bacteria can be viewed as unique entities, distinguishable from each other "even when they are the progeny of a single clone. . . . If you watch them closely . . . you can tell them from each other by the way they twirl, as accurately as though they had different names."

A second and equally amazing property of life is the continuity of basic genetic material, the underlying chemistry of life shared by all living things, from desert lizards and pond scum to deep-sea bacteria and primates. Until recently, the diversity of life in the sea was thought to be relatively sparse compared with rain forests, where a single tree may harbor several dozen species of ants and hosts of other insects. Now, new interest and new access to the sea is changing that perspective. Invertebrates actually far outnumber and outweigh animals with backbones on the land and in the sea. Land plants—flowers, trees, mosses, ferns, and their relatives—are more numerous and larger in mass than those in the sea, but they are more than matched in terms of annual productivity and possibly in diversity by the ocean's abundant photosynthetic organisms—until recently also regarded as "plants"—from sea grasses that *are* plants, large kelps, and other algae to the enormous numbers and kinds of microscopic diatoms, dinoflagellates, coccolithophorids, cyanobacteria, and others.

Holger Jannasch, microbiologist at the Woods Hole Oceanographic Institution, viewed every spoonful of ocean as home for complex assemblages of microbes—as many as a million bacteria and on the order of a hundred million viruses. Billions of individuals can exist in a cupful of water, most in resting stages that might persist quiescently for decades, centuries, or even millennia. The convergence of the right combination of temperature, nutrients, oxygen, or other factors could awaken dormant forms to an active state. Using new techniques for analyzing genetic material, researcher Craig Venter has found thousands of new forms in small scoops of water taken from surface waters around the world. Similar techniques were used by other scientists to analyze the DNA of microbes living around hydrothermal vents off the coast of Oregon, where thousands of new kinds were reported in 2007. There is little overlap in the species found in each sample, and the volume of ocean examined so far would not fill a small pond.

The Census of Marine Life has a growing global network of 2,000 researchers in more than 80 nations engaged in a comprehensive global ocean survey. A complementary project, the All

Where Life Lives

The biosphere is all the area on our planet—on land, in the air, and underwater—where there is life. It includes rain forests, deserts, caves, wetlands, coral reefs, the seafloor, and countless other habitats. But surprisingly, about 97 percent of the biosphere is in the ocean. This is a simple matter of numbers. Only 30 percent of the Earth's surface is covered by land, and no species live permanently in the air above it. But the ocean is a huge volume—70 percent of the Earth's surface, and an average of four kilometers deep—and all of it is full of life. Biodiversity is the range of life forms found in any part of the biosphere. The ocean predominates here, too. There are more broad categories of life in the ocean than on land. And because we have seen so little of the seas, it is likely that a high percentage of the biodiversity on Earth still lies undiscovered in the ocean.

Age of Maturity: *On land, large amounts of biomass are retained in long-lived trees and other vegetation; in the sea, large amounts of biomass drift as plankton and are bound up in the tissues of large numbers of long-lived predators such as sharks, tunas, and whales. Larger, older fish generally produce more offspring than smaller members of the same species. Ironically, the animals most prized for market are the big, old fish—the individuals with the greatest potential to produce more fish.*

Atlantic Bluefin Tuna, maturity 5-10 years, lifespan 20+ years

Horseshoe Crab, maturity 9-12 years, lifespan 20+ years

American Lobster, maturity 5-8 years, lifespan 50+ years

Patagonian Toothfish (Chilean Sea Bass), maturity 6-9 years, lifespan 50+ years

Australian Orange Roughy, maturity 27-32 years, lifespan 150+ years

Bowhead Whale, maturity 20 years, lifespan 200+ years

Species Inventory, aspires to document every living species on Earth, combining traditional methods of sorting out differences among organisms with advanced genetic techniques, and to make the information universally available through the Internet.

WEB LINK: marine species databases

New molecular data may provoke a substantial rearrangement of the relationships among broad categories of animal life. In May 2008, 18 scientists reported in *Nature* their findings from the examination of 29 animals belonging to 21 phyla, including 11 phyla previously lacking genomic data. It appears that mollusks may constitute more than one phylum, and there appear to be close relationships among several of the "worm" phyla—Annelida, Sipunculida, Echiura, Nemertea, and Phoronida—and the brachiopods. The resulting "tree of life" will no doubt continue to be refined as research continues, while new explorations will surely add twigs, if not new branches, to the present concepts.

Based on the rate of new discoveries, new methods of assessment, and the vast area of ocean yet to be explored, it is certain that thousands, perhaps millions, of new forms of marine life will be found, even as the rate of destruction of broad areas of the ocean takes place. There is a widely held view that species in the sea are not as vulnerable to extinction as those on the land, a concept that relates to the notion that habitats in the sea are more or less homogeneous. Waves of extinction in the sea as well as on the land have characterized geological eras of the past, and it is evident that human activities are provoking an equivalent wave of rapid loss through habitat destruction and deliberate taking of species on the land and in the sea.

Biologist Marjorie Reaka-Kudla observed in *Biodiversity II* that many marine organisms have a localized home range and that the loss of coral reefs and other marine habitats can lead to the disappearance of species "before they are even discovered." Recent broad changes in ocean chemistry, temperature, predator-prey relationships, and other factors can exacerbate losses on a grand scale.

Hope for new life begins with a puff of sperm from a mushroom coral on the Great Barrier Reef, Australia.

Although extinction is inevitable for most species, the current rate is unprecedented in the history of humankind. Lower diversity translates to lower resistance to change; simplified ecosystems are correspondingly more vulnerable. Preserving as many letters of the biological alphabet as possible provides greater likelihood of maintaining stability of the natural systems on which humankind depends. □

Key

Age of Reproductive Maturity | Lifespan

Categories of Life in the Sea

Nearly all of the major divisions, or phyla, into which organisms are organized occur in the ocean; only about half are terrestrial. At the species level, it is estimated that there may be 1 million to 10 million kinds of organisms in the sea, although fewer than 2 million total species have been named for the land and sea combined. What constitutes a species for microbes is debatable, but an estimated 10^{30} distinctive forms are thought to exist. Beyond species, the next level of organization is a genus, a group of closely related species. Above that in the hierarchy is the family, a group of genera, and above that comes an order, a collection of related families. Families are grouped into classes, and one or more classes represent a phylum or, with plants, a division, the highest level below the broad category of kingdom. Decades of research on the nature of life has resulted in recognition of seven kingdoms within three great domains. Considered here are the major groups of life, from domains to the phyla of marine Eukaryota.

WEB LINK: animal facts

Domain Archaea

Organisms in this domain superficially resemble bacteria—microscopic and with no organized nuclei within their cells—but their genetic makeup is so different from bacteria and all other forms of life that a new domain and kingdom have been designated.

KINGDOM ARCHAEABACTERIA

Microbiologist Carl Woese and colleagues from the University of Illinois determined that certain microorganisms living in hot-water springs at Yellowstone National Park and deep-sea hydrothermal vents were genetically and biochemically so different from known organisms that a new category was designated. Archaea, once thought to be exotic organisms living only in high-temperature areas, are now known to be abundant as plankton in the open sea, as well as being methane-producing inhabitants of environments ranging from the digestive tracts of cows and termites to extremely saline habitats, in anoxic muds of marshes, in deep-ocean vents, and in petroleum deposits deep underground.

Domain Monera

This group includes single-celled or colonial organisms in the kingdom Monera.

KINGDOM MONERA

Bacteria are the principal representatives of this group, mostly extremely small organisms that perform the functions of life within individual cells that do not have organized nuclei. As recently as the early 1990s, only about 4,000 bacteria had names, and few were thought to exist in the ocean. Now, the actual number is thought to be many millions of distinctively different kinds, including a great many that exist in relatively small numbers in a dormant state, with the ocean far and away their largest habitat.

At least a dozen major groups of bacteria exist, including the cyanobacteria, once classified as blue-green algae. The blue-greens share with plants the ability to photosynthesize, and have the distinction of having the longest known fossil record—3.5 billion years. Early in Earth's history, cyanobacteria generated much of the oxygen in the atmosphere, consuming and displacing carbon dioxide, a process that continues even now. Another important attribute of these organisms is their ability to convert inert nitrogen from the atmosphere into an organic form used by photosynthetic organisms for their growth.

Opposite: *Silvery* Salema *warily eye the Galápagos sea lion in their midst.*

Domain Eukaryota

All Eukaryota, from microscopic plankton to sponges to scuba divers, have one thing in common: a membrane-bound nucleus within their cell or cells that contains genetic material organized into chromosomes. Five kingdoms are recognized here. Other arrangements are given in various texts, and all will surely change as new biochemical techniques are used to gain better understanding of the true relationships among this highly diverse domain.

KINGDOM PROTISTA

The kingdom Protista is a heterogeneous collection of organisms that include small, single-celled protozoa, photosynthetic plankton, and many multicellular organisms. The photosynthetic members of this group, together with marine cyanobacteria, generate most of the oxygen in the atmosphere and fix the sun's energy through photosynthesis, thus driving the ocean's food webs and ultimately providing sustenance for a large portion of animal life in the sea, enormous numbers of seabirds, as well as numerous land dwellers with culinary connections to the sea.

Phylum Ciliata. Covering the surface of these single-celled but complex animals is a full or partial coating of short, dense, hairlike cilia that beat for propulsion and for engulfing food. Common in liquid water, fresh and marine, these small organisms grow rapidly in a wide range of environments.

Phylum Dinoflagellata. Single-celled but highly diverse, dinoflagellates are notorious as the organisms responsible for red tides and for creating some of the most brilliant displays of shallow-water bioluminescence. About half are photosynthetic; the rest consume other organisms or are parasitic. All have a characteristic pair of flagellae used for propulsion.

Phylum Foraminifera. Single-celled and shelled, foraminifera form intricate structures made of calcite, organic compounds, or sand grains cemented together. Enormous quantities of their shells form deep sediments on the seabed, and in places such as the Bahamas contribute substantially to the charactertistic white sand beaches.

Phylum Chlorophyta. The green algae include numerous freshwater species, some terrestrial kinds, and a large number of ancient and unusual marine species. Most occur in the upper 30 meters of the ocean, but some are adapted through special light-gathering pigments in addition to two kinds of chlorophyll that enable them to thrive in depths greater than 200 meters. Several groups incorporate calcium carbonate into their cell walls, including species of *Halimeda* that are so abundant in some tropical areas that their remains make up the principal ingredient of the region's sand.

Phylum Choanoflagellata. Some regard the tiny, flagellated, single-celled choanoflagellates as the group "where it all began for animals." Resembling certain cells of sponges, these minute mobile organisms are entirely aquatic, feeding on even smaller creatures in marine and freshwater environments.

Phylum Euglenophyta. This group of minute, mobile, mostly one-celled photosynthetic organisms sometimes causes greening or reddening of salt ponds and saline lagoons with their prodigious numbers. Each cell bears a single whiplike flagellum.

Phylum Myxomycota. Referred to as "slime molds," these have common characteristics with fungi, animals, and other protists. *Labyrinthula zosterae* is considered a pathogen of various sea grasses.

Phylum Radiolaria. Greatly admired for the intricate symmetry of their glassy shells, the single-celled radiolarians are as well-known to geologists as they are to biologists because their skeletons have endured in ocean sediments for millions of years and provide important clues concerning the nature of ancient seas.

Phylum Rhodophyta. The red algae are a highly diverse assemblage of more than 4,000 species, mostly marine, all with distinctive reddish-pink pigments and complex alternating life history phases. Some are thin, flat, or tubular; others grow in crusts, nodules, or upright clusters of branches and precipitate calcium carbonate from surrounding seawater and incorporate it into their cell walls. As much as 90 percent of the stony matrix of coral reefs is actually made up of coralline red algae. The red pigments effectively gather blue light in deep water, enabling some coralline species to thrive in depths well below 250 meters, carpeting the seafloor with stony pink nodules.

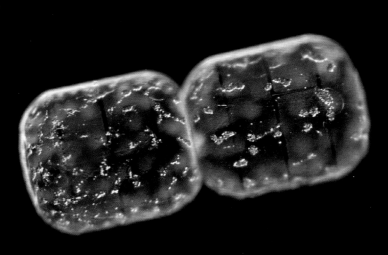

PHYLUM BACILLARIOPHYTA: A DIATOM

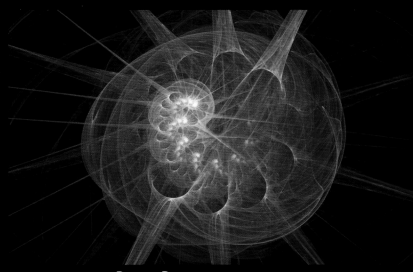

PHYLUM RADIOLARIA: A RADIOLARIAN

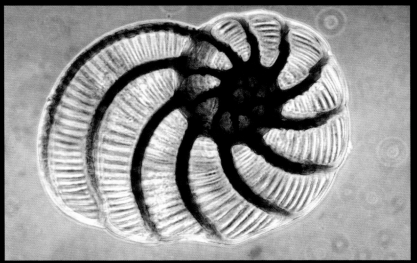

PHYLUM FORAMINFERA: A FORAMINFERAN

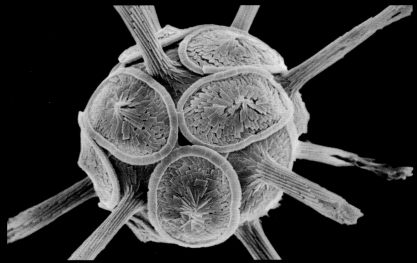

PHYLUM HAPTOPHYTA: A COCCOLITHOPHORID

PHYLUM CHLOROPHYTA, *CAULERPA RACEMOSA*: A GREEN ALGA

PHYLUM CHLOROPHYTA, *HALIMEDA*: A CALCAREOUS GREEN ALGA

PHYLUM RHODOPHYTA: A LEAFY RED ALGA

PHYLUM RHODOPHYTA: A CALCAREOUS RED ALGA

PHYLUM PHAEOPHYTA, *PADINA*: A BROWN ALGA

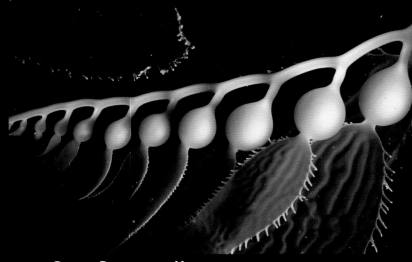

PHYLUM PHAEOPHYTA, *MACROCYSTIS PYRIFERA*: A BROWN ALGA

PHYLUM SPERMATOPHYTA, *THALASSIA TESTUDINUM*: A SEA GRASS

PHYLUM SPERMATOPHYTA, *THALASSIA TESTUDINUM* FLOWER: A SEA GRASS

PHYLUM PORIFERA: BARREL SPONGE

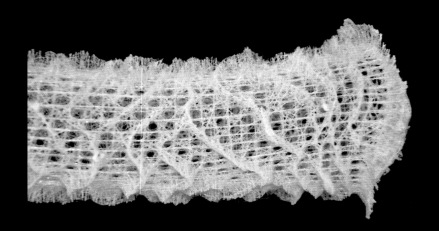

PHYLUM PORIFERA: GLASS SPONGE

PHYLUM CNIDARIA: A GORGONIAN CORAL

PHYLUM CNIDARIA: A JELLYFISH

Kingdom Chromista

Sometimes lumped with the kingdom Plantae, this varied group of organisms differs from them by having chlorophyll c, lacking in plants, and by not storing their energy in the form of starch. They differ from protists in having distinctive pigments that give them their characteristic brown or golden color. One group, the Oomycota, lacks pigments but in other ways is allied to this group.

Phylum Bacillariophyta. Diatoms are renowned not only for the beauty of their lacy, glassy shells, but also for their critical role as photosynthesizers and producers of food in the sea and in freshwater systems globally. Typically, two shells, one slightly smaller than the other, encase a single cell like a minute jewel box. Well-known in the fossil record, some rocks are formed almost entirely of diatom shells, and diatomaceous earth is often used for filtration.

Phylum Chrysophyta. The golden brown chrysophytes are microscopic, usually photosynthetic, sometimes colonial organisms, some with siliceous scales. Freshwater and marine, they are abundant in the fossil record and common now in plankton or attached to a surface.

Phylum Phaeophyta. The brown algae are nearly all ocean dwellers, most luxuriant and conspicuously developed in cool or cold coastal waters. Some form wispy clusters of filaments, while others resemble delicate ribbons or leafy, golden brown shrubs. Largest of all photosynthetic organisms in the sea, some kelps, notably California's *Macrocystis pyrifera,* may grow a foot a day and attain lengths as great as 30 meters.

Phylum Haptophyta. Numerous fossil species of this group are known, with about 500 living species that contribute significantly to photosynthetic activity in the sea, coccolithophorids among them. The delicate calcareous shells of coccoliths have accumulated in enormous sedimentary deposits over broad areas of the seafloor and are a common component of chalk.

Kingdom Fungi

At least four phyla of fungi are recognized, including many common marine species that, owing to their cryptic nature, are rarely seen by most people. Many are small, some are parasitic, and none photosynthesize. Of the 100,000 or so kinds of fungi known, only a few hundred marine species have been identified.

Kingdom Plantae

Historically, almost any organism that photosynthesized was regarded as a "plant," but as currently defined, plants are multicellular, photosynthetic organisms with cell walls containing cellulose, nuclei within the cells containing genetic material, and typically, a life cycle that involves a generation with a single set of chromosomes (haploid) and a generation involving a joined set or sets of chromosomes (diploid). Diploid embryos retained within female organs for development as seeds are characteristic of flowering plants, but methods of reproduction vary widely in other groups.

About a dozen phyla of organisms comprise about 250,000 mosses, ferns, liverworts, club mosses, horsetails, conifers, flowering plants (including most trees), and several extinct groups. A few ferns, shrubs, and marsh grasses live in brackish or salty water, but the best known and most widespread marine plants are 60 or so flowering plants in the phylum Spermatophyta known as sea grasses that typically occur as vast undersea meadows.

Kingdom Animalia (Metazoa)

This kingdom includes multicellular, non-photosynthetic organisms with cells that lack walls and have genetic material contained within nuclei. Most form tissues organized into specialized organs and have diploid embryos with two sets of chromosomes. The phyla of animals are sometimes lumped or subdivided into more or fewer categories as new insights are gained about relationships. No evolutionary ranking is intended for the following phyla, but in general, those with relatively simple structures are followed by those with increasing complexity.

Phylum Porifera. More than 5,000 living species of sponges represent three categories of these ancient, mostly marine "hole-bearing" animals. The Hexactinellida (glass sponges), the Calcarea, and the Demospongia have distinctive calcareous or siliceous spicules held within a spongy or soft matrix. One family of sponges snare crustaceans with Velcro-like spicules, then digest them with special cells that migrate to the site of capture. Reefs of glass sponges were common in warm, shallow seas during the Jurassic period, but were thought to exist in modern times only as fossils until large living reefs were found in the 1990s.

Phylum Placozoa. One minute (0.5 millimeter) species of this category of animals was discovered in the 1880s adhering to the glass of a marine aquarium. Beyond that, little is known.

Phylum Rhombozoa. Celebrated by virtue of having the smallest number of cells—8 to 40—of any animal, these entirely marine minute parasites live only in the kidneys of certain octopuses and squids.

Phylum Orthonectida. About 20 species of these small, ciliated marine parasites occur internally in various invertebrate animals.

Phylum Myxozoa. These minute parasitic animals use marine invertebrates and some vertebrates as hosts. They have distinctive multicellular spores and are regarded as relatives of the phylum Cnidaria.

Phylum Cnidaria. Thousands of jellyfish, corals, anemones, hydroids, and sea pens are included in this group, as well as a small number of freshwater species, all known for specialized stinging cells embedded within tentacles of various shapes and sizes. Cnidarians are distinctive in having only two basic cell layers, ectoderm and endoderm, with a soft material, the mesoglea, in between that may make up the bulk of large jellies and anemones. Corals form an external calcium carbonate enclosure around individual polyps, with many species together forming enormous stony structures.

Phylum Ctenophora. Eight distinctive bands of iridescent cilia adorn the sides of comb jellies, sea gooseberries, venus girdles, and sea walnuts, usually translucent, bioluminescent, entirely marine carnivores. Most live in the water column, but a few creep along the seafloor. Unlike the cnidarians that they superficially resemble, ctenophores have three distinctive cellular layers and have no stinging cells, although some have retractable tentacles armed with sticky cells useful in capturing prey. All consume other creatures, however, sometimes engulfing other jellies as large as they are.

Phylum Platyhelminthes. Of the three groups of flatworm known, two—the cestoda and the trematoda, or flukes—are parasitic, with complex life histories sometimes involving several hosts. Most notable in the ocean are the free-living turbellaria, including some that are brilliantly colored and swim with the grace of aquatic butterflies. Most are a few millimeters long, but some can reach 15 centimeters.

Phylum Nemertea. Nearly a thousand species of ribbon worms, soft, unsegmented animals that live throughout the ocean in sandy, muddy, and rocky places, use an extendable proboscis to gather food, sometimes wrapping prey with their sleek body. Most are a few centimeters long, but one species reaches 30 meters.

Phylum Rotifera. Of the 2,000 or so species of rotifers known, a few hundred live lightly attached to seaweed or other substrates or as plankton in the sea. Tiny (1 to 2.5 millimeters long), translucent, and often occurring in great numbers, these predators have a circular cilia-covered organ that propels smaller organisms into their gullet.

Phylum Gastrotricha. About 400 kinds of gastrotrichs, animals less than 1 millimeter long with characteristic hairy undersides, have been discovered living in muddy sand in aquatic places worldwide.

Phylum Kinorhyncha. From intertidal sand and the fronds of seaweed to the deep sea, the minute entirely marine 13-segmented, spiny, cylindrical, mostly transparent kinorhynchs are common but not often seen owing to their inconspicuous size and cryptic habits.

Phylum Nematoda. The long and narrow shape of these organisms is suggested by their name based on the Greek word *nema,* meaning "thread." Longitudinally aligned muscles enable the animal to bend side to side, but not in other directions. Free-living species thrive on bacteria in moist soil

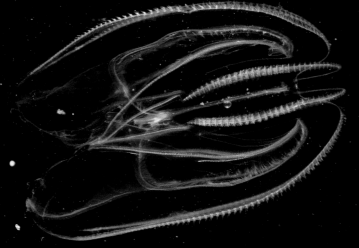

PHYLUM CTENOPHORA: A COMB JELLY

PHYLUM PLATYHELMINTHES: A FLATWORM

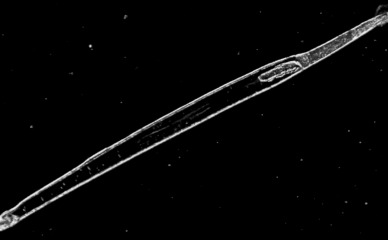

PHYLUM CHAETOGNATHA: AN ARROW WORM

PHYLUM NEMERTEA: A RIBBON WORM

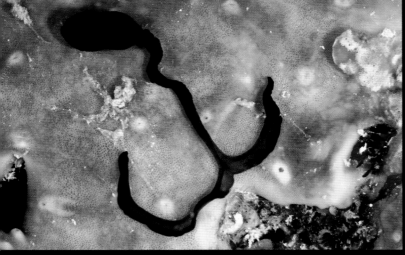

PHYLUM ECHIURA: A SPOON WORM

PHYLUM SIPUNCULIDA: PEANUT WORMS

PHYLUM ANNELIDA: A POLYCHAETE WORM

PHYLUM POGONOPHORA: TUBEWORMS; **PHYLUM ARTHROPODA:** A SPIDER CRAB

PHYLUM BRACHIOPODA: LAMP SHELLS

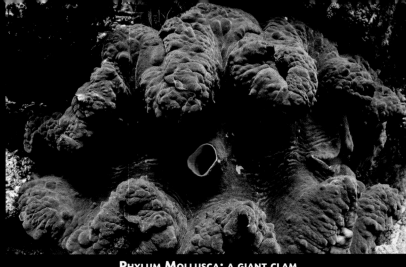

PHYLUM MOLLUSCA: A GIANT CLAM

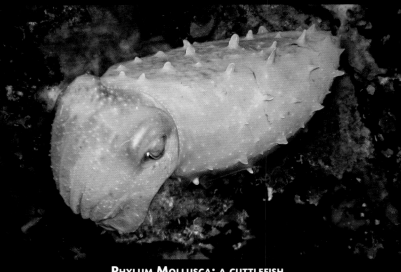

PHYLUM MOLLUSCA: A CUTTLEFISH

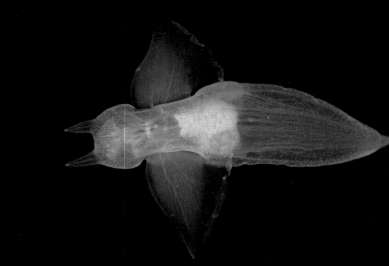

PHYLUM MOLLUSCA: A PTEROPOD

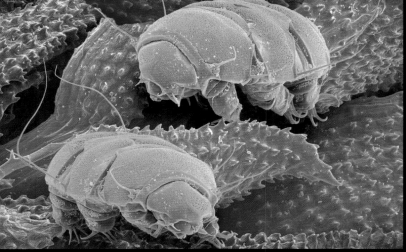

PHYLUM TARDIGRADA: WATER BEARS

PHYLUM CHELICERATA: A SEA SPIDER

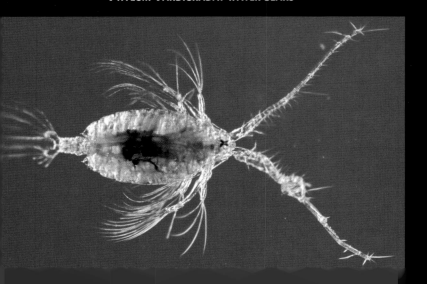

deep-sea mud, polar ice, hot springs, and essentially everyplace where food and water are available, whereas parasitic forms live on or in almost every other kind of organism known, including a 13-meter-long species that inhabits the gut of sperm whales. About 15,000 species are recognized, but it is estimated that there may be half a million yet to be discovered, thus rivaling arthropods in diversity and most likely exceeding them in sheer mass.

Phylum Nematomorpha. Most of the 240 species of long, slender horsehair worms live in fresh water, but some parasitize marine crabs. Related to nematodes with larvae that are invertebrate parasites, the adults of these organisms do not feed, but invest their short lives in producing eggs and fertilizing them to ensure the future of their kind.

Phylum Acanthocephala. These prickly-headed worms as adults are entirely parasitic in vertebrate animals, mostly freshwater fish, with larval stages parasitic in crustacea or other arthropods that must be eaten by an appropriate host for the larvae to mature.

Phylum Entoprocta. About 170 species of these tiny stalked animals occur widely in the oceans of the world; 1 lives in fresh water. Some are solitary, most link together in colonies, and all have a distinctive crown of tentacles with which they capture small prey.

Phylum Gnathostomulida. Entirely marine, about 100 kinds of these small, wormlike animals with paired jaws have been discovered living in shallow and deep mud and among sand grains worldwide.

Phylum Priapula. Small spiny "cactus worms" with about 20 species, entirely marine, constitute this distinctive and widespread but inconspicuous group of organisms.

Phylum Loricifera. These minute, translucent, barrel-shaped totally marine creatures with a characteristic sheath of spines and scales were first discovered amid grains of sand in several locations in the Atlantic. Currently, about 50 species are known to live in depths from 10 to at least 500 meters.

Phylum Cycliophora. Discovered in 1994, just one species is known of these small animals that adhere to the lips of Norwegian lobster whiskers and filter feed with cilia surrounding their mouth.

Phylum Sipunculida. About 330 entirely marine species of peanut worms are known, all muscular, bulbous, smooth, unsegmented creatures elongated at one end with a frill of tentacles surrounding a small mouth used to feed on detritus. Some are tiny, 2 millimeters or so long, but some are nearly as big as a baseball bat. Most live in sand or mud, but some burrow into rock or coral or nestle among the holdfasts of large seaweeds.

Phylum Echiura. About 150 species of entirely marine tube-dwelling spoon worms are widely distributed in the ocean, each with an extendable feeding proboscis at one end of the body and spiny hooks on the other. A Pacific species is known as the innkeeper because numerous small shrimp, crabs, polychaetes, and other creatures move into the spoon worm's burrow.

Phylum Annelida. About 9,000 kinds of marine annelids are known, mostly polychaetes—segmented creatures that live up to their name by typically having many bristles or spines. Enormously diverse and widespread, polychaetes live in sand, mud, on and in sponges and corals, or free swimming as plankton. The tiny planktonic trochophore larvae are distinctively top shaped and fringed with cilia.

Phylum Pogonophora. Entirely marine, about 80 species of bearded worms, mostly small animals with no mouth or stomach, occur from intertidal areas to the deep sea, the most spectacular representatives living in association with cold seeps and hot vents in the deep sea. Some exceed 2 meters in length.

Phylum Onychophora. Once abundant in ancient oceans, about 100 species of the small, caterpillar-like velvet worms today live in moist forest habitats, mostly in the Southern Hemisphere.

Phylum Tardigrada. Some 800 species of tardigrades are known, about half of them in marine places ranging from deep-sea sand to the surface of certain seaweeds. Some are predatory, but many simply suck the juices from other organisms. Resembling small, stubby-legged bears, usually a millimeter long or less, these mostly translucent creatures share with certain microbes the ability to become dormant for long periods.

Phylum Arthropoda. Arthropods have jointed legs, a segmented body, compound eyes, and an exoskeleton that is typically shed periodically during growth. In this most diverse group of animals, embracing about 80 percent of all known species, insects dominate, except in the ocean, where only a few have become established. In the sea, about 30,000 kinds of crustacea have been discovered, including species of crabs, shrimp, barnacles, copepods, ostracods, stomatopods, and many others.

Phylum Chelicerata. Closely related and sometimes lumped with arthropods, chelicerates—sea spiders, horseshoe crabs, spiders, and scorpions—are regarded here as a group distinguished by having four pairs of walking legs and two pairs of specialized mouthparts including the distinctive clawlike chelicerae. An ancient group originating in the ocean, *Chelicerata*'s marine species today include four or five kinds of horseshoe crabs and about 600 kinds of sea spiders. Extinct chelicerates, the eurypterids, grew to be as large as grizzly bears, nearly 3 meters long.

Phylum Mollusca. Most of the nearly 50,000 kinds of mollusks known are marine, including more than 600 kinds of cephalopods, 700 tooth shells, 1,000 or so chitons, and 2 kinds of mono placophorans that are entirely marine, and pelecypods (clams) and gastropods (snails) that are largely so. All are highly organized into tissues and organs, and most have an internal or external shell or shells, but cephalopods are especially well developed with sensory organs, eyes structured much like those of vertebrates, and a complex nervous system.

Phylum Phoronida. About 15 entirely marine species make up the horseshoe worms, small, widely distributed tube-dwelling filter-feeding animals.

Phylum Ectoprocta (Bryozoa). Far more abundant and diverse as fossils, about 5,000 filter-feeding bryozoan, or "moss animal," species currently live in the sea, as well as a few in freshwater, where they typically grow as lacy colonial crusts, sometimes in upright clusters.

Phylum Brachiopoda. An ancient group of entirely marine filter-feeding animals, lamp shells superficially resemble clams, once including thousands of species so abundant that they paved the seafloor during the Paleozoic. Now far less common and diverse, they mainly occur in cold deep water.

Phylum Echinodermata. This entirely marine group of "spiny skinned" animals—starfish, crinoids, sand dollars, sea cucumbers, brittle stars—have distinctive planktonic larvae and adults with calcareous plates embedded in their skin. All have five-part radial symmetry, even sea cucumbers when viewed in cross section, and all have tube feet powered by a specialized water vascular system.

Phylum Chaetognatha. About 125 species of arrow worms are known. They are small, entirely marine, usually transparent predators that often dominate planktonic communities, where they consume small crustaceans, larval fish—and other arrow worms.

Phylum Hemichordata. Entirely marine, sometimes classed with chordates but more closely related to echinoderms, these soft-bodied acorn worms include several hundred species, mostly burrowers, with many fossil forms.

Phylum Chordata. Chordates include some of the most conspicuous forms of life in the sea—about 17, 000 kinds of fish; 70 or so species of dolphins, whales, seals, sea lions, and otters; 8 to 10 kinds of sea turtles; several species of crocodilians; about 80 kinds of sea snakes; 1 semimarine toad; and hundreds of species of seabirds. Less well known are numerous kinds of salps, sea squirts, and small leaf-shaped lanclets.

One chordate species, *Homo sapiens,* is technically not marine, but owing to the dominant place humans occupy as predators in ocean ecosystems, extracting more than 100 million tons of ocean wildlife annually and profoundly altering the physical and chemical nature of the ocean, it is appropriate to include humankind here. Some humans have succeeded in becoming temporary marine mammals by diving, and a few have engaged technologies enabling them to live under the sea for days, weeks, and even months in underwater laboratories or encased in var-

Phylum Echinodermata: a seastar

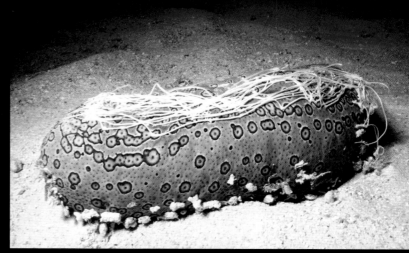

Phylum Echinodermata: a sea cucumber

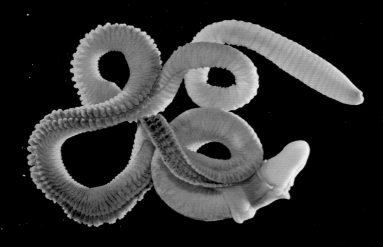

Phylum Echinodermata: a coinoid

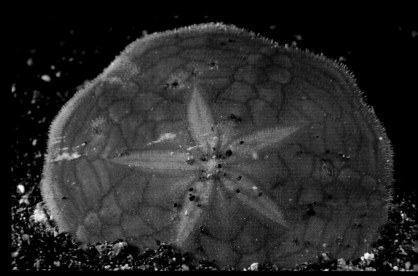

Phylum Echinodermata: a sand dollar

Phylum Hemichordata: an acorn worm

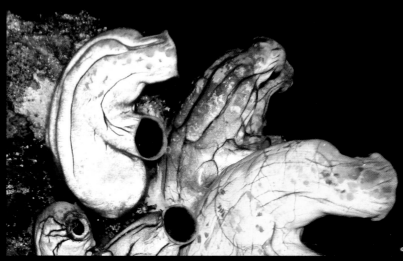

Phylum Chordata: a sea squirt

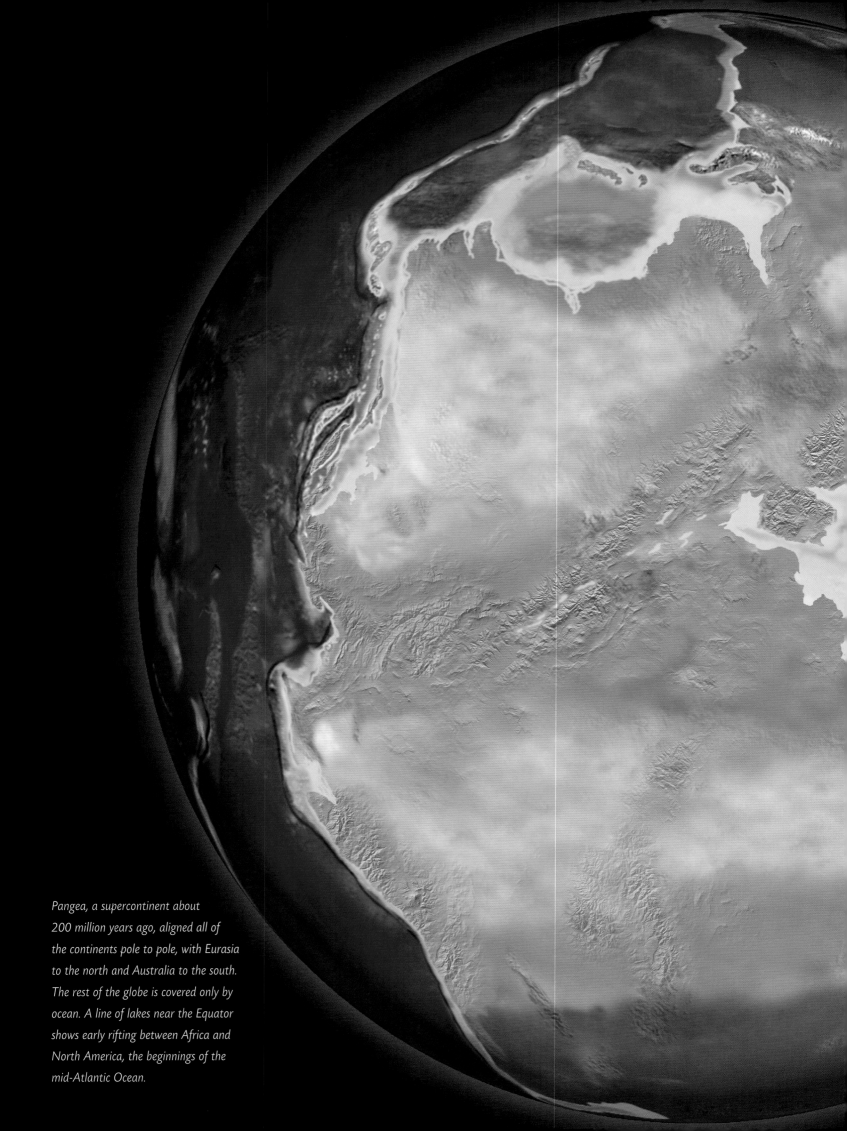

Pangea, a supercontinent about 200 million years ago, aligned all of the continents pole to pole, with Eurasia to the north and Australia to the south. The rest of the globe is covered only by ocean. A line of lakes near the Equator shows early rifting between Africa and North America, the beginnings of the mid-Atlantic Ocean.

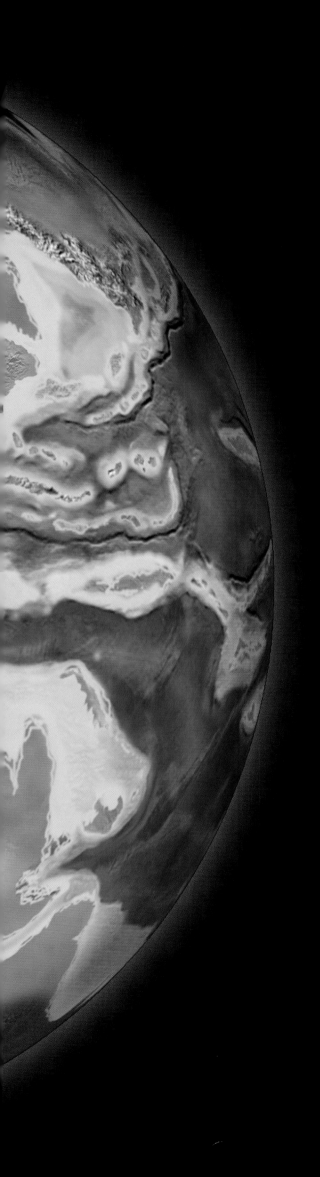

Chapter 3

OCEAN PAST

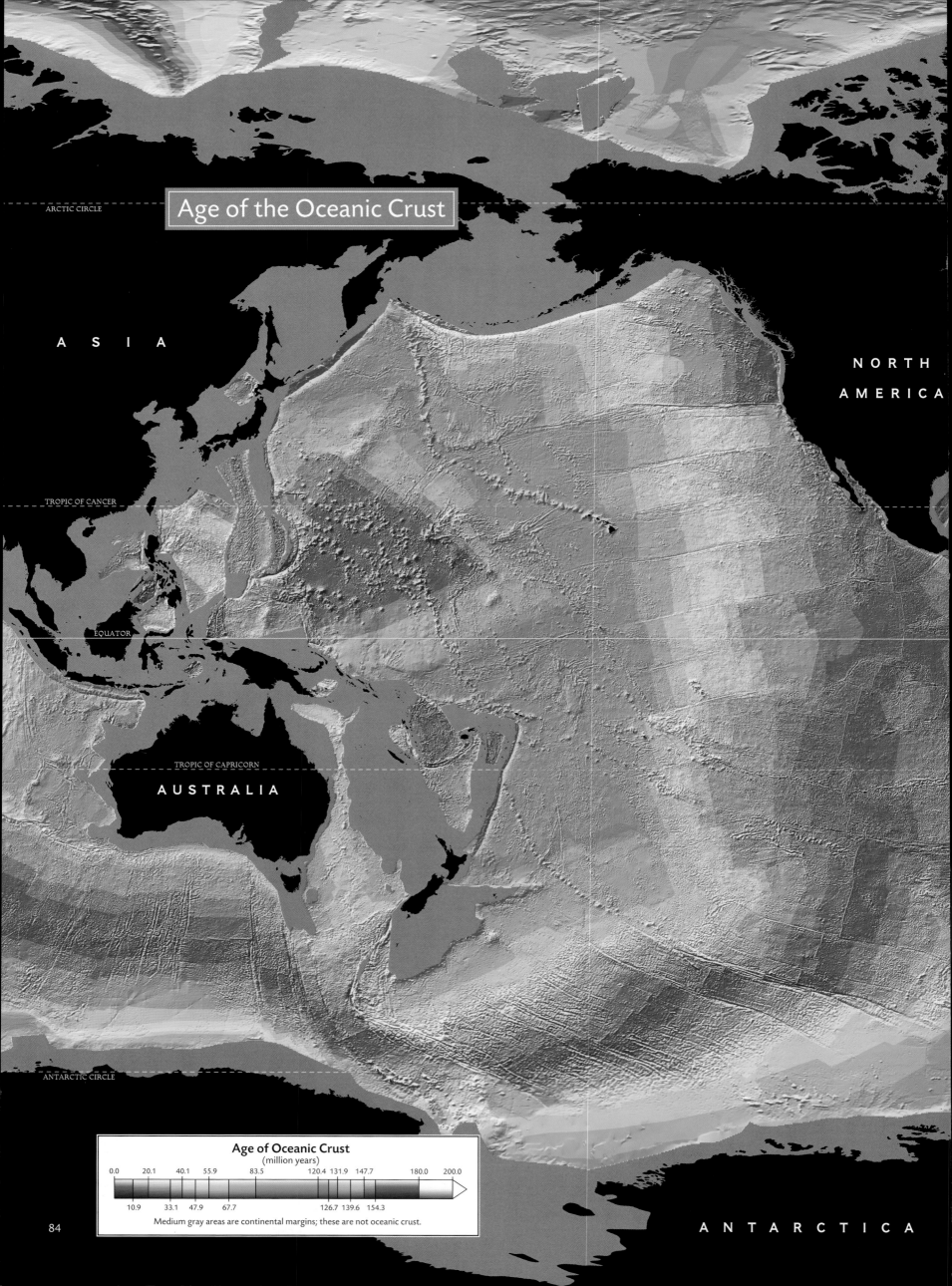

ARCTIC CIRCLE

A S I A

NORTH

AMERICA

TROPIC OF CANCER

EQUATOR

TROPIC OF CAPRICORN

AUSTRALIA

ANTARCTIC CIRCLE

Age of Oceanic Crust
(million years)

0.0   20.1   40.1   55.9   83.5   120.4 131.9 147.7   180.0   200.0

10.9   33.1 47.9   67.7   126.7 139.6 154.3

Medium gray areas are continental margins; these are not oceanic crust.

A N T A R C T I C A

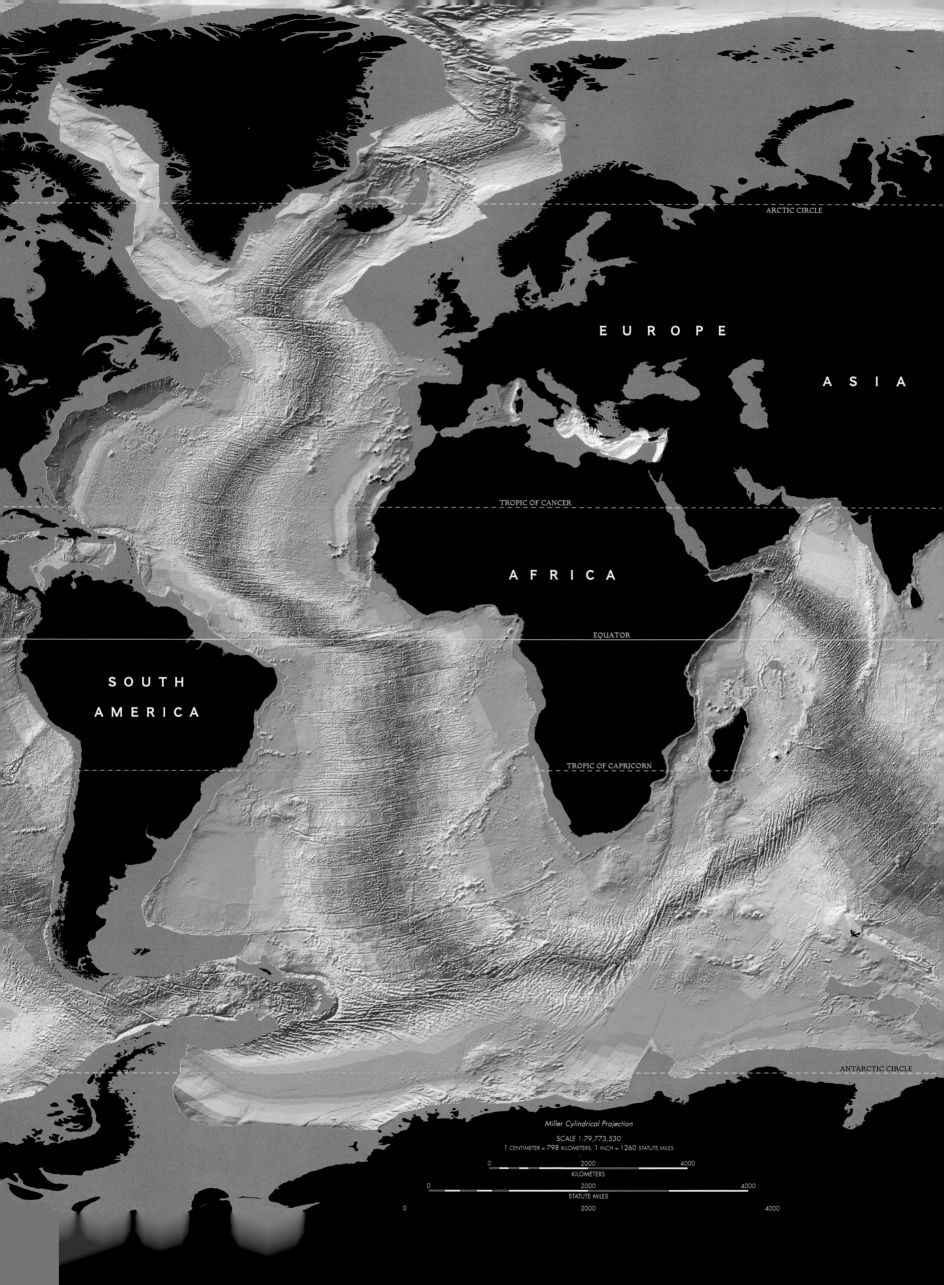

EUROPE

ASIA

AFRICA

SOUTH
AMERICA

TROPIC OF CANCER

EQUATOR

TROPIC OF CAPRICORN

ANTARCTIC CIRCLE

Miller Cylindrical Projection

SCALE 1:79,773,530

1 CENTIMETER = 798 KILOMETERS; 1 INCH = 1260 STATUTE MILES

0   2000   4000
KILOMETERS

0   2000   4000
STATUTE MILES

2000   4000

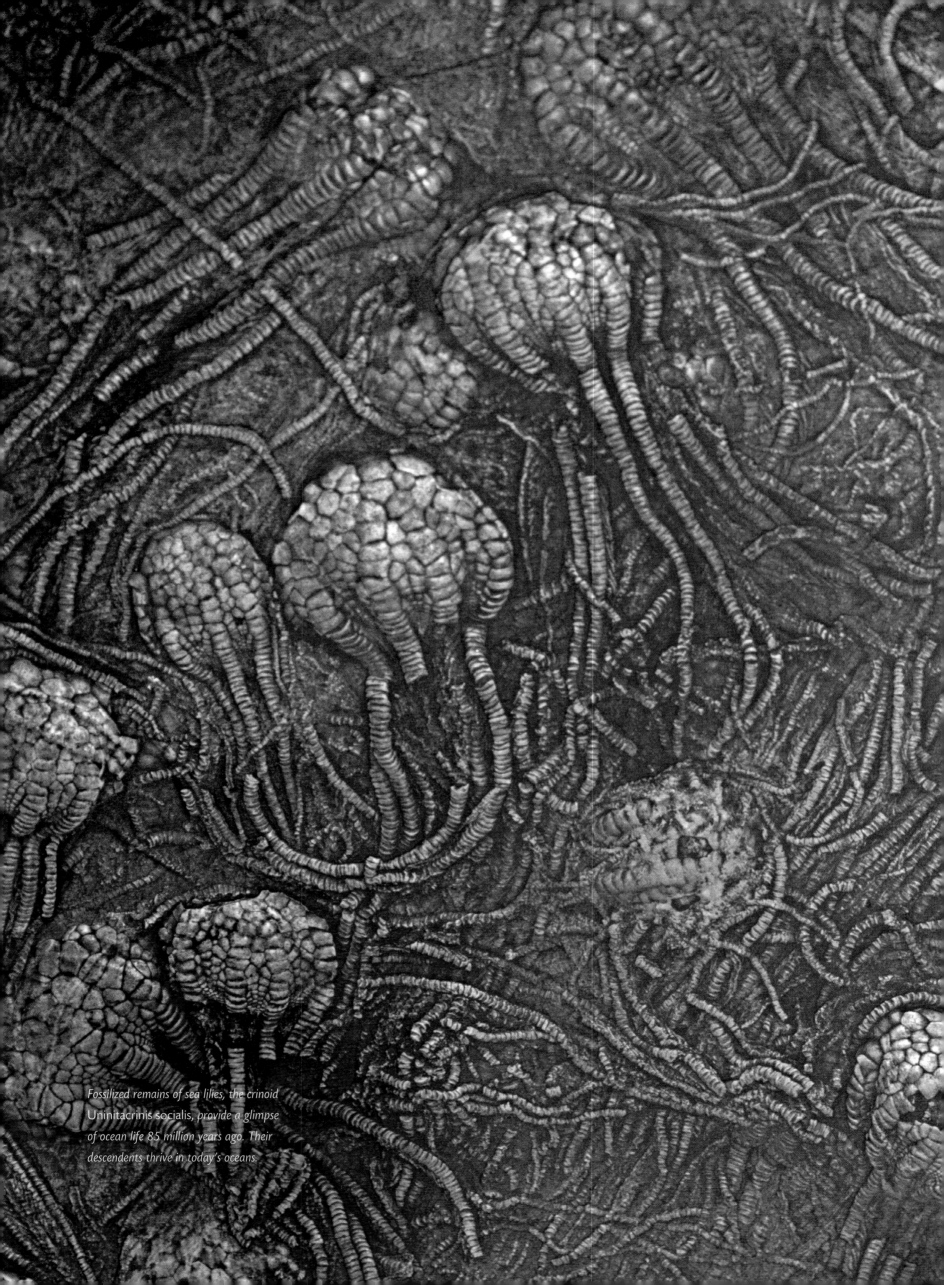

Fossilized remains of sea lilies, the crinoid *Uninitacrinis socialis, provide a glimpse of ocean life 85 million years ago. Their descendents thrive in today's oceans.*

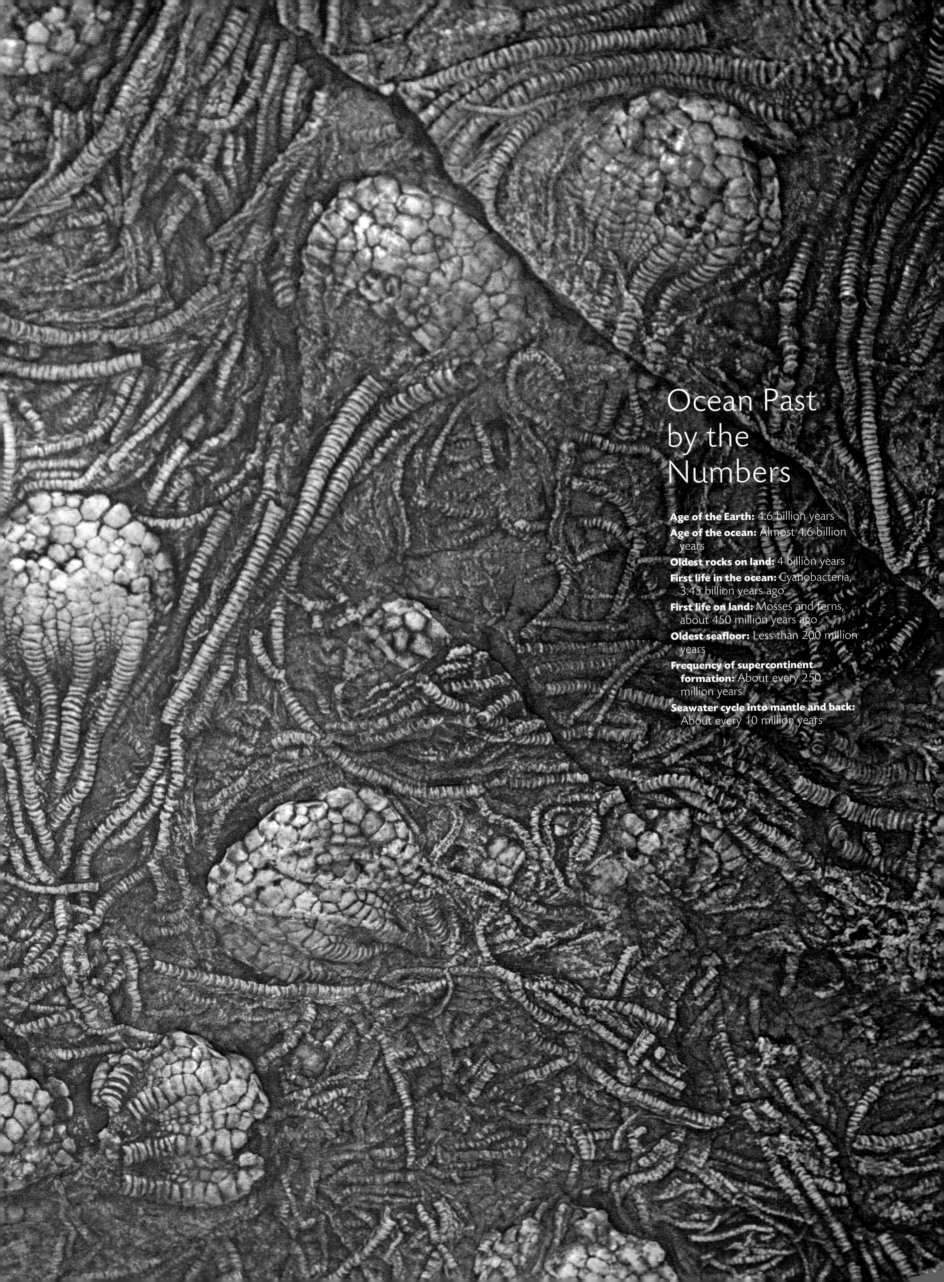

Ocean Past by the Numbers

Age of the Earth: 4.6 billion years

Age of the ocean: Almost 4.6 billion years

Oldest rocks on land: 4 billion years

First life in the ocean: Cyanobacteria, 3.45 billion years ago

First life on land: Mosses and ferns, about 450 million years ago

Oldest seafloor: Less than 200 million years

Frequency of supercontinent formation: About every 250 million years

Seawater cycle into mantle and back: About every 10 million years

"Nothing lasts long under the same form.

I have seen what once was solid earth changed into sea,

and lands created out of what once was ocean.

Seashells lie far away from ocean's waves. . . ."

—Ovid, *Metamorphoses,* Book XV

C omprehending the magnitude of geologic time is daunting yet vital for a perspective on the short but influential effects of humankind on the distillation of all preceding Earth history. Geologist John McPhee comments in *Basin and Range,* "Any number above a couple of thousand years—fifty thousand, fifty million—will with nearly equal effect awe the imagination to the point of paralysis." He also suggests a way to grasp the vastness of time: Stand with your arms held straight out to each side and let the extent of Earth's history be represented by the distance between the tips of your fingers. Running a file across the tip of the nail of your right middle finger would erase all of the time that humans have existed on Earth.

Another geologist Don L. Eicher in his slim volume *Geologic Time* presents the history of Earth in terms of a single imaginary year. In very early spring of Eicher's year, life began in the sea and continued as entirely microscopic marine forms until early fall—nothing was yet alive on land. Suddenly there was an explosion of new life within a few hours or days in November when the astonishing, distinctive, and enduring categories of multicellular life were established. Dinosaurs abounded in mid-December but were gone by the 26th. In the last minute of the year, the enormous ice sheets of the last ice age began to recede, marking the beginning of agriculture and the earliest stages of modern human civilization. Our generation is living in the last fraction of the last second.

The Geologic Time Scale

UNITS OF TIME WERE DEVISED by geologists more than a century ago to describe changes in the Earth, based mostly on the types of life found in fossils worldwide. The organization of the geologic time scale changes with new discoveries and varies by the source. Some scientists recognize only two great eons—the roughly 4-billion-year Precambrian before multicellular life developed on Earth and the Phanerozoic, from the time multicellular animals evolved about 570 million years ago to the present.

Some recognize four eons, splitting the Precambrian into three—the Priscoan (4.6 billion to 3.8 billion years ago), before the evidence of any life; the Archaean (3.8 billion to 2.5 billion years ago), marking the emergence of life; and the Proterozoic (2.5 billion to 57 million years ago), when oxygen levels rose on Earth and one-celled animals diversified greatly. Three great and distinctive ages of life on Earth, each ending with a mass extinction, are recognized within the Phanerozoic eon—the Paleozoic, Mesozoic, and Cenozoic eras. These eras are subdivided into periods and then epochs. This is the time scale used in this atlas.

Knowledge of the world in past times is obscured through burial and erosion of rocks over time; most of what has been learned comes from portions of continents once covered by ocean. So far, the oldest rocks found on Earth were formed about 4 billion years ago. The oldest fossils known are of cyanobacteria determined to be 3.45 billion years old. And the oldest remaining seafloor on Earth was created nearly 200 million years ago. The whole ocean floor, including mighty underwater

These giant ichthyosaurs are thought to have traveled the ocean in pods, similar to modern-day whales. Little was known about these ancient creatures before Canadian paleontologist Elizabeth Nicholls discovered in 1999 a massive specimen, measuring nearly 21 meters from nose to tail, along the Sikanni Chief River in British Columbia—the largest ichthyosaur ever discovered.

mountains, is destroyed—by subduction and melting or by being thrust up onto the land through continental collisions—roughly every 200 to 300 million years.

New methods for dating old rocks and fossils use the rate of decay of some radioactive elements and the ratios of heavy to light isotopes. Drilling techniques extract samples from hundreds of meters down in abyssal muds and the bedrock beneath; new acoustic methods map what we cannot see; and powerful computers allow the synthesis and analysis of data in unprecedented ways. As new evidence is discovered and data are correlated, the time scale will continue to be refined.

Pieces of the Puzzle

DRIFTING CONTINENTS, A VAST OCEAN, changes in atmosphere and climate, and evolving life have all worked together, influencing one another, as Earth's history has unfolded.

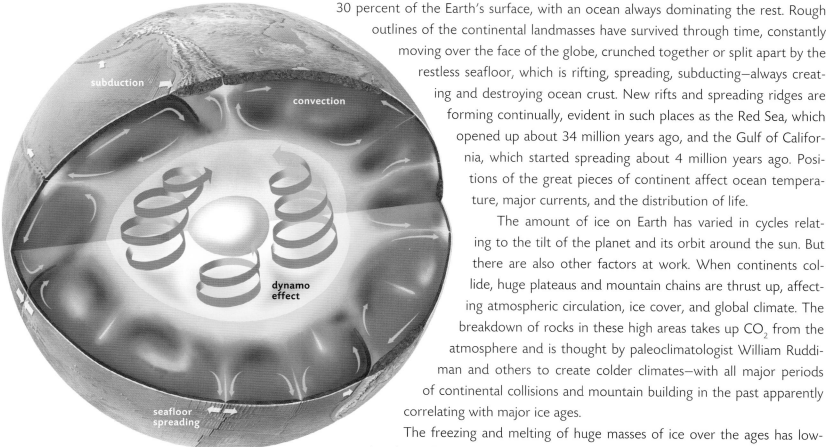

The amount of continental crust has been relatively constant since early time, covering about 30 percent of the Earth's surface, with an ocean always dominating the rest. Rough outlines of the continental landmasses have survived through time, constantly moving over the face of the globe, crunched together or split apart by the restless seafloor, which is rifting, spreading, subducting—always creating and destroying ocean crust. New rifts and spreading ridges are forming continually, evident in such places as the Red Sea, which opened up about 34 million years ago, and the Gulf of California, which started spreading about 4 million years ago. Positions of the great pieces of continent affect ocean temperature, major currents, and the distribution of life.

The amount of ice on Earth has varied in cycles relating to the tilt of the planet and its orbit around the sun. But there are also other factors at work. When continents collide, huge plateaus and mountain chains are thrust up, affecting atmospheric circulation, ice cover, and global climate. The breakdown of rocks in these high areas takes up CO_2 from the atmosphere and is thought by paleoclimatologist William Ruddiman and others to create colder climates—with all major periods of continental collisions and mountain building in the past apparently correlating with major ice ages.

The freezing and melting of huge masses of ice over the ages has lowered and raised sea level by hundreds of meters. Changing sea levels affect the size of shallow seas, which, in turn, influence the extent of nursery grounds for marine life and the amount of land exposed. Such changes affect erosion, which, in turn, alters the chemical composition of seawater—and so on. Two things are now confirmed: First, the planet has undergone continuous change—and is changing still—and, second, the knowledge needed to unravel these processes is still fragmentary.

Earth's Core: *Processes deep in the planet's molten core set up convection cells within the mantle that propel the crust's tectonic plates in their perpetual dance of seafloor spreading and subduction, forming supercontinents—that embrace all the land on Earth—then splitting and dispersing them again, about every 250 million years.*

Supercontinents

AT LEAST FIVE TIMES IN EARTH'S HISTORY—about every 250 million years—the continents have been brought together in one great "supercontinent," with all land joined in a single immense landmass, then split apart by new seafloor spreading. Evidence for early supercontinents is sparse, but four such events have been identified during Precambrian times—Vaalbara (3.1 billion to 2.8 billion years ago), Kenorland (2.7 billion to 2.5 billion years ago), Columbia (1.8 billion to 1.5 billion years ago), and Rodinia (1 billion to 750 million years ago). There have probably been two major supercontinents since the Precambrian: the Pannotia, roughly 600 million to 540 million years ago, and the most recent, Pangaea, about 300 million to 180 million years ago.

A comparison of two recent supercontinents—Rodinia and Pangaea—reveals great differences that highlight the complexity of the Earth's interacting systems. During the Proterozoic era, Rodinia aligned all of the Earth's land east to west along the Equator, but despite the tropical latitude, much of Rodinia was covered by ice in one of the earliest and coldest ice ages. By contrast, the Paleozoic supercontinent Pangaea was aligned north to south from Pole to Pole but had no ice cover for about a hundred million years. This land configuration disrupted globe-encircling currents and gave birth to two great gyres in the Northern and Southern Hemispheres—precursors of today's gyres in the northern and southern Atlantic and Pacific Oceans.

THE PRECAMBRIAN OCEAN—4.6 BILLION TO 570 MILLION YEARS AGO

More than 90 percent of Earth's history—roughly 4 billion years—is embraced by the Precambrian. Earth was formed 4.6 billion years ago, and the ocean has been a prominent feature for all but the earliest fraction of that time, when the planet was so hot that all water was held as water vapor in the atmosphere. In January 2001 a cover story in the journal *Nature* provided strong evidence that a nascent ocean was present on the Earth's surface 4.3 billion years ago. Several grains of a mineral called zircon were found in Australia and shown to have a special composition of oxygen isotopes that could be formed only in liquid water at the ocean surface. About 4 billion years ago, it appears that barren masses of land projecting through Earth's young but enormous Proterozoic ocean were engulfed by a toxic atmosphere rich in carbon dioxide, with nitrogen, some hydrogen, and ammonia, and probably laced with methane. The sun was 20 to 25 percent less bright than today, and surface temperature of the planet was probably about 70°C.

Ocean Magnetic Anomalies:

A symmetrical pattern of positive and negative magnetic values is found in bands of seafloor on either side of all spreading ridges. When molten material from the magma rises and cools along the ridge, the ferrous materials in it take on the form of tiny magnets pointing to the positive pole in the Earth's magnetic field, currently the North Pole. Only about half of these magnets point north, though, because the Earth's magnetic field has reversed from time to time, with positive polarity often at the South Pole. The pattern of reversed polarity found in oceanic crust is the same worldwide, giving clues to seafloor spreading rates and the age of oceanic crust.

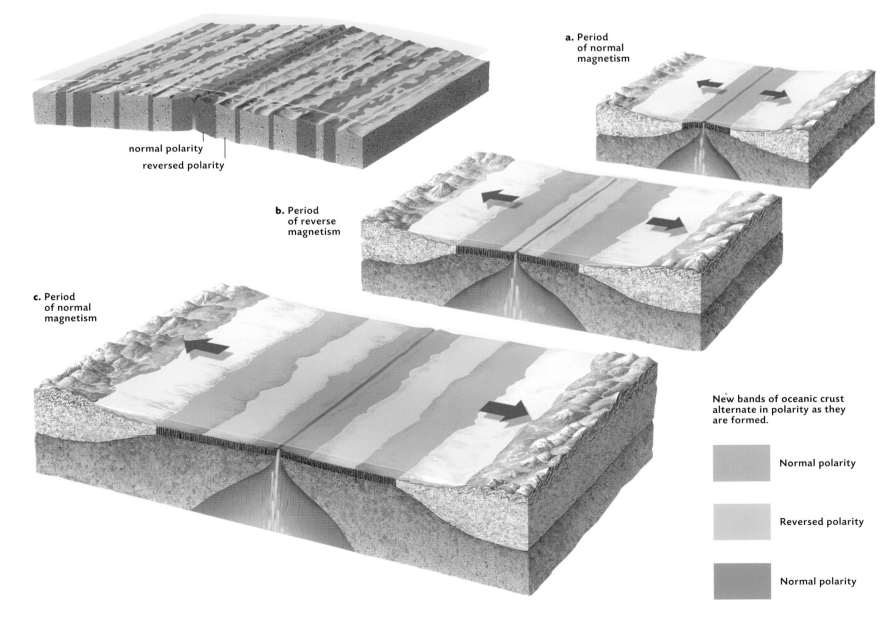

normal polarity
reversed polarity

a. Period of normal magnetism

b. Period of reverse magnetism

c. Period of normal magnetism

New bands of oceanic crust alternate in polarity as they are formed.

Normal polarity

Reversed polarity

Normal polarity

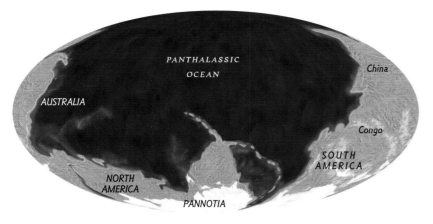

600 MILLION YEARS AGO

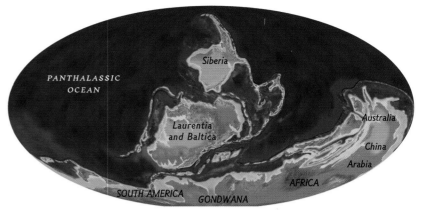

400 MILLION YEARS AGO

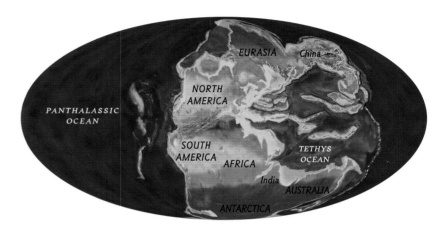

250 MILLION YEARS AGO

Continents Adrift: *Seafloor spreading has constantly moved continents around the face of the Earth. At 600 million years ago (Ma), Pannotia concentrated much of the land—including North and South America—around the South Pole. This broke into Laurentia and Gondwanaland at about 400Ma, then all land was rammed together into the supercontinent Pangea about 250Ma. Pangea split apart about 180Ma, and over the past 90 million years the current map has taken shape. Over the next 50 million years, the East African Rift valley will widen, Australia will collide with Asia, the Caribbean Sea will narrow, and the Mediterranean Sea will close up.*

SEE ALSO: modern-day CO$_2$ levels, pages 39, 270, and 317

WEB LINK: alternate plate reconstructions

The Archaean seas spawned the oldest fossils ever found—photosynthetic cyanobacteria that date from 3.45 billion years ago. But these organisms surely were not the first and were not alone, as microbial life advanced and extended throughout the world, following the water. Photosynthetic microbes gradually began to alter the mix of atmospheric gases by taking up CO$_2$ and churning out free oxygen. Bacteria proliferated massively, transforming the very rocks that gave them sustenance and leaving behind mineral deposits. Some have concentrated radioactive materials that today are mined as uranium deposits; others gathered iron, silver, and gold from the sea and deposited them as great veins of ore now being mined. The archaea, eubacteria, and eukaryotes emerged, paving the way for greater complexity.

Stromatolites were abundant in Archaean waters. Layered limestone rock formations found in Michigan, Wisconsin, Africa, and Australia were long thought simply to be mineralized deposits of mud. But in 1957 they were recognized as fossilized creations of ancient microorganisms growing in dense mats, primarily cyanobacteria, whose slimy cell coatings trapped layers of rock and sand, building dome-shaped structures a meter wide and several meters high. Stromatolites were later found alive in Shark Bay, western Australia, and in a channel with high current off Lee Stocking Island in the Bahamas. The few living lumps of rock and cyanobacteria alive today are hundreds of years old, but represent life as it was in shallow waters worldwide from 3 billion years ago to well into the Proterozoic.

Rocks and fossils from the Proterozoic have been identified at more than 30 localities on five continents, often bearing important sources of metallic ores—iron, gold, copper, nickel, and uranium. Abundant fossils mark this period—mostly bacteria, but organisms with organized nuclei in their cells developed during this time as well. Oxygen levels continued to rise with the proliferation of photosynthetic organisms, and this oxygen buildup appears to correlate with the appearance—then explosion—of multicellular life, from various forms of algae to the first animals. Fossil impressions of multicellular animals and frondlike organisms from the very late Proterozoic, about 600 million years ago, were found first in 1946 in sandstone deposits in the Ediacara Hills of South Australia. Some resemble small sponges, jellyfish, soft corals, sea pens, and annelid worms, as well as seaweed up to a meter long. By 590 million to 580 million years ago, calcareous algae were present, as well as animals with a number of hard parts—denticles, plates, tubes, and shells.

THE PALEOZOIC OCEAN—570 MILLION TO 240 MILLION YEARS AGO

The Paleozoic era includes two of the most significant events in the history of animal life. First came an explosion in diversity, with almost all animal phyla currently known appearing within a few million years. At the end, the largest mass extinction known eliminated more than 90 percent of all marine animal species, although representatives of most of the major divisions remained. The Paleozoic era embraces six periods—from oldest to youngest, the Cambrian, Ordovician, Silurian, Devonian, Carboniferous (sometimes separated into Mississippian and Pennsylvanian), and Permian periods—whose time ranges are shown on page 95.

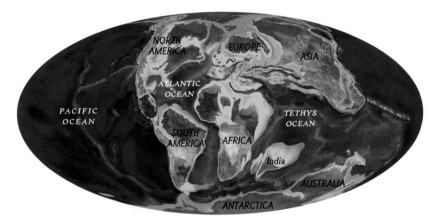

90 MILLION YEARS AGO

65 MILLION YEARS AGO

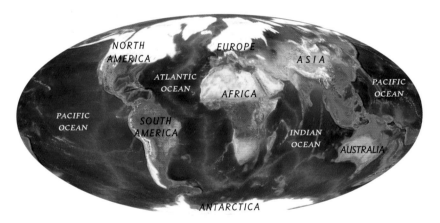

18,000 YEARS AGO

PRESENT

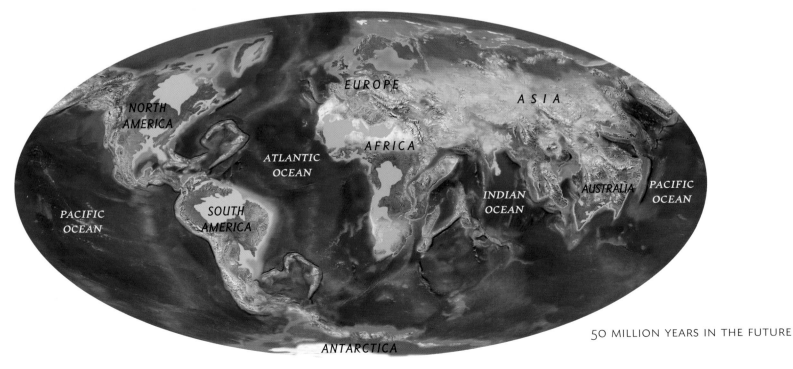

50 MILLION YEARS IN THE FUTURE

Right: *In life a jet-propelled predator, in death an opalescent fossil, this ammonite is one of many kinds of extinct mollusks that shaped the nature of ocean ecosystems during thousands of millennia.*

During the Cambrian, the ocean abounded in what paleontologist Peter Douglas Ward refers to as "creepers and burrowers and feeble swimmers," notably the ubiquitous crawling trilobites. Thousands of fossil sites all over the world provide glimpses of Cambrian creatures, but the Burgess Shale high on a mountainside in British Columbia is legendary for its richness and abundance of clues about life from this time. Discovered in 1909 by Smithsonian Institution scientist Charles D. Walcott, the area has yielded more than 60,000 unique fossils, many with rarely preserved soft parts.

Found in the Burgess Shale are a few curiously elongated, jawless creatures distinguished by the presence of a firm rodlike structure along the back, making them chordates, the ancestors of

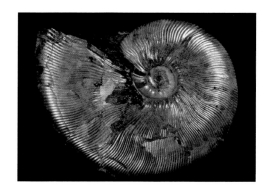

Relics from ancient seas, these Indian Ocean chambered nautiluses, Nautilus pompilius, *are living relatives of a large group of extinct cephalopods, the ammonites, that were abundant during the Paleozoic and Mesozoic eras, 400 million to 65 million years ago.*

A New Geologic Age?

Geologic eras are divided mostly according to the plants and animals living during each time span. Many scientists are arguing for designation of a new epoch in the Quaternary, called the Anthropocene (*anthro* being the Greek root for human), because humankind has clearly dominated the globe in ways that have affected all of its plants and animals in recent centuries.

Geologic Time: *This timeline is used by geologists to describe the sequence of and relationships between events that have occurred during the 4.5-billion-year history of the Earth.*

fish and other vertebrates (including humans) having backbones. A few types of chordates still live in shallow tropical seas today. The remains of arthropods are also common in the shale, along with numerous crinoids, sea cucumbers, worms, brachiopods, macroscopic algae, microscopic dinoflagellates, cyanobacteria, and other protists—typical life of this period before flowering plants, fish, amphibians, reptiles, birds, and mammals appeared on the scene.

Early in the Ordovician, the lands now known as southern Europe, Asia, South America, Africa, Antarctica, and Australia were gathered around the South Pole forming the giant continental mass Gondwanaland. North America straddled the Equator, largely submerged, and great carbonate formations built up through accumulation of the skeletons of countless minute marine organisms.

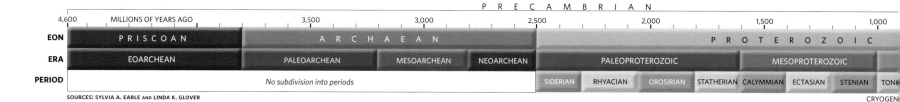

PRECAMBRIAN

MILLIONS OF YEARS AGO 4,600	3,500	3,000	2,500		2,000	1,500		1,000
EON PRISCOAN	ARCHAEAN				PROTEROZOIC			
ERA EOARCHEAN	PALEOARCHEAN	MESOARCHEAN	NEOARCHEAN		PALEOPROTEROZOIC		MESOPROTEROZOIC	
PERIOD	No subdivision into periods			SIDERIAN	RHYACIAN	OROSIRIAN	STATHERIAN CALYMMIAN ECTASIAN STENIAN	TON

SOURCES: SYLVIA A. EARLE AND LINDA K. GLOVER

CRYOGEN

While mosses and ferns began to green the land, life in the ocean continued to diversify. Mollusks appeared, with variations on the theme of bivalves and nautiluses. Fossils of corals, echinoids, crinoids, and starfish abound in Ordovician limestone formations in China, North America, and Argentina. In places, massive reefs of large sponges and bryozoans sheltered complex assemblages of invertebrates. This period gave rise to a great diversity of bony fishes, the Ordovician ostracoderms, armored with bony head shields, scales, a slitlike mouth, and no jaws. Some made their way into inland rivers, lakes, and streams, where much of the development of bony fishes followed. About 440 million years ago, a mass extinction eliminated more than a fifth of the known families of organisms and brought a close to the Ordovician.

During the Silurian period, 430 million years ago, a great but short glaciation occurred in Africa, which was then at the South Pole as part of Gondwanaland. When the large ice sheets melted, the resulting rise in sea level caused shallow flooding over large coastal areas, depositing vast layers of sediment. Later withdrawal of the water left oxidized "red beds" of rusty iron and salt deposits distinctive to the Silurian. The ocean sheltered the first reefs of coral, and evidence of true sharks appeared.

The Devonian is sometimes called the age of fishes, because land and ocean waters teemed with creatures recognizable as fish. Most of them—jawless predators armored with protective head plates–have long since disappeared. Another group, the placoderms, emerged as the earliest known bony fish with jaws; their mouths were like those of turtles—sharp edged, with no teeth. The armored fish, the first sharks, the first fish with fin rays, and the first lobe-finned fish lived during this time and gave rise to the enormous diversity of fish in today's waters. One type of lobe-finned fish, the coelacanth, is abundant in fossils from 300 million years ago until about 65 million years ago, with many widely distributed species. Because it was long believed extinct, the discovery of one alive in South Africa in 1938 (described in Chapter 6) was the marine equivalent of coming upon a live *Tyrannosaurus rex*. Other, less celebrated survivors are modern hagfishes, sleek, slippery eel-like animals notorious for generating copious amounts of gelatinous goo. Fossils of their forebears from more than 300 million years ago look much like the more than 60 species living today. Unrelated but similar in looks are the lampreys, also modern creatures with ancestry dating back to the Devonian.

On the land, tropical forests flourished, then were buried and compressed, forming immense coal deposits in what is now the Canadian Arctic and southern China. Among the rich diversity of invertebrates in seas at that time—sea scorpions, sea lilies, cephalopods, jellyfish, and sponges—were many kinds of horseshoe crabs, some venturing into fresh water and even onto the land. The four surviving species appear little changed from ancestors that left their mark on rocks more than 350 million years ago. Near the end of the Devonian, most disappeared along with about a fifth of all known families of organisms in another broad extinction.

Early in the Carboniferous period, the climate was much warmer than today, as the present Northern Hemisphere continents joined to form the landmass Laurentia and slipped toward the Equator. Shallow seas covered many regions now far inland and high above sea level, their former existence as aquatic realms evidenced by abundant marine fossils of many invertebrates, protists, and numerous early kinds of fish. During this period, the heavily armored fish species of the Devonian were largely replaced by ancestors of bony fish that ever since have been the principal vertebrate animals on Earth. A breakthrough—the amniote egg, protected from drying out when laid on land—allowed reptiles to reproduce and settle away from the sea. Four-legged animals evolved as well.

Pressed for time in the Burgess Shale, this trilobite is one of a group of arthropods that prospered from 570 million to 240 million years ago, when they and numerous other forms of life were victims of the Permian Extinction.

An artist's concept of what a living trilobite may have looked like, belly-side up.

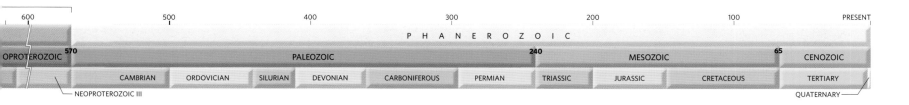

Prehistoric Marine Animals:

Working from the fossil record, a team of specialized scientists and artists recreated what some ancient sea creatures from the late Cretaceous period might have looked like. Represented above are, clockwise from top right, a Thalassomedon, Nothosaur, Shonisaur, Archelon, and a croc-like Tylosaur. One Shonisaurus specimen found in Nevada measured an incredible 15 meters in length.

WEB LINK: prehistoric animals

Birth and Death in the Mesozoic

Global warming in the Mesozoic era supported not only the emergence of dinosaurs, but also encouraged the widespread growth of tropical forests and spawned a massive blossoming of minute planktonic organisms in the sea. Buried remains of the forests created massive coal deposits, and the death, burial, and compression of trillions of tiny ocean creatures created widespread oil deposits. Thus, birth and death in the long-distant Mesozoic is now supporting the heating, energy, and economic needs of the human species that emerged millions of years later.

During the Permian, the climate became less stable, with sea level fluctuating many times over millions of years, reflecting periodic formation of ice at the Poles. Creatures particularly identified with the 50-million-year Permian period are ammonites, brachiopods, and a wide array of other marine invertebrates. Various bony fish, as well as sharks, expanded their numbers and types, and reptiles developed further both on land and in aquatic realms. The Permian ended with the largest mass extinction known, eliminating more than 90 percent of marine species. The cause remains controversial, but the devastating decline in the abundance and diversity of life opened the way for new types to flourish.

THE MESOZOIC OCEAN—240 MILLION TO 65 MILLION YEARS AGO

The Mesozoic era—the age of reptiles—includes the Triassic, Jurassic, and Cretaceous periods. Widely known as the time when dinosaurs ruled, large predatory reptiles also prospered in the ocean. Overall, the climate remained warm, with no ice crowning either Pole. Distinctive phyla of protists, fungi, plants, invertebrate animals, and fish continued to develop, including the first-known skates and rays. Diatoms, coccolithophorids, and dinoflagellates arose in the sea during the Mesozoic, dominating the phytoplankton, driving ocean food webs, shaping ocean chemistry, and contributing to oxygen production in the atmosphere—then and ever since.

Near the Equator during the Triassic, the great supercontinent of Pangaea embraced the small, warm Tethys Sea, ancestor of the Mediterranean and home for the first shallow-water coral reefs. Dinosaurs roamed the land, and the world's ecosystems thrived under a relatively mild and stable regime with no ice ages for almost a hundred million years—through the Triassic and much of the Jurassic period. Most of the major groups of Triassic sea creatures are still in the ocean today—jellyfish, sponges, crustaceans, polychaete worms, mollusks, starfish, crinoids, bryozoans, and others—but the species and their proportions have changed. The coccolithophorids are thought to have originated during this time—minute photosynthetic protists with calcium carbonate shells that make up enormous chalk formations on land today. Evolutionary biologist Gary Vermeij suggests that the Triassic decline of certain widespread and abundant marine mollusks was caused by the arrival of new predators. Many clam relatives perished, but some survived by developing ways to burrow into the sand or mud, with only a snorkel-like siphon exposed to obtain food, water, and oxygen. Other Triassic mollusks that abound in the fossil record are ammonites and nautiloids, shelled relatives of today's octopuses and squids.

Starting about 180 million years ago, during the Jurassic period, the supercontinent Pangaea began to split into the large northerly landmass Laurasia (which later became Europe, Asia, and North America) and the southerly landmass Gondwanaland (which became South America, Africa, India, Australia, and Antarctica). Except for a shallow sill between northern Africa and southern Europe, water flowed uninterrupted around the Earth's Equator. Creation of the Indian Ocean began, causing India to separate from Australia and Antarctica and begin its journey northward.

Brian Huber
THE SUPERGREENHOUSE OCEAN

Imagine the ocean being as warm as bathwater from the surface to the bottom and from Pole to Pole. Imagine, too, the polar areas being warm, free of ice, covered in luxuriant forests, and supporting a wide variety of animal life. Such a world existed during a phase of global climatic warmth called the Cretaceous "Supergreenhouse," which began about 94 million years ago and lasted about 11 million years. The configuration of Earth's surface then was much different, with the ocean covering about 7 percent more of the planet than today. Much of Europe, North Africa, and southern Asia was covered by the Tethys Ocean, a seaway that stretched continuously around the globe at the Equator. And Southern Hemisphere continents were either connected by land or separated by narrow seaways.

ago—reveal that sea-surface waters ranged between 34°C and 42°C near the Equator (compared with today's average of 27°C), and between 28°C and 32°C at 60° south latitude (compared with about 2°C today). Ocean waters at depths of between 1,500 and 500 meters ranged from 15°C to 25°C during the Supergreenhouse period, compared with 2°C to 5°C today. The ocean was warmer everywhere, on the surface and at depth. The extremely warm climate in the Cretaceous Supergreenhouse was most likely related to a period of major global volcanism events, which spewed out a large amount of carbon dioxide (CO_2) into the atmosphere. Using our present-day climate models to try to simulate the extremely warm ocean conditions does not work, however; even assuming an unre-

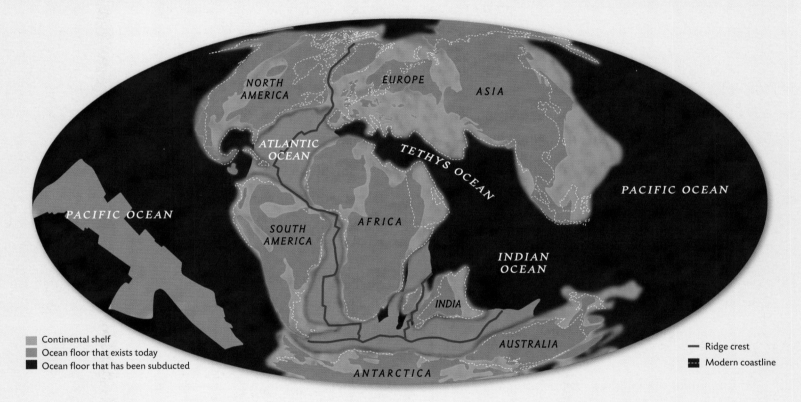

This map of the continental plates from 90 million years ago reveals the small area of oceanic crust available for deep-sea drilling of sediments from that time.

A record of ocean temperature change before, during, and after the Cretaceous Supergreenhouse has been constructed from countless chemical analyses of foraminifera shells found in deep-sea cores worldwide. As these tiny creatures make their shells, the ratio of $^{18}O/^{16}O$ oxygen isotopes incorporated is determined by the oxygen isotope composition of seawater at the time, and the ratio of oxygen isotopes in seawater depends on the water temperature at the time. Temperatures of the ocean during ancient times can thus be determined from shells that fall to the seafloor, are buried and preserved, and are later drilled up for analysis. Comparing the oxygen isotope temperature records from benthic (bottom-dwelling) and planktonic (surface-dwelling) foraminifera is especially valuable as a monitor of how sea-surface and bottom-water temperatures have varied over the past 120 million years.

Analyses of benthic and planktonic foraminifera from peak warmth in the Cretaceous Supergreenhouse—at 94 million and 90 million years

alistic level of six times more than today's CO_2 still can't reproduce the Supergreenhouse polar temperatures indicated from the deep-sea cores. This suggests that the ocean and climate mechanisms that transport heat toward the Poles and the global dynamics of ocean-climate interactions were very different during the Cretaceous Supergreenhouse than they are today.

Only 10 percent of the ocean crust that existed during the Cretaceous Supergreenhouse period remains available for drilling and study today, however, because most of it has been destroyed by subduction under the continents during seafloor spreading and plate tectonics. Finding the remaining Cretaceous sediments for drilling and analysis is necessary to help us better understand the Cretaceous climate and to help us better predict environmental changes that will occur in a future "greenhouse" world, with increasing temperatures caused by increased CO_2 concentrations.

William B. F. Ryan
THE DISAPPEARING TETHYS

As the two continental landmasses of Africa and Europe separated from the Americas beginning some 200 million years ago, a vast new seaway appeared called the new Tethys (in Greek mythology, the wife of Zeus and goddess of the ocean). Evidence of it has practically disappeared as the engine that drives the Earth's plates carries it back into our planet's interior. Just a little piece survives intact in the eastern Mediterranean Sea. Scraps of Tethys's sediment cover and volcanic bedrock lie scattered among the contorted rocks of the Alpine mountain system stretching from Spain to Persia.

quarters of Tethys had vanished. Continued convergence also brought the northwestern tip of Africa (today's Morocco) into collision with the Iberian prong of Europe 6 million years ago.

Cut off entirely at both ends, the trapped remainder of the Tethys Sea dried up and its deep floor was transformed into salt pans, lakes, and deserts. A layer of salt more than 1 kilometer thick accumulated as the seawater evaporated. Suddenly, a stretch of the Rif-Betic mountain belt at the western end collapsed. Atlantic water poured into this Gibraltar breach to produce the largest known flood event in the history of our solar system.

Although the modern Mediterranean Sea is young west of Italy, it contains remnants of the ancient Tethys beneath the deeper floors of its eastern region.

The reason the sea did not continue to spread, as is happening in the Atlantic and Indian Oceans, is only now being deciphered from calculations of past tectonic plate motions. Changes in plate movements are seen in the ocean's crust as reversals in the direction of the Earth's magnetic field. Over the past five decades oceanographic ships have charted in remarkable fidelity the magnetic pattern produced by these reversals.

Recently the pattern has shown that there was a major alteration in global plate movements starting 80 million years ago when Australia began to separate from Antarctica. As a consequence of the resulting plate motion reconfiguration, Africa and Eurasia switched from a diverging to a converging path. Tethys found itself caught in the jaws of a closing vise, initially thousands of kilometers wide but destined to shut tight. About 20 million years ago, around the time of the appearance of the horse, contact was made between the Arabian promontory of Africa and the belly of Eurasia in the vicinity of today's Zagros Mountains of Iraq and Iran. By then, three-

The filling of what remained of the Tethys Sea took no more than a decade and gave birth to the sea we know today as the Mediterranean. But the vise still tightens.

Consequently, as the Tethys seafloor slips under the Aegean and Tyrrhenian Seas, the grinding of plates past each other rattles Portugal, Spain, Italy, Greece, and Turkey, shaking cities such as Lisbon, Messina, and Istanbul during great earthquakes. The arrival of Tethys's water deep into the mantle beneath the southern edge of Europe triggered the eruptions of Vesuvius and Santorini, which buried the towns of Pompeii and Akrotiri under volcanic ash. As the Tethys seafloor continues to descend into our planet's interior, its skin is dragged along. This skin stretches and tears along monstrous detachment faults, bringing to the surface materials formerly buried at great depths and subjected to high temperatures. Such geological stretching exposes marble whose quarries in Greece and Italy supplied the illustrious sculptors of antiquity.

In the Jurassic ocean, great seagoing lizards competed with sharks, a growing array of bony carnivorous fish, and meat-eating invertebrates, from cephalopod mollusks to large crustaceans. Dinosaurs were conspicuous in forests on the continents, and the first birds appeared. In the Gulf of Mexico, enormous salt deposits accumulated, some hundreds of meters high and about a kilometer across, indicating prolonged periods of seawater evaporation. These salt domes, as well as organic-rich shales in the North Sea, are today associated with vast oil and gas reserves buried during the Jurassic.

Pangaea continued to break apart during the Cretaceous, and seafloor spreading built the North and South Atlantic Ocean Basins to about half their current width. Meat-eating snails developed, and ammonites flourished, gradually declined, and then disappeared by about 70 million years ago. The nature of life during the Cretaceous is recorded in numerous areas around the world, including the chalky, 90-meter-high White Cliffs of Dover in southeastern England. Made of the shells of the minute coccolithophorids that drifted eons ago in an ocean covering great portions of what is now land, the cliffs represent millions of years of history. The remains of many marine reptiles, fish, and thousands of other kinds of animals are embedded in the world's great limestone formations.

The Cretaceous period ended abruptly in another of Earth's momentous mass extinctions at what geologists call the K-T Boundary, with K from *Kreide,* the German word for Cretaceous, and T for Tertiary, the first period of the dawning Cenozoic era. The cause of the demise of the dinosaurs and about 75 percent of other forms of life on the planet was hotly debated for decades, but most scientists now agree that the impact of a huge asteroid caused the massive extinctions. In 1980, physicist Luis Alvarez and his geologist son Walter discovered an unusually high level of the element iridium—characteristic of asteroids—in layers of clay dated 65 million years old at several sites around the world. Subsequently, an enormous crater was discovered underwater near Mexico's Yucatán Peninsula. At 145 to 180 kilometers across, this crater, called Chicxulub, is one of the largest impact structures known on Earth. Simulations suggest an event 6 million times as energetic as the 1980 Mount St. Helens volcanic eruption, with resulting magnitude 10 or 11 earthquakes—stronger than anything experienced in human history—literally rocked the world. The many results of the impact—earthquakes, a massive burning of forests, a tremendous tsunami inundating the continents, and dust and soot blocking the sun for months—together created an event that forever changed the nature of life on Earth.

The Oldest Ocean Crust

Many clues to ancient marine life are to be found on land. Very old ocean deposits are preserved above water through lowering of global sea level, and especially by the thrusting up of the seafloor in mountain-building events when continents collide. In contrast, nothing more than about 200 million years old can be found on today's seafloor, because all the seafloor older than that has either been uplifted into mountains or thrust under the continents and melted in the mantle. Ocean crust from 165 million to almost 200 million years old is found on the margins of all the current ocean basins, but the oldest has been found in two places: in the western Pacific, in the Pigafetta Basin (part of the East Mariana Basin), just east of the Mariana Trench; and remnants of the Tethys Sea in the eastern Mediterranean.

Sulfur, salt, and other minerals color the crater of Dallol Volcano in Ethiopia.

THE CENOZOIC OCEAN—65 MILLION YEARS AGO TO THE PRESENT

Geologists divide the Cenozoic era into the Tertiary period (65 million to 1.8 million years ago) and the Quaternary period (1.8 million years ago to the present). The Tertiary, from oldest to most recent, is further broken down into the Paleocene, Eocene, Oligocene, Miocene, and Pliocene epochs. The Quaternary is divided into the Pleistocene and Holocene epochs.

In the early Tertiary Paleocene epoch, about 50 million years ago, drifting pieces of the former supercontinent Pangaea collided with each other, creating new mountain ranges: Africa and Italy pushed into western Eurasia raising the Alps; Spain moved toward France raising the Pyrenees; and the start of India's collision with Asia began the uplifting of the Tibetan Plateau and creation of the Himalaya, still rising today at about a centimeter a year. Most marine life resembled modern forms, birds diversified, and mammals evolved into creatures as small as 0.09-kilogram shrews and as large as 91-metric-ton whales. Small mammals diversified on land in the Paleocene epoch (65 million to 56 million years ago), the first marine mammals appeared during the Eocene (56 million to 35 million years ago),

Above: *Only four species of horseshoe crabs, three in Asia and one in the Atlantic, now represent a class of chelicerates that were abundant and widespread 200 million to 400 million years ago. This* Limulus polyphemus *from Cape Cod is part of a population that extends southward to parts of the Caribbean and the Gulf of Mexico.*

and the Oligocene (35 million to 23 million years ago) saw the appearance of the first anthropoid apes, as well as the proliferation of grasses, including the great marshes bordering shallow seas in temperate and tropical areas.

In the late Tertiary Neocene epoch, flowering plants and mammals diversified, including the ancestors of humankind, and whales, dolphins, and other sea mammals flourished in the oceans. The arrangement of land and water was much like today, but with some significant differences that affected marine life. Late in the Miocene epoch (23.8 million to 5.3 million years ago), about 6 million years ago, a lowering of sea level sealed off the Mediterranean Sea from the waters of the Atlantic Ocean. The deep Mediterranean dried up completely several times, destroying marine life, and today's inhabitants came in from the Atlantic when its waters flowed back over the shallow sill at the Strait of Gibraltar. By the middle of the Pliocene epoch (5.3 million to 1.8 million years ago), a land bridge—the Isthmus of Panama—developed between North and South America, isolating the Gulf of Mexico and effectively blocking exchange between the life-filled waters of the Atlantic and the Pacific. Also in the middle Pliocene, 2.5 million years ago, hominids were making tools. By the end of this epoch, the movement of continents encircled the waters of the high Arctic with land, water completely surrounded the continent of Antarctica, and ice caps that persist today formed at both Poles.

The Pleistocene epoch (1.8 million to about 11,000 years ago) was the great ice age, with as many as 30 to 50 successive episodes when huge continental ice sheets more than a kilometer high spread south across the continental landmasses, and nearly half the world ocean was full of sea ice and icebergs. Each successive glacial event locked up so much water that sea level was lowered as much as 200 meters, alternately exposing and inundating broad coastal areas. The last major advance of ice in the Northern Hemisphere occurred 18,000 years ago, carving valleys, leveling hills, and creating the Great Lakes. Humankind emerged during these great ice age fluctuations in climate, and half a million years ago early humans mastered the use of fire.

Ever since the beginning of the Holocene epoch (about 11,000 years ago), Earth has been gradually warming, with ice melting, sea levels rising to today's familiar shorelines, and conditions being created that have favored the prosperity of humankind. By 3,000 years ago, crops were being planted, calendars devised, and the moon and stars relied upon to guide early ocean navigators. Our species co-evolved with numerous now extinct land animals. They and entire ecosystems gave way to changes in climate, loss of habitat, and the increasingly effective predator *Homo sapiens*, as humankind steadily advanced in territory, sophistication, and numbers.

Drawing on the past as prelude, it is clear that the same processes that have shaped the Earth and its cargo of creatures are continuing. The ability to understand the natural systems that support humankind provides the best hope for charting a prosperous, enduring future within complex and ever-changing systems. ◻

Opposite: *Clues etched on stone, the 145-million-year-old spiraling track and remains of one of the hundreds of kinds of now-extinct horseshoe crabs provide a glimpse of life in an ancient ocean.*

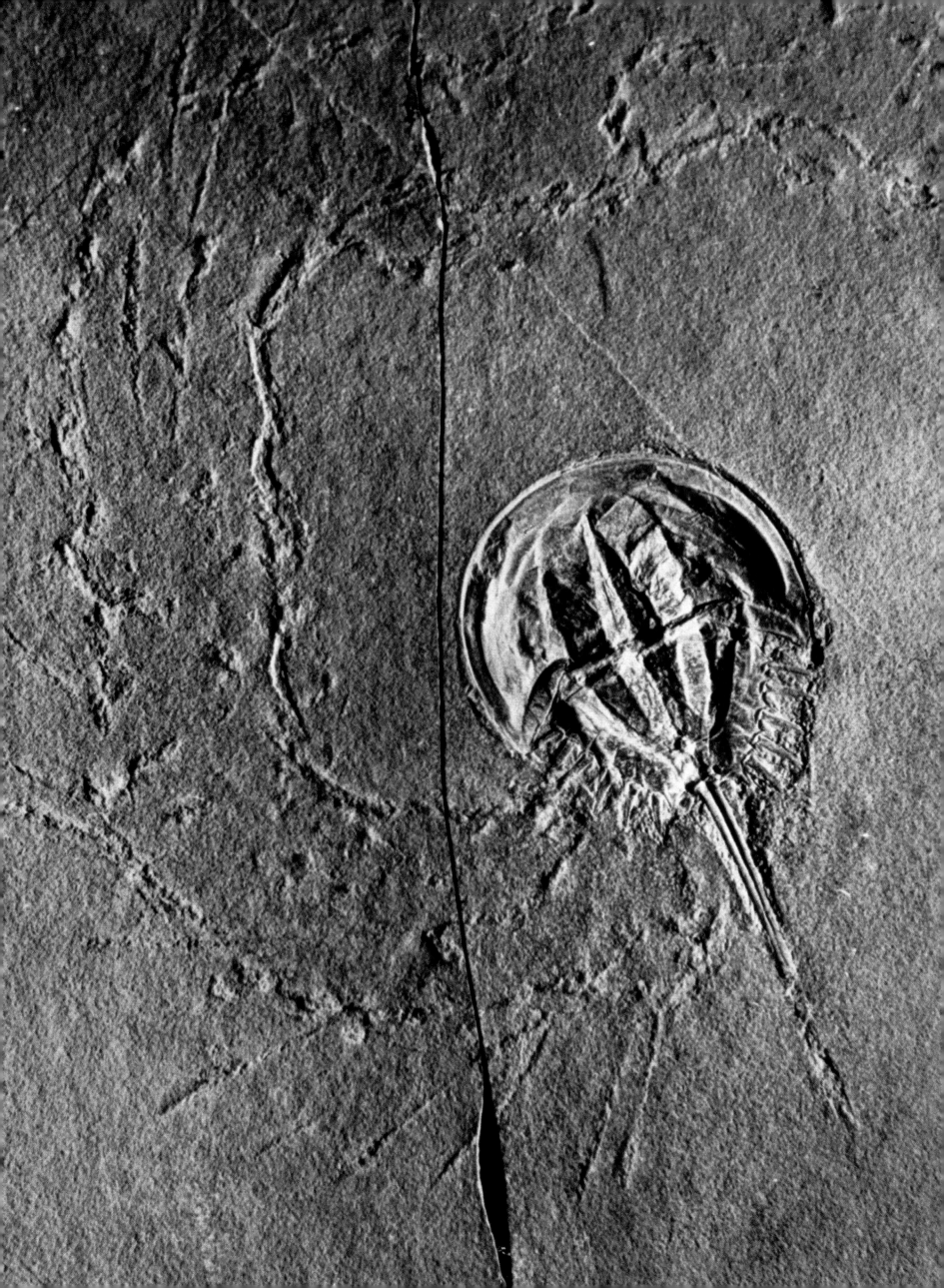

The highest concentrations of chlorophyll (yellows to reds) tend to be found along coastlines, supported either by nutrients in run-off from the land or upwelling along arid coastlines. In the North and South Atlantic, warm tropical waters resist mixing with deeper water where nutrients are more abundant and thus the abundance of phytoplankton is low (purples and deep blues).

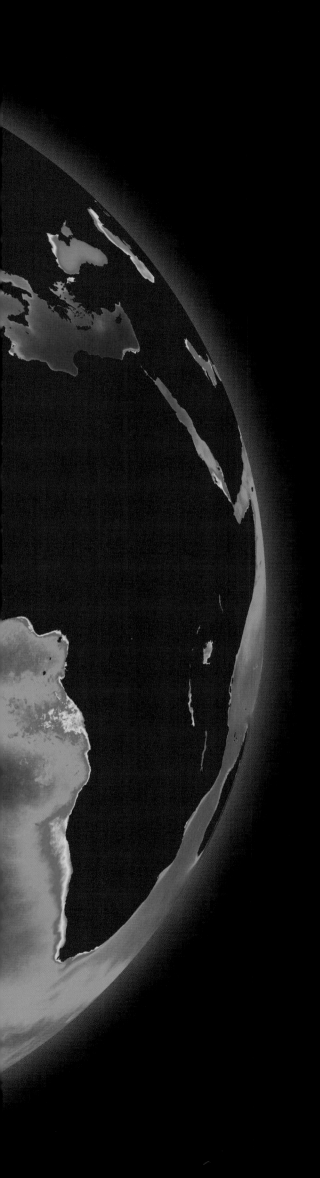

Chapter 4

ATLANTIC OCEAN

Atlantic Ocean Seafloor

J K L M N P Q R

11 10 9 8 7 6 5 4 3 2 1

AFRICA

EQUATOR

TROPIC OF CAPRICORN

ANTARCTIC CIRCLE

ANTARCTICA

Guinea Terrace

Skeleton Coast

Niger Fan · Bioko · Principe · São Tomé

GULF OF GUINEA

Grain Coast · Ivory Coast · Gold Coast · Slave Coast

Cape Palmas

Du Chaillu Seamounts

Brazza Seamounts

GUINEA PLAIN

GUINEA BASIN

GAMBIA PLAIN

ANGOLA PLAIN

ANGOLA BASIN

Congo Canyon

Congo Fan

Orange Fan

Cape of Good Hope
Cape Agulhas

Agulhas Bank

AGULHAS PLATEAU

AGULHAS BASIN

CAPE PLAIN

CAPE BASIN

WALVIS RIDGE

St. Helena

Wyandot Seamount

Vema Seamount

Meteor Rise

Herdman Seamount

Metz Seamount

Meteor Seamount

Discovery Tablemount

Spiess Seamount

ATLANTIC–INDIAN RIDGE

Bouvet

BOUVET FRACTURE ZONE

CONRAD FRACTURE ZONE

ATLANTIC–INDIAN BASIN

ENDERBY PLAIN

COSMONAUT SEA

Astrid Ridge

Gunnerus Bank

Richardson Seamount

METEOR FRACTURE ZONE

AGULHAS FRACTURE ZONE

AMERICA–ANTARCTIC RIDGE

MAUD RISE

WEDDELL PLAIN

WEDDELL SEA

Tristan da Cunha Group

SIERRA LEONE BASIN

Sierra Leone Rise

SIERRA LEONE FRACTURE ZONE

VERNADSKY FRACTURE ZONE

DOLDRUMS FRACTURE ZONE

CEARA PLAIN

DEMERARA PLAIN

Demerara Plateau

GUIANA BASIN

CAPE VERDE BASIN

GUATEMALA BASIN

LESSER ANTILLES

Trinidad

COCOS RIDGE

PANAMA BASIN

GALÁPAGOS ISLANDS

GALÁPAGOS RIFT

CARNEGIE RIDGE

PERU BASIN

NAZCA RIDGE

MENDOZA RISE

GALÁPAGOS RISE

De Gerlache Seamounts

Peter I Island

Juan Fernández Islands

San Ambrosio · San Félix I.

VALDIVIA FRACTURE ZONE

CHILE FRACTURE ZONE

CHILE RISE

CHILE BASIN

PERU–CHILE TRENCH

SOUTH PACIFIC OCEAN

SOUTHEAST PACIFIC BASIN

HUMBOLDT PLAIN

SOUTH AMERICA

St. Peter and St. Paul Rocks

Fernando de Noronha

Point Calcanhar

Abrolhos Seamounts · Hotspur Seamount

Columbia Seamount

Jaseur Seamount

Martin Vaz Islands

TRINDADE SEACHANNEL

Abrolhos Bank

Ferraz Ridge

Amazon Fan

Ceara Ridge

PERNAMBUCO PLAIN

Stocks Seamount

BRAZIL BASIN

ROMANCHE FRACTURE ZONE

CHAIN FRACTURE ZONE

ASCENSION FRACTURE ZONE

Ascension

FOUR NORTH FRACTURE ZONE

ROMANCHE GAP

ATLANTIC FRACTURE ZONE

MID-ATLANTIC RIDGE

Romanche Gap

Cape Frio

Santos Plateau

River Plate

San Matías Gulf

Gulf of San Jorge

Grande Bay

Patagonia

PATAGONIAN SHELF

Tierra del Fuego

Cape Horn

Staten I.

DRAKE PASSAGE

SOUTH ATLANTIC OCEAN

RIO GRANDE RISE

Bromley Plateau

Moore Gap

Columbia Seamount

ARGENTINE BASIN

ARGENTINE PLAIN

ARGENTINE RISE

Zapiola Ridge

FALKLAND ESCARPMENT

FALKLAND PLATEAU

FALKLAND TROUGH

Maurice Ewing Bank

FALKLAND

East Falkland · West Falkland · FALKLAND ISLANDS

Burdwood Bank

YAGHAN BASIN

SOUTH SHETLAND ISLANDS

ANTARCTIC PENINSULA

Jason Pen.

Larsen Ice Shelf

Joinville Island

ONA BASIN

Islas Orcadas Rise

South Georgia Rise

Northwest Georgia Rise

South Georgia

SOUTH GEORGIA RIDGE

WEST SCOTIA BASIN

SCOTIA SEA

PROTECTOR BASIN

EAST SCOTIA BASIN

South Sandwich Islands

SOUTH SANDWICH TRENCH

Sandwich

SOUTH SANDWICH TRENCH

24,317 ft / 7,412 m Southern Ocean's deepest point

Discovery Gap

Endurance Ridge

Bruce Ridge

South Orkney Islands

POWELL BASIN

Herdman Seamount

105

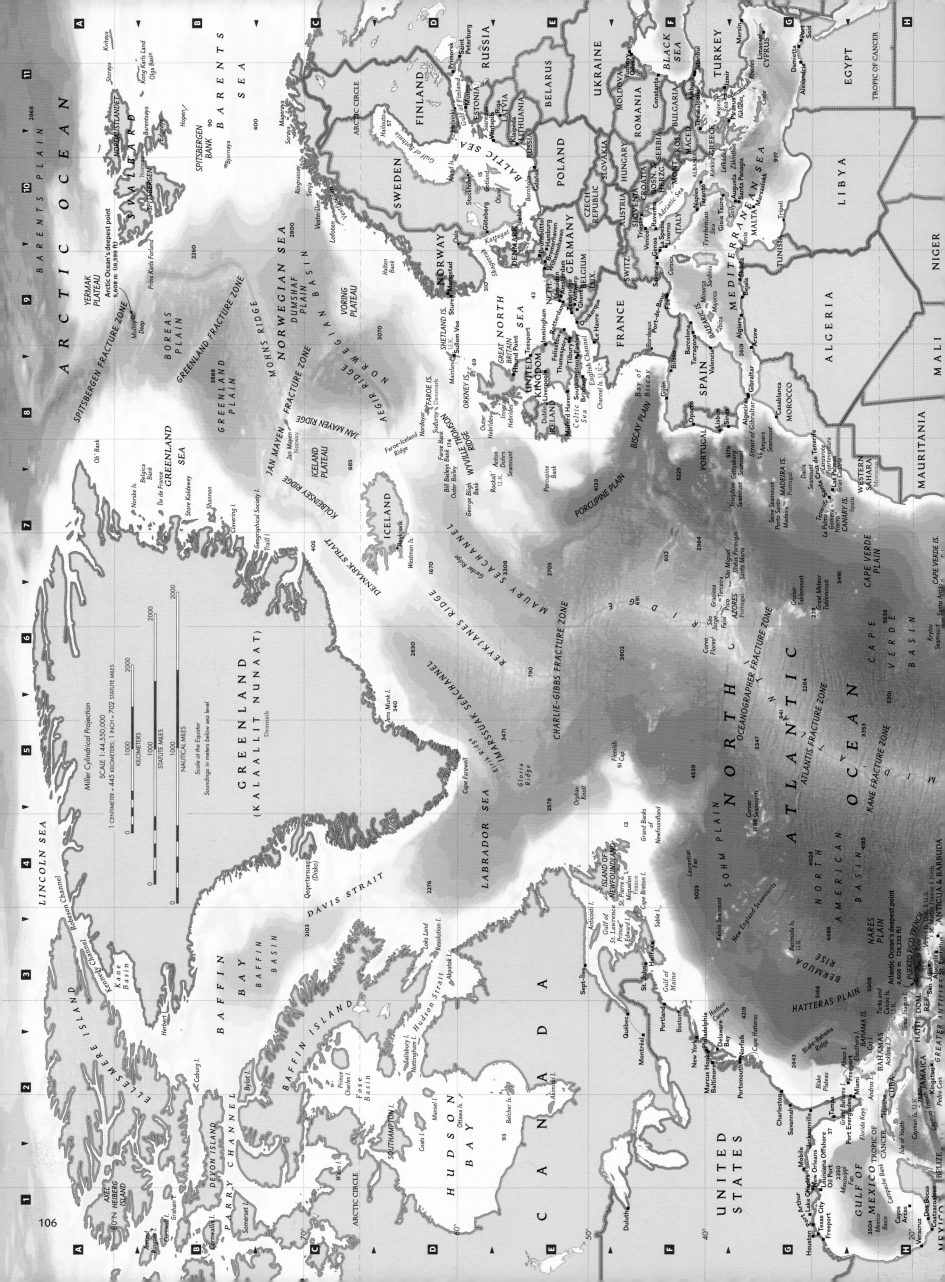

Atlantic Ocean
Political Map and
Depth Contours

107

EUROPE

ARCTIC CIRCLE

TROPIC OF CANCER

Degrees Celsius

| -10 | -3 | 6 | 9 | 12 | 15 | 18 | 21 | 24 | 27 | 30 |

| -30.2 | 32 | 42.8 | 48.2 | 53.6 | 59 | 64.4 | 69.8 | 75.2 | 80.6 | 86 |

Ice

Degrees Fahrenheit

Miller Cylindrical Projection
SCALE 1:44,550,000
1 CENTIMETER = 445 KILOMETERS; 1 INCH = 702 STATUTE MILES

2000
1000
KILOMETERS
0

2000
1000
STATUTE MILES
0

2000
1000
NAUTICAL MILES
0

Scale at the Equator
Soundings in meters below sea level

ARCTIC CIRCLE

N O R T H

A M E R I C A

TROPIC OF CANCER

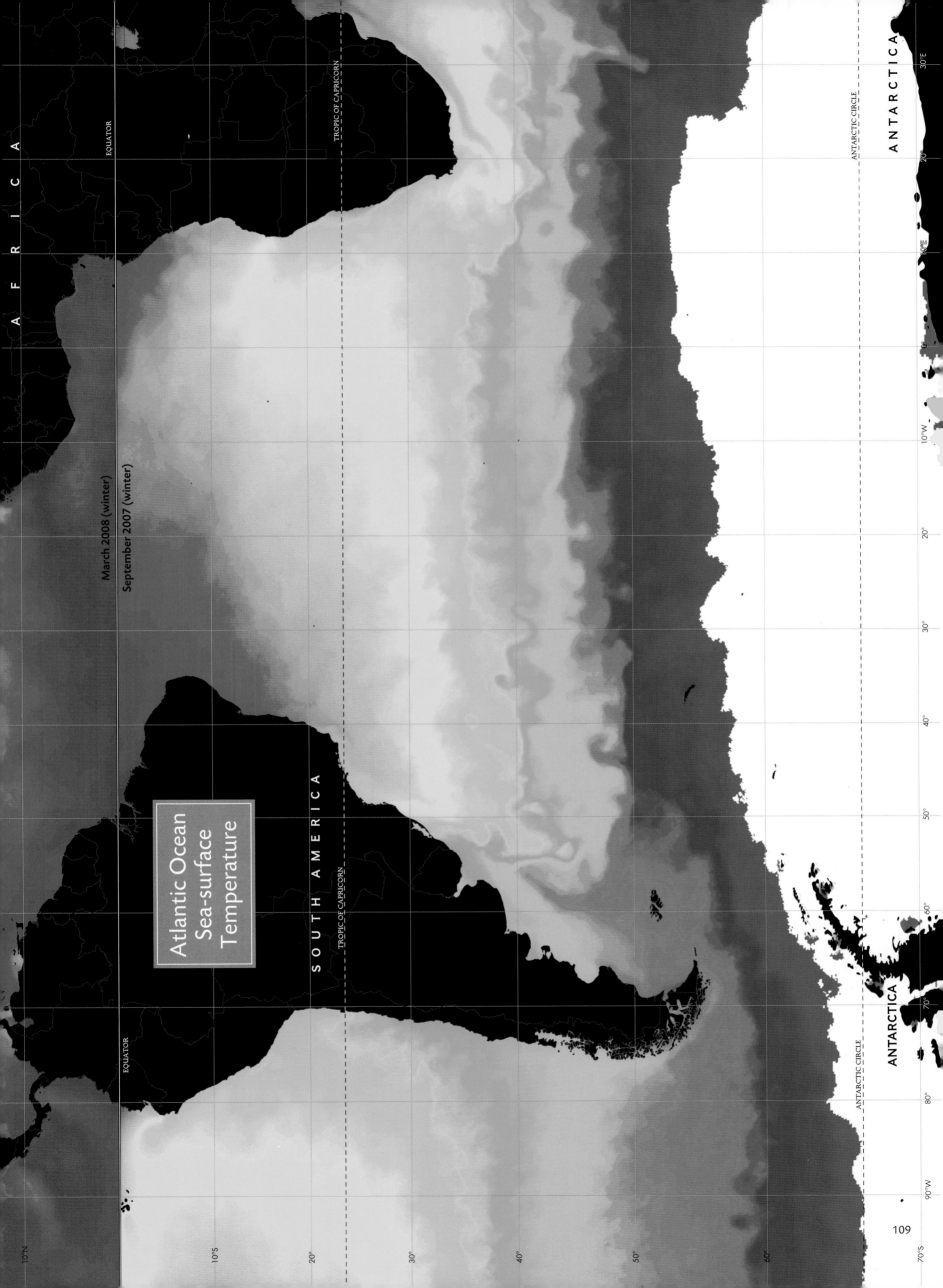

Atlantic Ocean
Sea-surface
Temperature

March 2008 (winter)

September 2007 (winter)

AFRICA

SOUTH AMERICA

ANTARCTICA

ANTARCTICA

EQUATOR

EQUATOR

TROPIC OF CAPRICORN

TROPIC OF CAPRICORN

ANTARCTIC CIRCLE

ANTARCTIC CIRCLE

30°E

20°

10°W

20°

30°

40°

50°

60°

70°

80°

90°W

10°N

10°S

20°

30°

40°

50°

60°

70°S

The Atlantic Ocean by the Numbers

(excludes North Sea, Baltic Sea, Mediterranean Sea, and Irish Sea)

Total area: 81,705,396 square kilometers

Total volume: 307,923,430 cubic kilometers

Greatest depth: 8,605 meters (Puerto Rico Trench)

NORTH ATLANTIC

Geographic boundaries: Equator to 60° N / 98° W to 2° W

Area: 41,258,837 square kilometers

Volume: 146,089,938 cubic kilometers

Average depth: 3,408 meters

SOUTH ATLANTIC

Geographic boundaries: Equator to 60° S / 70° W to 20° E

Area: 40,446,560 square kilometers

Volume: 161,833,492 cubic kilometers

Average depth: 3,967 meters

- Includes 25 percent of Earth's water area.
- World's greatest tides—16 meters—are found in the Bay of Fundy, Nova Scotia, Canada.
- The underwater Mid-Atlantic Ridge, Earth's longest mountain range, is as long as the Andes, Rocky Mountains, and Himalaya combined.

Hundreds of 10- to 20-year-old horseshoe crabs, Limulus polyphemus, scramble ashore to deposit and fertilize eggs in the moist sand. Vital to the future of Limulus, the eggs also provide critical sustenance for millions of migrating shorebirds en route to northern nesting areas.

"The wonders of the sea are as marvelous as the glories of the heavens. . . . Could the waters of the Atlantic be drawn off so as to expose to view this great sea gash . . . [it] would present a scene most rugged, grand and imposing. The very ribs of the solid earth, with the foundations of the sea, would be brought to light."

—Matthew Fontaine Maury, *The Physical Geography of the Sea*

The Atlantic Ocean, named by the Greeks the Sea of Atlas, is the second largest body of water on the planet—about half as large as the Pacific Ocean—occupying almost 25 percent of the Earth's surface and holding almost 25 percent of the world's water, and receiving more freshwater runoff from rivers than any other ocean. The Equator marks the division between the North and South Atlantic Oceans, and within each are subdivisions based on undersea topography and adjacent landmasses. The Mediterranean Sea, Gulf of Mexico, Caribbean Sea, Baltic Sea, and Hudson Bay are large, conspicuous seas within the Atlantic realm. Other, smaller embayments marking the shoreline include the North Sea, English Channel, Irish Sea, Gulf of St. Lawrence, and Chesapeake Bay.

One of the most dramatic features of the planet is the Mid-Atlantic Ridge, a huge underwater mountain range that extends from the edge of the Arctic down the center of the ocean to Antarctic waters. Exploration of the deep Atlantic half a century ago yielded major breakthroughs in understanding physical processes that shape the world, and more recent research on climate and weather has brought into focus the critical role the Atlantic plays in governing global temperature, climate, and chemistry. The Atlantic is the best known part of the global ocean, the most traveled for trade and pleasure, and the most exploited for mineral and living resources. Notorious as the host of some of Earth's most ferocious storms, seasonally sprinkled with icebergs in the far northern and far southern parts of the ocean, the Atlantic, not surprisingly, is the resting place for many thousands of sunken ships. New technologies are accelerating the pace of discovery, but below surface waters most of the Atlantic remains a mystery.

Formation of the Atlantic

WEB LINK: Alfred Wegener

FOR HUNDREDS OF YEARS, starting with 17th-century explorers and mapmakers, people were perplexed by the jigsaw puzzle–like fit between landmasses on opposite sides of the Atlantic. In 1912, German scientist Alfred Wegener formally proposed that these distant landmasses had once been joined and was roundly ridiculed. Over the next 150 years, however, he was vindicated as evidence grew for what is known as continental drift, including the discovery of similar plant and animal fossils along coastlines on opposite sides of the Atlantic. The remains of shallow-water marine animals typical of Europe were found laced within the matrix of sedimentary rock in eastern New England, and fossils characteristic of North America turned up in Norway, Ireland, and Scotland. Other fossils and geological similarities showed that parts of South Carolina and Florida were once in contact with what is now northern Africa.

Nonetheless, the idea of ancient connections between the eastern and western margins of the Atlantic remained highly controversial, because no known geological mechanism could explain the kind of massive rearrangements of land and sea required to separate these continents across a

Swimming in sunlit waters off the coast of Ireland, this Pelagia noctiluca *jellyfish gleams with its own bioluminescent light by night.*

Right: *With a tip-to-tip fin-span that can exceed 5 meters, manta rays,* Manta birostris, *such as this graceful swimmer at the Flower Garden Banks in the Gulf of Mexico, occur worldwide in warm seas. They may live for decades.*

Compasses Pointing South

Molten iron in the planet's core is forced to circulate by the Earth's rotation, and this spinning of magnetic material makes the whole planet into a huge magnet. When lava from volcanoes cools into rock, the iron in it aligns with Earth's magnetic field, leaving small "compasses" showing which way is north at the time. In many places on land, and throughout the seafloor, these basaltic rocks show the Earth's magnetic field has reversed—north became south, then switched back again—dozens of times. One of the first examples of this was found in the 1960s around the Mid-Atlantic Ridge south of Iceland, where parallel bands of north-aligned, then south-aligned, ocean crust are perfectly matched on either side of the ridge. These patterns exist in all ocean crust worldwide. The last reversal was about 785,000 years ago, during the Pleistocene. The Poles reverse on a very irregular basis, from tens of thousands to several million years, but no one knows why.

SEE ALSO: Tethys Sea, page 98

mighty ocean. Although now well documented, seafloor spreading, continental drift, and plate tectonics were not confirmed until the 1960s, with a site in the Atlantic Ocean playing a key role. The Reykjanes Ridge—part of the Mid-Atlantic Ridge, just south of Iceland—turned out to be an area that clearly demonstrates these processes. Scientists have pieced together compelling evidence in recent years that provides insight into what happened as continents were shoved apart by tectonic forces, leaving bits and pieces of each mass "stuck" to the other.

Formation of the present Atlantic Ocean basin began at least 170 million years ago when the infant Atlantic began spreading out from its center and grew along lines resembling the giant "S" between landmasses now recognized as western Europe and eastern North America, western Africa and eastern South America. Birds, mammals, and flowering plants were not yet flourishing on Earth during this period, but horseshoe crabs, crustaceans, sea stars, sponges, jellyfish, mollusks, fish, and many other creatures familiar in the sea today were around in abundance to witness the early growth of the present Atlantic Ocean.

That event marked an Atlantic Ocean *reborn*. There had been an earlier Atlantic separating the Americas from Europe and Africa and closing some 450 million years ago through the action of shifting tectonic plates. In the shift, oceanic crust of this earlier Atlantic was destroyed when it was squeezed by the growing Pacific Ocean. The colliding of continents along its margin formed the Shenandoah Mountain Range in present-day North America.

About 200 million years ago, volcanic action beneath the Earth's crust forced Pangaea to split into a large northerly landmass, Laurasia, that would later divide into Europe, Asia, and North America, and a southerly landmass, Gondwanaland—the future South America, Africa, India, Australia, and Antarctica. A continuous superocean, Panthalassa, encircled the planet. Except for a narrow but pivotal connection joining what is now northern Africa and southern Europe near the present Strait of Gibraltar, water flowed uninterrupted around the midsection of the Earth before the present major ocean basins formed.

Between Laurasia and Gondwanaland lay the Tethys Sea, a large body of water since replaced by the current Mediterranean Sea and the developing Indian Ocean. Sixty-five million years ago, the Atlantic Ocean was only about 40 percent of its present width, and configuration of the continents at that time allowed water to flow freely from the Pacific into what is now the Caribbean Sea. Then, about 10 million years ago, the gap between North and South America began closing. And during just the past 4 million years, there has been a narrow band of forested land—only 80 kilometers across—that has separated the Atlantic from the Pacific Ocean. Construction of the Panama Canal in the early 1900s reestablished a slender connection through a series of locks designed to allow ships to pass back and forth while maintaining a barrier against catastrophic flow through the canal and providing a freshwater protection against unwanted movement of sea plants and animals from one ocean to another.

Mid-Atlantic Ridge

THE U.S. NAVY OCEANOGRAPHER Lt. Matthew Fontaine Maury speculated in the mid-1800s that there might be a chain of mountains beneath the Atlantic. Yet years later, in 1874, Charles Wyville Thomson, chief scientist for H.M.S. *Challenger,* wrote in *The Depths of the Sea:* "According to our . . . information, we must regard the Atlantic Ocean as covering a vast region of wide shallow valleys and undulating plains with a few groups of volcanic mountains, insignificant . . . in height and extent." Despite the many brilliant discoveries of the *Challenger* expedition, it is amazing how much its members missed concerning the depths and complexities of the ocean floor.

Because visibility through even the clearest ocean water is limited to several dozen meters, the ocean floor is still not as well imaged or mapped as the moon or the surface of Mars. It took the advent of acoustic techniques—spurred by the World War II development of sonar (sound navigation ranging) to hunt for submarines—to lay the foundation for scientific techniques for seafloor mapping. Scientific advances identified optimal acoustic frequencies for ocean surveying. These were 12 kHz to 15 kHz frequency beams to find the depth of the seafloor; 3.5 kHz for looking down about 50 meters into sediments lying on the seafloor; and very low frequency seismic blasts at typically 10 to 50 Hertz to reverberate through and show structure in sediment layers up to 10 kilometers thick on the seafloor.

These acoustic techniques made it possible to visualize the depths below by "seeing with sound" and to begin scoping out the geography of the ocean floor. Using sonar, it was discovered that the Mid-Atlantic Ridge runs continuously from about 65° north latitude (just south of Iceland) to about 55° south latitude (close to the southern tip of South America), a straight north–south distance of about 13,000 kilometers. But because the ridge follows the same S shape as its surrounding continents, the actual meandering length of the ridge is closer to 20,000 kilometers—the longest mountain range on Earth. Today, the Mid-Atlantic Ridge is recognized as one of Earth's most dramatic features, the defining backbone of the Atlantic, where sharp-sided canyons rival the greatest cliffs and valleys on land.

SEE ALSO: sound in the ocean, page 311

Rift Valleys on the Ridge:

Character of the rift down the center of the mid-ocean ridge varies depending on the seafloor spreading rate. The Mid-Atlantic ridge (left), spreading at 2.5 cm per year, has a noticeably wide and deep cleft with sheer walls on either side. In contrast, the East Pacific Rise (right), spreading almost 10 times as fast, has a much narrower rift raised up above the surrounding seafloor.

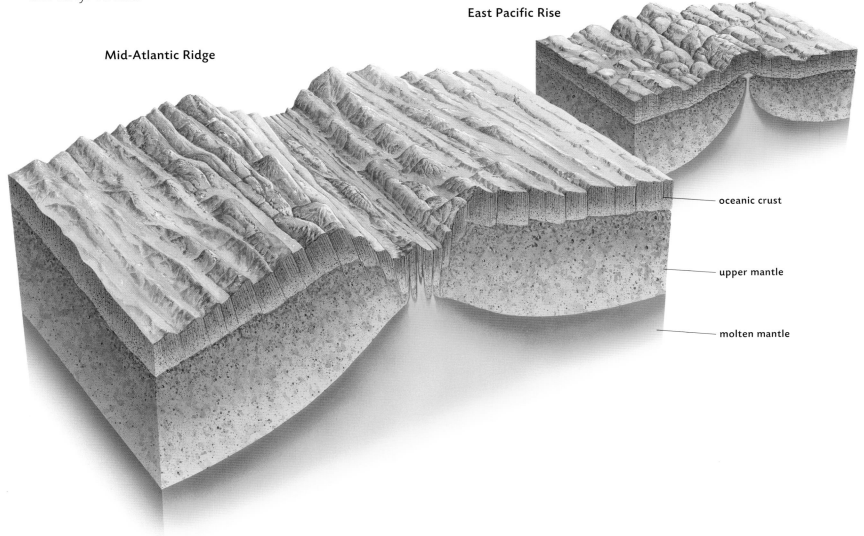

East Pacific Rise

Mid-Atlantic Ridge

oceanic crust

upper mantle

molten mantle

Amid billowing clouds of smoke and ash, an underwater volcano explosively emerged as the island of Surtsey off the coast of Iceand in 1963.

WEB LINK: National Geographic archives

Occupying about one-third of the Atlantic Ocean floor, the Mid-Atlantic Ridge is cleft down the middle by a continuous rift valley, with mountains on either side, from Iceland in the north to the edge of the Antarctic Ocean in the south. This valley is the boundary between the eastern and western Atlantic and is the place where hot lava rises up from Earth's mantle and cools, creating new seafloor that slowly pushes the two sides of the still-growing Atlantic Basin apart. Currently, the Atlantic is spreading at an average rate of 2.5 centimeters a year.

The ridge breaks the sea surface in Iceland not far from the capital, Reykjavík, as a narrow volcanic fissure. Forces that relentlessly cause the formation of new ocean crust and the spreading of the Atlantic Basin can be seen on land here, adding about 2.5 centimeters of width a year to the landmass of Iceland.

In 1963, amid outpourings of lava, steam, and ash, a new island called Surtsey grew up from the Mid-Atlantic Ridge and erupted from the sea 113 kilometers southeast of Reykjavík. Hundreds of kilometers south of Iceland and 2,743 meters down, scientists first witnessed the ongoing process of the growing Atlantic during a three-year project in the early 1970s called FAMOUS (French-American Mid-Ocean Undersea Study). They mapped and sampled a 155-square-kilometer area of the Mid-Atlantic Ridge Rift Valley and surrounding terrain near the Azores. Some 20 ships, 3 submersibles, and several towed underwater camera arrays gathered images that revealed the ocean floor as never seen before. They discovered that the rift valley is less than 3 kilometers across, with astonishingly sheer walls rising more than 300 meters from the seafloor.

The expedition's chief scientist, J. R. Heirtzler, put the discoveries in perspective in a 1975 *National Geographic* article: "For the first time in history, men have gone down in the sea to prowl and study first-hand . . . a system greater than the Rockies, the Andes, and the Himalayas combined. . . . We're at a watershed in the understanding of our planet. . . . [T]he theory of plate tectonics has turned earth science upside down, one of the major upheavals in the history of man's knowledge."

Seafloor and Vents

THE HIGH MOUNTAINS OF THE MID-ATLANTIC RIDGE fall away to plains much broader than Spain. Giant basins east of the ridge include, from north to south, the Porcupine, Biscay, Tagus, Cape Verde, Gambia, Angola, and Cape Plain; to the west, the Baffin, Hudson, Labrador, Newfoundland, and the Atlantic's largest, the North American Basin, which extends from the Grand Banks to waters east of Puerto Rico; and south of the Equator, the Brazilian and Argentine Basins.

The processes that form these flat abyssal plains were first reported in the northwest Atlantic. A large earthquake (7.2 on the Richter scale) occurred on November 18, 1929, on the Grand Banks off the coast of Nova Scotia. The energy from this underwater quake severed numerous underwater telegraph cables—progressively from north to south—over a period of 13 hours, but scientists could not explain how for two decades. In 1952, Bruce Heezen and Maurice Ewing of the Lamont Geological Observatory proposed the new mechanism of turbidity currents, or underwater avalanches, that jettison large quantities of sediments down the continental shelves and out onto the rough terrain below, until it is smoothed into flat, sediment-filled abyssal plains. The proposed speed and sediment load of these turbidity currents explained the 13-hour delay in the cable breaks and ultimately led to the understanding of countless sedimentary deposits on land, named turbidites, that had originally formed underwater.

First discovered in 1977 two and a half miles deep near the Galápagos Islands in the eastern Pacific, hot springs known as hydrothermal vents were initially thought not to exist in the Atlantic. That view changed in 1985 during an expedition led by geologist and geophysicist Peter Rona when plenty of hydrothermal action was discovered 2,897 kilometers east of Miami, Florida, 4 kilometers down. Subsequently, during a joint U.S.-Soviet expedition, reported in *National Geographic* in 1992, Rona witnessed "billowing black clouds" and observed that "red, yellow, and green—bright chunks of minerals—marked the Astrodome-size mound with its jetting

Holes in the Seafloor

Since the 1950s scientists have tried to drill holes kilometers deep through the Earth's crust to reach the mantle below. Imagine their surprise when they discovered places under the ocean where there is no crust at all: The mantle actually lies exposed on the seafloor. In 1979, U.S. Navy scientists studying the Gakkel Ridge (often called Nansen Ridge) in the Arctic proposed a startling explanation for some unexpected data—the crust, usually about 6 kilometers thick, seemed to be missing. Scientists have since found similar places along other slow-spreading ridges in the southwest Indian Ocean and just north of the Equator in the Atlantic.

Rimicaris exoculata shrimp perch at the edge of a hydrothermal vent on the Mid-Atlantic Ridge, where hot mineral-laden water favors development of bacteria that line the shrimp's gills and provide a built-in source of sustenance.

geysers . . . warm water seeped up and, meeting cold water, shimmered like heat waves on desert sand."

Rona is drawn to research concerning the physical processes that shape the planet, but he could not resist wondering about a biological phenomenon—the delicate balancing act performed by thousands of 5-centimeter-long shrimp swarming over black smoker chimneys in the vent area. Each tiny crustacean, *Rimicaris exoculata* ("the dweller in the rift without eyes"), maintains a precarious hold on life, perched between near-freezing water just beyond the vents and the spurting jets of mineralized water heated to 454.4°C. Where eyes should be, each tiny creature has two reflective oval patches that are thought to be sensors that enable the shrimp to find vents, then to keep a respectable distance from water hot enough to cook them.

In nearby sediments Rona spotted mysterious animals the size of a little cookie marked with a checkerboard pattern. The closest relative appears to be an invertebrate, *Paleodictyon nodosum*, previously known only from fossils in rocks that were underwater between 50 million and 340 million

Rising as much as 60 meters above the seafloor and hosting unusual hydrothermal activity, the delicate, pale carbonate pinnacles discovered in 2000 at 30° N at the summit of the Atlantis Massif on the Mid-Atlantic Ridge inspired the name, "Lost City." The craggy spire shown here, called Nature Tower, was photographed in 2003 by scientists in the submersible Alvin.

years ago. This creature, found alive, joins horseshoe crabs, sharks, sponges, mollusks, sea stars, and numerous other marine organisms that have mastered the art of survival in a relatively unchanged form for hundreds of millions of years, while many others perished.

Vents in the deep sea spurting plumes of metal-bearing "smoke" have, over the ages, given rise to rich ore deposits. Most deposits are still underwater, but many are now on land. In *Mapping the Deep*, Robert Kunzig points to copper mines on the Mediterranean island of Cyprus as evidence. The mines "tap an 800-square-mile [2,072-square-kilometer] block of ore . . . known as an ophiolite: a vertical slice of mid-ocean ridge that was beached on land when two plates collided. . . ." A band of ophiolites runs from Cyprus and Turkey, through Iran, and across the Persian Gulf into Oman. In a copper mine in Oman, fossils of tube worms similar to those that thrive around hot-water vents today were found amid the remains of a 95-million-year-old vent.

In December 2000, while exploring an unusual 3,660-meter-high mountain at 30° N on the Mid-Atlantic Ridge, scientists from several research institutions encountered a spectacular hydrothermal vent field unlike any previously observed. They named the area the Lost City, owing to the cathedral-like appearance of hollow, steep-sided pillars and spires as much as 55 meters high and up to 9 meters across. Along the sides, delicate white flanges composed of carbonates and silica appear like shelf fungi on giant tree trunks, awash in mineral-rich water with a temperature as great as 160°C. Few large organisms are present, but dense mats of microbes prosper in warm pools trapped under the flanges. Margaret Leinen, then assistant director for geosciences at the National Science Foundation, reported: "We thought we had seen the entire spectrum of hydrothermal activity on the seafloor, but this major discovery reminds us that the ocean still has much to reveal."

A hexagonal puzzle, Paleodictyon nodosum, *a trace fossil of an animal thought to be extinct 50 million years ago, was first discovered alive by geologist Peter Rona along the Mid-Atlantic Ridge in 1975, but the kind of animal responsible for the distinctive patterns remains a mystery.*

WEB LINK: Lost City Expedition

Seamounts and Islands

LIKE ICEBERGS, ISLANDS HAVE MOST OF THEIR MASS UNDERWATER; seamounts are mountains 1,000 meters or more high, largely of volcanic origin, that are entirely submerged. Most of the thousands of seamounts thought to exist in the Atlantic often in clusters equidistant from the spreading ridge on either side are associated with the slow-moving African, Eurasian, and North and South American plates. Many occur in and near the Mid-Atlantic Ridge. Nearly all remain unexplored, but many have been targeted for commercial fishing owing to the abundance of life they host.

The most studied seamounts in the Atlantic are the New England Seamounts, a submerged line of extinct volcanoes that stretches 1,500 kilometers east-southeast off Cape Cod halfway across the western Atlantic, and the Great Meteor Tablemount. The many peaks of the New England chain rise about 3,500 meters above the seafloor in depths of about 5,000 meters. This chain is one of the increasing number of seamount sites in the ocean where deep (1,000 to 2,000 meters) cold-water corals have been studied. Fish-egg casings discovered among these corals indicate that the seamounts may be an important deepwater fish hatchery.

The Great Meteor Tablemount, located just north of the Equator in the eastern Atlantic, is sometimes called a tablemount because of its size and shape. It is one of the largest known submerged features that is not part of the mid-oceanic ridges. Many of the studies on this feature focused on "Taylor" cells, the unique circular ocean rotation found around the tops of seamounts, which may concentrate nutrients and small sea life around these great underwater mountains.

Giants among ostracod crustacea, grape-sized species of Gigantocypris *live in deep water globally.*

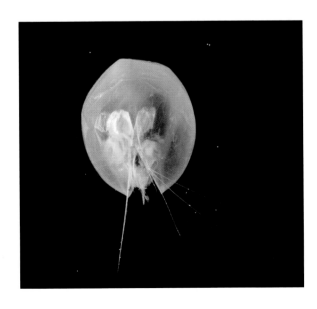

WEB LINK: Bermuda Atlantic Time-Series Study

Most of the islands in the Atlantic are continental in origin, including the British Isles, Falkland Islands, Canary Islands, Newfoundland, Cuba, and Trinidad, as well as many small coastal islands bordering large landmasses. Other Atlantic islands, including Iceland, the Azores, St. Peter and St. Paul Rocks, Ascension, and Tristan da Cunha, are parts of the mid-ocean ridge that extend above sea level. The Bahamas are upward extensions of the broad Blake Plateau, crowned with thousands of years of accumulated coral growth.

Bermuda, a 40-kilometer chain of mini-islands located 1,100 kilometers off the mid-Atlantic coast of the United States, has provided a base for the longest-running continuous measurements of oceanographic conditions that exist, through the efforts of researchers working at the Bermuda Biological Station, founded in 1903 (now the Bermuda Institute of Ocean Sciences).

Of the many Caribbean islands, more than 30 have developed as independent countries, including the largest, Cuba. Nearly all are characterized by extensive coral reefs, fringing mangroves, and sea grass meadows in shallow water, and most are surrounded by water thousands of meters deep close to shore.

Land, sea, and sky merge as storm clouds gather over the ocean at Bahia Honda State Park, Florida.

A dazzling diversity of life crowns ancient shorelines off the coast of Georgia, now protected as the Gray's Reef National Marine Sanctuary.

Continental Margins

HUGGING THE CONTINENTS IS THE CONTINENTAL SHELF, a border of submerged land—narrow in some places, hundreds of kilometers wide in others—that has been periodically inundated or dry, depending on whether the planet is going through a warm or a cold phase. Ice ages have come and gone repeatedly, and in the process have tied up water in glaciers or released it during meltdowns in quantities sufficient to significantly lower or raise sea level globally. At the height of the most recent great ice age, about 18,000 years ago, sea level was about 100 meters lower than it is now, and coasts along the Atlantic extended farther offshore than at present. Florida was about twice the size it is today, as was the eastern tip of South America. It would have been possible to walk or ski from Boston to the Grand Banks, and from Savannah to submerged islands such as Gray's Reef 30 kilometers or more beyond Georgia's famous fringing marshlands.

Currently, broad shelves with depths less than 200 meters occur in the North Sea around the British Isles, the Grand Banks of Newfoundland, and the northeastern United States, the northeastern coast of South America, and the extensive and highly productive shelf region along the coast of Patagonia. Along the west coast of Florida and in parts of the submerged coast offshore from Yucatán in the Gulf of Mexico, it is so shallow that it is possible in some places to stand on the bottom with your head out of the water while several kilometers offshore. In these broad, sunlit regions, plants, including benthic algae and sea grass meadows, and numerous benthic invertebrates prosper, providing habitat and sustenance for enormously abundant and diverse populations of fish and other animals.

Ancient rivers carved deeply into some now flooded coastal areas, and all rivers have carried masses of minerals, silt, and sediment from far inland to the sea. Flowing into the Atlantic are the world's greatest rivers—their greatness measured in terms of water volume, length, and extent of area drained—the Hudson, St. Lawrence, Mississippi, Amazon, Orinoco, and Paraná empty into the western Atlantic; the Orange, Congo, Niger, and (via the Mediterranean Sea) the Nile flow into the eastern Atlantic. Their influence is obvious far out into the sea, with reduced salinity, the scouring of the seafloor, and the massive buildup of sediments in abyssal plains farther offshore.

Anthony Knap
THE BERMUDA ATLANTIC TIME-SERIES

The Sargasso Sea is an anticyclonic gyre (clockwise rotating body of water) in the central North Atlantic Ocean. It is considered to be oligotrophic (desertlike), with low nutrients, and is representative of most of the oceanic gyres, which cover 80 percent of the ocean surface (about 60 percent of the globe). Traditionally the boundaries of the Sargasso Sea were defined by the presence of the free-floating pelagic plant sargassum weed. Today the Sargasso Sea is defined in terms of physical oceanography boundaries—the Gulf Stream to the west, the North Atlantic Current to the north, the Canaries Current to the east, and the North Equatorial Current to the south.

Perhaps one of the most important features of this area is the longest-running continuous time-series of ocean measurements in the world. Started by the late Henry Stommel in 1954 at Station S, almost 20 kilometers southeast of Bermuda, the series has provided insight into the changing conditions of the deep ocean for more than 50 years.

In 1988, under the auspices of the Joint Global Ocean Flux Study, a more detailed time-series was added to understand the time-varying changes of the biogeochemistry of the ocean focusing on cycling of carbon, nitrogen, and phosphorus.

This Bermuda Atlantic Time-series Study (BATS) site was centered approximately 80 kilometers southeast of Bermuda to minimize any effects from the island and was co-located with the Ocean Flux Program (OFP) sediment trap mooring. The OFP was initially started in 1978 by Werner Dueser from Woods Hole Oceanographic Institution and continues today at the Bermuda Institute of Ocean Sciences (BIOS) under the supervision of Maureen Conte. This is the longest continuous measurement program of the transport of material from the surface of the ocean to the deep (3,200 meters) and provides insights into how the major nutrients in the ocean are cycled from the surface to the deep.

At this site is an additional array called the Bermuda Testbed Mooring, also a collaborative program with many participants. This, though, is a bottom-to-surface mooring with a large surface float. Scientists participate by adding new and emerging technologies to the mooring line to provide new sensors to measure the ocean. This mooring is coordinated by Tommy Dickey of the University of California at Santa Barbara. To date, optical instruments, automated nutrient sensors and samplers, carbon dioxide sensors, trace metal samplers, and others have been added to the mooring over time, providing insights into the variability of the surface and deep ocean.

The BATS program consists of monthly five-day cruises to the BATS site, where water samples are taken. In addition, surface particle flux measurements are made, as well as a whole suite of ancillary measurements. In this area of the ocean there is a strong seasonal cycle called the spring bloom, which is responsible for a substantial removal of carbon from the surface ocean to the deep. Shorter cruises are added during these spring periods to try to define these events in more detail.

These measurement programs in the Sargasso Sea—funded by multiple agencies, primarily by the National Science Foundation, and managed through BIOS in collaboration with other key marine institutions—have created a key observatory for changing climate in this modern world. The Bermuda time-series programs can truly be considered one of the main barometers of global climate change.

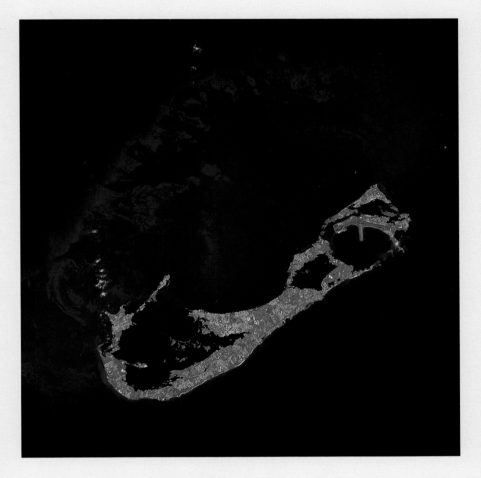

Anchored on rock bottom thousands of meters below the surface, the Bermuda Islands emerge as a series of mostly submerged mountains 1,100 kilometers east of the United States.

Bermuda Facts

• Longest continuous record of ocean measurements in the world
• More known about the changing ocean over time than any other open ocean site • Longest record of sediment trap deployments in the world
• Saharan dust plays a role in ocean productivity at Bermuda • The spawning of European and American eels at depth is still a great mystery
• The history of leaded gas in the United States is stored in the skeletons of Bermuda corals • Acid rain from the United States reaches Bermuda and affects rainfall chemistry

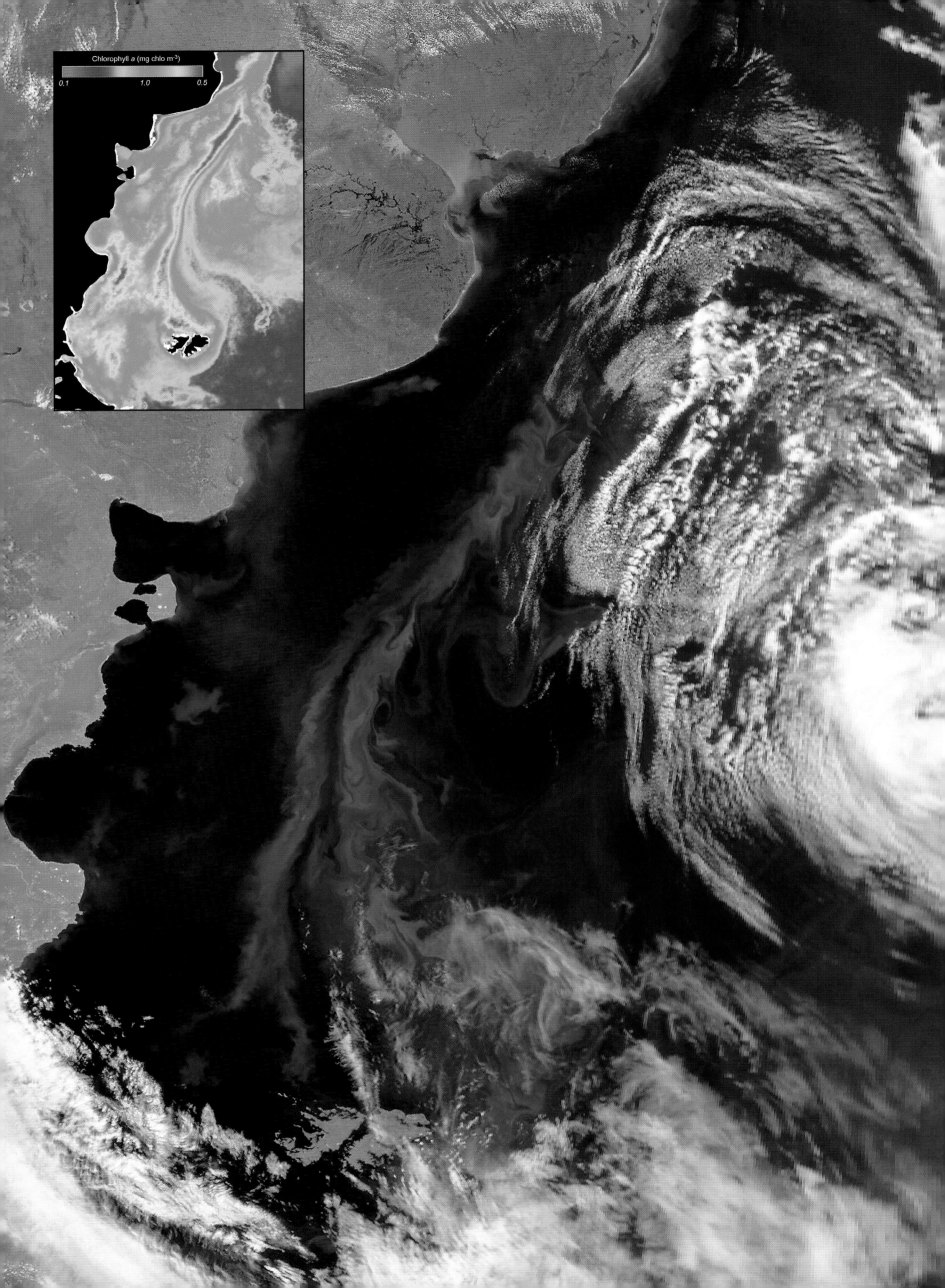

Chlorophyll a (mg chlo m⁻³)

0.1   1.0   0.5

Where fresh water meets the sea and mingles long enough to develop sustained low salinity and high nutrients, estuaries may form, among them the famously productive Chesapeake Bay, Florida's historic seaport Tampa Bay, the Mississippi Delta, shallow waters around the Netherlands, coastal marshes of the British Isles, and the Amazon Delta. These living fringe areas trap much of their rivers' mineral and organic outpouring, then tidal surge and ocean currents sweep cleansing waters into them—along with many marine species that use the wetlands as aquatic nurseries.

Continental margins are likely sites for the accumulation of hydrocarbons, and some of the richest fields in the world occur along the present and ancient borders of the Atlantic Ocean: the coast of Brazil, the Gulf of Mexico, eastern Canada, the North Sea, the Mediterranean Sea, western Africa. In the past few years, enormous quantities of oil and gas have been extracted from such deposits, first in shallow coastal areas, but increasingly in deep water as well. In a 1973 *Scientific American* article, Peter Rona predicted: "It is reasonable to expect the petroleum accumulation will extend seaward under the continental shelf, the continental slope, and the continental rise, to water depths of about 18,000 feet along large portions of both the eastern and western margins of the North and South Atlantic." To date, commercial extraction is feasible to more than half that depth, and new technologies are taking operations ever deeper.

Atlantic Tides and Currents

IN RESPONSE TO THE TUG OF THE MOON AND THE SUN, tides move the ocean twice a day throughout most of the Atlantic, creating rhythmic cycles of shoreline ebb and flow and generating forces that gnaw away or replenish the coastline within an intertidal area that may span a few centimeters or many meters. The tides are influenced by the position of the Earth relative to the sun and moon, the shape of the shoreline, the topography of the seafloor, and the direction and strength of the local winds. Semidiurnal, or twice daily, tides are most common, resulting from the natural tidal forcing period of 12 lunar hours (12 hours 25 minutes of our usual solar time). However, in some areas of the Atlantic, notably the Gulf of Mexico and along the middle to lower parts of South America's east coast, diurnal tides predominate, with one high and one low in a period of 24 hours and 50 minutes.

The places where rivers meet the sea, and where the sea reaches inland, tend to have the highest tidal range. In the Severn Estuary in Britain, the tides sweep through a spectacular 12-meter range. On the other side of the Atlantic in New Brunswick's Bay of Fundy, the location and configuration

Opposite: *Like a fast-flowing river, the Malvinas current sweeps along the Patagonian coast of Argentina bearing cold, nutrient-rich water onto the well-illuminated region along the edge of the continental shelf. The inset image illustrates the concentration of phytoplankton, with highest level of chlorophyll and nutrients indicated in red.*

Above: *The weather of northern Europe has dramatic swings every 5-10 years in association with the North Atlantic Oscillation. Contours show air pressure over the ocean's surface, tan being high and blue low. When the air pressure north of Portugal becomes higher than that over Iceland, westerly winds in the Atlantic become strong and bring warm and wet marine air to northern Europe for a mild winter. The opposite brings a colder, drier winter.*

Left: *In Canada's Bay of Fundy a swift tidal current rushes past the edge of New Brunswick's Provincial Park.*

The Gulf Stream, one of the most powerful and well-defined ocean currents, appears a warm red-orange against a silhouette of eastern North America as it flows into the cooler blue-green waters of the North Atlantic. The meandering of the stream and some of the circular eddies it has thrown off are visible.

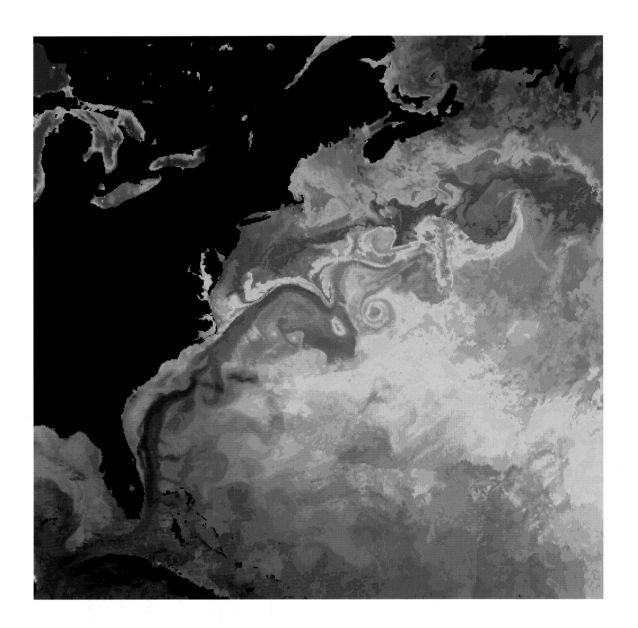

Eddies Win the Race . . . Sometimes

The Bermuda Race—from Newport, Rhode Island, to Bermuda—sends sailing yachts right through one of the strongest ocean current systems in the world. Once the Gulf Stream flows away from the coastline of the United States, it meanders far north and south of its path, and some meanders throw off large eddies, rotating clockwise north of the stream and counterclockwise to the south. Currents in the area can cross the rhumb line (shortest direct distance) of the race from many directions. In the 2002 race, boats that moved slightly west of the line rode favorable currents—from a large Gulf Stream meander and two eddies—to victory.

SEE ALSO: The Gulf of Mexico, pages 136-139

WEB LINK: The Gulf Stream

of the bay set the stage not only for a truly magnificent tidal range—up to 16 meters—but also for a phenomenon known as a tidal bore. Twice a day the bore surges more than a billion cubic meters of water—a meter-high wall—into the narrowing arms of the bay at high speed.

The principal surface current flow in the Atlantic consists of two great, roughly circular gyres, the North Atlantic gyre moving clockwise, and the South Atlantic gyre flowing counterclockwise. In the Southern Hemisphere, the gyre includes the southbound Brazil Current, which sweeps along the coast of South America, then bends eastward near the Patagonian Shelf toward southern Africa. The cold Benguela Current moves northward along the coast of Africa, spinning off the northbound Guinea Current and then continuing on a westward course back toward Brazil. The southern leg of the North Atlantic gyre, flowing westward toward the West Indies, piles up against Mexico's Yucatán Peninsula, and thus blocked, surges around the Gulf of Mexico, then around Florida, and into the warm, fast-moving Gulf Stream. It races through the Straits of Florida as fast as 8 kilometers an hour, then slides by the Bahamas before moving up the coast past Cape Hatteras and veering eastward across the Atlantic toward Europe, where warm water supports a relatively balmy climate, complete with palm trees in southwest England. From there, the current bends south toward the Equator, then turns west, completing a great wheel-like movement of surface waters.

While serving as deputy postmaster of the American Colonies in 1769, Benjamin Franklin researched the nature of this mysterious ocean highway, drawing upon knowledge supplied by sea captains and whalers as well as his own observations. He produced what are thought to be the first maps of the Gulf Stream and distributed them widely in an effort to speed up transits to and from England. In broad strokes, Franklin grasped the importance of understanding such ocean currents, but he lacked refined means to survey and track them. His efforts were the basis for Maury's charts a hundred years later.

WEB LINK: Monaco Museum

In the 1800s, Prince Albert, an ocean scientist as well as monarch of Monaco, discovered that the Gulf Stream splits as it sweeps past Newfoundland. One branch of warm water arches northeast toward Ireland and Great Britain, providing a profoundly mellowing influence on the region's climate; the other part curves south to form the eastern portion of the great gyre flowing past Spain and northern Africa. The method the prince used for his investigations was exquisitely simple, a variation on the theme of putting a message in a bottle. Glass bottles, wooden barrels, and copper balls were stuffed with a request in ten languages to advise him when and where any of the missives were recovered; enough were returned to reveal the current's pathways. Today, more sophisticated ocean drifters, floats, and even anchored buoys loaded with instruments measure temperature, salinity, depth, current speed, and other data about the ocean either for storage and later retrieval or for periodic transmissions to satellites for relay to ship- or shore-based researchers.

In the 1950s, Henry Stommel, an ocean scientist from the Woods Hole Oceanographic Institution with uncanny insights about how the ocean works, set out to determine whether his hunch about the existence of a countercurrent flowing south under the Gulf Stream was correct. Teaming with John Swallow, who had designed ingenious instruments that would float not on the surface, but suspended deep in the sea, Stommel deployed hundreds of Swallow floats and had the satisfaction of watching them flow south along the eastern seaboard in what came to be called the Deep Western Boundary Current. Since then, deep currents have been discovered throughout the ocean and their important role acknowledged as transporters of heat and nutrients and as inner-ocean corridors for marine life.

Adrift near Bermuda and looking like its seaweed namesake, this Sargassum fish, a kind of angler, entices potential prey with a tasty-looking lure on its nose.

Meanwhile, sea turtle expert Archie Carr deployed hundreds of floating drifters into the ocean to solve another mystery: Where do tens of thousands of hatchling sea turtles go after they run pell-mell into the ocean from nesting sites high on sandy beaches in Central America? Carr suspected that green and loggerhead turtles might make their way to the Sargasso Sea. This great, quiet mass of water occupies a space in the North Atlantic gyre that is about the size of the United States. It is a vast system of light winds and little rain with waters flowing slowly west to east along its northern border and east to west along its southern edges.

The Gulf Stream defines the western and northern borders of the Sargasso. In their book *The Sargasso Sea,* John and Mildred Teal describe the sea near the edge of the continental shelf of North America: "[T]he slope, which grades down from shallow seas, finally gives way to the deep sea, the abyss, the sea of eternal night waters. . . . Only a few bits of land break the Sargasso's deep blue waters, the Bermuda Islands, which protrude, isolated in the middle of the Sea." Bermuda is so remote from other land (the nearest is the United States' Carolina coast 1,100 kilometers to the west) and so far off major ocean currents that when British settlers bound for the American colonies in 1609 were shipwrecked on Bermuda during a storm, there were no native humans living there nor had there ever been.

WEB LINK: Christopher Columbus

In the Sargasso, long known to sailors as a legendary place where ships might languish for weeks for want of favorable winds, Christopher Columbus apparently found pleasure. On September 16, 1492, he wrote, "The weather is like April in Andalusia." And later he noted, "The air is soft as April in Seville, and it is a pleasure to be in it, so fragrant it is." Perhaps Columbus liked the aroma of seaweed. Millions of tons of ever-drifting, golden-brown seaweed prosper there, mostly two species of brown algae, *Sargassum natans* and *Sargassum fluitans,* that resemble small, leafy shrubs with no roots, flowers, or seeds but with numerous berry-like floats. The floats reminded Portuguese sailors of a kind of small grape called *sargaço,* and the name stuck.

Many millions of small plants, fishes, shrimp, crabs, hydroids, sea slugs, barnacles, and other organisms abound within their tangled branches, a sumptuous feast for young and hungry turtles. Carr said it was the only place he could think of where "there might be a concentration of small soft-bodied animals that baby turtles could find with no more finding power than they appear to have."

While Carr's experiments with drifters were not particularly helpful in determining turtle migrations, his uncanny ability to "think like a turtle" was vindicated when young turtles were eventually discovered grazing in large numbers in the Sargasso Sea's drifting pastures.

Images from space, new sensors, and the use of computer technologies have greatly enhanced concepts about the ever-changing nature of the Gulf Stream and other ocean currents, including new insights about eddies. These curious swirls or rings of water routinely entrap warm water north of the stream or colder water south of the stream. These aquatic "islands" may stay intact for many months, carrying their original plants and animals into areas not otherwise hospitable to their growth.

Satellite tags are now being applied to the backs of natural "drifters"—sea turtles that are tracked for weeks or months. New acoustic techniques that bounce sound off the seafloor and the use of submersibles have revolutionized knowledge of the ocean's bottom. But what of the space between the surface and the bottom? Although by far the largest continuous habitat on Earth, the mid-water realm of the world ocean remains the least known part of the planet.

Hurricanes and Global Warming

The intensity of hurricanes in the western Atlantic has increased in recent years. The picture is complex, with sea-level rise and coastal population density contributing to the damage caused by hurricanes striking land. But it is clear that sea-surface temperature has risen globally over the past 25 years, and this one factor seems to be a major influence in causing more frequent and more intense hurricanes.

WEB LINK: Atlantic storms

Atlantic Weather Phenomena

THE ATLANTIC, ESPECIALLY THE CARIBBEAN SEA, maintains its notoriety as the home of some of Earth's most spectacular and deadly storms—hurricanes, named for a god of the Carib Indians, Huracan. These frightening tropical storms have been documented for more than 500 years. They generate winds that rage from 117 to more than 322 kilometers an hour, enough to uproot roofs, flatten buildings, toss cars and boats around like toys, force huge walls of storm surge water onto the land, and churn the ocean into a sailor's nightmare.

Born in an area near the Equator known as the Intertropical Convergence Zone, tropical storms rotate counterclockwise in the Northern Hemisphere and clockwise in the Southern. Starting as a diffuse area of low pressure, a storm builds in intensity through complex interactions with the sea-surface temperature. In the North Atlantic, above the Equator, nascent storms are caught up by easterly trade winds—blowing east to west—and are sent spinning into the Caribbean Sea. Drawing energy from heat released by the condensation of vapor in the air just above the water's surface, a hurricane builds or dissipates depending on the temperature of the ocean surface beneath it. The warmer the air, the greater the capacity of a storm to hold water vapor and the greater the energy released when that vapor condenses. When water temperature is highest, as in late summer, the potential for powerful storms is greatest.

New technologies, including satellites, reconnaissance aircraft, ships at sea, land stations, radar, data buoys, high-speed computers, and complex communications networks combine with firsthand observations made by humans—on land and at sea—to assess, track, advise, and understand these enormous displays of power. The "great hurricane" of 1780, thought to be the most violent of the 18th century, struck Barbados and left neither trees nor dwellings standing. An English fleet anchored off the island of St. Lucia disappeared, and more than 6,000 people were lost in the storm's wake.

A century later, in Galveston, Texas, the sky was crimson at dawn over the Gulf of Mexico. Those who knew the old sailors' rhyme "Red sky in the morning, sailors take warning" were concerned, but no one knew how bad the 1900 Galveston hurricane would be. By nightfall, winds raced at 190 kilometers an hour, and giant combers washed over what had been a thriving seaport city of 40,000 people. Half the buildings were destroyed, more than 5,000 people were injured, and at least 6,000 were dead. At sea, such storms are equally terrifying. The 600 passengers aboard the S.S. *Central America* returning from the California gold rush in September 1857 ran into a hurricane 320 kilometers off North Carolina. Two-thirds aboard were lost in one of the worst sea disasters in American history. Storm predictions are improving, but the humbling power of hurricanes remains undiminished.

Four Storms in 2004

Above: This composite image, using visible and infrared data from the GOES-12 weather satellite, shows the relative sizes and differing pathways of four major hurricanes that hit the southeastern coast of the United States. From left to right, they are Ivan, Charley, Jeanne, and Frances. Hurricane Charley, the smallest of them, devastated parts of southwestern Florida. The largest was Ivan, a category-five hurricane that spawned 117 tornadoes in the eastern United States.

Katrina in 2005

Below, left: Warm water in the Gulf of Mexico, shown in red, intensified Katrina as it passed over. *Center:* A 3-D cutaway through Katrina's eyewall tower, 16 kilometers high, flanked by two isolated taller towers shown in red, indicates intensification. *Right:* Katrina is shown at full strength, on August 29. Storm surge more than 6 meters high breached canal levees in Louisiana and caused disastrous flooding in Mississippi and Alabama, forcing thousands from their homes.

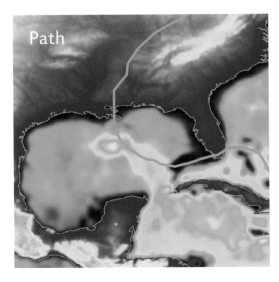

Path

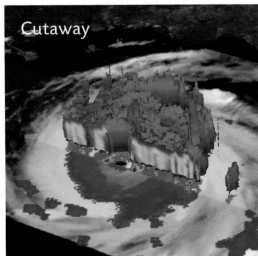

Cutaway

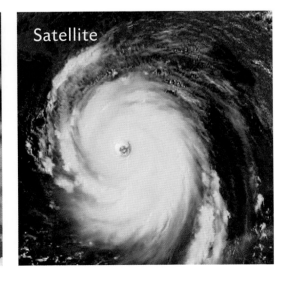

Satellite

Atlantic Marine Life

ALTHOUGH NOT AS OLD NOR AS LARGE AS THE
Pacific Ocean, the Atlantic is home for spectacularly abundant and diverse life, ranging from the
world's largest mammals—the great blue whale
and related cetaceans—and the largest invertebrates—giant squids and 20-meter-long chains
of the jellyfish-like siphonophores—to countless
millions of microscopic microbes, some of the
smallest creatures on Earth.

William Beebe, zoologist and explorer,
working in the Atlantic off Bermuda was the first to bring back news of what it is like to be
suspended thousands of meters under the Atlantic. Using a cranky but effective submersible
called a bathysphere, he and the sub's designer, Otis Barton, descended repeatedly far below
where sunlight penetrates, dangling by a cable from a makeshift surface support ship. In *Half
Mile Down*, Beebe writes:

> As I looked over the tossing ocean . . . and realized what I had been permitted to see . . . I knew
> that I should never again look upon the stars without remembering their active, living counter-
> parts swimming about in that terrific pressure . . . delicate and fragile. . . . When once it has been
> seen, it will remain forever the most vivid memory . . . solely because of its cosmic chill and isola-
> tion, the eternal and absolute darkness and the indescribable beauty of its inhabitants.

WEB LINK: J. Craig Venter Institute

Half a century ago, it was thought that microbes in the sea were uncommon, but recent explorations by a seagoing geneticist, Craig Venter, have proved how mistaken that belief was. In four small
samples of water taken in 2002 near Bermuda in the Sargasso Sea—long considered an ocean "desert" with very low levels of biological life because of its open-ocean location and enclosed gyre of
water—Venter discovered more than 1.2 million new genes in floating microbes, representing roughly
1,800 new species. Almost 1,000 of the new genes are photoreceptors, suggesting an unexplained
role for sunlight—beyond photosynthesis—in the lives of these microbes, including the possibility that
some may be converting sunlight directly into other types of energy.

A few days after the first full moon of summer, living clues to the ancient origins of marine life can
be witnessed in certain coastal areas of the
western North Atlantic. Thousands of horseshoe crabs, glistening like polished leather,
each roughly the size of half a soccer ball,
plow their craggy undersides into wet sand
and release billions of sperm and jade-col-
ored eggs. Flocks of shorebirds cascade from
the sky to gorge on much needed crab-egg
sustenance, stopping off on their journey of
many thousands of kilometers from the tip
of South America to nesting sites in Canada's
distant northern marshes.

Despite urgent searching for each
morsel by droves of turnstones, plovers,
gulls, red knots, and sanderlings, some eggs
remain safely in place, and over the next
few weeks they transform from amorphous
jelly to a miniature version of the parent

Prince Albert of Monaco
OCEANOGRAPHIC MUSEUM OF MONACO

An impressive white stone structure overlooking the Mediterranean Sea from a height of 90 meters, the Oceanographic Museum is the founding work of a prince who was both a great scholar and a great humanist, defender of peace and patron of the arts and sciences. Born in 1848, Prince Albert I of Monaco dedicated much of his life to the study of the sea and ocean. After a long period of military and maritime training and several years of travel on the seven seas, the prince embarked on an oceanographic career.

One of the major discoveries from observations made during his explorations was the phenomenon of anaphylaxis from the study of *Physalia*. Anaphylaxis is a cataclysmic physiological allergic-type reaction to certain toxins. Thus, understanding anaphylaxis began as an oceanographic discovery!

Albert I of Monaco was also the "instigator and promulgator" of the oceanographic science he contributed to. This is why he founded in 1906 the Institut Océanographique, which has two establishments located in Paris and Monaco.

Monaco's Oceanographic Museum and Aquarium was inaugurated on March 29, 1910. It displays in its exhibition halls and aquarium the wonders of life in the seas and the latest discoveries in marine biology and oceanography. Its missions are raising broad awareness of the importance of the seas and ocean, greeting international researchers and publishing the results of their work, and preserving and enhancing collections to form an exceptionally rich scientific and artistic heritage.

The most important of the museum's collections is the one made up of natural history samples and specimens collected during Prince Albert I's campaigns, which includes a large number of type specimens used by scientists to describe new species. Today researchers come to Monaco from all over the world to consult the type specimens in the collection, a key reference for determining the justification for defining new species. Thus, the Oceanographic Museum brings together art and science in one place.

Applying archaeological protocols to underwater sites, a diver observes an 11th-century shipwreck in the Aegean Sea off Serce Limani, Turkey.

The aquarium displays more than 6,000 specimens belonging to 400 fish species and 200 invertebrate species from the Mediterranean and tropical seas. These animals are shown in their magnificently recreated natural settings. This unique presentation is made possible thanks to highly sophisticated techniques based on the implementation of natural ecological processes. Living coral reefs are this aquarium's great innovation, with 90 tanks reconstructing the true image of the different marine ecosystems as they exist in the wild.

The reef ecosystems reconstructed in aquaria are truly natural laboratories in which a range of different studies can be carried out by the museum itself or affiliated independent laboratories such as the Scientific Center of Monaco. Work is carried out on hard coral ecophysiology, notably on calcification, photosynthesis, respiration, and response to ultraviolet radiation.

Experiments conducted in the past two decades in Monaco on Red Sea hard corals demonstrate several important points. Through the rigorous management of culturing conditions and stocking efforts, it is possible to maintain even reputedly sensitive hard corals under long-term culture for as long as 19 years, and up to 29 years for one *Turbinaria* species. These experiments also show the possible application of these techniques to large volumes: 40 cubic meters in 1989 with the Djibouti reef, and 130 cubic meters in 2000 with the construction of a shark lagoon. The current production system fully satisfies the aquarium's needs for hard corals, in terms both of quantity and quality.

Coral ecosystems, especially when they are well stocked and vibrant, have a powerful impact on the public. The reactions are quite varied, ranging from amazement to curiosity to reflection. The majority of visitors are overcome by an emotion that encourages a willingness to observe and understand. A particular emphasis is placed on threats to these ecosystems (acidification, sea-level rise, increasing seawater temperature) and on the need for citizens to adopt a conservation ethic.

crabs. Not crabs, really, but rather close relatives of long-extinct ancestors of spiders, scorpions, and their seagoing kin, horseshoe crabs existed more than a hundred million years before the super-continent Pangaea began to break apart giving birth to the present Atlantic Ocean.

WEB LINK: Biosphere animation

Among the air-breathing creatures that are at home diving into the Atlantic's twilight zone are several kinds of whales: humpbacks, Sei, Bryde's blue, right, sperm, grampus, and other toothed whales. Right whales, once common in coastal waters throughout much of the cooler Atlantic, were among the first to be decimated by whalers, starting in the 1500s. Slow-moving and gentle by nature, they have ample blubber that causes them to float when killed, making them relatively easy for whalers to catch and process. Although fully protected for decades, only about 300 right whales survive in the North Atlantic today, and their reproduction is not keeping pace with the loss from boat collisions, entanglement in fishing nets, and the effects of water pollution. In the South Atlantic, numbers appear to be increasing slowly, but there are still so few that zoologist Roger Payne, who has studied southern right whales since the 1970s, recognizes individually most of those that breed along the shores of Patagonia.

Perhaps the most stunning surprise the sea has given humankind so far relates not to storms or seamounts or new communities of life yet to be discovered. Rather, it is that for all of the ocean's great size and proven capacity for resilience, it is possible for the actions of humankind to alter the nature of systems and processes that have been developing for hundreds of millions of years. Nowhere is evidence more compelling than in the North Atlantic Ocean. In the nearly half century since the Mid-Atlantic Ridge was first mapped definitively, hundreds of millions of tons of crabs, lobsters, oysters, clams, and other marine wildlife have been removed from the North Atlantic's once richly productive waters. At the same time, hundreds of millions of tons of sewage, garbage, and other wastes have been added.

SEE ALSO: global overfishing, pages 312-314

Cod, once so abundant that it provided a key part of the economy of several nations for 500 years, has become so severely depleted by overly aggressive fishing that some believe that its very survival is in doubt. In the Atlantic, bluefin tuna, swordfish, haddock, menhaden, several species of grouper and snapper, summer flounder, and many other fish taken commercially have been reduced drastically within a few decades. Of the enormous populations of menhaden, oysters, and clams that once filtered the entire contents of the Chesapeake Bay in a matter of days, providing clean and healthy waters for all of the other inhabitants, only about 2 percent remain.

Special Places of the Atlantic

THE MEDITERRANEAN

The Mediterranean Sea supported early life and commerce for humans starting thousands of years ago. Some of this ancient history is being found through marine archaeology. During a lifetime of exploring sunken ships, marine archaeologist George Bass has seen ample evidence of the many ways that anything designed to travel on the surface of the ocean may ultimately wind up under it. In his 1975 account *Archaeology Beneath the Sea*, Bass explores a ship that sank in the Aegean Sea with a cargo of curiously shaped copper ingots near Bodrum, on the southern coast of Turkey, around 1200 B.C. during the time of Ulysses. Through careful application of research techniques comparable to those developed for terrestrial digs, Bass and his team of scuba divers have discovered many personal effects and habits of the ship's

Bottles resembling those of Muslim craftsmen yield a treasure of history in the Aegean Sea off Serce Limani, Turkey.

captain and crew. The ship apparently struck jagged rocks along the shore and sank, to lie undisturbed for nearly 3,200 years.

The Mediterranean is connected to the Indian Ocean via the Red Sea through the man-made Suez Canal and to the Atlantic by the narrow but natural channel that now exists at Gibraltar. Although more than 1.6 kilometers deep, the Mediterranean dried up completely 6 million years ago. During a long, global ice age, so much water was taken out of the ocean to form massive ice sheets that sea level was lowered below the natural dam at Gibraltar and the Mediterranean was cut off from Atlantic waters. Like the Great Salt Lake of North America, supersaline Mediterranean lakes formed. Made increasingly salty through evaporation, they created thick layers of gypsum, halite, and other salts as they dried. Subsequent warming melted the Earth's glaciers enough to raise sea level and cause Atlantic waters to spill back into the Mediterranean. For the past 5 million years, the Mediterranean has been a liquid blue jewel separating Europe from the continent of Africa.

THE GULF OF MEXICO AND CARIBBEAN SEA

The Gulf of Mexico has some unusual features. In addition to its many buried oil and gas reserves, it has: salt diapirs, huge vertical structures of salt that push up into the overlying sediments; underwater brine lakes, large, shallow bowls of very salty water on the seafloor; and hydrocarbon seeps, where petroleum products bubble up naturally from the seafloor.

Cold seeps support communities of chemosynthetic animals that depend on chemicals from the seafloor, instead of photosynthesis from sunlight, as their food and energy source. Such communities are common on relatively shallow upper continental slope sites in the northern Gulf, and are surprisingly similar to the animals found around the extremely hot hydrothermal vents in the deep ocean.

In 2006, a group of scientists from a number of American and European universities made dives in the submersible *Alvin* at sites deeper than 1,000 meters along the lower continental slope to see if the cold-seep communities exist in deeper waters of the Gulf. Though the cold-seep animals at greater depth were made up of slightly different species, the strange communities were present at every place they explored.

The small Caribbean tectonic plate was formed about 80 million years ago. To the northeast and east, this plate is undergoing subduction, being pushed under the Atlantic oceanic plate off the island of Puerto Rico, forming the Puerto Rico Trench, which is the deepest area in the Atlantic Ocean. Subduction of the Caribbean plate to the east has formed the Lesser Antilles. This collection of small volcanic islands is arranged in a long, curved line—a classic volcanic island arc formation over a subduction zone. Beneath these islands, the Caribbean crust is being pushed down, heated, and melted, creating forces that release some of the tension and melted materials back to the surface through the occasionally active volcanoes in the island chain. There are more islands in the Caribbean than anywhere else in the Atlantic.

About 65 million years ago, a large asteroid, almost 10 kilometers in diameter, struck the Earth on the western margin of the Atlantic just off today's Yucatán Peninsula in the Gulf of Mexico and created the Chicxulub Crater, about 240 kilometers in diameter. The impact created huge tsunamis and earthquakes, and threw so much dust and carbon gases into the atmosphere that it reduced sunlight and air temperatures globally. Most scientists believe this was the great disaster that caused the end of the Cretaceous era and the reign of dinosaurs on Earth.

Along the Atlantic–Caribbean coastline of Central America lies an enormous barrier reef of corals, second in size and length only to the Great Barrier Reef of Australia. Mark Spalding, who studies coral reefs around the world, estimates that the Caribbean Basin holds about 7 percent of the world's shallow coral reefs. Spalding and a colleague, Phil Kramer, have also studied the number of different species of marine animals in the Caribbean. They found the highest levels off the coast of Venezuela and, surprisingly, around the busy, heavily traveled southern and eastern coasts of Florida. ☐

Strange Creatures at Cold Seeps

Biologists were stunned in 1977 when hydrothermal vent communities were found on the seafloor thriving in very hot water, with no sunlight and no obvious way to get food. Some of the tiny organisms that take energy from hot vent minerals are so unusual that a whole new kingdom of life, Archaea, was named to describe them. Then these microbes were found on land in hot springs and geysers—right under our noses for centuries. Almost a decade later came another stunning breakthrough: Similar strange creatures also live around cold seeps on the seafloor, but these communities use methane bubbling up from the sediments for their sustenance.

Kemps Ridley sea turtle hatchlings make a dash for the sea at Rancho Nuevo, Mexico.

John W. Tunnell, Jr.
GULF OF MEXICO

The Gulf of Mexico is the ninth largest body of water in the world, and it is economically and ecologically one of the most productive and important. Geographically, it is located in the southeastern part of North America, and it is surrounded by three countries—the United States to the north, Mexico to the west and south, and the island of Cuba to the east. The Gulf occupies a surface area of about 1.5 million square kilometers. It measures 1,570 kilometers in its maximum east-west dimension and 900 kilometers from north to south between the Mississippi Delta and Yucatán Peninsula. The shoreline, extending from Cape Sable, Florida, to Cabo Catoche, Quintana Roo, is about

Warm, tropical water enters the Gulf of Mexico from the Caribbean Sea between the Yucatán Peninsula and Cuba via the Yucatán Channel, where it forms the predominant Gulf current, known as the Loop Current. Large eddies sometimes spin off of this major current and move westward. After looping into the eastern Gulf, it exits via the Florida Straits between Florida and Cuba and forms one of the world's strongest and most important currents, the Gulf Stream, sending warm water up the eastern seaboard of the United States and making the United Kingdom a habitable climate rather than a frozen landscape. As a large receiving basin, the Gulf of

Land and sea converge in a network of marshy islands and shallow water at the mouth of the Mississippi River, fed by dozens of smaller rivers flowing from the heartland.

5,700 kilometers long, with another 380 kilometers of Gulf shoreline in Cuba from Cabo San Antonio in the west to Havana in the east.

The Gulf of Mexico Basin resembles a bowl, or large pit, with a shallow rim. The shallow continental shelves (less than 200 meters) are narrow and terrigenous (riverborne clay, silt, and siliceous sand) in the west; moderate widths and terrigenous in the north; and wide, carbonate (biogenic) platforms in the east, adjacent to the Florida and Yucatán Peninsulas. They occupy about 32 percent of the Gulf. The continental slope (200 to 3,000 meters) occupies about 41 percent, and the abyssal plain (greater than 3,000 meters) covers the remainder. The deepest depth, known as the Sigsbee Deep, is more than 3,658 meters, but the exact depth is uncertain (estimates range from 3,658 to 4,148 meters).

Mexico receives extensive river drainages from five countries (the United States, Canada, Mexico, Guatemala, and Cuba), including more than two-thirds of the U.S. watershed. The Mississippi River dominates drainage in the north, and the Grijalva-Usumacinta river system dominates in the south. On the positive side, the Mississippi River drainage has created the largest coastal wetland in the United States, with its attendant high productivity of fish and wildlife in coastal Louisiana. On the negative side, however, that same drainage, with a huge load of nutrients from America's heartland, causes tremendous algae blooms in the Gulf of Mexico, which have led to one of the largest hypoxic (low oxygen) or dead zones in the world's ocean.

Biologically, the shallow waters of the northern Gulf are warm temperate, and those in the south are tropical. Oyster reefs and salt marshes are the dominant habitat type in the northern Gulf, with low-salinity estuaries and sea grass beds common in clearer, more saline bays. In the tropical southern Gulf, mangroves line bay and lagoon shorelines with oyster reefs, salt marshes, and sea grasses distributed in conditions of similar salinity as the northern Gulf. In the western Gulf, wedged between two wet regions, the Laguna Madre of Texas and Tamaulipas exists as the most famous of only five hypersaline lagoons in the world. This highly productive lagoon has extensive wind-tidal flats and shallow sea grass beds in a semi-arid region. Offshore, coral reefs are common in the Florida Keys, Cuba, and the southern Gulf off the state of Veracruz and on the Campeche Bank. The Flower Garden Banks off the Texas-Louisiana border represent the only coral reefs in the northern Gulf, and they are the most northerly coral reefs on the North American continent.

An amazing array of marine life, including more than 15,000 species, exists in the Gulf of Mexico, making it one of the most biodiverse oceanic water bodies on Earth. In addition to the thousands of invertebrates, including almost 2,500 mollusks, there are almost 1,500 species of fish, 5 sea turtles, nearly 400 species of birds, and 30 species of marine mammals. Recent findings off the northern Yucatán reveal one of the world's largest summer aggregations of whale sharks, between 800 and 1,000 individuals. The Kemp's ridley sea turtle is the most endangered in the world, but its numbers are now increasing after decades of decline. In addition to the only wild population of whooping cranes in the world along the Texas coast, vast numbers of colonial waterbirds nest on rookery islands along Gulf shores and on the Campeche Bank, and hundreds of thousands of migrating shorebirds, songbirds, raptors, and

Ancient residents of the planet, jellyfish have been pulsing in the ocean for more than half a billion years, but individuals such as this Cassiopea in the Florida Keys is likely to survive for less than a year.

waterfowl (ducks and geese) use Gulf flyways. The most common coastal marine mammal, the bottlenose dolphin, has a population near 45,000 along the Gulf coast.

Most visitors to the northern Gulf of Mexico have a mistaken conception of this grand aquatic ecosystem. Their visits to Corpus Christi, Galveston, Biloxi, or Mobile often reveal brown, turbid waters in the Gulf with oil and gas platforms on the horizon and oil refineries on the mainland. However, just a short distance offshore and all the way to Mexico and Cuba are some of the bluest waters on Earth, with a rich diversity of marine life and habitats.

Beyond the productive economies and ecologies are some underlying concerns or impacts to both the Gulf and to human health. However, more institutions, organizations, businesses, and individuals are realizing that stewardship and conservation are the best tools for protecting both the ecology and the economy of this vast resource for future generations.

The Harte Research Institute for Gulf of Mexico Studies at Texas A&M University in Corpus Christi is focused on providing research and policy that will support and advance the long-term sustainability and conservation of the Gulf of Mexico. A unique hallmark of this institute is collaborative partnerships in all three Gulf countries.

Establishing and encouraging working relationships, partnerships, and stewardship around the Gulf of Mexico, as well as raising the awareness of Gulf resources and issues and working toward solutions to problems, will be the key to restoration and conservation of a healthy and productive Gulf of Mexico for future generations.

Resources of the Gulf

• Seven of the nation's top 10 ports • 93 percent of U.S. offshore oil production • 98 percent of U.S. gas production • $77.7 billion annual oil and gas revenue • Oil and gas revenue or leases second only to income tax in revenue generated for the U.S. • $44.2 billion annual recreational/tourism industry • Largest shrimp and oyster production in the U.S. • Over 50 percent of U.S. coastal wetlands • $1.1 billion fishing industry • Padre Island, longest barrier island in the world

Human Impacts on the Gulf

• Loss of critical habitat • Degradation of water quality • Overfishing • Oil spills • Marine debris • Nutrient enrichment with dead zones or low-oxygen zones • Invasive species • Beach/shellfish closures • Coastal development • Harmful algae blooms • $1.1 billion fishing industry

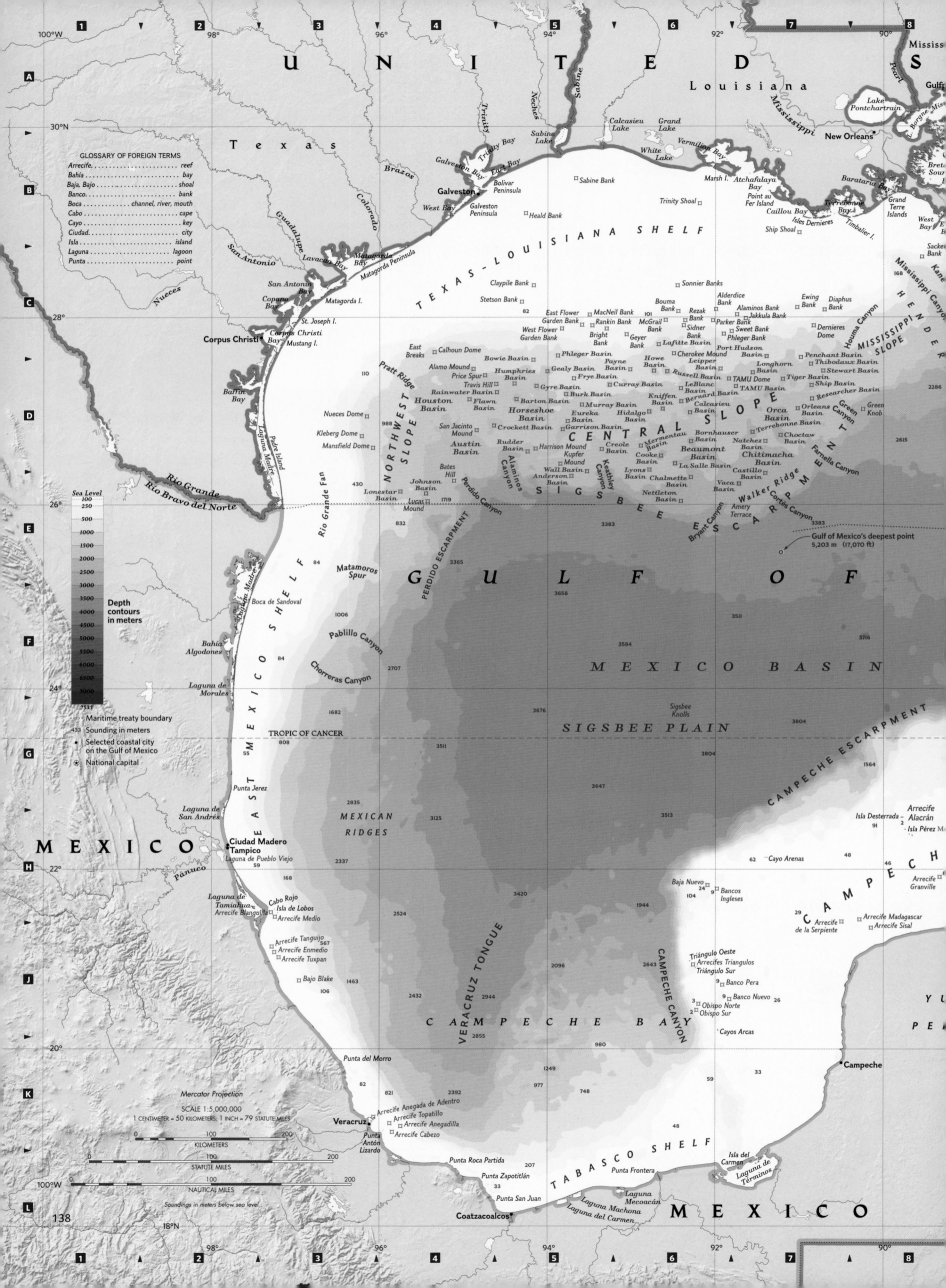

U N I T E D   S

Louisiana

Gulf

Lake
Pontchartrain

New Orleans

L. Borgne Miss

30°N

Texas

Brazos

Trinity
Bay

Sabine
Lake

Calcasieu
Lake

Grand
Lake

Vermilion Bay

White
Lake

Marsh I.

Atchafalaya
Bay

Point au
Fer Island

Barataria Bay

Bret
Sour

Neches

Sabine

Trinity

Mississippi

Pearl

GLOSSARY OF FOREIGN TERMS
Arrecife . . . . reef
Bahía . . . . bay
Baja, Bajo . . . . shoal
Banco . . . . bank
Boca . . . . channel, river, mouth
Cabo . . . . cape
Cayo . . . . key
Ciudad . . . . city
Isla . . . . island
Laguna . . . . lagoon
Punta . . . . point

Galveston
Bay

Trinity Bay

East Bay

Bolivar
Peninsula

Galveston

West Bay

Galveston
Peninsula

Heald Bank

Sabine Bank

Trinity Shoal

Caillou Bay

Isles Dernieres

Ship Shoal

Timbalier I.

Terrebonne
Bay

Grand Terre
Islands

West
Bay

Sacket
Bank

Kane

168

San Antonio

Guadalupe

Colorado

Lavaca Bay

Matagorda
Bay

Matagorda Peninsula

T E X A S – L O U I S I A N A   S H E L F

Claypile Bank

Sonnier Banks

Ewing
Bank

Diaphus
Bank

Mississippi Canyon

H E N D E R

San Antonio
Bay

Copana
Bay

Matagorda I.

Stetson Bank

82

East Flower
Garden Bank

MacNeil Bank

Bouma
Bank

Rezak
Bank

Alderdice
Bank

Alaminos Bank

Houma
Canyon

2286

M I S S I S S I P P I   S L O P E

St. Joseph I.

Corpus Christi

Corpus Christi
Bay

Mustang I.

West Flower
Garden Bank

Rankin Bank

McGrail
Bank

Sidner
Bank

Parker Bank

Sweet Bank

Dernieres
Dome

Calhoun Dome

Bright
Bank

Geyer
Bank

Lafitte Bank

Port Hudson
Basin

Baffin Bay

East
Breaks

Bowie Bank

Phleger Bank

Phleger Basin

Cherokee Mound
Leipper
Basin

Penchant Basin

Thibodaux Basin

Pratt Ridge

Alamo Mound

Humphries
Basin

Gealy Basin

Payne
Basin

Howe
Basin

Longhorn

Stewart Basin

Price Spur

Travis Hill

Gyre Basin

Frye Basin

Curray Basin

Russell Basin

TAMU Dome

Tiger Basin

Ship Basin

110

Rainwater Basin

Burk Basin

Kniffen
Basin

LeBlanc
Basin

TAMU Dome

Researcher Basin

Houston
Basin

Flawn
Basin

Barton Basin

Murray Basin

Bernard Basin

N O R T H W E S T   S L O P E

Horseshoe
Basin

Eureka
Basin

Hidalgo
Basin

Calcasieu
Basin

Orca
Basin

Nueces Dome

988

San Jacinto
Mound

Crockett Basin

Garrison Basin

C E N T R A L   S L O P E

Choctaw
Basin

Green
Knob

Kleberg Dome

Austin
Basin

Rudder
Basin

Harrison Mound
Kupfer
Mound

Creole
Basin

Mermentau
Basin

Beaumont
Basin

Bornhauser
Basin

Terrebonne Basin

2615

Mansfield Dome

Anderson
Basin

Cooke
Basin

Chitimacha
Basin

Orleans
Basin

430

Bates
Hill

Alaminos
Canyon

Keathley
Canyon

La Salle Basin

Castillo
Basin

Natchez
Basin

Farnella Canyon

Johnson
Basin

Wall Basin

Lyons
Basin

Chalmette
Basin

Vaca
Basin

Walker Ridge

Cortes Canyon

3383

Lonestar
Basin

Lucas
Mound

1719

Nettleton
Basin

S I G S B E E

S C A R P M

Amery
Terrace

Bryant Canyon

3383

832

Perdido Canyon

Gulf of Mexico's deepest point
5,203 m (17,070 ft)

Rio Grande

Río Bravo del Norte

Padre Island

26°

Sea Level
100
250
500
1000
1500
2000
2500
3000
3500
4000
4500
5000
5500
6000
6500
7000

Depth
contours
in meters

7535

Maritime treaty boundary

Sounding in meters

Selected coastal city
on the Gulf of Mexico

National capital

Laguna Madre

Laguna de
Morales

R I O   G R A N D E   F A N

Matamoros
Spur

Boca de Sandoval

Perdido Escarpment

2365

2707

1006

3365

G U L F   O F

M E X I C O   B A S I N

3658

3511

3584

3716

Pablillo Canyon

84

Bahía
Algodones

84

Chorreras Canyon

1682

3676

3804

TROPIC OF CANCER

808

55

3511

SIGSBEE KNOLLS

S I G S B E E   P L A I N

3804

1564

Laguna de
San Andrés

Punta Jerez

2835

M E X I C A N
R I D G E S

3125

3647

3513

CAMPECHE ESCARPMENT

Ciudad Madero
Tampico

Laguna de Pueblo Viejo

59

2337

Isla Desterrada – Arrecife
Alacrán
Isla Pérez Ma

91

M E X I C O

Pánuco

Laguna de
Tamiahua

Cabo Rojo
Isla de Lobos
Arrecife Blanquilla

168

2524

3420

1944

62

Cayo Arenas

48

Baja Nuevo

24

Arrecife
Granville

46

Arrecife Enmedio
Arrecife Medio

567

104

9

Bancos
Ingleses

C A M P E C H

Arrecife Tanguijo

Arrecife Tuxpan

2096

2643

29

Arrecife
de la Serpiente

Arrecife Madagascar

Arrecife Sisal

Bajo Blake

1463

106

V E R A C R U Z   T O N G U E

2432

2944

2855

2524

Triángulo Oeste
Arrecifes Triangulos
Triángulo Sur

9

Banco Pera

Banco Nuevo

26

Obispo Norte
Obispo Sur

Cayos Arcas

980

Y U

P E

Punta del Morro

2392

1249

977

748

33

59

Campeche

82

821

Arrecife Anegada de Adentro
Arrecife Topatillo

Veracruz

Punta
Antón
Lizardo

Arrecife Anegadilla
Arrecife Cabezo

T A B A S C O   S H E L F

Punta Roca Partida

207

Isla del
Carmen

Laguna de
Términos

Punta Zapotitlán

Punta Frontera

Punta San Juan

Laguna
Mecoacán

Coatzacoalcos

Laguna Machona

Laguna del Carmen

M E X I C O

E A S T   M E X I C O   S H E L F

Mercator Projection

SCALE 1:5,000,000
1 CENTIMETER = 50 KILOMETERS; 1 INCH = 79 STATUTE MILES

KILOMETERS

STATUTE MILES

NAUTICAL MILES

Soundings in meters below sea level

138

18°N

C A M P E C H E   B A Y

CAMPECHE CANYON

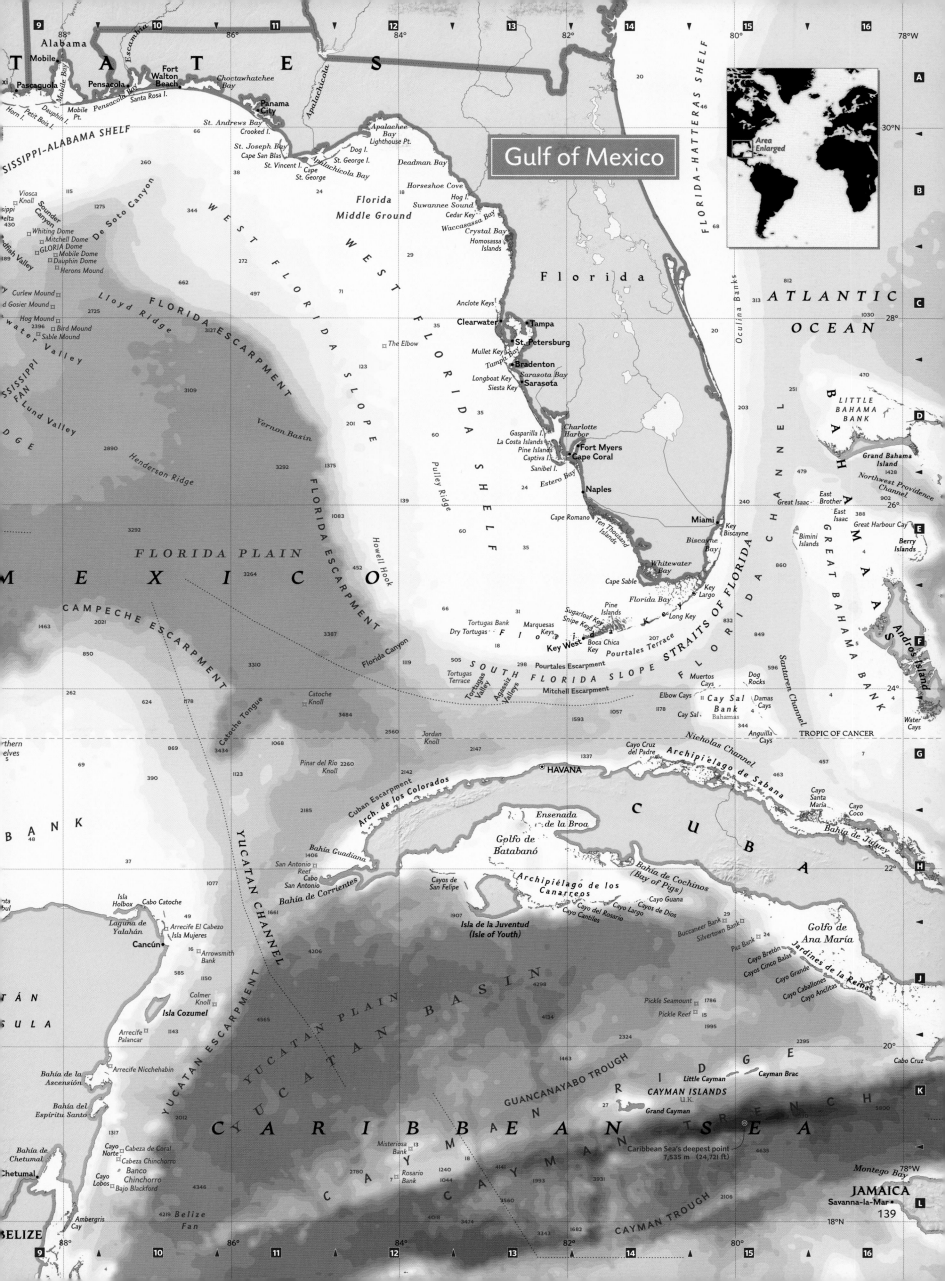

The same physics governing chlorophyll distribution in the Atlantic also operates in the Pacific Ocean, resulting in chlorophyll-poor central gyres and elevated chlorophyll along the equator, coastlines, and higher latitudes. The central North Pacific receives more nutrient input than the South through wind-borne Asian dust and volcanic emissions from the Ring of Fire.

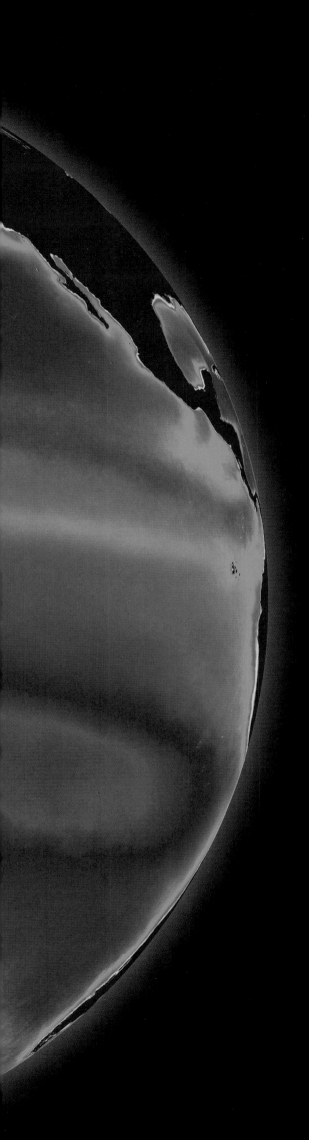

Chapter 5

PACIFIC OCEAN

Pacific Ocean Seafloor

A

ARCTIC CIRCLE

B

C

D

E

F

G

H

J

K

L

ALASKA

GULF OF ALASKA

Alaska Peninsula
Kodiak
Island
Kodiak
Seamount
2289
Pratt
Seamount
729
708
Welker
Seamount
44
Bowie
Seamount
Gilbert
Seamount
Queen
Charlotte
Islands
Alexander
Archipelago

Vancouver
Island

JUAN
DE FUCA
RIDGE

Eickelberg
Seamount

CASCADIA
BASIN

TUFTS PLAIN

Comstock
Seamount

Harris
Seamount

NORTHEAST

MENDOCINO FRACTURE ZONE

PIONEER FRACTURE ZONE

MURRAY FRACTURE ZONE

WEST

Mendelssohn Seamount

Musicians
Seamounts

Moonless
Mountains

Fieberling
Tablemount

Channel
Islands

Guadalupe I.

Henderson
Seamount

PATTON ESCARPMENT

Baja California

Gulf of California

NORTH AMERICA

HUDSON
BAY

Great Lakes

Gulf of
Maine

Cape Hatteras

NORTH
ATLANTIC
OCEAN

Bermuda

Blake
Plateau

GULF OF
MEXICO

MEXICO
BASIN

Campeche Bank

Yucatán
Peninsula

BAHAMA
ISLANDS

Cuba

GREATER ANTILLES

CAYMAN TRENCH

CARIBBEAN SEA

Hispaniola

Puerto
Rico

8,605
(28,232 ft)
Atlantic Ocean's
deepest point

LESSER ANTILLES

Miller Cylindrical Projection

SCALE 1:49,470,000
1 CENTIMETER = 495 KILOMETERS; 1 INCH = 781 STATUTE MILES

0   1000   2000
KILOMETERS
0   1000   2000
STATUTE MILES
0   1000   2000
NAUTICAL MILES

Scale at the Equator
Soundings in meters below sea level

TROPIC OF CANCER

HAWAIIAN RIDGE

O'ahu

Hawai'i

MOLOKAI FRACTURE ZONE

CLARION FRACTURE ZONE

CLIPPERTON FRACTURE ZONE

PACIFIC BASIN

Revillagigedo
Islands

Mathematicians
Seamounts

MIDDLE AMERICA TRENCH

COCOS TRENCH

Palmyra Atoll

LINE ISLANDS

Kiritimati
(Christmas I.)

Jarvis I.

GALÁPAGOS FRACTURE ZONE

GUATEMALA BASIN

GALÁPAGOS RIFT

GALÁPAGOS
ISLANDS

COCOS RIDGE

PANAMA
BASIN

CARNEGIE RIDGE

EAST PACIFIC RISE

EQUATOR

MANIHIKI
PLATEAU

Manihiki Atoll

MARQUESAS
ISLANDS

MARQUESAS FRACTURE ZONE

TUAMOTU ARCHIPELAGO

Pukapuka

COOK ISLANDS

Manuae

Tahiti

SOCIETY
ISLANDS

Mangaia
Iles
Maria

AUSTRAL ISLANDS

Neilson Reef
Marotiri

President Thiers
Bank

Morane

Pitcairn I.

Iles Gambier

Ducie I.

Sala-y-Gómez

Easter Island
(Isla de Pascua)

EASTER FRACTURE ZONE

SALA Y GÓMEZ RIDGE

NASCA RIDGE

PERU BASIN

GALÁPAGOS RISE

PERU-CHILE TRENCH

SOUTH
AMERICA

TROPIC OF CAPRICORN

San Félix I.
San Ambrosio I.

CHILE
BASIN

SOUTH PACIFIC OCEAN

SOUTHWEST PACIFIC BASIN

CHALLENGER FRACTURE ZONE

AGASSIZ FRACTURE ZONE

MENARD FRACTURE ZONE

EAST PACIFIC RISE

VALDIVIA FRACTURE ZONE

CHILE RISE

Juan Fernández
Islands

SOUTHEAST

PACIFIC

BASIN

HUMBOLDT
PLAIN

ELTANIN FRACTURE ZONE

UDINTSEV FRACTURE ZONE

Pacific Ocean Political Map and Depth Contours

ARCTIC CIRCLE

RUSSIA

MONGOLIA

CHINA

Qinhuangdao
Xingang · Bo Hai · Dalian
NORTH KOREA
Qingdao · Incheon · Daesan · Pohang
SOUTH KOREA · Gwangyang · Yeosu · Ulsan · Busan
Rizhao
Lianyungang
Yellow Sea · Jeju I.
58
Shanghai
Ningbo
EAST CHINA SEA
Yaku Is.

SEA OF OKHOTSK
SAKHALIN ISLAND
Tatar Strait
KURIL BASIN
HOKKAIDO
Habomai
Kunashir
Iturup
Urup
Simushir
Ketoy
Matua
Rasshua
Shiashkotan
Onekotan
Paramushir

SEA OF JAPAN (EAST SEA)
JAPAN
HONSHU · 3053
Tokyo · Kashima
Kawasaki · Chiba
Kobe · Nagoya · Yokohama
Osaka
Oita · Shikoku · 3839
KYUSHU
Amami Is.
Okinawa
2929

St. John I.
131
Shantar Is.
830

Shelikhov Gulf
Karaginskiy I.
3703
Bering I.
Commander Is. · Mednyy I.

Gulf of Anadyr
St. Law
St. Matthew I

BERING
ALEUTIAN BASIN
SHIRSHOV RIDGE
ALEUTIAN
ALEUTI
Attu I. · Near Is.
Agattu I. · Kiska I.
Andreanof Is. · Seguam I.
Tanaga I. · Adak I. · An
Delarof
7568
Detroit Seamount
7619 · Amchitka

KAMCHATKA
JAPAN TRENCH
KURIL ISLANDS
KURIL TRENCH
9750
NAMPO SHOTO
Sumisu
9695
Sofu Gan
Bonin Is.
Moko Jima Retto
Chichi Jima Retto
Haha Jima Retto
Volcano Is.
Kita Iwo To
Iwo To (Iwo Jima)
Minami Iwo To

NORTHWEST PACIFIC BASIN
SHATSKIY RISE
3510
5982
4362
5831

NORTH PAC
EMPEROR SEAMOUNTS
CHINOOK T
Jimmu Seamount
Suiko Seamount
Nintoku Seamount
2194 · Jingu Seamount
Ojin Seamount
HESS RISE
4453
Isakov Seamount
Makarov Seamount · 1471
Yuryaku Seamount
Kammu Seamount
Judge Seamount
Ferguson Seamount · 5996 · Mellish Seamount · 5319
Grosvenor Seamount
Guadeloupe Seamount · MAPMAKER SEAMOUNTS
Kure Atoll · Pearl and
Midway Is. · Hermes I.
Salmon Bank
1218
Lisianski I.
Minami Tori Shima · Japan · 1133

MID-PACIFIC MOUNTAINS
Wake I.
U.S.
NECKER
881

Huangpu · Xiamen
Shenzhen
Chiwan
Zhanjiang
Hainan

Chilung
Sakishima Islands
Jiehung
Mai-Liao
Hong Kong · TAIWAN · Kaohsiung
3529
Babuyan Is.
Batan Is. · 3098
2195

RYUKYU ISLANDS
Kita Daito I.
Daito Is.
Okino Daito I.

KYUSHU-PALAU RIDGE
KYUSHU TRENCH
RYUKYU TRENCH

Parece Vela · Japan
4392
Farallon de Pajaros
Asuncion
Agrihan
Pagan
Alamagan
NORTHERN MARIANA ISLANDS
Sarigan
Anatahan
Saipan
Tinian · Rota
Guam · U.S.

WEST MARIANA BASIN
EAST MARIANA BASIN
5811
MAGELLAN SEAMOUNTS
1330
Taongi Atoll

Bikar Atoll
5231
Bikini Atoll · Utirik Atoll
Enewetak Atoll · Rongelap Atoll · Ujelang Atoll
Kwajalein Atoll
Ailinglapalap Atoll · Namorik Atoll
Jaluit Atoll
Pingelap Atoll
Maloelap Atoll
Wotje Atoll
Arno Atoll · Mili Atoll
Majuro Atoll
MARSHALL ISLANDS
RATAK CHAIN
RALIK CHAIN
CENTRA
Magellan Rise · 2981

PHILIPPINE BASIN
1902
Benham Seamount · 2621
LUZON
Manila
Paracel Is.
SOUTH CHINA SEA
Mindoro
Panay
22
Negros
Palawan
5082

PHILIPPINE SEA
PHILIPPINE TRENCH

World's greatest ocean depth
(35,827 ft) 10,920 m
Challenger Deep
10057
Yap Is.
Ngulu Atoll
Fais
Ulithi Atoll

CAROLINE ISLANDS
Namonuito Atoll
Gaferut · Hall Is.
Faraulep Atoll · Pikelot
Pulusuk · Chuuk · Losap Atoll
Woleai Atoll · Satawal · Pulap · Oroluk
Eauripik Atoll · Namoluk · Mortlock Is.

Senyavin Is.
Ailinglapalap Atoll
Ngatik Atoll
Kosrae
Ebon Atoll

4533

Babelthuap
Sonsorol Is.
Pulo Anna
Merir
Tobi
Helen I.
PALAU
WEST CAROLINE BASIN
EAST CAROLINE BASIN

FEDERATED STATES OF MICRONESIA
Nukuoro Atoll
2553
Kapingamarangi Atoll

MALAYSIA
BRUNEI
Natuna Is.
Balabac
Spratly I.
Con Son
GREATER
BORNEO

Sangihe Is.
Talaud Is.
Morotai
Halmahera
Waigeo
Yapen

EAURIPIK RISE
Mapia Is. · 3908

Abaiang · Marakei
Bairiki · Maiana
Tarawa
Abemama · Nonouti
Beru · 4788
Aranuka · Tamana
Arorae
GILBERT ISLANDS

Butaritari
Howland I. · U.S.
Baker I. · U.S.

CENTRA
BASIN
McKean I.
Birnie
Nikumaroro
Orona
PHO
ISLA
TOKELAU
N.Z.
Nukunono
Faka

NIKITIN SEAMOUNT

EQUATOR
Simeulue
Nias
Siberut
Mentawai Is.
Singapore
Pulau Bukom
SUMATRA

Bangka
Belitung
Jakarta
JAVA
Madura
Surabaya

Sula Is.
Buru
Buton
Muna
Selayar
Ceram
Ambon
Banda
Kai Is.
Aru Is.
Dolak

Celebes Sea
5484
Makassar Str.
SULAWESI
LESSER SUNDA ISLANDS

INDONESIA
Java Sea
Bali · Lombok · Alor
Sumbawa · Flores · Savu Sea
Sumba · Sawu · Roti
Banda Sea
Wetar
Moa · Babar
Tanimbar Is.
Timor
TIMOR-LESTE
Timor Sea
Arafura Sea

NEW GUINEA
PAPUA
NEW GUINEA
Admiralty Is.
Manus
Mussau Is.
New Hanover
New Ireland
Nukumanu I.
Bismarck Sea
New Britain
NAURU
1582
Bougainville
New Georgia
Buka
Choiseul
Santa Isabel
SOLOMON ISLANDS
Woodlark Is.
Solomon Sea
Guadalcanal
Malaita
San Cristobal
Rennell
1628

Nanumea
Niutao
Nukufetau · Vaitupu
Funafuti
Nukulaelae
Niulakita
TUVALU

Nanumanga
NZ

SAMO

MID-INDIAN BASIN
Nicobar Is. · India
ANDAMAN SEA
Andaman Is. · India

BAY OF BENGAL
INDIA
SRI LANKA
BANGLADESH
NEPAL · BHUTAN
MYANMAR (BURMA)
LAOS
THAILAND
CAMBODIA
VIETNAM
Gulf of Tonkin
Gulf of Thailand
Bangkok
Laem Chabang
Map Ta Phut
TROPIC OF CANCER

Thursday I.
Torres Str.
D'Entrecasteaux Is.
Louisiade Archipelago
Tagula I.
Misima I.

NINETYEAST RIDGE

INVESTIGATOR RIDGE

EAST INDIAMAN RIDGE

JAVA TRENCH

Cocos (Keeling) Is.
Australia
Christmas I.
Australia
Indian Ocean's deepest point
(23,376 ft) 7,125 m

Osborn Plateau

Wallaby Plateau
Cuvier Plateau

EXMOUTH PLATEAU

NORTH AUSTRALIAN BASIN

Ashmore and Cartier Is.
Australia
Melville I.
Joseph Bonaparte Gulf

Gulf of Carpentaria

Great Barrier Reef

Santa Cruz Is.
Tikopia
VANUATU
Banks Is.
Torres Is.
Espiritu Santo
Maewo
Malakula
Pentecost
Ambrym
Shepherd Is.
Efate
Erromango
Tanna
Futuna
Anatom
2669
Matthew
Hunter
4168
VITYAZ TRENCH
NEW HEBRIDES TRENCH

Wallis Is.
France
Rotuma
Fataka
Tikopia
Îles de Horne
France
Niuafo'ou
Savai'i
SAMO
Niuatoputapu

FIJI ISLANDS
Vanua Levu
Viti Levu
Kadavu
Lau Group
Vatoa
Ono-i-Lau
Ceva-i-Ra
TONGA
Vava'u Group
Ha'apai Group
Tongatapu Group
Ata

CORAL SEA BASIN
4477
Willis Islets
Tregrosse Islets
Îles Chesterfield
2011
Îles Bélep
NEW CALEDONIA
France
Île Huon
Loyalty Islands

CORAL SEA

LORD HOWE RISE
NORFOLK RIDGE
NEW CALEDONIA BASIN

SOUTH FIJI BASIN
4572

LAU RIDGE

KERMADEC TRENCH
TONGA TRENCH
LOUISVILLE R

AUSTRALIA

Hay Point
Gladstone
1464
Fraser I.
Brisbane
MIDDLETON BASIN
Middleton Reef
Lord Howe I.
Australia
Newcastle
Sydney
Botany Bay
Port Kembla
Ball's Pyramid

Norfolk I.
Australia · Phillip I.
2976
Three Kings Is.
N.Z.
L'Esperance Rock
Macauley I. · N.Z.
Curtis I.
Raoul I.
1318
Gascoyne Tablemount
Taupo Tablemount
Auckland
1952
Tauranga
NEW ZEALAND
NORTH ISLAND
Great Barrier I.

TROPIC OF CAPRICORN
WHARTON BASIN
PERTH BASIN
BROKEN RIDGE
Naturaliste Plateau
Shark Bay
Spencer Gulf
Great Australian Bight
Kangaroo I.

SOUTH AUSTRALIAN BASIN

TASMAN PLAIN
660
SOUTH TASMAN RISE
3398

DIAMANTINA FRACTURE ZONE
TASMAN FRACTURE ZONE

INDIAN OCEAN

King I.
Bass Strait
Furneaux Group
TASMANIA
East Tasman Plateau
4831
TASMAN SEA

2892
CHATHAM RISE
Chatham Is.
N.Z.
SOUTH ISLAND
BOUNTY TROUGH
Bounty Is.
N.Z.
The Snares
N.Z.
CAMPBELL PLATEAU
Auckland Is.
N.Z.
Campbell I. · N.Z.
3901
Antipodes Is.
N.Z.
Bollons Tablemount
EMERALD BASIN

Miller Cylindrical Projection
SCALE 1:49,470,000
1 CENTIMETER = 495 KILOMETERS; 1 INCH = 781 STATUTE MILES

0   1000   2000
KILOMETERS
0   1000   2000
STATUTE MILES
0   1000   2000
NAUTICAL MILES

Scale at the Equator
Soundings in meters below sea level

Longitude East 130° of Greenwich

146

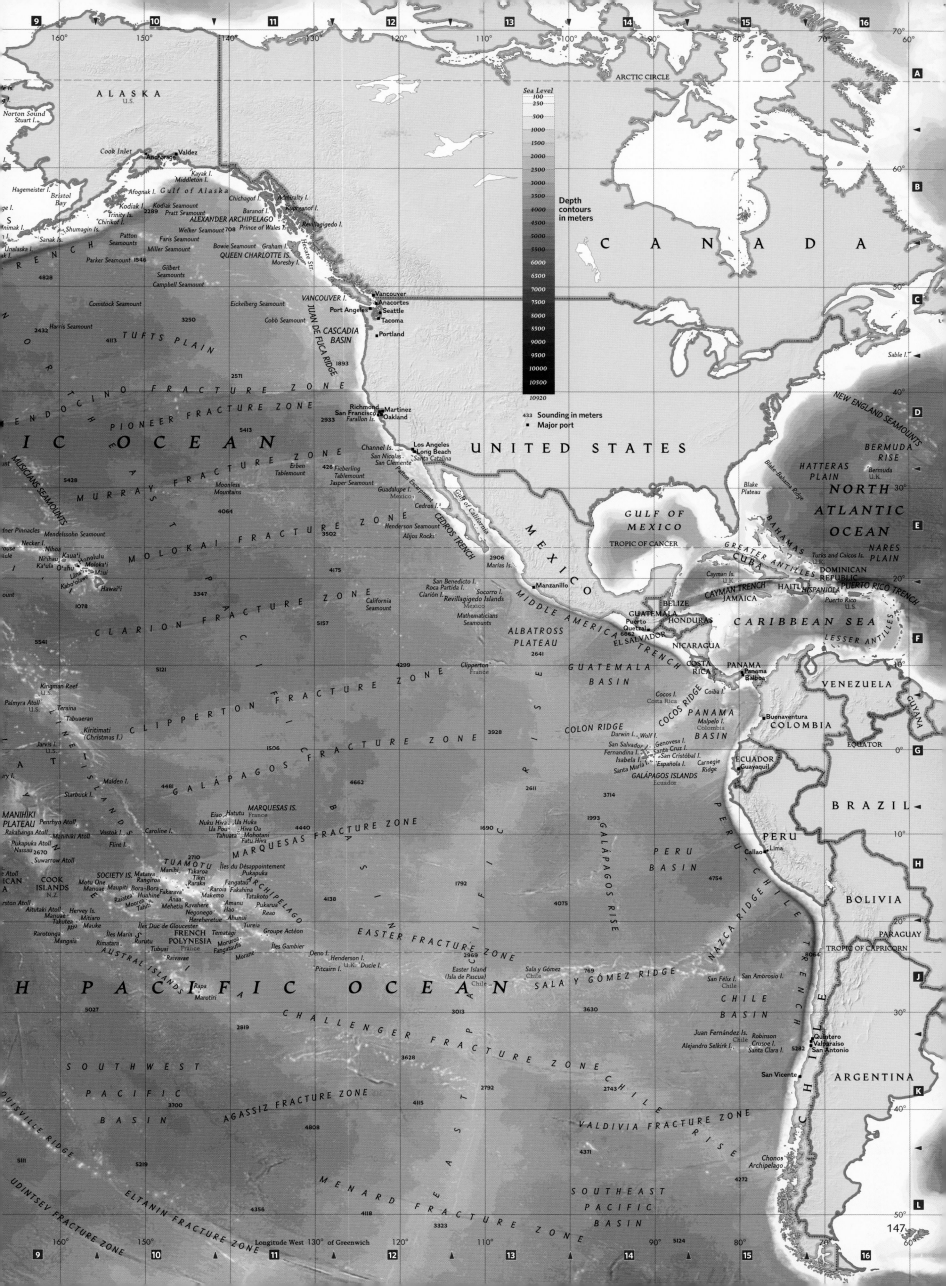

Pacific Ocean Sea-surface Temperature

ASIA

Degrees Celsius

-1 0 3 6 9 12 15 18 21 24 27 30

Ice

-30.2 32 37.4 42.8 48.2 53.6 59 64.4 69.8 75.2 80.6 86

Degrees Fahrenheit

ARCTIC CIRCLE

TROPIC OF CANCER

EQUATOR

AUSTRALIA

TROPIC OF CAPRICORN

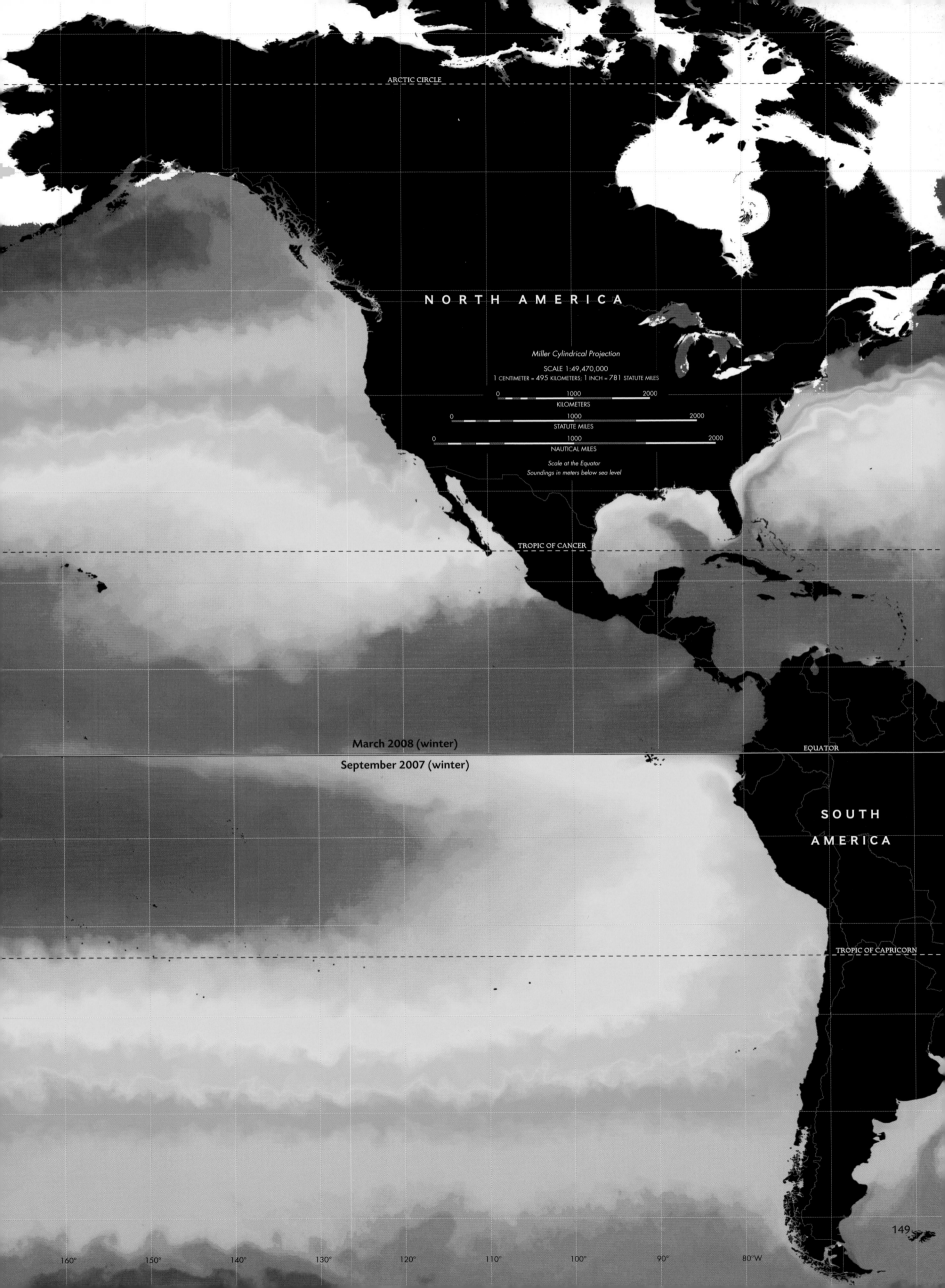

NORTH AMERICA

Miller Cylindrical Projection

SCALE 1:49,470,000
1 CENTIMETER = 495 KILOMETERS; 1 INCH = 781 STATUTE MILES

0   1000   2000
KILOMETERS

0   1000   2000
STATUTE MILES

0   1000   2000
NAUTICAL MILES

Scale at the Equator
Soundings in meters below sea level

ARCTIC CIRCLE

TROPIC OF CANCER

March 2008 (winter)

September 2007 (winter)

EQUATOR

SOUTH

AMERICA

TROPIC OF CAPRICORN

160°   150°   140°   130°   120°   110°   100°   90°   80°W

Stripe-tail aholehole, Kuhlia taeniura,
glide in unison on the underside of
turbulent waves at Roca Partida,
Revillagigedos Islands, Mexico.

The Pacific Ocean by the Numbers

(excludes East Asian and Bering Seas)

Total area: 152,617,159 square kilometers

Total volume: 645,369,567 cubic kilometers

Greatest depth: 10,920 meters (Challenger Deep, in the Mariana Trench, North Pacific)

NORTH PACIFIC

Geographic boundaries: Equator to 64° N / 130° E to 30° W

Area: 68,907,910 square kilometers

Volume: 315,690,574 cubic kilometers

Average depth: 4,573 meters

SOUTH PACIFIC

Geographic boundaries: Equator to 60° S / 145° E to 70° W

Area: 83,709,249 square kilometers

Volume: 329,678,993 cubic kilometers

Average depth: 3,935 meters

• Includes 46 percent of the Earth's water area, the largest water expanse.
• Half of the Pacific seafloor has been subducted.
• Still spreading off South America but shrinking overall.

"A chaos of waves . . . rushed upon us and hurled us round and sideways. . . . High waves and low waves, pointed waves and round waves, slanting waves and waves on top of other waves . . . the weeks passed . . . the whole sea was ours, and with all the gates of the horizon open, real peace and freedom were wafted down from the firmament itself."

—Thor Heyerdahl, *Kon-Tiki: Across the Pacific by Raft*

Viewed from afar, astronauts see the Pacific Ocean as Earth's glistening blue face, a broad expanse of water that more than any other feature might justify calling this planet "Ocean." It takes superlatives to describe the Pacific: the largest, deepest, oldest, most seismically active, most biologically diverse, the widest, wildest mass of liquid water on Earth, in the solar system, or as far as we know, in the universe. Large enough to swallow all of the continents, or two Atlantic Oceans, the Pacific is blessed with more undersea mountains, more islands, more coral reefs and more deep trenches than any other body of water. It is the great blue heart of the planet, the place where much of the heavy lifting occurs with respect to biological processes that churn out oxygen, take in carbon dioxide, produce food for the enormous diversity of life in the ocean, and otherwise shape the chemistry of Earth as a whole. Separating North and South America from Asia and Australia, the Pacific's average depth is about 4 kilometers, and its deepest place is Challenger Deep in the Mariana Trench, more than 10 kilometers below the sea surface.

During his around-the-world voyage in 1520, it took the Portuguese navigator Ferdinand Magellan more than a month to sail westward from the Atlantic to the Pacific through the notoriously stormy passage at the tip of South America since named the Strait of Magellan in his honor. When he emerged into relatively calm seas on the western side of the passage, he described a "beautiful, quiet ocean"—and named this newly seen body of water "Pacific," meaning peaceful.

Although in some places it can be as flat and reflective as a mirror, the Pacific has every conceivable variation on the theme of ocean storms, from short, punchy squalls to monstrous typhoons in every way the equivalent of hurricanes. Even during times of placid weather, the wide Pacific delivers consistently high waves beloved by surfers along beaches in California, Hawaii, Australia, Peru, and beyond. The power of winds and currents across the extraordinarily long, broad reach of the Pacific give rise to enormous, destructive "rogue" waves, sometimes attaining more than 50 meters in height, legendary for their size and power, and greatly feared by mariners. Owing to the high level of seismic activity in the Pacific undersea terrain, especially in the regions where ocean crust dives under continental masses, sizable earthquakes are common, as are the tsunami waves they sometimes generate.

Far from being peaceful, the Pacific Ocean, from the undulating waters above to the mountain-studded depths below and rivers of current between, is an extraordinarily lively, ever-changing, often wildly tempestuous arena.

Liquid rock lights the night and spills into the sea as Law'apuliu erupts in January 2000 in Hawaii's Volcanoes National Park.

Formation of the Pacific

THE PRESENT PACIFIC IS THE OLDEST AND WIDEST OCEAN BASIN, the enduring heart of the once all-encompassing ocean Panthalassa. Pacific Ocean crust dates from brand new, just forming, to

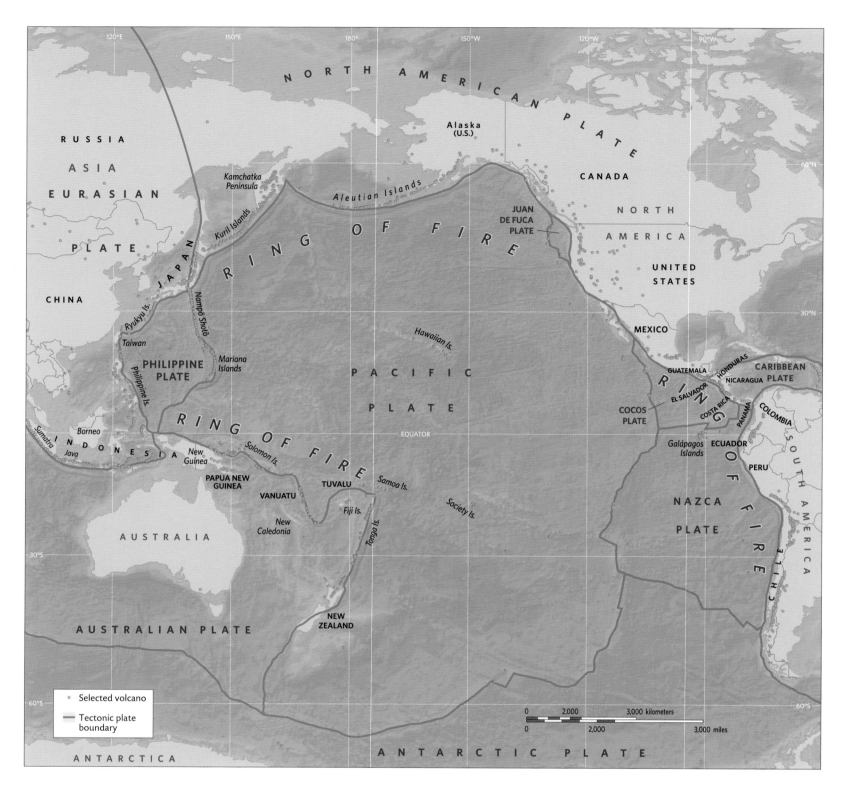

Edges of the gigantic Pacific Plate form the notorious "Ring of Fire," home to 70 percent of the world's earthquakes and most of its volcanic eruptions.

nearly 200 million years old. Compared with the relatively quiet spreading ridges in the Atlantic Rift system, the volcanic action is robust along the remaining spreading centers of the Pacific's seafloor plates, spilling out enough magma along the East Pacific Rise to cause an overall increase of almost 20 centimeters a year. The Earth remains the same size, as do the continental landmasses that drift around. What gives in this dynamic system is the ocean floor. Although the Pacific seafloor is still spreading, the size of the Pacific has grown steadily smaller over the past 100 million years as other ocean basins have formed and forced their way across the face of the planet. More seafloor is destroyed in subduction zones under deep-ocean trenches along the Pacific Rim than is created at its spreading ridges, causing the overall size of the Pacific to gradually shrink.

Geologist Harry Hess points out that the Atlantic, Indian, and Arctic Oceans are surrounded by the trailing edges of continents moving away from their spreading ridges, whereas the Pacific plate is all ocean crust, colliding with and being forced under advancing continents from all directions.

Nowhere on Earth is there more evidence of the powerful processes that continually reshape the planet than in and around the Pacific Ocean's broad blue belly. Where continents and oceanic plates collide, there is a necklace of active volcanoes behind deep-sea trenches aptly called the Ring of Fire. There, the thin seafloor crust is swallowed under adjacent landmasses. East of Japan, the great Pacific plate crunches into, and is forced beneath, the Asian continent along the Japan Trench, sending more than a thousand perceptible tremors a year across the nearby islands, including an occasional catastrophic quake. Enormous forces are at play around the margins of the Pacific, caused mostly by the continuous grinding of oceanic plates against each other. This produces more than a million small, medium, and sometimes very large earthquakes and volcanic eruptions every year, as the forces of seafloor spreading and plate tectonics rearrange the pattern of land and sea worldwide.

Mid-Ocean Ridge

RUNNING NORTH-SOUTH ROUGHLY PARALLEL to the western coast of South America is the Pacific's primary spreading ridge, the East Pacific Rise, whose spreading rate of 20 centimeters a year is one of the fastest in the world. It runs north right into the Gulf of California. Baja California split from the mainland about 5 million years ago, creating the Gulf of California. Today, it is a deep, narrow gash of water more than 1,000 kilometers long and up to 160 kilometers wide. The spreading ridge here, as elsewhere, is creating new seafloor and spreading apart—causing the gulf to widen by about 3 centimeters a year. As it continues to widen, some believe that a large piece of coast will gradually slip westward, creating a long, slim island that will take with it California's seaboard cities from San Diego to San Francisco. The Pacific spreading ridge then disappears beneath the North American continent, where its underlying forces still create havoc along the San Andreas Fault, where the gigantic Pacific and North American plates grind past each other.

Only Half an Ocean

The Pacific is the deepest ocean mainly because it has no mid-ocean ridge. Today's Pacific seafloor is just the western half of the original Pacific Basin. Only small pieces of the eastern half remain off the west coasts of North and South America. The rest of the eastern Pacific crust and the Mid-Pacific Ridge have been subducted under the North American continent and melted. About 180 million years ago, when all the continents were joined in the supercontinent Pangaea, the mighty Pacific, then the Panthalassa Ocean, was twice as wide as today.

Subduction: *Pacific Ocean crust is being subducted on both sides of the basin. The deepest ocean trenches on Earth surround the western Pacific, where oceanic crust is thrust down into the mantle. To the east, subduction under South America creates trenches, volcanoes, and earthquakes. And most of the ancient mid-Pacific ridge has been entirely subducted under North America creating raised terrain and active volcanoes along the west coast of the United States.*

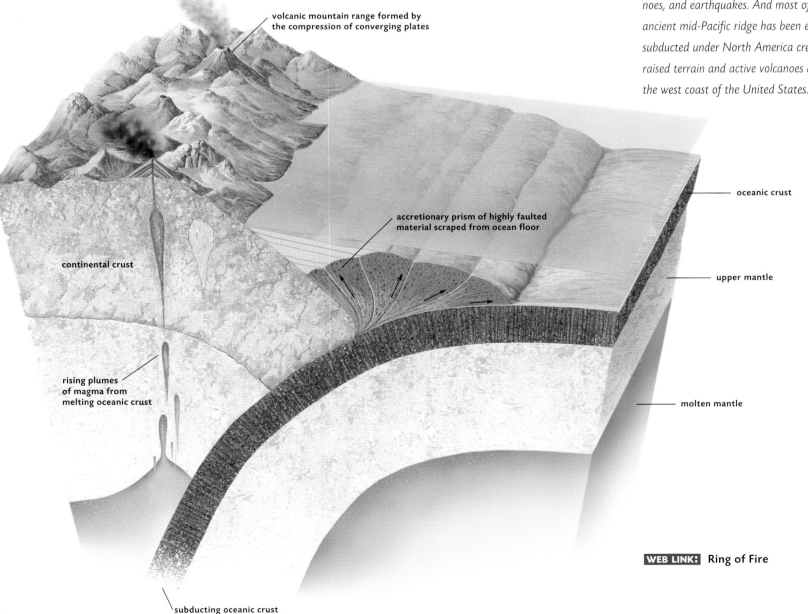

volcanic mountain range formed by the compression of converging plates

accretionary prism of highly faulted material scraped from ocean floor

continental crust

rising plumes of magma from melting oceanic crust

oceanic crust

upper mantle

molten mantle

subducting oceanic crust

WEB LINK: Ring of Fire

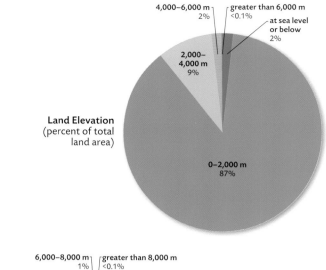

4,000–6,000 m
2%

greater than 6,000 m
<0.1%

at sea level
or below
2%

2,000–
4,000 m
9%

Land Elevation
(percent of total
land area)

0–2,000 m
87%

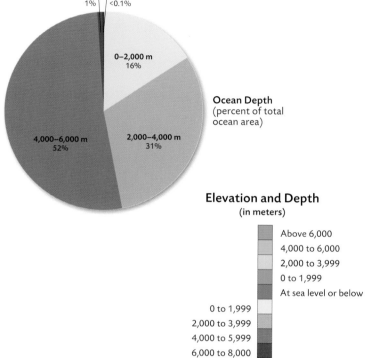

6,000–8,000 m
1%

greater than 8,000 m
<0.1%

0–2,000 m
16%

Ocean Depth
(percent of total
ocean area)

4,000–6,000 m
52%

2,000–4,000 m
31%

Elevation and Depth
(in meters)

Above 6,000
4,000 to 6,000
2,000 to 3,999
0 to 1,999
At sea level or below

0 to 1,999
2,000 to 3,999
4,000 to 5,999
6,000 to 8,000
Below 8,000

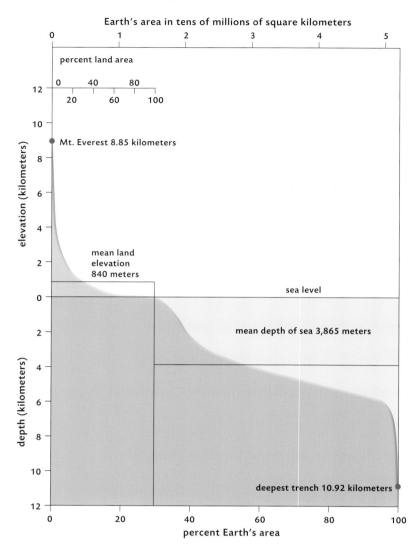

Earth's area in tens of millions of square kilometers

percent land area

Mt. Everest 8.85 kilometers

mean land
elevation
840 meters

sea level

mean depth of sea 3,865 meters

deepest trench 10.92 kilometers

percent Earth's area

Land vs. Ocean: *A comparison of land and sea are shown here, including the greatest height above sea level (Mount Everest) and the greatest depth below (Mariana Trench) as well as the average elevation above sea level (840 meters) and mean depth below (3,795 meters). The curve in the diagram portrays the overall distribution of heights and depths. Most of the Earth's total area—about 96 percent—is at elevations below 2,000 meters. The majority of the oceanic area lies between 4,000 and 5,000 meters.*

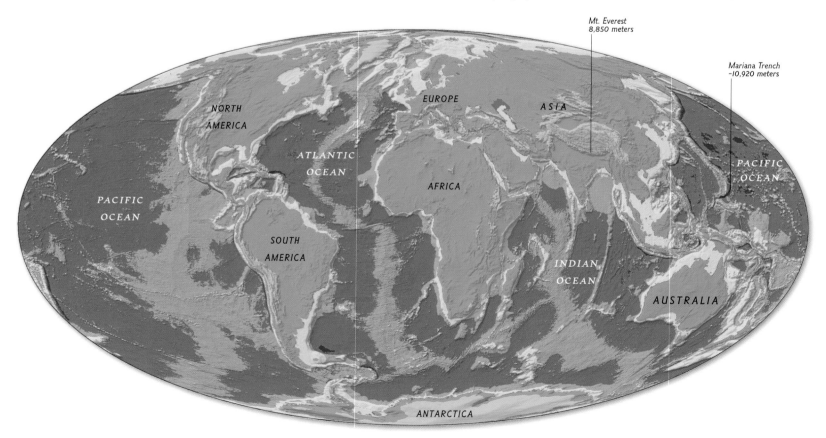

Mt. Everest
8,850 meters

Mariana Trench
-10,920 meters

The Pacific is unique in that almost the entire ocean basin is made up of a huge, deep central depression, the Central Pacific Trough. Unlike other oceans that have broad, raised areas down their middles caused by their mid-ocean ridges, with troughs down either side, the Pacific has only half this typical basin shape. Its eastern half has been almost completely destroyed under North America and is still disappearing under South America; only the old, deep western half of the original Pacific Ocean Basin remains.

Left: In the Galápagos Rift, far below the reach of sunlight, a sea cucumber appears tinged with fuchsia when illuminated by the lights of a submersible. Below: East of the Mariana Islands is the deepest gash on the planet's surface, the Mariana Trench, shown here in dark blue, formed where the Pacific Plate collides and dives under the Philippine Plate. The Challenger Deep, near the southern end, was confirmed by the Japanese ROV Kaiko in 1995 to be 10,911 meters deep—2,000 meters deeper than Mount Everest is high.

The Seafloor

RELATIVELY FLAT ABYSSAL PLAINS occupy large expanses of the deep Pacific Ocean floor, covered by sediments accumulated from the water column above. Over vast areas, fist-size lumps of rock, manganese nodules—actually "poly-metallic" sulfides that contain many metals in addition to manganese—carpet the seafloor in immense numbers, sometimes appearing as dense as cobblestones on a street. First discovered in the Kara Sea off Siberia in 1868, these curious formations were subsequently encountered in deepwater samples taken from the Atlantic, Indian, and Pacific Oceans during the H.M.S. *Challenger* expedition in the 1870s.

The mineral composition of the nodules varies, but most contain varied amounts of iron, manganese, nickel, copper, cobalt, silicon, and aluminum, as well as small amounts of hydrogen, oxygen, titanium, sodium, and other elements, sometimes including silver and platinum. Formed around a central object—a shark's tooth or a very small shell—concentric layers of minerals are slowly deposited, precipitated from the surrounding seawater, a process that appears to involve the action of microbes and may take millions of years for growth of a potato-size lump. In recent years, they have attracted considerable interest as a possible source of valuable metals, but the economic and environmental issues involved with mining at sea are still proving to be major constraints.

The Mariana Trench, about 640 kilometers east of the Philippines, is the deepest known chasm in the ocean. In 1960, Swiss engineer Jacques Piccard and Lt. Don Walsh of the U.S. Navy descended in the bathyscaphe *Trieste* 11 kilometers to the bottom of the trench and for half an hour observed the nature of life where pressure is a crushing 1,125 kilograms per square centimeter. Life also observed them when a flounder-like fish (or, some biologists believe, a strange sea cucumber) reacted to their presence. Not until 1997, though, was this most magnificent of

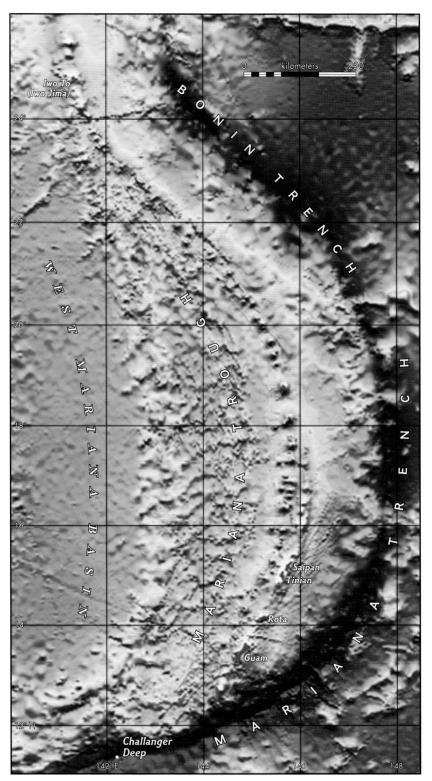

Depth in meters

900
0
-1,000
-2,000
-3,000
-4,000
-5,000
-6,000
-7,000
-11,000

Hydrothermal Vents: *Along seafloor spreading ridges, seawater seeps down through cracks in the seafloor and spews back up from the mantle in very hot underwater geysers laden with chemicals and minerals that sustain unusual assemblages of animals. Black smokers are the hottest (over 400°C) bringing dark iron and sulfides from deep in the mantle. White smokers are cooler (100-300°C) bringing barium, calcium, and silicon from shallower sources in the mantle.*

depths reached again. Then, a Japanese robot, *Kaiko,* trailing a tether linked to a surface ship, made the first of several dives to explore the geologic character of the ultimate subduction zone and further document the kinds of creatures that live in the deepest of the deep places in the ocean.

Hydrothermal Vents

THOUGH THE EXISTENCE OF HYDROTHERMAL VENTS had been predicted for years, they had not actually been seen in the deep sea until 1977, as John Corliss and Robert Ballard, with three ships, a submersible, and several dozen other researchers, explored a promising part of the Galápagos Rift 320 kilometers off shore from the Galápagos Islands. In *National Geographic*, they wrote: "Shimmering water streams up past giant tube worms, never before seen by man. A crab scuttles over lava encrusted with limpets, while a pink fish basks in the warmth." The researchers said the

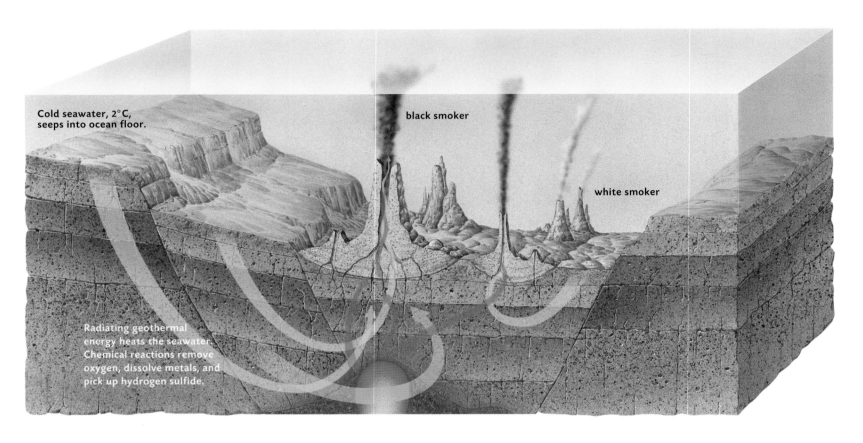

Cold seawater, 2°C, seeps into ocean floor.

black smoker

white smoker

Radiating geothermal energy heats the seawater. Chemical reactions remove oxygen, dissolve metals, and pick up hydrogen sulfide.

creatures and other life found at these vents, "like lush oases in a sunless desert, are a phenomenon totally new to science."

Crouched inside the research submersible *Alvin* 2.4 kilometers under the sea, they gazed with unabashed wonder at glassy mounds of pillow lava and plumes of hot water laden with hydrogen sulfide. These geophysicists savored the experience of being literally immersed in their research. But there was an unexpected bonanza for biologists—a virtual metropolis of strange-looking creatures unknown to humans. Fish could be identified as fish, and crabs, although odd-looking, were clearly crabs. But what were those stringy white things laced over the rocks that pulled back when touched? Was there a name for the gelatinous blobs oozing in all directions? And what were those 2-meter-tall stalked things crowned with brilliant red plumes?

WEB LINK: hydrothermal vents

Right: Hot, white smokers (greater than 100°C) jet mineral-laden water from the champagne vent chimneys in the western Pacific Ocean.

Peter Rona
LIFE AT DEEP-SEA HOT SPRINGS

Traveling in a human-occupied submersible to observe the otherworldly vent ecosystems that exist at deep-ocean hot springs, one is cramped in a metal sphere as wide as the occupant's outstretched arms, accompanied by a pilot, copilot, and racks of electronic instrumentation. Depending on the locality, a descent of 1.5 to 4 kilometers will take one to two and a half hours, and the sphere will become icy cold quickly in the near-freezing temperature of the deep ocean. Yet all thought of discomfort is forgotten once the seafloor appears in the submersible's floodlights.

Near the mouth of the Gulf of California, off Mexico on the East Pacific Rise, lies a submerged volcanic mountain range that extends some 55,000 kilometers and along whose axis hydrothermal vents generally lie. Cold, heavy seawater penetrates kilometers downward through cracks in the volcanic rocks that underlie the seafloor; is heated up by the upwelling molten rocks; expands; becomes lighter and buoyantly rises; dissolves metals and other elements from the surrounding rocks; and discharges up from the seafloor. Black smokers, which were first discovered here in 1979, were so named because the solutions they vent crystallize in chimney-like structures that spew dark clouds of metallic mineral particles, thus resembling factory smokestacks belching black smoke. They occur at widely spaced sites, each typically up to the size of a football field. The surrounding deep seafloor is like a desert covered with freshly frozen lava flows, their glassy surfaces glaring like ice in the submersible's floodlights.

Here one finds an oasis of life—clusters of tube worms with red plumes containing blood similar to ours protruding from white stalks the height of a person; crabs clinging to the stalks and grazing on the plumes, which retract in response. Rows of giant white clams, each up to 0.3 meter long, filter microbes from warm water pouring from cracks in the dark lava seafloor. Clusters of yellow-shelled mussels hang from the rocks like large grapes on a vine. Mats of microbes resemble splashes of whitish paint on the dark rocks. The chimney is coated with the excrement of worms, each several centimeters long, with their heads darting in and out of tubes that tap hot water through the chimney wall.

When black smokers and their ecosystems were discovered at this Pacific site, the scientific community thought that such hot springs could only occur in the Pacific because it is the most volcanically active of all ocean basins ("Ring of Fire") and volcanoes heat hot springs. My role was to lead the discovery of hot springs and their life in the Atlantic. After years of exploration we found in a valley at the center of the Mid-Atlantic Ridge, midway between the coasts of North America and northwestern Africa, a mound the size of the Houston Astrodome built of metallic minerals deposited by hot springs and spouting black smokers swarming with a new variety of shrimp unlike any at the hot springs in the eastern Pacific.

While exploring the Mid-Atlantic Ridge in 1975, before finding the vents at this site, my deep-sea camera tows imaged thousands of striking six-sided forms, each slightly larger than a poker chip. The hexagonal forms occurred on thin sediments that cover an area of one wall of the central valley. The leading marine biologists were initially unable to identify the form from the photographs, but it was soon discovered that the seafloor forms appeared identical to a fossil, named *Paleodictyon nodosum*, found in ancient sediments that had been uplifted from the seafloor more than 50 million years ago.

To the east, at the portion of the mid-ocean ridge that extends into the Indian Ocean, shrimp that appear identical to the Atlantic vent shrimp are discernible swarming over the active black-smoker chimneys. In a basin to the west of the Mariana Islands can be found snails the size of golf balls, grazing on microbes that cover active chimneys; a luminous white whelk with a shell like porcelain; and even shrimp like those at the vents in the Atlantic and Indian Oceans. The shrimp may have been able through time to migrate along the mid-ocean ridge between the Atlantic, Indian, and western Pacific.

The discovery of vent ecosystems based on microbes that use chemical energy from the Earth's interior is like finding life on another planet and may indeed guide us to life in our solar system and beyond. Future dives will take us to vents in the Arctic and Antarctic Oceans, where exploration is only beginning and the mysteries of life at hydrothermal vents continue to unfold.

Vent shrimp, Rimicaris exoculata

Brachyuran crab

Deepsea lizardfish, Bathysaurus

Sea-Vent Life Facts

• An ecosystem of animals new to science exists at deep-sea hot springs.
• The animals of this ecosystem differ at hot springs in different oceans.
• Microbes are at the base of the food chain at all the hot springs in the deepsea. • Microbes at hot springs use chemicals dissolved in the hot seawater as a source of energy to manufacture their food.

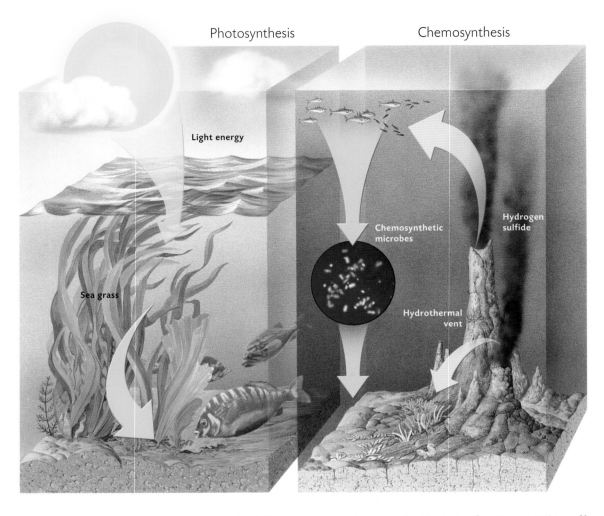

Photosynthesis

Chemosynthesis

Light energy

Sea grass

Chemosynthetic microbes

Hydrogen sulfide

Hydrothermal vent

Chemosynthesis vs. Photosynthesis: *Sunlight, water, and carbon dioxide in the presence of chlorophyll and other pigments drive photosynthesis (left), yielding oxygen and simple sugar, which is converted into more complex carbohydrates, fats, and proteins. More than 95 percent of photosynthesis in the sea is accomplished by microbes, but some is from sea grasses and algae such as those illustrated here. In the absence of light, certain microbes can produce food through chemosynthesis (right) by converting hydrogen sulfide, carbon dioxide, and water into glucose, sulfur, and sulfur compounds. Other microbes utilize methane, carbon dioxide, and water to produce food.*

SEE ALSO: photosynthesis, page 57

WEB LINK: Woods Hole Oceanographic Institution

Biologists clamored to participate in follow-up expeditions to the East Pacific Rise at 21° N off the mouth of the Gulf of California in 1978; to the Galápagos Rift in 1979; and, later, to the Juan de Fuca Ridge off the coast of Oregon and Washington. Fred Grassle was one of those who couldn't resist the chance to be among the first to explore the nature of the very lively deep-sea vent communities. A marine biologist who for years had studied life in the soft, muddy seafloor areas of the Atlantic, Grassle had made discoveries about the abundance and diversity of life in depths below 3,000 meters that had astonished and confounded his colleagues.

The giant clams, foot-long mussels, and fields of tube worms as tall and densely packed as an Iowa cornfield dazzled early observers with their enormous size. The very existence of these large, exotic-looking animals posed some basic problems. At such depths, there is no sunlight, and thus no plants to generate food; so what sustains these lush communities? Textbooks written before 1977 suggest that life in the deep sea is totally dependent on the nutritious "rain" of organisms from the ocean's sunlit surface waters, and that it is logical to expect a scarcity of creatures deep down because not much of the sustenance can make it all the way to the bottom. Creatures around the vents obviously had not read the books. But the question remained: How did they make a living?

Answers began emerging when attention shifted from the larger creatures to the microscopic ones, especially the thick clouds of sulfur-loving bacteria. The giant clams, mussels, and other filter feeders were straining bacteria from the seawater. And they, in turn, were eaten by crabs and other small predators that then became prey for larger ones. Holger Jannasch, a microbiologist at the Woods Hole Oceanographic Institution, pioneered studies on these hydrothermal microbes, examining the pathways whereby some of them, taking advantage of sulfur compounds ejected from the vents and oxygen from the surrounding seawater, convert carbon dioxide into organic matter. This process, chemosynthesis, is an ancient way of supporting life on Earth, but it was unknown until the late 1970s. In a 1977 article for the *Annual Review of Microbiology,* he wrote:

> It was an overwhelming experience to "fly," 2,550 meters deep, over dense beds of large mussels or . . . stands of hundreds of snow-white tube worms (up to two meters long) crowned with

feather-like blood-red plumes. . . . Here solar energy, which is so prevalent in running life on our planet, appears to be largely replaced by terrestrial energy—chemolithoautotrophic bacteria taking over the role of green plants. This was a powerful new concept and, in my mind, one of the major biological discoveries of the 20th century.

And the giant tube worms? Careful inspection revealed that they have no mouth, no stomach, no digestive system at all. How do creatures so large and so numerous gain the energy required to live, grow, and reproduce without these fundamentals? The mystery was solved by Colleen Cavanaugh, a scientist at Woods Hole who proposed, then proved, that the worms harness energy from chemosynthetic bacteria living inside their tissues. The worms are fed, the bacteria are housed, and all benefit, a symbiotic relationship comparable in some ways to the partnership between reef corals and the photosynthetic algae growing within their tissues.

Another group of microbes found thriving around hydrothermal vents initially were thought to be bacteria, but years of careful analysis proved that the basic genetic makeup of these minute organisms is so different from all other forms of life that a new biologic kingdom was proposed, the Archaea. It is astonishing that about half of the genome of the Archaea is different from all other plants, animals, and bacteria on Earth. Given the extreme environment in which they live, it is equally amazing that these strange microbes have as much in common with other forms of life as they do.

Genome scientist Craig Venter intensively studied one kind, *Methanococcus jannaschii*, and found himself beguiled by the tiny organism's weirdness. It lives at temperatures from 48°C to 94°C and at pressures 200 times as high as those found at sea level; oxygen kills it; it generates sustenance from carbon dioxide, nitrogen, and hydrogen, and it produces methane. In a 1996 *Science* article, Venter remarked, "It's like something out of science fiction. Not so long ago, no one would have believed you if you'd told them such organisms existed on Earth." Those seeking life beyond Earth's atmosphere are heartened by the discovery of *M. jannaschii* and other microbes that thrive under circumstances that may have prevailed on Earth in its formative years—and that may exist now on Mars; Jupiter's moon, Europa; or on planets in other solar systems where water can be found and volcanism occurs.

Where Hydrothermal Vents Are Found

First discovered in the Pacific in 1977—to the amazement of the scientific world—hydrothermal vents and their strange communities, dependent on chemicals gushing up from the seafloor, turn out to be a fairly widespread phenomenon, since found in all ocean basins. They occur mostly along active seafloor spreading ridges, around fracture zones along those ridges, along subduction zones where ocean crust is being pushed down under a continent, and sometimes on isolated seamounts—in other words, in most places in the ocean that experience volcanism. Based on the discoveries of hydrothermal vents so far, and on the fact that only about 10 percent of the 64,000-kilometer mid-ocean ridge has been studied so far, at least 500 sites worldwide are estimated to exist.

Standing more than 2 meters high, giant tube worms, Riftia pachyptila, *lack mouth and stomach but are well-fed with nutrition derived from symbiotic sulfide-oxidizing bacteria harbored within the tissues of their feathery red plumes. This image was captured during an* Alvin *dive in 2002 on the East Pacific Rise.*

Seamounts and Islands

WEB LINK: seamount biology

WEB LINK: virtual fly-throughs of the Mariana Arc

Structure of a Seamount:

An undersea perspective prepared by NOAA's Vents Program of a submarine volcano, East Diamante, Mariana Islands, rising from 2,744 meters depth to within 127 meters of the sea surface, viewed toward the south-southwest. The shallowest black smoker hydrothermal activity known is located here on the central dome of the volcano at depths of only a few hundred meters.

Lines of Islands— Running Parallel

Look closely at a bathymetric map of the Pacific, and you'll notice something odd about its many chains of islands and seamounts. Many of them, moving north-to-south—Hawaiian Islands, Mid-Pacific Mountains, Caroline Islands, Solomon Islands, French Polynesian (Society) Islands, Samoa Islands, Tuamoto Archipelago, most of the Cook Islands, the Austral Islands, even the Galápagos—have something in common. They are arranged in parallel lines, trending west-northwest/east-southeast over hundreds of kilometers. The whole, huge, old Pacific Ocean Basin has moved for 150 million years over several hot spots deep in the mantle. These hot spots create one seamount or island at a time as the crust is pushed over them by seafloor spreading. Other island chains—Kurils, Bonins, Tongas, Kermadecs, Fijis, and Marianas—are volcanic islands trending roughly north-south over western Pacific subduction zones.

ACROSS THE PACIFIC, hundreds of undersea volcanoes tap into Earth's molten core, some rising thousands of meters to break the surface as the Galápagos, the Hawaiian Islands, the Aleutians, and many island chains in the South Pacific. More than 25,000 islands and many more islets break the surface of the Pacific Ocean; at least 30,000 seamounts, essentially undersea islands, are fully submerged. Most of these, whether underwater or extending above, are in the Pacific's great middle section, between 30° N and 30° S latitudes. The islands here are called Oceania. Australia is typically regarded as part of Oceania, along with three major island groups: Melanesia, Micronesia, and Polynesia.

Melanesia, the most populated island region, includes New Guinea (Papua New Guinea and the Indonesian provinces of Papua and West Irian Jaya), New Caledonia, Vanuatu, Fiji, and the Solomon Islands. Micronesia includes not only the Federated States of Micronesia but also the Marianas, Guam, Wake Island, Palau, the Marshall Islands, Kiribati, and Nauru. New Zealand is considered part

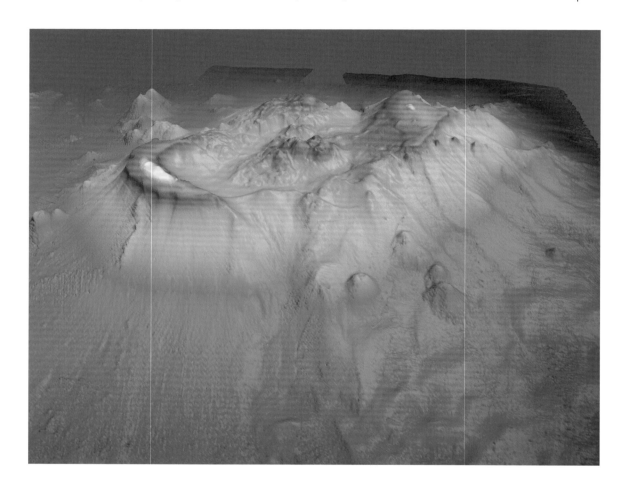

of Polynesia, along with the Hawaiian Islands, Rotuma, the Midway Islands, Samoa, American Samoa, Tonga, Tuvalu, the Cook Islands, French Polynesia, and Easter Island.

Culturally more connected to nearby continents are thousands of other islands not regarded as part of Oceania: most of the islands of Indonesia; Japan, including the Ryuku Islands; Taiwan; the Philippines; the islands of the South China Sea; the Galápagos; and the Aleutian Islands, as well as those within the intricately dissected coastal waters of Alaska, western Canada, and southern Chile.

Three oceanic plates converge in the region where the western Pacific meets the Indian Ocean, with dynamic processes giving rise to more than 13,000 islands that make up Indonesia; more than 7,000 Philippine islands; and many others in New Guinea, Malaysia, and nearby waters. Borneo, the third largest island in the world, and Taiwan arise from the shelf that borders continental Asia, along with arcs of islands including Java, Sumatra, Bali, and the Lesser Sunda Islands.

New Zealand, with its two major and numerous small islands, arises from a continental plate, and the island country of Australia, which lies half in the Pacific Ocean and half in the Indian Ocean, is a large continental piece of what was Gondwanaland, once joined to Antarctica. Curved island chains such as the Marianas Islands along the western margin of the Pacific are volcanic island arcs

SEE ALSO: **Northwest Hawaiian Islands National Monument, pages 166-167**

fringing a trench and subduction zone, where oceanic crust pushed beneath a continental block is melted by the heat and pressure at depth, and some of it spews back up to the surface through island-arc volcanoes. Long, straight chains of islands in the Pacific are created from single hot spots that continue to form volcanic islands as the spreading crust moves over them, in a process originally identified in 1967 by Jason Morgan of Princeton University. The Hawaiian and French Polynesian (Society) island groups, for example, line up in a similar southeast-to-northwest orientation as the Pacific plate moves in that direction over their respective hot spots.

Long before hot spots were recognized, James Dana, a geologist working with the United States Exploring Expedition to the Pacific Islands in 1840, concluded that in the Hawaiian Islands there was an increasing degree of erosion, and thus greater age, among the islands to the northwest—Molokai, Kauai, and the distant Midway Islands—than in the volcanically active islands of Hawaii and Maui to the southeast. Mauna Kea, the highest peak on the youngest island of Hawaii, if measured from its deeply submerged base on the seafloor to its fiery top, exceeds

Mount Everest in overall height. Recent observations have confirmed that the Hawaiian Islands to the northwest are progressively older, including a long line of now submerged seamounts that extend far beyond those seen above sea level. The hot spot that created the Hawaiian archipelago is at work today constructing an island-in-the-making called Loihi, a fast-growing volcanic mound that now rises from the deep to within an eighth of a kilometer below the sea surface near Oahu. Alex Malahoff, a geologist from the University of Hawaii, and Terry Kirby, pilot of several submersibles that transport Malahoff and other observers, are using Loihi as a rare natural laboratory. They have tracked the rise of this growing volcanic subsea mountain and its associated geological processes for more than two decades.

The remnants of what was once an active volcano form the underpinnings of this atoll and its semi-enclosed lagoon in Palau.

Islands of Oceania

Top coordinate markers: 1 2 3 4 5 6 7 8

120° 130° 140° 150° 160° 170°

TROPIC OF CANCER

TAIWAN
KAOHSIUNG

Luzon Strait
Batan Is.
Babuyan Is.

LUZON

⊛ MANILA

Mindoro

Iwo To
(Iwo Jima)
Minami Iwo To

Volcano Islands
(Kazan Rettō)
Japan

Parece Vela

Okino Daitō Jima
Japan

Farallon de Pajaros

Asuncion
Agrihan
Pagan
Alamagan
Sarigan
Anatahan

WEST
MARIANA
BASIN

4392

1453

Minami Tori Shima
(Marcus)
Japan

Wake Island
U.S.

MID-PACIFIC MOUNTAINS

N O R T

Taongi Atoll

Bikar Atoll

Bikini
Atoll

Rongelap Atoll

Utirik Atoll
Ailuk Atoll
Wotje Atoll

MARSHALL
ISLANDS

NORTHERN
MARIANA
ISLANDS

Tinian
Rota
Guam U.S.

Saipan

EAST
MARIANA
BASIN

Enewetak Atoll

Ujelang
Atoll

Kwajalein
Atoll

Maloelap Atoll

PHILIPPINE
SEA

PHILIPPINE
BASIN

Benham
Seamount

2621

PHILIPPINES

Samar
Leyte
Negros
Panay

Sulu
Sea

MINDANAO
DAVAO

Sulu
Archipelago

Sangihe
Islands

Celebes Sea

KYUSHU-PALAU RIDGE

MARIANA TRENCH

Magellan Seamounts

Challenger Deep
World's greatest ocean depth
10920 m (35827 ft)

5082

Ulithi Atoll

Yap Islands

Ngulu Atoll

PALAU

Melekeok
Babelthuap

Sonsorol Is.
Pulo Anna

Merir

Tobi
Helen I.

WEST
CAROLINE
BASIN

Fais

Gaferut
Faraulep
Atoll

Sorol Atoll

Woleai Atoll

Eauripik Atoll

Pikelot

Satawal

Namonuito Atoll

Hall Is.

Pulap
Atoll

Chuuk
(Truk Is.)

Puluwat Atoll

Pulusuk

Minto Reef

Oroluk Atoll

Losap Atoll

Mortlock Is.

Senyavin Is.

Pohnpei (Ponape)
⊛ Palikir

Ngatik Atoll

Kosrae
(Kusaie)

Pingelap Atoll

Ebon Atoll

Ailinglapalap Atoll

Namorik
Atoll

Jaluit Atoll

Majuro

Arno Atoll

Mili Atoll

Kili I.

M I C R O N E S I A

CAROLINE ISLANDS

FEDERATED STATES OF MICRONESIA

EAST
CAROLINE
BASIN

Nukuoro Atoll

2553

Kapingamarangi Atoll

4533

Butaritari

Abaiang
Maiana

Marakei

GILBERT

Tarawa (Bairiki)
Abemama

ISLANDS

Banaba
(Ocean I.)

Nonouti

Tabiteuea

Beru

Tamana

Aro

NAURU

RALIK CHAIN

RATAK CHAIN

YAP TRENCH

PHILIPPINE TRENCH

PALAU TRENCH

Ngulu Atoll

Talaud
Islands

Morotai

Halmahera

Asia Is.

Waigeo

Mapia Is.

3908

EQUATOR

SULAWESI
(Celebes)

Teluk Tomini

Peleng

Sula Is.

Buru

Selayar

Buton

Banda
Sea

Ceram
Ceram Sea

MOLUCCAS

MOLUCCA SEA

INDONESIA

Biak
Yapen

Teluk Cenderawasih

NEW GUINEA

Jayapura

Admiralty
Islands
Manus

Mussau Is.

New Hanover

BISMARCK
ARCHIPELAGO

New Ireland

1628

Bismarck Sea

Rabaul

New Britain

8940

Green Islands

Bougainville

Nukumanu Islands

1582

SOLOMON ISLANDS

Choiseul

Santa Isabel

New Georgia

Honiara

Malaita

M E L A N E S I A

Duff Islands

Santa Cruz Islands

Nupani

Nendo
(Ndeni)

Utupua

Anuta (Cherry I.)

Fataka (Mitre I.)

VITYAZ TRENCH

Nanume

Nanumanga

Nui

Nukufe
Fu

T U V A L U

Flores

Lomblen

Alor Wetar

Moa

Babar

Dili
TIMOR-LESTE
Timor

Savu Sea

Roti

Lesser Sunda Islands

Kai Islands

Aru
Islands

Tanimbar Islands

Dolak

Arafura Sea

Port Moresby

PAPUA NEW GUINEA

Huon G.

D'Entrecasteaux Is.

Trobriand Is.

Woodlark Is.

Solomon Sea

Louisiade Archipelago

912

Rennell

Guadalcanal

San Cristobal

Vanikoro Is.

Tikopia

Torres Islands

Banks Islands

Espiritu Santo

Malakula

Shepherd Is.

Maéwo
Pentecost
Ambrym

Rotuma
Fiji

NORTH
FIJI
BASIN

Vanua

Yasawa Group

FIJI ISLA

Su

Viti Levu

Kada

Timor Sea

Ashmore and
Cartier Islands
Australia

Melville I.

Joseph
Bonaparte
Gulf

Cape York

Torres Strait

Gulf of
Carpentaria

Willis
Islets

Tregrosse
Islets

CORAL SEA
BASIN

4477

2011

CORAL
SEA
ISLANDS
TERRITORY
Australia

Port-Vila Éfaté

Île Huon

Îles
Chesterfield

Erromango

Tanna
Anatom

Futuna

VANUATU

Ouvéa

Lifou

Loyalty Is.

Maré

1586

NEW
CALEDONIA
France

Nouméa

Île des Pins
(Kunié)

Matthew

Hunter

Ceva-
i-Ra

NEW HEBRIDES TRENCH

SOUTH
FIJI
BASIN

4572

Cairns

Great Barrier Reef

Great Dividing Range

TROPIC OF CAPRICORN

AUSTRALIA

Fraser Island

1464

BRISBANE

MIDDLETON
BASIN

Middleton
Reef

Lord Howe I.

Ball's Pyramid
Australia

2976

C O R A L   S E A

LORD HOWE RISE

NEW CALEDONIA RIDGE

NORFOLK RIDGE

NEW CALEDONIA BASIN

Norfolk Island
Australia

Phillip Island

Three Kings Islands

Cape Maria van Diemen

North Cape

GREAT
AUSTRALIAN
BIGHT

Spencer
Gulf

ADELAIDE

Kangaroo I.

SOUTH
AUSTRALIAN
BASIN

Great Dividing Range

Taupo
Tablemount

SYDNEY

Canberra

MELBOURNE

Wilsons Promontory

King I. Bass Strait

Furneaux Group

TASMANIA

Hobart

South East Cape

EAST
TASMAN
PLATEAU

4831

Gascoyne
Tablemount

1318

TASMAN PLAIN

T A S M A N

S E A

Auckland

NORTH ISLAND

Cook Strait

Cape Farewell

Wellington

SOUTH ISLAND

Great Barrier

Bay
Ple

CHAT

NEW ZEALAND

INDIAN OCEAN

TASMAN FRACTURE ZONE

660

SOUTH
TASMAN
RISE

Puysegur Point

Foveaux Strait

Stewart Island/Rakiura

The Snares

1952

Longitude East 170° of Greenwich

BOU

TRO

Bounty I

120° 130° 140° 150° 160° 170°

Bottom coordinate markers: 1 2 3 4 5 6 7 8

Left row markers: A B C D E F G H J K L

20° 10° 0° 10° 20° 30° 40°

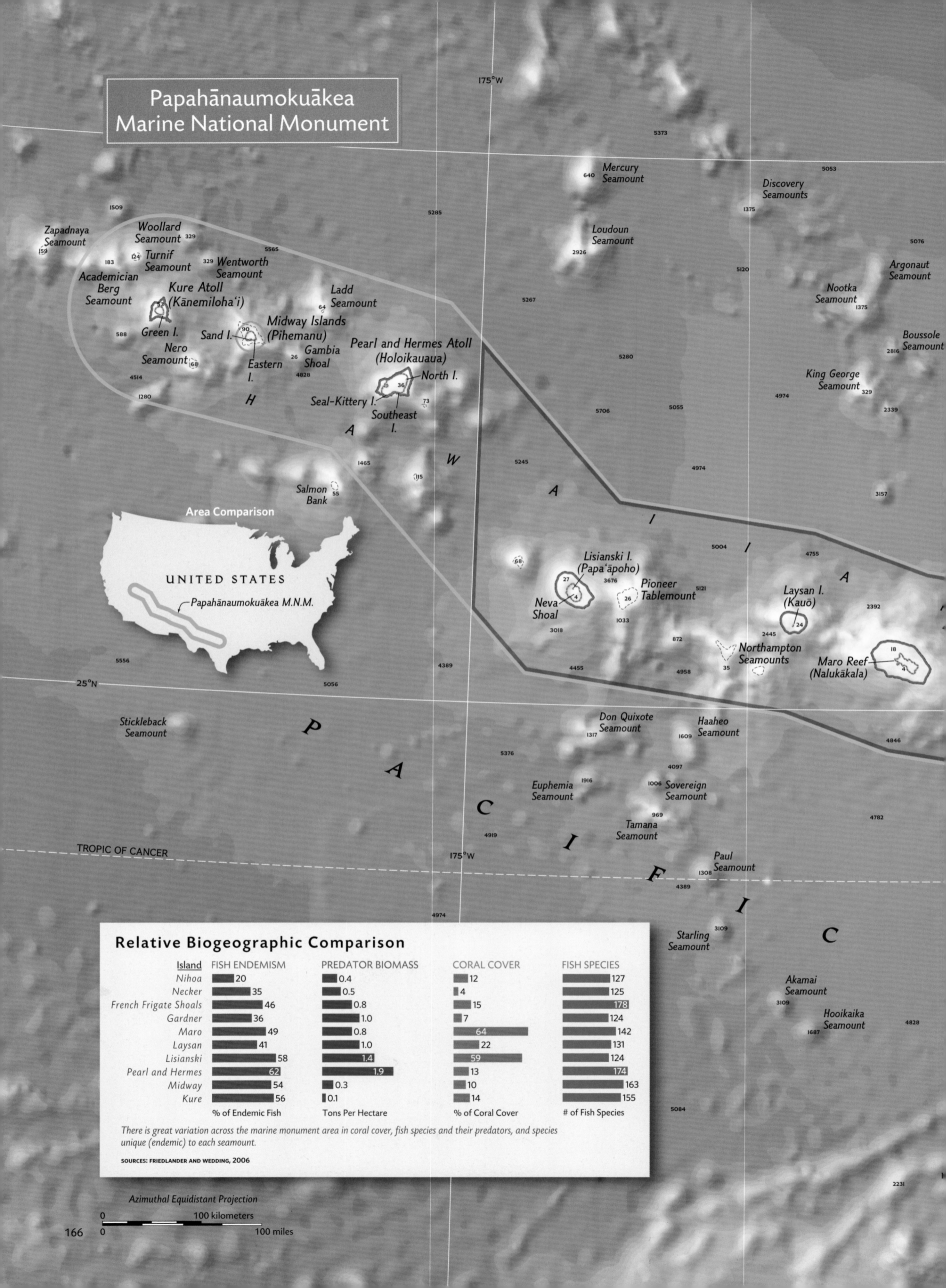

Papahānaumokuākea
Marine National Monument

175°W

Zapadnaya Seamount
159

Woollard Seamount 329
1509
Turnif Seamount
183 24
Academician Berg Seamount
329 Wentworth Seamount
5565
Kure Atoll (Kānemilohaʻi)
Green I.
588
Nero Seamount 68
4514
1280

Ladd Seamount 64
Midway Islands (Pihemanu)
Sand I. 90
Eastern I.
Gambia Shoal
26
4828

H

Pearl and Hermes Atoll (Holoikauaua)
North I.
36
Seal-Kittery I.
Southeast I.
73

A

W

1465
115

Salmon Bank 55

Area Comparison

UNITED STATES
Papahānaumokuākea M.N.M.

5556

25°N

5056

Stickleback Seamount

P

A

C

TROPIC OF CANCER 175°W

I

F

I

C

Mercury Seamount 640

Discovery Seamounts
5053

Loudoun Seamount
2926

5285

5373

5120

5267

5280

5076

Argonaut Seamount

Nootka Seamount
1375

5076

Boussole Seamount
2816

King George Seamount 329
4974

2339

5706

5055

5245

4974

3157

A

I

I

68

Lisianski I. (Papaʻāpoho)
27
3676
4
Neva Shoal
3018

Pioneer Tablemount
26
1033

5121

5004

4755

A

Laysan I. (Kauō)
24

2392

872

2445

Northampton Seamounts
35

Maro Reef (Nalukākala)
18
4

4455

4958

4389

Don Quixote Seamount
1317

Haaheo Seamount
1609

4846

5376

4097

Euphemia Seamount
1916

Sovereign Seamount
1006

969

4919

Tamana Seamount

4782

Paul Seamount
1308

4389

4974

Starling Seamount
3109

Akamai Seamount
3109

Hooikaika Seamount
1687
4828

5084

2231

Relative Biogeographic Comparison

Island	FISH ENDEMISM	PREDATOR BIOMASS	CORAL COVER	FISH SPECIES
Nihoa	20	0.4	12	127
Necker	35	0.5	4	125
French Frigate Shoals	46	0.8	15	178
Gardner	36	1.0	7	124
Maro	49	0.8	64	142
Laysan	41	1.0	22	131
Lisianski	58	1.4	59	124
Pearl and Hermes	62	1.9	13	174
Midway	54	0.3	10	163
Kure	56	0.1	14	155
	% of Endemic Fish	Tons Per Hectare	% of Coral Cover	# of Fish Species

There is great variation across the marine monument area in coral cover, fish species and their predators, and species unique (endemic) to each seamount.

SOURCES: FRIEDLANDER AND WEDDING, 2006

Azimuthal Equidistant Projection

0 — 100 kilometers
0 — 100 miles

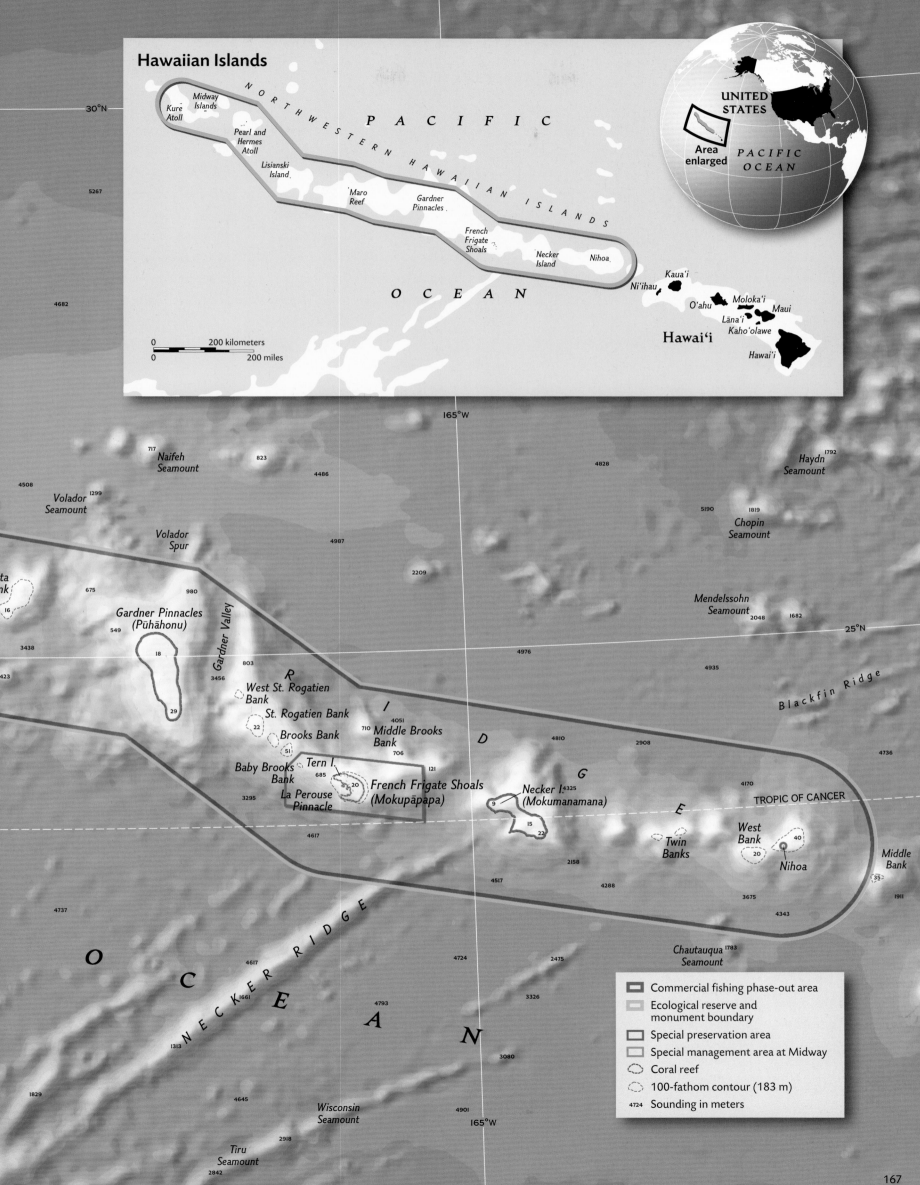

Hawaiian Islands

NORTHWESTERN HAWAIIAN ISLANDS

PACIFIC OCEAN

Kure Atoll
Midway Islands
Pearl and Hermes Atoll
Lisianski Island
Maro Reef
Gardner Pinnacles
French Frigate Shoals
Necker Island
Nihoa

Kaua'i
Ni'ihau
O'ahu
Moloka'i
Lāna'i
Kaho'olawe
Maui
Hawai'i

Hawai'i

30°N
5267
4682

0   200 kilometers
0   200 miles

UNITED STATES
Area enlarged
PACIFIC OCEAN

165°W

717
Naifeh Seamount
823
4486
4828
Haydn Seamount
1792

4508
Volador Seamount
1299
5190
1819
Chopin Seamount

Volador Spur
980
4987
2209

Gardner Valley
Mendelssohn Seamount
2048
1682

aita ank
16
675
Gardner Pinnacles (Pūhāhonu)
549
18
3438
3456
803
R
4976
25°N
4935
Blackfin Ridge
4736

1423
29
West St. Rogatien Bank
St. Rogatien Bank
22
Brooks Bank
51
Baby Brooks Bank
685
3295
La Perouse Pinnacle
Tern I.
20
I
710 Middle Brooks Bank
4051
706
121
French Frigate Shoals (Mokupāpapa)
D
4810
2908
G
Necker I. 4325 (Mokumanamana)
9
4170
TROPIC OF CANCER
E
West Bank
40
20
Nihoa
Middle Bank
35
1911

4617
15
22
2158
Twin Banks
3675
4343

O
4737
NECKER RIDGE
1661
4617
C
1313
4793
E
3080
A
3326
N
2475
Chautauqua Seamount
1783

1829
4645
Wisconsin Seamount
2918
4901
165°W

Tiru Seamount
2842

4517
4288

165°W

	Commercial fishing phase-out area
	Ecological reserve and monument boundary
	Special preservation area
	Special management area at Midway
	Coral reef
	100-fathom contour (183 m)
4724	Sounding in meters

Jean-Michel Cousteau
THE RECOVERY OF CORAL REEFS

When the Papahanaumokuakea Marine National Monument was designated in the northwestern Hawaiian Islands in 2006, it was the largest protected area in U.S. territory and the largest protected marine area in the world. This national monument covers 362,000 square kilometers and is 100 times as large as Yosemite National Park, larger than 46 of the 50 states, and more than 7 times as large as all existing national marine sanctuaries combined. These 11,655 square kilometers of coral reef habitat also make up the largest remote reef system in the world. At a time when coral reefs worldwide are under siege, it was a stunning and wise decision. It was based on the fact that we now know that protection—forbidding all human impact within certain areas—enables the natural system to recover.

There were two things I found particularly striking while diving the northwestern Hawaiian Islands. First, these remote islands are at the northern limit of coral reefs and could predictably be under stress and impoverished. In fact, they were diverse and healthy. Second, there was an abundance of large predators, particularly jacks and sharks. It may be that these two observations are connected.

Predators are important in maintaining a balance of species on a reef, and the effect of large predators can ripple through the entire ecosystem, directly affecting an incredible diversity of life. So these predators have contributed to the health and vitality of these reefs, and their absence on other reefs worldwide is a bad sign. The remoteness of the National Monument reefs also means that there are fewer stresses from human impact and less fishing to deplete these large predators. Compared with other reefs I have visited in the Pacific, these reefs were abundantly healthy. About 30 percent of the world's reefs are now estimated to have been seriously degraded, and a much greater percentage are threatened, particularly in areas adjacent to human populations.

The greatest threats to coral reefs are climate change, resulting in coral death and a reduced ability to construct their skeletons; overfishing; and excessive nutrient enrichment from deforestation, agriculture,

runoffs, and poor or no sewage treatment. Many of these originate on land, far from the sea. Ultimately, overpopulation is the most important contributing factor, since the magnitude of and damage caused by these abuses increase directly with the rapidly rising human population and its modifications to the environment.

Because the threats to coral reefs are so varied, there is no single solution to the problem. Protecting and restoring reefs will require a broad spectrum of actions—a global effort spanning countries and villages, industries and individuals. We all contribute to the destruction of reefs through our use of fossil fuels. Carbon dioxide from energy use contributes to global warming that is killing entire reef systems and reduces their ability to create new reefs. Reducing and modifying our reliance on fossil fuels will also reduce these devastating effects.

If we could make a global commitment to only these three actions—reducing greenhouse gas emissions, stopping the release of nutrients into the sea, and establishing more marine protected areas (MPAs)—we could positively affect coral reefs. I have seen over and over that MPAs can restore the ecological balance of species on a reef, particularly large predators, and help reefs return to a healthy state in a relatively short time.

For example, MPAs of a range of sizes, from the Dry Tortugas in Florida, to the Anacapa Islands in California, are uniformly successful not only in protecting a variety of species but also in fostering their abundance. Documented studies show that, on average, the mass of animals and plants in MPAs increased 446 percent; the number of plants or animals (the density) increased 166 percent; the body size of animals increased in MPAs an average of 28 percent; and the number of species increased by 21 percent.

So I remain optimistic. We are on the brink of an exciting experiment in watching our new marine monument, and for now, some of our greatest hopes for the world's coral reef system lie in the northwestern Hawaiian Islands.

Hundreds of tiny tentacles along the branches of this giant sea fan snare passing plankton while sheltering fish and many small creatures.

Craggy seamounts pepper the Pacific, providing island-like havens for high-seas marine life and plenty of puzzles for geologists who debate the origin and fate of submarine mountains. All seamounts in the Pacific appear to be volcanic, but there is a flat-topped version called guyots that defy easy explanation. Some speculate that they were once above water and were flattened by wave action over time, but most guyots today are several thousand feet below the surface. Harry Hess proposes that they may indeed once have been islands when they were closer to a mid-ocean spreading area, but the Pacific crust sank deeper as it moved away from the ridge and toward the trenches, and the wave-flattened mountains were moved into deeper water.

One of the highest mountains on Earth—8,123 meters—is perched underwater on the seaward edge of one of the deepest trenches, the Tonga, which plunges nearly 11 kilometers deep. The mountain is leaning, as it is being gradually drawn over the edge into the subduction zone—as Hess puts it, "down into the jaw crusher." Presently, beyond the reach of most ocean scientists, technologies are being developed that will provide access to these deep areas.

Continental Margins

MAPS OF THE LANDMASSES IN THE PACIFIC OCEAN usually show only the region above the sea, a coastline about 135,650 kilometers long, not including the countless indentations and small embayments that crinkle most shores. What is not apparent from this perspective are the submerged shelves bordering the land, an area usually 200 meters deep or less, where sunlight can penetrate and drive productivity in the water column and on the seafloor below. The continental margins of western North and South America tend to be narrow, with some exceptions, including areas along the shore of southern Alaska, western Canada,

Jutting from the central California coast, the great 3.6-kilometer-deep Monterey Canyon is shown here in bathymetric detail with adjacent terrestrial topography.

and parts of Central America and Ecuador, as well as the southern half of Chile. In the western Pacific, the margins are broader, notably along the coasts of China, Korea, and eastern Australia.

Numerous rivers flow along continental margins into the Pacific, creating local coastal estuaries and marshes as well as providing corridors for certain species that travel between land and sea. In the North Pacific rivers of Russia and North America, salmon and some kinds of sturgeon are among the animals that have evolved as creatures that typically live as adults in the sea but move upstream into fresh water to spawn. Despite the high economic value of continental margins for human occupation and other activities, many coastal regions have not been fully mapped, let alone explored. The islands and fjords of southern Chile are examples of parts of the Pacific continental margin that are rapidly being developed for various human uses, coincident with new discoveries in the few areas studied that indicate unusual and highly vulnerable assemblages of plants and animals. Once converted into fish farms and other uses, the unique ecosystems and endemic species are compromised or lost.

Brilliant and feisty, this Garibaldi, Hypsypops rubicundaya, *patrols its territory in a forest of giant kelp,* Macrocystis pyrifera, *near Catalina Island in the Channel Islands, California.*

Tides and Currents

PACIFIC TIDES GENERALLY HAVE A SMALL RANGE, within a foot or two, and are mostly diurnal, with only one high and one low tide a day. But along the western coast of North America, a combination of daily and twice-daily tides is common, with a large range in successive high and low water heights. The most notable tides around the Pacific coasts is the upper part of the Gulf of California, with a tidal range as great as 12 meters. Overall, the surface pattern of water flow in the Pacific is comparable to the Atlantic. Two great gyres move in opposite directions, one clockwise in the Northern

Hemisphere, and one counterclockwise in the Southern. But the wide currents and countercurrents of the equatorial Pacific are much more complex.

At the Pacific's midsection, the warm North Equatorial Current flows from east to west in an unbroken 14,500-kilometer sweep. Along its western edge, the flow turns north where it narrows into the Kuroshio, a fast-moving current along the coast of Japan. A western boundary current like the Gulf Stream of the North Atlantic, the Kuroshio, moves north straight and fast for hundreds of kilometers, then meanders and spins off circular eddies to the north and south of the main current. The warm Kuroshio converges with the cold Oyashio Current moving south along the coast of Siberia, and the merged flow moves eastward across the ocean as the North Pacific Current. The northeastern edge of the gyre bends south along the coast of Oregon and continues moving south as the cool California Current. North of the great clockwise North Pacific gyre is the smaller, colder, deeper counterclockwise subarctic gyre, which flows north and west along the coasts of Canada, Alaska, and the Aleutians, then turns south as the Oyashio to join the North Pacific Current.

Circulation of currents south of the Equator is a rough mirror image of circulation to the north. The South Equatorial Current flows east to west across the ocean and bends south along the eastern coast of Australia, where it bathes the Great Barrier Reef and Coral Sea in warm water. This great counterclockwise South Pacific gyre then moves eastward toward New Zealand and across the Pacific until it reaches the tip of South America. Here it turns north along the coasts of Chile and Peru as the cold Humboldt Current, which turns into the Peru Current near the Equator.

At the Pacific's Equator, about 180 meters below the surface, and beneath the two strong east-to-west equatorial surface currents, a powerful undercurrent flows in the opposite direction—west to east. Understanding the interplay between these cold and warm watermasses, between surface and deep currents, and between the waters below and the atmosphere above, has proved to be a monumental challenge. Not until the latter part of the 20th century, with the creative use of observations from satellites, research ships, drifting buoys, and sophisticated new computer models to analyze the masses of data gathered, did the impact of ocean currents on climate and weather, rainfall and drought, and human health, wealth, and safety begin to come into focus.

WEB LINK: Pacific currents

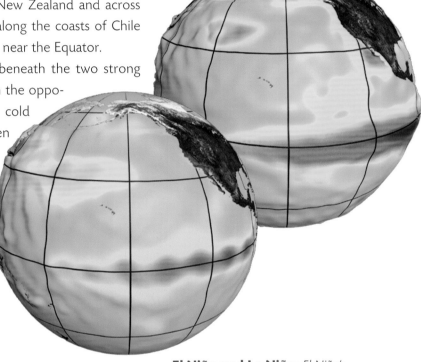

Weather Phenomena

WHAT DO DROUGHT IN BRAZIL AND AFRICA, flooding in the American Midwest, famine in the Sudan, forest fires in Indonesia, the spread of disease in Bangladesh, the failure of crops, the price of corn, and ups and downs in global stock markets have in common with fishermen, cormorants, and anchovies in Peru? The fishermen call it El Niño, named for the Christ child because the phenomenon, when it happens, begins around Christmastime. Others call it the Callao Painter, a reference to the way white buildings of Callao, a coastal city just west of Lima, Peru, sometimes blacken with bacteria from an acid fog generated by rotting fish and elements in the atmosphere that intensify when El Niño comes.

Every two to seven years, warm water sweeps close to Peruvian shores, displacing the cold Peru Current and drastically affecting the lives of anchovies, herrings, squid, and other cold-loving creatures that cannot tolerate the higher temperatures. Fishermen, sea lions, and cormorants and other seabirds suffer as the creatures they normally depend on for sustenance disappear. Rain, normally rare in this area, comes in deluges. Ages ago, the Inca of Peru knew to build their cities and store their food on the tops of hills, away from rivers, to avoid the consequences of cyclical flooding in their land. But it took the advent of satellites, especially those showing trends over time in sea temperature patterns, ocean currents, and cloud distribution, for the rest of humankind to recognize that El Niño packs a global punch.

El Niño and La Niña: *El Niño's equally terrible twin, La Niña, arrives when winds push warm surface waters along the Pacific Equator farther west than usual, impacting upper-air winds and creating a hurricane-friendly atmosphere in the Atlantic. Sea-surface heights and temperature (red, above normal; blue, below normal) recorded by satellites help predict such events. The image above shows El Niño in November 1997; below, La Niña in January 2000.*

WEB LINK: El Niño

Antonio J. Busalacchi, Jr.
EL NIÑO

The largest interannual signal of the Earth's air-sea climate system is the El Niño/Southern Oscillation (ENSO) phenomenon. The strongest and most direct of ENSO climate variations occur in the tropical belt. Along the coast of Ecuador and Peru, El Niño brings torrential rains to a region that is normally semiarid. A prerequisite to understanding the effects of human activities on climate requires an understanding of natural variability, such as that caused by El Niño, and that due to human influence, such as global warming. El Niño has its origin in the equatorial Pacific Ocean,

but its effects have worldwide implications. El Niño appears every two to seven years as a result of coupled interactions between the tropical Pacific Ocean and the atmosphere above it. Anomalous changes in the equatorial Pacific trade winds cause changes in the equatorial Pacific Ocean circulation. The resultant perturbations in the ocean give rise to changes in sea-surface temperatures (SST). These fluctuations, in turn, induce changes in the surface wind field, and the cyclical atmosphere-ocean interaction begins anew. An indicator of El Niño is a shift of the

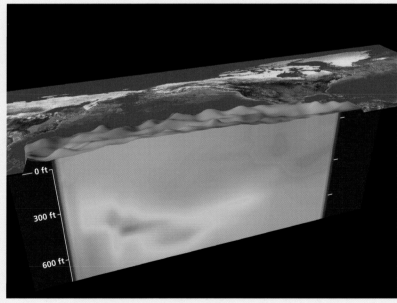

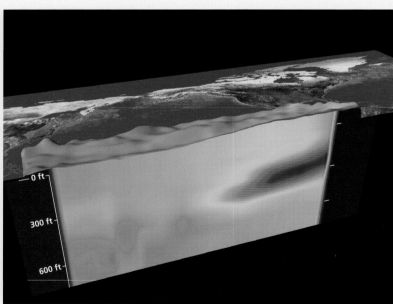

JANUARY 1997

Prior to the onset of El Niño, sea level is higher in the western tropical Pacific and lower in the eastern tropical Pacific in response to the normal trade winds blowing from east to west. Sea-surface ocean temperatures were cooler in the upper ocean to the east and warmer at greater depths in the west. During this time the trade winds started to weaken (not shown) in the far western tropical Pacific.

JUNE 1997

In response to relaxation of the tradewinds, sea level has decreased in the west and increased in the east, by way of an eastward-propagating sea-level signal along the Equator—known as an equatorially trapped Kelvin Wave. In relation to this propagating feature, there is a noticeable west-to-east increase in temperature at depth in the ocean.

warmest water in the global ocean from the dateline in the Pacific Ocean eastward by about 5,000 kilometers, inducing sea-surface temperature changes of 2°C to 4°C. This eastward migration of a critical atmospheric heat source changes global patterns of precipitation and temperature far beyond the equatorial Pacific. The 1982-83 El Niño cost global economies more than $13 billion. Since then, an ocean observation system has been deployed to predict and monitor future ENSO events. Moreover, a series of remote-sensing satellites has been launched to supplement and enhance the in situ observations. The 1997-98 "El Niño Event of the Century" was the first major El Niño to be measured from start to finish with space-based observations of sea-surface temperature, sea-surface topography, sea-surface winds, and precipitation.

Top row (globes): Departures from normal sea-surface height, as measured from the TOPEX/Poseidon radar altimeter satellite, are reflected in the colors on the globes: red indicates high, with white being the highest; blue indicates low, with purple being the lowest. Bottom row (cutaways): These depth-versus-longitude sections along the Equator in the Pacific Ocean depict a combination of actual sea-surface topography, as measured from the TOPEX/Poseidon satellite, with ocean temperature departures from normal measured by a series of NOAA moored ocean buoys. Blue represents cooler temperatures; red indicates warmer temperatures.

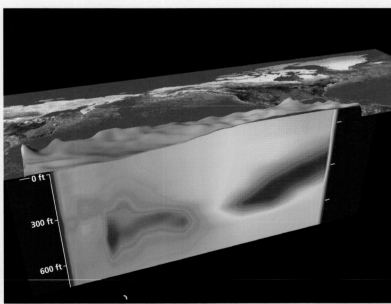 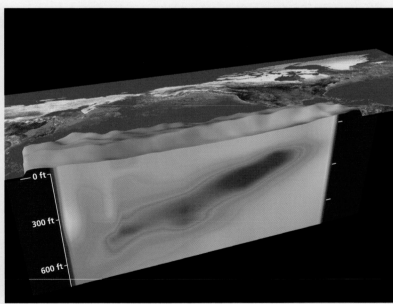

NOVEMBER 1997

By late 1997 the El Niño event has reached a mature phase. Sea level is 20 to 30 centimeters higher than normal in the east and depressed by a similar amount in the west, resulting in a complete reversal of the normal sea level gradient along the Equator. This reversal is reflected at depth with colder than normal temperatures in the western equatorial Pacific and warmer than normal temperatures in the eastern equatorial Pacific.

MAY 1998

The El Niño event is nearly over, and there are signs that the opposite phase of the El Niño/Southern Oscillation, known as La Niña, may be forthcoming. By May 1998 sea level and sea-surface temperatures had returned to close to normal values in the eastern equatorial Pacific Ocean. Colder than normal temperatures at depth from west to east in the equatorial Pacific Ocean signal a rapid reversal from El Niño to La Niña conditions for the latter part of 1998.

**Typhoons in the
Western Pacific
2004–2007**

Storm Tracks

◄━ Category 5

◄━ Category 4

*Sister storms to Atlantic hurricanes,
typhoons speed across the western Pacific
after forming near the Equator, moving
westward with tradewinds in an elliptical
pattern. Eventually they fade over land or
curve northeastward or southeastward,
losing power over the cooler water in the
middle latitudes.*

WEB LINK: **Tropical Atmosphere
Ocean array**

Gradually, as data showed a recurrent sequence of events, it seemed possible to predict, and thus prepare for, the effects of El Niño. It begins when equatorial trade winds from the western Pacific subside or disappear. The usual patterns of air pressure reverse, creating an abnormally low-pressure area near Tahiti coupled with a high-pressure area over northern Australia. Nudged by these new wind patterns, warm surface water from the western Pacific spreads eastward. The result is a broad, warm-water band spanning the equatorial Pacific, and more clouds than usual develop above it. These increase the frequency of storms in the eastern Pacific, as well as in the southern part of North America. This changed wind pattern also shears the tops off westbound Atlantic storms, decreasing the potential for Atlantic hurricanes during an El Niño year. However, some areas experience drought, including Indonesia, eastern Australia, New Guinea, the southern part of West Africa, and northern South America. Drought in one region of India during a spectacular El Niño period starting in 1789 is thought to have cost the lives of 600,000 people. The dryness contributes to large-scale wildfires. The arena where El Niño forms occupies only about one-fifth of the Earth's circumference, yet it transforms weather and dramatically affects lives globally.

Despite growing awareness of the nature and importance of El Niño, a surprise occurrence of the phenomenon in the winter of 1982-83 had devastating consequences. More than 2,000 people were killed and hundreds of thousands displaced by the effects of related floods and storms in the United States, Peru, Ecuador, Bolivia, and Cuba; by unusually strong typhoons in Hawaii and Tahiti; and by droughts and fires in Australia, southern Africa, Central America, Indonesia, the Philippines, South America, and India. Moreover, this extreme year was followed by another in reverse as El Niño's terrible twin, La Niña, took over in 1984. La Niña events are times when warm surface waters along the Pacific Equator are pushed farther west than usual, affecting upper air winds in a way that increases the likelihood of hurricanes in the Atlantic. But where flooding occurs during El Niño, drought comes during La Niña; where there was drought, La Niña brings downpours. Anticipating these events can save thousands of lives and billions of dollars.

The devastation wrought by the El Niño/La Niña sequence of the early 1980s had at least one positive outcome: There was a redoubling of efforts to understand and predict when the state of tropical Pacific waters and atmospheric conditions above them would once again spell trouble. To supplement observations from satellites and research vessels, an unprecedented array of 70 moored buoys equipped with scientific instruments was deployed across the tropical Pacific in 1994, an early warning system known as the Tropical Atmosphere/Ocean (TAO) array. Instruments on the buoys monitor ocean temperature from the surface down to almost 500 meters, as well as winds, air temperature, and relative humidity. Satellites receive data transmitted from buoys and send the information to the National Oceanic and Atmospheric Administration's Pacific Marine Environmental Laboratory in Seattle for the use of scientists worldwide.

Top predators in the sea, southern bluefin tuna, Thunnus maccoyii, *have become such popular prey for humans that they and their northern hemisphere counterparts,* Thunnus thynnus, *have declined by more than 90 percent in less than half a century.*

Increased quality and quantity of data, and the collaboration of many scientists, made it possible for the first time in 1997 to anticipate an El Niño/La Niña cycle months in advance and to make preparations to limit the damage. But it took more than raw data to do this. The advent of supercomputers has made possible a far greater understanding of the weather, and our ability to predict what will happen—and when. The fundamental laws of oceanic and atmospheric physics are incorporated into software, and climate models are generated that simulate various scenarios, depending on the nature of the data provided. The resulting predictions are becoming impressively accurate.

Even before trade winds off the coast of Peru began to diminish in 1997, the computer models had predicted the most severe El Niño of the century. Although the damage brought about by that year's cycle of drought and flood was huge—more than 30 billion dollars' worth of damage and the loss of more than 2,000 lives worldwide—widespread warning and preparation avoided or diminished damage in many areas. Hundreds of lives were saved in Peru, for example, where emergency supplies were stockpiled in anticipation of coping with floods that arrived as predicted.

Marine Life

THE PACIFIC IS HOME to the largest number of atolls in the world. Young, high volcanic islands are often fringed with reefs, and as land subsides and is worn away, a circle of coral may remain around a shallow lagoon, creating an atoll. Charles Darwin accurately deduced the origin of these encircling reefs during his worldwide expedition aboard H.M.S. *Beagle* in the early 1800s. Although living reefs are among the liveliest places imaginable, Darwin, in highlighting their history, referred to atolls as "shining white gravestones marking the sites of sunken, dead volcanoes."

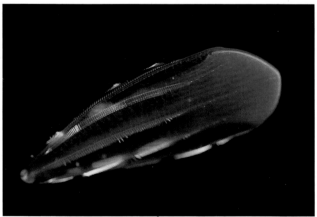

Eight iridescent bands of shimmering cilia propel a glow-in-the-dark comb jelly, Beroe, *that dines on other jellies in the mid-water realm.*

The Pacific also holds the largest expanse of coral reef—the Great Barrier Reef—stretching more than 2,000 kilometers along the northeastern coast of Australia. The Great Barrier Reef is home to at least 400 kinds of corals, 1,500 species of fish, 4,000 species of mollusks, 240 species of birds, and representatives of essentially all the major biological divisions of animal life on Earth. Elsewhere in the Pacific, the diversity of species is even higher for some categories of marine life. Within the warm waters of Palau, a small archipelago in the western Caroline Islands, more than 700 species of hard and soft corals live, and about 2,500 kinds of fish have been discovered in and around the reefs of the Philippine Islands.

WEB LINK: SeaWiFS Biosphere Data over the North Atlantic

Long-Distance Swimmers

An innovative way to determine where open-ocean creatures spend their time is to put tags on them that collect or report their locations over time. Whales, tunas, sharks, seals, and turtles have been tagged in recent years and their wanderings around the Pacific mapped. The distances covered have been a surprise, especially for leatherback turtles, which swim all the way across the Pacific Ocean and back, a journey of some 20,000 to 30,000 kilometers. In some cases, the animals carry instruments that also measure underwater temperature, salinity, and other factors in areas where there is little data from ships. Some creatures carry underwater cameras that unwittingly document what they are chasing—or being chased by—as they swim in the depths.

Richard Pyle, an intrepid ichthyologist based at Hawaii's Bernice P. Bishop Museum, has ventured deep into "the twilight zone" that borders many coral reefs to better understand connections between the sunlit surface waters, where most observations are made, and the adjacent deep habitats, where few have ever ventured, even in submersibles. Pyle uses a rebreather, a device that recycles oxygen and other gases needed for underwater breathing, and chemically scrubs out exhaled carbon dioxide. He descends into the realm of almost dark/almost light and is repeatedly rewarded by the discovery of new species and fresh insights about the deepwater underpinnings of coral reef systems. Some of the reef fish he observes remain deep down where the brightest light is a soft indigo. Others, especially those who live away from the reef in mid-water areas, tend to migrate up and down, ascending at night to feed amid the downward drift of food generated in sunlit surface waters, and descending by day into darker, deep water, where they are less vulnerable to being eaten themselves.

The mid-water realm of the Pacific Ocean is the largest continuous habitat on Earth. There are few places to hide, but the creatures that live there have developed ingenious strategies for survival. Many organisms have countershading: their top sides are dark; their undersides are light. Flying fish, mackerel, and many other open-ocean fish seem to disappear when viewed from below—silvery white bellies merging with illuminated water above—or dark fish against dark water when seen from above. Having mirror-like skin or scales provides camouflage for some species, but one of the most effective ways to avoid detection in an aquatic medium is simply to look like water. Many mid-water and open-ocean creatures are transparent, barely visible blobs of water stitched together with fragile living threads, wisps of tissue, membranes, veils, or strands of jelly. Some have clusters of feathery bristles, globules of lighter-than-water oil, or preposterously long antennae that inhibit sinking. Life abounds in the Pacific's seafloor sediments, largely small invertebrates, including numerous burrowing worms and large numbers of sea cucumbers and brittle stars.

In 2000, during National Geographic's Sustainable Seas Expedition, teams of scientists explored populations of bioluminescent krill, small crustaceans that abound along the coast of California and provide a critical source of food for creatures as small as juvenile rockfish and as large as 70-metric-ton blue whales. Baldo Marinovic, a marine biologist who has followed the ways of krill in Monterey for several years, uses side-scan sonar to locate large krill swarms. They appear as shadowy patches in 180- to 300-meter depths on acoustic maps derived as a ship travels back and

Glowing like opals, the waters around One Tree Island, a part of the Great Barrier Reef National Marine Park in Australia, are celebrated for their abundance and diversity of marine life.

forth across the bay. Next, Marinovic deploys three plankton nets simultaneously in a single set, positioned in such a way that they will capture plankton at a certain depth upon a signal from the surface. Samples taken this way enable him to determine what kind of creatures are living within the krill swarms, and at what depth.

But the next phase—deploying an observer in a submersible to be in the middle of a krill swarm 300 meters underwater—helps validate the other observations and provides real-time knowledge of krill behavior and visual confirmation of their predation by squid, rockfish, eels, and other creatures. Returning from a night dive along the edge of the Monterey Canyon in the summer of 2000, photographer Kip Evans tried to explain what it was like to sit alone in the dark, miles offshore, watching sparkles of blue light from clouds of krill dancing overhead. On deck, when asked "Were you afraid?" Evans said, "No. It was like the Fourth of July!" On the horizon just then, a shower of green sparks and bright flashes over the coastal city of Santa Barbara reminded him of the date: it was, in fact, the Fourth of July.

Recent explorations on the flanks of Pacific seamounts and islands have offered startling revelations of previously unknown marine life there. A newly discovered species called Christmas tree coral—in white, golden, pinkish orange, and reddish brown colors and growing as high as 3 meters— was discovered in 1995 and confirmed in 2005 in depths of 90 to 300 meters in the cold waters off the coast of California. A study of seamounts in the Coral and Tasman Seas published in 2000 discovered 850 new species, with more than 30 percent apparently unique to individual seamounts. A deep submersible study in 2005, down to 2,700 meters on the flanks of the Kodiak-Bowie Seamount Chain off Alaska, discovered a surprising abundance of red-tree, bubblegum, bamboo, and black corals in very deep waters, with some species of crab, brittle star, and shrimp found only on these corals and nowhere else on the seafloor. A 2003-2004 set of deep video transects down the sides of the central Aleutian Islands found deepwater corals clinging to rocks as deep as 3,000 meters and large areas of sea pen and gorgonian corals growing in soft, muddy areas. Near British Columbia, Canada, researchers found a reef of glass sponges covering 700 square kilometers, with individual sponges more than a century old, and the entire reef structure dating 9,000 years old. Few such reefs are known, but they are presently at risk because of recent commercial fishing operations using bottom-scraping trawls.

Stark white sand above, a blaze of living color below, this section of the Great Barrier Reef off Australia harbors far greater diversity of animal phyla than all of the world's rain forests combined.

Special Places of the Pacific

THE GALÁPAGOS

Caught in the middle of virtually every El Niño/La Niña cycle—and probably to a large extent shaped by the constant changes in wet and dry, warm and cold—are the Galápagos Islands, home and haven for some of the most wondrous wildlife in the world. The air is generally warm, rarely dropping below 24°C at sea level, and rarely going above 30°C. Tropical elements are obvious: large dark lizards lounge on and seem to merge with black rocks; weird variations on the theme of prickly pear cacti sprout like trees on some islands and on others spread like shrubs; flamingos filter small insects and crustaceans from shallow, warm lakes; parrotfish, surgeonfish, angelfish, moray eels, barracuda, and other coral reef residents abound, as do a few species of hard corals.

But as happens nowhere else on Earth, side by side with these tropical creatures are penguins and fur seals. Below a few meters of relatively warm surface water, cold water surrounds fish, invertebrates, and algae that are typically found in cool water seas.

Although it might seem that the Galápagos archipelago could host extensive coral reefs, sprawled as it is right across the Equator, the presence of the cold Peru Current coming from the east and a cool equatorial countercurrent coming from the west are numbing inhibitors to underwater tropical creatures. When the waters around the Galápagos are cooler than usual, as happens during a La Niña event, the reproduction of some species is favored, while others decline in numbers. Penguins and fur seals like it cold; parrotfish like it hot; and lack of rain puts stress on many terrestrial species. El Niño years tend to spell disaster for all that depend on large schools of small fish for food, because the great silver whirlpools of anchovy-like species are scarce when the water is warmer than usual. In the winter of 1997-98, thousands of sea lions and sea birds starved and many algae-eating iguanas perished, along with their favorite seaweeds. One creature's famine is another's feast, however. El Niño rains mean better times for mockingbirds, some insects, and many plants that often suffer for lack of water. In the ocean, certain tropical species, such as the grapelike seaweed *Caulerpa racemosa*, prosper.

In normal years—the times between El Niño and La Niña extremes—the seas around the Galápagos are generally warm in the upper 30 meters or so, 22°C to 26°C. This warm layer is lighter than the cool water below and floats more or less intact, a wide if not deep habitat for tropical species. At times, scuba divers can feel a touch of the Arctic with their toes while keeping head and shoulders in the tropics. Moving down through the water several hundred meters, a range of temperatures that would normally stretch over thousands of miles laterally is found in a narrow ver-

Chlorophyll (mg / m³)

≤0.05　0.1　　0.3　0.5　　1　　　3　　5　　10　　　30　≥60

tical band here. Although a number of distinctly warm water species of reef corals occur in the main islands of the Galápagos, periodic upwelling of cold water appears to doom the development of large coral-reef formations commonly present around many islands in the usually balmy waters between 30° N and 30° S. Greater diversity and abundance of tropical organisms, including corals, prosper in the warmer waters around the northern Galápagos Islands, Darwin and Wolf.

Like certain turtles and crocodilians, marine iguanas are adapted to swimming and diving in salt water, but their range is restricted to the Galápagos Islands where they graze on submerged species of algae.

THE SOUTH CHINA SEA

A warm arm of the western Pacific Ocean, the South China Sea combines a deep, rich heritage of ancient life on land and sea. What the Galápagos Islands were for Charles Darwin—a natural laboratory that gave rise to the concept of evolution through natural selection—islands in the South China Sea proved to be for Alfred Russel Wallace, who concurrently developed similar ideas. Wallace, regarded as the father of animal geography, was inspired while observing the nature of birds, beetles, mammals, mollusks, and other wildlife on the islands of Southeast Asia. In particular, he was struck by the sharp difference in the birds living on the island of Bali, which were related to those on the large islands of Java and Sumatra, whereas those just 32 kilometers away on Lombok were allied with those of New Guinea and Australia. He designated each area as a distinct zoogeographic region, and over time recognized a natural biogeographical dividing line extending northward between Borneo and Sulawesi, today known as Wallace's Line.

WEB LINK: Charles Darwin Foundation

Regarded as one of 64 Large Marine Ecosystems by the World Conservation Union (IUCN), the tropical South China Sea is bordered by eight countries—Vietnam, China, Taiwan, the Philippines, Malaysia, Thailand, Indonesia, and Cambodia—with Brunei claiming portions as part of its Exclusive Economic Zone. The ownership of the 400 or so rocky reefs and small islands scattered over an 800,000-square-kilometer area known as the Spratly Islands, as well as the Paracel Islands and Macclesfield Bank, was not contested until the 1970s, when the region became targeted for oil and gas exploitation. This, coupled with perceived strategic advantages and access and claims to the area's abundance of fish and other marine wildlife, has continued to provoke conflict among nations in the region.

WEB LINK: World Conservation Union

Extensive natural forests of coastal mangroves have largely been destroyed to support human activities, but sea grass meadows and coral reefs, although substantially degraded in recent years, still occupy broad expanses of shallow water that extend far across much of the South China Sea. The remaining stands of mangroves host the greatest diversity of mangrove species known, and the complex tangle of prop roots and associated shrubs provide home for numerous species including many that exist nowhere else.

A sponge plays host to a roaming feather star on a reef in the southeastern part of the South China Sea.

Although subject to extremely intensive and destructive fishing practices, the coral reefs that remain in good condition provide haven for some of the richest assemblages of life known. More than 2,000 species of reef fish occupy waters of the Philippine Islands alone, and the deep waters beyond the coastal areas, although largely unexplored, have yielded numerous previously unknown forms of life. The South China Sea embraces about half of the celebrated "coral triangle"—a relatively small portion of the tropical coral reefs known to exist, but home to a disproportionately large number of the world's reef fish species as well as corals, echinoderms, and other invertebrate groups. ◻

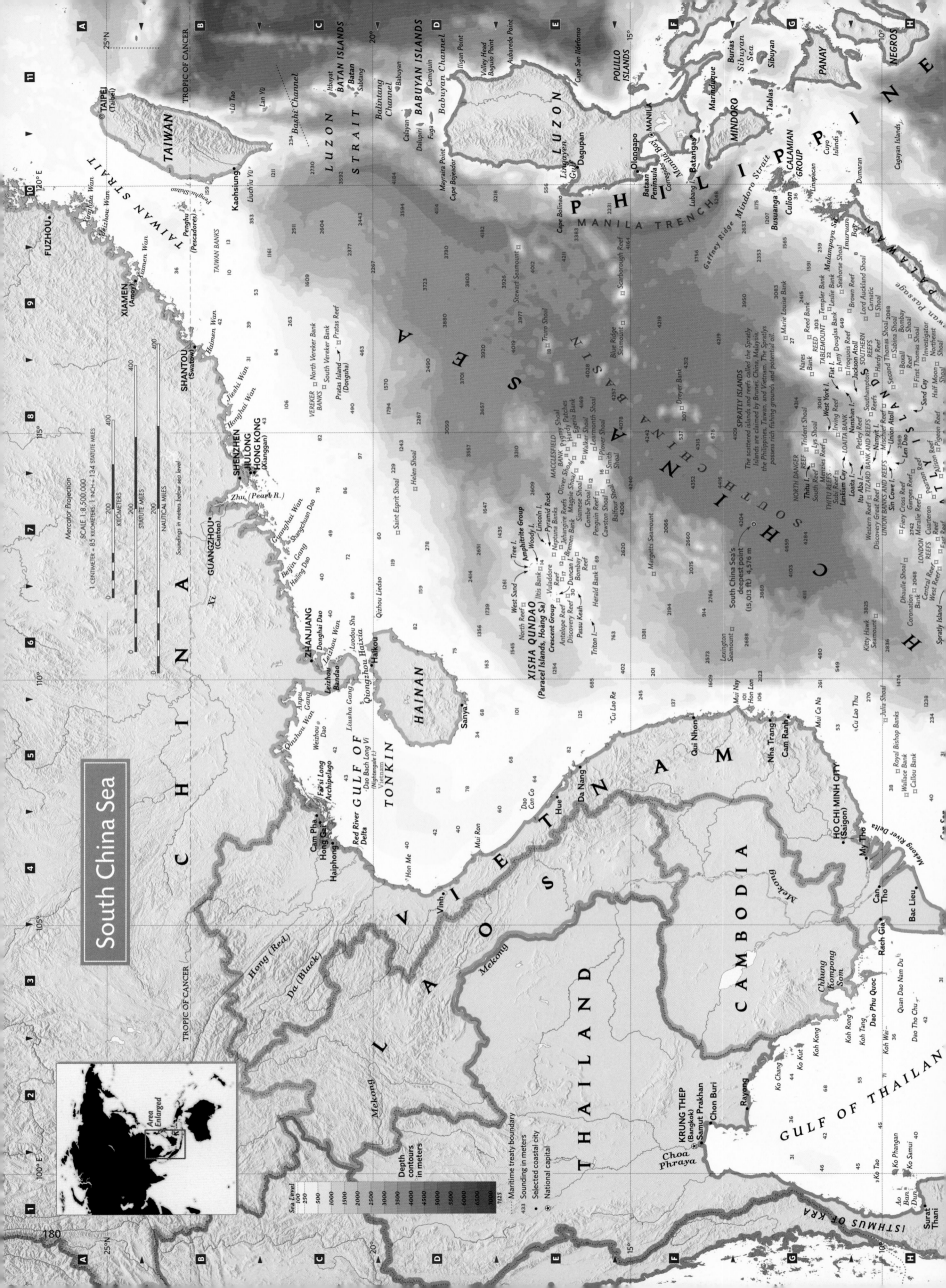

The land-locked Indian Ocean has a strong upwelling of cold, nutrient-rich water along the Horn of Africa and the Arabian Peninsula during the summer months, which fuels rapid phytoplankton growth. Along the southern end of the basin, part of the Agulhas Current joins the Antarctic Circumpolar Current and supports a band of higher biomass that stretches eastward from the southern tip of Africa.

Chapter 6

INDIAN OCEAN

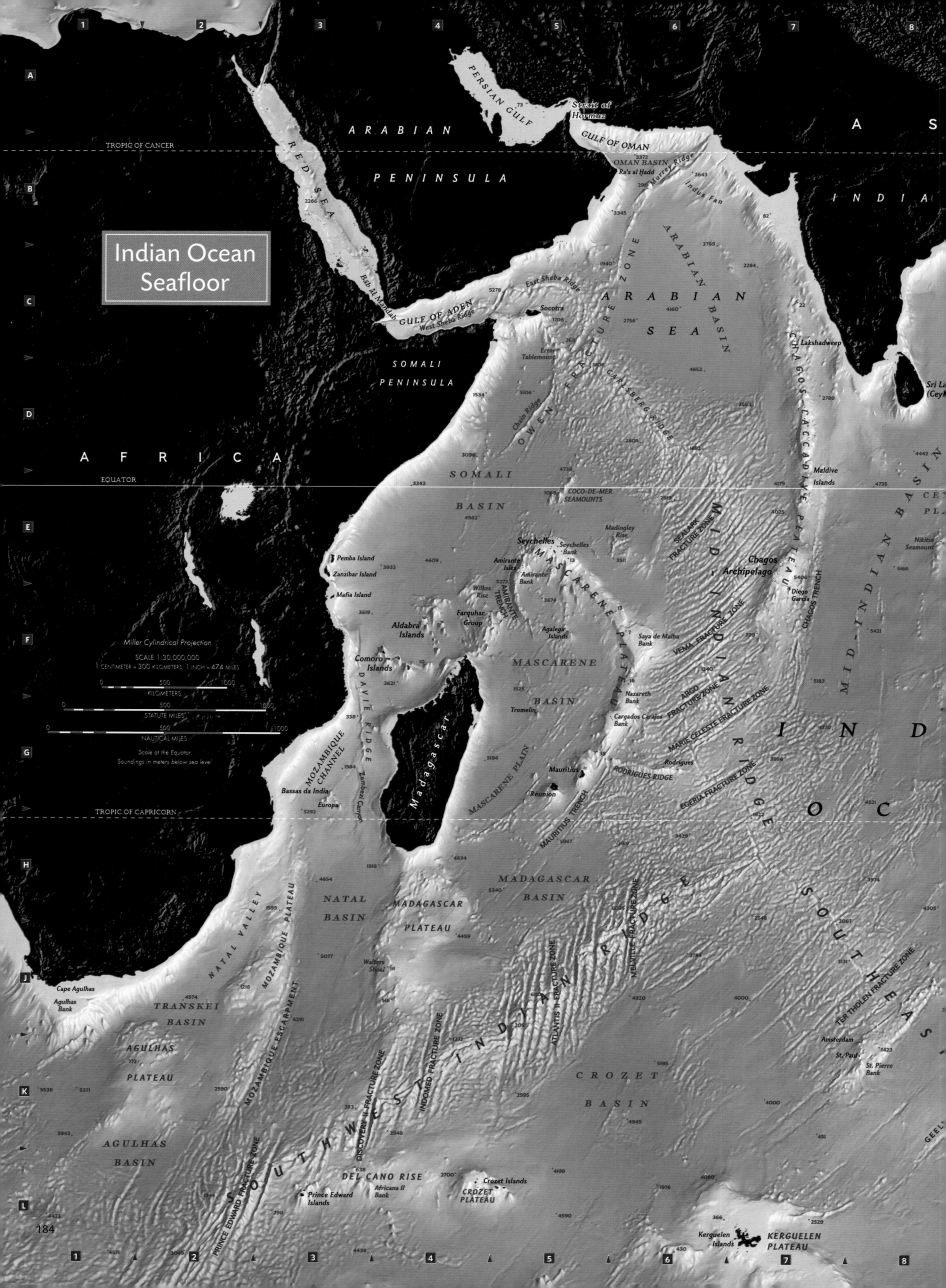

A

EAST
CHINA
SEA

Kyushu

3106
Isokov
Seamount

B

TROPIC OF CANCER

Bonin
Islands

5982

RYUKYU ISLANDS

5202

Taiwan
Taiwan Strait

RYUKYU TRENCH

Daitō Is.

2936

9016

BONIN TRENCH

IZU TRENCH

I A

59

Ganges Fan
2577

INDOCHINA
PENINSULA

73

3529

3098

PHILIPPINE
SEA

4392

KYUSHU-PALAU RIDGE

MARIANA TROUGH

C

AY OF
ENGAL

2821

ANDAMAN
SEA

31

Gulf of
Thailand
73

1902

20

PHILIPPINE
BASIN

458

WEST
MARIANA
BASIN

1663

1020

Mariana Islands

Guam

MARIANA TRENCH

Luzon

2028

16

Andaman
Islands

ANDAMAN
BASIN

1311

Malay Peninsula

22

Palawan

PHILIPPINE
ISLANDS

SULU
BASIN

Mindanao

10057

PHILIPPINE TRENCH

5082

9051

4527

PALAU TRENCH

YAP TRENCH

Palau

16

Chuuk

D

Nicobar
Islands

1842

Strait of Malacca

PALAWAN TROUGH

Challenger
Deep
-10,920 m
(35,837 ft)
World's greatest
ocean depth

CAROLINE ISLANDS

EAURIPIK RISE

COCOS
BASIN

4113

38

Sumatra

SOUTH CHINA SEA

SUNDA SHELF

NATUNA
SEA
EQUATOR

Borneo

CELEBES
BASIN
5484

5722

WEST
CAROLINE
BASIN
3908

EAST
CAROLINE
BASIN

EQUATOR *7248*

E

2302

2352

Mentawai Ridge

JAVA RIDGE

805

361

I N D O N E S I A

Sulawesi

4575

7250

BANDA SEA

27

New Guinea

BISMARCK SEA

BISMARCK
ARCHIPELAGO

4547

INVESTIGATOR RIDGE

5576

GREATER
SUNDA ISLANDS
JAVA SEA

Java

Bali

FLORES
SEA

Lesser Sunda Islands

Timor

ARU SEA

490

F

1517

Christmas I.

SUNDA TROUGH

JAVA TRENCH

LOMBOK BASIN

7,125 m
(23,376 ft)
Indian Ocean's
deepest point

TIMOR SEA

ARAFURA SHELF
ARAFURA SEA

Torres Strait

1884

CORAL SEA
BASIN

4362

Cocos Is.
(Keeling Is.)

718

Vening Meinesz
Seamounts

2725

NORTH
AUSTRALIAN
BASIN

5728

SAHUL SHELF

68

Gulf of
Carpentaria

Great Barrier Reef

CORAL
SEA

G

OSBORN PLATEAU

4547

5678

GASCOYNE
PLAIN

777

ROWLEY SHELF

EXMOUTH
PLATEAU

WHARTON BASIN

907

NINETYEAST RIDGE

WALLABY
PLATEAU

2540

CUVIER
BASIN

TROPIC OF CAPRICORN

H

Zenith Plateau

East Indiaman Ridge

Zeewyk Dutchmen Ridge

1582
Batavia
Seamount

CUVIER
PLATEAU

5468

A U S T R A L I A

Guilden Draak
Seamount

1125

847

BROKEN RIDGE

946

HARTOG RIDGE

PERTH BASIN

3650

5060

J

4321

2370
NATURALISTE
PLATEAU

GREAT AUSTRALIAN
BIGHT

73

499

4680

DIAMANTINA FRACTURE ZONE

4285

4068

SOUTH AUSTRALIAN
BASIN

5018

5850

60

Bass Strait

K

URE ZONE

I N D I A N

2315

397

3902

4990

35

Tasmania

4813

RIDGE

3861

2770

4111

3290

4008

EAST TASMAN
PLATEAU

660

SOUTH TASMAN RISE

L

185

Indian Ocean Political Map and Depth Contours
EGYPT
ISRAEL
JORDAN
IRAQ
IRAN
AFGHANISTAN
PAKISTAN
INDIA
KUWAIT
SAUDI ARABIA
BAHRAIN
QATAR
U.A.E.
OMAN
YEMEN
ERITREA
DJIBOUTI
SOMALILAND
ETHIOPIA
SUDAN
SOMALIA
UGANDA
KENYA
RWANDA
BURUNDI
DEMOCRATIC REPUBLIC OF THE CONGO
TANZANIA
ANGOLA
ZAMBIA
MALAWI
MOZAMBIQUE
ZIMBABWE
NAMIBIA
BOTSWANA
SWAZILAND
LESOTHO
SOUTH AFRICA
MADAGASCAR
COMOROS
SEYCHELLES
MAURITIUS
MALDIVES
SRI LANKA
TROPIC OF CANCER
EQUATOR
TROPIC OF CAPRICORN
Suez Canal
Port Said
Suez
Ain Sukhna
Gulf of Suez
Elat
Aqaba
Gulf of Aqaba
Basra
Bandar-e Khomeini
Bubiyan
Khārk I.
Mina Al Ahmadi
PERSIAN GULF
Jubail
Juaymah
Ra's Tannūrah
Ad Dammām
Gulf of Bahrain
Umm Sa'id
Zirkūh I.
Dās I.
Jebel Dhanna
Ruwais
Dubai
Jebel Ali
Qeshm
Bandar-e 'Abbās
Strait of Hormuz
Khor Fakkan
Fujairah
GULF OF OMAN
Mīnā' al Faḩl
Sonmiani Bay
Karachi
Yanbu
Jeddah
RED SEA
2266
Port Sudan
Suakin Archipelago
Farasan Islands
Dahlak Archipelago
Jabal Zuqar Islands
Bab el Mandeb
Aden
GULF OF ADEN
5278
Abd al Kuri
Socotra
Yemen
The Brothers
Cape Xaafuun
Masira
Gulf of Masira
Sawqirah Bay
Kuria Muria Islands
Salalah
Al Qamar Bay
Kandla
Gulf of Kutch
Sikka
Gulf of Khambhat
Mumbai (Bombay)
Jawaharlal Nehru
Marmagao
Mangalore
Chennai (Madras)
Vishakhapatnam
Tuticorin
Gulf of Mannar
Colombo
Palk Strait
291
INDUS FAN
ARABIAN SEA
ARABIAN BASIN
4652
368
22
LAKSHADWEEP
India
Amindivi Is.
Kavaratti
Nine Degree Channel
Minicoy
Eight Degree Channel
LACCADIVE SEA
Ihavandiffulu Atoll
Tiladummati Atoll
North Malosmadulu Atoll
Miladummadulu Atoll
Fadiffolu Atoll
Male Atoll
South Male Atoll
Ari Atoll
Mulaku Atoll
Kolumadulu Atoll
Haddummati Atoll
CHAGOS-LACCADIVE PLATEAU
Suvadiva Atoll
Addu Atoll
4735
OWEN FRACTURE ZONE
CARLSBERG RIDGE
5106
Mogadishu
Coco-de-Mer Seamounts
1066
SOMALI BASIN
4962
Pate I.
Pemba I.
Zanzibar
Dar es Salaam
Mafia I.
Denis
Praslin
Silhouette
Mahé I.
Frigate
13
Amirante Isles
Desroches
Platte I.
Coetivy I.
Fortune Bank
5273
Alphonse I.
AMIRANTE TRENCH
MASCARENE PLATEAU
Cosmoledo Group
Aldabra Is.
Assumption I.
St. Pierre I.
Providence I.
Cerf I.
Astove I.
Farquhar Group
Agalega Islands
Mauritius
Glorieuses Is.
France
Njazidja
Mwali
Nzwani
10
Mayotte
France
Nosy Mitsio
Nosy Be
Paisley Seamount
Mozambique Channel
338
Juan de Nova I.
France
Nosy Vao
Nosy Barren
Nosy Ste. Marie
Bassas da India
France
Europa I.
France
Saya de Malha Bank
MASCARENE BASIN
1525
Nazareth Bank
Tromelin
France
Cargados Carajos Shoals (St. Brandon)
Mauritius
Soudan Bank
RODRIGUES RIDGE
Rodrigues
Mauritius
Réunion
France
MAURITIUS TRENCH
CHAGOS ARCHIPELAGO (OIL ISLANDS)
United Kingdom
Peros Banhos
Salomon Is.
Three Brothers
Nelsons I.
Danger I.
Egmont Is.
Diego Garcia
5406
VEMA FRACTURE ZONE
6402
799
CHAGOS TRENCH
5421
MID-INDIAN RIDGE
EGERIA FRACTURE ZONE
INDIAN OCEAN
MID-INDIAN BASIN
Maputo
Richards Bay
Durban
Cape Town
Port Elizabeth
Cape Ste. Marie
MADAGASCAR BASIN
5340
MADAGASCAR PLATEAU
MOZAMBIQUE PLATEAU
1216
18
Walters Shoal
516
205
TRANSKEI BASIN
Agulhas Bank
MOZAMBIQUE ESCARPMENT
6291
NATAL BASIN
772
AGULHAS PLATEAU
INDOMED FRACTURE ZONE
SOUTHWEST INDIAN RIDGE
ATLANTIS II FRACTURE ZONE
5195
CROZET BASIN
2067
SOUTHEAST INDIAN RIDGE
Île Amsterdam
France
Île St.-Paul
AGULHAS BASIN
PRINCE EDWARD FRACTURE ZONE
638
Prince Edward I.
Marion I.
PRINCE EDWARD ISLANDS
South Africa
Îles des Apôtres
Île aux Cochons
Îles des Pingouins
CROZET ISLANDS
France
Île de la Possession
Île de l'Est
Crozet Plateau
4590
ATLANTIC-INDIAN BASIN
KERGUELEN PLATEAU
Îles Nuageuses
Île de l'Ouest
Îles de Boynes
KERGUELEN ISLANDS
France
Grande Terre
Roches Salamanca
430

Indian Ocean
Sea-surface
Temperature

TROPIC OF CANCER

30°N

20°

10°N

AFRICA

EQUATOR   0°

March 2008 (winter)

September 2007 (winter)

Miller Cylindrical Projection

SCALE 1:30,000,000
1 CENTIMETER = 300 KILOMETERS; 1 INCH = 474 MILES

0   500   1000
KILOMETERS

0   500   1000
STATUTE MILES

0   500   1000
NAUTICAL MILES

Scale at the Equator
Soundings in meters below sea level

10°S

20°

TROPIC OF CAPRICORN

30°

40°S

30°E   40°   50°   60°   70°   80°

I A

EQUATOR

EQUATOR

A U S T R A L I A

TROPIC OF CAPRICORN

Degrees Celsius

| 0 | 3 | 6 | 9 | 12 | 15 | 18 | 21 | 24 | 27 | 30 |

| 32 | 37.4 | 42.8 | 48.2 | 53.6 | 59 | 64.4 | 69.8 | 75.2 | 80.6 | 86 |

Degrees Fahrenheit

90°   100°   110°   120°   130°   140°E

Distinctive mushroom shapes mark the reefs of Aldabra, a World Heritage Site 680 kilometers north of Madagascar. Part of the Seychelles, Aldabra hosts numerous endemic species, including a giant land tortoise similar to those living in the Galápagos Islands half a world away.

The Indian Ocean by the Numbers

(excludes major seas around Indonesia and northern Australia)

Geographic boundaries: 25° N to 60° S / 20° E to 145° E

Total area: 67,469,539 square kilometers

Total volume: 261,519,545 cubic kilometers

Average depth: 3,897 meters

Greatest depth: 7,125 meters (Java Trench, south of the Indonesian arc of islands)

- Includes 20 percent of Earth's water area.
- Contains the world's longest linear feature, the Ninetyeast Ridge, a chain of submerged peaks.
- Underwater temperatures 1.6 kilometers deep are hottest, 22°C, in the Red Sea, an active spreading center.

"[W]e watched . . . school after school of jacks; 500 batfish,
their silver sides reflecting afternoon light; five fat, bomberlike
dog-tooth tunas; a hammerhead shark high overhead,
silhouetted against the path of the sun; a school of shuri
swimming in a loose funnel shaped like an emerging tornado.
. . . To my left was Asia, to my right, Africa. Between them,
I had at my back the richest reef I'd ever seen."

—David Doubilet, *Light in the Sea*

To sea turtles and whales, the Indian Ocean is a vaulted blue home and highway, flowing over canyons and mountain peaks, bordering reefs, shallow meadows of sea grass, rocky shores, and long sand beaches. To certain elephants of the Andaman Islands, this largely tropical sea is a gargantuan spa, a salty but refreshing place to escape equatorial heat, where pachyderms can seem as weightless as ballerinas. To sea captains, the Indian Ocean is a place of many moods, at times a serene seascape mirroring clouds by day, stars by night; at others an ocean notorious for seasonally strong winds, monstrous monsoons, and towering freak waves preceded by deep troughs that can snap ships and sink them without a trace. To marine biologists, this ocean is a place of rich opportunities for research on environments ranging from mangrove swamps, coral reefs, and atolls to submerged walls, valleys, and steep, deep trenches—and all of the life-filled liquid in between.

Geologically, the Indian Ocean is the youngest ocean but a place still mysterious and largely unexplored. The third largest body of water on Earth, the Indian Ocean covers about 67.5 million square kilometers, stretching some 10,000 kilometers at its widest point. To the west, it is bounded by the landmasses of Africa and the Arabian Peninsula; to the north by Iran, Pakistan, India, and Bangladesh; to the east by the Malay Peninsula, the Sunda Islands of Indonesia, and western Australia; and to the south by Antarctica.

Shrouded with the mystique of ancient trade routes and lost civilizations, beguiling in its range of diverse peoples, wildlife, and undersea environments, the Indian Ocean has its own exotic character, while serving as a connecting bridge between the Atlantic on one side, the Pacific on the other, and the frigid Southern Ocean surrounding Antarctica to the south. Roughly triangular, only the warm-water apex of this mostly tropical ocean crosses the Equator into the Northern Hemisphere. Like all other oceans, though, the entire Indian Ocean is distinctly cold—from 4°C to 5°C—about 4,000 meters down.

Six centuries ago, Chinese traders made their way across the oceans with remarkably sophisticated sailing ships, venturing into the Indian Ocean and bringing to Arab countries knowledge of ocean navigation and instruments, including the first magnetic compass. In 1498, Portuguese explorer Vasco da Gama helped open long-distance sea travel from Europe when he sailed, with guidance from local navigators, around the southern tip of Africa and into the Indian Ocean. Others entered the Indian Ocean by the Red Sea, a seaway known as the Route of Spices.

Formation of the Indian Ocean

Glassy sweepers, Parapriacanthus ransonnet, *flow like liquid silver in a Red Sea cave.*

WHEN GONDWANALAND BEGAN BREAKING APART about 180 million years ago, the Indian subcontinent began its steady drift northward, propelled by the seafloor spreading that created the new Indian Ocean crust. India collided with Asia 50 million to 60 million years ago, and the force of that impact

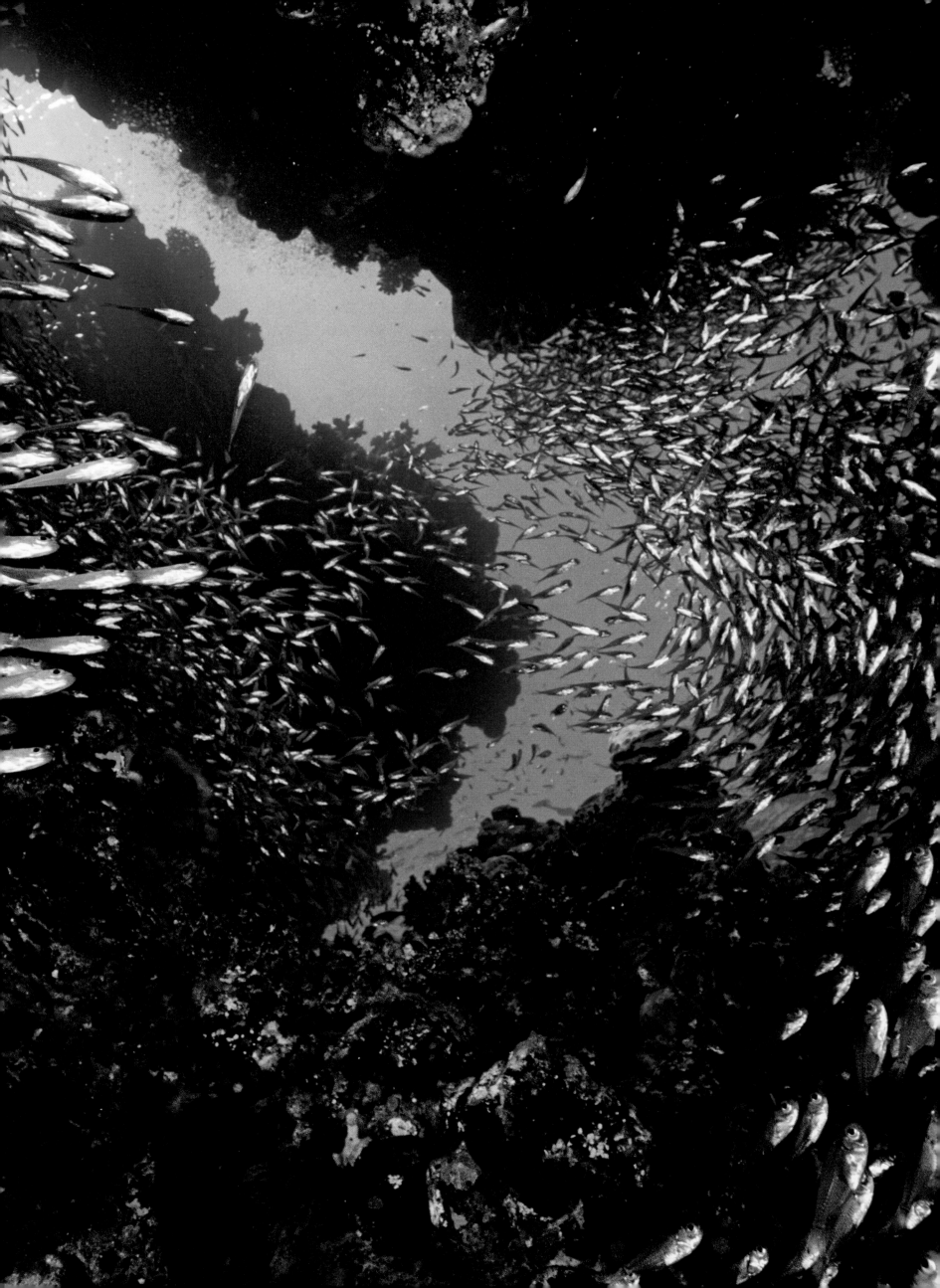

buckled the Earth, gradually pushing crust skyward and creating the Himalaya—the world's youngest and tallest major mountain chain—about 10 million years ago.

Evidence of India's northward journey is apparent as giant "skid marks" on the seafloor today, including the longest linear feature on Earth. The Ninetyeast Ridge, aligned north to south along the 90° E meridian of longitude, was created as a chain of volcanoes formed one by one over a stationary hot spot in the Earth's mantle as the Indian plate moved north. The Chagos-Laccadive Plateau running north-south off the western coast of India is another such remnant of the northern drift of the Indian plate. As Arabia separated from Africa and drifted northeastward, it pushed against Asia—giving rise to the Zagros Mountains of Iran and the Hajar Range of Oman. The easterly side of the small Arabian plate was shoved down under the Asian plate, sliding below sea level and forming the shallow Persian Gulf. Here, as sediments accumulated and eventually compressed into rock, salt formations in this area trapped carbon deposits and created the Middle East oil fields, the largest known on Earth.

With a dancer's grace and a built-in snorkel, an Andaman Islands elephant cools off in the northern Indian Ocean. Given a chance, elephants plunge into the sea for a bath or swim just as they do in freshwater lakes and rivers.

Mid-Ocean Ridge

THE SEISMICALLY ACTIVE, RUGGED MID-INDIAN RIDGE forms a massive inverted-Y shape in the western half of the ocean. The spreading ridge begins in the Arabian Sea along the Carlsberg Ridge in the upper northwestern part of the ocean, where the first evidence of seafloor spreading was demonstrated scientifically in 1963. It then ranges south past the Chagos-Laccadive Plateau off southwestern India, where it becomes the Central or Mid-Indian Ridge. The mid-ocean ridge then splits into two branches at roughly 25° S, just north of the Tropic of Capricorn. The Southwest Indian Ridge continues southwestward, curling around the southern tip of Africa and merging with the Atlantic-Indian Ridge. The Southeast Indian Ridge slants southeastward, joining with the Pacific-Antarctic Ridge south of the island of Tasmania, off the southeastern coast of Australia. The Indian Ocean's spreading ridges rise an average of 3,000 meters above the seafloor, with a few of their peaks (Rodrigues, Amsterdam, and St. Paul) rising above sea level to form isolated islands.

The Seafloor

AMONG THE RIDGES, ISLANDS, AND SEAMOUNTS are basins from 320 to 9,000 kilometers wide, layered with thick sediment, and with abyssal hills (less than 1,000 meters high) poking up from the seafloor in abundance. The largest of these basins is the Central Indian Basin, and to the east the Wharton, Perth, and South Australian Basins. To the west are a number of areas named for nearby land areas: the Arabian Basin off the Arabian Peninsula; the Somali Basin near the coast of Somalia; and the Mascarene Basin, Madagascar Plain, and Madagascar Basin seaward of the eastern coast of Madagascar. There is also the Natal Basin off southern Africa, and the broad Crozet Basin occupies much of the space between the long, sweeping arms of the Southwest and Southeast Indian Ridges in the southern part of the ocean.

The abyssal plains within these basins generally appear smooth and flat, owing to the deep blanket of fine-grained sediment formed from the steady rain of minute skeletons and shells of planktonic organisms mixed with clay particles and other debris accumulated over many thousands of years. As in other ocean basins, some areas host enormous fields of manganese nodules that have varying concentrations of iron, nickel, cobalt, and copper as well as manganese. Animals that thrive in soft sediment, from sea cucumbers to burrowing mollusks, are also abundant.

The Java Trench—the second longest deep-sea trench in the ocean—arcs for more than 4,500 kilometers along the coast of southwestern Java. It continues northward with a new name, the Sunda Trench, off Sumatra, extending along the Andaman and Nicobar Islands into the northern Indian Ocean.

Few earthquakes occur along the Ninetyeast Ridge and several smaller ridges in the Indian Ocean, including those on the plateaus around Madagascar and Mozambique, and the Chagos-Laccadive Plateau. There is noteworthy seismic activity at times in the Indian Ocean, however.

The Longest Straight Line on the Globe

Not discovered until 1962, the 2,700-kilometer-long Ninetyeast Ridge under the Indian Ocean runs along a line so curiously straight it appears to be drawn with a ruler along the 90° E line of longitude, thus its name. Formed like many island chains in the Pacific Ocean—by a crustal plate being moved over a volcano-producing hot spot in the Earth's mantle—it is the longest linear ridge of mountains on Earth, quite obvious when looking at a bathymetric map of water depths around the globe.

SEE ALSO: Mariana Trench, page 157

WEB LINK: tsunamis

With a patch of constantly glowing bacteria under each eye that is covered or revealed by a movable flap, flashlight fish, Photoblepheron palpebratus, signal other flashlight fish and attract light-loving prey.

On December 26, 2004, a violent earthquake on the seafloor just west of Sumatra was measured at a magnitude of 9.1—the second strongest and the longest earthquake ever recorded. It caused a massive slump of seafloor sediment, which in turn caused a sudden movement of huge volumes of overlying water that generated a devastating series of tsunamis. These tsunami waves—as high as 30 meters when they swept over the coast of Sumatra—caused more than 220,000 deaths in 14 countries around the entire perimeter of the Indian Ocean and wrought coastal devastation in 6 others, as far away as South Africa and western Australia. Although most tsunamis occur in the Pacific Ocean, this Indian Ocean event was the most destructive tsunami in history in terms of lives and property lost.

Krakatau, a mountainous island that long ago emerged from the sea in the channel between Java and Sumatra, literally blew apart in August 1883 with a series of explosions estimated to exceed 200 megatons. The blasts were heard 3,200 kilometers away, and only a third of the volcano was left above sea level. The eruptions set in motion nine enormous tsunamis, and a series of walls of dark water as much as 400 meters high engulfed the northwestern tip of Java. The cloud of ash ejected into the sky rose 80 kilometers and encircled the globe. The ash layer was so dense that it cooled world climate for five years and filtered the sun's rays so much that the sun appeared to be blue or green, rather than yellow, for many months.

Hydrothermal Vents

WHEN FIRST DISCOVERED IN THE PACIFIC in the late 1970s, hydrothermal vents were for a while thought to occur only in the Pacific. That changed in 1983 when similar formations were discovered in the Atlantic. The prominence of hydrothermal activity in the deep sea as a fundamental part of ocean dynamics worldwide was reaffirmed in 2001 when scientists from a dozen institutions aboard the Woods Hole research vessel *Knorr* were exploring the Indian Ocean's "triple junction," where three enormous crustal plates converge. They confirmed what an earlier Japanese team of scientists had discovered: the presence of chimney-like structures 4 kilometers underwater and two stories tall spewing plumes of superheated, mineral-laden water.

The location of this Kairei vent field, high on the rift-valley wall at 25° 19.2′ S and 70° 1.8′ E, proved to be home to fuzzy white sea anemones, mussels, crabs, pale shrimp resembling those known from Atlantic vents, and armor-plated snails unlike any mollusk ever seen before. When biologist Anders Waren examined the strange snail in his laboratory at the Swedish Museum of Natural History in Stockholm, he was puzzled when the interlocking scales that covered the body and base of the animal's foot kept sticking to his forceps. Like a coat of medieval armor, the scales proved to be iron based and magnetic. They were built by the animals from the iron sulfide minerals spewing from nearby metal-laden hydrothermal plumes. No other creature on Earth is known to use iron sulfides to build its own outer structure.

Four years later, a hydrothermal "megaplume" 70 kilometers long was discovered in the Indian Ocean. Bramley Murton of the British National Oceanography Centre said, "[T]his thing is at least 10 times—or possibly 20 times—bigger than anything of its kind that's been seen before." Once thought to be rare, hydrothermal vents are now believed to be widespread in the Indian Ocean, and in certain deep-sea areas of volcanic activity throughout the world ocean. Current thinking is summed up by geophysicist Robert Reves-Sohn: "I'd be surprised if in the next five years we didn't experience a mini-revolution in terms of finding these [fields] in places where they are not supposed to exist."

Seafloor Spreading Built Mount Everest

Seafloor spreading constantly moves the same pieces of continental crust around the surface of the Earth, and mountain ranges are built when they collide. When two continental plates are pushed together, each is too thick to be pushed beneath the other, so there is nowhere to go but up. The faster the spreading, the faster and higher the continental edges are uplifted into mountains and high plateaus. And, the more recent the mountain building, the less time there has been for erosion, so the higher the mountains. The Indian plate was pushed north from near the South Pole to a collision with Asia both quickly and recently, in geologic terms, which created Mount Everest as the highest peak on Earth.

Seamounts and Islands

NUMEROUS SEAMOUNTS HAVE BEEN PREDICTED in the Indian Ocean in recent times using satellite sensors, but almost none have been mapped in detail using acoustic surveying techniques, and most have yet to be confirmed, let alone explored. Many appear to occur between Réunion and the Seychelle Islands in the Central Indian Basin, and another large number rise from the seafloor in the Central Indian Basin and in the Vening Meinesz group near the Wharton Basin in the far eastern Indian Ocean.

Although much of the Indian Ocean is open sea, the numerous islands that do occur are rich with natural and cultural significance. Many islands are of volcanic origin. Among their number are the Christmas, Cocos, Farquhar, Prince Edward, St. Paul, and Amsterdam Islands; the Amirante, Nicobar, Chagos, Crozet, and Kerguélen groups; and Comoros, Lakshadweep (Laccadive, Minicoy, and Amindivi Islands), Mauritius, and Réunion. The Andaman and Sunda Islands, also volcanic, are subduction island-arc systems, bordered by deep-ocean trenches. Others—the Maldives, Seychelles, Socotra, Sri Lanka, and Madagascar—are continental fragments. The fourth largest island in the world at 1,600 kilometers long and 530 kilometers wide, Madagascar is an ancient block of continental crust that was once sandwiched between Africa and Australia but broke free about 150 million years ago and began drifting to its present location off the southeast coast of Africa. Isolated from the mainland for so many millions of years, Madagascar became an independent Eden, home and haven for an astonishing array of creatures that occur nowhere else on Earth.

The Seychelles, a group of more than a hundred tropical islands that have been an independent republic since 1976, lie 1,600 kilometers south of India and about the same distance east of Africa. The larger, central islands are primarily granitic fragments left over from the ancient landmass of Gondwanaland. Like Madagascar and the island of Mauritius, where dodos once prospered, the Seychelles are known for many species of ancient origins that have become, or are about to become, extinct.

The Maldives is a glistening blue-green necklace of about 1,200 islands in 26 atolls—the crowns of a vast mountain range stretching over thousands of kilometers of seabed southwest of India—with its mountaintops just barely emerging above sea level. At the end of the last ice age, when sea level was about 100 meters lower than at present, there was significantly more land exposed above the water. Today, the Maldives is a nation of sea more than land: The highest point above the sea is barely greater than the height of a man—about 2 meters. Even a modest increase in global sea level is a matter of critical concern to the more than 300,000 people who live in these islands and could irrevocably lose their home.

Coral reefs wreath the low-lying lands of the Maldive Islands, shown here in a gull's-eye view.

Continental Margins

WEB LINK: Indian Ocean coral reefs

MOST OF THE 66,500 KILOMETERS of coastal shores in the Indian Ocean are tropical or subtropical, with a great diversity of estuaries, salt marshes, mangroves, coral reefs, beaches, barrier islands, lagoons, dunes, cliffs, and river deltas. Major estuaries and extensive mangrove forests have formed at the mouth of the Ganges River and in the Bay of Bengal where the Hugli River meets the sea near Kolkata (Calcutta). The broad Indus River Delta of Pakistan is a haven for shorebirds, with rich fare in the huge mudflats that extend for kilometers along the shore. The coast of Somalia is largely bordered by massive sand dunes, and half of the coastline of India is fringed with beaches. In southern India, northern Sri Lanka, and other parts of the upper Indian Ocean, beach sands are mined for their rich content of minerals, including monazite, ilmenite, rutile, and zircon.

Around the margins of the Indian Ocean, the continental shelf is narrower than most places in the Atlantic and Pacific Oceans, with an average width of only 120 kilometers. The broadest continental shelf areas occur off the coast of India at Mumbai (Bombay) and off the northwestern shores of Australia. Typically around the islands there is a sheer drop-off into deep water within only about 300 meters of the shore. Submarine canyons cut into the break between the continental shelf and continental slope, with especially large gouges where major rivers, notably the Zambezi and the Ganges, flow into the sea. Massive sediment deposits fan out across the continental shelves from the major rivers, extending far offshore, down through the canyons, and out across the abyssal plains. The most extensive accumulation of river-derived sediment in the world lies underwater off the mouth of the Ganges River.

Cyanobacteria growing in the sea 3.5 billion years ago trapped sediment and deposited layers of limestone in lumps of rocks such as these modern stromatolite counterparts living in Hamelin Pool, Shark Bay, western Australia.

Tides and Currents

Tidal ranges in the Indian Ocean are generally smaller than in the Atlantic and Pacific Oceans, largely because the Indian basin is smaller. Twice-daily tides are characteristic around most of the Indian Ocean, but there are once-daily tides along parts of the southwestern coast of Australia, the shores of Thailand, in the Andaman Sea, and along the southern shore of the Persian Gulf. A mix of diurnal and semidiurnal tides occur in the Arabian Sea and the Persian Gulf. The tidal range there is generally small, but the configuration of the seafloor and shoreline and the pattern of prevailing winds cause tides to be much higher in some areas. The greatest tides around the Indian Ocean are in the Gulf of Khambhat along the western coast of India, with a tidal range of as much as 12 meters, and in the Gulf of Kachchh in the northeastern reaches of the Arabian Sea, where the tidal range is greater than 7 meters.

At the southernmost tip of Africa, the cool gray-green waters of the Atlantic collide with the tropical blue of the Indian Ocean, creating a place known to sailors as the Sea of Storms. Seafarers have followed the winds and currents along these coasts for ages, although few records remain prior to the 1400s. Arabian sailors are believed to have sailed dhows (small open boats powered by triangular sails) throughout the Indian Ocean for at least a thousand years. The Maldives, located as a crossroad on sea routes between southern Arabia, Ceylon, and the Far East, appear to have served as a strategic port. From 1405 to 1433, the Chinese admiral Zheng Ho led seven expeditions to the Indian Ocean with various ships of the famous Treasure Fleet, establishing largely peaceful connections along the way through trade in India, Ceylon, and various parts of Africa.

The Indian Ocean is strikingly different from the Atlantic and Pacific in that little of it lies in the Northern Hemisphere, and what does is largely enclosed by land. As a result, there is no grand, steady clockwise gyre like those of the North Atlantic and North Pacific Oceans. But south of the Equator, the Indian Ocean has a well-developed, great counterclockwise current—comparable to those in the South Atlantic and South Pacific Ocean Basins. The South Equatorial Current travels east to west just south of the Equator, then swings south, where it proceeds down both sides of the large island of Madagascar. Between Madagascar and the mainland of Africa the flow, called the Mozambique Current, is constricted and complex, but most of it rejoins the main flow south of Madagascar to form the Agulhas Current south of 30° S latitude. The Agulhas, which continues down to the southern tip of Africa, is one of the strong, western boundary currents in the world ocean, with average speeds of 3 to 5 knots. This current flows straight into the direction of prevailing winds blowing up from the southern tip of Africa, and because of this opposition of winds and currents, storms in this area are infamous for creating giant and destructive rogue waves.

Tracing a swirl in the sea, tidal currents flow around the Lacepede Islands in western Australia.

The south-flowing Agulhas turns east at about 40° S latitude and joins the Antarctic Circumpolar Current as it sweeps eastward toward Australia. Part of the Antarctic Current flow then angles back toward the north as the cold West Australia Current, and this current turns west and merges with the South Equatorial Current, completing the gyre.

In the northern Indian Ocean, the constricted land area, and the resulting interplay between land and sea climates, creates a complex, seasonal current pattern driven by monsoon winds. A clockwise movement of currents characteristic of other Northern Hemisphere oceans occurs only during the summer months, with the Somali Current moving north along the western edge of the basin, flowing generally west to east along the Asian coastlines, with a generalized return flow from east to west about 10° south of the Equator. Between November and April each year, the currents shift radically. Most of the waters north of the Equator move east to west, dominated by the North Equatorial Current. On reaching the coast of Africa, this turns into the Somali Current, which moves south along the coast this time of year. Some flow crosses the Equator into the Mozambique and Agulhas Currents, but much of it turns into the Equatorial Countercurrent, which flows west to east along the Equator.

WEB LINK: Indian Ocean currents

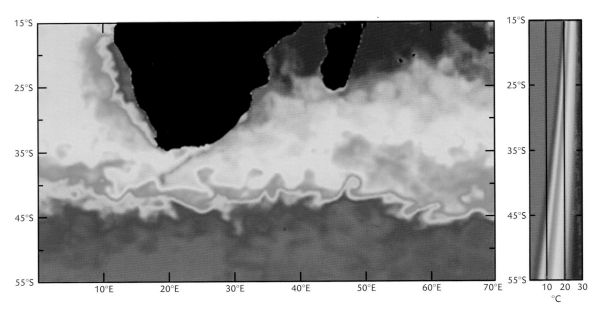

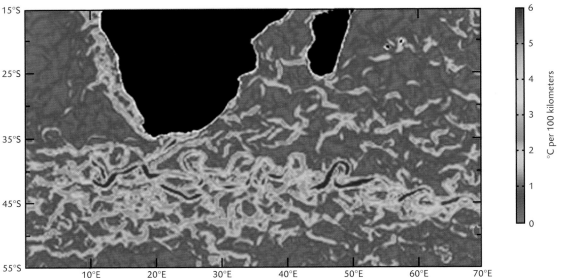

Sea Temperatures off Southern Africa: *In the region of the Agulhas Current off the tip of southern Africa, sharp patterns of color indicate water temperature measured by NASA and NOAA during a three-day period in April 2005, keyed on the bar graphs to the right. Red indicates warm; violet is cold. The upper figure illustrates the dynamic range of sea-surface temperature at each latitude; the figure below shows the magnitude of spatial gradient in sea-surface temperature associated with these ocean currents.*

In recent years, it has been discovered that there is an Indian Ocean counterpart to the Pacific's El Niño/La Niña events. Normally water temperatures along the Equator are warmer in the eastern Indian Ocean and cooler to the west. In some years, this pattern reverses, with surface waters of the eastern Indian Ocean being cooler and its sea level lower. This type of event, last documented in 2006, is called the Indian Ocean Dipole. Scientists have deployed an array of moored buoys across the Indian Ocean Basin to study this phenomenon.

Weather Phenomena

FOR ITS SIZE, THE INDIAN OCEAN has remarkably complex climate and weather. In the cold, subantarctic, southern region, gale-force westerly winds prevail. In the warm, temperate region between 30° S and 45° S, air temperatures average from 20°C to 22°C in the summer months, and 16°C to 17°C in the winter. Steady southeasterly trade winds prevail between 10° S and 30° S, where steady southeasterly winds blow much of the year. In this area, as well as in the broad region north of latitude 10° S, fierce storms tend to be born in the hot, late Southern Hemisphere summer, January through March.

On February 22, 1845, a small sailing craft called the *Charles Heddles* was shipping cattle between Mauritius and Madagascar when it encountered such a storm one day out of port. The captain ran with the wind, and with increasing violence it drove the ship before it, stripping its sails. When the sky cleared five days later, the captain took a bearing and discovered that the ship was essentially back where it started, a few miles off Mauritius, having been blown in a giant circle.

WEB LINK: ocean wind

In the narrow, land-constrained area of the Indian Ocean north of the Equator, the winds and weather, as well as the sea-surface currents, follow a seasonal pattern unique to this ocean. They are called monsoons, a word derived from the Arabic *mawsim,* meaning "season." During the Northern Hemisphere winter months, November through April, landmasses are cooled faster than the sea, and the wind blows steadily from land to sea from the northeast, forming the northeast monsoons. During the summer months there, the air over the hot landmasses rises, which pulls in moisture-laden winds that have blown across the ocean from the southwest. This southwest monsoon brings torrents of rain across India, Bangladesh, and Pakistan.

Other rhythms are also correlated with the monsoons. Twice a year, in the Northern Hemisphere's late spring and summer, outbreaks of cholera, one of mankind's most devastating diseases, soar in parts of Bangladesh and other coastal areas of the northern Indian Ocean. There is a direct correlation between seasonal warm water in the Bay of Bengal and the prevalence of cholera. It has taken scientists years to recognize that cholera is common in the waters of many coastal areas of the world, but the microbes become infectious only when conditions favor their rapid proliferation. A Bangledeshi scientist, K. M. S. Aziz, explained that increased water temperature accelerates the growth of tiny planktonic plants that provide food for minute animals—zooplankton such as copepods, barnacle larvae, and small shrimp—that harbor cholera bacteria, usually harmlessly. The southwest monsoons drive these plankton-rich waters into estuaries, where the bacteria contaminate local supplies of drinking water. Boiling drinking water kills cholera, but in Bangladesh firewood and other energy sources are in short supply. Rita Colwell, a microbiologist who has been tracking the mysteries of cholera for decades and who first identified marine zooplankton as a cause, has

Killer Cyclone

Major storm systems at sea fed by high temperature, high moisture, and inward-spiraling winds—spinning clockwise in the Northern Hemisphere and counterclockwise in the Southern—are called hurricanes in the Atlantic, typhoons in the Pacific, and cyclones in the Indian Ocean. On May 3, 2008, a killer cyclone named Nargis struck the mouth of the low-lying Irrawaddy River Delta in the country of Myanmar. The 3-meter-high storm surge rushed 40 kilometers inland, killing tens of thousands of people. One factor contributing to the destruction and death toll appears to be removal over the past half century of most of the mangrove forests (to create shrimp farms and rice paddies), which could have provided a natural barrier to some of the storm waters.

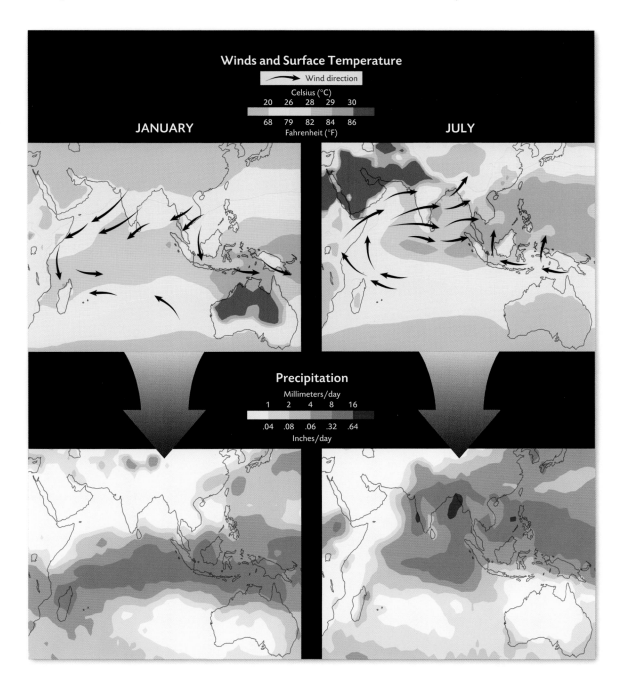

Monsoon Patterns: *The seasonally changing winds of the monsoon system blow back and forth over the northern part of the Indian Ocean, flowing from cold regions to warm. In the Northern Hemisphere winter, Asian land cools faster than the sea. The cool, dry land air sinks and flows to the sea in a large counterclockwise wind pattern. In the Northern Hemisphere summer, land heats more rapidly than the ocean. The hot air over India and nearby countries rises and is replaced by cooler, moister air moving clockwise up from the southern Indian Ocean. Water vapor in the rising air condenses forming clouds and rain, driving the monsoons across India, Bangladesh, and Pakistan.*

Diego Arcas
TSUNAMIS

On the morning of December 26, 2004, a massive seismic event took place along the Java Trench off the northern coast of Sumatra. The Indo-Australian tectonic plate slipped under the Eurasian plate, releasing stress accumulated over hundreds of years and generating the third largest earthquake ever recorded at a moment magnitude, $M_w = 9.1$. Devastation from the earthquake was widespread throughout the island of Sumatra, and reports of ground shaking came from places as remote as India to the west and Thailand to the east.

The enormity of the havoc wreaked by the earthquake was only to be dwarfed a few hours later, however, by the destruction brought to thousands of kilometers of coastline by the ensuing tsunami. The Sumatran earthquake caused an area approximately 1,200 kilometers long by 100 kilometers wide and lying 2,000 meters under the waters of the Indian Ocean to rise by an estimated 20 meters. This seismic dislocation resulted in the displacement of the ocean surface by a similar amount, and triggered a series of tsunami waves that propagated throughout all of the world's ocean, bringing destruction and death to almost every coastline of the Indian Ocean.

Tsunami waves differ from other more conventional waves in their size and travel speed. The dynamics governing their propagation throughout the ocean are also different from those of higher-frequency waves. Due to the large extent of the deformation undergone by the ocean surface during a tsunami-generating earthquake, the waves created are characterized by a very long wavelength when compared to the depth of the ocean they travel in. This peculiarity endows tsunami waves with a particular, and at times unintuitive, behavior.

The main difference in dynamics of long-period waves when compared with the more conventional wind-generated or shorter-period waves, is that the propagation speed of the wave fronts for long waves can accurately be determined by the depth of the water they travel in, via a simple relation: the square root of $g \times h$, where g is the acceleration of gravity and h is the ocean depth. This means that all wave frequencies present in a wavetrain travel at the same speed, as long as they "feel" the same ocean depth.

When waves exhibit this type of behavior in which wave speed does not depend on wave frequency, they are called "non-dispersive" waves. This is, however, not the case for shorter-period waves, whose

A new appreciation for the destructive power of tsunamis came with the advent of satellite imagery: **left top,** *a satellite image of Banda Aceh on June 23, 2004, before a massive tsunami struck;* **left bottom,** *a true-color satellite image of Banda Aceh along the northern border of the area after the tsunami, showing eroded shoreline, browned vegetation, and destruction of buildings.*

Scale varies in this perspective. Distance from northern Sumatra to Somalia is 4,830 kilometers.

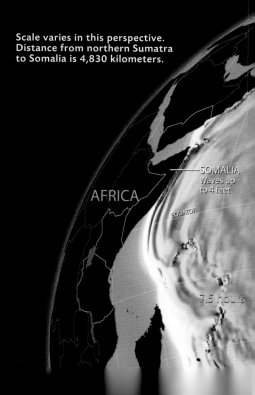

SOMALIA
Waves up to 4 feet

AFRICA

EQUATOR

7.5 hours

speed of propagation is dominated by their frequency and are known as "dispersive" waves.

Propagation of nondispersive waves does not conform to the intuitive and frequently observed circular pattern described by their dispersive counterparts. When a stone is dropped in a pond of stagnant water, dispersive waves travel out from the disturbance equally fast and equally far in all directions. In contrast, nondispersive tsunami waves exhibit a pronounced directionality, branching out from their source along preferred directions and focusing their energy along well-defined paths, while minimizing their wave height along other directions defined by the seafloor topography. Computation of this energy distribution pattern is crucial to tsunami forecasters, who can use this information to predict the preferred travel directions of a tsunami and identify coastal areas that are at higher risk of focusing the wave energy than others.

Tsunami warning centers use sophisticated wave propagation models in combination with real-time data reported by a network of 39 tsunami sensors called DART (Deep-Ocean Assessment and Reporting of Tsunamis), presently deployed in the Pacific, Indian, and Atlantic Oceans, to produce a forecast of tsunami wave amplitude and arrival time along the coastline. The DART stations are sophisticated devices positioned at strategic locations in the ocean and capable of reporting sea-level changes as small as 1 millimeter. Every 15 seconds the DART sensors monitor the sea surface for any unusual and potential tsunami-creating changes in elevation.

When a potential tsunami event is detected by one of the sensors, the information is transmitted via satellite to the Alaska and West Coast Tsunami Warning Center as well as the Pacific Tsunami Warning Center, which is currently also responsible for warning operations in the Indian Ocean. The warning centers then analyze and combine these deep-water sea-level data with seismic and coastal tide gauge observations to generate a tsunami forecast and to determine the level of alert that should be issued for different areas.

Unfortunately, no warning or alert system was deployed in the Indian Ocean on December 26, 2004, which resulted in massive loss of human life and property. Even knowing a few minutes before immanent danger can make the critical difference between life and death. Since the 2004 disaster, a great amount of effort and resources have been dedicated to expanding the operations of the warning centers to other oceans and to improving their capabilities in order to produce more precise and detailed forecasts. Public awareness and education of at-risk populations on tsunami hazard response and mitigation is another front where major efforts have been invested to ensure that no future tsunami results in the massive destruction brought to the shores of the Indian Ocean on that fateful Sunday morning.

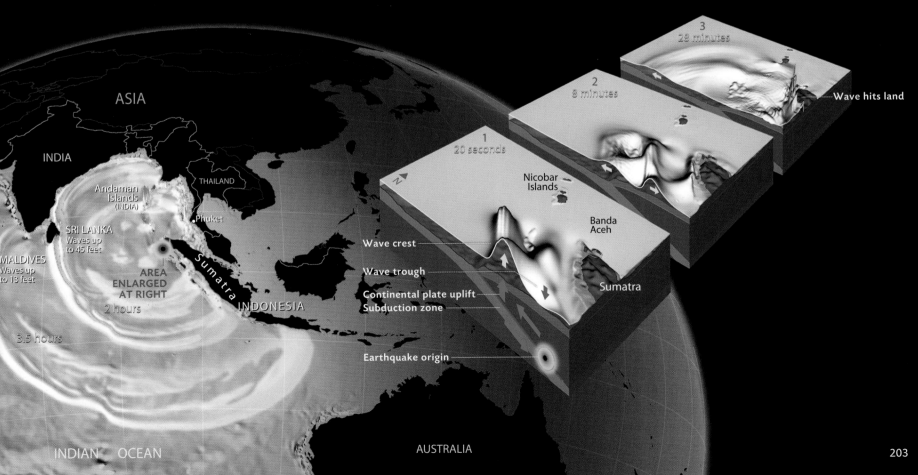

In the time series shown below, the tsunami's leading wave, just over half a meter tall, races west across the ocean at more than 800 km per hour. Barely noticeable while traveling, the wave attained enormous energy and surged to a height of about 15 meters when it hit shallow water.

Block 1 (20 seconds): A magnitude 8 earthquake lifts the seabed by nearly 5 meters and initiates the tsunami wave.

Block 2 (8 minutes): Energy pulses speed eastward toward the Sumatra coast and west across the open sea.

Block 3 (28 minutes): The giant wave gains height as it nears the coast and smashes into the shore.

ASIA

INDIA

THAILAND

Andaman Islands (INDIA)

Phuket

SRI LANKA
Waves up to 45 feet

MALDIVES
Waves up to 13 feet

AREA ENLARGED AT RIGHT

Sumatra

2 hours

INDONESIA

3.5 hours

INDIAN OCEAN

AUSTRALIA

1
20 seconds

2
8 minutes

3
28 minutes

Nicobar Islands

Banda Aceh

Sumatra

Wave hits land

Wave crest

Wave trough

Continental plate uplift

Subduction zone

Earthquake origin

SEE ALSO: human health and the ocean, page 307

shown how filtering contaminated water through layers of cloth (the same soft, light material used by the women for saris, their normal attire) can greatly reduce the risk of infection.

Indian Ocean Marine Life

WHEN NATURALIST DAVID ATTENBOROUGH described Madagascar as "a place where antique . . . forms of life that have long disappeared from the rest of the world still survive in isolation," he was referring mostly to the extraordinary life on land, but there are counterparts in the surrounding sea. Extensive coral reefs and coastal mangrove forests lace Madagascar's shores, and preliminary surveys of its surrounding waters reveal sufficiently unusual assemblages of plants and animals—of such diversity, character, and biological significance—that large marine areas have been designated for protection.

Using sight as well as sound to maneuver in the open waters of the Indian Ocean, a sperm whale, Physeter catodon, *is safe from commercial whaling. The Indian Ocean north of 55° S latitude was declared off limits to commercial whaling in 1979 by the International Whaling Commission, a ban that is now global.*

WHALES

The Indian Ocean was historically home to numerous kinds of toothed and baleen whales, from the small, dolphin-like minkes to the great blue whales, the largest creatures ever to live. Whalers from Europe, Russia, and America joined those from Indian Ocean countries in an era of comprehensive slaughter. By the latter half of the 20th century, the numbers of all the large species had declined to the point of biological collapse for the whales, and economic collapse for the whalers. Nonetheless, whaling continued out of South Africa, Australia, and several other countries. Although too late to save any intact social groups of whales, representatives from 16 Indian Ocean countries met in the Seychelle Islands in 1981 to organize a brilliant, if belated, plan to declare the entire Indian Ocean a sanctuary for whales, a concept that subsequently was adopted as policy and remains so today.

WEB LINK: whaling

GREAT WHITE SHARKS

Like coelacanths, great white sharks have close relatives in the fossil record from the distant past 300 million years ago. Although sharks swim in all oceans, the Indian Ocean is home year-round to large numbers of this predator of predators. In the southern winter, many great whites gather in a small area off the coast of South Africa near the Cape of Good Hope, where the warm Agulhas Current sweeping down

With the exception of humans, great white sharks, Carcharodon carcharias, *are regarded as the ocean's ultimate predator. Beautifully adapted for ranging thousands of kilometers, this great white eyes lunch in the Neptune Islands off southern Australia.*

the east coast of Africa meets and mixes with the cold Benguela Current, which flows up the west coast. The attraction for the sharks may simply be lunch, lots of it, in the form of thousands of young fur seals attracted by the abundance of small fish.

Although attacks on humans are rare, it is hard to dispel the perception, popularized in Peter Benchley's novel *Jaws,* that great whites are always on the lookout for a tasty primate. Despite the shark's aggressive reputation, Benchley and photographer David Doubilet teamed to document great whites at their winter gathering off the Cape of Good Hope and investigated a persistent rumor that these giants could be mesmerized by just the right kind of nose squeezing. Their guide Andre Hartman demonstrated his shark-charming technique by luring a great white to the side of the boat where Benchley and Doubilet sat. Benchley described what happened next in a *National Geographic* story: "There, in an instant, was the mouth, the most notorious mouth in nature. . . . Andre's hand cupped the snout, almost caressing it. . . . No one spoke. No one breathed . . . until Andre pulled his hand back . . . then—easily, gracefully—it half-slid, half-fell backward, [and] slipped beneath the surface."

Oblivious to its rarity, this hawksbill, Eretmochelys imbticata, *pauses on a reef for a jellyfish snack. Prized for their glossy shells, hawksbills, like other sea turtles, are endangered worldwide.*

GREEN TURTLES

In the western part of the Seychelles lies Aldabra, a volcanic island with a coral-and-mangrove-fringed lagoon about 64 kilometers long—a favored nesting place for green turtles. Reports from the late 1800s told of as many as 500 females coming ashore to lay eggs on one strip of sand there. Aldabra and its neighboring islands are thought to have had the greatest concentration of breeding turtles in the Indian Ocean in modern times, and perhaps in antiquity. Over the years, hundreds of thousands were taken for export to Europe and America in response to an insatiable market for turtle soup, turtle steaks, and turtle shells for decoration. By 1970, a careful inventory of nesting female turtles among all the Aldabran islands yielded fewer than a dozen.

CORAL REEFS

Although coral reefs are absent or poorly developed along the shores of Somalia, mainland India, and Malaysia, the clear and warm waters in most of the Indian Ocean provide the right setting for reef-building corals to prosper, some as atolls, some as fringing reefs, others forming barrier reefs. Shallow coral reefs, some of them spectacular in size, are common along the coasts of the Red Sea; the East African coasts of Kenya, Tanzania, and Sumatra; the coast of northwestern Australia;

WEB LINK: coral reefs

Tony Ribbink
WINDOWS TO THE PAST

Waters of the western Indian Ocean are home to a remarkable fish, the coelacanth, a strange, dark, steel-blue fish, one and a half meters long with luminous blue eyes. Almost 100 species were long known only from fossils of the Devonian geological period, about 360 million years ago, and all were thought to have become extinct about 65 million years ago, at about the time of the dinosaur extinctions. In 1938 a single specimen turned up alive and well in the net of a fishing trawler off the Chalumna River on the east coast of South Africa. It was named *Latimeria chalumnae* in honor of Marjorie Courtenay-Latimer, the young woman who recognized the fish as something out of the ordinary, saved what she could of it, and notified fish expert J. L. B. Smith about the discovery. Smith and his zoologist-artist wife, Margaret, spent years searching for another coelacanth and in 1952 were rewarded by news of one caught off Anjouan, one of the Comoro Islands.

More than a hundred live coelacanths—sometimes called old four legs, because their lobed fins suggest a primitive version of the arms and legs of land vertebrates—were later captured around the Comoros, believed to be the primary home for these living fossils. In 1990, a German expedition discovered and documented several living coelacanths sheltered within caverns at a sea-depth of 200 meters, along steep, undersea cliffs off the Comoros. Then, in 1998, zoologist Mark Erdmann and his bride, Arnaz Mehta, were walking through a fish market in Sulawesi, Indonesia, thousands of miles from the Comoros. Arnaz spotted what she knew right away was a coelacanth. Later, Erdmann swam eye-to-eye with a dying 30-kilogram, 1.2-meter-long coelacanth caught by fishermen and released for observation in shallow water. The Indonesian coelacanths have since been designated as a distinct species, but no one knows whether they or the east African animals are widespread or rare. Fewer than 400 animals have been found alive in recent decades, nearly all taken from deep water by fishermen or observed using submersibles.

More than 60 years after the original 1938 discovery off South Africa, divers pushing the limit of scuba observed and photographed several coelacanths at depths of more than 100 meters some 900 kilometers north of where the first specimen was captured. Research expeditions led by the African Coelacanth Ecosystem Program since 2002 have engaged hundreds of researchers, students, and public officials from nine countries and provided new insight into the ecology, distribution, and behavior of these ambassadors from ancient times as well as new oceanographic and geological data concerning the nature of environmental conditions over much of their known range in the western Indian Ocean.

However, many of the fundamental questions asked initially in the late 1930s—life history, breeding behavior, gestation period (the baseball-size eggs of coelacanths are fertilized internally, where the young grow until they are about 30 centimeters long before being born), where the young are born, whether parental care is practiced or whether the young hide until they are large enough to join adult groups—remain unanswered. The growth rate and longevity are imprecisely known. When, where, how often, and upon what coelacanths feed is known from scanty information for which conclusions are somewhat inferential.

Coelacanth research is continuing under the auspices of the Sustainable Seas Trust in the canyons and caves of Kenya, Tanzania, Mozambique, Madagascar, the Comoros, and South Africa. As such, the coelacanth has become an icon for conservation and a symbol of hope for the countries of the western Indian Ocean and also in Indonesia.

Although they were once protected by their inaccessibility, increasing fishing pressure by fishermen who venture into deeper water to set gill nets makes the future uncertain for these enduring relics of the Devonian period. A species that has remained essentially unchanged, surviving the extreme stresses for more than 65 million years, is now vulnerable to extinction owing to deep-water fishing. Trade in coelacanths is prohibited by the Convention on International Trade in Endangered Species (CITES), so these fish, mostly by-catch, are of little value to the coastal communities. Alive these ancient fish provide an enduring door to the past and a window to the future, inspiring us to forge a more harmonious relationship between ourselves and the rest of the living world.

One of more than 120 of the coelacanth species that prospered from 360 to 65 million years ago, the fish that made this fossil is believed to have lived in the sea 150 million years ago in what is now Germany.

"Old Four Legs" is the nickname given to the coelacanth, Latimeria Chalumnae, *by J. L. B. Smith, the ichthyologist who described the one captured in South African waters in 1938, 65 million years after they were believed to be extinct. The one shown here was discovered in the Comoro Islands in 1987.*

and around many of the Indian Ocean islands including Aldabra, Christmas Island, Madagascar, the Seychelles, and the Mascarenes. The diversity of coral species is relatively low in the reefs of the Persian Gulf owing to higher salinity and greater temperature swings than many species can tolerate. There are also more than 140,000 square kilometers of submerged reefs that do not reach the surface today and most likely were islands when sea level was lower a few thousand years ago. The Seychelles Bank alone extends over an area of more than about 43,000 square kilometers.

Submerged in the Mozambique Channel between Madagascar and Mozambique, a seamount rising from the seafloor more than 2,000 meters deep has a summit that comes to within 20 meters of the sea surface. Its sunlit coralline crown, known as Lazarus Reef, was observed during low-altitude flights by explorer and ecologist J. Michael Fay. "It's a jewel, " he said, "infinite shades of pale blue, turquoise and green, that seem to glow in stunning contrast against the blue-black of the deep water all around." In recent years, industrial trawling has scoured the top of the reef, but the steep sides presently retain much of their pristine nature.

Flashes of crimson mark a school of scalefin anthias, Pseudoanthias squamipinnis, *over Egyptian reefs in the Red Sea.*

Special Places of the Indian Ocean

THERE ARE SEVERAL LARGE SEAS along the margins of the Indian Ocean. In the northwest are the large Gulfs of Aden and Oman; in the northeast lies the Bay of Bengal; and to the southeast, the Great Australian Bight sculpts the western coast of Australia. To the north, the Red Sea and Persian Gulf are both semi-enclosed seas where salinity rises as a consequence of high evaporation and low rainfall. As their more saline, and thus denser, waters flow through the Arabian Sea, each watermass retains a distinctive temperature and salinity signature that can be tracked as far as the western coast of Indonesia and beyond.

THE RED SEA

The deep trough of the Red Sea is part of an active rift system—a seafloor spreading center that marks the beginnings of a new ocean. This spreading system also extends 5,600 kilometers to the southwest through the East African Rift Valley—seen on the map as a line of East African lakes—which are also early spreading centers working to form a new ocean. In a classic triple junction in seafloor spreading and plate tectonics, the Gulf of Aden angles off to the northeast from the southern end of the Red Sea in another branch of seafloor spreading. This ridge then angles southeast at the mouth of the Gulf of Aden and turns into the Carlsberg Ridge, where seafloor spreading was first proved.

The immense tectonic complexities of this region are demonstrated by the fact that another, smaller triple junction lies at the northern end of the Red Sea, where the Gulf of Suez, oriented toward the northwest, is slowly opening up, and the narrow Gulf of Aqaba is another incipient spreading center that angles toward the northeast, creating the depression filled by the Dead Sea.

Daniel J. Fornari and Timothy M. Shank

BIRTH OF AN OCEAN: THE RED SEA

Many times during Earth's history, continental landmasses have been pulled apart by forces operating in the mantle below. Evidence of continental rifting can be found today in many places, most notably in the Gulf of California off western Mexico, in the East African rift valleys, and in the Red Sea. Rifting events occur over relatively short geologic time spans of about 1 to 3 million years. They cause thinning of the continental crust and major cracks, known as faults, in the rocks to produce an incipient rift valley system. At times, the process moves only so far before the global push-and-pull of plate tectonic movements stops it. But if the process continues, magma rises into the rift from the mantle below causing eruption of basaltic lavas onto the rift floor. With continued spreading, the rift eventually breaks the thinned continental crust apart and new oceanic crust is created from the continued emplacement of gabbroic rocks at depth and basalts in the upper crust. Over time, the rift opens and a narrow gulf or sea forms.

The Red Sea is a prime example of recently rifted continental crust and a growing, young ocean basin. The long, narrow Red Sea formed about 3.5 to 5 million years ago. It is roughly 1,800 kilometers long and 250

Lake
Victoria

kilometers wide with an average depth of about 560 meters and maximum depth of 2,900 meters. Magnetic anomalies in the new seafloor crust indicate the spreading rate is about 1.5 centimeters per year—about half the average growth of a human fingernail.

Nearly 60 years ago, the Swedish vessel *Albatross* reported highly unusual measurements of seawater temperature and salinity in deep areas in the middle of the Red Sea, and from about 1960 to 1980, many expeditions investigated these unique "hot brine" settings and their metal-rich sediments. The Red Sea's central rift zone is now known to contain more than twenty deep places filled with very hot, very salty waters full of dissolved metals escaping from the mantle below. Four of these basins, named the Shaban, Kebrit, Atlantis II, and Discovery Deeps, have been sampled

and examined in some detail, with the young Atlantis II Deep, only 1.8 million years old and 2,200 meters deep, perhaps the best studied.

In contrast to most seafloor spreading areas with hydrothermal activity (where extremely hot waters full of dissolved metals and hydrogen sulfide escape up from the mantle, through the crust, and into the waters above), the Red Sea areas are more complex. The unique chemistry of fluids in the Red Sea's deep brine pools results not only from normal hydrothermal reactions of seawater with basalts, but is complicated by interactions with a thick layer of sediments full of salts from seawater that evaporated in the Miocene Epoch, more than 5 million years ago, that now underlies the entire Red Sea area. These salt-rich sediments are called evaporites.

Hydrothermal vents all along the global mid-ocean ridge system sustain unique communities of organisms that derive their sustenance from the unusual mix of chemicals released from beneath the seafloor. The evolutionary history of organisms unique to deep-sea hydrothermal vent areas is a matter of high scientific interest, including how the development of these strange communities is linked with the history of regional seafloor spreading, and how the development of such strange, but similar, communities could take place in areas along the mid-ocean ridge that are so geographically separated. Recent findings indicate that dozens of vent species evolved during the Miocene Epoch, and we now believe that the Red Sea and Gulf of Aden—as part of the ancient Tethys Sea—may have been key conduits during the late Miocene for the spread of these organisms along different parts of the global mid-ocean ridge.

Observations from shallow submersible dives by the Russians in 1979-1980 near the Red Sea deeps revealed an abundance of animals including bivalves, crabs, shrimp, amphipods, and eel-like fish. But over the past 25 years, because of political problems in gaining international scientific access to the Red Sea, there has been little progress in studying these sites with modern oceanographic methods and deep submergence technologies. A joint expedition between Saudi and American investigators at the Woods Hole Oceanographic Institution in the fall of 2008 will study the water characteristics and water circulation patterns in the Red Sea and will try to locate, sample, and photograph hydrothermal vent communities in Red Sea hot brine environments. It is hoped that these studies will shed light on the relationships of Red Sea vent fauna with the global biogeography of hydrothermal vent fauna along the mid-ocean ridge.

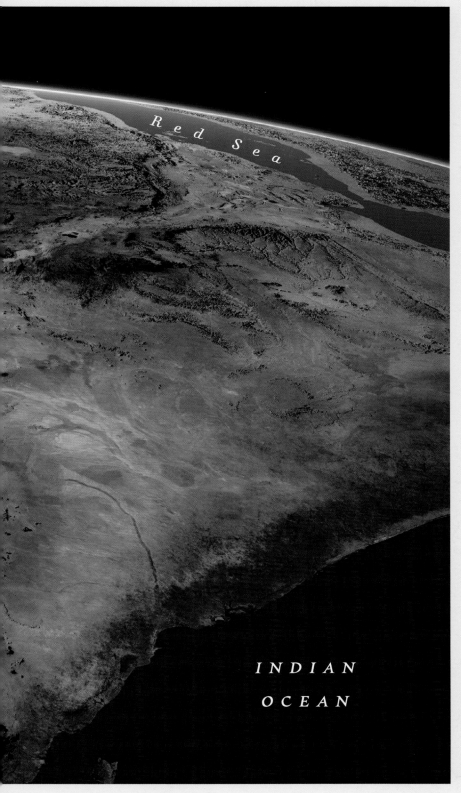

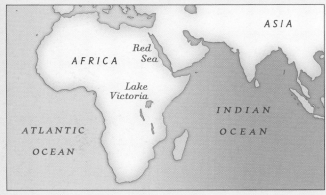

Lake Victoria appears as a dark blue oval east of a line of lakes that have filled the breach in Earth's crust as the continent slowly splits along the East African Rift Valley.

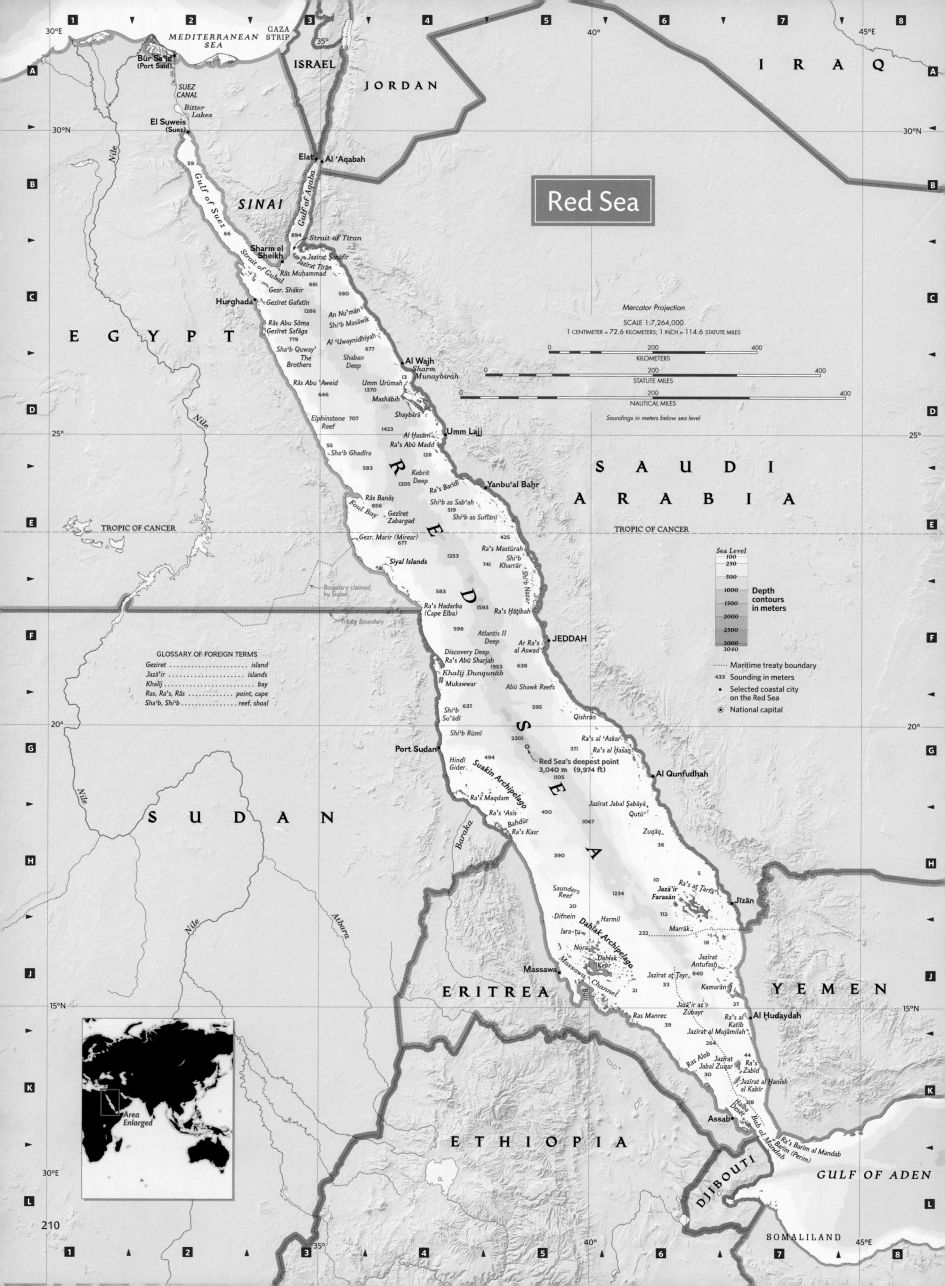

The Red Sea is thus actually an ocean—a very young but growing one—that could in 150 million years or so rival the Atlantic. Born of the divergence about 35 million years ago when Arabia began to break away from Africa, this deep, narrow blue gash in the desert should properly be regarded as a continuation of the Mid-Ocean Ridge, a place where Earth's deep lava spills forth, gradually adding inches to the width of the seafloor.

About a kilometer and a half down in the Red Sea the temperature can be a balmy 22°C and even warmer near deep thermal springs of hot, supersaline, mineral-laden brine. In the 1960s, scientists from the Woods Hole Oceanographic Institution discovered rich deposits of iron, manganese, zinc, and copper—some as much as 90 meters thick—more than 1,800 meters underwater in places that are rich in hydrogen sulfide and low in oxygen. The commercial potential of the Red Sea's deep, metal-rich muds has sparked considerable interest, but economically feasible techniques for extraction remain elusive.

As valuable as the deep muds may be, some regard the Red Sea's coral reefs, glittering fish, and violet blue waters as the region's greatest treasures. In *Lady with a Spear,* marine biologist Eugenie Clark shared a glimpse of what she experienced there:

Near the end of summer, steady winds from the southwest drive an upwelling of deep water nutrients to the surface, nourishing blooms of plankton along the coast of Oman, shown here in satellite images of the area.

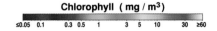

> *At one moment I stood on the hot sands of the barren desert; the next moment I found myself in one of the most beautiful places I have ever seen . . . a submarine coral garden of brilliant colors and teeming with life . . . corals of the most graceful, delicate, and unusual forms. Some grew like clusters of pink and lavender flowers. . . . And you could see a thousand fishes at a glance.*

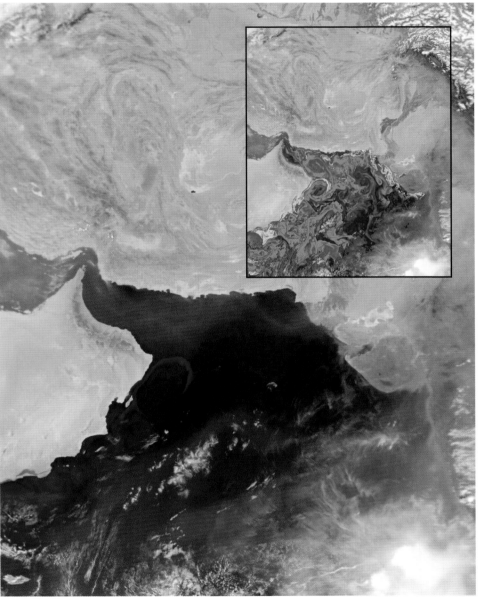

PERSIAN GULF

Formed at the mouth of the Tigris and Euphrates Rivers, the Persian Gulf has a rich human heritage, a focal point in the lives of people since the early Stone Age, more than half a million years ago. At the height of the last global ice age 18,000 years ago, sea level was significantly lower than at present, the climate was much wetter, and the Persian Gulf was lush with freshwater marshes fed by river waters as they meandered toward the Strait of Hormuz and into the Indian Ocean. Hippopotamuses, lions, elephants, zebras, and other large animals thrived. As the climate changed and sea level rose, deserts displaced the fertile landscapes, and salt water flooded the gulf from the Indian Ocean. With the encroaching sea came the ingredients that made possible a new kind of ocean "fertility"—meadows of sea grasses and algae that provided food and shelter for dugong, sea turtles, corals, and other tropical marine creatures.

People also prospered, despite increasing desertification. Under the dunes, the peculiarities of Arabian geology trapped not only oil but also great quantities of water. Aquifers formed over thousands of years, holding priceless but nonrenewable "fossil water" that is tapped today to provide a critical resource to the region's growing human population. When huge oil and gas reserves were found in the gulf and later on the Arabian mainland in the 1930s, the discoveries set in motion the quest for—and the source of—unprecedented modern wealth for several nations. ☐

WEB LINK: natural resources of the Persian Gulf

Persian Gulf

GLOSSARY OF FOREIGN TERMS

Bandar	anchorage, port
Dawḥat	bay, cove, inlet
Damāgheh	cape
Fasht	shoal, bank, reef
Ḥayr, Ruqq	shoal
Jazāʾir, Jazīrat, Jazīreh	island
Jūn	bay
Kasr	reef
Khalīj	bay, gulf
Khawr, Khowr	bay, channel, inlet
Mīnāʾ	port
Raʾs	point, cape

Depth contours in meters

Sea Level
100
250
500
1000
1500
2000
2500
3000
3500

.... Maritime treaty boundary
62 Sounding in meters
• Selected coastal city on the Persian Gulf
✪ National capital

IRAN

Sheyū
Khalīj-e Nakhīlū
Bandar-e Maqām
Khowr-e Nakhīlū
Raʾs-e Nakhīlū
eh-ye Lāvān
Jazīreh-ye Shatvar
Bandar-e Chārak
Jazīreh-ye Hendorābī
Sar-e Chīrū
Khowr-e Māsheh
Charak Bay
Raʾs-e Yarīd
Raʾs-e Shāvar
Sambarūn Bank
Khalīj-e Moghūyeh
Khowr-e Kish
Bandar-e Lengeh
Jazīreh-ye Kīsh
Stiffe Bank
Raʾs-e Shenās
Khalīj-e Shenās
North Bank
Basa ʿĪdū
Raʾs-e Dastakān
The Flat
Forūr Shoal
Jazīreh-ye Forūr
Mariner Shoal
Coote Rock
Greater Tunb
Lesser Tunb
Jazīreh-ye Banī Forūr
The Tunb Islands are administered by Iran; claimed by U.A.E.

Bandar-e ʿAbbās
Bandargāh-e Bandar ʿAbbās
Torʾeh-ye Khvorān (Clarence Strait)
Bandar-e Khoemir
Qeshm
Jazīreh-ye Hormoz
Jazīreh-ye Lārak
Tyab
JAZĪREH-YE QESHM
Bandar-e Sūzā
Torʾeh-ye Khvorān
Jazīreh-ye Hengām
Patrick Stewart Bank
Maundrell Shoal
Strait of Hormuz
Ṭāhrūʾī
As Salāmah
Ennerdale Rock
As Salāmah wa Banātuhā
Dīdāmar
Persian Gulf's deepest point 119 m (344 ft)
Jazīrat Umm al Ghanam
Raʾs Musandam
Kumzār
Raʾs Qabr al Hindī
SHIBH JAZĪRAT MUSANDAM
Raʾs Khayseh
Khaṣab
Jazīrat Umm al Fayyārīn
Raʾs Shaykh Masʿūd
Raʾs Dillah
Khawr Ḥabalayn
Ash Shaʾm
Raʾs Sarkān
Raʾs-e Shīr

GULF

Sīrrī
Abu Musa
Abu Musa is claimed by Iran and U.A.E. and jointly administered by them.
Khawr al Khuwayr
Līmā
Raʾs Līmāʾ
OMAN
Khawr Ḥulaylān
Raʾs-e Shīr
Raʾs Ḥaffah
GREAT PEARL BANK
Raʾs-al-Khaimah
Mīnāʾ Saqr
Jazīrat al Ḥamrāʾ
Khawr al Madfaq
Jazīrat as Siniyah
Bayʿah
Dawḥat Dibā
Umm al-Qaiwain
Khawr al Baydah
Dibā
Raʾs Dibā
Nadd Manīʿ
Khawr Jufrah
Dadnā
Şīr Bū Nuʿayr
Al Ḥamrīyah
Jazīrat Zawrah
Palm Deira (under construction)
Khawr Zawrah
Khawr ʿAjman
MADHA Oman
Sharjah (Ash Shāriqah)
Khawr Fakkān
The World (under construction)
Khawr ash Shāriqah
Khawr Fakkān
DUBAI
NAHWA U.A.E.
Al Fujairah
Palm Jumeirah
Kalbā
Palm Jebel Ali
Jabal Alī
Mīnāʾ Jabal Alī
RUQQ ʿAZ ZUKUM
Raʾs Ḥaṣyān
Jazīrat aṭ Ṭawīlah
Raʾs Ḥanyūrah
Khawr Ghanāḍah
Ḥadd aṭ Ṭallah
Jazīrat Raʾs Ghurāb
Dawḥat Hanyurah
Raʾs al Ghurāb
As Saʿdīyat
Jazīrat Ḥayl
Jazīrat Abū Ẓaby
Khawr Faridah
Al Fuʿayt
Khawr Fahid
ABU DHABI
Ṭīnah
Khawr al Baṭīn
Mubarraz
Jazīrat Marawwaḥ
Ḥālat al Hayl
Raʾs Bū Kuskayshah
Khawr Qirqishān
Janānah
Şalāḥah
Qaşşabī
Jazīrat ar Rafīq
Abū al Abyaḍ
Bandar Maria
Khawr al Mughayrā
Ṭarīf
Al Mughayrā

Ḥālat al Bahrānī
Bū Kuskayshah

ARAB EMIRATES

OMAN

GULF OF OMAN

Khowr-e Mobārak
Damāgheh-ye Kūh
Jāsk
Mason Shoal
Khalīj-e Sharqī-ye Jāsk
Raʾs Jagīn
Damāgheh-ye Meydānī
Ra's al Hijārī
Ra's Şallān
Ra's Suwādī
Jazāʾir Daymānīyāt
Ghubbat al Ḥayl
Jazīrat al Faḥl
Raʾs Masqaṭ

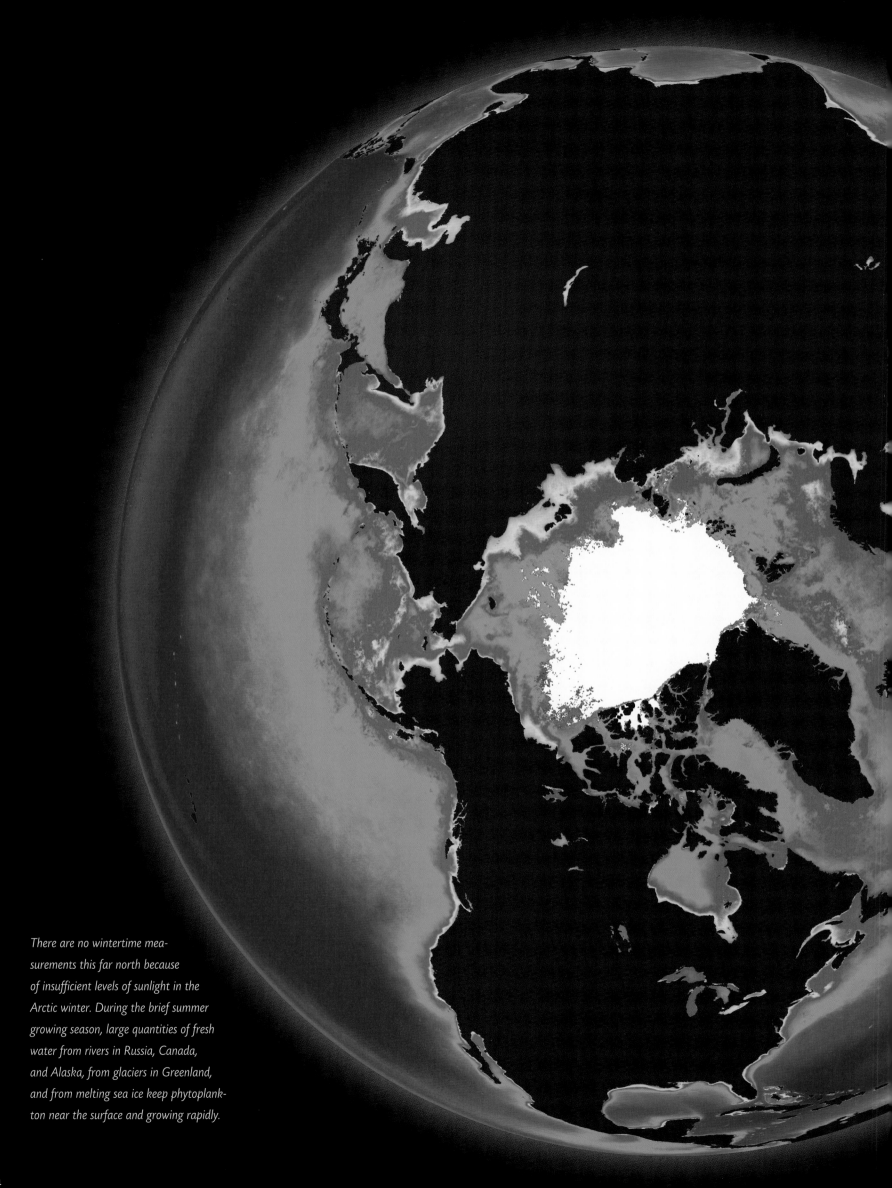

There are no wintertime measurements this far north because of insufficient levels of sunlight in the Arctic winter. During the brief summer growing season, large quantities of fresh water from rivers in Russia, Canada, and Alaska, from glaciers in Greenland, and from melting sea ice keep phytoplankton near the surface and growing rapidly.

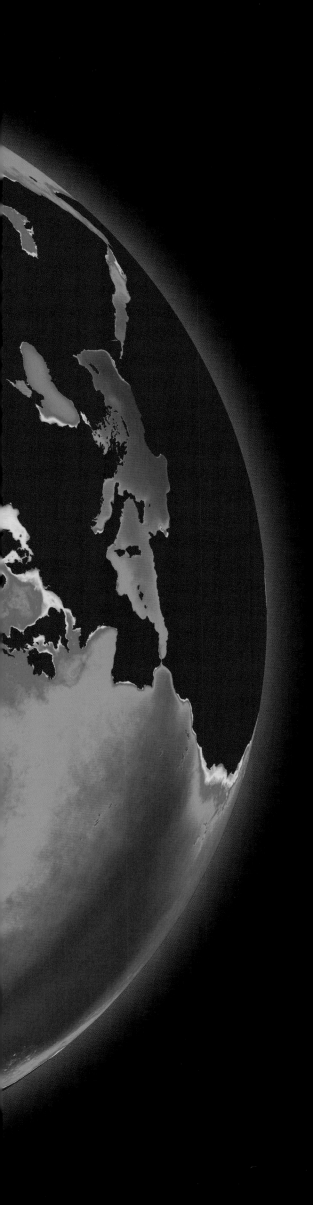

Chapter 7

ARCTIC OCEAN

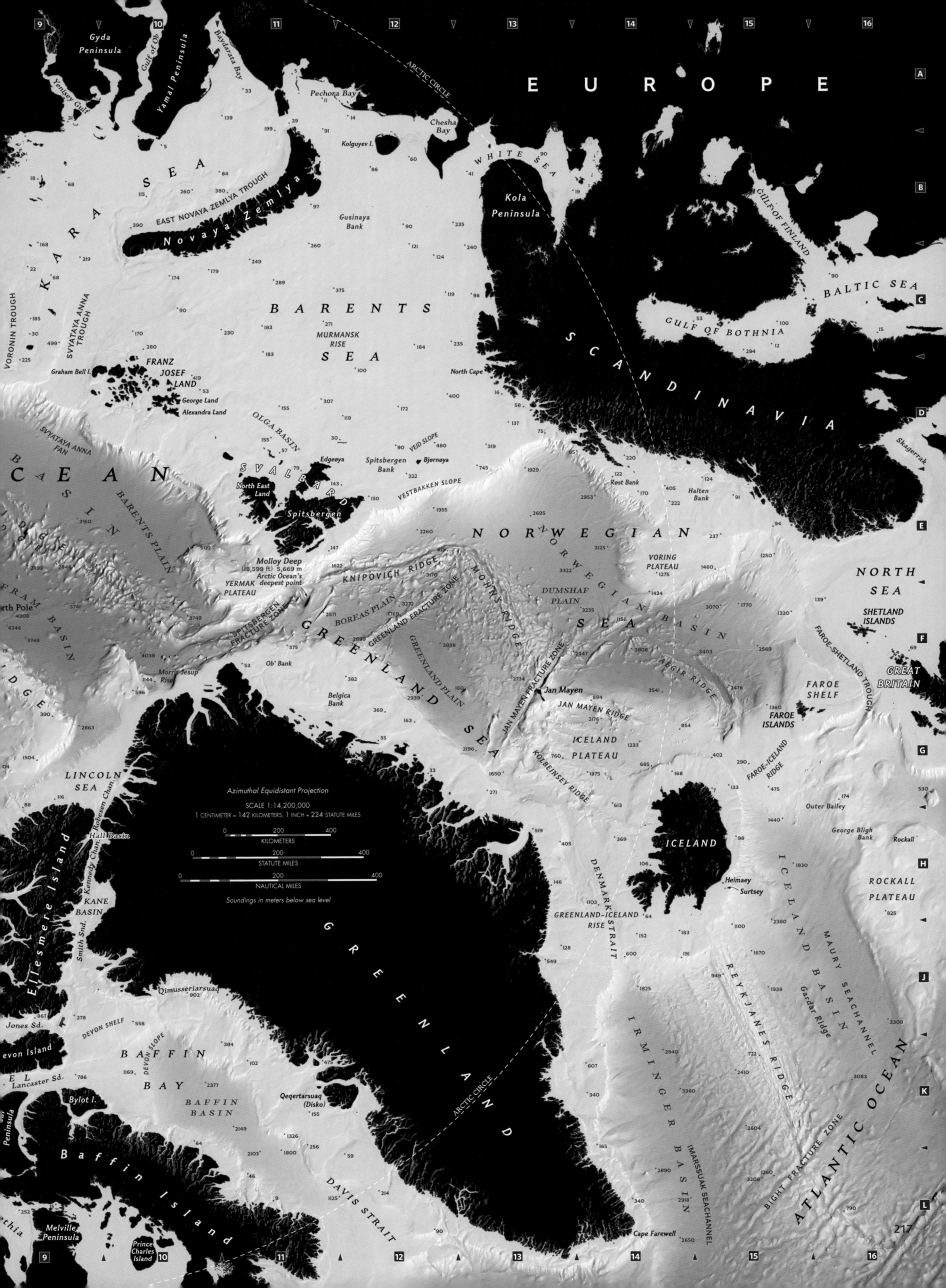

A

SEA OF
OKHOTSK

B

Buor-Khaya Bay

Gulf of Yana

BOL'SHOY
BEGICHEV I.

Russk

LAPTEV SEA

Cape Chelyuskin

NORTH LA

C

RUSSIA

35

LYAKHOV IS.

1399

Bol'shevik
Island

October Revolution
Island

Komsomolets
Island

N

2879

Karaginskiy
Island

ANJOU ISLANDS

15

60

A

N
S
E
N

Sea Level
100
250
500
1000
1500
2000
2500
3000
3500
4000
4500
5000
5500
5669

Depth
contours
in meters

268 Sounding in meters

D

SHIRSHOV RIDGE

Bear Is.
13

NEW SIBERIAN ISLANDS

Bennett I.

Zhokhova

3449

N
A
N
S
E
N

P
O
L
E

P
L
A
I
N

Henrietta I.
Jeannette I.

1900

A   R   C   T   I   C

E

B
E
R
I
N
G

9
Ayon I.
Chaun Bay

29

77

WRANGEL
PLAIN
2830

3130

L
O
M
O
N
O
S

EAST SIBERIAN SEA

MAKAROV BASIN

F

Gulf of
Anadyr

11

53

2070

MENDELEYEV   RIDGE

2487

WRANGEL
ISLAND

SARGO
PLATEAU

CHUKCHI
PLAIN 2242

MENDELEYEV PLAIN

S
E
A

St. Matthew Island
Alaska

CHUKCHI
SEA

48

CHUKCHI
PLATEAU
268

2653

3879

1047

MARVIN SPUR

ALPHA CORDILLERA

G

ST. LAWRENCE
ISLAND
Alaska

40

Mys Dezhneva (East Cape)

NORTHWIND PLAIN

North Magnetic Pole
3700   2009 ✳

Cape Prince of Wales

Bering Strait

Point Hope

NORTHWIND RIDGE

3819

620

22 Kotzebue Sound

Cape Lisburne

NORTHWIND ESCARPMENT

NUNIVAK
ISLAND

Norton
Sound

Point
Barrow

CANADA PLAIN

Peary Chan.

Helb
Isl

H

BARROW
CANYON
3990

C
A
N
A
D
A
   B
A
S
I
N

Borden
Island

Prince
Gustaf
Adolf Sea

647

SVERDRU

2305

Ballantyne Str.

Ellef
Ringnes
Island

ISLAND

B
E
A
U
F
O
R
T

S
L
O
P
E

29

Prince
Patrick
Island

Mackenzie
King I.
Hazen
Str.

Belcher
Channel

BEAUFORT
SHELF

3530

Borden
ALASKA
United States

371

QUEEN ELIZABETH I

M'Clure Strait

Melville Island

545

PARRY ISLANDS

J

913

MACKENZIE
TROUGH

BEAUFORT
SEA

Banks Island

46

488

Bathurst
Island

P   A   R   R   Y

Cornwalls

Viscount Melville Sound

C   H   A

ALASKA PENINSULA

Amundsen Gulf

K

Kodiak
Island

356

M'Clintock Channel

Somers
Island

GULF OF ALASKA

Prince
of Wales
Island

Gulf

Victoria
Island

L

PACIFIC
OCEAN

CANADA

223

Boothia
Peninsula

218

101

King
William
Island

Arctic Ocean
Sea-surface
Temperature

ASIA

ARCTIC CIRCLE

60°N

70°N

80°N

80°N

70°N

North

North Magnetic Pole ✳
2009

ARCTIC CIRCLE

NORTH AMER

140°E

130°E

120°E

110°E

100°E

150°E

160°E

170°E

180°

170°W

160°W

150°W

140°W

130°W

120°W

110°W

100°W

60°N

EUROPE

Azimuthal Equidistant Projection

SCALE 1:14,200,000

1 CENTIMETER = 142 KILOMETERS; 1 INCH = 224 STATUTE MILES

KILOMETERS

STATUTE MILES

NAUTICAL MILES

Soundings in meters below sea level

March 2008 (winter)

Degrees Celsius

-1 0   3   6   9   12

Ice

-30.2 32   37.4   42.8   48.2   53.6

Degrees Fahrenheit

*Floating lumps of ice provide this polar
bear a place to rest between long swims
in the Arctic Ocean.*

The Arctic Ocean by the Numbers

(excludes major seas of North Asia
and North America)

Geographic boundaries: 66°33' N to
90° N / circumpolar

Total area: 8,676,520 square kilometers

Total volume: 16,787,461 cubic
kilometers

Average depth: 990 meters

Greatest depth: 5,669 meters
(Molloy Deep)

• The smallest ocean includes 3 percent
of the Earth's water area.

• Produces up to 50,000 icebergs
per year.

"On a frigid afternoon in May, I slipped through a crack in the sea ice and dropped into the Arctic Ocean. . . . At one point I looked back up at the ice, expecting it to appear as it most often does . . . blue, featureless, lifeless. But . . . it moved. . . . I was watching a massive cloud of amphipods, tiny shrimplike crustaceans, as they fed on phytoplankton that grow on the underside of the ice. . . . I was seeing the foundation of the ecosystem . . . upon which all the bigger animals—polar bears, whales, birds and seals—depend."

—Paul Nicklen, "Life at the Edge," *National Geographic*

T he top of the world gleams starkly white with a crown of frozen water drifting slowly around the surface of the Arctic, the Earth's smallest ocean. Essentially landlocked, the Arctic Ocean is surrounded by the northernmost reaches of Canada, Greenland, Russia, Norway, and the United States. It is connected with the Pacific Ocean by the narrow Bering Strait, and with the Atlantic along the coasts of Greenland through the Davis and Denmark Straits. The deepest place found so far is 5,669 meters, but because of the unusually broad continental shelf areas surrounding the Arctic, the average depth is only about 990 meters, much shallower than all the other oceans. At the North Pole, continuous light or darkness lasts up to six months each year.

WEB LINK: Arctic animations

Some define the Arctic as the high-latitude region where the average daily summer temperature does not rise above 10°C; others regard the Arctic as the area north of the tree line, the limit of upright tree growth. Geographically, the Arctic is defined as the area within the Arctic Circle, north of latitude 66° 33' N. North of this boundary, the sun does not rise above the horizon on the winter solstice, about December 21, or set on the summer solstice, about June 21. Small changes in the tilt of the Earth cause even the delineations known as the Arctic and Antarctic Circles to change. Every 40,000 years or so, they gradually move north or south about 300 kilometers.

Defining the magnetic poles—the north and south points around which the Earth's magnetic field or magnetosphere is arranged—is also tricky. Since the Earth is not really quite round, its magnetic field is irregular. As a result, the magnetic poles are offset more than 1,600 kilometers from the geographic poles. The needle on a compass does not point to "true geographic north," and it also is not fully controlled by the magnetic pole. The needle points in a direction influenced by the combined magnetic effects of all parts of the Earth. To find the geographic poles using a compass, it is necessary to factor in a magnetic variation, which differs based on your position on the globe.

The Arctic Ocean is a place connected to people from several countries, where humankind and wildlife have interacted and flourished for at least 5,000 years, probably much longer. Explorer Barry Lopez says, the Arctic "is organized like Australia, around an inland desert sea, with most of its people living on its coastal periphery. . . . It has the heft, say, of China, but with the population of Seattle." Lopez observes that the familiar Mercator projection used for many maps gives a misleading perception of the Arctic, which on paper appears to stretch from one edge of the world to the other, as wide as the Equator. It is possible at the North Pole, however, literally to dance in a circle around the world, in a few steps moving through all longitudes and all 24 of the world's time zones.

Dim summer light enables diatoms to flourish on the underside of Arctic sea ice and swarms of amphipods flourish by consuming them.

Not until the end of the 19th century was it confirmed that an ocean, not land, underlies the high Arctic. Even now, the region remains largely unknown, unexplored, a tantalizing goal for those seeking a wealth of new scientific discoveries, as well as those hoping for tangible bounty in terms of minerals, oil, gas, and populations of fish and other marine wildlife heretofore protected by their inaccessibility. However, as concerns grow about the profound consequences of accelerated global

warming and climate change, the greatest value of the Arctic may prove to be its role as the planet's primary regulator of temperature, its cool presence critical to maintaining the nature of the Earth as a place hospitable for humankind.

Formation of the Arctic Ocean

SEE ALSO: global mid-ocean ridge, page 30

ABOUT 66 MILLION YEARS AGO the Arctic's present mid-ocean spreading ridge, called the Nansen (or Gakkel) Ridge, formed beneath a part of the Eurasian continent. As magma flowed up and out from this new rift zone, forming new ocean crust, a large fragment of the ancient continent split off from what is now the continental shelf of Russia under the Kara and Barents Seas. As it was rafted away from the continent by seafloor spreading, this continental fragment, known as the Lomonosov Ridge, sank deeper beneath the water toward its current location under the North Pole.

Mapping and sampling of the Arctic seafloor is expensive, difficult, time-consuming, and sometimes dangerous, because of the constant ice cover. Expeditions in recent years have focused on the Nansen spreading ridge and have made surprising discoveries there. But the basics about formation of Arctic seafloor on the side closer to the Pacific are still mostly a mystery.

Mid-Ocean Ridge and Hydrothermal Vents

WEB LINK: Arctic mapping and imaging

THE MID-ATLANTIC RIDGE SPLITS through the middle of Iceland, is offset through several major fracture zones, continues north as Mohns Ridge toward the Arctic Basin, and connects with the Nansen (Gakkel) Ridge, the deepest and slowest-spreading ridge in the world ocean. The Nansen spreading ridge is 3 to 5 kilometers deep and stretches in a straight line for 1,800 kilometers across the Arctic Ocean from the Greenland Sea north of the Atlantic to the Laptev Sea midway along the northern coast of Russia. The rate of spreading and creation of new seafloor has been calculated to be 1 centimeter per year, about 20 times slower than spreading at the East Pacific Rise.

Many predicted there would be little or no volcanic activity along the Nansen Ridge. That changed in 2001 when rocks were dredged up by the U.S. Coast Guard cutter *Healy* and the German research icebreaker *Polarstern* during the nine-week Arctic Mid-Ocean Ridge Expedition (AMORE), designed to study how the Earth's oceanic crust forms. The first sampling station brought up fresh volcanic rock, and high-resolution maps obtained during the expedition revealed large, young volcanoes dominating the end of the ridge nearest Greenland.

University of Texas geologist Hedy Edmonds and her colleagues attached a device to the cable of a rock sampler to record temperature and sense the presence of distinctive chemicals associated with hydrothermal activity. Nine hydrothermal vent sites and three additional likely vent areas were identified, provoking Edmonds to comment, "I never in my wildest dreams thought we would see the extent of activity we saw in the Arctic Ocean."

A 2003 *Geophysical Research Abstracts* report noted, "For this slowest-spreading mid-ocean ridge, (MOR), predictions were that magmatism and crustal thickness should progressively diminish as the spreading rate decreases progressively eastward along the ridge and that hydrothermal activity should be rare. Instead, magmatic variations are irregular and hydrothermal activity is abundant."

Chief scientist for AMORE, Peter Michael, from the University of Tulsa, summed up the importance of exploration in the Arctic and beyond in 2003: "What we found could not be extrapolated from decades of previous studies of the ocean ridge system. It shows that there is still much to be discovered from exploratory science, and testing hypotheses in new regions. Discovery often happens when we put ourselves in conditions where we are likely to be surprised."

In 2005, an international team of scientists used a remotely operated vehicle to explore, document, and sample the nature of hydrothermal vents at 71° N, north of Iceland, along the Mohns

Where's the Spreading Ridge?

Maps of the Arctic seafloor show three huge mountain ranges coursing across it. The Lomonosov Ridge cuts right through the middle of the Arctic Basin, but it isn't the Arctic's mid-ocean ridge, because it isn't part of the nearly continuous, globe-encircling spine of seafloor spreading ridges. The Arctic's spreading center, Nansen (or Gakkel) Ridge, is offset far over toward Europe and Russia. So where did the Lomonosov Ridge come from? It is an old mountain range that used to be above water, but was separated from the Eurasian continent, moved north, and gradually sank through millions of years of seafloor spreading along the Nansen Ridge.

Ridge between northern Greenland and Norway. "There were huge numbers of chimneys . . . 50 or more," commented Rolf Pedersen of the University of Bergen. Temperatures in one field reached as high as 260°C, but life—shrimp, anemones and bacterial mats, and a type of tube worm, perhaps related to those known from Pacific vent systems—abounds nearby. Adam Schultz, a geophysicist from Oregon State University, noted the presence of a vast low-temperature vent field as well. Schultz said that "the fluids coming out of these vents come out at temperatures only a fraction of a degree above the temperature of the background seawater and that is very cold—below zero Celsius—which is only possible in the Arctic." These cold vent fields also support diverse communities of life, including large sea lilies that, according to Schultz "sit atop mineral/bacterial chimney-like structures that look . . . like pineapples."

A multinational expedition in 2007 led by geophysicist Robert Reves-Sohn from Woods Hole Oceanographic Institution focused on obtaining additional data, samples, and images from Nansen Ridge's deep vents using three newly designed autonomous underwater vehicles. Because Nansen Ridge has been isolated from other ecosystems for millions of years, research almost certainly will include discovery of many unique organisms and new insights into geological processes.

The Seafloor

THE FLOOR OF THE ARCTIC OCEAN is subdivided by three great ridges that run almost parallel to one another like long, bony fingers across the top of the Earth between Greenland and Siberia.

Starting nearest to the Eurasian coast, north of the high Arctic islands of Spitsbergen and Franz Josef Land, is the actively spreading Nansen (Gekkel) Ridge, with the

A giant sun star ambles over crustose coralline algae and anemones on this submerged rock in the Arctic.

Nansen Basin lying between it and the islands. On Nansen Ridge's other flank, toward the Pole, lies the Fram Basin. On the other side of the Fram Basin, and running almost directly under the North Pole, is the 1,800-kilometer-long Lomonosov Ridge, a submerged mountain range that rises an average of 3,050 meters above the seafloor and in places comes to within 800 meters of the surface. On the other flank of this great ridge lie the Wrangel Plain, the Fletcher Plain, and the Makarov Basin. Closer to the Pacific side of the Arctic, the Alpha Cordillera and Mendeleyev Ridge run in a curved but almost continuous line from northern Canada to East Siberia. Between this underwater mountain range and the lands of Canada, Alaska, and East Siberia lies a complex topography that includes the Mendeleyev Plain, the Chukchi Plain, and the large Canada Basin, a broad, sweeping abyssal plain with an average depth of 3,660 meters.

The deepest point on the Arctic seafloor is the Molloy Deep. Lying along the Molloy transform fault, west of Spitsbergen, the small basin drops to a depth of 5,669 meters.

Seamounts and Islands

LITTLE IS KNOWN ABOUT SEAMOUNTS on the floor of the deep Arctic. This is partly because most seamount locations in the world ocean are actually predicted from satellite altimetry data showing

Peter Vogt
GEOLOGY OF THE ARCTIC OCEAN

The Arctic Ocean seafloor, like the rest of the world ocean, can be readily divided into a hard crust and a softer blanket of sediments lying above it that have drifted down from surface waters or avalanched down through underwater canyons from the continental margins. All margins of the Arctic shallower than 1,000 meters, except those around Iceland, are underlain by ancient, complex continental crust up to 30 kilometers thick. In deeper waters and around Iceland, the crust is oceanic in nature—topped by dark, iron- and magnesium-rich volcanic basalt.

Although typical ocean crust is 7 kilometers thick, the Arctic offers a wild range of thicknesses—from 25 kilometers or more under the Greenland-Iceland-Faroe Ridge and the mysterious but probably similar Alpha-Mendeleev Ridge, to no crust at all along the very slowly spreading Nansen (Gakkel) Ridge where the viscous mantle itself oozes up to the seafloor in places. The current boundaries of the Arctic tectonic plate range from 1,000 meters above sea level in Iceland to almost 5,700 meters deep along parts of the Nansen Ridge, and the Arctic hosts oceanic crust ranging in age from 130 million years old under the Canada Basin to brand new, just forming, along the Nansen Ridge.

Apart from its iciness, the marine Arctic stands out as unusual. First, fully half the area of the Arctic Basin is made up of shallow continental shelves, many exposed by low glacial-age sea levels. There are also three "microcontinents"—small pieces of continental crust separated from their original continents by seafloor spreading long ago, lying under Arctic waters. The 1,800-kilometer-long Lomonosov Ridge was split away from Eurasia starting 66 million years ago to mark the birth of the Eurasia Basin; the Jan Mayen Ridge split away from west Greenland 35 million years ago; and the Chukchi Plateau was separated from Canada by a seafloor spreading process that is no longer active. The Arctic also holds three "abandoned" spreading ridges—places where new seafloor was being created, but the spreading has stopped long ago. The extinct Aegir Ridge in the Norway Basin stopped spreading 25 million years ago; the Mid-Labrador Sea Ridge, which died 40 million years ago, left the Greenland plate closely connected to the North American; and an unnamed extinct ridge now buried under the Canada Basin long ago separated northern Alaska from Canada.

The Arctic's Nansen (Gekkel) Ridge is the planet's slowest spreading center, imaged here by the University of New Hampshire's Center for Coastal and Ocean Mapping with a new data compilation from the International Bathymetric Chart of the Arctic Ocean.

Sediments lying on the Arctic seafloor hold a record of ancient Arctic environments, and because the enclosed Arctic Basin surrounding the North Pole has long been sensitive to climate change, scientists are eager to read this "diary." Sampling these records requires lowering core pipes into the seafloor sediments from research ships with icebreaking hulls. Scientists then study the layers of sediment—a mix of glacial detritus melted from floating ice above, and the tiny skeletons of planktonic creatures that drifted in the near-surface waters of the Arctic in ages past. The species of plankton, and the composition of their skeletons, provide an accurate measure of temperature and salinity in the surface waters at the time they lived, and studying each layer buried through time provides a climate history.

Finding good cores with an undisturbed climate record can be a challenge, though. In the deep, flat-floored Arctic basins, we find thick accumulations of turbidites, layers of sediment scattered across the seafloor by underwater avalanches of material from nearby continental margins—up to 10 kilometers thick off the mouth of the Mackenzie River delta. Such sediments provide too disturbed a record to be used for climate history. An international icebreaker expedition in 2004 collected a core of undisturbed sediments 428 meters deep on top of the Lomonosov Ridge, recovering a reasonably continuous record of Arctic climate changes over the past 56 million years.

The story that has emerged from these sediment records shows great variations in past climates in the Arctic. Despite winter darkness, warm stormy air from the south kept the Pole ice free for millions of years. Around 55 million years ago, the Pole was 5°C to 10°C in winter and 10°C to 15°C in summer, much like modern Ireland. Stepwise global cooling began about 51 million years ago; sands carried by sea ice show up in the sediment record about 46 million years ago; and 18 million years ago, the growing separation between the North American and Eurasian plates first admitted oxygen-rich Atlantic water through the Fram Strait into the previously isolated deep Arctic. Perennial sea ice cover began 13 to 14 million years ago, synchronous with the expansion of Antarctic glaciers, and year-round pack ice has covered the North Pole area ever since.

permanent rises in sea-level heights over these underwater mountains. Permanent ice cover in the Arctic prevents the aerial viewing of these localized sea-height phenomena, and seafloor surveys from ships or ice islands are expensive and time-consuming. A handful of seamounts have been surveyed on the margins of the Arctic, and according to the National Science Foundation's Seamounts Online database, there are two in the Greenland Sea that have been sampled to determine the nature of the creatures living there.

Novaya Zemlya Island, a 1,600-kilometer-long feature, is a seaward extension of Russia's Ural Mountains. Notorious as the site of nuclear testing and dumping of thousands of metric tons of radioactive wastes by the Soviet Union in the latter half of the 20th century, the island and surrounding waters provoke continuing concern about their long-term toxic character.

West of Novaya Zemlya Island, the Barents Sea embraces Franz Josef Land, an icy archipelago of nearly 200 islands and islets marking the northernmost territory of Russia. The islands were a single landmass during the Jurassic period more than 100 million years ago, but severe faulting has

WEB LINK: Seamounts Online database

Seasonal meltwater gushes from an Arctic glacier in 2007, a year of precipitous decline in ice cover.

shattered the land into steep-sided pieces, with deep straits separating individual islands. Although today it is populated along the usually frozen shores by polar bears, arctic foxes, numerous birds, and many marine mammals, its harsh climate has discouraged human habitation. Summer visitors are common, though, and permanent Russian weather stations are maintained.

Moving west to east across the Russian Arctic coast, the largest ice cap in the Russian Arctic tops Komsomolets Island, part of the Severnaya Zemlya group. The eastern margins of the Laptev Sea are enclosed by a remote island group variously called the Anjou Islands or the East Siberian Islands. Wrangel Island, known also by its Russian name Vrangelya, is the easternmost of Russia's major islands, just 140 kilometers off northeastern Siberia, near the opening to the Pacific Ocean. Wrangel Island remained relatively mild during the most recent glaciation and today has much more diverse and abundant wildlife and vegetation than most other Arctic islands. Numerous other small island groups occur in the Russian Arctic—Ayon Island, Belyy, Kolguyev, the New Siberian Islands, and Vaygach all have extensive ice cover and are lightly vegetated with lichens and mosses.

On the Western Hemisphere side of the basin lie the Queen Elizabeth Islands of Canada. Situated north of 74° N, well above the Arctic Circle, this triangular collection of islands covers roughly 400,000 square kilometers, with about one-fifth of that being ice-covered year-round, and most of the rest covered with barren tundra. Almost completely uninhabited, these islands have been host to extensive oil drilling operations since the 1960s. The mountainous Ellesmere Island is the largest and northernmost of the archipelago and the tenth largest island in the world. It is home to Barbeau Peak—at 2,616 meters the highest mountain in eastern North America.

Awkward-looking on land but graceful in the sea, a walrus moves under the Arctic's shifting pack ice with powerful tail thrusts.

Continental Margins

THE OCEAN SURROUNDING THE NORTH POLE has the world's broadest continental shelves, which take up almost one-third of the area of the Arctic Ocean. Along the Alaskan, Canadian, and Greenland coasts, the shelf extends between 80 and 200 kilometers seaward, but along the Russian shoreline it ranges from about 500 kilometers to more than 1,800 kilometers wide in the Barents Sea.

The shallow continental shelves are marked by strange tracks in many images of the seafloor around the margins of the Arctic Basin. These distinct features are furrows gouged into the sediments by the underside of moving icebergs, scars sometimes as wide as 20 meters and as much as 2 meters deep. Millions of square kilometers of permafrost underlie the tundra-covered land areas surrounding the Arctic, and recently, the presence of widespread underwater permafrost layers was discovered under the sediments of many of the Arctic's shelves and marginal seas where they were trapped during the last ice age. Oil and gas deposits occur in parts of this vast area, but extraction has been focused on relatively few places, notably Prudhoe Bay in northern Alaska, where oil was discovered in 1968; in Canada's Queen Elizabeth Islands; and in the Gulf of Ob, an area of the Russian shelf from which gas has been extracted.

A number of marginal seas are delineated by island groups and peninsulas jutting across the relatively shallow continental shelves of the Arctic. Moving east to west, starting from the opening of the Pacific Ocean into the Arctic, they are the Chukchi, East Siberian, Laptev, Kara, Barents, Greenland, and Beaufort Seas. The extremes of underwater topography are represented by the shallow Kara Sea, with nearly half of its depth at less than 50 meters, and the Barents Sea, with an average depth of about 230 meters where it flanks Novaya Zemlya Island.

The margins of the Arctic Ocean are fed with fresh water from melting ice and, especially, from Russia's rivers. Three great rivers course northwest over Siberia, their mouths frozen in the winter but flowing freely into the Arctic Ocean during the summer months. From east to west, these are: the Lena River flowing into the Laptev Sea; the mighty Yenisey, fed by thousands of smaller rivers and ultimately emptying into the Kara Sea; and the Ob River carrying melted glacier water from the Altay Mountains into the Kara Sea. The enormous influx of fresh water makes the Arctic the least salty of the world's oceans.

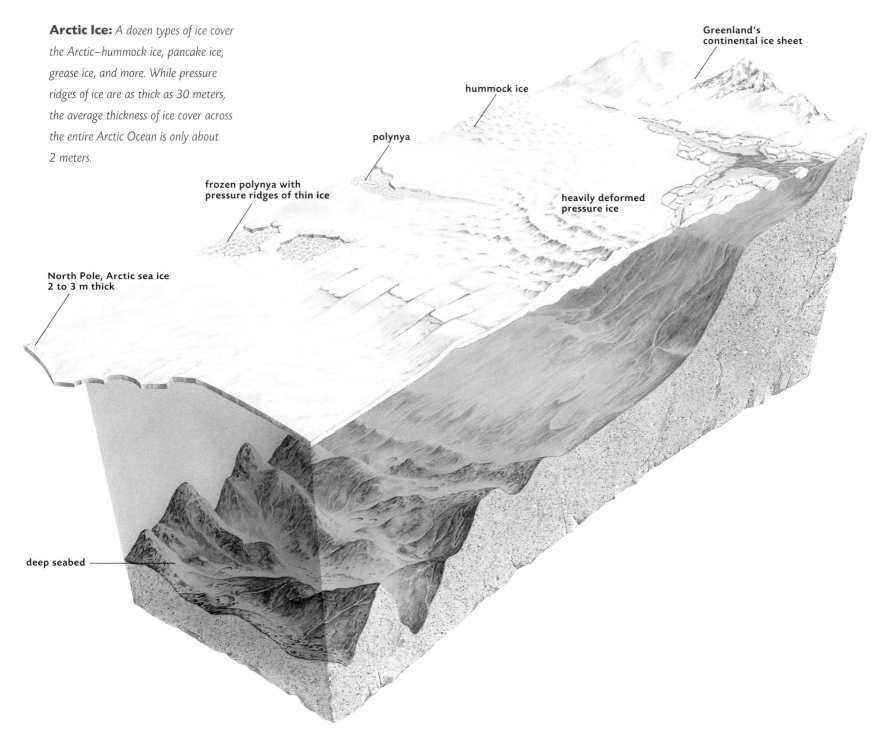

Arctic Ice: *A dozen types of ice cover the Arctic—hummock ice, pancake ice, grease ice, and more. While pressure ridges of ice are as thick as 30 meters, the average thickness of ice cover across the entire Arctic Ocean is only about 2 meters.*

Greenland's continental ice sheet

hummock ice

polynya

frozen polynya with pressure ridges of thin ice

heavily deformed pressure ice

North Pole, Arctic sea ice 2 to 3 m thick

deep seabed

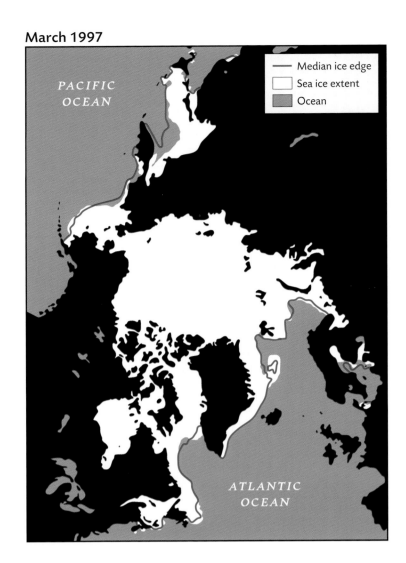

——	Median ice edge
☐	Sea ice extent
▨	Ocean

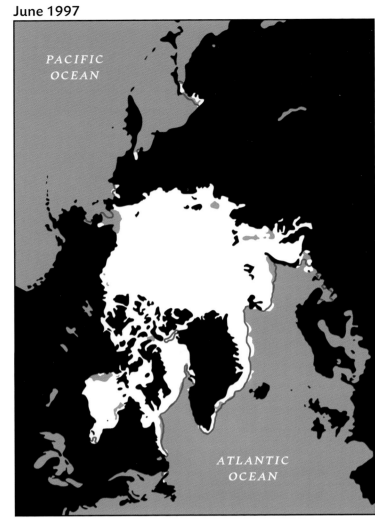

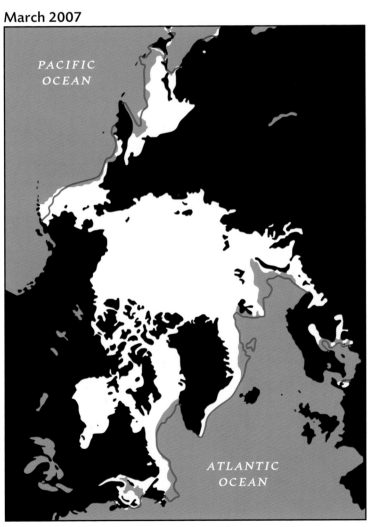

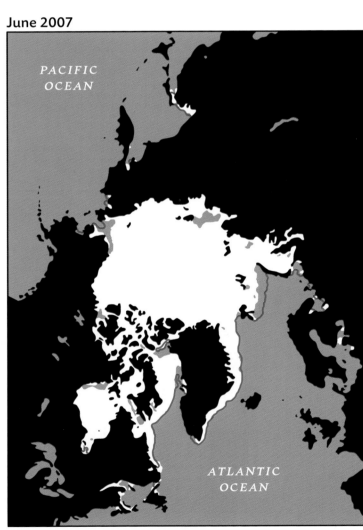

Seasonal Fluctuations of Sea Ice: *These maps show the seasonal cycle of sea-ice cover in the Northern Hemisphere for both 1997 and 2007. In both years, ice cover reaches its maximum in March and its minimum in September. The overall decrease in Northern Hemisphere sea ice over the decade from 1997 to 2007 can be seen clearly in each month shown (March, June, September, and December), although it is most*

September 1997

December 1997

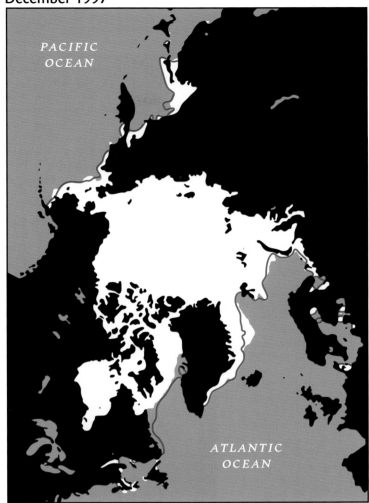

September 2007

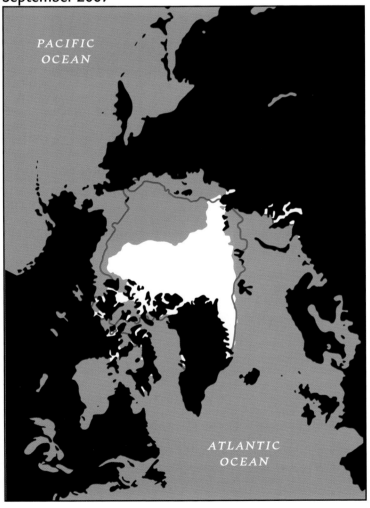

December 2007

prominent in the September images. The values mapped are the area covered by sea ice in each season, and can be compared with the mean ice cover averaged over all years since 1979, when satellite observations began. Images courtesy of Claire Parkinson and Nick DiGirolamo, NASA Goddard Space Flight Center.

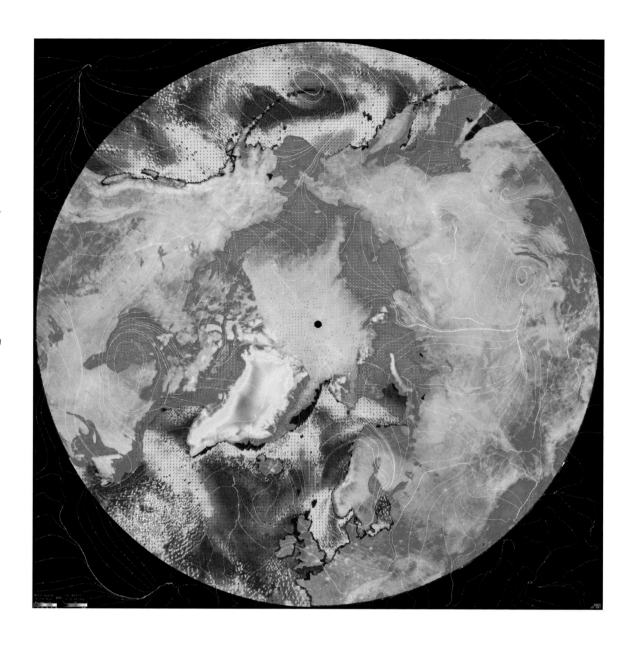

This false-color image captures some of the dynamics of the Arctic in February 2003 using NASA's SeaWinds scatterometer, a specialized satellite radar that measures winds over the ocean and detects sea ice and snow melt. The white streamlines show surface wind computed using a numerical weather model at noon on February 19, 2003. Wind blows along the lines in the direction of the arrows. The brightest areas on Greenland in light pink and light blue appear where the snow melts each summer. In the Arctic, multiyear sea ice is blue, while freshly frozen (first-year) ice is dark blue and red. In the open ocean wind speeds are depicted with lightest colors for the highest winds and darkest colors for the calmest winds (legend on page 271).

Tides and Currents

THE ARCTIC OCEAN SURGES WITH A RHYTHM of tides that enhances the mixing of dissimilar water-masses and contributes to the fracturing and movement of sea ice. To complement insights gained from satellite radar observations, hundreds of tide gauges have been established in the Arctic in recent years, providing new insights into the diurnal and semidiurnal tides of the region. New models of Arctic tides are being used to integrate data and lead to more accurate predictions. Scientists with NASA's Polar Research Program have been able to draw on recent measurements to demonstrate how the tides promote mixing in shallow waters, drive circulation in the relatively sluggish deep Arctic, and influence the formation and duration of polynyas—narrow open-water channels in the ice—along the Eurasian Shelf.

During a February 2007 expedition to Baffin Island, Arctic explorer Will Steger witnessed the effects of tidal surge at close range:

> *Over the past few days we've noticed that at high tide the ocean water rises up from underneath the pack ice and inundates the shore. The snowmobile road that skirts that shore gets flooded up to three feet deep.... The riders get soaked and almost bogged down.... With this unseasonably warm weather, the water takes many hours to refreeze and even at low tide it remains soft and slushy.*

Arctic currents were first explored and studied by a distinguished Norwegian scientist Fridtjof Nansen. In 1884 he was struck by the appearance off the coast of Greenland of a ship that had been crushed in 1881 in the ice on the other side of the Arctic in the Laptev Sea. Nansen commissioned the construction of a wooden ship, the *Fram,* with a hull specially designed to remain intact when frozen into pack ice. He sailed from Norway with 11 men in June 1893 to test his ideas, and by the end of September, the *Fram* was solidly locked into the ice—just north of the New Siberian Islands in the Laptev Sea—as he intended. As they drifted farther north, Nansen left the ship in 1895 and with sled dogs made a heroic but unsuccessful attempt to reach the North Pole. For almost three years the ship was carried by the drifting ice as it slowly but surely moved east to west past the northern-most islands of Russia and Europe to Spitsbergen (Svalbard). *Fram's* captain, Otto Sverdrup, brought the ship safely out of the ice and into the Greenland Sea in August 1896, confirming Nansen's theory of Arctic circulation.

Putting the ice to work as a slowly drifting laboratory, with a research station frozen in place much like Nansen's *Fram,* is a concept pioneered by the Soviets in 1937–38, when *Severnyy Polyus* was manned as an ice-camp research base. The *SP-2* was developed in 1950, and others have followed. The United States began adopting the concept in 1952 and continues to have effective ice-based stations adrift in the Arctic. Only in recent years have enough data been pieced together to begin to clarify the interactions among ice, air, water, and living systems, and to describe basic phenomena in the Arctic, including water movement.

The currents that flow into, out of, and within the Arctic Ocean are all strongly influenced by interactions between water temperature and salinity. Conditions under the ice vary depending on the ice thickness, on periodic freezing and melting of the ice, and on the inflow of fresh water from rivers. About 3.5 percent of ocean water consists of dissolved minerals—mostly salt—that lower the freezing point from the norm of 0°C to –3°C. When the temperature reaches this point, ice crystals containing only fresh water form, and they leave behind a heavier and increasingly salty brine that sinks away. Newly frozen sea ice may be a tenth as salty as seawater, and as the ice grows older, more salt escapes, leaving the uppermost ice increasingly fresh. People of the Arctic take advantage of this phenomenon, melting snow and surface ice for drinking and cooking water.

Circulation of water on the Russian side of the Arctic Ocean flows from the Chukchi Sea to the Greenland Sea in the long, east-to-west sweeping arc of the Transpolar Drift. On the Canadian side of the great Arctic Basin, water moves in a wide, clockwise swirl larger than the Gulf of Mexico known as the Beaufort Gyre. Fresh water from ice melt and from northern rivers accumulates in the gyre—sometimes more, sometimes less, depending on the temperature of the air above and the water below. Increased flow of fresh water from the gyre spilling out of the Arctic over the more saline, warmer waters of the North Atlantic can block the release of heat from the warmer waters to the atmosphere, thus inhibiting the tempering effect of the ocean on winters in Europe and North America.

Called the flywheel of the Arctic climate engine by Andrey Proshutinsky, an oceanographer from the Woods Hole Oceanographic Institution, the Beaufort Gyre is also referred to by some as

WEB LINK: Fram Museum

On Thin Ice

Since about 3 million years ago, when permanent ice cover first formed over the Arctic Ocean, the ice has always been remarkably thin. There are ice "keels" in places that reach more than 30 meters below the sea surface, but at the North Pole the ice has averaged only about 2 meters thick. Now the ice is melting, and quickly. Over the past 30 years, the average extent of sea ice has decreased by about 9 percent per decade, but in 2007 the summer sea-ice cover declined much more than ever seen before in 50 years of measurement. Scientists were predicting an Arctic Ocean completely free of ice in summers by mid-century, but this is now expected to happen in fewer than ten years. The impact on global climate—with open water in the Arctic absorbing more CO_2 and warming methane in permafrost sediments of coastal waters releasing more CO_2—will be complex and almost certainly profound.

Pressure ridges and cracks sculpt the frozen surface of the Arctic Ocean. The ever-moving ice temporarily opens up water areas called leads, or polynyas.

WEB LINK: Arctic research buoys

WEB LINK: The Beaufort Gyre

the great white black hole, owing to the vast unknowns that remain concerning its nature. Joining an international team of researchers from Canada, Japan, and the United States, Proshutinsky has been leading recent research efforts to explore above, below, and within this vast system.

Instrument-laden moorings deployed under the ice in the Beaufort Gyre are anchored to the seafloor at depths of 3,800 meters; extend up to within 50 meters of the ocean's ice cap; they measure water temperature, chemistry, and currents. Other 800-meter-long lines have been dangled through holes in the ice with instruments that travel up and down the line daily, taking measurements and sending data, including precise location, via satellite, back to Woods Hole. These data complement information from hundreds of other water samples taken between moorings. The waters in the Beaufort Gyre appear to make one grand, clockwise revolution around the basin roughly every four years.

Some Arctic Ocean water moves through channels among the Queen Elizabeth Islands into Baffin Bay and the relatively shallow Davis Strait west of Greenland, and there is relatively modest flow through the narrow and shallow Bering Strait between Alaska and Russia. The principal movement of water into and out of the Arctic Basin, about 80 percent, streams through the channel between Greenland and Spitsbergen. This is also the only deepwater connection between the Arctic and other oceans. Deepwater circulation in the Arctic Basin is not well understood, but all of the densest, deepest waters seem to enter from the Atlantic. About 2 percent of the water escaping annually from the Arctic Ocean does so as chunks of frozen ice, traveling this same route through the Greenland Sea. Near Spitsbergen, and to the south and southeast of Greenland, cold winds, evaporation, storms, and the outflow of briny water from sea ice formation in the Arctic create very cold, dense watermasses that sink and move south. This North Atlantic Deep Water is so salty that it can be traced near the seafloor all the way to the Southern Ocean around Antarctica, and is a major driver of ocean currents globally. The present global warming trend is speeding up the melting of the Greenland ice cap and other Arctic ice, and the resulting influx of low-salinity water could interfere with this critically important process, with profound consequences to global climate.

Warm bodies in a near-freezing sea, these narwhals, Monodon monoceros, *gather in a narrow break in the ice-covered Arctic Ocean.*

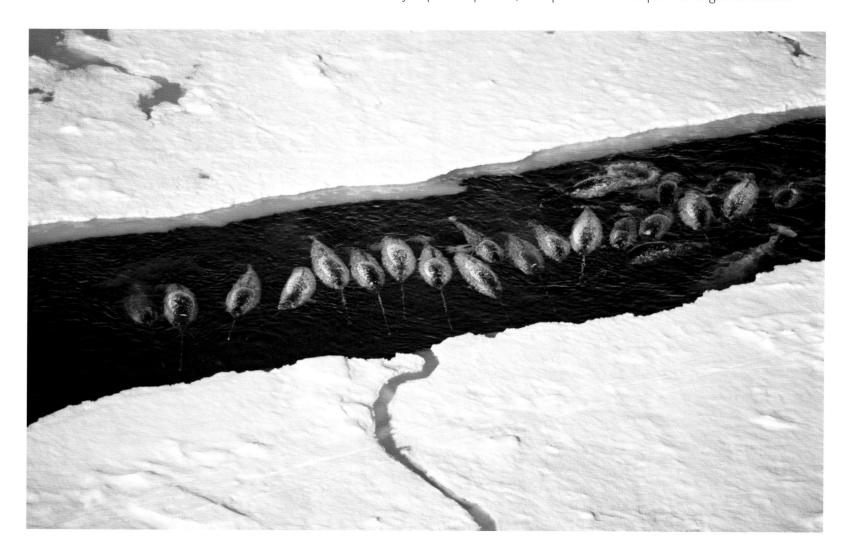

Dale Andersen
ICE AND LIFE

Sea ice is an ephemeral phenomenon, its presence and thickness dictated by the prevailing climate. At the sea surface, ice is subject to large swings in temperature and light. Ice temperature will equilibrate to the local air temperature, so that in the deep winter the ice may be −60°C. During the summer, the ice temperature will move back toward the melting point as the air above it warms. Sea ice is often bathed in intense sunlight, including exposure to ultraviolet radiation, and is transported by currents and wind. The ice pack is subject to numerous collisions between rafting ice floes, forming cracks, pressure ridges, and overturned ice.

It is not surprising, then, that it is hard for life to establish itself on the surface of sea ice. The surface does, however, serve as an important place for a variety of mammals to rest, give birth, or move from region to region in search of food or reproductive mates. Sea ice has large gradients in temperature, light, dissolved gases, and nutrients, so any organism that does live there must be able to adapt to these changing conditions.

The light penetration through sea ice can be quite variable—clear ice allowing some light to penetrate, although not if snow, an effective barrier to light transmission, covers the surface. Numerous microorganisms, including bacteria, archaea, algae, viruses, protists, flatworms, and small crustaceans such as small copepods, live within this ice. Some of the microorganisms have adapted to the cold and are able to remain metabolically active down to −20°C. Little is known of these ice inhabitants and the intricate food webs with which they are associated.

Farther down, a variety of microorganisms house themselves in the ice's pore space and a network of brine channels. During formation of the sea ice, when salts and dissolved gases in the seawater are forced out of the ice crystal lattice, concentrated brine that forms does not freeze, but instead flows down through the ice, collecting in ever larger sets of tubules and finally flowing out beneath it. As the supercooled, salty water enters the ocean, it forms "brine tubes" that resemble stalactites in caves and caverns.

The bottom surface of sea ice, which is an undulating, billowing landscape, has a very large surface area owing to the formation of platelet ice crystals that stack upon and next to one another. This large surface area is very important to life, because it provides a place for attachment, and a great number of nooks and crannies in which to live that afford some protection against predation. Many planktonic organisms, including algae, bacteria, small crustaceans, and small fish, find refuge under the ice or are caught up in it during each season's freeze-up. Pennate diatoms able to form filaments several centimeters long colonize the underside of ice and may cause large sections of it to take on a golden brown color.

Below the ice, creatures of the water column ranging in size from the smallest microbes to whales can be found. On the seafloor are animals such as anemones, tunicates, sea stars, sea cucumbers, sea urchins, clams, fish, and a host of others largely dependent upon the productivity of life associated directly with the ice above.

While there is significant inter-annual variability, a generally downward trend in the amount of perennial ice begins in the early 1970s. This trend appears to coincide with a general increase in the Arctic-wide, annually averaged surface air temperature, which also begins around 1970.

With mean global temperatures rising, the polar ice of the Arctic may, in the not too distant future, form only during winter months, with a completely ice free Arctic Ocean in the summer. Any changes to the distribution, extent, or thickness of sea ice will undoubtedly have a major impact on the distribution, seasonal feeding, and reproductive behaviors of many key organisms in the Arctic web of life. The discovery only in recent years of picobiliphytes, very small but abundant eukaryotic algae found in and beneath the ice, underscores the need to study further and understand the tremendous biodiversity occurring in and around polar ice before the ice is lost on a global scale.

Ablaze with life, this nudibranch clambors over the Arctic seafloor landscape.

Polar Ice Facts

• 2007 recorded a new record minimum for sea ice extent, 39 percent below the long term average from 1979-2000. • Measurements of the seasonal and coastal ice cover do not indicate any statistically significant change in thickness in recent decades. • Older, thicker ice is concentrated in the western Arctic basin in the region of the Beaufort Gyre.

Weather and Climate

To measure and monitor conditions throughout the Arctic, stations have been established on and under the ice by Russia, Canada, Norway, Denmark, and the United States, with other countries participating in international research in places such as the International Arctic Research Center at the University of Alaska in Fairbanks. High in the Alaskan Arctic at Barrow, NOAA's northern-most weather station measures year-round temperature, wind, and moisture, as well as pollutants released in northern Europe and blown across the top of the world. Canada maintains a permanent weather station at Eureka on Ellesmere Island, just above 80° N, only 1,100 kilometers from the North Pole.

In recent years, official Arctic measurements indicate an average temperature range from −17.8°C to −6.7°C, with a maximum low of −67.8°C recorded at both the northern end of Greenland and in northern Siberia, and 51 to 102 centimeters of precipitation annually. As many as 50 cyclones a year sweep across the Arctic Ocean, appearing on satellite images as furiously swirling aerial whirlpools much like hurricanes, with winds as powerful as their tropical counterparts. The dark winter months over the Arctic Ocean tend to be cold and stormy (winter cyclones are stronger but less frequent than summer storms) and dominated by inversions—warm air layered over the top of cold.

During the long Arctic summer days, despite the frequency of overcast skies and weeks of high wind, sunlight powers the production of phytoplankton and coastal wetlands vital to life in the sea as well as to many land creatures. High winds increase the movement of broken ice, stir up waves in open water, create mixing between different watermasses, drive forceful currents, and enhance the impact of the tides.

During breaks between storms, under clear summer skies, in subzero temperatures, flat, white seascapes can produce spectacular optical phenomena. Sometimes a white glare—an "ice blink"—appears on the undersides of clouds, indicating the presence of ice beyond the range of vision. Mirages shimmer at the horizon, with objects appearing to float above their actual locations due to the downward refraction of light in cold, dense air. A form of mirage, a *fata morgana,* may cause a distant, flat object to appear to have tall cliffs, columns, and pedestals. A halo may form around the sun when light is refracted through ice crystals high in the sky, and sometimes, in a dense fog, a soft, silvery version of a rainbow devoid of color—a "fog bow"—may arch luminously across the sky.

The one phenomenon most responsible for both cause and effect in Arctic weather and climate is the vast expanse of ice. More than 14 million square kilometers of sea ice usually cover the Arctic Ocean in the early spring, diminishing by about half during the summer and re-forming during winter months. Driven by winds, currents, and tides, the enormous mass of pack ice rotates clockwise at a stately but erratic pace. All the while, its gleaming surface reflects most of the summer sunlight back into space. Immobile multiyear ice frozen to the coastlines is bordered by

Chlorophyll (mg / m³)

≤0.05 0.1   0.3 0.5   1   3   5   10   30   ≥60

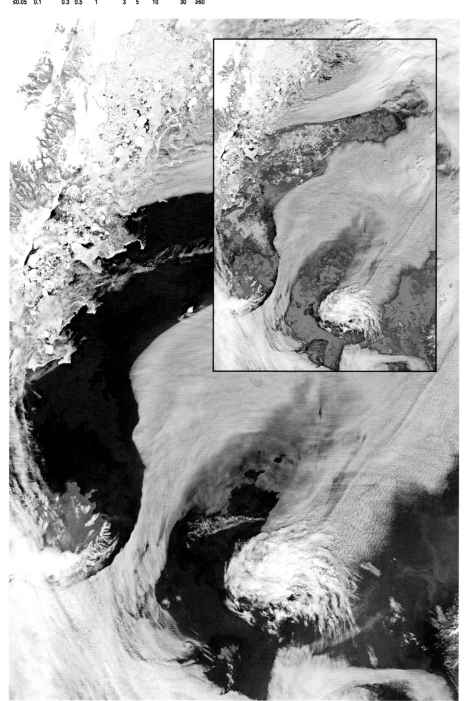

WEB LINK: Arctic weather

a perennial "circumpolar flaw lead"—a narrow ribbon of open water between the fast ice and drifting ice—that supports a great deal of life and is a source of significant heat exchange between the ocean and the atmosphere. Fringing the ice pack's edges is a partly frozen filigree of ice floes, ice islands, and icebergs. Every year, hundreds of small icebergs flake off from Greenland's ice shield and Canada's glaciers, where they may drift for decades as glistening islands. Some tabular icebergs that have broken away from the northern edge of Ellesmere Island are larger than some nations—as much as 700 square kilometers in area and 50 meters thick.

Over the millennia, the Arctic has at many times been ice free and at others has been frozen over with far greater ice cover than at present. There is abundant evidence that at least part of the Arctic Ocean was relatively warm more than 40 million years ago. Little is known about the conditions that created the present year-round ice cover, but it is believed to have occurred about 3 million years ago, with today's Arctic ice pack a frozen remnant from the most recent Pleistocene ice age. There is compelling evidence that during the last ice age—about 18,000 years ago—the formation of mile-high glaciers on the continents drew so much water out of the ocean that worldwide sea level was lowered about 200 meters, and a large part of the shallow Bering Sea between Asia and North America was exposed as dry land.

The Bering Land Bridge provided a route for creatures large and small—saber-toothed cats, woolly mammoths, horses, camels, short-faced bears, and other now extinct creatures, as well as humans—to move from Asia to the Western Hemisphere, though humans and other creatures also arrived by sea. The lowered sea level, and emergent land connections, limited the movements—underwater and near the sea surface—of certain marine animals of the time. There is evidence that in more recent times—about 5,000 years ago—Earth may have been somewhat warmer than today, with the tree line advanced far north over Arctic plains now covered with tundra.

Clearly, climate has changed over the ages, sometimes colder, sometimes warmer than the current era. However, an unusually rapid trend toward warming has been recorded in recent years, enhanced by humankind's industrial activities. According to a 2007 report in *Nature,* the minimum extent of sea ice in the Arctic typically occurs in September, with an average since 1979 of more than 7 million square kilometers. In 2002, this was reduced to less than 6 million square kilometers, and the extent of Arctic ice cover has continued to stay low or decrease to record low levels every year since. In 2007, the Arctic's ice cap shrank to its smallest size in the past century. Submarine and radar surveys indicate that the ice is also becoming thinner. The rate of ice loss in the Arctic polar ice cap appears to have been about 9 percent per decade over the past 30 years. As the white ice cover that reflects the sun's radiation diminishes, the amount of darker seawater that absorbs the radiation and heat increases. This, in turn, is increasing water temperatures and hastening further melting of the ice, in a classic feedback loop. Some climate models predict a completely ice free Arctic in the autumn by the year 2040, but based on the unexpectedly sharp decline of ice in 2007 and 2008, late-summer ice could be gone within a decade.

These dramatic changes in the Arctic are raising serious concerns about the potential impact further loss of ice may have on global climate. In the 2007–2009 International Polar Year, extensive research is being focused on the Arctic's past and present, with the goal of better understanding future trends.

A low pressure system comparable to circumstances that give rise to hurricanes here forms swirls of water vapor over the frozen Arctic Ocean near Canada's Queen Elizabeth Islands.

Lodged on an icy ledge in cool Canadian waters, this Arctic cod, Boreogadus saida, *ranges widely in the Arctic feeding on plankton and being consumed by numerous other animals. With natural antifreeze proteins in their blood, these fish can thrive in water temperature below 0°C.*

Arctic Marine Life

THE ARCTIC IS FAMOUS for its abundance and diversity of mammals and birds—from polar bears, whales, and walruses to snow geese and arctic terns as well as the diverse dwarf plants and lichen that form the unique tundra. Far less is known about the multitudes of other forms of life that abound in the cold, mostly dark underwater realm—less visible but no less important as components of the vast and varied Arctic ecosystem. Amphipods, copepods, numerous kinds of small crabs and krill, arrowworms, polychaete worms, salps, and many more create a vital, living matrix within Arctic waters.

As in other oceans, the Arctic is home to microbes and minute planktonic organisms that capture energy through either of the two basic energy sources of life—photosynthesis or chemosynthesis—providing the fuel that powers creatures that consume them. Some seaweeds prosper on the Arctic Ocean's broad continental shelf in depths where there is suitable sunlight and substrate. Most of the basic food production, though, happens at the micro level and continues among very small crustaceans and the juvenile larval stages of creatures that later grow large, from jellies and starfish to crabs and cod.

Plankton beware! With a 5-meter-wide mouth and enormous baleen plates, the gentle bowhead or ice whales, Balaena mysticetus, *may engulf two tons of minute crustaceans each day. The longest-lived mammals known, individual bowhead whales may thrive for more than two centuries, but the species was nearly exterminated by Yankee whalers before commercial hunting for them ceased in 1946. A few thousand—a small fraction of the original number—now live close to the Arctic ice pack.*

Two species of fish—Arctic cod, *Boreogadus saida,* and capelin, *Mallotus villosus*—are particularly significant in the Arctic food chain because they feed directly on plankton and convert these minute organisms into something that can be captured as food by seals, birds, bears, whales, and humans. Arctic cod may grow to 30 centimeters long, sleek and silvery with beautiful large eyes, golden brown speckles on the back, and a single small barbel under the lower lip. As babies, they are part of the plankton too, and although millions of eggs are released during

annual spawning, only one or two from each spawning pair may survive the many mouths that are eager to swallow them on their perilous journey to maturity.

Like the arctic cod, capelin translate the sun's energy packed in small crustaceans into fish-size bites that can be captured by larger creatures. Beautiful in their own right, silvery capelin gather for spawning along sandy shores to deposit and fertilize huge numbers of eggs that are themselves consumed by countless creatures. Beautiful, too, is their fine-tuned role in Arctic ecosystems. Capelin and cod are cornerstone species whose abundance or scarcity have a magnified impact on all who share Arctic waters.

Consider the dynamics of the Arctic food chain: A polar bear, a giant at the top of the food chain, may eat a seal. That seal has eaten hundreds of fish in the previous three years. And each of those fish has fed over the previous ten years on numerous smaller fish and crustaceans. Those small creatures will have consumed millions of minuscule crystalline diatoms that bloomed years ago as a golden sheen on the bottom of ice faintly illuminated by sunlight filtering through 2 to 3 meters of Arctic ice.

The ever-present ice, in its various forms, provides unique habitats in the Arctic Ocean. Cracks form in the constantly moving ice pack, opening "leads" or open-water channels called polynyas. These areas are full of life and provide vital open-water breathing spaces for whales and seals, particularly in summer months. Icebergs sometimes provide a haven for birds, bears, and seals. But below the water, they also host clouds of hitchhiking microorganisms and other creatures that bore into, ride upon, or gather around their frozen upside-down mountain of ice.

The Arctic's vast, frozen underbelly of ice is a unique and critically important habitat for diatoms, crustaceans, worms, and many other marine organisms. For some, it is their only home. It is a richly populated surface year-round, but especially during spring and summer, when sunlight that does not reach the seafloor far below penetrates to the bottom of the thin Arctic ice cover, providing energy for photosynthesis and the complex food chains that depend on it.

Known for melodious flute-like vocalizations, ringed seals such as this plump individual in Lancaster Sound, Canada, stay warm in near-freezing water and below freezing air with a built-in jacket of fat under smooth, furry skin.

Crossing the Arctic

SOME HAVE VENTURED INTO THE ARCTIC for wealth derived from the region's wildlife—whales and walruses for oil, and seals, foxes, and polar bears for their fur. Others have been drawn by the indefinable lure to explore; more than a few wanted to be the first to reach the North Pole. Sir William Parry, a British explorer, tried reaching the Pole in 1827 with specially designed boats mounted on runners. Like Nansen, many used dogsleds, including Robert E. Peary, who made four attempts to reach the North Pole between 1900 and 1909, and who on the last trip is credited with having been the first to succeed. In 1969, Sir Wally Herbert, using the tried-and-true dogsled technique, was successful in being the first person to travel all the way across the Arctic Ocean's icy surface.

Starting in the 1500s, many attempts were made to find a "Northwest Passage"—a sea way from the Atlantic to China across the top of the world, rather than one through the stormy waters around the tip of South America and across the Pacific. One of the most famous attempts was made in 1845 by British Rear Adm. Sir John Franklin, who proved the existence of a sea passage through the North American Arctic. In the process, though, he became trapped and perished in the ice with his ships, *Terror* and *Erebus,* and all of their crew. Year-round sea ice and numerous islands thwarted all attempts to successfully achieve passage via the fabled northwesterly route until 1906

WEB LINK: Northwest Passage

Edward Cassano
NORTHWEST PASSAGE

The fabled Northwest Passage leading from Europe to Asia through or around North America has been sought for centuries. This search was described by James Delgado in his book *Across the Top of the World,* as "an epic tale of tragedy, determination and human struggle to best nature in one of history's greatest enterprises." This quest lasted for more than four centuries and was considered by some the holy grail of maritime achievements.

In the early 15th century, decreasing access to the Orient using traditional overland routes prompted European nations to seek a different route via the sea by exploring to the west across the Atlantic. Columbus's voyages

Across the centuries, how these initial explorers related to the Inuit people still holds important lessons for human stewardship of our planet and interrelationships with the Earth's diverse communities today. The Inuit's very existence was, until very recently, inextricably linked to their understanding and relationship with the natural world. Those European explorers who recognized the ageless wisdom and knowledge of the Inuit people quickly learned to survive, even thrive, in the Arctic. Others, who viewed the Inuit as savages, an inferior race, suffered untold hardships and death in this unforgiving land. The greatest Arctic tragedy, the loss of the Franklin

Ships such as the one above already venture far into the Arctic Ocean. Given present warming trends, the top of the world may soon be ice free during the summer months.

and many that followed probed the north and south along both the North and South American continents. As Delgado describes in his book, Spanish control of Central and South America drove British explorers to the north, seeking the fabled shortcut to the Orient.

From the 16th to the early 20th centuries, dozens of expeditions were launched to penetrate the northern latitudes, ready to discover the Northwest Passage that all assumed to be there. As these explorers ventured farther and farther to the north into the high Arctic, they "discovered" a race of people fully adapted to life in one of our planet's harshest climates.

expedition in the mid-19th century, and the first successful transit of the Northwest Passage by Roald Amundsen between 1903 and 1906, illustrate the dichotomy of these two worldviews.

When John Franklin set sail in 1845 aboard the *Terror* and the *Erebus,* everything one needed to successfully survive in the Arctic had been learned, forgotten, relearned, and then ignored. *Terror* and *Erebus* were state-of-the-art polar exploration vessels, even equipped with some of the first marine engines. However, as countless others had learned, the ships were too big, they required too many men to operate, and they were ill-suited to the type of navigation required to penetrate the maze of passages in the heart of the high Arctic. In their profound belief in the superiority of European technology, the Franklin crew ignored the lessons of Inuit methods of dress, transportation, food, and survival in the Arctic climate, opting instead for heavy wool clothes, man-hauling of sleds, canned food, large ships, and large crews. Upon entering the Arctic in 1847, Franklin and his men, along with his two ships, disappeared, never to be seen alive again.

Roald Amundsen took a different approach to seeking the passage in the early 1900s. An avid student of Polar exploration, he realized the formula for success in conquering the Northwest Passage was not in massive ships and large crews but in an expedition that was small, nimble, and crewed with highly experienced, talented individuals. His ship, *Gjoa*, was small and shallow drafted. His crew totaled seven, including himself. Amundsen quickly learned the other key to success in the Arctic during his first winter. Anchored in what has been named the Gjoa Haven on King William Island, the ship quickly attracted a large group of Inuit. Amundsen, ever the student of the Arctic, recognized and respected the wisdom of this complex human community. He immersed himself in the Inuit culture and was welcomed by this gregarious community. He appreciated the critical innovations this Arctic people had made to thrive in this place. It was here that he learned how to drive a dog team, to dress for the Arctic winters, and to work and play in one of the harshest environments on the planet. Eighteen months after anchoring at Gjoa Haven, Amundsen was guided by his new Inuit friends through the complex islands and shoals of Simpson Strait, to complete the first transit of the Northwest Passage.

When the Northwest Passage was finally mapped in the mid-19th century, one explorer remarked that the Northwest Passages (there are three main passages) "are without significance and useless for navigation as long as the climate in these parts is so severe and the sea covered with ice 50 to 60 feet thick." Today, though, the Arctic polar cap is melting and the fabled Northwest Passage is likely to be ice free during summer months in the coming decade, perhaps as early as in the next five years. The route sought for centuries will now be a reality—owing to global warming.

The significance of a feasible commercial route across the top of North America cannot be overestimated. The opening of the Northwest Passage to commercial traffic will change global shipping patterns dramatically, resulting in a global economic impact on a scale not seen since the industrial revolution. Today, the most direct route from Europe to Asia is through the Panama Canal, a distance of 23,300 kilometers. By contrast, passage via the Northwest Passage is only 14,600 kilometers. This means it would take a ship traveling at 25 knots about 12.5 days compared with 21 days, translating to a savings of close to 40 percent in time and fuel. It could also almost double the transits a ship could make in a year. Of almost equal significance, there would be no size restriction on the vessels as there is now for ships that transit the Panama Canal.

Up until the dramatic reduction in sea ice, ownership of the Northwest Passage was not really an issue. It has been claimed by Canada as sovereign waters and thus under its sole control, and the United States has long supported Canada's position, but most of the rest of the international community views the passage as an international strait. Today Canada is proposing to build six new Arctic patrol vessels dedicated to "protecting" its northern interests. Once again, the Northwest Passage is in the news as the tension over who controls this route resonates across the international community.

Equally dramatic is the rush to claim territories beyond the 200-mile Exclusive Economic Zone recognized for coastal nations in the United Nations Convention on the Law of the Sea (UNCLOS), the governing international treaty of the world's ocean. Provisions within UNCLOS allow for an extension of a coastal nation's claim to the natural resources on and under the seafloor up to 350 nautical miles, if that nation can prove its continental shelf extends beyond the existing 200-nautical-mile limit. Russia's submersible dive and planting of its flag on the "real" North Pole and the geographic feature it lies on, the Lomonosov Ridge, is part of its claim that the Russian continental shelf extends well beyond the 200-nautical-mile boundary. The Russians are not the only Arctic coastal state to rush to extend its boundaries—the United States, Denmark, and Canada all have science teams working to document and bolster their claims for extending their continental shelf claims.

As the frenzy and rush for resources inevitably begin with the opening of the Northwest Passage, it is essential that we act with the knowledge and wisdom we have gained over the millennia on how to live in balance with nature. We must act immediately to stem and reverse the dramatic rise of human-produced greenhouses gases, especially CO_2. As global citizens we must also act as wise stewards to one of the last great areas of our planet, the Arctic, in an effort to protect this key element of our planetary ecosystem.

A changing Arctic means a dramatically changing planet that will affect all of us. Sheila Watt-Cloutier, who was nominated for the Nobel Peace Prize in 2007 for her work on climate change, reminds us that the Arctic is a homeland to the Inuit people. She has stated that to effectively address global warming we must acknowledge that "we are all one; that we are a shared humanity; and we all have a shared responsibility to each other."

Environmental Facts

• The Northwest Passage passes through areas of three Canadian territories: Nunavut, the Northwest Territories, and the Yukon. • The northern coast of the state of Alaska comprises the "western" entrance to the Northwest Passage. • The population of these three territories is a little more than 100,000. • The Inuit make up a large portion of the coastal population for both Canada and the United States in these northern areas.

Socio-Economic Facts

• Industrial activities include government, tourism, oil and gas, military, commercial fishing, subsistence hunting and fishing, and mining. • The opening of the Northwest Passage represents a potential economic boom to this environmentally sensitive region. • Dramatic increases in shipping, coastal development, oil and gas activities, and tourism are likely to occur as the passage opens.

when Norwegian explorer Roald Amundsen traveled by ship through Lancaster Sound south of Victoria Island, eventually emerging through the Bering Strait.

In 1969, the U.S. icebreaking supertanker *Manhattan* made its way through the 4,800-kilometer-long Northwest Passage, from the North Atlantic to Prudhoe Bay in Alaska and back, demonstrating the feasibility—but not the economic practicality—of transporting oil across the top of the world. Moving oil via pipelines across the Arctic proved more cost-effective. Other goods have been shipped through the frozen waters since World War II, when the Soviet Union used icebreakers to reach its harbors along the polar sea during summer months. Starting in 1991, the Russians used enormous nuclear-powered icebreakers to guide cargo ships and tankers in convoys across the pack ice in another Arctic sea route, the Northeast Passage, a coast-hugging route from the Atlantic to the Pacific across the frozen north coast of today's Russia.

Crossing the Arctic Ocean in commercial passenger-carrying aircraft following fuel-saving "great circle" routes is common today, but was not until the latter part of the 20th century. Richard Byrd pioneered the use of aircraft for Arctic exploration in 1926. In the same year, Roald Amundsen, the first person to reach the South Pole, became the first to cross the Arctic Ocean in an airship, the *Norge*. Writing in 1935, Anne Morrow Lindbergh described a trip in a single-engine aircraft with her husband, aviator Charles Lindbergh, from New York across the margins of the Arctic Ocean to China. "Our route was new; the air untraveled; . . . the stories mythical; the maps, pale, pink, and indefinite. . . ."

Over the decades, a few intrepid scuba divers have plunged into the waters under the ice at the North Pole. Among those who have viewed Arctic ice from the standpoint of ringed seals and polar bears—from underneath looking up—are the former chairman of the board of the National Geographic Society, Gilbert M. Grosvenor, and his diving companions, Canadian explorer Joseph MacInnis and photographer Al Giddings. MacInnis recalls swimming directly beneath the North Pole, where all meridians meet and every direction is south, where "translucent plates of ice glittered . . . a huge rampart of white loomed . . . plunging deep into violet waters and gradually disappearing into purple nothingness far below."

Some have crossed the Arctic Ocean by deliberately pointing their ships downward—underwater. Amid great secrecy in 1958—an era of *Sputnik* and the beginnings of the U.S.–Soviet space race and the Cold War—the U.S. Navy's nuclear submarine *Nautilus* transited under the Arctic ice cap, stopping to surface through the ice at the North Pole. In a 2008 book on Arctic exploration, Alfred McLaren describes how U.S. Navy submarines went on to chart unknown waters of the Laptev, East Siberian, and Chukchi Seas.

Many explorers noted that the real North Pole—not the one constantly moving around on surface drift ice, but the fixed location deep below on the Arctic seafloor—had never been reached. On the ocean bottom more than 4,219 meters below, just east of the Lomonosov Ridge in the Fram Basin, it is pitch-black all the time. In August 2007, explorers in two Russian submarines, *Mir I* and *Mir II*, reached this previously inaccessible deep and frigid destination for the first time.

Success in crossing the Arctic Ocean by ships awaited the arrival of powerful icebreakers such as the Soviet *Arktika* in 1977. Since 1991, regular excursions have been made to the North Pole and beyond aboard nuclear-powered icebreakers such as the giant Russian vessel *Sovetskiy Soyuz*, sometimes with a hundred or more well-fed, warmly clad visitors from all over the world, calmly sipping vodka while crashing through 2 meters of ice at a speed of 14 knots. Given present warming trends, Arctic icebreakers may soon become obsolete. ☐

Arctic Ice Loss: *The graph above illustrates the steady loss of ice in the Arctic from 1979 to 2007. According to satellite data, the old, thick ice is declining faster than ever before recorded, with a precipitous drop in 2007 and continuing the trend into 2008.*

Arctic Sea Routes and Continental Claims

PACIFIC OCEAN

Aleutian Islands

ALASKA
U.S.

Prudhoe Bay

CHUKCHI SEA

Wrangel Island

ARCTIC OCEAN

New Siberian Islands

LAPTEV SEA

BEAUFORT SEA

B

CANADA

Bathurst Island

Resolute

Ellesmere Island

Arctic sea ice reached its record minimum extent in 2007

Severnaya Zemlya

KARA SEA

RUSSIA

UNITED STATES

HUDSON BAY

Baffin Island

BAFFIN BAY

Franz Josef Land

Svalbard
Norway

A

Novaya Zemlya

BARENTS SEA

GREENLAND
Denmark

New York

LABRADOR SEA

ICELAND

NORWEGIAN SEA

FINLAND

SWEDEN

NORWAY

ATLANTIC OCEAN

NORTH SEA

DENMARK

UNITED KINGDOM

IRELAND

London

Bering Strait

Sea of Okhotsk

JAPAN

Tokyo

+ **North Pole**
Russia leaves its flag on the seabed in 2008, 4,000 meters beneath the surface, as part of its claims for oil and gas reserves.

◌ Lomonosov Ridge
Russia argues that this underwater feature is an extension of its continental territory.

— EEZ boundary
200-nautical mile (370 kilometers) line shows how far countries' agreed economic area extends beyond their coastline. This is often set from outlying islands.

- - - Potential continental shelf claims
Countries can claim up to 350 nautical miles (403 miles, 638 kilometers) if the area proves to be a direct extension of the continental shelf.

A Russian-claimed territory
Area disputed by Russia and Norway

B New claim
Russia claims it has geological evidence to prove that this vast area, which stretches all the way to the North Pole, is part of its continental structure.

▪▪▪ London to Tokyo (via Northeast Passage)
13,000 kilometers

▪▪▪ New York City to Tokyo (via Northwest Passage)
14,000 kilometers

London
Tokyo

Tokyo
New York

—— **London to Tokyo via Northeast Passage**
13,000 kilometers

—— **London to Tokyo via Suez Canal**
20,900 kilometers

—— **New York City to Tokyo via Northwest Passage**
14,000 kilometers

—— **New York City to Tokyo via Panama Canal**
18,200 kilometers

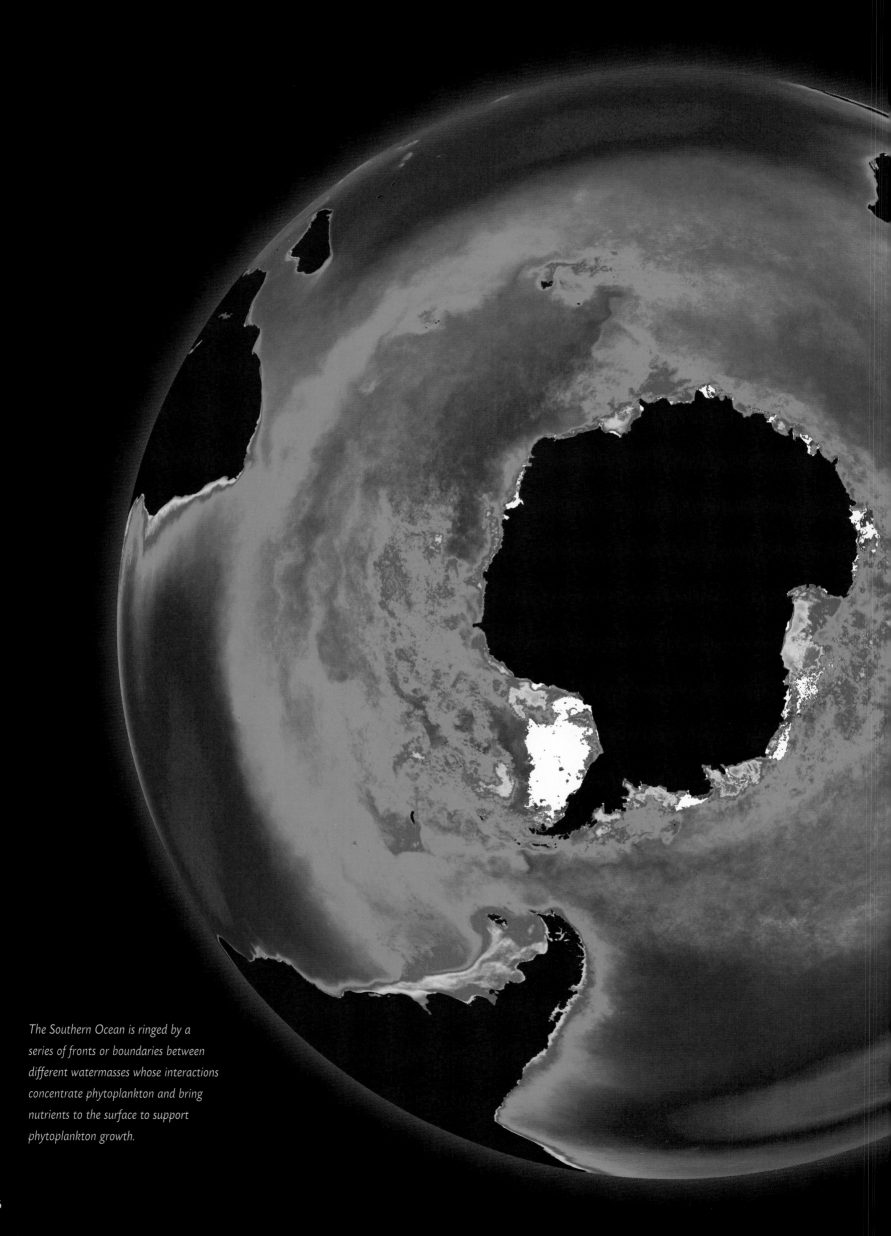

The Southern Ocean is ringed by a series of fronts or boundaries between different watermasses whose interactions concentrate phytoplankton and bring nutrients to the surface to support phytoplankton growth.

Chapter 8

SOUTHERN OCEAN

Southern Ocean Seafloor

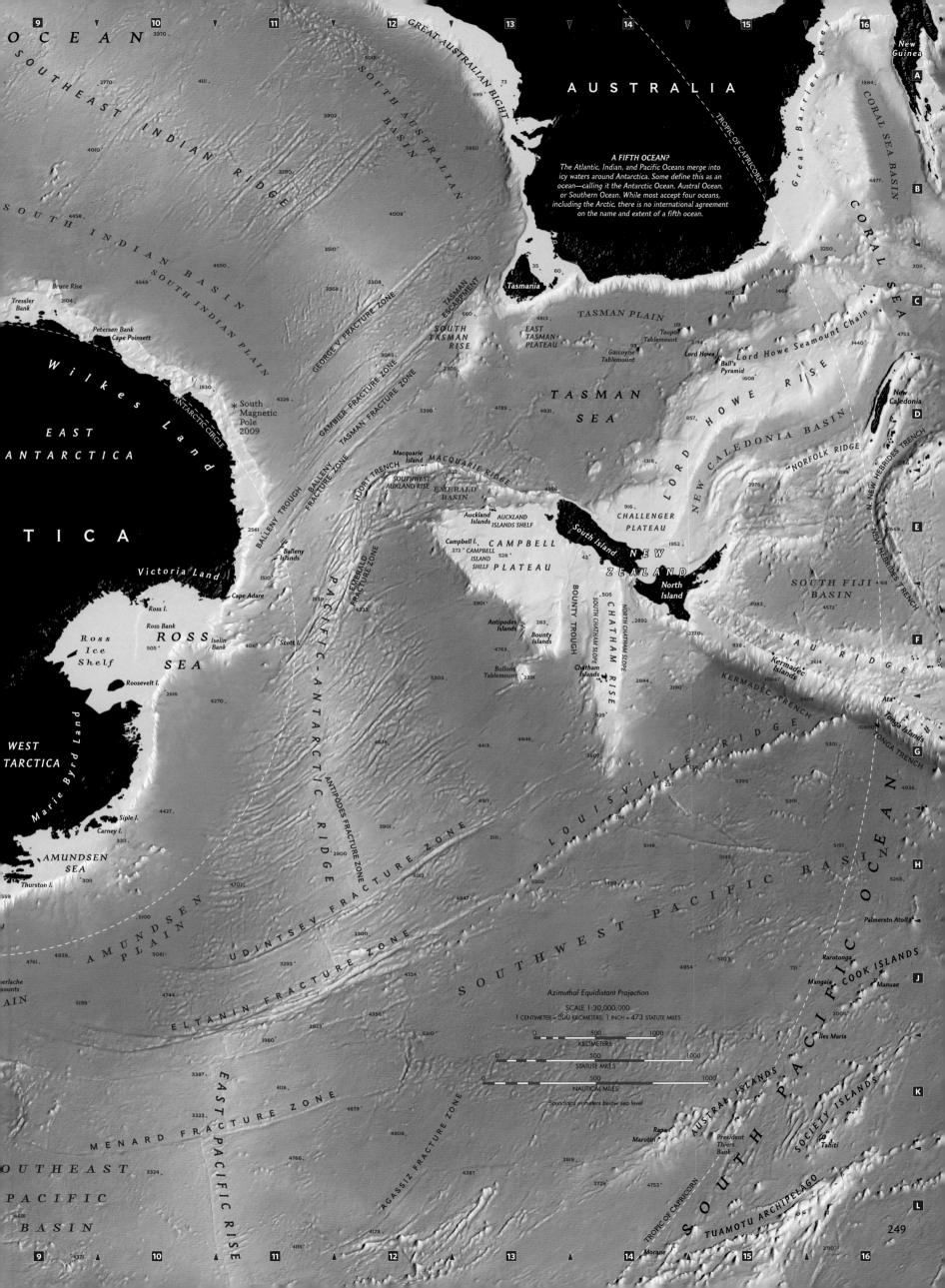

OCEAN

SOUTHEAST INDIAN RIDGE

SOUTH INDIAN BASIN

SOUTH INDIAN PLAIN

2770
4111
3970
5018
3902
4010
3290
4650
4458
3510
4549
1968
2508
4226
3045
3398
4785
4008
4990
4831
5850
4813
4956

Bruce Rise
2104
Tressler Bank
Petersen Bank
Cape Poinsett

Wilkes Land

EAST ANTARCTICA

ANTARCTIC CIRCLE

1830
* South Magnetic Pole 2009

TICA

Victoria Land

2561
1510
1839

Cape Adare

Ross I.
Ross Bank
505
Iselin Bank
406
Scott I.

ROSS SEA

Ross Ice Shelf

Roosevelt I.
2616
4270
4427

WEST TARCTICA

Marie Byrd Land

Siple I.
Carney I.
3311

AMUNDSEN SEA
3011
Thurston I.

559

BALLENY TROUGH
BALLENY FRACTURE ZONE

GEORGE V FRACTURE ZONE

GAMBIER FRACTURE ZONE

TASMAN FRACTURE ZONE

HJORT TRENCH

Macquarie Island
322
Macquarie Ridge
SOUTHWEST AUKLAND RISE
EMERALD BASIN

Auckland Islands
AUCKLAND ISLANDS SHELF

Campbell I.
272
CAMPBELL ISLAND SHELF
528
CAMPBELL ISLAND PLATEAU

3901

Antipodes Islands
283
Bounty Islands

4763

Bollons Tablemount
2391
5303

EMERALD FRACTURE ZONE

PACIFIC-ANTARCTIC RIDGE

ANTIPODES FRACTURE ZONE

Balleny Islands

AUSTRALIA

GREAT AUSTRALIAN BIGHT

73
499
35
60

SOUTH AUSTRALIAN BASIN

TROPIC OF CAPRICORN

A FIFTH OCEAN?
The Atlantic, Indian, and Pacific Oceans merge into icy waters around Antarctica. Some define this as an ocean—calling it the Antarctic Ocean, Austral Ocean, or Southern Ocean. While most accept four oceans, including the Arctic, there is no international agreement on the name and extent of a fifth ocean.

Tasmania

TASMAN ESCARPMENT
660
SOUTH TASMAN RISE
2305

EAST TASMAN PLATEAU

TASMAN PLAIN
119
Taupo Tablemount
Gascoyne Tablemount

TASMAN SEA

New Guinea

Great Barrier Reef
1884

CORAL SEA BASIN

CORAL SEA

4477
2011
3250
402
1464
4753

Lord Howe
Lord Howe Seamount Chain
1440
Ball's Pyramid
1608

New Caledonia

LORD HOWE RISE

NEW CALEDONIA BASIN

"NORFOLK RIDGE"

2976

-1318

857

916
CHALLENGER PLATEAU

South Island

NEW ZEALAND
1952
42
North Island

BOUNTY TROUGH

SOUTH CHATHAM SLOPE
NORTH CHATHAM SLOPE
CHATHAM RISE
Chatham Islands
.505
929
.2892
2844

SOUTH FIJI BASIN
4168
4572

N. NEW HEBRIDES TRENCH
2266
NEW HEBRIDES TRENCH
2669

LAU RIDGE
938
Kermadec Islands
2614

KERMADEC TRENCH
10041
Ata
6409
Tonga Islands
10800
TONGA TRENCH

4936

5301

5393

5148
784
1846

SOUTHWEST PACIFIC BASIN

PACIFIC OCEAN

SOUTH PACIFIC OCEAN

Palmerstn Atoll

Rarotonga
731
Mangaia
Manuae
COOK ISLANDS
2005
Iles Maria

Rapa
Marotiri
President Thiers Bank

AUSTRAL ISLANDS

SOCIETY ISLANDS
Tahiti

TUAMOTU ARCHIPELAGO
Morane

5268
5155
5027
4954

4625
4413
4846
4917
3901
5111
2607
2800
5012
5505
1499
4847
3300
3293
4724
4356
5210
2923
1980
3387
4118
4879
4808
4766
4387
2819
3729
4753
4115
4173
3323
3324
4691
5199
4744
4761
4939
5081
5100
297
552

AMUNDSEN PLAIN

ELTANIN FRACTURE ZONE

UDINTSEV FRACTURE ZONE

AGASSIZ FRACTURE ZONE

EAST PACIFIC RISE

MENARD FRACTURE ZONE

SOUTHEAST PACIFIC BASIN

LOUISVILLE RIDGE

4732
4707

Azimuthal Equidistant Projection

SCALE 1:30,000,000
1 CENTIMETER = 300 KILOMETERS; 1 INCH = 473 STATUTE MILES

```
0          500         1000
KILOMETERS

0          500         1000
STATUTE MILES

0          500         1000
NAUTICAL MILES
```

Soundings in meters below sea level

Southern Ocean Political Map and Depth Contours

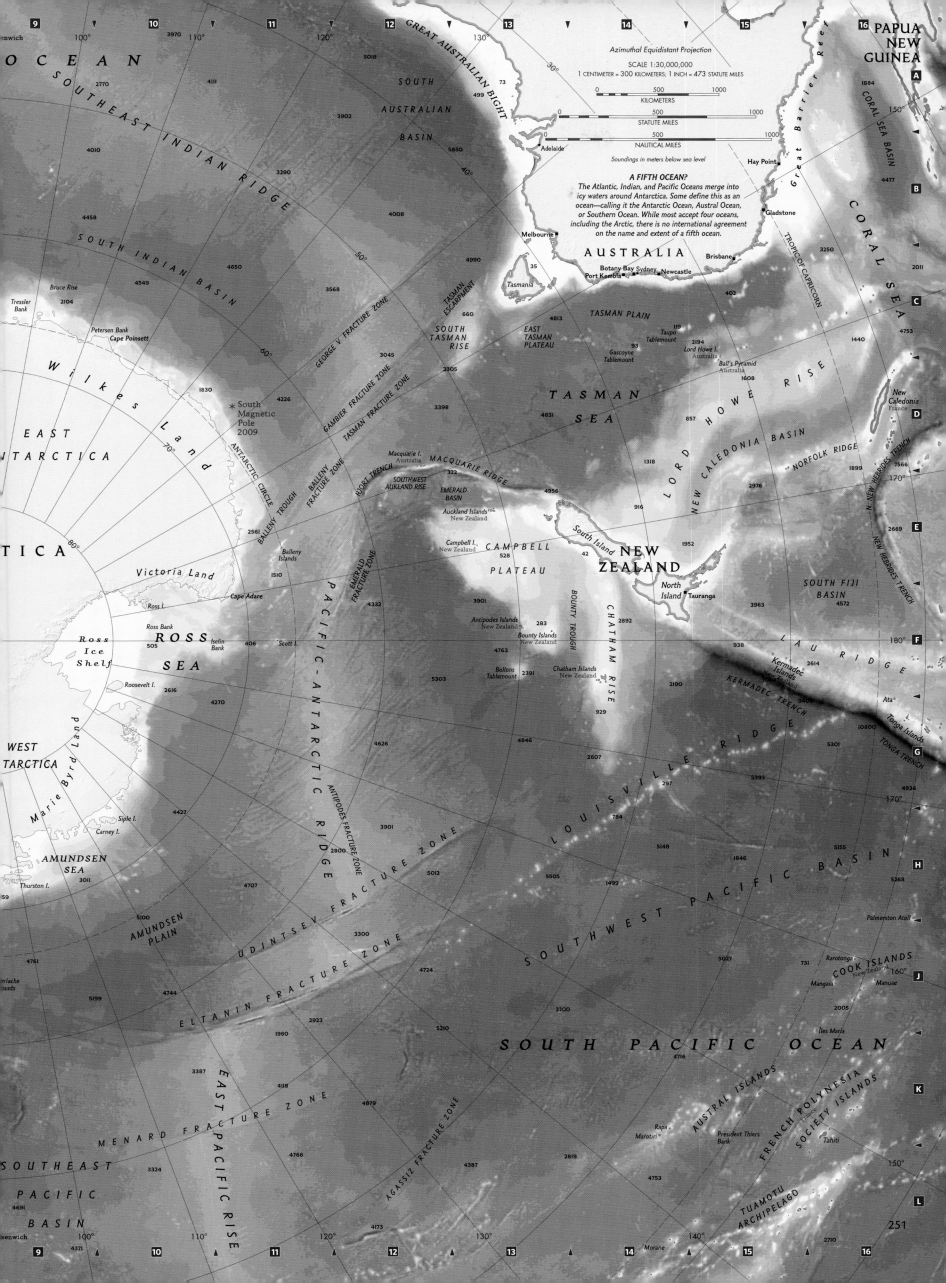

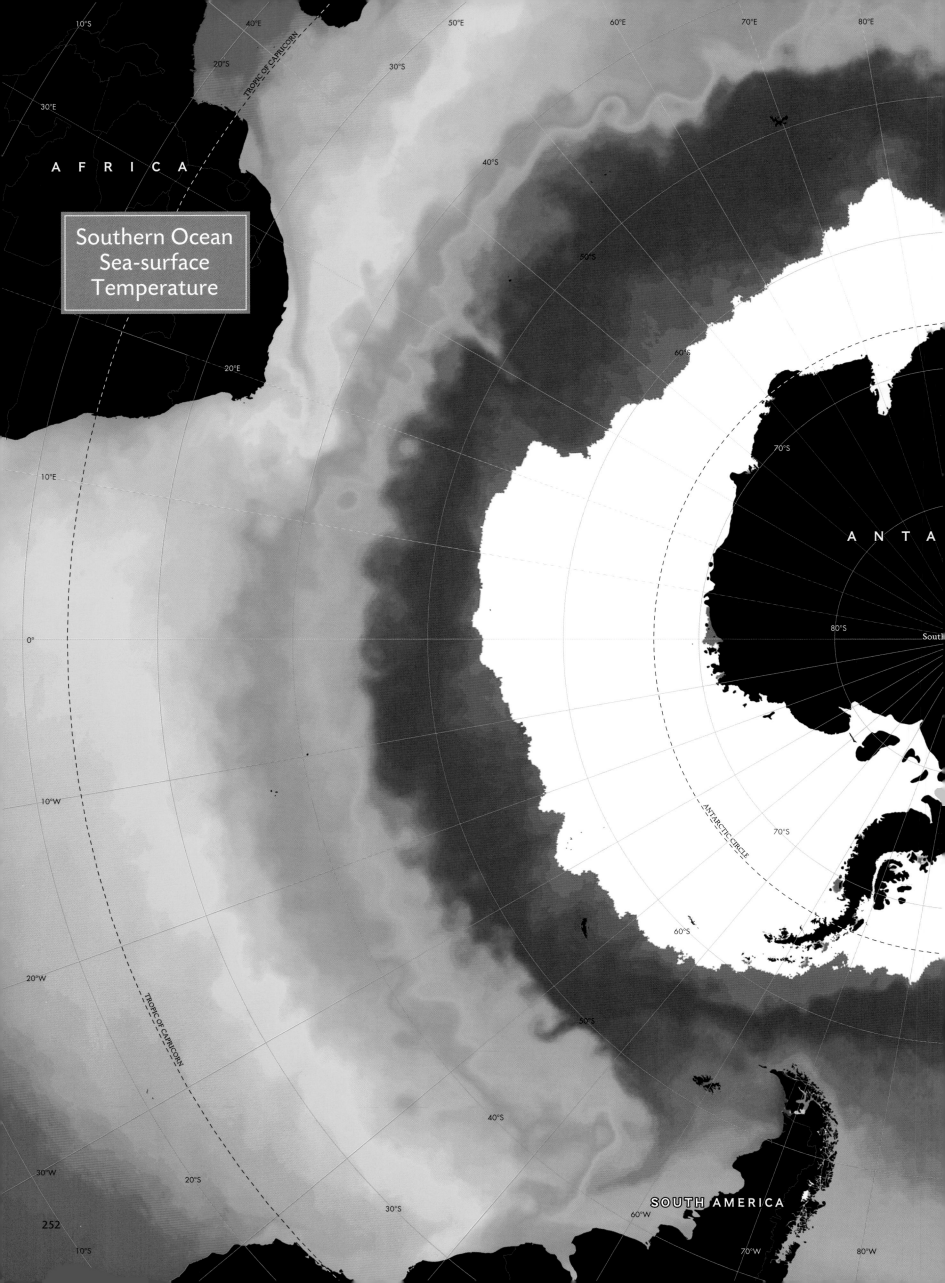

Southern Ocean
Sea-surface
Temperature

AFRICA

ANTA

ANT

SOUTH AMERICA

September 2007 (winter)

Degrees Celsius

-1 0   3   6   9   12   15   18   21   24   27

Ice

-30.2 32 37.4 42.8 48.2 53.6 59 64.4 69.8 75.2 80.6

Degrees Fahrenheit

A U S T R A L I A

A FIFTH OCEAN?
The Atlantic, Indian, and Pacific Oceans merge into
icy waters around Antarctica. Some define this as an
ocean—calling it the Antarctic Ocean, Austral Ocean,
or Southern Ocean. While most accept four oceans,
including the Arctic, there is no international agreement
on the name and extent of a fifth ocean.

ANTARCTIC CIRCLE

✳ South
Magnetic
Pole
2009

T I C A

Azimuthal Equidistant Projection

SCALE 1:30,000,000
1 CENTIMETER = 300 KILOMETERS; 1 INCH = 473 STATUTE MILES

0   500   1000
KILOMETERS

0   500   1000
STATUTE MILES

0   500   1000
NAUTICAL MILES

Soundings in meters below sea level

TROPIC OF CAPRICORN

TROPIC OF CAPRICORN

Chinstrap penguins look on as high winds churn near-freezing seas at Candelmas Island, South Sandwich Islands.

The Southern Ocean by the Numbers

Geographic boundaries: 60° S to 85° S / circumpolar

Total area: 20,973,318 square kilometers

Total volume: 71,515,351 cubic kilometers

Average depth: 3,239 meters

Greatest depth: 7,412 meters (south end of the South Sandwich Trench)

- Includes 6.5 percent of Earth's water area.
- Approximately 98 percent of the Antarctic continent lies under permanent ice sheets.
- If all ice on Antarctica were to melt, sea levels worldwide would rise more than 60 meters.
- Coldest temperature on Earth, recorded at Vostok Station, Antarctica, on July 21, 1983, was −89°C.
- Contains the largest ocean current, the Antarctic Circumpolar, which transports 130 million cubic meters of water per second, a hundred times the flow of all the world's rivers.

"[T]he breakers were white on a dark grey sea and the ice only had its whiteness broken with the most exquisitely shaded blues and greens . . . slabs the size of kitchen tables . . . so frozen, with every hollow and crack and crevice a perfect miracle of blue and green light."

—Edward A. Wilson, *Diary of the "Discovery" Expedition to the Antarctic Regions 1901–1904*

WEB LINK: International Hydrographic Organization (IHO)

Like a moat around a frozen castle, 21 million square kilometers of turbulent, near-freezing water churns around the continent of Antarctica in a roughly circular course, effectively forming a liquid barrier between waters at the cold southern reaches of the world and the warmer oceans to the north.

Once regarded as the southernmost waters of the Atlantic, Pacific, and Indian Oceans, this mass of water is sometimes referred to as the Antarctic Ocean. In 2000, the International Hydrographic Organization (IHO) declared the region reaching from the edges of the Antarctic continent up to 60° S latitude all around the globe to be the Southern Ocean. When asked about the need to formally designate the Southern Ocean as the world's fifth, Commodore John Leech, then director of the IHO, said, "Thinking of this body of water as various parts of the Atlantic, Pacific and Indian Oceans makes no scientific sense. New national boundaries arise for geographical, cultural or ethnic reasons. Why not a new ocean, if there is sufficient cause?" Although the term is now widely used in the Southern Hemisphere, it is not yet universally recognized.

Other oceans are largely confined by land, but the northern boundary of the Southern Ocean is fluid and flexible. The 60° S limit was chosen to coincide with the northern boundary of influence of the original United Nations Antarctic Treaty of 1959, but the watermass itself often ranges well north of this line. The natural boundary where the cold polar current collides with the warmer waters of the great oceans to the north is known as the Antarctic Convergence, a 40-kilometer-wide ring of rich biological activity and distinctive air and water temperature that sometimes flows as far north as 50° S or more. A later international treaty dealing with the marine life of the Southern Ocean—the Convention on the Conservation of Antarctic Marine Living Resources of 1982—recognized this phenomenon of marine animals following the frigid waters of the Antarctic Circumpolar Current north of the 60° S line and set its limits of influence to range from 60° S up to 45° S latitude in various sectors surrounding Antarctica.

WEB LINK: Antarctica animation

The encircling Southern Ocean is strongly influenced by the continent of Antarctica—the coldest, highest, windiest, driest landmass in the world—14.2 million square kilometers of frigid, largely ice-covered land at the southernmost end of the planet. Antarctica has the highest average elevation of any continent, the lowest average temperature recorded, and the deepest depression on the planet's land surface. The incredible weight of Antarctica's 3.2-kilometer-high ice sheet actually pushes much of the continent below sea level, with a downward depression of more than 3,400 meters.

More than 90 percent of Earth's fresh water is contained in the permanent ice sheet of Antarctica—a 225-million-cubic-kilometer, diamond-bright slab of frozen water. It reflects as much as 83 percent of the sun's radiation back to space, and is substantially chillier than its counterpart at the North Pole, where ice partly melts in the summer months and resulting dark waters absorb solar heat. Penguins, terns, seals, and sea lions are the most conspicuous forms of life dwelling on the Antarctic continent, but they spend a lot of time on and under the sea where they share space with an abundance and diversity of life comparable to tropical reefs.

Fragile but fiercely armed with defensive chemicals, a dorid nudibranch, Tritoniella belli, approaches the crown of a tube-dwelling polychaete worm, anchored on the seafloor in Antarctic waters.

Right: *A natural boundary, the Antarctic Convergence shown here is as effective as a corral for temperature-sensitive creatures. Ranging around the Antarctic continent between 45° S and 60° S, it marks the shifting edge of the cold Antarctic Circumpolar Current where it encounters the more temperate Atlantic, Pacific, and Indian Ocean waters. Cold Southern Ocean water sinks and moves north beneath the lighter, warmer waters, helping to drive the great ocean conveyor belt.*

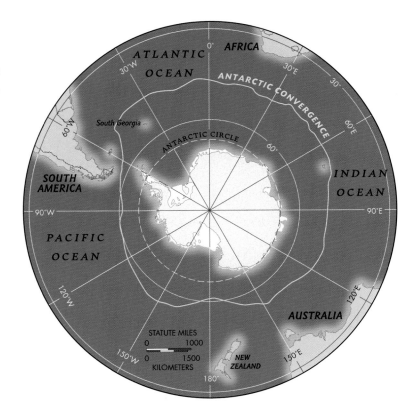

Below: *The Antarctic Treaty, signed in 1959, acknowledged overlapping claims from seven nations, but bound its members to preserve the continent for peaceful scientific uses only. In 1982, as part of the Treaty, the Convention on the Conservation of Living Antarctic Resources came into effect to regulate exploitation of marine life in the region.*

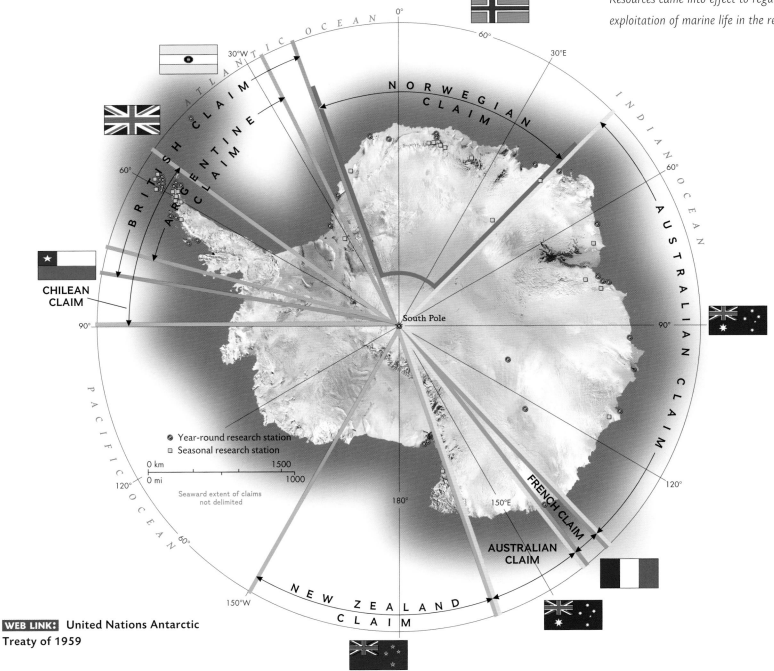

WEB LINK: United Nations Antarctic Treaty of 1959

Formation of the Southern Ocean

ANTARCTICA WAS ONCE A PART of the much larger landmass called Gondwanaland. According to fossil evidence from the Jurassic period, not only was Antarctica much farther north than at present, it was also warm enough to host lizards, giant ferns, and mosses. The remains of several dinosaurs and other animals characteristic of warm or temperate climates have been discovered on the Antarctic continent, including one fossilized dinosaur found only 640 kilometers from the South Pole. As South America, Africa, India, Australia, and New Zealand were broken off from Gondwanaland about 180 million years ago by the forces of seafloor spreading and continental drift, Antarctica gradually began moving to its present location at the Earth's southernmost extreme. The southerly location of Antarctica's air and watermasses, receiving heat from the sun only obliquely, is believed to have initiated formation of the Antarctic ice sheet about 35 million years ago.

WEB LINK: Mosaic of Antarctica

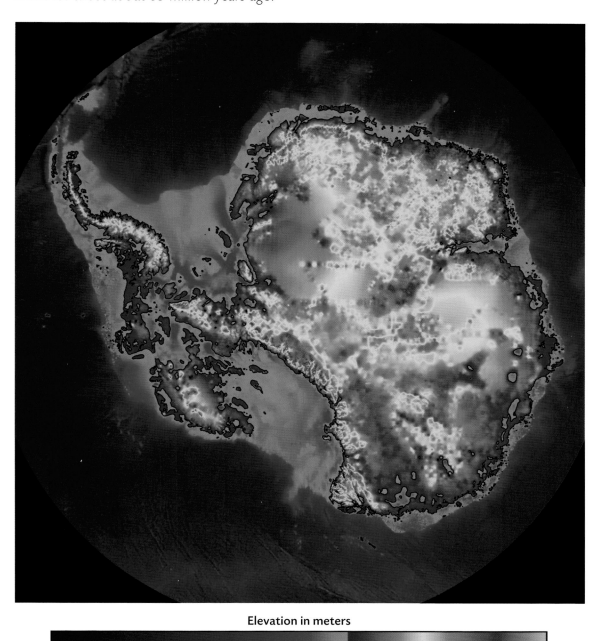

Take away the ice, and the archipelago of Antarctica, would appear as a single large island fringed by hundreds of smaller ones. Elevation is indicated by the color bar below.

Elevation in meters

-6,000   -4,000   -2,000   0   2,000   4,000

The Southern Ocean was formed in its present globe-encircling configuration when South America and Antarctica were pulled apart by plate tectonics, and Drake Passage formed and grew deeper sometime between 49 million and 17 million years ago. This opening allowed the Antarctic Circumpolar Current to flow unimpeded from west to east around the continent of Antarctica. During the southward drift of the Antarctic landmass, water temperatures in the Southern Ocean gradually decreased from a temperate environment in the late Cretaceous to its present frigid temperatures, ranging in surface waters to the seafloor from 2°C to −1.8°C.

Mid-Ocean Ridges and Hydrothermal Vents

UNDERLYING THE SOUTHERN OCEAN and essentially surrounding the Antarctic continent are various seafloor ridges. In the far south of the Atlantic Ocean there is a seaward extension of three continental plates—Antarctic, South American, and African—abutting at a place near Bouvet Island (at 54° 26′ S and 3° 24′ E) known as the Bouvet Triple Junction. Three active seafloor spreading ridges angle away from this dynamic juncture. To the north, the Mid-Atlantic Ridge is spreading at about 3 centimeters per year. The American-Arctic Ridge, angling to the west roughly parallel to the Antarctic coast, has continued for the past 9 million years to spread and move Antarctica and South America farther apart by about 1.45 centimeters per year. The dynamics of the eastern arm—variously called the Atlantic-Indian Ridge or the Southwest Indian Ridge—are more complicated. For about the past 1 million years, spreading along this ridge has stopped, and spreading has jumped slightly north to a new Speiss spreading ridge. Over time, this will probably move the triple junction to a new location, with a broad, diffuse, confused plate tectonics zone in the area until this resolves.

The Southwest Indian Ridge continues up into the middle of the Indian Ocean Basin, where it joins with the Mid-Indian Ridge and the Southeast Indian Ridge in another triple junction, forming the notable inverted Y seen as the central backbone of this ocean. It is at this point (at about 25° S latitude) where mid-ocean ridges range the farthest away from the Antarctic continent and the Southern Ocean. The immensely long Southeast Indian Ridge extends south from this junction and proceeds, between Antarctica and Australia, all the way to the Pacific. A graphic demonstration of seafloor spreading and continental drift—much like matching up the shape of coastlines on either side of the Atlantic—is the perfect symmetry of the Australian and Antarctic coastlines equidistant from this ridge.

Moving farther east across the southern margin of the South Pacific, the Pacific-Antarctic Ridge, is spreading and creating new ocean crust between Antarctica and New Zealand. As this ridge approaches the eastern Pacific, it is offset by a number of huge transform faults between 150° W and 120° W longitude, then turns north along the coast of Argentina and becomes the East Pacific Rise. Between this turn north into the East Pacific Rise and the American-Arctic Ridge on the other side of Drake's Passage, thousands of kilometers to the east, the seafloor is complex but lacking in spreading ridges.

Upcoming research is aimed at locating and exploring hydrothermal vents, mud volcanoes, and beds of methane ice. It is thought that communities of life around such habitats could be significantly different from those known elsewhere owing to isolation, but there is also the possibility that there may be links to other areas through deep currents. Mud volcanoes near the Sandwich Islands, hydrothermal vents in the East Scotia Sea, in the Bransfield Strait, and gas hydrates north of King George Island are targeted for investigation as a part of the Census of Marine Life Program, a global study of chemosynthetic communities. Better understanding of the nature of the Southern Ocean's ridge systems and vents is expected as a consequence of extensive research in the waters surrounding Antarctica during the International Polar Year (IPY) 2007-2009.

The Seafloor

THE SEAFLOOR AROUND THE ANTARCTIC CONTINENT was once thought to be a more or less continuous trough, like a deep moat around the land. But over the years, data have been pieced together demonstrating great complexity, including basins separated by ridges extending radially from the continent, deep channels, submarine canyons, and extensive outer banks.

South of the Atlantic, there are a number of abyssal plains lying under the Southern Ocean. Between the Bouvet Triple Junction area and the coast of Antarctica lies the Weddell Plain, flat-bottomed with an average depth of almost 5,000 meters except for numerous seamounts in its northern reaches. Most of the plain is covered in fine sediment from the rain of plankton from

Is There a Southern Ocean?

In the Northern Hemisphere, where the ocean basins are clearly defined by surrounding landmasses, deciding their limits is fairly straightforward. But in the Southern Hemisphere, with much more water than land and a strong current running right around the Earth between Antarctica and South America, Africa, and Australia separating ocean waters into defined basins is more difficult. The United Nations' International Hydrographic Organization says there is a separate Southern Ocean, and it ranges from Antarctica up to 60° S latitude. A major conservation treaty agrees, giving it a boundary that ranges between 60° S and 45° S, based on the habitat of marine animals they are trying to manage and protect. Nations are actually voting on the existence and naming of a separate Southern Ocean. Whatever the outcome of this great geographic debate, there are unquestionably distinct currents, water characteristics, and biological communities in the ocean surrounding Antarctica and even active spreading ridges growing new seafloor between Antarctica and all of its surrounding continents.

above, interspersed with layers of volcanic and coarser material from turbidity currents coursing down the continental slope. To the east, south of Madagascar, is a similar, slightly deeper basin, the Enderby Plain. The very large Kerguélen Plateau, about twice the size of Madagascar, angles southeast to northwest from near the Antarctic coast toward the great triple junction in the Indian Ocean. It appears to be a volcanic chain, like so many in the Pacific, caused by the crust moving across a hot spot in the Earth's mantle. With an average depth of about 2,500 meters, this huge underwater feature impedes the deeper flow of the Southern Ocean's Antarctic Circumpolar Current.

East of Kerguélen is the immense South Indian Basin south of Australia, and the narrower Bellingshausen Plain south of the Pacific Ocean, separated by an underwater ridge system that connects Tasmania and New Zealand to the Balleny Islands just off the Antarctic continent. Both average between 4,000 and 5,000 meters deep and display the usual flat characteristics of abyssal plains filled with sedimentary debris from the water above and from nearby continents.

An underwater ridge known as the Scotia Arc links South America's southern tip, Cape Horn, to the Antarctic Peninsula. The South Sandwich Trench lies mostly north of 60° S and arcs around the islands of the same name between 26° W and 33° W longitude. The trench is caused by subduction of the South American tectonic plate underneath the small Scotia Plate. It drops to a depth of 8,325 meters at its northern end, but the deepest place within the geographically defined Southern Ocean, south of 60° S, is 7,412 meters at the southern end of this trench.

During the Pliocene era about 2 million years ago, one of the largest meteorites known to have collided with Earth—a stupendous chunk of rock thought to be 1,000 meters in diameter traveling at 70,000 kilometers an hour—slammed into the Bellingshausen Sea west of the Antarctic Peninsula. Called the Eltanin meteorite, it was the only asteroid impact yet found in a deep ocean basin, one that is likely to have triggered enormous global tsunamis but seems not to have resulted in a wave of widespread extinctions.

SEE ALSO: subduction diagrams, pages 29 and 155

Dwarfed by an immense grounded Antarctic iceberg, a diver beams light across the seafloor where clusters of polychaete sponges, Isodictya erinacea, *thrive.*

Soviet charts from the 1970s include useful bathymetry surrounding Antarctica, but overall, because of its extremely cold, stormy, remote, and dangerous ice-filled waters, the Southern Ocean has had fewer ship surveys—and therefore less detailed information on the nature of the seafloor—than any other ocean basin. In 1980, the Canadian Hydrographic Service published depth charts of the Antarctic Ocean, a continuation of the Generalized Bathymetric Chart of the Oceans (GEBCO) series established in 1903 by an International Geographic Congress Commission on Sub-Oceanic Nomenclature, chaired by Monaco's Prince Albert I. An indication of how much Antarctic waters remain to be explored is illustrated by spaces left blank on current maps owing to lack of sufficient data.

WEB LINK: International Polar Year 2007-2008

That will change, however, based on data from new research and surveys in connection with the International Polar Year 2007-2009. Nearly all of the many ships deployed for the IPY surveys are equipped with precise positioning systems and sophisticated multibeam systems to enhance the bathymetry of what, for now, remains the least explored of all the oceans.

Fire and ice coincide in the South Sandwich Islands, as Mount Belinda spews ash, dusting a nearby iceberg and its cargo of penguins.

Seamounts and Islands

SEAMOUNTS ARE THOUGHT TO BE SCARCER in the Southern Ocean than in other basins—with an estimated 4.3 seamounts per million square kilometers. Little is known about them, and few have been well surveyed or even named.

Many islands and island groups are swept by the waters of the Southern Ocean. The climate of these mostly snow- and ice-covered rocky islands is influenced by their proximity to mainland ice, the surrounding ice pack, or the cold waters of the Antarctic Circumpolar Current. Circling around the Antarctic continent west to east, starting south of the southern tip of South America, the largest archipelago is the South Shetland Islands, rising from the seafloor about 120 kilometers north of the Antarctic Peninsula, in Drake's Passage. Eleven major islands and nine islets span out across more than 500 kilometers of ocean. Most are volcanic in origin, and one—Deception Island—is still an active caldera.

The South Orkney Islands are 600 kilometers northeast of the tip of the Antarctic Peninsula. Centered at 60° 35' S, and 45° 30' W, this is a group of four major islands and numerous smaller islets that are largely surrounded by pack ice during winter months. The largest of the sub-Antarctic islands—technically outside the Southern Ocean because they lie north of 60° S but encompassed by the circumpolar current—is South Georgia, at 54° 22' S, 36° W. It is about 161 kilometers long, much of it permanently covered with ice and snow. Just to the east are the South Sandwich Islands, a classic volcanic island arc created by the subduction trench that bears the same name.

Several peaks on the large Kerguélen Plateau pierce the sea surface to create islands at its northern end. A number of small islands and island groups dot the rest of the Antarctic coastline. Bechervaise and Magnetic Islands—along the coast near 62° E and 78° E, respectively—are sites where wildlife is monitored for the international Convention on Conservation of Antarctic Marine Living Resources (CCAMLR), as are the Shirley Islands at about 130° E. Another group, the Balleny Islands, stretching 160 kilometers across the Antarctic Circle northwest of Cape Adare at 163° E, is made up of heavily glaciated, low-lying islands of volcanic origin. Scott Island in the Ross Sea, very near 180° longitude, is the remains of a volcanic crater, only 50 meters high and completely ice-covered in winter.

Ross Island is the closest to the South Pole of any island not permanently covered with thick shelf ice. It lies in the Ross Sea at 77° 51' S on McMurdo Sound at the edge of the Ross Ice Shelf. Because of its proximity to the Pole, this island was used as a provisioning base by two of the most courageous Antarctic explorers—Robert Falcon Scott in 1903 and 1911, and Ernest Shackleton in 1907-08. The very cold, dry air has preserved the huts and their contents remarkably well for a hundred years since they were abandoned. Very nearby to these old exploration huts, also on Ross Island, is the largest scientific research facility in Antarctica, McMurdo Station, a permanent U.S. base since 1955 for local research and for logistical support to the South Pole Station. Four giant volcanoes—Erebus, Terror, Bird, and Terra-Nova—form the basis of Ross Island. Erebus is the largest, most active volcano on the continent, harboring within its fiery heart a red lake of molten lava 250 meters across. The Mount Erebus Volcano Observatory now monitors the volcano year-round, keeping track of phenomena first observed at the crater's rim by members of the famous 1908 expedition led by Shackleton. Lava bombs sometimes erupt as high as 1,000 meters, landing on snowy slopes surrounding the crater in a magnificent blazing display of fire and ice.

WEB LINK: U.S. McMurdo Station

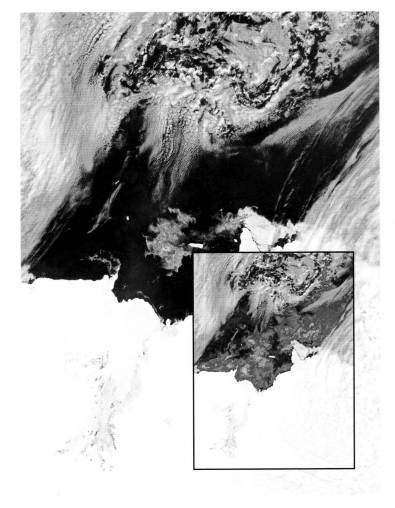

The world's largest glacier, the Lambert Glacier, flows northward from the bottom left of the image to the edge of the Amery Ice Shelf. Massive summer blooms of phytoplankton are indicated in shades of yellow and red.

Chlorophyll (mg / m³)

≤0.05 0.1   0.3 0.5   1   3   5   10   30   ≥60

Continental Margins

THE CONTINENTAL SHELF SURROUNDING ANTARCTICA is relatively narrow and unusually deep, ranging from 360 to 500 meters before it drops to the continental slope, descending to the seafloor between 4,000 and 6,000 meters down. The Weddell Sea and Ross Sea form two bays, each nearly as large as France, cutting deeply into the Antarctic continent—dividing it into East and West Antarctica on either side of the Antarctic Peninsula, which juts north toward the southern tip of South America. The continental shelf under both of these two seas is generally shallower and broader than elsewhere around Antarctica. Under the Weddell Sea, the shelf in most places is not deeper than 900 meters and fans seaward for 240 to 480 kilometers. The Ross Sea, situated between Marie Byrd Land and Victoria Land, is much shallower, with all of it less than 750 meters, and the eastern portions less than 250 meters deep.

March 1997

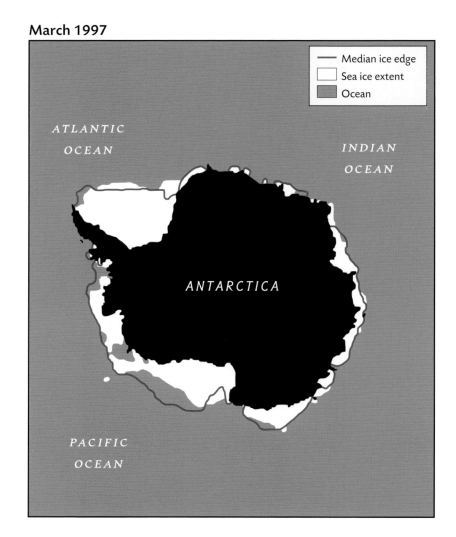

Legend:
— Median ice edge
☐ Sea ice extent
■ Ocean

ATLANTIC OCEAN

INDIAN OCEAN

ANTARCTICA

PACIFIC OCEAN

June 1997

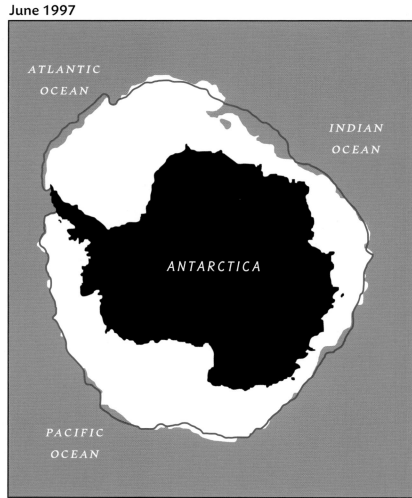

ATLANTIC OCEAN

INDIAN OCEAN

ANTARCTICA

PACIFIC OCEAN

March 2007

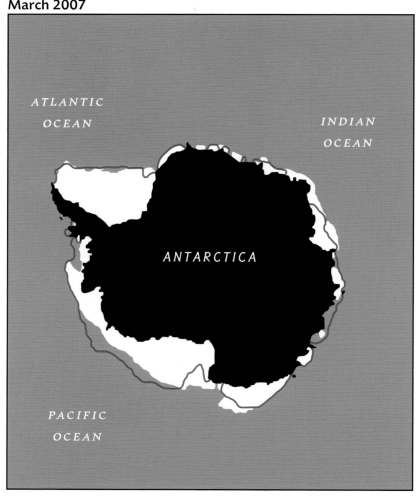

ATLANTIC OCEAN

INDIAN OCEAN

ANTARCTICA

PACIFIC OCEAN

June 2007

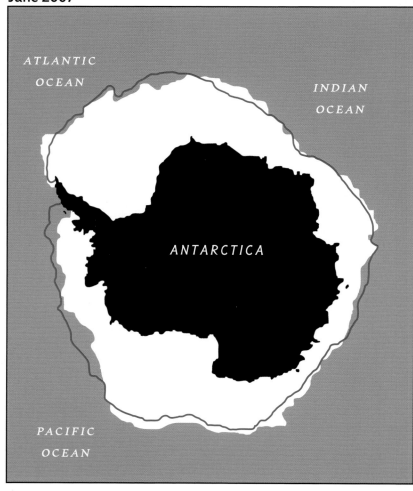

ATLANTIC OCEAN

INDIAN OCEAN

ANTARCTICA

PACIFIC OCEAN

Seasonal Fluctuations of Sea Ice: *Seasonal cycle of sea-ice coverage in the Southern Hemisphere in 1997 and 2007, from satellite passive-microwave data. In both years, ice coverage reaches its minimum in February and its maximum in September. In sharp contrast with the Northern Hemisphere, Southern Hemisphere sea-ice cover increased overall during the decade, although not by as much as Northern Hemisphere ice cover*

September 1997

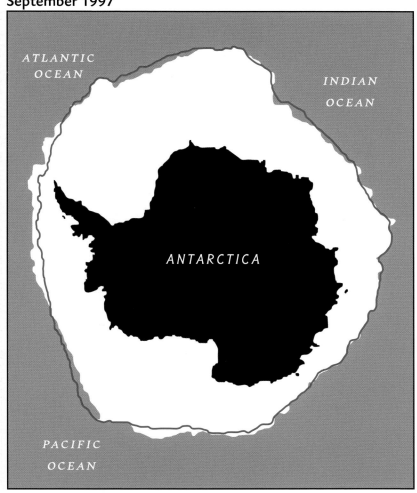

December 1997

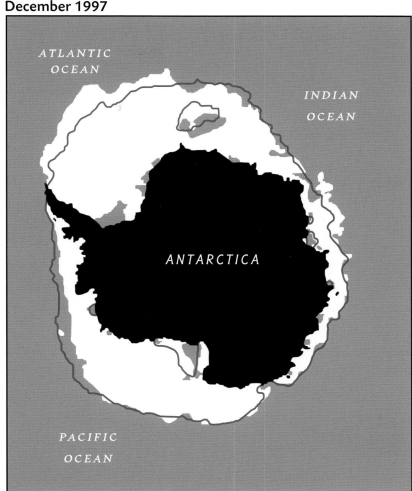

September 2007

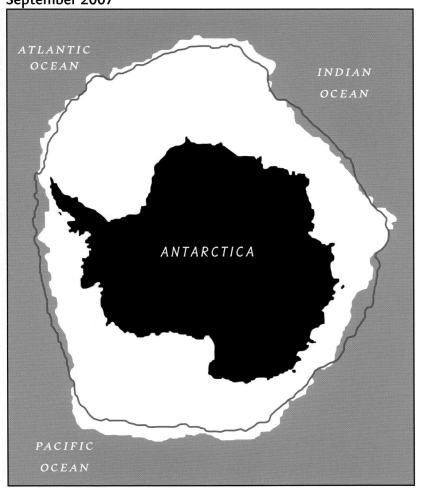

December 2007

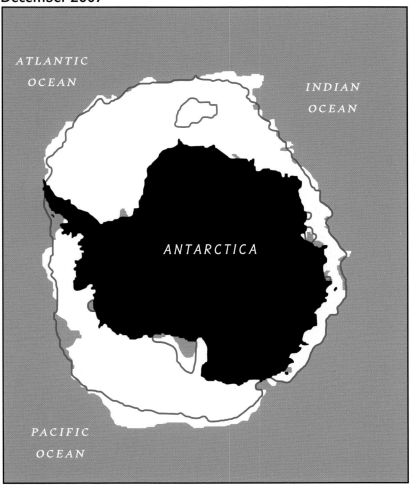

decreased. In each pair of Southern Hemisphere images (for March, June, September, and December), there are some regions where there was less ice cover in 2007 than in 1997 and others where there was more. The values mapped are the area covered by sea ice in each season. Images courtesy of Claire Parkinson and Nick DiGirolamo, NASA Goddard Space Flight Center.

Much of what appear to be the continental margins of Antarctica are actually frozen ice shelves—the seaward extension of the great continental ice sheet. The immense weight of the 3-kilometer-high inland ice continually pushes the coastal fringe outward, toward—and out over—the surrounding ocean. Accompanied by an intermittent symphony of deep rumbling groans, cracks, and high-pitched screeching, ice flows in slow motion via "rivers" of deforming, stretching, cracking ice, inexorably shunting the accumulation of thousands of years of frozen water toward the sea. Most fringing ice sheets floating above the Southern Ocean rise as much as 100 meters above sea level and change size, shape, and thickness seasonally and over long periods of time. Huge masses of shelf ice engulf much of the Ross Sea (the Ross Ice Shelf) and the Weddell Sea (the Ronne and Filchner Ice Shelves). Pack ice surrounds the ice shelves, and beyond that is a moving flotilla of small, medium, and sometimes very large chunks of drifting ice that have broken away.

Every year, thousands of icebergs break away, typically tabular or flat-topped giants 1.5 kilometers or more long that calve with loud, booming sounds as they plunge into the ocean. Some are colossal, more than 160 kilometers from one end to the other, encompassing thousands of square kilometers. Once adrift, the ice crystals within the bergs—some frozen for thousands of years—eventually melt and return to the sea as fresh water or to the atmosphere as water vapor. Although the size and shape of the ice surrounding Antarctica has always been in flux, the recent sloughing off of large masses of long-frozen areas is unprecedented in human history.

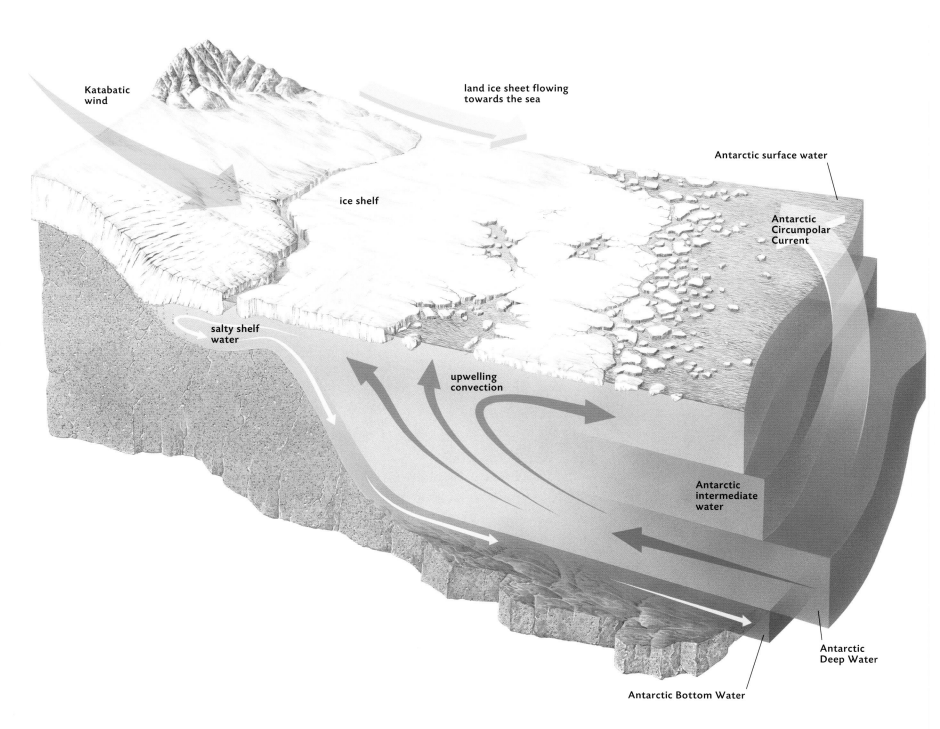

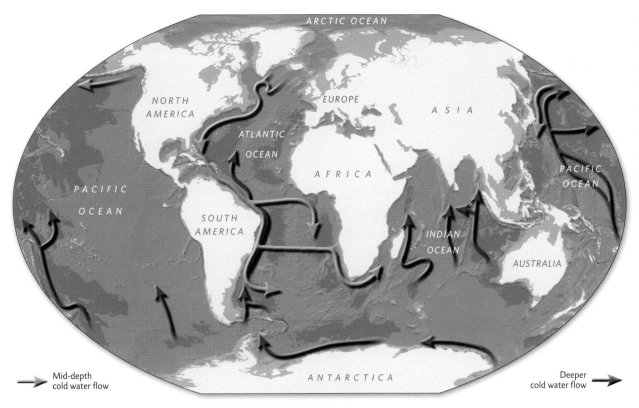

ARCTIC OCEAN

NORTH
AMERICA

EUROPE

ASIA

ATLANTIC
OCEAN

AFRICA

PACIFIC
OCEAN

PACIFIC
OCEAN

SOUTH
AMERICA

INDIAN
OCEAN

AUSTRALIA

ANTARCTICA

→ Mid-depth
cold water flow

Deeper →
cold water flow

SEE ALSO: Grace Mission, page 30

Subsurface Currents: *The dense, cold water of the Southern Ocean sinks and spreads northward into the Atlantic, Pacific and Indian Oceans as Antarctic Bottom Water, shown in the diagram below. As it travels, the deep, cold flow gradually mixes with overlying water, growing warmer, less dense, and rising to the surface. Via the global system of currents, a parcel of Antarctic Bottom Water that leaves the Southern Ocean will return in a thousand years or more and then begin the journey again.*

Tides and Currents

DATA OBTAINED FROM THE SATELLITE-BASED Gravity Recovery and Climate Experiment (GRACE) mission, from August 2002 to June 2004, suggest that tidal action not only causes very broad-scale up-and-down movements of the great ice shelves, but may also chew away at the underside of the ice. Both of these processes are likely to contribute to the slippage and breakup of shelf ice.

The Antarctic Circumpolar Current is the world's largest ocean currents. Mostly driven by wind, it sweeps slowly but powerfully around Antarctica from west to east in a giant globe-encircling ring 21,000 kilometers long and as much as 3,000 meters deep. Unlike all other major ocean currents, it is uninterrupted by any continental landmasses. In places as fast-moving as 1.5 meters per second, its surface flow generally moves at less than 0.3 meters per second. The current is so wide and deep that it carries about 120 million metric tons of water a second, more than twice as much as the Gulf Stream and about 100 times as much as all of the world's rivers combined.

Despite its appearance as an enormous mixer churning at full tilt, measurements of temperature and salinity within this circumpolar mass of water reveal three distinct layers. At the top floats a layer about 180 meters thick of cold, low-salinity water diluted by melted ice. A slightly warmer but saltier layer lies underneath this and extends down to about 1,500 meters. Beneath Antarctica's ice shelves, particularly in the Weddell and Ross Seas, the formation of sea ice takes up fresh water from the sea and leaves salty, dense waters that sink to the bottom. Cold and very salty water also flows in along the seafloor all the way from the North Atlantic. Becoming even more chilled as it reaches the far southern latitudes, this coldest, saltiest, densest watermass on Earth moves around Antarctica between 1,500 meters and the seafloor and then makes its way back north along the bottom into the other ocean basins.

The existence of a previously unknown large, deep current was discovered in 2007. It flows south down the eastern coast of Australia and around the island of Tasmania, and then moves west past Australia's coast, at a depth of about 800 to 1,000 meters, into the Indian Ocean. K. R. Ridgway and J. R. Dunn from Australia's Commonwealth Scientific and Industrial Research Organization (CSIRO) identified the current—which they named the Tasman Outflow—based on an analysis of data collected over 50 years from satellites, ships, and ocean monitoring stations. This flow serves as a "supergyre" that connects the mid-depth waters of the Pacific, Indian, and Atlantic Oceans near the margins of the Southern Ocean. The discovery provides a critical missing link in our understanding of the great global ocean conveyor belt that carries currents—and heat—around the world ocean.

WEB LINK: Commonwealth Scientific and Industrial Research Organization

Chris McKay
SPACE STUDIES OF ANTARCTICA

Liquid water is the one ecological requirement that all life on Earth has in common, and the first step in the search for life beyond the Earth is to find water. As it happens, the worlds in our solar system that may contain liquid water are cold and the water below the surface is in contact with ice. The planet Mars and the icy moons of Jupiter and Saturn are the likely targets. We are searching for possible life in cold, ice-covered waters, so we turn to the ice-covered oceans and lakes of Antarctica as the best example on Earth of these conditions. In the Antarctic Ocean there is a surprising richness of life below the ice, where nutrient-rich water is carried up by

lakes in the past. The presence of heavily cratered terrain juxtaposed next to large rivers and lakes indicates that the climate on Mars was cold, with a snow-based hydrological cycle. Rain, if present, would have caused enough erosion to erase the craters. The Antarctic dry valleys provide the only example on Earth of rivers and lakes without rain. Seasonal melting of glaciers provides the water input to sustain perennially ice-covered lakes. Beneath the 5-meter-or-so-thick ice cover of these lakes we find photosynthetically based microbial ecosystems. Could similar systems have functioned on Mars in ice-covered lakes billions of

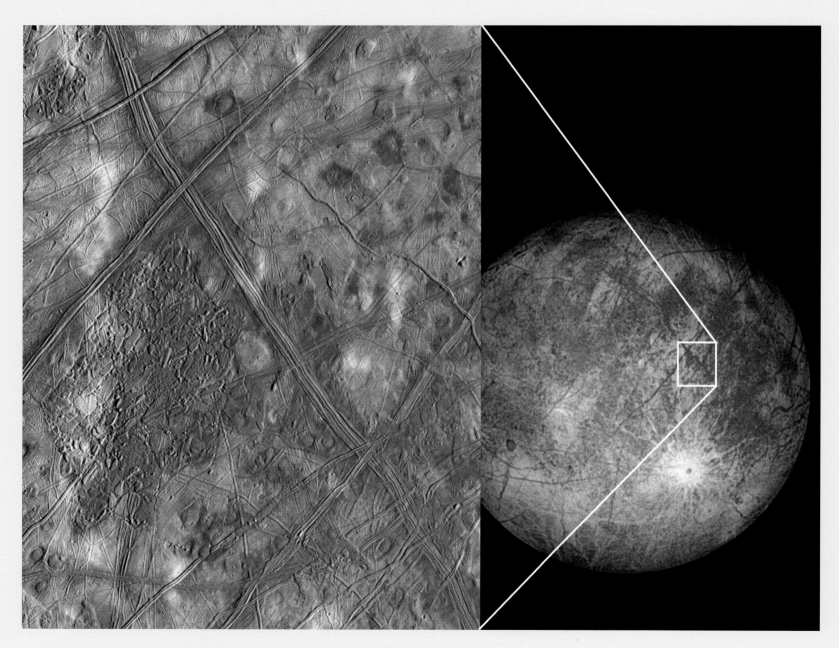

Europa, Jupiter's fourth largest moon (slightly smaller than Earth's moon), may have an ocean under its icy surface. Blocks of ice appear to have rafted over the surface.

cold currents. In the summer, light penetrates the relatively thin one-year ice and powers photosynthesis. Studying these systems on Earth, we seek to understand if similar processes might be occurring in cracks in the surface ice on Europa—a moon of Jupiter with an ocean under its icy surface.

There does not appear to be liquid water on the surface of Mars today, but there is considerable evidence that there were rivers and

years ago, and if so, can we find evidence of these ecosystems in the preserved sediments?

Enceladus, a tiny moon of Saturn, may be the easiest target for sampling liquid water environments on other worlds. From the south pole of Enceladus a geyser sprays a shower of ice and water vapor into space. The source of this ice is thought to be a pressurized subsurface aquifer.

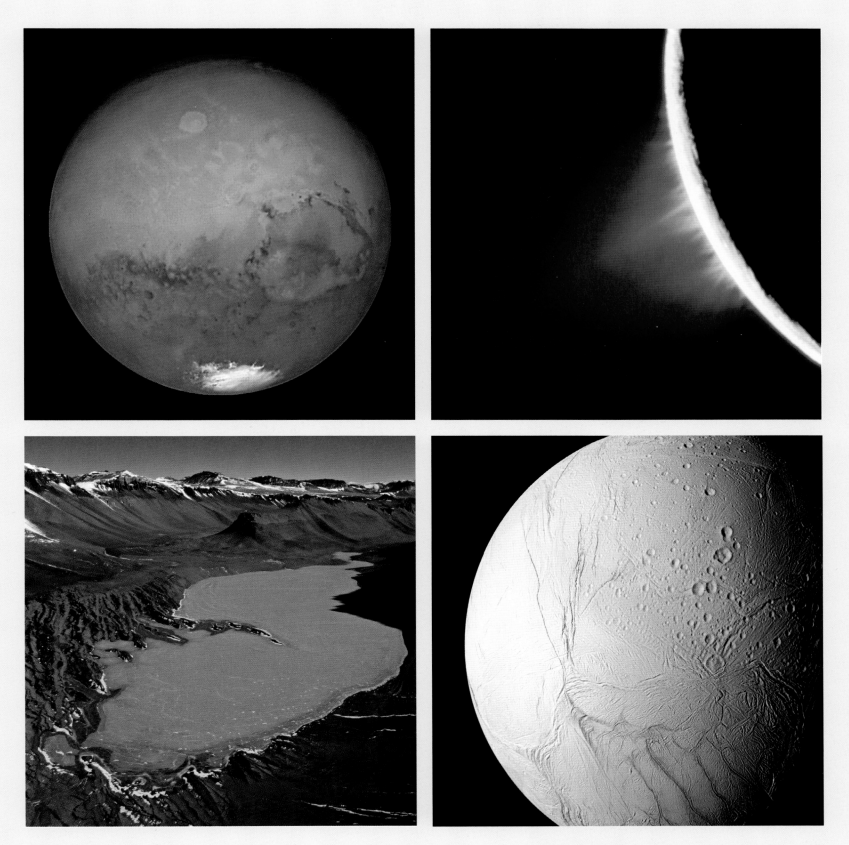

Mars (top left), a cold dry world with polar caps of dry ice in winter, may have been wet but still cold early in its history. Lake Vanda in Victoria Land, Antarctica (bottom left), is a perennially ice-covered lake and a possible model for early Mars. Enceladus (bottom right) an icy moon of Saturn has a jet of ice and methane (top right) rising from its south pole. A subsurface liquid water aquifer may be the source of this ice and methane. Could the methane be biological in origin?

Methane and nitrogen, but not ammonia, are present in the plume. Methanogens (organisms that produce methane as a metabolic by-product in oxygenless conditions) are known to survive in ice-covered waters in the Antarctic, and these compounds could be a model for subsurface life on Enceladus. The plume we sample may contain the evidence of such life. Looking at the systems on Earth may tell us what to look for when we send probes to fly through and sample the plume on Enceladus. The aquifer on Enceladus may be similar to Lake Vostok and other lakes known to exist deep below the polar plateau in Antarctica but are as yet unexplored.

As we explore other water worlds, we cannot say in advance what we will find. We may find only organic molecules and no life, or we may discover life that is identical to Earth life. Most interesting of all, we may find life that is truly alien—evidence for a second genesis. If in our own solar system life originated twice, then surely the universe is full of life. The ice-covered lakes and ocean of the Antarctic provides a place to test the instruments we plan to send to icy worlds beyond.

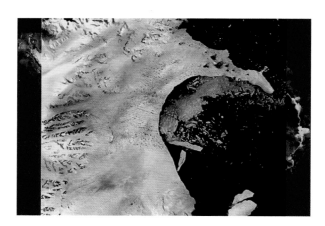

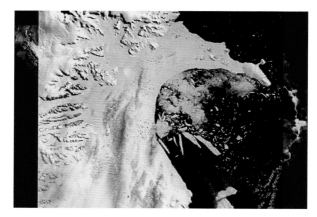

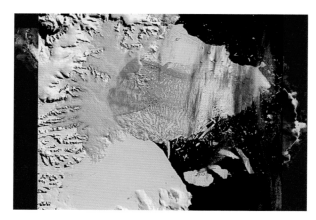

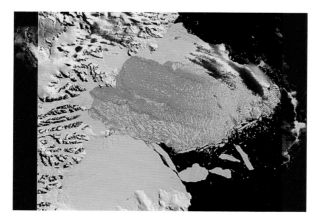

Weather and Climate

THE COLDEST TEMPERATURE EVER SEEN on the Earth's surface, −89.2°C, was recorded on July 21, 1983, at Russia's Vostok Station, which sits atop ice 3.5-kilometers thick about 1,300 kilometers away from the geographic South Pole in the direction of Australia. The most consistently cold place on the planet documented so far was at Plateau Station, a temporary research and provisioning station occupied from 1965 to 1969, 1,130 kilometers from the geographic South Pole south of Africa and the Indian Ocean. The *average* temperature recorded there for three years was −56.7°C. Along the coasts of Antarctica, the annual mean temperatures are a relatively mild −33°C.

Blistering cold winds and high seas characterize the 1,130-kilometer-wide strip of wild ocean between the tip of South America and the long, curved finger of the Antarctic Peninsula, the notoriously raucous waters known as Drake Passage. In the latitudes called the furious fifties, and the savage or screaming sixties, storms often create 15-meter waves and winds of almost 200 kilometers an hour. As upper-level air circulates toward Antarctica from the tropics, much of the moisture is lost. Extremely cold, the air descends over the central polar plateau, flowing downhill across the Antarctic ice sheet with increasing speed until it blasts the coasts with hurricane force—up to 290 kilometers an hour. Average air temperatures for areas around the Antarctic coastline range from −8°C to −20°C in the winter, and from −3°C to 11°C in the summer months.

More than half of the Southern Ocean surface freezes over each Southern Hemisphere winter, from May until August. Even during the sunlit summer months, about 4 million square kilometers of ice cover remains. Large variations in ice cover during the year involve transfer of heat and moisture from the ice and seawater to the atmosphere, influencing winds and, ultimately, weather and climate over broad areas of the globe. The Southern Ocean strongly influences global climate, weather, temperature, and chemistry, as roughly one-third of the carbon dioxide absorbed from the atmosphere by the ocean occurs in the cold waters of the region. Taken together, the Antarctic continent, the surrounding ocean, and the atmosphere above make up about 10 percent of the Earth, a relatively small but highly influential part of what makes the world function as it does.

Through the ages, snow falling on the ice sheet has accumulated, frozen, and trapped evidence of the prevailing climatic conditions of the time. The ice is a vast storehouse of historic information available for those who are willing and able to obtain and read it. Cores drilled into Antarctic ice have yielded insight into Earth's past, including records of temperature, atmospheric chemistry, and evidence of volcanic eruptions. A 2004 report in *Nature* described analysis of a 3 kilometer long ice core composed of compressed snowfall from the past 740,000 years high on East Antarctica's plateau.

French scientists analyzing deep-ice cores have found a correlation between rising temperature and carbon dioxide levels in ancient times, and in so doing, discovered important clues to natural causes of global warming. But the uppermost strata contain indications of significant human-induced events, such as traces of pollution starting with the industrial revolution and the detonation of the first atomic bomb. Along with methane and other greenhouse gases, carbon dioxide (CO_2) helps trap solar heat in the Earth's atmosphere that would otherwise be reflected back into space. The level of CO_2 has risen from 280 parts per million by volume (ppmv) at the start of the industrial revolution about 200 years ago to more than 384 ppmv in 2007. The increase in CO_2 is linked to the increased burning of fossil fuels that in turn is tied to the present unusually swift increase in global warming.

One of the most dramatic demonstrations of warming in the world was seen recently on the margins of Antarctica when the Larsen B ice shelf cracked and collapsed very suddenly. The northeastern coast of the Antarctic Peninsula is lined by a long, fringing ice shelf that covers three embayments where the Weddell Sea cuts into the land. Segments of the ice shelf have been named to reflect the separate bays that hold them. They are designated A, B, and C, ranging from north to south, and this also reflects their size, from smallest to largest. The small, northernmost Larsen A ice shelf cracked and moved away from the coast during the Southern Hemisphere summer of 1995. Then, in the summer of 2002, scientists witnessed the spectacularly rapid disintegration of the Larsen B ice shelf, which was 220 meters thick and 3,275 square kilometers in area, and had been in place continuously for 12,000 years since the last great ice age. Over a period of only 35 days, the entire Larsen B ice sheet shattered and sent 650 billion metric tons of ice in thousands of icebergs drifting into the Weddell Sea, destined to melt in the Southern Ocean beyond.

This false-color image captures some of the dynamics of the Antarctic using NASA's SeaWinds scatterometer, a specialized satellite radar that measures winds over the ocean and detects sea ice and snow melt. The white streamlines show surface wind computed using a numerical weather model at noon on July 18, 1999. Wind blows along the lines in the direction of the arrows. The darker pink and blue sea ice field surround the bright white and pink of the continent of Antarctica in this microwave backscatter image. The large bright region to the lower right of the pole in the center of the image is the "mega-dune" region of enormous snow dunes that are a kilometer wide and hundreds of kilometers long, but perhaps only a meter or two high. In the open ocean, wind speeds are depicted with lightest colors for the highest winds and darkest colors for the calmest winds.

Marine Life

SEVERE CLIMATE PROHIBITS MOST TERRESTRIAL LIFE on the Antarctic continent: microscopic algae occur in the Dry Valleys east of McMurdo Sound; several kinds of mosses and lichens have found places to their liking; and two species of flowering plants, a pink and a grass, grow in a few places on the northern Antarctic Peninsula. Other than birds and seals that are essentially marine, there are no land animals larger than mites, springtails, and tiny flightless flies. Captain James Cook, the first to step ashore on South Georgia Island in 1775, reported it as barren: "Not a tree or shrub was to be seen, no not even big enough to make a tooth-pick." Yet, this remote, rocky island, marked with deep fjords, huge glaciers, and a shoreline hugged by towering icebergs, is the single most important nesting and breeding ground in the world for millions of seabirds. Among birds that take to the air are fulmars, petrels, a type of prion, storm petrels, a cormorant, skuas, a gull, a tern, and a scavenging shorebird known as the sheathbill. The large albatrosses are wind-loving birds that may stay at sea for years at a time, feeding on squid and small fish. Seven species of flightless marine penguins breed on the continent and nearby islands, including the Adélie, chinstrap, gentoo, macaroni, and emperor penguins.

Life *under* the Southern Ocean, however, is rich, diverse, and extremely abundant, including representatives of nearly all of the major phyla, or divisions, of animal life on Earth. Many of the islands around Antarctica provide rookeries for prodigious colonies of seals and other marine mammals. Although temporary, icebergs—some a few meters across, others much larger than many of Antarctica's islands—provide havens for seals and birds above water, and a thriving menagerie of life within and around the frozen surfaces below.

In March 2000, an 11,650-square-kilometer tabular berg known as B-15 cracked away from the Ross Ice Shelf and plunged into the Ross Sea, soon splitting into several large fragments and thousands of smaller chunks of floating ice. A National Geographic expedition headed by New

Elegant on land and exquisitely adapted for swift maneuvers underwater, these emperor penguins, Aptenodytes forsteri, *trailing plumes of exhaled bubbles, can hold their breath for twenty minutes while diving up to 200 meters deep.*

England Aquarium biologist Gregory Stone and photographer Wes Skiles set out in 2001 to explore the underside of some of these floating ice-islands, plunging into −1.4°C water. Stone reported, "We wore two layers of underwear, dry suits, electric heaters, and two hoods. Still, most of the time in the water, our hands and feet throbbed with pain. It took several months after returning home for some of us to recover complete feeling in faces, fingers, and toes." Hostile for humans but hospitable for millions of sea creatures, B-15 provided homes for thriving communities of life that require a surface to grow upon, and a movable feast for roaming predators.

Herbert Ponting, photographer on Robert Scott's expedition to the South Pole, was among the first to record observations of Antarctica's unusual marine life. Through a crevice in the ice at McMurdo Sound, he noted swarms of codlike fish of a special family, the Nototheni-idae. "They have large heads, with bodies that taper off rapidly to the tail, and large wing-like

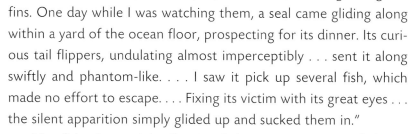

fins. One day while I was watching them, a seal came gliding along within a yard of the ocean floor, prospecting for its dinner. Its curious tail flippers, undulating almost imperceptibly . . . sent it along swiftly and phantom-like. . . . I saw it pick up several fish, which made no effort to escape. . . . Fixing its victim with its great eyes . . . the silent apparition simply glided up and sucked them in."

The fish observed by Ponting belongs to a group of closely related species that, according to marine biologist Richard Miller, composes a unique fauna that has been evolving "even as the Antarctic Ocean itself has evolved, in an area of the world where most other fishes have been excluded. The zone encompassed . . . is marked by the encircling sharp change in water temperature at the Antarctic Convergence." Some 20 families of fish, including 75 genera and more than 200 species, are known from the Southern Ocean and Antarctica's continental shelf. Among species so far identified, 76 percent of the genera and 90 percent of the species are notothenioids endemic to the Antarctic—that is, they are not known to occur anywhere else on Earth. These remarkable animals have developed amazing diversity, but the so-called ice fish are exceptional in that within their bloodstream courses a unique antifreeze compound that enables them to prosper at low temperatures lethal to other fish. The large fish known as the Antarctic cod is so adapted to the cold that its body temperature is maintained at 1.9°C; it dies when water temperature rises above 5.6°C. Although the seas of Antarctica are hostile to even the hardiest of humans, many creatures find the frigid Southern Ocean precisely to their liking.

Less than 15 years after Captain James Cook reported, "Seals or Sea Bears were pretty numerous . . . the Shores swarm'd with young cubs," sealers from Europe and North America rushed to convert the animals into furs and oil. In 1792, one vessel alone sailed away with 50,000 fur seal pelts and 45.4 metric tons of elephant seal oil. Within a decade, taking seals was no longer profitable, but hunting continued until all but a small relict population were killed.

Whaling began in the early 1900s, with a processing center at South Georgia Island, the industry hub. Between 1904 and 1965,

Blending with ledges of ice, this bald Notothenid or Borch, Pagothenia borchgrevinki, *avoids becoming a frozen fish owing to special glycoproteins in its blood that serve as antifreeze.*

Penguins vs. Polar Bears

Photographs of both Poles are defined by stark, white ice, but the life found around the two polar ice caps is very different. Seventeen species of penguins live around the margins of Antarctica; on the southern tips of South America, Africa, Australia, and New Zealand; and surprisingly in the Galápagos Islands near the Equator, but there are no penguins in the northern hemisphere or around the Arctic. On the other hand, iconic species of the Arctic—polar bears and the tusked and whiskered walrus—do not occur in the Southern Hemisphere. Very few plants or animals live above the ice around Antarctica, but beneath the ice life abounds.

Glowing like crystal, Antarctic krill,
Euphausia superba, *may live for more than a decade if not eaten by fish, squid, birds, seals, whales, jellies, and other dwellers in the Southern Ocean, or captured by humans who extract millions of tons annually for export to distant markets.*

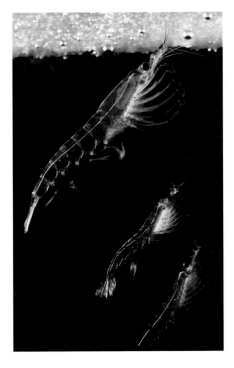

WEB LINK: Census of Antarctic Marine Life

Opposite: Under a canopy of frozen ocean, sea stars prosper on nutrient-rich deposits made on the seafloor by Weddell seals as they visit a breathing hole carved in the ice.

some 175,000 whales were taken—southern right, humpback, sperm, blue, sei, fin, and minke. The pace accelerated with the introduction of factory whaling ships in the 1920s, but by 1965 the last whaling station in Antarctica had closed. In a belated effort to give the whales a chance to recover from near annihilation, the International Whaling Commission created the Southern Ocean Whale Sanctuary in 1994. It included the environs of South Georgia Island and most of the Southern Ocean, but Japan continues to take hundreds of minke whales supposedly for research but really for food.

One of Earth's most abundant organisms is a translucent red crustacean about as long as a human thumb, commonly known as krill. Individually, krill are exquisitely beautiful, with large, dark eyes; a slender, glasslike body; numerous feathery legs; and brilliant blue-green luminescent markings, extremely useful for creatures that live in the dark most of the time. Collectively, krill are critical to maintaining the integrity of the Southern Ocean ecosystem. They feed on the rich blooms of minute phytoplankton that explode during the four-month season of bright sunlight; in turn, they are fed upon by numerous other creatures, from juvenile fish not much larger than they are to Earth's colossus, the great blue whale.

Krill are rarely found alone. More than 80 species are known worldwide, but the one most important to life in Antarctic seas, *Euphausia superba,* typically aggregates in dense swarms, many millions gathering in highly concentrated patches several hundred meters across and as many meters deep. The baleen whales—blue, sei, right, and minke—rely on large masses of krill as a primary food source, as do many fish, birds, squid, and seals. About half of the diet of the notoriously carnivorous leopard seal consists of krill. This little creature is the cornerstone of the entire Antarctic ecosystem, and depletion or disruption of its populations will resound throughout the Southern Ocean.

There is great uncertainty about how many krill there are, and many mysteries remain concerning basic aspects of their life history, including their whereabouts and behavior during the winter months, when research in Antarctic seas is the most difficult for humans. Studies so far suggest that, from egg to adult, krill pass through 18 stages, a process that may take more than two years; lucky individuals may live six to eight years, possibly more.

Looking after the future of marine creatures was not a feature of the 1959 Antarctic Treaty. By the 1970s, exploratory trawling for fish began before information existed concerning their population size, age, life history, or other data vital for fishery management. With no authority to regulate or even guide exploitation, industrial-scale fishing ensued. Within two years the fishery crashed. Proposals for controls were initiated in 1979 by scientists of the concerned nations, in cooperation with United Nations research and fisheries organizations, and in 1982 they entered into the CCAMLR Treaty, establishing broad powers for study and calls for protection of all biota of the Southern Ocean. A further agreement by Antarctic Treaty nations took effect in 1982, aimed at preventing overfishing of all living marine resources of the area.

As a part of the IPY 2007–2009, scientists from 30 countries and 50 institutions embarked on an expedition under the auspices of the Census of Antarctic Marine Life (CAML), which has resulted in the discovery of numerous new forms of life, from microbes to previously unknown species of sponges, corals, pteropods, jellyfish, and fish. The search for knowledge about the diversity, distribution, and abundance of life is now coupled with a sense of urgency about how ecosystems in the southernmost seas may be changing as climate changes and, in turn, how human impacts on these systems may influence production of atmospheric oxygen and absorption of carbon dioxide—matters of significance to all life on Earth. ☐

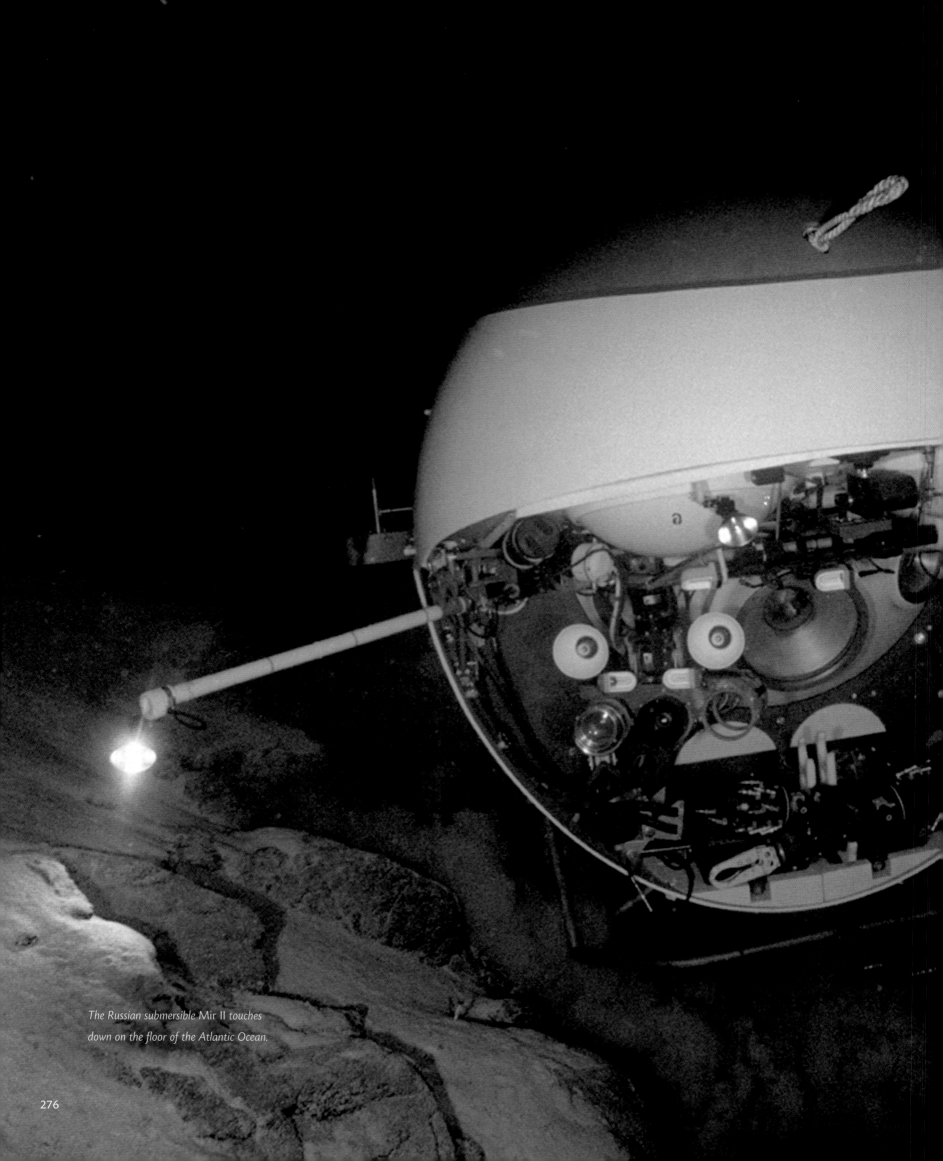

The Russian submersible Mir II touches down on the floor of the Atlantic Ocean.

Chapter 9

OCEAN EXPLORATION

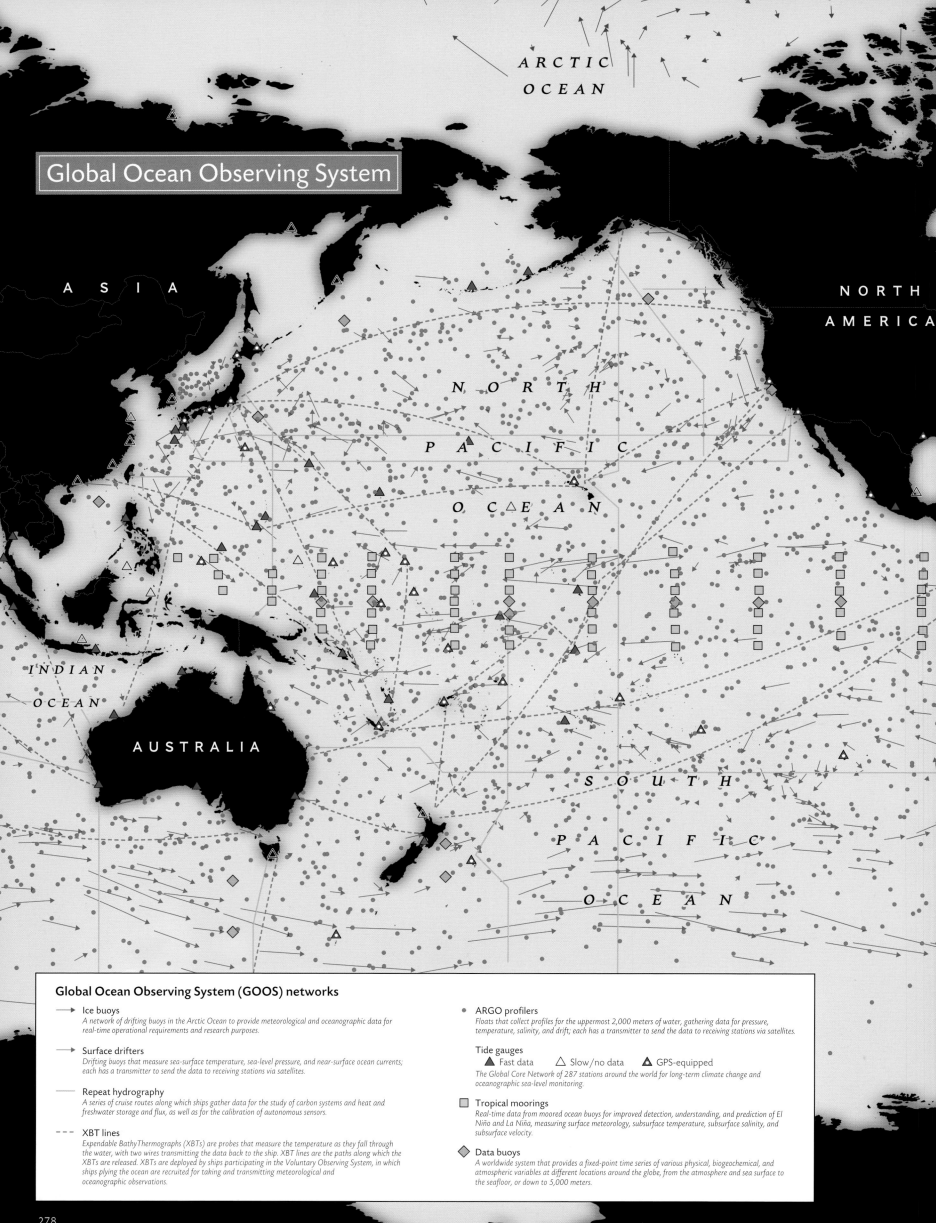

Global Ocean Observing System

ARCTIC OCEAN

ASIA

NORTH AMERICA

NORTH

PACIFIC

OCEAN

INDIAN

OCEAN

AUSTRALIA

SOUTH

PACIFIC

OCEAN

Global Ocean Observing System (GOOS) networks

→ Ice buoys
A network of drifting buoys in the Arctic Ocean to provide meteorological and oceanographic data for real-time operational requirements and research purposes.

→ Surface drifters
Drifting buoys that measure sea-surface temperature, sea-level pressure, and near-surface ocean currents; each has a transmitter to send the data to receiving stations via satellites.

— Repeat hydrography
A series of cruise routes along which ships gather data for the study of carbon systems and heat and freshwater storage and flux, as well as for the calibration of autonomous sensors.

--- XBT lines
Expendable BathyThermographs (XBTs) are probes that measure the temperature as they fall through the water, with two wires transmitting the data back to the ship. XBT lines are the paths along which the XBTs are released. XBTs are deployed by ships participating in the Voluntary Observing System, in which ships plying the ocean are recruited for taking and transmitting meteorological and oceanographic observations.

● ARGO profilers
Floats that collect profiles for the uppermost 2,000 meters of water, gathering data for pressure, temperature, salinity, and drift; each has a transmitter to send the data to receiving stations via satellites.

Tide gauges
▲ Fast data   **△ Slow/no data**   **▲ GPS-equipped**
The Global Core Network of 287 stations around the world for long-term climate change and oceanographic sea-level monitoring.

■ Tropical moorings
Real-time data from moored ocean buoys for improved detection, understanding, and prediction of El Niño and La Niña, measuring surface meteorology, subsurface temperature, subsurface salinity, and subsurface velocity.

◆ Data buoys
A worldwide system that provides a fixed-point time series of various physical, biogeochemical, and atmospheric variables at different locations around the globe, from the atmosphere and sea surface to the seafloor, or down to 5,000 meters.

ARCTIC
OCEAN

EUROPE

ASIA

NORTH

ATLANTIC

OCEAN

AFRICA

SOUTH
AMERICA

INDIAN

OCEAN

SOUTH

ATLANTIC

OCEAN

Miller Cylindrical Projection

SCALE 1:79,770,000

1 CENTIMETER = 798 KILOMETERS; 1 INCH = 1260 STATUTE MILES

0   2000   4000
KILOMETERS

0   2000   4000
STATUTE MILES

0   2000   4000
NAUTICAL MILES

Scale at the Equator

ANTARCTICA

Ocean Exploration by the Numbers

Amount of the ocean explored: about 5 percent

Amount of the ocean mapped in detail: about 5 percent

TIMELINE

First use of diving bell: Alexander the Great, 4 B.C.

First global exploratory expeditions: Chinese Admiral He, 1403-1433

First global ocean research expedition: H.M.S. *Challenger,* 1972-1874

First research descent to 1,000 meters: zoologist William Beebe and engineer Otis Barton, Bermuda, 1934, in a tethered submersible called the Bathysphere

Invention of Self-Contained Underwater Breathing Apparatus (SCUBA): Jacques Cousteau and Emile Gagnan, 1943

Successful descent to and return from the deepest place in the sea, the Mariana Trench: Don Walsh and Jacques Piccard in January 1960, in the bathyscaphe *Trieste*

First research submersible: *Alvin,* launched by Woods Hole Oceanographic Institution and the U.S. Navy in 1964, the start of nearly half a century of global ocean undersea exploration

First comprehensive census of marine life undertaken: 2000

First descent to the North Pole under Arctic Ocean ice: August 2, 2007, by two Russian Mir submersibles, each with three men on board

First global 3-D maps of the ocean and marine life available on-line through Google Earth: 2008

The ocean flows into the heart of the
Earth in Chandelier Cave, Palau.

The lure of the unknown, the search for new territory, trade routes, conquest, and new sources of food—all have been powerful motives throughout history for developing the ways and means to venture onto and under the ocean. In so doing, great truths have been revealed: those who sailed over the horizon would not careen off the edge of the Earth; no man-eating monsters lurked amid the waves; all landmasses are essentially islands on a planet dominated by water; and—perhaps most significantly—there is but one ocean. In the 20th century, the fundamental role of the ocean in driving the way the world works came into focus, as did the awareness that, despite its vast size and resilience, the ocean is not infinite in its capacity to accept what we put in or take out of it. Currently, the ocean is being surveyed with spacecraft, new instruments, and a growing array of undersea technologies that complement surface vessels; knowledge is being gathered, compiled, linked, and communicated in a new era of swiftly accelerating exploration and discovery.

Venturing Across the Ocean

WEB LINK: history of ocean exploration

AGES AGO, ALERT TO THE MOVEMENTS OF STARS, waves, and currents, and other subtle signs, people of the Pacific Islands collectively known as Oceania navigated across great distances in small, open craft without the benefit of charts, compasses, or sextants. There is evidence that people lived in New Guinea more than 50,000 years ago during an ice age when lowered sea levels narrowed the sailing distance among islands. Somehow humans reached Australia by sea about 40,000 years ago, and other areas of the South Pacific were gradually found as people developed increasingly effective means of traveling by sea. The Solomon Islands were populated at least 25,000 years ago, and following the end of the most recent ice age 18,000 years ago, new migratory waves fanned out over the Pacific's many islands. People became established on some islands of western Polynesia—Fiji, New Caledonia, Vanuatu, Samoa, Tonga, and the Marianas—3,500 years ago. Within two millennia, people had arrived at virtually all of the major islands of Melanesia, Micronesia, and Polynesia, owing to the mastery of the sea with vessels powered by wind and ocean currents. A little less than 2,000 years ago, by A.D. 300, the major eastward migration eventually included New Zealand, the Hawaiian Islands, and Easter Island—a tiny speck of land more than 4,000 kilometers west of the South American continent. When Captain James Cook explored Polynesia in the late 1700s, he encountered cultures whose means of transport was by wooden canoe with outriggers and double canoes equipped with triangular sails. It was, he said, "extraordinary that the same Nation should have spread themselves all over the isles of this Vast Ocean."

Based on locations and dating of man-made tools, it has long been thought that humans first reached North America 14,000 to 16,000 years ago by walking across the Bering Strait between today's eastern Siberia and Alaska on land exposed by a lowered sea level during the last ice age.

Twin prows of the Hokule'a, a traditional Hawaiian voyaging canoe, slice through Pacific swells on a 22,500-kilometer round trip between Hawaii and Easter Island in 1999.

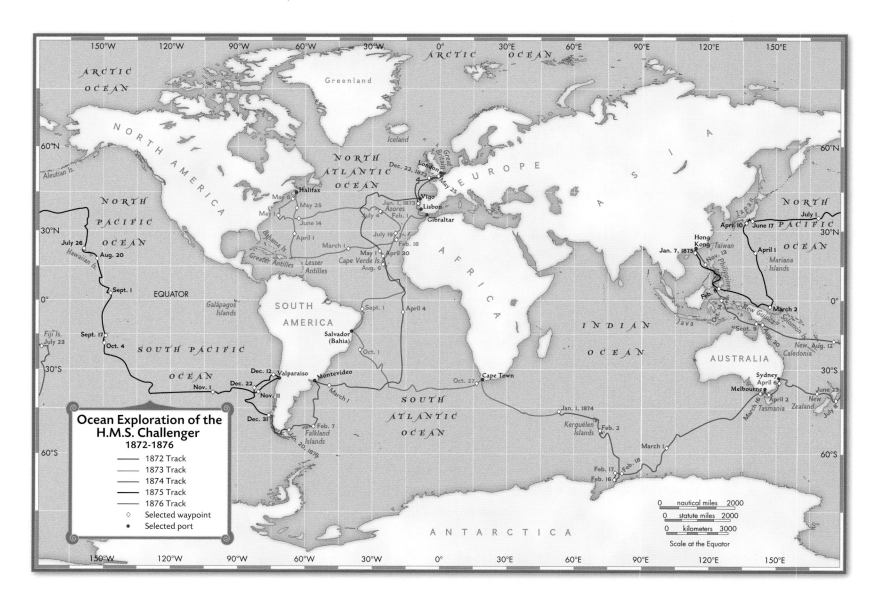

Ocean Exploration of the H.M.S. Challenger 1872-1876

---- 1872 Track
---- 1873 Track
---- 1874 Track
---- 1875 Track
---- 1876 Track
◇ Selected waypoint
● Selected port

The first global expedition dedicated to ocean research and exploration, the 1872-76 voyage of the H.M.S. Challenger marked the beginning of oceanography as a recognized scientific discipline. Scientists aboard discovered thousands of new species and recorded volumes of data about ocean tides, temperatures, currents, depths, and much more during 111,000 kilometers of travel at sea.

WEB LINK: **H.M.S. Challenger expedition**

New archaeological finds and more accurate dating provide evidence that humans may also have arrived in the New World by boat—across both the Pacific and Atlantic Oceans. Much of the history of these early voyages and settlements probably lies on the continental shelf, once exposed above sea level but now submerged.

Early methods of open-ocean travel likely involved tree trunks hollowed out as single-hulled dugout canoes or bound together as rafts. Above the Arctic Circle, the earliest seagoing craft were probably fashioned as they are today from animal skins artfully stretched over a frame of bone or minimal wood. Open versions, called umiaks, and kayaks with watertight enclosures have been used for thousands of years. The Phoenicians traveled into the Atlantic from ports with stone piers such as those from 6000 B.C. that are still being used in Essaouira, Morocco. Bundles of papyrus bound together in various forms were used for boatbuilding by Egyptians by about 4000 B.C., and sails assisted Egyptian boats with wooden hulls as long ago as 3200 B.C. Although largely confined to rivers, Egyptian vessels were also used for transport into the Red Sea and Mediterranean, and possibly into the ocean beyond.

About 3,000 years ago, variations on the concept of wooden seagoing galleys appeared, vessels equipped with both sails for cruising and oars for maneuvering in battle. For centuries, the Phoenicians, Greeks, Romans, Egyptians, Arabs, and others used such craft for warfare and trade. In the Mediterranean and later in the northwest Indian Ocean about 1,400 years ago, Arab wooden-hulled feluccas and dhows emerged, vessels with one or more triangular lateen sails. These progressive fore-and-aft rigs proved more nimble than the old square sails and were widely used until the 1960s, when trade between East Africa and the Persian Gulf was largely replaced with motorized ships.

A thousand years ago, the Vikings reached Greenland in open longboats with high bows and sterns, a single broad sail, and as many as 60 oarsmen, and they preceded Christopher Columbus to North America by several centuries. There is some evidence that the Chinese explorer Admiral

Cheng Ho may also have reached America before Columbus, during one of his seven voyages to the Western world between 1405 and 1433. The now famous European explorers—Vasco da Gama, Ferdinand Magellan, Sir Francis Drake, Captain James Cook, and Columbus—had little but their wits to guide them on their extraordinary voyages of discovery centuries ago.

The 1800s marked a significant era of ocean exploration, including the historic global voyage of H.M.S. *Beagle,* from 1831 to 1835, that took Charles Darwin to the Galápagos Islands and resulted in a quantum shift in scientific thinking. By 1872, when H.M.S. *Challenger* set sail from England for the four-year global expedition that effectively marks the beginning of the science of oceanography, a steam-powered engine complemented her sails and helped stabilize the ship during sampling in depths as great as 8,200 meters. By the 1900s, motorized ships became common, and by the 20th century, sails had essentially disappeared from commercial vessels. Never in the history of the Earth has the ocean been host to anything so large, fast, or numerous as the millions of watercraft now plying the world's oceans, from military aircraft carriers longer than skyscrapers are high to supertankers transporting millions of barrels of oil; passenger ships accommodating more people than some cities; and modern research vessels capable of forging deep into the polar ice, drilling deep into the seafloor, and extracting data from the surface to the greatest depths of the sea.

NAVIGATION

Before development of the compass, early explorers found their way around the ocean by dead reckoning, estimating position simply by time, speed, distance, and direction of travel from the last known position. Arabian navigators used a device called a *kamal,* a small wooden rectangle about one or two finger widths wide, held at arm's length to sight the position of the North Star, Polaris, relative to the horizon. Quadrants followed and upgraded the same type of readings. Astrolabes—instruments that show how the night sky looks at a specific place at a given time—originated nearly 2,000 years ago and were highly developed in the Islamic world by the year A.D. 800. Arabs introduced the astrolabe and quadrant to Europeans, who took the principles and developed the sextant, which also measures the angle of elevation of a celestial object above the horizon, and printed catalogs of star positions in the night sky. Based on concepts originating in China in the fourth century B.C., magnetic compasses pointing roughly toward the North Pole have also been used widely since the 12th century A.D.

Latitude—the position of a ship or place north or south of the Equator—could be estimated based on the angular height of the sun above the horizon at about midday or the height of the North Star above the horizon during the night. However, determining longitude—the distance east or west of a fixed point on Earth—relied on knowing the precise time, and no existing clocks could work on the rolling decks of a ship at sea. Englishman John Harrison, over 40 years of obsessive determination, devised precise chronometers that could measure time aboard a ship at sea and thus provided the key to accurate calculations of longitude. Captain James Cook used one of Harrison's creations in the mid-1770s to discover and map the locations of islands in the South Seas, and in the 1850s, twenty-two marine chronometers were aboard H.M.S. *Beagle* to assist in calculating longitude in foreign areas.

Despite advances, determining position at sea was challenging until late in the 20th century. In the 1950s, Loran, a network of radio-transmitting stations—along with equivalent systems called Decca in Europe, and Chayka in the Soviet Union—gave ships enhanced accuracy in coastal waters with signals that enabled them to triangulate their position among stations. By 1960, a U.S. electronic navigation system called Omega used similar theories and huge land-based towers emitting very low frequency radio signals to provide rough estimates of at-sea positions for ships

Below, top: An early aid to navigation, this quadrant has an arm that points to an arc of a marked circle.

Below, bottom: A critical precursor to modern navigation was the development of a way to tell the time precisely. Although large, delicate, and 40 years in the making, several supremely well-engineered chronometers were developed in England by John Harrison. One is shown here.

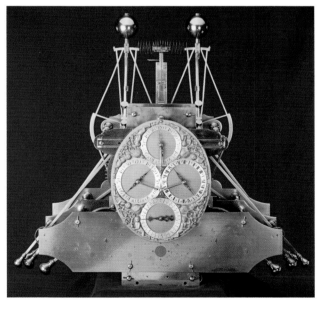

Still Using the Stars

There are many fancy new navigation systems that give precise positions using the global positioning system (GPS), with small units in cars, kayaks, even on wristbands. Positioning is based on where your unit is compared to the location of several GPS satellites at any given time. But what are the satellite positions based on? The heavens. Precise positions of man-made objects in space are based on the known positions of star-like objects called quasars millions of light-years away in deep space.

and aircraft globally. Also in the 1960s, the U.S. Navy developed and launched the first space-based global navigation system: Navsat (navigation satellite system), also called Transit. In recent decades, a satellite-based global positioning system (GPS) provides increasingly precise time, navigation, and positioning, making it possible to know exactly where on the planet you are anytime, anywhere, on land and at sea—a technological breakthrough that would dazzle seafarers of even half a century ago.

Exploring the Depths

OVER THE AGES, PEOPLE HAVE DIVED to gather food, precious coral, sponges, and pearls during descents while holding their breath. In Japan and Korea, for more than a thousand years, women divers called *ama* have free-dived for seaweed and shellfish. Pressing the limits of human physiology, a few hardy humans have descended briefly on a single breath of air to more than 150 meters.

Among the first to try capturing air to breathe underwater was Alexander the Great, reputed to have used a diving bell of sorts in 433 B.C. Aristotle described Greek sponge divers breathing air trapped in overturned kettles lowered into the water. Edmond Halley, best known as an astronomer, designed a diving bell used in depths to 15 meters. By 1715, the first diving suit—the Lethbridge barrel—enabled its occupant to descend to 18 meters for about 20 minutes. Owing largely to designs by Augustus Siebe, practical diving suits supplied with compressed air were in common use for commercial salvage and construction by the mid-1800s. But the first recorded use of diving for scientific observations was in 1844 when biologist Henri Milne-Edwards and a naturalist friend plunged beneath the Strait of Messina off the shores of Italy. To "pursue animals in their most hidden retreats," they took turns using breathing equipment designed by the Paris Fire Brigade for use in flooded cellars.

By 1943, the French naval officer Jacques Cousteau and engineer Émile Gagnan devised the first fully automatic compressed-air Aqua-Lung. The success of the Aqua-Lung, now referred to as scuba—for self-contained underwater breathing apparatus—has enabled millions to experience what Cousteau longed for and expressed in his classic book *Silent World:* "I reached the bottom in a state of transport. . . . To halt and hang attached to nothing, no lines or air pipes to the surface, was a dream. . . . Now I flew without wings."

Nitrogen in compressed air is absorbed into the bloodstream while diving; the greater the depth and time, the more nitrogen is taken up. The buildup of nitrogen in the blood must be expelled through decompression—a gradual process of pressure reduction that allows nitrogen to escape over time. If a diver returns to the surface too soon or too fast, the trapped nitrogen forms bubbles resulting in "the bends"—pain, trauma, paralysis, and sometimes death. To increase depth and time, various gas mixes have been tried, usually replacing or reducing nitrogen with another gas.

A concept for rebreathing air in a closed system that chemically scrubs carbon dioxide and replenishes depleted oxygen was developed in 1879 by inventor Henry Fluess primarily to rescue miners trapped underwater. Military versions using various gas mixes were in use by World War II, with University of Pennsylvania scientist Christian Lambertsen acknowledged as "the Father of the Frogmen" for his improvements of rebreathers and other diving systems. Now in use by a wide range of sport divers, scientists, and military and commercial divers, as well as sky-walking astronauts, rebreathers greatly extend excursion time, and the lack of bubbles reduces the likelihood of being seen by or disturbing marine life.

Living underwater for days, weeks, even months at a time seemed impossible until the 1960s, when Jacques Cousteau and engineer Edwin Link in parallel pioneered saturation diving, a technique that involves staying submerged long enough for tissues to become saturated with the gases being breathed. Once saturated, decompression time is the same, whether a dive lasts for 24 hours or 24 days. Successful dives hundreds of feet down were made in various underwater habitats—Cousteau's Conshelf I, II, and III; Link's Man-in-Sea program; and the U.S. Navy's Sealab project. In 1969 and 1970, while the first footprints were being planted on the moon, more than fifty civilian scientists and engineers demonstrated the advantages of

Named for Jim Jarrett, the person who tested the 1920s prototype, "Jim" is piloted here by author Sylvia Earle 400 meters deep in Hawaiian waters in 1979.

Bruce Robison
USING SUBMERSIBLES TO FIND LIFE

New technologies often serve to advance science, and deep-sea research is no exception. In the case of undersea vehicle technology, the scientific progress it enables is showing spectacular results. When it comes to exploration and the discovery of new kinds of organisms, submersibles—both remotely operated vehicles (ROVs) and human-occupied vehicles (HOVs)—have revolutionized the field.

Among their most important discoveries are the communities of animals found at deep hydrothermal vents, first observed by the HOV *Alvin* near the Galápagos Islands but now known to occur in most oceans. These assemblages contain species that derive nutrition from symbiotic bacteria that use chemical energy rather than solar energy to power the food web. Their discovery has had a profound impact across the biological sciences.

One of the great advantages provided by submersibles is that they allow scientists to see animals in the context of their natural habitats. For the vent species, it would have been very difficult to understand them, or their biology and ecology, if they had been brought up in nets with no clue to the geological and chemical setting they came from. Likewise, animals that are observed directly often look very different from those hauled up, usually dead, from the depths by a net. Many clues to the identity of a specimen lie in its dynamic characteristics, like color, shape, and behavior. Usually, these characteristics can be seen accurately only with the animal alive in its natural surroundings. A good example is the giant siphonophore *Praya*, which can reach lengths of more than 40 meters. Siphonophores are colonial predators that occur in chains easily fragmented by contact with nets. The random pieces we used to find in our trawl samples gave no hint of the huge creatures that awaited us when we were finally able to see them with our own eyes.

Another important discovery enabled by submersibles is the great abundance and diversity of gelatinous animals in the deepwater column. Traditional sampling methods employed nets, which typically turn these delicate animals into unrecognizable mush. When it became possible to make direct observations in the habitat using submersibles, it quickly became apparent that jellies are far more numerous and varied than was ever thought possible. The ctenophores *Kiyohimea usagi* and *Lampocteis sanguiniventer* are

The submersible Alvin *explores the seafloor at Cayman Trough in the Caribbean Sea.*

examples of species prominent in their deep, watery habitat but that are too fragile to be collected by traditional sampling gear. It was not until we could dive into their realm that they were discovered and described. Even today there are no preserved specimens in museums, only images recorded by undersea vehicles.

A further advantage conferred by submersibles is that they can be steered to follow an agile specimen that might easily avoid a net that is being towed blindly along a straight path. Fragile specimens can be collected with precise movements by a well-piloted submersible, and often these animals reach the surface alive and in perfect condition. Submersibles allow selective sampling instead of indiscriminate collecting.

As I write this I am sitting in the darkened control room of a mother ship, while an ROV flies through the water column 3,000 meters below us. High-definition video fills a large screen in front of me, and to either side are screens with readouts from instruments measuring environmental conditions and showing the status of the ROV and its subsystems. Microwave links connect us in real time to experts around the world.

The number of new life-forms yet to be discovered is very high; we have made thousands of dives deep into Monterey Bay and yet we are still finding new ones. These are not just new species, but new genera and new families of animals as well. My guess is that submersibles already have tripled the number of animals we know from the deep and that in the next ten years or so that number will increase by an order of magnitude. Without a doubt, the greatest era of ocean exploration has just begun.

Characterizing the deep ocean's enormous diversity of species is an important challenge if we are to be effective stewards of our planet. The principal problem for the scientists and conservation biologists who hope to expand our knowledge of deep-sea ecology is limited access to the tools they need. The technology of HOVs and ROVs is well developed, and the promise of autonomous underwater vehicles (AUVs) is growing. But the number of vehicles available for scientific research is very small. When every ocean-going research vessel carries a dedicated undersea vehicle, the age of deep-ocean discovery will have truly begun.

living underwater during projects using the Tektite underwater laboratory in the U.S. Virgin Islands. The Soviet Union, Germany, Japan, Canada, Norway, and other countries developed their own systems, with the U. S.-built Hydrolab eventually used by more than 300 researchers until it was retired in 1985. The technique is currently valued for commercial and military applications, but only one facility, *Aquarius,* remains in active use by scientists. Located in 18 meters of water about 5 kilometers offshore of Key Largo, Florida, it has been operated with funding from NOAA since 1992.

ATMOSPHERIC DIVING

The idea for staying dry and maintaining surface pressure within a submarine has ancient origins, but the first workable design was produced in 1620 by a Dutch inventor Cornelius van Drebbel. Numerous military systems evolved starting in the 1800s, mostly to operate undetected in a few hundred meters. Diesel-electric-powered systems dominated during two world wars, but the advent of nuclear power marked a new era. The first U.S. nuclear sub, the *Nautilus,* set records for distance and time, crossing from the Pacific to the Atlantic under the Arctic ice pack in 1954.

Laboratory and home, Aquarius *has enabled hundreds of scientists to stay underwater for a week or more in the U.S. Virgin Islands and here on Conch Reef, 5 kilometers offshore of Key Largo, Florida.*

U.S. nuclear systems and their equally sleek, fast, and hauntingly quiet counterparts, the Alpha-class Soviet submarines, traveled throughout much of the world in the latter half of the 20th century. Some engaged in exploration, notably the U.S.S. *Queenfish,* which charted unknown terrain under the Arctic ice in 1970. The U.S. Navy commissioned one special small, fast, and deep-diving nuclear sub, *NR-1,* deliberately designed for research. Since 1969, scientists have explored many parts of the world with *NR-1,* including the Mediterranean Sea, where Robert Ballard has used the sub's unique capabilities to find and document numerous ancient shipwrecks.

The search for treasure and scientific knowledge has driven development of numerous submersible systems. The German manufacturing firm Neufeldt and Kuhnke developed a one-man armored diving suit used in 1930 to recover 5 tons of gold bullion from the vessel *Egypt,* sunk in 130 meters of water off France. The same year, engineer Otis Barton and zoologist William Beebe descended in a hollowed-out steel ball, the Bathysphere, off the south shore of Bermuda, and later set a record for human exploration of the sea at a depth of 923 meters. Meanwhile, English engineer Joseph Peress developed a refined version of a one-atmosphere diving system, "Jim," named after his colleague Jim Jarrett who tested the suit. It was used successfully off the coast of Ireland to locate the remains of the vessel *Lusitania* in 100 meters of water; modern versions were later adopted for use in commercial and scientific diving.

One-atmosphere systems, from one-person suits to massive submarines, advanced significantly during the latter half of the 20th century. In 1948 Swiss engineer Auguste Piccard and Max Cosyns tested a deep-diving system they called a bathyscaphe and used it for dives to a record 4,050 meters near Dakar in 1954. Six years later, the bathyscaphe *Trieste,* with Piccard's son, Jacques, and U.S. Navy Lieutenant Don Walsh piloting, made the deepest dive possible—to the bottom of the Mariana Trench, 10,920 meters down. By the mid-1970s, twelve countries deployed more than a hundred small manned submersibles for various applications. The three-person *Alvin,* operated by Woods Hole Oceanographic Institution, was first launched in 1964, and, with numerous upgrades, continues in 2008 as the undisputed workhorse of research submersibles, but it soon will be replaced with a system capable of a 6,500-meter depth. Several Canadian-built Pisces subs have supported ocean exploration for more than three decades, and in the same time frame, two four-person Johnson-Sea-Link research subs designed by ocean pioneer Edwin Link and operated by

Rear Admiral Timothy McGee
MAPPING THE OCEAN

The U.S. Navy and naval officers throughout history have been closely associated with—and have led—the science and technologies connected with navigation, astronomy, precise time, charting, meteorology, and oceanography. Today, an important focus of the Navy is understanding the inner workings and hidden mechanisms of our remarkable ocean.

From a line with a lead weight cast from the bows to obtain water depth, to single-beam acoustic sounders, to digital multi-beam arrays and high-resolution side-scanning sonars, technology is helping our picture of the ocean floor come increasingly into focus. As those technologies have improved, so have navigation accuracies—from latitude estimates to true celestial navigation with a chronometer to electronic systems (such as long-range navigation, or Loran, and Omega) and the global positioning system (GPS).

Now the Navy's ocean survey fleet looks at high-resolution multibeam "swaths" of the ocean's floor, as wide as three times the ocean depth, and accurately correlates the sounding from each beam with a precise position on Earth's surface.

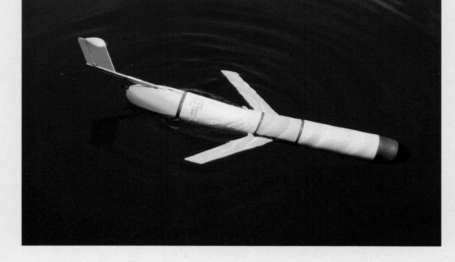

Autonomous battery-powered ocean gliders such as this one assist in ocean surveys.

These data form the baseline for charting to support surface and submarine navigation and, notably, become the bottom boundary for the Navy's numerical ocean models.

But technology's many advantages are always tempered with challenges. The representative data sets have leaped from single-point data to trillions of bits of data per survey. The classic image of a cartographer agonizing over the veracity of a single sounding has given way to one of modern professionals registering millions of soundings at a glance through a three-dimensional visualization process. Substantial upgrades to shipboard networks and communication systems were required to handle the huge data flow and storage. And despite these amazing advances in technological capabilities, only about 10 percent of the ocean floor has been adequately mapped.

Beyond understanding the seafloor, mapping the ocean means first understanding the complexity of what is going on in the ocean, and then learning how to predict what will happen in the future. This has been the Navy's focus for many years, and we are beginning to see the fruits of that labor through the recent and significant success of our numerical ocean-modeling program.

The high-resolution bottom-mapping data provide a lower boundary to the problem of forecasting ocean circulation. Each day we also describe the sea-surface height variation (altimetry) and sea-surface temperature with data from multiple satellites, and computer models force the surface with winds and heat transfers from high-resolution weather models. We adjust the modeled vertical water column by assimilating data from drifting and profiling buoys, autonomous undersea vehicles, and, most recently, ocean gliders.

This latest sensing technology has truly enabled a renaissance in the way we understand the ocean. The gliders "fly" up and down in the water column, changing their ballast and attitude, using their own density for propulsion. They are persistent (stay on station for months); they are adaptive (can be steered to where we want them to observe); they communicate as frequently as we want them to; and they can be commanded via satellite from anywhere in the world.

For the first time, our numerical ocean models can start with an accurate depiction of the physical ocean structure. All these data are fed into our high-resolution ocean models running on tera-scale supercomputers, currently 32 in the list of top 500 supercomputers in the world. This computational power is required, as our "models" are solving multiple simultaneous differential equations across millions of four-dimensional grid points. Our first truly global operational model in 2001 resolved the world ocean into a 14-kilometer horizontal grid with only six layers describing the depths of the ocean. This was all the computers could handle at the time. With increases in computational capacity, we are now transitioning into operation a global model that will resolve the ocean at resolutions of 1 to 2 kilometers in the horizontal, less than a meter in the vertical, and seconds in time. Once we have computed the forecast fields, we then compare the predictions with what we observe with the gliders—and the results have been amazing.

First, in every instance, the real (and modeled) ocean has been vastly different from, and more dynamic than, our earlier, climatologically averaged view of the ocean would have led us to believe. Second, the gliders are verifying the accuracy of our forecasts well out beyond five days, and we are getting it right. We are now looking at an ocean that changes every day, just as we have long looked at daily changes in the atmosphere, through the Navy's investment in ocean science and technology and in operational oceanography at the Navy's Meteorology and Oceanography Command.

Now that we are refining our ability to understand and predict the physical processes (currents, temperature, and geophysics) in the ocean, we know there are coherent relationships between the physical structure and the chemical and biological structure. As we begin to unravel those relationships, we understand we are on the path toward effective and accurate ecosystem modeling—and that will be the right map of the ocean.

U.S.S. Queenfish *breaks through the ice during pioneering underwater explorations of bathymetry and marine life in the high Arctic.*

the Harbor Branch Oceanographic Institution have taken hundreds of scientists to depths as great as 1,000 meters. More than 50 scientists operated several one-person microsubmersibles, including the *Deep Rover,* able to descend to 1,000 meters, and smaller *Deep Worker* subs, with a 600-meter range, for research during the Sustainable Seas Expeditions from 1998 to 2003 sponsored by the Goldman Foundation, the National Geographic Society, and NOAA.

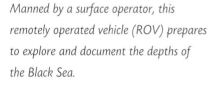

Two Russian subs, *Mir I* and *Mir II,* have repeatedly made history with dives to unusual destinations, including the remains of the ocean liner *Titanic* and an expedition to the seafloor 4,300 meters under the ice at the North Pole in August 2007. The *Mir*s are two of only four subs capable of taking people to nearly half of the ocean's depth. The others, the French *Nautile* and the Japanese *Shinkai 6500,* are currently the only manned subs available to explore the vast unknown ocean below 4,200 meters, although systems are in development, both manned and remotely operated, to return to full ocean depth, where *Trieste* briefly touched down in 1960.

REMOTELY OPERATED AND AUTONOMOUS UNDERWATER VEHICLES

New ways to remotely access the ocean began to be developed for military, scientific, and industrial uses in the 1960s. Towed camera arrays were engineered and used by various research institutions in the United States, the United Kingdom, Japan, and elsewhere to image the nature of the seafloor in deep water. The first discovery of hydrothermal vents near the Galápagos Islands was made possible by the use of such systems from both Scripps Institution of Oceanography in 1976 and Woods Hole Oceanographic Institution in 1977. The next step was to actively control cameras, instruments, and the movements of propellers—thrusters—on underwater vehicles from a surface station. One of the first such practical tethered camera systems was referred to as a flying eyeball and used in support of oil and gas operations in depths to 2,000 meters.

Manned by a surface operator, this remotely operated vehicle (ROV) prepares to explore and document the depths of the Black Sea.

Growing demand for unmanned systems that could service rigs, inspect pipelines, and otherwise support underwater activities provided incentive to develop vehicles with manipulators and specialized tools that performed operations comparable in some ways to tasks required of space station astronauts years later. By the late 1980s, ROVs were regarded as essential tools for inspection, construction, maintenance, and repair in the offshore oil and gas industry, and navies around the world developed or adapted their own versions of remotely operated systems for jobs including harbor monitoring and locating and removing mines.

Scientists began using ROVs in the 1980s to explore under the ice in Antarctica and in deep water everywhere, most often controlled from the deck of a ship, but sometimes from distant stations that guided the ROV's movements by a microwave or satellite link. At the University of Washington, scientists developed a long, slim, free-swimming autonomous vehicle, *Deep Glider,*

Kathryn Sullivan
OBSERVING THE OCEAN FROM SPACE

My first glimpse of Earth from a space shuttle was a stunning tableau of blue and white: the waters of the North Atlantic Ocean decorated with the most beautiful patches of white cloud. The scale of ocean and weather circulation patterns that were apparent at a glance from this vantage point was simply amazing! In the sun's glint, I saw major circulation features, like the wall of the Gulf Stream. I traced fine filaments of sediment far away from major rivers and marveled at the milky white swirls of huge plankton blooms. My spaceship was moving almost 1,300 times as fast as a typical oceanographic ship, letting me see almost all of the Atlantic

example, scientists can calculate the wind speed, direction, and wave height on the ocean surface. Other calculations using microwave pulses produce maps of seafloor topography and the gravity field. Such techniques yield global maps of seasonal changes in currents, sea-surface height, winds, waves, biological productivity, rainfall, sea ice, and sunlight reaching the sea. By blending satellite data with in situ measurements in global models of the combined ocean-atmosphere system, scientists now can predict phenomena like the El Niño/Southern Oscillation many months in advance and with considerable accuracy.

While flying high above the blue planet, the space shuttle Endeavor's *robotic arm appears to touch the sun during the STS-77 shuttle mission in 1996.*

Ocean in just a few hours. Imagine how well we'd know the ocean if we could measure everything at this speed!

The space-age ability to take measurements across Earth's immense oceans has launched a new era of ocean science and boosted public interest in the ocean and its role in weather and climate. Space-based observations have also contributed to great improvements in weather prediction. Today's five-day forecasts are as accurate as three-day predictions were just twenty-five years ago, thanks largely to satellite data that make up more than 90 percent of the input to numerical weather prediction models.

Modern satellite oceanography combines orbiting sensors, a global scientific community, and powerful supercomputers into a potent tool for research and prediction. Turning the raw signals from a sensor into data about the physical state of the ocean is a complex process. Using the amplitude and polarization of microwave energy backscattered from the sea, for

This ability to measure, map, and model critical physical parameters at global scale—one of the signal achievements of the space age—has transformed our ability to predict weather phenomena and understand long-term climate patterns. The practical benefits of this scientific advance are tremendous: earlier warnings of severe events like tornados and tsunamis can save lives. More precise forecasts of intense storms help communities prepare and respond more effectively. Reliable long-term seasonal forecasts give agricultural economies the chance to adapt plantings and avoid crop failures.

We have only just begun to understand our planet as an integrated suite of dynamic systems and to tap the potential of this new predictive ability. To achieve the next stage of progress, scientists and engineers will have to push the frontiers of our knowledge about the physical mechanisms of remote sensing, develop techniques and devices to store and retrieve immense data sets, and develop new sensor technologies.

to stay underwater for up to a year; dive to nearly 2,700 meters; and measure temperature, salinity, and other data across entire ocean basins. Several ROVs the size of small cars have been outfitted at the Monterey Bay Aquarium Research Institute (MBARI) to gather data, photographs, and selected specimens of marine life in the nearby Monterey Canyon. Hundreds of viewers share, in real time, what scientists are observing at sea via microwave transmissions from several kilometers offshore.

The ROV *Kaiko* was launched in 1995 by the Japanese oceanographic research institution JAMSTEC to the deepest place in the sea—the bottom of the Mariana Trench, almost 11,000 meters down. It was the first time since 1960 that any direct observations had been made of this remote location, and the first time that photographs and samples were taken from that stupendous depth. In 2003, the cable connecting *Kaiko* to its support ship snapped and the vehicle was lost, and with it, the only means then available in the world to gain access to the deepest ocean. China has recently undertaken construction of deep ROV systems, reflecting that nation's growing commitment to ocean exploration. Woods Hole Oceanographic Institution continues to develop and use new remotely operated and autonomous vehicles as well as hybrid systems, HROVs, that can swim without a tether but also can carry a light fiber optic cable for control and image transfer. One HROV in particular is destined to access the Mariana Trench in the near future.

George Bass, well-known for initiating scientific discipline in underwater archaeology, pioneered the use of subs and ROVs to explore and document ancient shipwrecks, including a Bronze Age vessel found along the southern coast of Turkey. No gold or jewels were aboard, but Bass commented, "We are salvaging the greatest of all treasures—the treasure of knowledge." Undersea explorer Robert Ballard spearheaded a cooperative U.S.-French expedition involving the U.S. Navy, the Woods Hole Oceanographic Institution, Institut Français de Recherche pour l'Exploitation de la Mer (IFREMER), and the National Geographic Society, to locate the R.M.S. *Titanic*, a British luxury liner that sank 4 kilometers deep in the Atlantic after colliding with an iceberg in 1912. After weeks of searching, on September 1, 1985, images of the ship's huge boiler, and then scattered debris, appeared via a live video transmission from a towed camera and sonar array. The *Argo* and *Jason* ROVs were then used to explore and photograph the remains of the sunken *Titanic*. More than a million ships that once traveled on the ocean's surface are now somewhere underwater, each a time capsule, some holding great wealth. According to Ballard, there is no doubt that "the ocean holds more artifacts about the history of humankind than all of the world's museums combined."

SEE ALSO: *Kaiko,* page 157

Do We Still Need Research Ships?

A hundred years ago, the only way to study the ocean was to go to sea. Fifty years ago, research ships discovered the basics of bathymetry, the mid-ocean ridges, seafloor spreading, gravity, magnetics, sediments and rocks below the seafloor, water chemistry, bottom currents, hydrothermal vents, and many new life-forms in the sea. Today new technologies study the ocean without humans on-scene: through sensors riding on satellites, increasingly sophisticated fixed and floating buoys, and gliders preprogrammed to "swim" underwater collecting information as they go. But we still need ships and scientists at sea. An increasing percentage of researchers in oceanography never go to sea, and their interpretation of data remotely collected or computer simulated can suffer from their lack of observing and experiencing the ocean firsthand. Satellite data need calibrating; automated surveys need to be augmented by those where human intuition reacts to the unexpected; and there are still some types of data and samples from the depths that can only be collected from ships.

WEB LINK: international ocean research

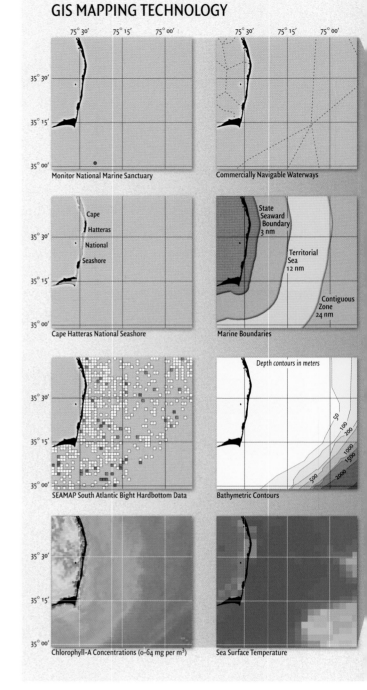

GIS MAPPING TECHNOLOGY

Monitor National Marine Sanctuary

Commercially Navigable Waterways

Cape Hatteras National Seashore

Marine Boundaries

SEAMAP South Atlantic Bight Hardbottom Data

Bathymetric Contours

Chlorophyll-A Concentrations (0-64 mg per m³)

Sea Surface Temperature

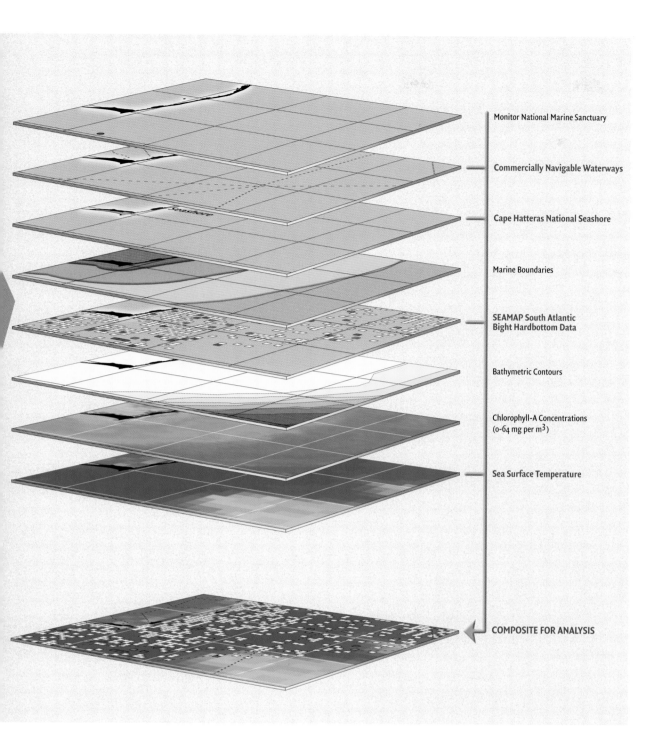

Monitor National Marine Sanctuary

Commercially Navigable Waterways

Cape Hatteras National Seashore

Marine Boundaries

SEAMAP South Atlantic
Bight Hardbottom Data

Bathymetric Contours

Chlorophyll-A Concentrations
(0–64 mg per m³)

Sea Surface Temperature

COMPOSITE FOR ANALYSIS

Mapping Technology: *Geographic Information System (GIS) technology allows cartographers and marine scientists to map, monitor, model, and display ocean resources and other phenomena and to overlay them on composite maps. GIS provides a referencing network by which satellite imagery and other data can be quickly registered to geographic locations and then fused in various combinations and analyzed. These results equip officials with timely, accurate information to make informed decisions.*

In this example, sea-surface temperature data enable the National Marine Fisheries Service (NMFS) to predict the impact of fishing on overwintering sea turtles off the coast of North Carolina's Outer Banks. Because sea turtles prefer waters that are within a particular temperature range, scientists are able to predict potential migratory patterns. Using a GIS, these data are laid over other related habitat data, protected areas, and vessel traffic to gauge the potential damage to turtles unintentionally trapped in fishing nets.

WEB LINK: Introduction to GIS

Studying the Ocean

OCEAN SCIENTIST MARGARET DAVIDSON recently remarked, "It covers two-thirds of the Earth's surface, yet little of the ocean environment has been charted to any level of detail. We struggle to understand the scope, depth, and definition of even our near-shore estuarine environments." Many are surprised to discover that maps of the Earth's surface under the ocean are far less accurate than those of the surface of the moon, Mars, or Jupiter. Limited visibility through seawater—rarely more than 30 meters or so—is the key. Dolphins and whales have overcome the problem of communicating beyond visual range by using sophisticated acoustic techniques, and starting in the 1950s, so have humans.

Methods for "seeing" with sound underwater were developed in World War II as sonar (sound navigation ranging)—sending a beam of sound into the water and using its echo to find objects—to hunt for submarines. Later advances identified the best sound frequencies for ocean mapping by determining the depth of the seafloor, as well as probing beyond, into several kilometers of sediments and rock structures underlying the seafloor. Seismic surveys by the oil and gas industry followed, enabling geologists to identify promising formations before undertaking expensive drilling operations. The U.S. Navy developed multibeam arrays, yielding surveys a hundred times more detailed than possible previously, and in 1995, declassified data from the Navy's Geosat satellite provided data about the seafloor in areas not yet surveyed by ships. Satellite data from Geosat predicted an astonishing number of previously undetected seamounts and other underwater features, including the first comprehensive visualization of the seafloor under the ice in the Arctic Ocean. Global satellite data released by Russian agencies provided similar information for much of the ocean.

The ability to obtain samples of the seafloor, the sediments, and underlying rocks has also advanced significantly in recent decades. Dredges have been used since the *Challenger* expedition to get a rough idea of what lies on the seafloor, but late in the 20th century, new methods evolved to hold ships steady while deep cores of sediments as much as 40 meters long were extracted by drilling into selected areas. Such samples help determine age and chemical and biological changes over time, and give insight into ancient climates.

In the 1990s, more than 500 research cruises with hundreds of scientists from 30 countries gathered information over a period of eight years about global ocean temperature and the ways of the world's ocean currents during a project called WOCE, the World Ocean Circulation Experiment. Ocean currents are measured with ocean drifters, floats, and anchored buoys loaded with instruments that record temperature, salinity, depth, current speed, and other data. Newly developed autonomous ocean gliders are programmed to follow a predetermined underwater course, rising to the sea surface periodically to transmit data via satellite. Sensors from satellites provide global views and new insights concerning surface currents, wave patterns, sea-surface temperature, salinity, biological productivity, the height of the sea surface, and even the nature of the seafloor beneath the ocean.

LOOKING AHEAD

Since the 1950s, more has been learned about the nature of the aquatic realm that dominates Earth than during all preceding human history— and the pace is picking up. In 1999, the U.S. government twice convened a panel of ocean explorers, scientists, and educators to consider developing a strategy for "discovering Earth's final frontier." After much deliberation, the panel called for "mapping of the physical, geological, biological, chemical, and archeological aspects of the ocean . . . exploring ocean dynamics and interactions at new scales . . . developing new sensors and systems for ocean exploration." These are mandates much like those given to scientists aboard H.M.S. *Challenger* more than a century ago—"to explore all aspects of the ocean." In 2008, a new NOAA vessel, *Okeanos Explorer*, was launched with similar lofty goals. Globally, a network of observing stations—the Integrated Ocean Observing System (IOOS)—is gaining the support of many nations.

Early in the 21st century, new technologies have made the perspective from space widely available to the public at large through the Internet. Hundreds of millions of people now look at the world from an astronaut's point of view, turn the Earth at will, explore mountains and valleys, careen down the Grand Canyon, zoom into cities and towns, peer into backyards. It will soon be possible to cross the ocean vicariously, seeing not just waves of blue, but geo-referenced features— located precisely on the Earth—including underwater mountains; huge deepwater plains; submerged canyons; ocean currents; the migrations of certain large sea animals; and the location of coral reefs, kelp forests, and other marine ecosystems below the surface. □

Armed with instruments to document temperature, wind, and other information, this giant buoy off the Yucatan Peninsula, owned and maintained by the National Data Buoy Center, is part of a growing network of Integrated Ocean Observing System (IOOS) monitoring stations.

Opposite: An egg yolk jellyfish, Phacellophora camtschatica, *and biologist Bruce Robison cross paths in the depths of the Carmel Bay, within the Monterey Bay National Marine Sanctuary.*

The red border around landmasses in this view of Earth, created by NOAA's Science on a Sphere Project, indicates how much of today's global shoreline will be underwater if sea level rises 6 meters.

Chapter 10

OCEAN FUTURE

Human Impact on the World Ocean

Above: *A rigorous analysis published in 2008 in* Science *by Benjamin Halpern and his colleagues looked at the impacts from 17 different human activities, including various types of pollution, fishing, shipping, offshore oil and gas, and climate change, on 20 kinds of coastal and ocean regions ranging from coastal mangroves to coral reefs to deep seamounts. They found the highest impacts in coastal areas, but also found that no part of the world ocean, however remote, is free of negative human impacts.*

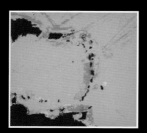

Left: *The eastern Caribbean and waters surrounding the Lesser Antilles islands show surprisingly high impacts from a matrix of human activities despite their remoteness.*

Right: *The North Sea also shows high impacts from fishing, pollution, shipping, and offshore industrial operations.*

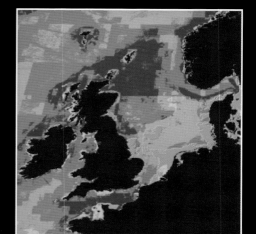

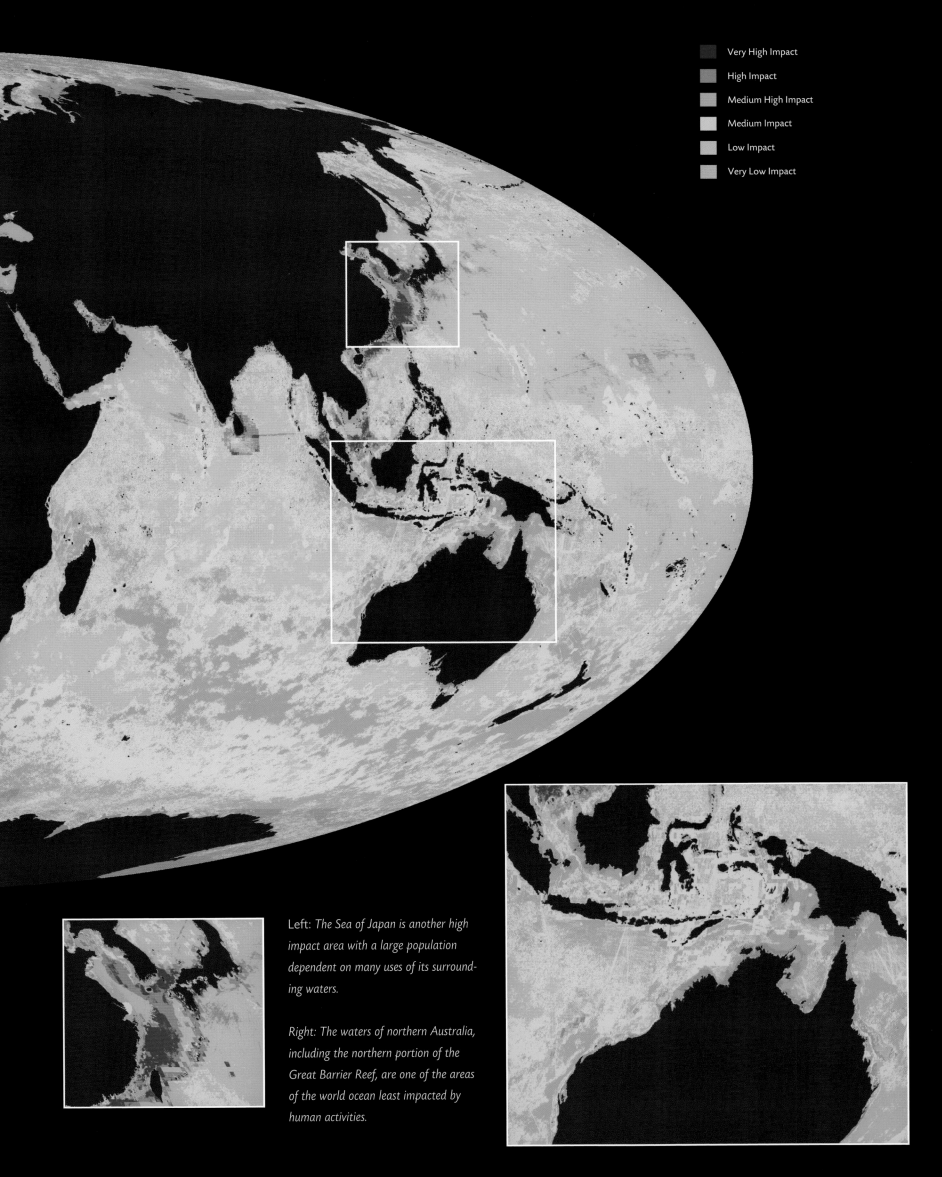

Very High Impact

High Impact

Medium High Impact

Medium Impact

Low Impact

Very Low Impact

Left: *The Sea of Japan is another high impact area with a large population dependent on many uses of its surrounding waters.*

Right: *The waters of northern Australia, including the northern portion of the Great Barrier Reef, are one of the areas of the world ocean least impacted by human activities.*

Every year more than 300,000 marine mammals die in active or lost fishing gear, including these California sea lions, Zalophus californicus, *snared in a gill net near the Coronados Islands, Baja California.*

Ocean Future by the Numbers

World population in 1800: 1.6 billion

World population in 2008: 6.7 billion

Percent of people living within 100 kilometers of the sea: about 50 percent

Plastic debris in the ocean in 1900: none

Plastic debris in the ocean in 2000: hundreds of millions of metric tons

Global marine wildlife marketed in 1900: nearly 3 million metric tons

Global marine wildlife marketed in 1990: nearly 82 million metric tons

Amount of ocean protected from the extraction of wildlife: 0.005 percent

What will the ocean be like in the centuries, millennia, and eons to come? No one knows, of course, but based on knowledge of the past, some predictions can be made with reasonable certainty. Geological processes established over the ages will continue, with ocean basins spreading or shrinking and continents continuing to glide across the globe atop the crust, driven by tectonic forces deep within the Earth. Sea life will continue to evolve and be affected, sometimes catastrophically, by changes in the ocean and the atmosphere. Climate and weather will continue to change, in an ages-old cycle of cooling and warming, ice ages will come and go, sea level will fall and rise. But where does humankind fit in? Will the changes now under way work in our favor?

Until recently, it was widely believed that nothing we did could alter the processes that govern climate, weather, or the broad systems that support life as we know it. The sea seemed especially remote, beyond our capacity to influence. The English poet Lord Byron expressed this view nearly two centuries ago in *Childe Harold:*

> *Roll on, thou deep and dark blue Ocean—roll!*
> *Ten thousand fleets sweep over thee in vain;*
> *Man marks the earth with ruin—his control*
> *Stops with the shore . . .*

Ocean scientist and writer Rachel Carson echoed the theme in *The Sea Around Us,* published in 1951: "Eventually man . . . found his way back to the sea. . . . And yet he has returned to his mother sea only on her own terms. He cannot control or change the ocean as, in his brief tenancy on earth, he has subdued and plundered the continents."

Events and scientific advances during the latter half of the 20th century, however, have shattered the notion that the ocean is so vast, so resilient, there is little humans can do to alter its nature. In a few decades, human activities have brought about changes of geological magnitude—changes usually wrought over millennia through natural forces—to the atmosphere, to wildlife, to the land, and to the world's waters, fresh and marine, with consequences that will have a profound influence on the future of the ocean and, in turn, on the future of mankind. Nineteen scientists collaborated in a study of human impacts on 20 marine ecosystems around the world and reported in *Science* in February 2008 that no area is free of human influence. In fact, a large number of areas (41 percent) are strongly affected by multiple direct and indirect human effects.

What has provoked the swift and devastating changes to the chemistry of the sea, to global climate and weather, and to life in the sea? Humankind is now facing choices concerning the radical decline of numerous commercially exploited species and ecosystems, the rapid increase of ocean pollution, acidification of the ocean, the acceleration of global warming, and potentially devastating sea level rise. Ocean policy and governance—including international treaties that attempt to

Oil smothers mangroves, marshes, and sea grass meadows of the Persian Gulf. During conflicts in 1990 between Iraq and Kuwait, more than 800 oil wells were set afire and 12 million barrels of crude oil were released into the Gulf.

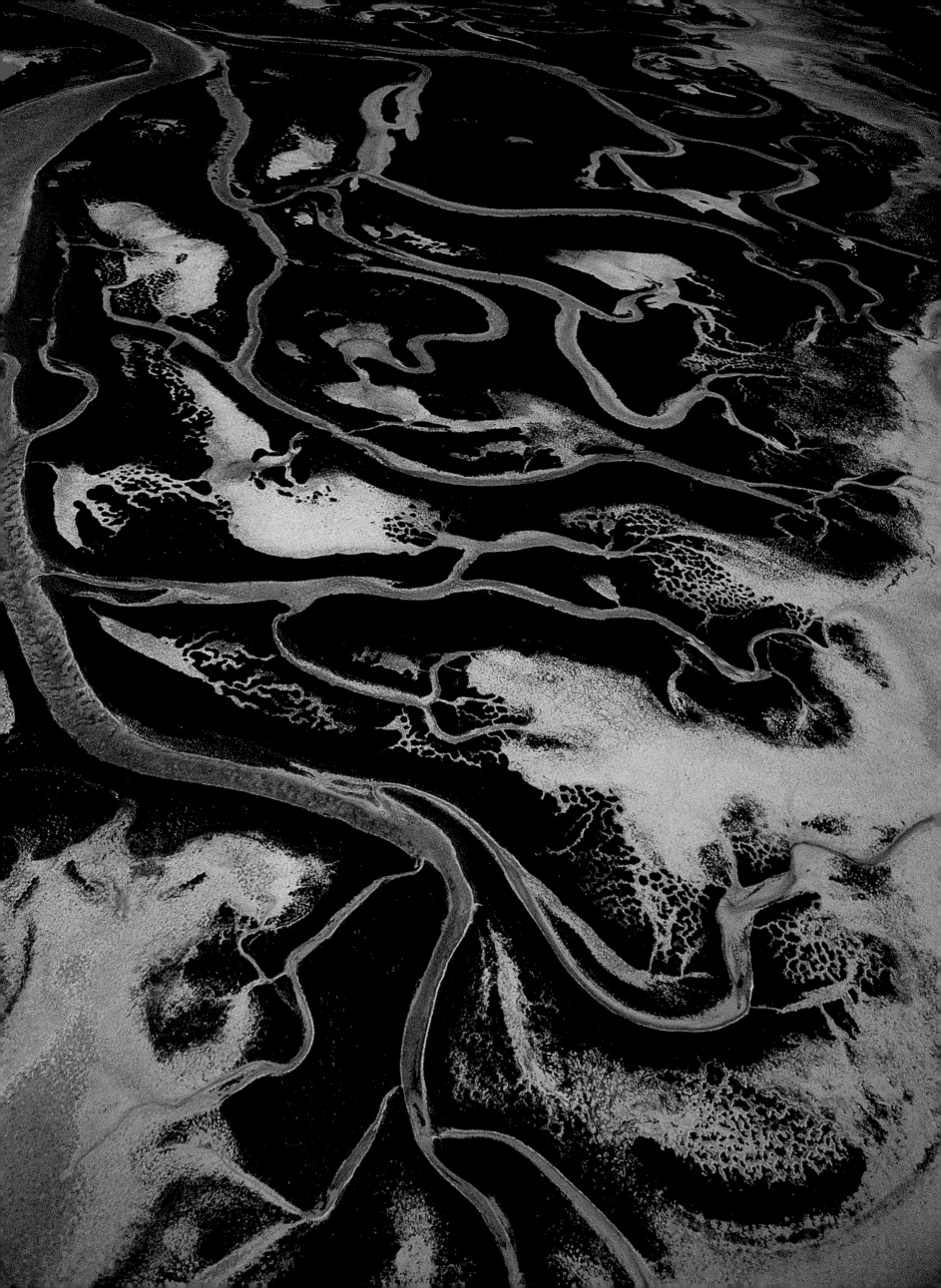

control the uses and abuses of the ocean and its resources—are evolving, but not as quickly as the swift changes that threaten human health; global, regional, and local economies; security; and, some believe, the very existence of humans on this planet.

Ocean Policy and Governance

THE OPEN OCEAN WAS FOR MILLENNIA a place outside the laws of any land. Since the end of World War II, the United Nations and its subsidiary institutions have developed many international treaties that provide a balance between the age-old free-for-all and new national responsibilities on the seas. These include restrictions on slavery, piracy, and drug trafficking at sea, but the world community has also given increasing focus to ocean conservation issues over the past six decades, including the killing of whales (the International Convention for the Regulation of Whaling of 1946); the

Economic Claims of Coastal and Island Nations: *In the late 1950s, the United States, Chile, Peru, and Ecuador claimed fishing rights along their coasts and offshore to 200 nautical miles. This practice became the basis, through the late 1960s and 1970s, of the concept of 200-nautical mile Exclusive Economic Zones, or EEZs, included in the 1982 United Nations Convention on the Law of the Sea. Island nations particularly expand their resources by establishing an EEZ.*

WEB LINK: Law of the Sea

commercial taking of certain fish species (the International Convention for the Conservation of Atlantic Tuna of 1966, among others); the dumping of wastes in the ocean (the Convention on the Prevention of Marine Pollution by Dumping of Wastes and Other Matter of 1972); and contamination of the ocean by oil, chemicals, packaged goods, sewage, and garbage (the Marine Pollution, or MARPOL, International Convention for the Prevention of Pollution from Ships of 1973). Today, dozens of regional and international conventions and treaties—often unclear or conflicting in their provisions—govern various aspects of human behavior relating to the sea.

In 1972, the United Nations adopted the Stockholm Declaration on Human Environment as a nonbinding policy based on several fundamental principles that included: "The natural resources of the earth, including the air, water, land, flora and fauna and especially representative samples of natural ecosystems, must be safeguarded for the benefit of present and future generations through careful planning or management, as appropriate." The Stockholm Declaration was a starting point for many international actions concerning the ocean, including recommendations two decades later from the 1992 World Summit on Sustainable Development (WSSD) that called for action by governments to protect the world's marine life and to ensure "sustainable development."

The premier international policy and governance mechanism for the behavior of nations with respect to the ocean is the United Nations Convention on the Law of the Sea of 1982. It was drafted by many nations in the 1970s; opened for signature in 1982; signed by 119 countries that year; ratified by the requisite 60 nations needed to bring the treaty into force in 1993; and is now binding on all nations that have ratified it—currently 155 plus the European Union countries.

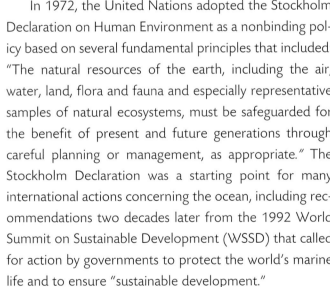

The Law of the Sea Convention provides a comprehensive international legal framework governing activities on and in the world's ocean. It includes the rights of military mobility on the high seas, through international straits and in coastal waters; ensures the free movement of global commerce; clarifies high-seas freedoms for laying cables and pipelines; establishes an international framework for maritime law enforcement, marine environmental protection, and marine scientific research; and creates a mechanism for settling international disputes. A provision of the convention with profound significance allows coastal states to declare jurisdiction over living and nonliving marine resources in a zone up to 200 nautical miles off their shorelines. In 1983, President Ronald Reagan claimed such an Exclusive Economic Zone (EEZ)—an area of 8.8 million square kilometers—for the United States, extending U.S. sovereignty over resources within an aquatic realm significantly larger than all of the nation's landmass. Many countries were similarly enhanced, including island nations that suddenly had a much larger presence in the world.

Trouble arose around Part XI "The Area"—the deep seafloor beyond all nations' jurisdiction. A group of developing nations known as the Group of 77 insisted that any taking of resources from this area, such as from ocean mining, should be governed by a United Nations office and that all technologies used and profits made must be shared with all nations. A number of industrialized nations, concerned about such an international precedent that undercut free-market forces,

WEB LINK: Exclusive Economic Zones

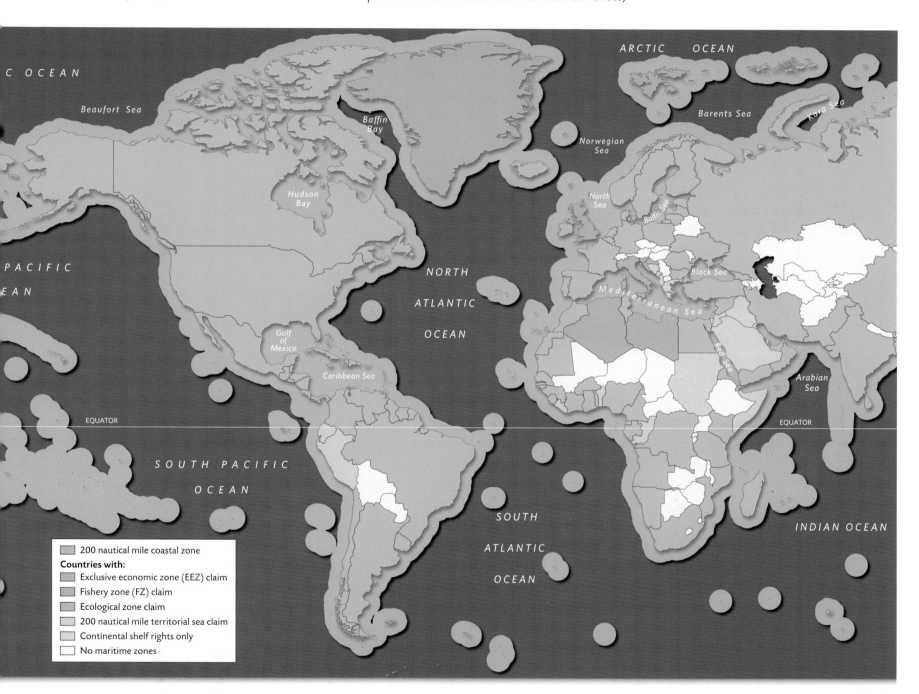

refused to sign the treaty. In 1983, President Reagan issued a proclamation announcing the United States would comply with all aspects of the treaty except Part XI. In the late 1980s, the United States drafted and negotiated a new treaty that amended the Part XI deep seabed mining parts of the Law of the Sea Convention. This solution was widely accepted; many industrialized nations finally ratified the Convention; and in 1998 President Bill Clinton signed the Law of the Sea Treaty for the United

States. By 2008, the U.S. Senate had still not ratified the convention, thereby making the United States the only major maritime power that, despite its key role in framing the Law of the Sea, is still not officially a party to the convention.

Another provision of the Law of the Sea has taken longer to emerge—the potential to extend seabed resource claims up to 350 nautical miles offshore—based on sophisticated and costly surveys proving the seabed is part of a natural extension of the continental shelf. Claims are proliferating, some of them overlapping among different countries.

Perhaps the most noteworthy of these were made in 2007 in polar areas where commercial exploitation is not feasible—yet. In June 2007, Russia was the first to descend to the seafloor under the North Pole, planting the Russian flag and announcing its claim to a huge triangle of underwater terrain from the Pole to the widely separated margins of Russia. Also in 2007, the United Kingdom ran counter to long-standing international agreements against commercial exploitation of Antarctica by preparing a claim to extend its 1908 British Antarctic Territory to the seabed offshore.

In the United States, the new millennium saw a renewed focus on the oceans. Formed in 2001 at the direction of the Oceans Act of 2000, a National Ocean Commission began the first comprehensive review of U.S. ocean policy since the 1960s. Simultaneously, an independent nongovernmental U.S. initiative, the Pew Oceans Commission, considered major threats to the health and integrity of ocean systems, with special consideration given to fisheries issues. Among its recommendations, released in 2003, were improved management of commercial fishing and the establishment of many more marine reserves. Its report, *America's Living Oceans: Charting a Course for Sea Change,* underscored many of the findings of the national commission, and in due course, the two came together in a Joint Ocean Commission Initiative.

WEB LINK: Integrated Ocean Observing System

Working together, the two commissions undertook an annual U.S. Ocean Policy Report Card, aimed at assessing progress toward implementing the recommendations from both commissions. Although focused on the United States, the issues and solutions are relevant globally. Among the key recommendations, endorsed by ocean scientists around the world, is the implementation of a global Integrated Ocean Observing System (IOOS) to monitor and better understand the dynamic ocean processes that so profoundly affect the nature of the planet as a whole.

Concurrently with the two U.S. commissions, 150 scientists, policymakers, educators, economists, and business leaders from 70 organizations in 20 countries began assembling global data for a meeting in Los Cabos, Mexico, in May–June 2003 known as Defying Ocean's End (DOE). The goal of the DOE conference was to develop a global action plan—with priorities, timetables, and estimated costs—aimed at stabilizing and reversing the troubling trends in the world ocean. Key recommendations, published in *Defying Ocean's End* in 2005, included:

- Treat the 60 percent of the world ocean outside of national EEZs as a World Ocean Public Trust, with legal approaches concerning use of the high seas, including fisheries, under coordinated, international multi-use zoning regimes.
- Reform fisheries using market-based mechanisms, subsidy changes, and sustainable practices.
- Implement global and regional communications plans to educate the public.
- Create, consolidate, and strengthen marine protected areas into a globally representative network.
- Develop an expanded research program focused on top priority marine environments high in endemism and biodiversity.

WEB LINK: population figures

In a world where the human population has grown from about 1 billion in 1800, to 2 billion in the 1930s, 4 billion in the 1980s, and 6.6 billion early in the 21st century, there has been growing recognition that human demands on the land, fresh water, air, and sea are being stressed beyond what scientists recognize as the planet's "carrying capacity." Although policies, precedents, and treaties continue to grow governing the behavior of people in, on, over, around, and under the ocean, there continues to be a frontier attitude about the use of the sea. The current concern is that human influence is spreading beyond coastal areas, and the laws and treaties are not keeping pace.

Rita Colwell and Guillaume Constantin de Magny
CLIMATE, OCEAN, AND CHOLERA

Human health, climate, and the ocean are broadly correlated, with factors such as temperature, rainfall, flooding, the nature and abundance of disease-bearing organisms, and human activities linked in ways that can now be demonstrated. Like detectives solving the mystery of strange deaths, scientists have gathered evidence to understand enigmatic outbreaks of an ancient scourge—cholera. For this disease, recent insights have converged concerning ocean conditions, the abundance of marine plankton, and the occurrence of tiny marine crustacea. As a consequence, it is now possible to predict when outbreaks of the disease may occur and to reduce their impact.

Cholera, a potentially fatal illness, has long been known to be caused by a bacterium, *Vibrio cholerae*. In recent years it has been confirmed that these bacteria occur naturally in the aquatic environment, where they attach to copepods, small crustacean that live in fresh and marine waters worldwide. Thousands of individual *Vibrio* cells may adhere to a single animal, traveling with these hosts as the follow their food source, algae, and phytoplankton. Normally, the numbers of these bacteria are too small to cause human health problems, but under the right combination of temperature, salinity, and nutrients large blooms of phytoplankton can occur, followed by an abundance of *Vibrio*-laden copepods that, in turn, may lead to outbreaks of cholera in certain coastal areas.

Recent findings on the ecology of *V. cholerae*, coupled with new methods for surveying oceanographic conditions, are making it possible to predict the occurrence of the disease and to take precautionary measures. The discovery of these connections and their immense value for the protection of human health came about through studies of cholera outbreaks in Kolkata, India, and Matlab, Bangladesh. Satellite sensors were used to measure chlorophyll-concentration and sea-surface temperature. Rainfall data were gathered from a combination of satellite and in situ gauge measurements, and when analyzed, a statistically significant relationship was observed among epidemics of cholera, chlorophyll concentration in the Indian Ocean, and rainfall throughout the year.

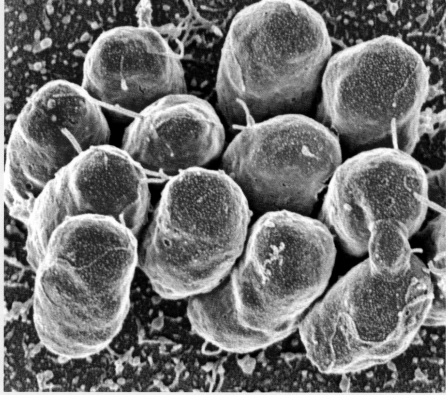

Small in size but giant in impact, Vibrio cholerae *bacteria, magnified here in an electron microscope image, usually live unnoticed and harmless to humans. Changes in ocean temperature and chemistry can trigger blooms of plankton that are linked to deadly Cholera outbreaks.*

Some doubted the importance of copepods in cholera transmission when the relationship was first discovered, but the correlation was conclusively demonstrated in a study where the number of cholera cases in Bangladesh villages was reduced significantly when copepods were removed from drinking water. The method used was simple but ingenious: The water was filtered through several layers of sheer but finely woven cloth of the traditional sari clothing worn by women of the region.

Now that the relationship is known between environmental and climatic factors that drive the prosperity of copepods and the *V. cholerae* bacteria, the dynamics of copepod populations can serve to estimate the abundance of *V. cholerae*. The idea of correlating the annual cyclic pattern of cholera epidemics with sea-surface temperature and sea-surface height by remote sensing, along with changes in coastal ecosystems, is an approach that was first tried only about a decade ago. Since then, mathematical models have been used to help understand cholera's seasonal cycle.

From September 1997 to December 2006, satellite-derived data were gathered from the closest coastal environment for Kolkata and Matlab, and the results show differences that appear to be related to local conditions. Predictions can be improved by using dynamic or statistical regional climate and ocean forecast models involving sea-surface temperature, rainfall, chlorophyll, and sea-surface height, now readily monitored with satellite-based sensors. In 2009, the Aquarius satellite mission will measure global sea-surface salinity, yielding data that may help put another piece of the puzzle in place.

In countries where drinking water is consumed without treatment, a better understanding of the factors underlying the occurrence of cholera should make it possible to provide preemptive public health measures. The variables related to local conditions will cause the lead time to estimate the number of cholera cases to vary, but even a short time to provide a warning will permit precautionary measures to be taken and thus save lives.

What We Put into the Ocean

FOR SOME PEOPLE, "FREEDOM OF THE SEAS" means using the ocean as the place to put whatever noxious things they don't want near them on land—from sewage to trash from ships, medical waste, industrial chemical wastes, nuclear waste from power plants, and even decommissioned nuclear submarines. The traditional notion of the vastness and immutability of the ocean led in the 1960s, 1970s, and 1980s to the idea that the "solution to pollution is dilution." Despite the fact that many scientists have since discredited this approach, enormous quantities of excess fertilizers, pesticides, and other contaminants still make their way into coastal waters and thus into the nursery areas for marine life and into open-ocean food chains. Pollutants work their way from prey to predator, directly affecting the health and productivity of marine life. This poses direct risks to humans through consumption of contaminated seafood. But, on a larger scale, it causes degradation of the critical interactions of biology and chemistry in the sea, and ultimately to the global systems that support us.

Upstream input of excess fertilizers, biocides, toxic chemicals, and other harmful substances from fields, farms, highways, and yards pollute freshwater systems before flowing out to pollute adjacent coastal waters.

Concerns over several major oil spills, notably the release of nearly 110,000 metric tons of oil cargo from the tanker *Torrey Canyon* in 1967, provoked action to address such accidents, although it was recognized that operational pollution, including discharge of oily ballast, was a greater and more persistent problem than the occasional spectacular spill. Protocols were modified in 1978, and numerous amendments have been added, including a provision in 1992 requiring double hulls on oil tankers. The accidental release of more than 42 million liters of crude oil into Prince William Sound in 1989 by the tanker *Exxon Valdez,* although far from the largest spill, caused enormous environmental damage—and swift public reaction. It led in 1990 to the passage of the federal Oil Pollution Act, with stiff new standards for prevention and emergency response.

WEB LINK: Oil Pollution Act

Most of what enters the sea via rivers, streams, and groundwater originates far upstream. Altering a river's natural flow—disrupting its floodplain through dams, harnessing it for hydroelectric power, diverting it for irrigation—is a common practice that changes what happens downstream and interferes with ancient land-sea interactions. Most rivers that flow into the Atlantic have been the recipients in the past half century of heavy loads of nontraditional materials—pesticides, herbicides, chemical fertilizers, and more—drastically altering the nature of coastal bays. Excess nutrients from the upstream application of fertilizers have caused an increase in the frequency and intensity of toxic algal blooms and the development of more than 300 so-called dead zones off river mouths of many countries. Excess nutrients, especially phosphate and nitrogen compounds, stimulate the rapid growth of certain algae that die, sink, and decay. This reduces the amount of dissolved oxygen available to other organisms—creating huge at-sea areas of little or no marine life.

SEE ALSO: map of river watersheds, pages 326-327

Plastic debris such as this abandoned crate adrift on the high seas of the Central North Pacific is choking the ocean. Rare in the sea half a century ago, plastic today accounts for the majority of tangible trash in the ocean.

As plastic degrades, most of it breaks into ever smaller pieces but does not disappear altogether. Broad areas of the ocean now contain more plastic than living plankton, as illustrated in this sample.

Wetland ecologist William Mitsch reported in 2000 that dissolved oxygen in the notorious dead zone off the mouth of the Mississippi in the Gulf of Mexico falls, in the late spring and summer, from the normal 5 parts per million to 2 parts per million over an area of about 18,000 square kilometers. "Humans levied the river to make it behave, while the river used to have the ability to naturally flood over its banks and spread nutrients over the landscape," Mitsch said. "When water naturally spills over the banks, it can drain through a riparian [river] corridor and come back as cleaner groundwater." Loss of such natural cleansing is one of the trade-offs for using rivers for other human purposes.

SEE ALSO: effects of carbon dioxide on the ocean, pages 39 and 92

The chemistry of the ocean is also being changed through the addition of a wide range of chemicals that fall from the atmosphere, flow from the rivers and groundwater, or are deliberately disposed of in the sea. As a consequence, mercury and other heavy metals, pesticides, herbicides, fire retardants, and numerous other synthetic chemicals have become a part of the ocean, and increasingly—a part of us as well. Most worrisome of all may be the addition of carbon dioxide from the atmosphere into the sea. The consequences relating to global warming, sea level rise, and ocean acidification are discussed elsewhere in this chapter.

The accumulation of plastic debris in the ocean has become a serious and growing concern. Discarded fishing gear—nets and thousands of kilometers of line—clogs the waters of the world, continuing for years to catch and kill fish and other marine animals, unseen, in the depths of the sea. Bags, foam, and hundreds of other plastic products choke countless marine creatures and birds and eventually degrade into tiny pieces that may outnumber living plankton in the near-surface waters of the sea by three times or more. Some places—notably the North Pacific gyre—accumulate enormous, thick, floating masses of plastic debris; such an area near the Hawaiian Islands in early 2008 was reported to extend over thousands of kilometers.

Not all forms of ocean pollution are visible; some are audible. For the past 200 years, the ocean has become an increasingly noisy place due to human-induced sounds—the thump and growl of boat engines; the ping of sonars for science, fish-finding, and military uses; and the thunder of seismic surveys for research and oil and gas exploration. Most fish, numerous crustaceans, other invertebrates, and all marine mammals produce and receive sounds that are integral to their lives in various ways, and the impacts on marine life of the new noises are of increasing concern.

A fatal diet of plastic is inadvertently gathered by albatross parents who travel hundreds of miles to find food for their single, waiting chick on Midway Island in the northwestern Hawaiian Islands. The mosaic of debris shown here was removed from a single chick, one of many thousands that have succumbed to death by plastic.

Peter Tyack
EFFECTS OF SOUND IN THE OCEAN

When you look out of your dive mask underwater, you are lucky to be able to see 10 meters in front of you, but you can hear ships that are far away. The physics of the ocean favors sound for long-distance communication. Many marine animals that swim over long ranges, such as some fish and mammals, have developed sensory systems that allow them to use sound to communicate, to find prey or predators, and to orient themselves. During their winter breeding season, some baleen whales use low-frequency sounds that can be heard hundreds of kilometers away to find mates. By contrast, elephants make some of the loudest and lowest-frequency calls of terrestrial animals, and these are thought to be audible "only" at ranges of 4 kilometers or so. Deep-diving toothed whales use high-frequency clicks to find and select prey in the dark a kilometer below the sea surface. Sperm whales are thought to detect squid at a range of 325 meters using clicks with a center frequency of 15 kHz, near the upper limit of frequencies that humans can hear. By contrast, a flying bat, producing pulses in the 20 to 50 kHz range, is thought to detect its prey at ranges of a few meters. These bat pulses would be well above the frequencies humans can hear. For both low-frequency communication and high-frequency echolocation, mammals in the ocean appear to exploit sound ranges about a hundred times lower and farther reaching than their counterparts on land.

When sound radiates from an animal, it may reflect from the ground or seafloor. On land, atmospheric conditions such as a temperature inversion can cause sound to refract back toward the ground. In these "ducting" conditions, an elephant call may be detected up to 10 kilometers away, and animals may time their calling to take advantage of these favorable sound propagation conditions. In the ocean, variations in temperature, salinity, and pressure also cause sound to refract. A deep-ocean sound channel is important for long-range propagation of the low-frequency sounds of whales and human sound sources such as ships. Sound energy in this channel is concentrated at depths of 1,000 meters or more in tropical oceans, becoming shallower at the Poles.

Over past century, humans have learned to use sound in ways that are similar to capabilities evolved by marine organisms over tens of millions of years. Some of the ways humans use sound may interfere with marine life, and vice versa. In addition, motorized shipping has elevated

The Sound Fixing and Ranging (SOFAR) channel is a layer of the ocean in which the speed of sound is minimum, owing to changes in water pressure and temperature. Within the channel, low-frequency sound waves may travel thousands of miles before dissipating.

noise levels in the world's oceans, especially in the low frequencies. This raises concern that baleen whales, whose populations were decimated by whaling, may not be able to communicate as far as they could when the oceans were quieter.

We know that intense sound can actually affect the hearing of marine mammals, reducing their sensitivity. But sound can harm marine mammals in other ways. An unusual pattern of mass strandings of the beaked whale, a toothed whale larger than a dolphin and smaller than a sperm whale, has been observed to coincide with naval sonar exercises. Until we know why whales strand when they hear these sounds, and what exposures cause the strandings, it will be difficult to protect these animals.

Although strandings are the most dramatic effect of sound, subtler effects may be more important for marine mammal populations. There is some evidence that exposure to human-produced sounds, such as air guns used in research and oil exploration, may change the distribution or behavior of fish and reduce the rate at which marine mammals can feed. Elevated noise may make it harder for a receptive female to find a calling male for breeding. Over long periods of time, these changes could affect growth and reproduction. Exposure to sound can also stimulate stress responses, which can lead to chronic problems.

The biggest problem for protecting marine life from adverse effects of noise is our ignorance of the effects of activities that are critical for commerce (shipping), for energy (seismic survey for oil exploration), and for defense (sonars used to find submarines). These activities are so important that it is unlikely humans will abandon them because of hypothetical impacts. We know it is a good idea to reduce exposure whenever possible, but effective protection of marine life will require a better understanding of how marine organisms respond behaviorally and physiologically to sound over the short and long term and how these responses affect the growth and stability of populations.

Until we have these answers, managers will have a hard time balancing the goal of protecting marine life with restricting global trade, offshore energy production, and defense. What is certain is that the ocean's natural tapestry of hauntingly beautiful, biologically vital sounds, reflecting interactions of complex and ancient ecosystems, has in less than a century been altered by the actions of a terrestrial mammal, a newcomer to the sea.

What We Take out of the Ocean

FISHING

As late as the 1960s it was widely held that "food from the sea" could fill a significant part of the world's growing need for protein as well as for oils and fertilizer. Some species—sardines in California, anchovies in Peru, cod and herring in the North Atlantic, and whales everywhere—already had declined significantly because of fishing and whaling, but many experts believed that a much higher level of taking could be sustained by targeting other species and that depleted populations would recover over time. A popular theory of "maximum sustainable yield" encouraged fishermen to believe it was all right to reduce unexploited populations by about half, and at that point the reproductive potential of those remaining would perpetually reproduce to a level that could be fished repeatedly. Now thoroughly discredited, the idea remains embedded in fisheries policy, encouraging unrealistic expectations and, inevitably, overexploitation.

New fishing fleets and technologies were developed globally in the 1970s, aided by government subsidies, in anticipation of bringing to market at least 100 million tons of marine life every year. That goal has never been attained. In 1989, about 90 million tons were taken, and world catch has since declined, despite new deep-water techniques targeting species not previously considered to be commercially valuable. Included are Patagonian toothfish (marketed as Chilean sea bass), orange roughy, monkfish, sharks, and Antarctic cod—all long-lived, slow-growing species. Increased effort and new methods for finding, catching, and transporting ocean wildlife failed to increase yields. Instead, the global catch fell 13 percent between 1994 and 2003.

Use of destructive gear exacerbated the decline of exploited species by ruining the ecosystems they depend upon. Trawls and draggers scrape the seafloor like bulldozers, flattening rugged terrain and destroying millions of tons of bycatch, the plants and animals that are killed and discarded.

Known to scientists as slimeheads, Hoplostethus atlanticus is marketed as orange roughy. It is a deep-dwelling fish that takes three decades to mature and can live to be 250 years old. The target of trawl-fishing in Australia, New Zealand, and elsewhere, the population has declined precipitously since commercial extraction began in the 1970s.

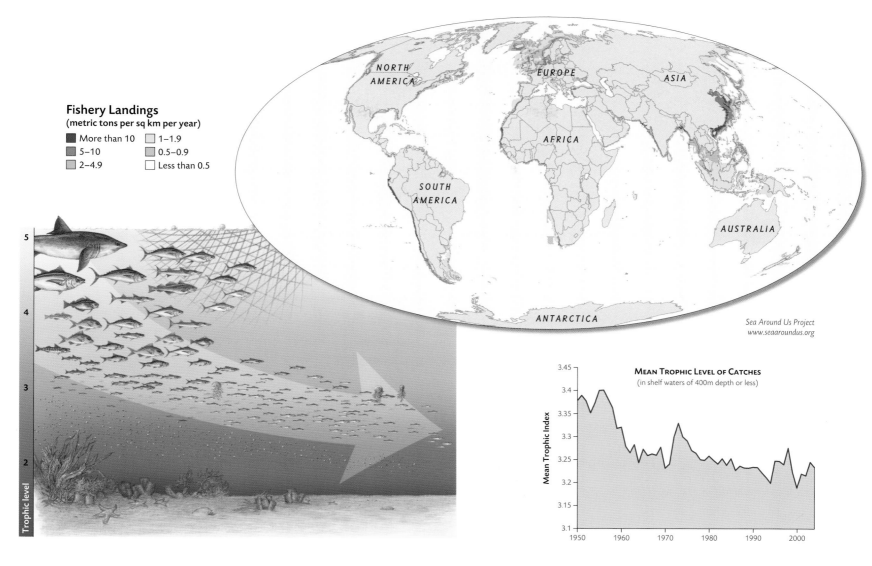

Fishery Landings
(metric tons per sq km per year)

- More than 10
- 5–10
- 2–4.9
- 1–1.9
- 0.5–0.9
- Less than 0.5

Sea Around Us Project
www.seaaroundus.org

MEAN TROPHIC LEVEL OF CATCHES
(in shelf waters of 400m depth or less)

Longlines, some exceeding 100 kilometers with thousands of baited hooks, lure sea birds, turtles, marine mammals, and nontargeted fish species to their death. Drift nets intercept and kill everything from turtles and dolphins to jellyfish and diving birds.

In 2003 Canadian scientists Ransome Myers and Boris Worm reported in *Nature* that after 50 years of increasingly aggressive industrial fishing only 10 percent of all large fish remain in the sea. Myers remarked in a report by SeaWeb, "From giant blue marlin to mighty bluefin tuna, and from tropical groupers to Antarctic cod, industrial fishing has scoured the global ocean. There is no blue frontier left." Worm added, "These are the mega-fauna, the big predators in the sea, and the species we most value. Their depletion not only threatens the future of these fish and the fisheries that depend on them, it could also bring about a complete reorganization of ocean ecosystems, with unknown global consequences."

Among the most sought-after fish in the sea are bluefin tuna. Millions of years of exacting pressures brought bluefins to the apex of complex food chains in the sea, but nothing in their history prepared the ultimate fish for the ultimate predator—humans equipped with sophisticated sonar, watchers in spotter planes, high-speed chase boats, powered harpoons, huge nets, and baited hooks deployed on lines many kilometers long. International regulations have failed to halt the slide of bluefins to near extinction.

Sharks also have felt the serious bite of industrial fishing. Promotion of sharks as "underutilized species" for human consumption led to increased taking in the 1980s, then rapidly escalated as new markets developed for an ancient delicacy, shark fin soup. What once was a highly prized specialty became a high priced but accessible luxury, especially in China, but appearing on menus globally. As with other large ocean predators, only about 10 percent of big sharks remain.

Even small species of fish have declined sharply since the middle of the 20th century. The Atlantic menhaden, a member of the herring family, is critically important as food for numerous birds, fish, and marine mammals and as a natural ocean filtration system. In his 2007 book, *The Most Important Fish in the Sea,* H. Bruce Franklin describes "dense schools of menhaden . . . their mouths agape, slurping up plankton, cellulose, and just plain detritus like a colossal submarine vacuum cleaner."

Global Overfishing: *Humans' growing appetite for marine wildlife has driven powerful new technologies to find, capture, and transport to market more than 70 million metric tons of ocean wildlife each year. Many once-common species have been taken in such large numbers that their future commercial value—and their future existence on Earth—may be in jeopardy. This has led to "fishing down the food web"—that is, catching species closer to the primary production level that converts sunlight into chlorophyll, the lowest trophic level. This practice could have disastrous effects on the entire ocean biologic system.*

Excessive taking of menhaden for fish meal and oil in recent decades has seriously disrupted menhaden-dependent food chains and diminished the natural cleansing of coastal waters in the western Atlantic and the Gulf of Mexico.

Fishermen today face an uncertain future. Large-scale industrial operations have so depleted ocean species that it is increasingly difficult for individual families and communities traditionally dependent on the sea to maintain a living. Curiously, many people are unaware of the urgent plight of such fishermen or of the marine animals they see in markets and restaurants. The available variety and apparent abundance suggests that fish, lobsters, crabs, oysters, and other ocean wildlife must abound. Part of the illusion derives from a phenomenon called "shifting baselines," a term coined by Canadian fisheries biologist Daniel Pauly in 1995. Zoologist Jeremy Jackson, with 18 coauthors, elucidated the concept in a 2001 article in *Science*, showing how each generation considers what they have experienced to be "normal," when, in fact, they are unaware that most of the exploited species were once larger and more abundant. Callum Roberts notes in *The Unnatural History of the Sea*, "Nobody alive

Tsukiji, the Tokyo fish market, annually processes more than a million tons of wildlife from global sources. Highly prized and highly endangered bluefin tuna, shown here, may have been swimming in an ocean half a world away. In less than half a century, their numbers have plummeted by more than 90 percent.

Fish Are Wildlife

Tigers are wildlife. So are ocean fish. Most of the food taken from the land is grown for that purpose: grains and vegetables are planted and harvested; chickens and livestock are raised to provide meat. It is generally understood that 6.5 billion people cannot be fed by animals taken from the wild, like tigers. Yet, millions of tons of wildlife are "harvested" from the ocean for food each year, with no cultivation. Much better approaches to aquaculture must be developed if the ocean is to feed the growing human population. A young orange roughy or Chilean sea bass in the market may be 20 years old but killed before it could reproduce young. Or a larger one on a restaurant menu could be 150 to 200 years old. Animals in the open ocean aren't just seafood, or "living marine resources," or fishery populations. They are ocean wildlife.

today has seen the heyday of cod or herring. No one has watched sporting groups of sperm whales five hundred strong or seen alewife run so thick up river there seemed to be more fish than water."

The decline of ocean wildlife has spurred increasing interest in farming marine species. For centuries, cultivation of freshwater carp, crabs, and other plant-eating species has been common in China, and pond farming of marine species has a long history in Hawaii and various Pacific island countries. In recent decades, some marine fish have been grown in coastal areas, including Atlantic salmon, striped bass, mahimahi, and several kinds of shrimp, oysters, clams, and scallops. Some operations are moving offshore with netted enclosures for fish. Most marine fish that are being farmed are carnivores, however, and feeding them usually involves catching four or five tons of small wild fish for every ton of farmed animals raised. Other problems include buildup of wastes around the farms, introduction of antibiotics and parasites to native populations, and the escape of nonnative species to nearby ecosystems. Shrimp aquaculture in Thailand, Malaysia, Mexico, Belize, and other countries has displaced thousands of acres of coastal mangroves and marshes, reducing the natural storm protection these systems provide with costly consequences.

Most of these thorny problems have solutions, however. Closed systems that recycle water and use biological filtration achieve "more crop per drop" and also avoid concerns about escapes and contamination. Selecting fast-growing plant-eating species rather than slow-growing carnivores follows the model established for terrestrial farm-raised animals. There is enormous potential for cultivating microbes for food, pharmaceuticals, edible oils, and even renewable sources of oil for fuel. The greatest potential for extracting wealth from the ocean may be embodied in the enormous diversity of living assets available for those with the foresight and wisdom to use them, without using them up.

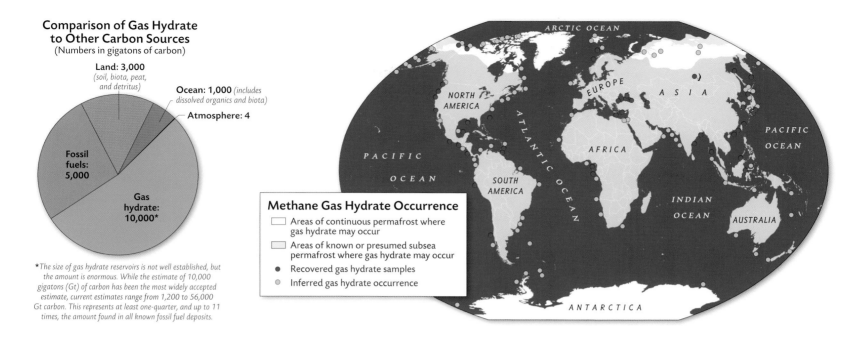

Comparison of Gas Hydrate to Other Carbon Sources
(Numbers in gigatons of carbon)

Land: 3,000 *(soil, biota, peat, and detritus)*

Ocean: 1,000 *(includes dissolved organics and biota)*

Atmosphere: 4

Fossil fuels: 5,000

Gas hydrate: 10,000*

*The size of gas hydrate reservoirs is not well established, but the amount is enormous. While the estimate of 10,000 gigatons (Gt) of carbon has been the most widely accepted estimate, current estimates range from 1,200 to 56,000 Gt carbon. This represents at least one-quarter, and up to 11 times, the amount found in all known fossil fuel deposits.

Methane Gas Hydrate Occurrence
- Areas of continuous permafrost where gas hydrate may occur
- Areas of known or presumed subsea permafrost where gas hydrate may occur
- ● Recovered gas hydrate samples
- ○ Inferred gas hydrate occurrence

OFFSHORE OIL AND GAS

The market for oil, "black gold," has prompted extensive searching underwater for new sources. The first offshore oil well was constructed in Summerland, California, in 1887, when H. L. Williams moved his oil-drilling operations from the beach to a pier about 100 meters offshore. Pressures for more oil sparked the beginning of the offshore oil industry, with installation in 1947 by Kerr-McGee of the first offshore drilling operation out of sight of land. Within two years, 11 oil fields were found underwater in the Gulf of Mexico, and 44 exploratory wells drilled. As the whole world has since edged toward an oil-based economy, oil and gas reserves have been discovered deeper and farther offshore in many parts of the world—the Gulf of Mexico, the Persian Gulf, the Caspian Sea, the North Sea, the bays of eastern China, and the coast of Brazil. Shell Oil is now drilling successful wells in water depths as great as 3,000 meters.

Operations are also moving farther offshore, in some places beyond 320 kilometers from the coast. In a recent review, the U.S. Geological Survey estimated "proven" world reserves at 1.1 trillion barrels. The actual amount is not easy to determine, and some oil-rich places are off limits because of political or environmental reasons.

OCEAN MINING

Many materials—salt, sand and gravel, fresh water, petrochemicals, diamonds, and metallic ores—are extracted from the ocean, mostly from coastal waters. Underwater vehicles specially designed for diamond mining have been used successfully in a few hundred meters in South African waters since the early 1990s and are viewed as a model for what might be used at much greater depths. Much of the technology needed for mining in water depths as great as 6,000 meters has already been developed for scientific research and for offshore oil and gas operations.

Interest in deep-sea mining of manganese nodules and mineralized crusts from hydrothermal vents has grown slowly since the 1980s, but the potential economic return has not yet been sufficient to inspire widespread investment. Nearly 400 deep-sea vent fields have been found, and some companies have explored the ways and means of extracting valuable metals from the surrounding crusts. Off Papua New Guinea, experimental surveys are under way to determine the economic and environmental consequences of full-scale mining operations for a wide range of underwater substances, proposed to begin in 2009. An Australian company is exploring for copper, silver, zinc, lead, and gold on the Kermadec Seamounts off northern New Zealand.

But just as there are environmental costs associated with mining operations on the land, there are also concerns about the impacts of deep-sea mining. Most plans call for scraping or cutting into metal-bearing rock and using pumps to bring a slurry of water and cuttings to a floating platform, where the rock would be separated for processing. Compounds typically used to separate

Methane Gas: *High concentrations of methane gas may be trapped in ice, permafrost, and in the deep sea. This map shows the methane content around the globe, indicating areas that are prone to methane concentrations. A pie chart illustrates the relationship of methane gas to other hydrocarbons, such as petroleum, natural gas, and coal. A huge amount of the Earth's carbon is now thought to be bound up in gas hydrates. Increasing temperature could trigger the release of enormous amounts of methane, further accelerating global warming and potentially upsetting the environmental balance that makes Earth hospitable to humans.*

the desired minerals from other materials have often resulted in significant pollution of waters near land-based mining operations, and those concerns also apply to mining operations at sea.

Although the regions of seafloor covered by manganese nodules are immense, virtually nothing is known about the nature of the deep-sea ecosystems that produced these mysterious formations, except that they evidently are of microbial origin, and typically formed over thousands of years around something organic—a bit of bone, shell, or a shark's tooth. The consequences of removing these ancient mineral formations, and the effects of disrupting whatever complex ecosystems have formed them, are unknown. But, given the centuries required to create them, it is clear they cannot recover quickly from mining operations.

In warm summer months, glacial ice normally thaws to some extent, spilling fresh water into the Arctic Ocean, but in recent years, the time of thawing has increased and the time of freezing decreased, one of many indications of a global warming trend.

Climate Change and the Ocean

THROUGHOUT EARTH'S HISTORY, climate has changed in concert with the ocean. Since ocean water holds about 1,000 times as much heat as the atmosphere, the primary driver of climate patterns is the interaction between ocean temperatures and currents and their global distribution of heat. The planet has been slowly warming since the end of the last ice age, but a significant increase in ocean temperature has been observed in the 20th century, with a global mean surface temperature rise of about 0.5°C. Also over the past century, sea levels have risen 18 centimeters, with an increase of nearly 4 centimeters between 1993 and 2003 alone. The warming trend is expected to cause accelerated melting of polar ice, with predictions that there will be little or no summer ice in the Arctic by the middle of the 21st century, or possibly much sooner.

Predictions about future climate change and its consequences are dependent on improved knowledge of both past and present conditions. Information about the past is being assembled through careful analysis of core samples taken from polar ice, lakes, deep-sea muds, coral reefs, and, for recent centuries, even from living trees. To increase the understanding of today's climate, there are satellite sensors, instruments regularly lofted into the atmosphere by balloons, a global network of on-the-ground weather stations, and a growing array of ocean observing systems, which are critical but difficult and expensive to deploy and maintain because of the great depths and expanses, remote locations, and often harsh conditions at sea.

There are concerns, based on recent projections, that global warming might shut down, or drastically change, the global, interconnected system of ocean currents that drives the planet's climate patterns. The system depends on a balance of temperature and salinity. If either changes significantly, the present pattern of circulation could collapse, with potentially disastrous effects to the climate patterns now favorable to human life on Earth.

Since the beginning of the industrial revolution, about half of all carbon released into the atmosphere by fossil fuels has been taken up by the ocean. Some carbon dioxide in the sea is vital for photosynthesis, but excessive amounts are transformed into carbonic acid. A trend toward increased acidification has been measured recently, and concerns are growing about the potential for a massive, worldwide dissolving of organisms with carbonate-based skeletons. These include corals, mollusks, larval fish, and many of the multitudinous planktonic organisms responsible for generating oxygen and absorbing carbon dioxide, thus keeping the Earth's atmosphere habitable for marine and land species, including humans.

Looking back over time, it is obvious that climate change is not new, it is inevitable, but the present wave of change is unique in that for the first time, a single species is rocking the planetary boat. Oceanographer John Knauss once observed that "no one knows why the dinosaurs went extinct, but dinosaurs were not to blame." Coupled with policies and technologies aimed at stabilizing climate changes—curbing emissions, capturing energy in ways that do not involve the release of greenhouse gases—it is critical also to maintain and restore what remains of the natural ocean ecosystems and the diversity of life within them that are the underpinnings for the global balance that holds the planet steady.

Is Global Warming Really a Problem?

The Earth has gone through natural climate cycles for hundreds of millions of years and was much warmer in the mid-Cretaceous about 80 million years ago than it is today. But during the Cretaceous warming, there were no humans, no political boundaries, no port cities, no farmland, no coastal real estate. A natural warming of that magnitude today, with huge sea-level rise, massive changes in areas that can grow crops, and constant monster storms, would be devastating to the homes, transportation, food sources, security, and other basic needs of human life. Some people still question the importance of human impacts—whether the burning of fossil fuels since the industrial revolution is making any difference. But almost all scientists are now convinced that human actions are significantly accelerating global warming with unfavorable consequences too profound to be ignored.

R. Steven Nerem
GLOBAL SEA-LEVEL RISE

Sea-level rise is an important aspect of climate change because it could have tremendous socioeconomic implications. The sea-level changes as the volume of the water in the ocean changes, much like the water level in a bathtub. Water expands or contracts as it gets warmer or cooler (like the mercury in a thermometer), causing the water level to go up or down. In addition, water is exchanged between the regional oceans, the continents, and the atmosphere. Over long periods, this water exchange is driven primarily by the melting of ice in mountain glaciers and the polar ice sheets and the subsequent runoff of that water via rivers and streams into the

that calculate the distance between the satellites and the ocean surface. The satellites show that sea level has been rising at a rate of 3.5 millimeters per year, nearly double the rate observed by the tide gauges over the past century. For the recent sea-level change, roughly a third is the result of warming of the oceans (thermal expansion), a third is caused by melting of mountain glaciers, and the rest is due to other sources, including melting of the polar ice sheets (about 0.3 millimeter per year). There is independent evidence (other satellite and aircraft measurements) that all of these contributions have accelerated over the past decade.

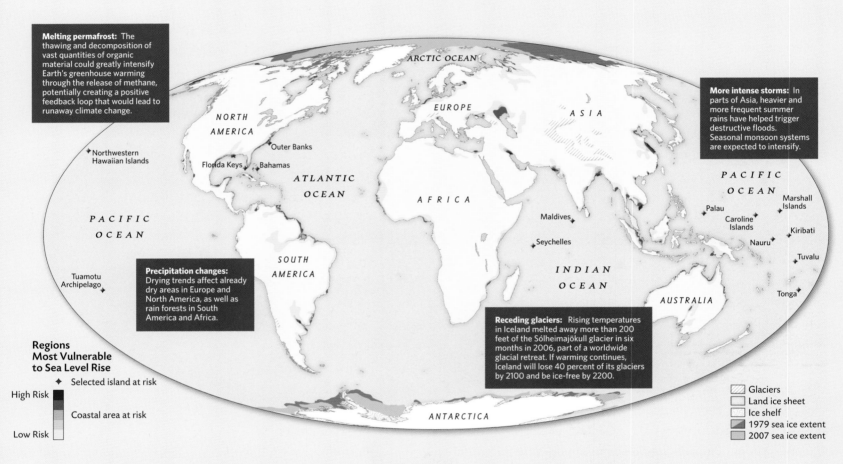

Melting permafrost: The thawing and decomposition of vast quantities of organic material could greatly intensify Earth's greenhouse warming through the release of methane, potentially creating a positive feedback loop that would lead to runaway climate change.

More intense storms: In parts of Asia, heavier and more frequent summer rains have helped trigger destructive floods. Seasonal monsoon systems are expected to intensify.

Precipitation changes: Drying trends affect already dry areas in Europe and North America, as well as rain forests in South America and Africa.

Receding glaciers: Rising temperatures in Iceland melted away more than 200 feet of the Sólheimajökull glacier in six months in 2006, part of a worldwide glacial retreat. If warming continues, Iceland will lose 40 percent of its glaciers by 2100 and be ice-free by 2200.

Regions Most Vulnerable to Sea Level Rise

✦ Selected island at risk

High Risk

Coastal area at risk

Low Risk

Glaciers
Land ice sheet
Ice shelf
1979 sea ice extent
2007 sea ice extent

Many islands and shorelines of the world are at risk from sea-level rise. Shoreline changes for a 6-meter rise are shown on pages 296-297.

oceans. (Think of a spigot adding water to the bathtub.) The ice stored on Greenland (7 meters of potential sea-level rise) and Antarctica (65 meters of potential sea-level rise) provides the greatest potential for catastrophic sea-level change (here defined as greater than 1 meter); water temperature changes and melting of mountain glaciers are important contributors as well. The oceans absorb most of the excess heat associated with climate change; thus, monitoring sea level is an important aspect of climate change science. And because sea level responds to many different factors, sea-level change is a sensitive yardstick of climate change.

Over the past century, tide gauge measurements (think of a yardstick on the end of a pier measuring the height of the water) have been our primary source of information on sea-level change, although they provide measurements only near islands and continental coastlines. Since the early 1990s, sea level has been measured globally by satellites using instruments

Predicting future sea-level change is very difficult. Even under the most pessimistic climate change scenarios, thermal expansion will contribute at most 1 meter of sea-level rise by 2100. The melting of mountain glaciers, which could disappear by 2100, could contribute an additional three-quarters of a meter. Although ice melt from Greenland and Antarctica currently contributes only about 10 percent of the observed sea-level rise, it is of most concern for future sea-level change because of the large amount of water stored there. Unfortunately, the dynamics of large ice sheets are poorly understood, and thus there is some uncertainty about how quickly they will respond to climate change. Satellite observations will be crucial for monitoring the ice sheets, and these observations suggest that large changes are already well under way in Greenland and western Antarctica. Significant melting of these ice sheets could have catastrophic effects on coastal population centers and wildlife.

Marine Protected Areas

In 1872, Yellowstone was designated as the first national park in the United States, and in the ensuing years, a number of individuals supported by the National Geographic Society and the administration of President Theodore Roosevelt worked to create what some call "the best idea America ever had"—the National Park System, established in 1916. Roosevelt's ethic is embodied in his comment: "The nation behaves well if it treats the natural resources as assets which it must turn over to the next generation increased, and not impaired, in value." As of 2008, nearly 400 places of natural, cultural, and historic importance are included under the jurisdiction of the National Park Service and protected to some degree as a critical part of the nation's heritage. In 1972, exactly 100 years after the designation of the first national park on land, the U.S. Congress authorized the establishment of protected areas in the sea. Over the past three and a half decades, this National Marine Sanctuary Program has grown to encompass 14 areas in U.S. waters.

WEB LINK: Marine Protected Areas

A living palette of corals, sponges, fish, and other wildlife prospers on this reef in Raja Ampat, Indonesia, a symbol of hope that the ingredients exist to brighten damaged systems with restored diversity and abundance of life.

Worldwide, more than 4,600 marine protected areas have been designated, mostly small, and with varying degrees of use and protection. Although the words "sanctuary," "park," and "protected area" may suggest that everything within is safe from harm, there is really little sanctity for wildlife in most marine sanctuaries. In most, both commercial and sport fishing are allowed, and all are subject to the flow of pollutants. Despite these shortcomings, some protected areas—especially

SEE ALSO: recovery of coral reefs, page 168

Dan Laffoley
MARINE PROTECTED AREAS

In 1962 John F. Kennedy said, "We are tied to the ocean. And when we go back to the sea, whether it is to sail or to watch it, we are going back from whence we came." Since John F. Kennedy spoke those words more than four decades ago, we understand much more about our connections to the ocean, not just as a place of enjoyment or a place to obtain food. And with climate change has come a dawning realization that the ocean does far more for us than is obvious to most people. Our ocean can be viewed as the principal property holder of our planet, with the human race squeezed onto the remaining 30 percent of our world that is made up of land. The

The good news is that many governments of the world have already signed up for ocean protection at a policy level. This is principally through the Convention on Biological Diversity and agreements such as those brokered at the 2002 World Summit on Sustainable Development. There are a variety of ways we can safeguard the seas, but the most important is by setting areas aside for special management of their wildlife and habitats—marine protected areas (MPAs). These commitments add up to countries committing to protect 10 percent of their sea areas through MPAs and building networks of MPAs by 2012. Since being introduced,

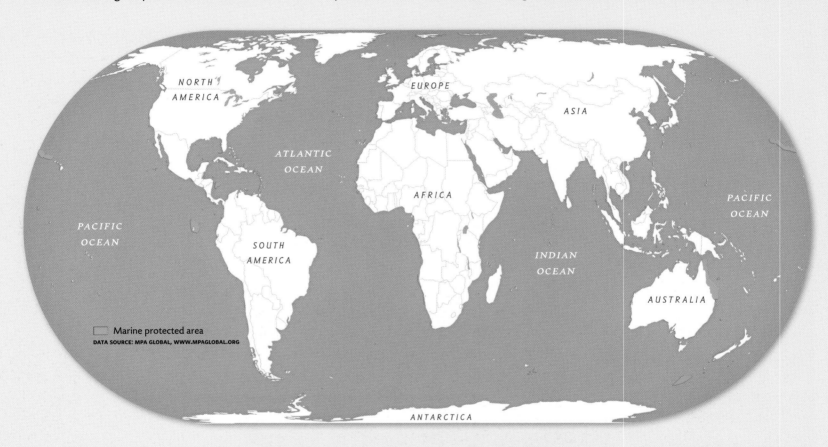

This map, created in 2008, is based on data from the MPA global database of the world's marine protected areas. It is the result of a formal collaboration between the Sea Around Us project, the World Wildlife Fund, the United Nations Environment Programme–World Conservation Monitoring Centre, and the World Conservation Union–World Commission on Protected Areas (www.mpaglobal.org).

ocean is essential to life on Earth: it shapes and regulates our climate, storing very significant amounts of the carbon from the air—the very carbon in carbon dioxide that is now causing such concern as our emissions continue to rise. The challenge with the ocean, given the critical part it plays in life on Earth, is to go beyond just recognizing its role and to ensure that our management and protection sustains it for the future. It is perhaps surprising that ocean protection doesn't resonate far more with all of us despite President Kennedy's words all those years ago. It may be because we live at the coastal margins and seldom venture far from land. It may be because most people's relation to the ocean these days is more about the blue bits they fly over in planes, and how many in-flight movies they can squeeze in, rather than anything that is real and wet and may swim in the sea or live deep down on the ocean floor.

this approach has been endorsed by countless groups, from the Group of Eight industrialized nations to many countries working individually or together at regional levels.

The bad news is that despite this unprecedented level of political support, progress is falling short of the promises. This is not so much the result of intentional or malicious neglect of the ocean, but more often than not the deferral of decisions to bow to the needs of a particular stakeholder group or to carry out "further studies." All of this uses up valuable time before the 2012 deadline. Despite political backing, less than 1 percent of the ocean is currently protected by MPAs, and only a fraction of that in an adequate manner. At the current rate of progress our best estimate is that it may not be until about the 2070s that we put in place what needed to be done by 2012.

We know more than ever before about what is needed to safeguard our ocean world. We know that MPAs are an effective management tool. If created with high levels of protection, they can recover the quality and abundance of marine wildlife. Often termed "marine reserves," this type of protected area shows that when we take the pressures of exploitation off our seas, even for very small areas, the wildlife and habitats bounce back. They also show us what we frequently fail to understand: how depleted the ocean is. This is known as the concept of shifting baselines, in which generation after generation views the state of the seas from its own perspective, not recognizing the slow, steady, and inexorable decline as quality, values, and benefits are serially lost across the decades.

Marine reserves show us there is still hope for our seas, and that local communities can be the first to benefit. They also tell us that recovery may take a long time to achieve—some species respond dramatically and quickly, but usually it takes decades for habitats and ecosystems to replenish themselves. This often comes down to a basic fact of life: The larger and older individuals in populations act as the seed bank for future generations. Yet year by year it is these large individuals that our selective exploitation targets. Thus, timescales are not on our side; the longer we deplete, the greater the risk of never being able to replace what has been lost, as population after population falls to all-time lows. Marine reserves are the control in a very large experiment. Marine reserves are in fact the only places where we are really starting to understand the potential of our seas. What is increasingly worrisome is the large-scale experimental way in which we manage the rest of the ocean, with few, if any, control sites that marine reserves represent. It is perhaps surprising that management of our seas in this respect falls so far behind other disciplines—from chemistry to medicine—where using controls to quantify effects is not just usual but expected, and a sign of good practice.

On top of these problems, what many people do not realize is that the ability to declare and manage effective MPAs is almost exclusively limited to waters that such countries have claimed as their economic zones, and therefore where their laws can apply. This leaves nearly two-thirds of the world ocean, the high seas, without any effective system to protect habitats and species. It may be tempting to think that, because they are remote, the high seas are in no need of protection. This could not be further from the truth. With the depletion of the cod fishery and so many other coastal fish stocks worldwide, the fishing industry has turned to the high seas to exploit their resources. Other industries, such as deep-sea mining, are not far behind. Fishing operations are now targeting the seamounts, ocean ridges, and plateaus of the deep ocean beyond national jurisdiction, where ownership and responsibility do not lie with any nation. In the course of a decade or more, we have caused significant damage to largely unknown ecosystems, depleted species, and probably doomed many others to extinction.

Every day, commercial fishing fleets, dispatched primarily from just 11 nations, venture onto the high seas to fish the deep ocean with seabed trawls. They deploy massive gear with names like canyon buster, which indicate the sheer scale involved and the damage they inflict. Everything in their path, from ancient corals and sponges to 200-year-old fish, is stripped away and caught in their nets. In a single trawl, lumps of sponges, corals, and other species, together weighing as much as 4,500 kilograms, can be trapped and destroyed.

The high seas are very special. Covering 64 percent of the surface of the planet, it is mostly here where you can find dense groupings of animals that derive their energy from sources other than the sun around volcanic vents on the deep-sea floor. It is here where you can find areas still free from non-native species, as in the seas around Antarctica. And it is here where you can find living organisms that are more than 8,000 years old, like many of the massive deep-sea corals. But what really sets the high seas apart from other areas we know is this overwhelming lack of protection for any of this natural heritage.

We marvel when a new species is discovered on land, yet it is quite humbling to consider that there is a 50 percent chance of finding a new marine species every time we venture into waters below 3,000 meters. On the high seas, with the absence of any proper management, a conservation tragedy of epic proportions is now unfolding. We need to move quickly. Given the fragility of these environments, we simply do not have the luxury of time, but we *can* act before it is too late.

As we continue to build our understanding of high-seas oceans and the life within, we must establish MPAs that extend beyond just the areas we know today to be valuable or threatened. We must place biodiversity conservation at the center of high-seas ocean governance; build the precautionary approach into the United Nations Convention on the Law of the Sea; and ensure that every activity in these areas beyond national jurisdiction is conducted in a sustainable manner that is fair to present and future generations. We must recognize that all of the geographical, geological, and biological parts of the ocean are interrelated and interdependent and equal one tremendously significant ecosystem.

Right now, we have this opportunity to prevent the extinction of countless species and ecosystems that are only just being discovered. The next few years will be critical in deciding whether we succeed or fail. Recalling President Kennedy's perspective, perhaps the ultimate question now for marine protected areas should not be whether we can afford, or should implement, such agreements. The question is surely much more about whether current and future generations will forgive us for not doing so, and quickly. We must stem the tide of loss—not only of wildlife, but of all the benefits we receive, realized or often unseen. This is not just in our inshore waters with which we may be most familiar, but throughout what is, in effect, not really planet Earth but much more planet Ocean.

....

MPA Facts

• Current protection targets aim to protect 10-30 percent of global marine habitats within the next 2-4 years. • So far, some 5,000 MPAs have been created worldwide. • About 2.58 million square kilometers—0.65 percent of the world ocean and 1.6 percent of the total marine area within Exclusive Economic Zones—are currently protected. • Only 0.08 percent of the world ocean and 0.2 percent of the total marine area under national jurisdiction is considered no-take, where extractive uses are prohibited.

Gathered together here to breed, these sleek swimmers, longfin inshore squid, Loligo pealeii, *often move offshore in waters from Newfoundland to the Gulf of Venezuela.*

those "no-take" or "reserve" areas where fishing is prohibited—are yielding positive results.

The largest area where all extractive activities except sport fishing are banned includes the 410,234-square-kilometer Phoenix Island Protected Area designated in 2007 in the waters of the Republic of Kirabati, a nation made up of numerous islands and reefs in the South Pacific Ocean. The next largest fully protected area is in the United States, the Papahanaumokuakea Marine National Monument, 362,072 square kilometers surrounding a large part of the northwestern Hawaiian Islands. Designated by President George W. Bush in 2006, it is larger than all the national parks in the United States combined. The largest "multiple-use" marine protected area remains Australia's Great Barrier Reef National Marine Park Authority, established in 1972, a vast network of deep and shallow reefs along Australia's eastern seaboard. In 2005, 33 percent of the 2,000 kilometers of reefs were designated for full protection, increased from what had been about 6 percent.

In January 2001, scientists from countries all over the world attending a meeting of the American Association for the Advancement of Sciences discussed the results of observations in fully protected areas. Consistently the research showed greater numbers of larger fish and greater diversity overall in the no-take areas after only five years.

Valuing the Living Ocean

THE FIRST ADMINISTRATOR of the National Oceanic and Atmospheric Administration, meteorologist Robert White, was mindful of the growing dangers to the oceans, the atmosphere, and the living systems that everyone uses but no one owns. He observed in 1994: "What is at stake in all of this is the fate of the global commons. We are all dependent on maintaining the habitability of the planet. . . . This is the quintessential challenge for mankind in the next century."

Included among the major discoveries of the latter part of the 20th century unknown or not well understood in the 1960s were some ocean basics: life occurs in the sea from the surface to the greatest depths; tectonic processes cause major shifts in the position of continents and watermasses; the ocean governs global temperature and therefore is the key to climate and weather; microbes abound in the sea and are critical to global chemistry; the sea takes up the majority of carbon dioxide that enters the atmosphere; and most of the oxygen in the atmosphere has been and continues to be generated by organisms in the sea. The most important discoveries, however, may have been the awareness that the ocean is not infinitely resilient and that the nature of the world—and thus its capacity to support humankind—is shaped by the state of the ocean.

Opposite: A humpback mother and calf, Megaptera novaeangliae, *pirouette within a nursery as wide and deep as the ocean itself. Born in the South Pacific, a youngster such as this may swim with its mother in its first year to feeding areas thousands of kilometers away.*

And now the next century is under way. Journalist Mark Lynas observes in *Six Degrees: Our Future on a Hotter Planet,* "We are already into a new geological era, the Anthropocene, where human interference is the dominant factor in nearly every planetary system." The deep and dark blue ocean will continue to roll—far into the future—but it is increasingly clear that it is unrealistic to take for granted the benefits it provides, the distillation of four and a half billion years of fine-tuning. Never before has there been a greater need to understand all aspects of the deep frontier and to provide a sound knowledge base for crucial decisions that will otherwise be made in ignorance. And never again will there be better opportunities to explore and protect the natural ocean systems that are crucial to the future of humankind on this ocean planet. □

The Last Word

Sylvia A. Earle

Immersed in darkness 390 meters underwater, I waited for the surface crew aboard American Marine's ship, *Islander,* to give me the signal to return to the realm of sunlight and air. As part of the National Geographic Society's Sustainable Seas Expeditions, photographer and biologist Kip Evans and I in two *Deep Worker* personal submersibles had explored for four hours the rugged volcanic terrain and deep stretches of sand between Lanai and Maui, Hawaii, but a storm was brewing and we had to end our observations for the day. Kip ascended first and was landed on deck safely, but just as I got ready to lift off, something large and dark drifted into view. My first thought was that it was trash, a garbage bag or a tangle of lost fishing gear, common sights on nearly every dive I have made in recent years. Curious, I aimed the sub's lights at the shadowy mass, and a glistening silvery red body with eyes and arms came into view. "A giant squid!" was my first thought. Well, maybe a small giant squid, or at least a cephalopod of some sort. Two meters long, hovering gently above the seafloor, the creature regarded me while I hurriedly readied the sub's camera to document whatever it was.

At the time, January 2002, no one had ever seen a giant squid alive in the deep sea, although there had been reports of creatures longer than a city bus grappling at the surface with sperm whales, the squid's only known predator. Numerous novels and films have fostered the myth of *Architeuthis dux* as a calculating people-eater, building on legends inspired by rare glimpses of these enormous mollusks, distant cousins of clams and snails. In recent years, there have been so many unsuccessful quests to find the giant squid that it has become a symbol of how ill-equipped humans are to access the deep ocean, and how little is truly known about a vast part of the biosphere.

In the 2001 *National Geographic Atlas of the Ocean,* I posed a question about what would most surprise scientists from the 1872-76 *Challenger* expedition. What would top the list? New technologies, new discoveries, new scientific breakthroughs? Flying high in the sky and looking back on Earth from space? Predicting weather, hearing news and seeing images via television, the Internet, and wireless telephones? Or would those early ocean explorers be most awed by what still remains to be discovered? Surely they would wonder how we could succeed in sending men to the moon, to the deepest sea, and to the top of Mount Everest and yet be unable to arrange a rendezvous with one of the largest animals on Earth.

In 2005, scientists from Japan's National Science Museum finally captured an *Architeuthis* on a baited hook at a depth of 650 meters about 1,000 kilometers south of Tokyo and filmed the giant, reddish creature alive before it was taken as a museum specimen. No one has yet encountered these amazing animals on their own terms, underwater, and little is known of their life history, their behavior, age, or maximum size. Actually, not much is known about most of the 700 or so kinds of living cephalopods—squids, octopuses, cuttlefish, and nautiloids—other than as ornaments or how they taste as calamari or sushi or how effective they are as bait or ground up as animal food. Scientists have discovered that they are exquisitely diverse, with eyes hauntingly structured like those of mammals; that many have complex signaling systems using flashes of color, shapes, and bioluminescence; that some appear to have intelligence and curiosity perhaps on a par with cats. All have a

Opposite: Reflecting the mystery and majesty of the sea and hundreds of millions of years of cephalopod history, this Humboldt squid flares its arms toward the light in the night waters of the Gulf of California. With care, cephalopods and humans will share a future as enduring as the big mollusks' past.

fundamental role in ocean ecosystems as effective predators, and some are critically important prey for marine mammals, fish, birds, and other hungry cephalopods.

From my perch in the depths, watching the silvery red creature swim toward me, I realized that I was being inspected not by a squid but rather a large, intensely curious octopus. Eight, not ten arms reached out to touch the mechanical arms of the sub, revealing a sheltered cluster of pale eggs. Officially, my dive was over, but I begged and got permission to remain nearly an hour, staying close as the octopus glided upward in the water column, stopping when she stopped, moving when she moved, keeping pace in a slow-motion dance until, finally, I had to pull away.

Seeing a creature unlike any I had ever seen before, knowing that she had never seen a creature such as I, inspired in me a sense of wonder and hope. Humans are newcomers on this ancient planet, the first and only species to so radically dominate Earth's natural systems—land, water, air, and biosphere—and the first and only to provoke changes that not only threaten our survival but could initiate Earth's sixth planetwide wave of extinction.

Cephalopods may have an advantage over us with their resilience, their half-a-billion-year lineage that has endured several waves of mass extinction, including the cataclysmic events 65 million years ago when dinosaurs faded into oblivion and mammals began a new era of prosperity. Some variation on the cephalopod theme will likely survive, one way or another, to swim in future seas. But we may have our own kind of advantage as the first and only species with the capacity to look back over the broad sweep of time, see our place in the greater scheme of things, and take actions that can ensure an enduring future for ourselves, for squids, and for all of the living components that have been fine-tuned over four and a half billion years to yield a planet that works in our favor. There is time, but not a lot, to use that wondrous capacity that humans have to dream, to anticipate the next decade, century, millennium, and beyond. If we so choose, we have the power to craft a world where we respect and live in peace with ourselves and with the mostly blue world that sustains us.

Ocean vs. Land

The Earth

Mass: 5,974,000,000,000,000,000,000 (5.974 sextillion) metric tons

Land Area: 148,647,000 square kilometers (57,393,000 square mi)

Population, as of July 2008: 6,707,580,000

Area of Each Ocean

	SQ KM	SQ MI	PERCENT OF EARTH'S WATER AREA
Total ocean area	331,441,932	127,970,446	100
Atlantic	81,705,396	31,546,630	24.6
Pacific	152,617,159	58,925,815	46.1
Indian	67,469,539	26,050,135	20.4
Arctic	8,676,520	3,350,023	2.6
Southern	20,973,318	8,097,843	6.3

Volume of Each Ocean

	CUBIC KM	CUBIC MI	PERCENT OF EARTH'S WATER VOL.
Total volume	1,303,115,354	312,634,001	100
Atlantic	307,923,430	73,874,760	23.6
Pacific	645,369,567	154,832,394	49.5
Indian	261,519,545	62,741,876	20.1
Arctic	16,787,461	4,027,526	1.3
Southern	71,515,351	17,157,445	5.5

Deepest Point in Each Ocean

	METERS	FEET
Challenger Deep, Pacific Ocean	-10,920	-35,827
Puerto Rico Trench, Atlantic Ocean	-8,605	-28,232
South Sandwich Trench (south end), Southern Ocean	-7,412	-24,318
Java Trench, Indian Ocean	-7,125	-23,376
Molloy Deep, Arctic Ocean	-5,669	-18,599

Largest Islands

		AREA	
		SQ KM	SQ MI
1	Greenland	2,166,000	836,000
2	New Guinea	792,500	306,000
3	Borneo	725,500	280,100
4	Madagascar	587,000	226,600
5	Baffin Island	507,500	196,000
6	Sumatra	427,300	165,000
7	Honshu	227,400	87,800
8	Great Britain	218,100	84,200
9	Victoria Island	217,300	83,900
10	Ellesmere Island	196,200	75,800
11	Sulawesi (Celebes)	178,700	69,000
12	South Island (New Zealand)	150,400	58,100
13	Java	126,700	48,900
14	North Island (New Zealand)	113,700	43,900
15	Island of Newfoundland	108,900	42,000

Largest Seas by Area

		AREA		AVERAGE DEPTH	
		SQ KM	SQ MI	METERS	FEET
1	Coral Sea	4,183,510	1,615,260	2,471	8,107
2	South China Sea	3,596,390	1,388,570	1,180	3,871
3	Caribbean Sea	2,834,290	1,094,330	2,596	8,517
4	Bering Sea	2,519,580	972,810	1,832	6,010
5	Mediterranean Sea	2,469,100	953,320	1,572	5,157
6	Sea of Okhotsk	1,625,190	627,490	814	2,671
7	Gulf of Mexico	1,531,810	591,430	1,544	5,066
8	Norwegian Sea	1,425,280	550,300	1,768	5,801
9	Greenland Sea	1,157,850	447,050	1,443	4,734
10	Sea of Japan	1,008,260	389,290	1,647	5,404
11	Hudson Bay	1,005,510	388,230	119	390
12	East China Sea	785,990	303,470	374	1,227
13	Andaman Sea	605,760	233,890	1,061	3,481
14	Red Sea	436,280	168,450	494	1,621
15	Black Sea	410,150	158,360	1,336	4,383

Ocean Extremes

Longest reef: Great Barrier Reef, Australia 2,300 kilometers (1,429 miles)

Greatest tidal range: Bay of Fundy, Canadian Atlantic Coast, 16 meters (52 feet)

Largest bay: Bay of Bengal, Indian Ocean, 2,173,000 square kilometers (839,000 square miles)

Hottest seawater: Persian Gulf, 35°C (95°F)

Oldest oceanic crust: Eastern Mediterranean Sea, almost 200 million years

World Port Rankings

RANK	PORT	COUNTRY	TEUs
1	Singapore	Singapore	24,792,000
2	Hong Kong	China	23,539,000
3	Shanghai	China	21,710,000
4	Shenzhen	China	18,469,000
5	Busan (Pusan)	South Korea	12,039,000
6	Kaohsiung	Taiwan (China)	9,775,000
7	Rotterdam	Netherlands	9,655,000
8	Dubai	United Arab Emirates	8,923,000
9	Hamburg	Germany	8,862,000
10	Los Angeles	United States	8,470,000
11	Qingdao	China	7,702,000
12	Long Beach	United States	7,289,000
13	Ningbo	China	7,068,000
14	Antwerp	Belgium	7,019,000
15	Guangzhou	China	6,600,000

Twenty-foot equivalent unit, or TEU, is a standard linear measurement used in quantifying container traffic flows.

Longest Rivers

	KM	MI
1 Nile, Africa	6,825	4,241
2 Amazon, South America	6,437	4,000
3 Chang Jiang (Yangtze), Asia	6,380	3,964
4 Mississippi-Missouri, North America	5,971	3,710
5 Yenisey-Angara, Asia	5,536	3,440
6 Huang (Yellow), Asia	5,464	3,395
7 Ob-Irtysh, Asia	5,410	3,362
8 Amur, Asia	4,416	2,744
9 Lena, Asia	4,400	2,734
10 Congo, Africa	4,370	2,715
11 Mackenzie-Peace, North America	4,241	2,635
12 Mekong, Asia	4,184	2,600
13 Niger, Africa	4,170	2,591
14 Paraná–Río de la Plata, South America	4,000	2,485
15 Murray-Darling, Australia	3,718	2,310
16 Volga, Europe	3,685	2,290
17 Purus, South America	3,380	2,100

Largest Lakes by Area

	AREA SQ KM	AREA SQ MI	MAXIMUM DEPTH METERS	MAXIMUM DEPTH FEET
1 Caspian Sea	371,000	143,200	1,025	3,363
2 Lake Superior	82,100	31,700	406	1,332
3 Lake Victoria	69,500	26,800	82	269
4 Lake Huron	59,600	23,000	229	751
5 Lake Michigan	57,800	22,300	281	922
6 Lake Tanganyika	32,600	12,600	1,470	4,823
7 Lake Baikal	31,500	12,200	1,637	5,371
8 Great Bear Lake	31,300	12,100	446	1,463
9 Lake Malawi	28,900	11,200	695	2,280
10 Great Slave Lake	28,600	11,000	614	2,014

Largest Drainage Basins

	AREA SQ KM	AREA SQ MI
1 Amazon, South America	7,050,000	2,721,000
2 Congo, Africa	3,700,000	1,428,000
3 Mississippi-Missouri, N. America	3,250,000	1,255,000
4 Paraná, South America	3,100,000	1,197,000
5 Yenisey-Angara, Asia	2,700,000	1,042,000
6 Ob-Irtysh, Asia	2,430,000	938,000
7 Lena, Asia	2,420,000	934,000
8 Nile, Africa	1,900,000	733,000
9 Amur, Asia	1,840,000	710,000
10 Mackenzie-Peace, N. America	1,765,000	681,000
11 Ganges-Brahmaputra, Asia	1,730,000	668,000
12 Volga, Europe	1,380,000	533,000
13 Zambezi, Africa	1,330,000	513,000
14 Niger, Africa	1,200,000	463,000
15 Chang Jiang (Yangtze), Asia	1,175,000	454,000

Mouth-Discharge Rates

	CUBIC METERS/SEC	CUBIC FEET/SEC
Amazon, S. America	174,998	6,180,000
Congo, Africa	38,992	1,377,000
Negro, S. America	35,000	1,236,000
Chang Jiang, Asia	32,196	1,137,000
Orinoco, S. America	25,202	890,000

Notes on Sources: Unless otherwise noted, the *National Geographic Family Reference Atlas of the World, 2nd Edition* (2007) served as the basis for these geographic comparisons. The areas and volumes for each ocean were calculated by the U.S. Naval Oceanographic Office in 2001 using the DBDB-5.0 bathymetric database. Ocean depths are from the *National Geographic Atlas of the World, 8th Edition* (2005), with the exception of the South Sandwich Trench depth which was provided by the National Geophysical Data Center. World port rankings are from 2006, based on data collected by the American Association of Port Authorities. Mouth-discharge rates are based on *Geodata* (2003).

Bibliography

General Reference

Columbia University. *Southern Ocean Atlas*. Columbia University Press, 1982.

Couper, Alastair, ed. *The Times Atlas of the Ocean*. Van Nostrand Reinhold Company, 1983.

Cramer, Deborah. *Smithsonian Ocean: Our Water, Our World*. Collins, 2008.

Earle, Sylvia A. *National Geographic Atlas of the Ocean: The Deep Frontier*. National Geographic Society, 2001.

Elder, Danny, and John Pernetta, eds. *The Random House Atlas of the Oceans*. Random House, 1991.

Leier, Manfred. *World Atlas of the Oceans*. Firefly Books, 2001.

National Geographic Society. *National Geographic Atlas of the World*, 8th ed. National Geographic Society, 2007.

National Geographic Society. *Satellite Atlas of the World*. National Geographic Society, 1998.

National Oceanic and Atmospheric Administration (NOAA). *Hidden Depths: Atlas of the Oceans*. Collins, 2007.

Rand McNally Atlas of the Oceans. Rand McNally, 1977.

Stow, Dorrik. *Oceans: An Illustrated Reference*. University of Chicago Press, 2006.

The Times Atlas and Encyclopedia of the Sea. Harper and Row, 1989.

The Times Atlas of World Exploration. HarperCollins, 1991.

Books

Anderson, J. B., and L. R. Bartek. "Cenozoic Glacial History of the Ross Sea Revealed by Intermediate Resolution Seismic Reflection Data Combined with Drill Site Information." In *Antarctic Research Series*, Vol. 56. American Geophysical Union, 1992.

Arms, Myron. *Riddle of the Ice: A Scientific Adventure into the Arctic*. Doubleday, 1998.

Balech, E., et al. "Primary Productivity and Benthic Marine Algae of the Antarctic and Subantarctic." In *Antarctic Map Folio Series*, No. 10. American Geographical Society, 1968.

Ballard, Robert D., with Malcolm McConnell. *Explorations: My Quest for Adventure and Discovery Under the Sea*. Hyperion, 1995.

Beaglehole, J. C. *The Exploration of the Pacific*, 3rd ed. Stanford University Press, 1966.

Beebe, William. *Half Mile Down*. Harcourt Brace, 1934.

Bering Sea Impacts Group. *Summary of the Main Implications of Global Change in the Bering Sea Region*. International Arctic Science Committee, 1998.

Botkin, Daniel, et al. *Forces of Change*. National Geographic Society, 2000.

Bowermaster, Jon. *Birthplace of the Winds: Adventuring in Alaska's Islands of Fire and Ice*. National Geographic Society, 2001.

Broad, William J. *The Universe Below*. Simon and Schuster, 1997.

Brosse, Jacques. *Great Voyages of Discovery: Circumnavigators and Scientists, 1764-1843*. Facts on File, 1983.

Collette, Bruce B., and Grace Klein-MacPhee. *Bigelow and Schroeder's Fishes of the Gulf of Maine*, 3rd ed. Smithsonian Institution Press, 2002.

Convention on the Conservation of Antarctic Marine Living Resources. *The Southern Ocean Convention Workshop on Management of Antarctic Marine Living Resources: Report and Recommendations*. Convention on the Conservation of Antarctic Marine Living Resources, 1980.

Cumston, J. S. *Macquarie Island*. Antarctic Division, Department of External Affairs, Melbourne, Australia, 1968.

Daily, Gretchen C., ed. *Nature's Services: Societal Dependence on Natural Ecosystems*. Island Press, 1997.

Darwin, C. *The Voyage of the Beagle*. P. F. Collier and Son, 1909.

Davidson, Osha Gray. *The Enchanted Braid: Coming to Terms with Nature on the Coral Reef*. John Wiley and Sons, 1998.

Davis, Lloyd Spencer, and Martin Renner. *Penguins*. Yale University Press, 2004.

Deacon, George. *The Antarctic Circumpolar Ocean*. Studies in Polar Research. Cambridge University Press, 1984.

Deacon, Margaret. *Scientists and the Sea 1650-1900: A Study of Marine Science*. Academic Press, 1971.

Earle, Sylvia A. *Sea Change: A Message of the Oceans*. G. P. Putnam's Sons, 1995.

Earle, Sylvia A., and Al Giddings. *Exploring the Deep Frontier: The Adventure of Man in the Sea*. National Geographic Society, 1980.

Earle, Sylvia A., and Wolcott Henry. *Wild Ocean: America's Parks Under the Sea*. National Geographic Society, 1999.

Ellis, Richard. *Deep Atlantic: Life, Death and Exploration in the Abyss*. Alfred A. Knopf, 1996.

El Sayed, S. Z., et al. *Chemistry, Primary Productivity and Benthic Algae of the Gulf of Mexico*. Serial Atlas of the Marine Environment, Folio 22. American Geographical Society, 1972.

Environmental Systems Research Institute. *ESRI Map Book: Implementing Concepts of Geography*, Vol. 14. Environmental Systems Research Institute, 1999.

Estes, James A., et al., eds. *Whales, Whaling, and Ocean Ecosystems*. University of California Press, 2006.

Everhart, Mike. *Sea Monsters: Prehistoric Creatures of the Deep*. National Geographic Society, 2007.

Fagan, Brian. *The Little Ice Age: How Climate Made History, 1300-1850*. Basic Books, 2000.

Firor, John. *The Changing Atmosphere: A Global Challenge*. Yale University Press, 1990.

Fisher, Mildred L. *The Albatross of Midway Island: A Natural History of the Laysan Albatross*. Southern Illinois University Press, 1970.

Fogg, G. E., and David Smith. *The Explorations of Antarctica: The Last Unspoilt Continent*. Cassell, 1990.

Food and Agricultural Organization of the United Nations. *State of World Fisheries and Aquaculture 2006*. Food and Agricultural Organization of the United Nations, 2007.

Fortey, R. A. *Life: A Natural History of the First Four Billion Years of Life on Earth*. Vintage, 1999.

Fortey, Richard. *Earth: An Intimate History*. Alfred A. Knopf, 2004.

Franklin, H. Bruce. *The Most Important Fish in the Sea: Menhaden and America*. Island Press, 2007.

Freiwald, André, et al. *Cold-Water Coral Reefs: Out of Sight—No Longer Out of Mind*. United Nations Environment Programme-World Conservation Monitoring Centre, 2004.

Freuchen, Peter, and Finn Salomonsen. *The Arctic Year*. G. P. Putnam's Sons, 1958.

Garrison, Tom. *Essentials of Oceanography*, 4th ed. Thomson Brooks/Cole, 2006.

Gianni, Matthew. *High Seas Bottom Trawl Fisheries and Their Impacts on the Biodiversity of Vulnerable Deep-Sea Ecosystems: Options for International Action*. World Conservation Union (IUCN), 2004.

Gladwin, Thomas. *East Is a Big Bird: Navigation and Logic on Puluwat Atoll*. Harvard University Press, 1970.

Gloerson, P., et al. *Arctic and Antarctic Sea Ice, 1978-1987: Satellite Passive-Microwave Observations and Analysis*, NASA SP-511. National Aeronautics and Space Administration, 1992.

Glover, Linda K., and Sylvia A. Earle, eds. *Defying Ocean's End: An Agenda for Action*. Island Press, 2004.

Gordon, A. L., and E. J. Molinelli. "Thermohaline and Chemical Distribution and the Atlas Data Set." In *Southern Ocean Atlas*. Columbia University Press, 1982.

Gore, Al. *An Inconvenient Truth: The Planetary Emergency of Global Warming and What We Can Do About It*. Rodale Books, 2006.

Gorman, James. *Ocean Enough and Time: Discovering the Waters Around Antarctica*. HarperCollins, 1995.

Gould, Stephen Jay. *Wonderful Life: The Burgess Shale and the Nature of History*. W. W. Norton, 1989.

Greenhood, David. *Mapping*. University of Chicago Press, 1964.

Grotzinger, John, Thomas H. Jordan, Frank Press, and Raymond Siever. *Understanding Earth*, 5th ed. W. H. Freeman, 2007.

Grupper, Jonathan. *Destination: Polar Regions*. National Geographic Society, 1999.

Gurney, Alan. *Below the Convergence: Voyages Toward Antarctica, 1699-1839*. W. W. Norton, 1997.

Haedrich, Richard, and K. O. Emery. "Growth of an Oceanographic Institution." In *Oceanography: The Past*. Springer-Verlag, 1980.

Hammer, W. R. "Triassic Terrestrial Vertebrate Faunas of Antarctica." In *Antarctic Paleobiology: Its Role in Reconstruction of Gondwanaland*. Springer-Verlag, 1990.

Hassol, Susan Joy. *Impacts of a Warming Arctic: Arctic Climate Impact Assessment*. Cambridge University Press, 2004.

Hazen, Robert M. *Genesis: The Scientific Quest for Life's Origins*. Joseph Henry Press, 2005.

Helvarg, David. *Blue Frontier: Saving America's Living Seas*. W. H. Freeman, 2001.

Henderson, Bruce. *Fatal North: Murder and Survival Aboard USS Polaris. The First U.S. Expedition to the North Pole*. New American Library, 2001.

Herring, Peter, et al., eds. *Light and Life in the Sea*. Cambridge University Press, 1990.

Hinrichsen, Don. *Coastal Waters of the World: Trends, Threats, and Strategies*. Island Press, 1998.

Humphries, Susan E., et al. *Seafloor Hydrothermal Systems: Physical, Chemical, Biological and Geochemical Interactions*, Geophysical Monograph 91. American Geophysical Union, 1995.

Jager, Jill, and Howard Ferguson, eds. *Climate Change: Science, Impacts and Policy. Proceedings of the Second World Climate Conference*. Cambridge University Press, 1991.

Jones, O. A., and R. Endean, eds. *Biology and Geology of Coral Reefs*, Vol. 3. Academic Press, 1973.

Kitchingman, Adrian, and Sherman Lai. "Inferences on Potential Seamount Locations from Mid-Resolution Bathymetric Data." In *Seamounts: Biodiversity and Fisheries*. Edited by Telmo Morato and Daniel Pauly. Fisheries Centre, University of British Columbia, 2004.

Knoll, Andrew H. *Life on a Young Planet: The First Three Billion Years of Evolution on Earth*. Princeton University Press, 2003.

Konvitz, Josef. "Changing Concepts of the Sea, 1550-1950: An Urban Perspective." In *Oceanography: The Past*. Springer-Verlag, 1980.

Lansing, Alfred. *Endurance: Shackleton's Incredible Voyage*. Carroll and Graf, 1959.

Laws, R. M., ed. *Antarctic Ecology*, 2 vols. Academic Press, 1984.

Lee, Milton Oliver, and George A. Llano, eds. *Biology of the Antarctic Seas*, publication number 1190. American Geophysical Union of the National Academy of Sciences-National Research Council, 1964.

Levinson, Thomas. *Ice Time: Climate, Science and Life on Earth*. Harper and Row, 1989.

Lewis, David, and Mimi George. *Icebound in Antarctica*. William Heinemann, 1987.

Liebes, Sidney, Elisabet Sahtouris, and Brian Swimme. *A Walk Through Time: From Stardust to Us—The Evolution of Life on Earth*. John Wiley and Sons, 1998.

Lindbergh, Anne Morrow. *North to the Orient*. Harcourt Brace, 1935.

Llano, George Albert, ed. *Biology of the Antarctic Seas II*, publication number 1297. American Geophysical Union of the National Academy of Sciences-National Research Council, 1965.

Long, John A. *The Rise of Fishes: 500 Million Years of Evolution*. Johns Hopkins University Press, 1995.

Lopez, Barry. *Arctic Dreams*. Bantam Books, 1986.

Lutjeharms, J. R. E. *The Agulhas Current*. Springer-Verlag, 2006.

Lynas, Mark. *Six Degrees: Our Future on a Hotter Planet*. National Geographic Society, 2008.

MacLeish, Sumner. *The Bering Sea Ecoregion: A Call to Action in Marine Conservation*. World Wildlife Fund Public Information Report. Beringia Conservation Program, 2000.

Margulis, Lynn, and Michael F. Dolan. *Early Life: Evolution on the Precambrian Earth*, 2nd ed. Jones and Bartlett, 2002.

Margulis, Lynn, and Dorion Sagan. *Acquiring Genomes: A Theory of the Origins of Species*. Basic Books, 2002.

Maury, M. F. *The Physical Geography of the Sea*. Harper and Brothers, 1855.

McLaren, Alfred S. *Unknown Waters: A First-Hand Account of the Historic Under-Ice Survey of the Siberian Continental Shelf*. University of Alabama Press, 2008.

McNeill. J. R. *Something New Under the Sun: An Environmental History of the Twentieth-Century World*. W. W. Norton, 2000.

Menard, H. W. *The Ocean of Truth: A Personal History of Global Tectonics*. Princeton University Press, 1986.

Miller, Richard Gordon. *History and Atlas of the Fishes of the Antarctic Ocean*. Foresta Institute for Ocean and Mountain Studies, 1993.

Mirsky, Jeannette. *To the Arctic! The Story of Northern Exploration from Earliest Times*. University of Chicago Press, 1970.

Mitchell, Barbara. *Frozen Stakes: The Future of Antarctic Minerals*. International Institute for Environment and Development, 1983.

Mitchell, Barbara, and Richard Sandbrook. *The Management of the Southern Ocean*. International Institute for Environment and Development, 1980.

Monterey Bay Aquarium. *Instrumentation and Measurements in the Polar Regions*. Proceedings of a workshop. San Francisco Bay Region Section of the Marine Technology Society, 1988.

Morato, Telmo, and Daniel Pauly, eds. *Seamounts: Biodiversity and Fisheries*. Fisheries Centre, University of British Columbia, 2004.

Morris, Simon Conway. *The Crucible of Creation: The Burgess Shale and the Rise of Animals*. Oxford University Press, 1999.

Myers, Robert F. *Micronesian Reef Fishes: A Comprehensive Guide to the Coral Reef Fishes of Micronesia*. Coral Graphics, 1999.

Nansen, Fridtjof. *Farthest North*, 2 vols. Harper and Brothers, 1897.

National Assessment Synthesis Team, U.S. Global Change Research Program, eds. *Climate Change Impacts on the United States: The Potential Consequences of Climate Variability and Change*. Cambridge University Press, 2000.

National Geographic Society. *The Wonders of the World*. National Geographic Society, 1998.

National Research Council. *An Assessment of Atlantic Bluefin Tuna*. National Academies Press, 1994.

———. *Managing Troubled Waters: The Role of Marine Environmental Monitoring*. National Academies Press, 1990.

———. *Oceanography in the Next Decade: Building New Partnerships*. National Academies Press, 1992.

———. *Sea-Level Change*. National Academies Press, 1990.

———. *Striking a Balance: Improving Stewardship of Marine Areas*. National Academies Press, 1997.

———. *Sustaining Marine Fisheries*. National Academies Press, 1999.

———. *Understanding Marine Biodiversity*. National Academies Press, 1995.

———. *Effects of Trawling and Dredging on Seafloor Habitat*. National Academies Press, 2002.

Naveen, Ron, Colin Monteath, Tui De Roy, and Mark Jones. *Wild Ice: Antarctic Journeys*. Smithsonian Institution Press, 1990.

Nybakken, James W., and Mark D. Bertness. *Marine Biology: An Ecological Approach*, 6th ed. Benjamin Cummings, 2005.

Parry, Martin, et al., eds. *Climate Change 2007: Impacts, Adaptation and Vulnerability*. Contribution of Working Group II to the Fourth Assessment Report of the Intergovernmental Panel on Climate Change. Cambridge University Press, 2007.

Pauly, Daniel, et al. "Marine Fisheries Systems." In *Ecosystems and Human Well-Being: Current States and Trend: Millennium Ecosystem Assessment,* Vol. 1. Island Press, 2005.

Pielou, E. C. *A Naturalist's Guide to the Arctic.* University of Chicago Press, 1994.

Prager, Ellen J. *Furious Earth: The Science and Nature of Earthquakes, Volcanoes, and Tsunamis.* McGraw-Hill, 1999.

Prager, Ellen J., with Sylvia A. Earle. *The Oceans.* McGraw-Hill, 2000.

Raitt, Helen, and Beatrice Moulton. *Scripps Institution of Oceanography: First Fifty Years.* Ward Ritchie Press, 1967.

Raven, Peter H., and Tania Williams, eds. *Nature and Human Society: The Quest for a Sustainable World.* Committee for the Second Forum on Biodiversity, National Academy of Sciences and National Research Council. National Academies Press, 1997.

Reaka-Kudla, Marjorie L., Don E. Wilson, and Edward O. Wilson, eds. *Biodiversity II: Understanding and Protecting Our Biological Resources.* Joseph Henry Press, 1997.

Richmond, R., ed. *Proceedings of the Seventh International Coral Reef Symposium,* Vols. 1 and 2. University of Guam Press, 1993.

Roberts, Callum. *The Unnatural History of the Sea.* Island Press, 2007.

Roberts, David, ed. *Points Unknown: A Century of Great Exploration.* Outside Books, 2000.

Robison, Bruce, and Judith Connor. *The Deep Sea.* Monterey Bay Aquarium Natural History Series. Monterey Bay Aquarium Press, 1999.

Rona, Peter A., et al., eds. *Hydrothermal Processes at Seafloor Spreading Centers.* NATO Conference Series. Springer-Verlag, 1984.

Rowell, Galen. *Poles Apart: Parallel Visions of the Arctic and Antarctic.* University of California Press, 1995.

Ruddiman, William F. *Earth's Climate: Past and Future.* W. H. Freeman, 2001.

Scientific American. *Continents Adrift: Readings from Scientific American.* W. H. Freeman, 1970.

Scott, Robert Falcon. *Scott's Last Journey.* Edited by Peter King. HarperCollins, 1999.

Sears, Mary, and Daniel Merriman, eds. *Oceanography: The Past.* Springer-Verlag, 1980.

Shackleton, Sir Ernest. *South: The Last Antarctic Expedition of Shackleton and the* Endurance. Lyons Press, 1998.

Simon, Alvah. *North to the Night: A Spiritual Odyssey in the Arctic.* Broadway Books, 1998.

Simpson, George Gaylord. *Penguins.* Yale University Press, 1976.

Smith, Walker O., Jr., ed. *Polar Oceanography, Part A: Physical Science.* Academic Press, 1990.

———. *Polar Oceanography, Part B: Chemistry, Biology and Geology.* Academic Press, 1990.

Stern, Paul C., Oran R. Young, and Daniel Druckman, eds. *Global Environmental Change: Understanding the Human Dimensions.* National Academies Press, 1992.

Sullivan, Walter. *Continents in Motion: The New Earth Debate.* American Institute of Physics Press, 1991.

Sumich, James L., and John F. Morrissey. *Introduction to the Biology of Marine Life,* 8th ed. Jones and Bartlett, 2004.

Sutton, George H., Murli H. Manghnani, and Ralph Moberly, eds. *The Geophysics of the Pacific Ocean Basin and Its Margins.* American Geophysical Union, 1976.

Sverdrup, K. A., Alyn C. Duxbury, and Alison B. Duxbury. *An Introduction to the World's Oceans,* 8th ed. McGraw-Hill, 2005.

Symon, Carolyn, et al., eds. *Arctic Climate Impact Assessment.* Cambridge University Press, 2005.

Talwani, Manik, and Walter C. Pitman III, eds. *Island Arcs, Deep Sea Trenches and Back Arc Basins.* American Geophysical Union, 1977.

Taylor, Peter Lane. *Science at the Extreme: Scientists on the Cutting Edge of Discovery.* McGraw Hill, 2001.

Thomson, C. Wyville. *The Depths of the Sea.* Macmillan and Co., 1874.

Thomson, C. Wyville, and John Murray. *Report on the Scientific Results of the Voyage of H.M.S. Challenger During the Years 1872-1876.* First Part. Eyre and Spottiswoode, 1895.

United Nations Environment Programme. *Global Environmental Outlook. GEO-4: Environment for Development.* United Nations Environment Programme, 2007.

Van Dover, Cindy Lee. *The Ecology of Deep-Sea Hydrothermal Vents.* Princeton University Press, 2000.

Wegener, Alfred. *The Origin of Continents and Oceans.* Translated from the 4th rev. German ed. by John Biram. Methuen, 1967.

Wilson, Edward O. *The Diversity of Life.* Harvard University Press, 1992.

———. *The Future of Life.* Alfred A. Knopf, 2002.

Wong, P. P. "The Coastal Environment of Southeast Asia." In *The Physical Geography of Southeast Asia.* Edited by Avijit Gupta. Oxford University Press, 2005.

Wood, Rachel. *Reef Evolution.* Oxford University Press, 1999.

Worsley, F. A. *Shackleton's Boat Journey.* W. W. Norton, 1977.

Magazines and Journals

Ackerman, Jennifer. "New Eyes on the Ocean." *National Geographic* (October 2000), 86-115.

Adkins, Jess F., Katherine McIntyre, and Daniel P. Schrag. "The Salinity, Temperature, and ^{18}O of the Glacial Deep Ocean." *Science* (November 29, 2002), 1769-1773.

Allen, John F., and William Martin. "Evolutionary Biology: Out of Thin Air." *Nature* (February 8, 2007), 610-612.

Allwood, Abigail C., et al. "Stromatolite Reef from the Early Archaean Era of Australia." *Nature* (June 8, 2006), 714-718.

Anbar, A. D., and A. H. Knoll. "Proterozoic Ocean Chemistry and Evolution: A Bioinorganic Bridge?" *Science* (August 16, 2002), 1137-1142.

Apotria, Theodore G., and Norman H. Gray. "Absolute Motion and Evolution of the Bouvet Triple Junction." *Nature* (August 15, 1985), 623-625.

Azam, Farooq. "Microbial Control of Oceanic Carbon Flux: The Plot Thickens." *Science* (May 1, 1998), 694-696.

Ballard, Robert D. 1998. "High-Tech Search for Roman Shipwrecks." *National Geographic* (April 1998), 32-40.

Ballard, Robert D., and J. Frederick Grassle. "Incredible World of the Deep-Sea Rifts." *National Geographic* (November 1979), 680-685.

Balmford, Andrew, et al. "The Worldwide Costs of Marine Protected Areas." *Proceedings of the National Academy of Sciences* (June 29, 2004), 9694-9697.

Bass, George F. "Oldest Known Shipwreck Reveals Splendors of the Bronze Age." *National Geographic* (December 1987) 693-733.

Beatty, J. Thomas, et al. "An Obligately Photosynthetic Bacterial Anaerobe from a Deep-Sea Hydrothermal Vent." *Proceedings of the National Academy of Sciences* (June 28, 2005), 9306-9310.

Bergquist, Derk C., Frederick M. Williams, and Charles R. Fisher. "Longevity Records for Deep-Sea Invertebrate." *Nature* (February 3, 2000), 499-500.

Boetius, Antje. "Lost City Life." *Science* (March 4, 2005), 1420-1422.

Bohannon, John. "Microbe May Push Photosynthesis into Deep Water." *Science* (June 24, 2005), 1855.

Bonner, W. Nigel. "The Krill Problem in Antarctica." *Oryx* (May 1981), 31-37.

Brandt, Angelika, et al. "First Insights Into the Biodiversity and Biogeography of the Southern Ocean Deep Sea." *Nature* (May 17, 2007), 307-311.

Brocks, Jochen J., et al. "Archaean Molecular Fossils and the Early Rise of the Eukaryotes." *Science* (August 13, 1999), 1033-1036.

Brower, Kenneth. "A Galaxy of Life Fills the Night." *National Geographic* (December 1981), 834-847.

Butterfield, Nicholas J. 2007. "Macroevolution and Macroecology Through Deep Time." *Palaeontology* (January 2007), 41-55.

Christensen, Villy, et al. "Hundred-Year Decline of North Atlantic Predatory Fishes." *Fish and Fisheries* (March 2003), 1-24.

Clarke, Andrew, and J. Alistair Crame. "The Origin of the Southern Ocean Marine Fauna." *Geological Society, London, Special Publications* (1989), 253-268.

Corliss, John B., et al. "Submarine Thermal Springs on the Galápagos Rift." *Science* (March 16, 1979), 1073-1083.

Corliss, J. B., J. A. Baross, and S. E. Hoffman. "An Hypothesis Concerning the Relationship Between Submarine Hot Springs and the Origin of Life on Earth." *Oceanologica Acta Supplement* (1981), 59-69.

Davy, Bryan. "Bollons Seamount and Early New Zealand-Antarctic Seafloor Spreading." *Geochemistry Geophysics Geosystems* (June 29, 2006).

Delaney, J. R., et al. "The Quantum Event of Oceanic Crustal Accretion: Impacts of Diking at Mid-Ocean Ridges." *Science* (July 10, 1998), 222-230.

DeLong, Edward F., et al. "Bacterial Rhodopsin: Evidence for a New Type of Phototrophy in the Sea." *Science* (September 15, 2000), 1902-1906.

Des Marais, David J. "Evolution: When Did Photosynthesis Emerge on Earth?" *Science* (September 8, 2000), 1703-1705.

———. "Sea Change in Sediments." *Nature* (October 6, 2005), 826-827.

Devine, Jennifer A., Krista D. Baker, and Richard L. Haedrich. "Deep-Sea Fishes Qualify as Endangered." *Nature* (January 5, 2006), 29.

Dickson, Robert R., and Juan Brown. "The Production of North Atlantic Deep Water: Sources, Rates and Pathways." *Journal of Geophysical Research* (June 1994), 12319-12341.

Ducklow, Hugh W., et al. "Marine Pelagic Ecosystems: The West Antarctic Peninsula." *Philosophical Transactions of the Royal Society* (January 29, 2007), 67-94.

Dunn, Casey W., et al. "Broad Phylogenomic Sampling Improves Resolution of the Animal Tree of Life." *Nature* (April 10, 2008), 745-749.

Eigenbrode, Jennifer L., and Katherine H. Freeman. "Late Archean Rise of Aerobic Microbial Ecosystems." *Proceedings of the National Academy of Sciences* (October 24, 2006), 15759-15764.

Ericson, Jason P. et al. "Effective Sea-Level Rise and Deltas: Causes of Change and Human Dimension Implications." *Global and Planetary Change* (February 2006), 63-82.

Eriksson, Cecilia, and Harry Burton. "Origins and Biological Accumulation of Small Plastic Particles in Fur-Seal Scats from Macquarie Island." *Ambio* (September 2003), 380-384.

Fabry, Victoria J. "Marine Calcifiers in a High-CO_2 Ocean." *Science* (May 23, 2008), 1020-1022.

Falkowski, P., et al. "The Global Carbon Cycle: A Test of Our Knowledge of Earth as a System." *Science* (October 13, 2000), 291-296.

Falkowski, P., T. Fenchel, and E. Delong. "The Microbial Engines That Drive Earth's Biogeochemical Cycles." *Science* (May 23, 2008), 1034-1039.

Finney, Ben. "Tracking Polynesian Seafarers." *Science* (September 2007), 1873-1874.

Fisher, Charles R., Ken Takai, and Nadine Le Bris. "Hydrothermal Vent Ecosystems." *Oceanography* (March 2007), 14-23.

Früh-Green, Gretchen L., et al. "30,000 Years of Hydrothermal Activity at the Lost City Vent Field." *Science* (July 25, 2003), 495-498.

Furnes, Harald, et al. "A Vestige of Earth's Oldest Ophiolite." *Science* (March 23, 2007), 1704-1707.

Gardner, Toby A., et al. "Long-Term Region-Wide Declines in Caribbean Corals." *Science* (August 15, 2003), 958-960.

Gebruk, A. V., et al. "Food Sources, Behaviour, and Distribution of Hydrothermal Vent Shrimps at the Mid-Atlantic Ridge." *Journal of the Marine Biological Association of the United Kingdom* (June 2000), 485-499.

Giribet, Gonzalo. "Current Advances in the Phylogenetic Reconstruction of Metozoan Evolution. A New Paradigm for the Cambrian Explosion?" *Molecular Phylogenetics and Evolution* (September 2002), 345-357.

Grebmeier, Jacqueline M., et al. "A Major Ecosystem Shift in the Northern Bering Sea." *Science* (March 10 2006), 1461-1464.

Halpern, Benjamin S., et al. "A Global Map of Human Impact on Marine Ecosystems." *Science* (February 15, 2008), 948-952.

Hammer, William R., and William J. Hickerson. "A Crested Theropod Dinosaur from Antarctica." *Science* (May 6, 1994), 828-830.

Han, Shin-Chan, C. K. Shum, and Koji Matsumoto. "GRACE Observations of M2 and S2 Ocean Tides Underneath the Filchner-Ronne and Larsen Ice Shelves, Antarctica." *Geophysical Research Letters* (October 29, 2005).

Harris, Peter. "High Seas and Marine Protected Areas." *AusGeo News* (June 2007).

Haymon, Rachel M., et al. "Volcanic Eruption of the Mid-Ocean Ridge Along the East Pacific Rise at 9°45-52'N: Direct Submersible Observation of Seafloor Phenomena Associated with an Eruption Event in April, 1991." *Earth and Planetary Science Letters* (1993), 85-101.

Heezen, Bruce, and M. Ewing. "Turbidity Currents and Submarine Slumps, and the 1929 Grand Banks (Newfoundland) Earthquake." *American Journal of Science* (December 1952), 849-873.

Hobbs, Carl H., III, et al. "Geological History of Chesapeake Bay, USA." *Quarternary Science Reviews* (March 2004), 641-661.

Hoegh-Guldberg, O., et al. "Coral Reefs Under Rapid Climate Change and Ocean Acidification." *Science* (December 2007), 1737-1742.

Hughes, T. P., et al. "Climate Change, Human Impacts, and the Resilience of Coral Reefs." *Science* (August 15, 2003), 929-933.

Huber, Julie A., et al. "Microbial Population Structures in the Deep Marine Biosphere." *Science* (October 5, 2007), 97-100.

Hutchings, Jeffrey A., and John D. Reynolds. "Marine Fish Population Collapses: Consequences for Recovery and Extinction Risk." *Bioscience* (April 1, 2004), 297-309.

Johnson, Claudia. "The Rise and Fall of Rudist Reefs." *American Scientist* (March-April 2002), 148-154.

Jørgensen, B. B., and S. D'Hondt. "A Starving Majority Deep Beneath the Seafloor." *Science* (November 10, 2006), 932-933.

Juniper, S. Kim, Javier Escartin, and Mathilde Cannat. "Monitoring and Observatories: Multidisciplinary, Time-Series Observations at Mid-Ocean Ridges." *Oceanography* (March 2007) 128-137.

Kelley, Deborah S., et al. "A Serpentine-Hosted Ecosystem: The Lost City Hydrothermal Field." *Science* (March 4, 2005), 1428-1434.

Kerr, Richard A. "Is Battered Arctic Sea Ice Down for the Count?" *Science* (October 5, 2007), 33-34.

———. "Stealth Tsunami Surprises Indonesian Coastal Residents." *Science* (August 11, 2006), 742-743.

Kleiven, H. F., U. S. Ninnemann, and A.-E. Førde. "The Role of Southern Ocean Dynamics in Abrupt Climate Change Revealed by Decadally Resolved Records of Sub-Antarctic Surface and Intermediate Water Property Changes 20 -70 ka." *Geophysical Research Abstracts* (2007).

Knowlton, Nancy. "The Future of Coral Reefs." *Proceedings of the National Academy of Sciences* (May 8, 2001), 5419-5425.

Kock, K.-H., et al. "Fisheries in the Southern Ocean: An Ecosystem Approach." *Philosophical Transactions of the Royal Society B* (December 2007), 2333-2349.

Koschinsky, A., et al. "Discovery of New Hydrothermal Vents on the Southern Mid-Atlantic Ridge (4°S-10°S) During Cruise M68/1." *InterRidge News* (2006), 9-14.

Kump, Lee R., and Mark E. Barley. "Increased Subaerial Volcanism and the Rise of Atmospheric Oxygen 2.5 Billion Years Ago." *Nature* (August 30, 2007), 1033-1036.

LeBoeuf, Burney J., Karl W. Kenyon, and Bernardo Villa-Ramirez. "The Caribbean Monk Seal Is Extinct." *Marine Mammal Science* (January 1986), 70-72.

Lewis, Adam R., et al. "The Age and Origin of the Labyrinth, Western Dry Valleys, Antarctica: Evidence for Extensive Middle Miocene Subglacial Floods and Freshwater Discharge to the Southern Ocean." *Geology* (July 2006), 513-516.

Lund, David C., Jean Lynch-Stieglitz, and William B. Curry. "Gulf Stream Density Structure and Transport During the Past Millennium." *Nature* (November 30, 2006), 601-604.

Lutz, Michael J., et al. "Seasonal Rhythms of Net Primary Production and Particulate Organic Carbon Flux to Depth Describe the Efficiency of Biological Pump in the Global Ocean." *Journal of Geophysical Research* (October 2007).

Lutz, Richard A., et al. "Rapid Growth at Deep-Sea Vents." *Nature* (October 20, 2002), 663-664.

Lyons, Timothy W. "Oxygen's Rise Reduced." *Nature* (August 30, 2007), 1005-1006.

MacKenzie, Brian R., and Ransom A. Myers. "The Development of the Northern European Fishery for North Atlantic Blue-Fin Tuna *Thunnus thynnus* During 1900-1950." *Fisheries Research* (November 2007), 229-230.

Marshall, Charles R. "Explaining the Cambrian 'Explosion' of Animals." *Annual Review of Earth and Planetary Sciences* (May 2006), 355-384.

Martinez, Fernando, et al. "Back-Arc Basins." *Oceanography* (March 2007), 116-127.

Maslanik, J. A., et al. "A Younger, Thinner Arctic Ice Cover: Increased Potential for Rapid, Extensive Sea-Ice Loss." *Geophysical Research Letters* (December 2007).

Matthews, Samuel W. 1981. "New World of the Ocean." *National Geographic* (December 1981), 792-832.

McAdoo, David, and Seymour Laxon. "Antarctic Tectonics: Constraints from an ERS-1 Satellite Marine Gravity Field." *Science* (April 1997), 556-561.

Mitchell, Neil C., and Roy A. Livermore. "The Present Configuration of the Bouvet Triple Junction." *Geology* (March 1998), 267-270.

Morato, Telmo, et al. "Fishing Down the Deep." *Fish and Fisheries* (March 2006), 24-34.

Mumby, Peter J., et al. 2004. "Mangroves Enhance the Biomass of Coral Reef Fish Communities in the Caribbean." *Nature* (February 5, 2004), 533-536.

Murton, Bramley J., et al. "Detection of an Unusually Large Hydrothermal Event Plume Above the Slow-Spreading Carlsberg Ridge: NW Indian Ocean." *Geophysical Research Letters* (May 2006).

Myers, Ransom A., and Boris Worm. "Rapid Worldwide Depletion of Predatory Fish Communities." *Nature* (May 15, 2003), 280-283.

Myers, Ransom A., et al. "Cascading Effects of the Loss of Apex Predatory Sharks from a Coastal Ocean." *Science* (March 30, 2007), 1846-1850.

National Geographic Society. "Changing Climate: A Special Report." *National Geographic* (April 2008).

Nghiem, S. V., et al. "Rapid Reduction of Arctic Perennial Sea Ice." *Geophysical Research Letters* (October 2007).

Nisbet, Euan. "The Realms of Archaean Life." *Nature* (June 8, 2000), 625-626.

O'Connell, David. "Viral Genomics: Small Is Beautiful." *Nature Reviews: Microbiology* (2005), 520.

Palumbi, Stephen R. "Germ Theory for Ailing Corals." *Nature* (April 7, 2005), 713-715.

Pandolfi, J. M., et al. "Are U.S. Coral Reefs on the Slippery Slope to Slime?" *Science* (March 18, 2005), 1725-1726.

Pinnegar, John K., and Georg H. Engelhard. "The 'Shifting Baseline' Phenomenon: A Global Perspective." *Reviews in Fish Biology and Fisheries* (February 2008), 1-16.

Pyle, Richard. "The Twilight Zone." *Natural History* (November 1996), 59-62.

Raloff, Janet. "Underwater Refuge." *Science News* (April 28, 2001), 264-266.

Ramirez-Llordra, E., T. M. Shank, and C. R. German. "Biodiversity and Biogeography of Hydrothermal Vent Species: Thirty Years of Discovery and Investigations." *Oceanography* (March 2007), 30-41.

Rasmussen, Birger. "Filamentous Microfossils in a 3,235-Million-Year-Old Volcanogenic Massive Sulphide Deposit." *Nature* (June 8, 2000), 676-679.

Reed, Christina. "Boiling Points." *Nature* (February 23, 2006), 905-907.

Reedy, Rear Adm. James R. "First Flight Across the Bottom of the World." *National Geographic* (March 1964), 454-464.

Reysenbach, Anna-Louise, and Everett Shock. "Merging Genomes With Geochemistry in Hydrothermal Ecosystems." *Science* (May 10, 2002), 1077-1082.

Ridgway, K. R., and J. R. Dunn. 2007. "Observation Evidence for a Southern Hemisphere Oceanic Supergyre." *Geophysical Research Letters* (July 2007).

Rignot, E., et al. "Southern Melt." *Nature* (January 17, 2008), 226.

Robbins, William D., et al. "Ongoing Collapse of Coral-Reef Shark Populations." *Current Biology* (December 5, 2006), 2314-2319.

Roberts, Harry, et al. "Alvin Explores the Deep Northern Gulf of Mexico Slope." *EOS: Transactions of the American Geophysical Union* (August 28, 2007), 341-342.

Roberts, J. Murray, Andrew J. Wheeler, and André Freiwald. "Reefs of the Deep: The Biology and Geology of Cold-Water Coral Ecosystems." *Science* (April 28, 2006), 543-547.

Robison, Bruce H., Kim R. Reisenbichler, and Rob E. Sherlock. "Giant Larvacean Houses: Rapid Carbon Transport to the Deep Sea Floor." *Science* (June 10, 2005), 1609-1611.

Roussel, Erwan G., et al. "Extending the Sub-Sea-Floor Biosphere." *Science* (May 23, 2008), 1046.

Sala, Enric, and Nancy Knowlton. "Global Marine Biodiversity Trends." *Annual Review of Environment and Resources* (November 2006), 93-122.

Sale, P. F. "Maintenance of High Diversity in Coral Reef Fish Communities." *American Naturalist* (March-April 1977), 337-359.

Schulte, Mitchell. "The Emergence of Life on Earth." *Oceanography* (March 2007), 42-49.

Sclater, J. G., et al. "The Bouvet Triple Junction." *Journal of Geophysical Research* (April 10, 1976), 1857-1869.

Serreze, Mark C., Marika M. Holland, and Julienne Stroeve. "Perspectives on the Arctic's Shrinking Sea-Ice Cover." *Science* (March 16, 2007), 1533-1536.

Shank, T. M., et al. "Temporal and Spatial Patterns of Biological Community Development at Nascent Deep-Sea Hydrothermal Vents (9°50'N, East Pacific Rise)." *Deep-Sea Research II: Topical Studies in Oceanography* (January 1998), 465-515.

Sharp, Gary D., and Douglas R. McLain. "Fisheries, El Niño/Southern Oscillation and Upper-Ocean Temperature Records: An Eastern Pacific Example." *Oceanography* (November 1, 1993), 13-22.

Snow, Jonathan E., and Henrietta A. Edmonds. "Ultraslow-Spreading Ridges: Rapid Paradigm Changes." *Oceanography* (March 2007), 90-101.

Sogin, Mitchell L., et al. "Microbial Diversity in the Deep Sea and the Underexplored 'Rare Biosphere.'" *Proceedings of the National Academy of Sciences* (August 8, 2006), 12115-12120.

Stanton, B. R. "Vertical Structure in the Mid-Tasman Convergence Zone." *New Zealand Journal of Marine and Freshwater Research.* (March 1975), 63-74.

Stone, Richard. "A World Without Corals?" *Science* (May 4, 2007), 678-681.

Stroeve, Julienne, et al. "Arctic Sea Ice Extent Plummets in 2007." *EOS: Transactions of the American Geophysical Union* (January 2008), 13-14.

Stroeve, J., et al. "Arctic Sea Ice Extent Plummets in 2007." *EOS, Transactions of the American Geophysical Union* (January 8, 2008), 13.

Strom, Suzanne L. "Microbial Ecology of Ocean Beigeochemistry: A Community Perspective," *Science* (May 23, 2008), 1043-1045.

Suttle, Curtis A. "Viruses in the Sea." *Nature* (September 15, 2005), 356-361.

Torsvik, Trond H. "The Rodinia Jigsaw Puzzle." *Science* (May 30, 2003), 1379-1381.

Van Dover, C. L., et al. "Evolution and Biogeography of Deep-Sea Vent and Seep Invertebrates." *Science* (February 15, 2002), 1253-1257.

Venter, J. Craig, et al. "Environmental Genome Shotgun Sequencing of the Sargasso Sea." *Science* (April 2, 2004), 66-74.

Vine, F. J. and D. Matthews. "Magnetic Anomalies over Oceanic Ridges." *Nature* (1963) 947-949.

Warén, Anders, et al. "A Hot-Vent Gastropod with Iron Sulfide Dermal Sclerites." *Science* (November 7, 2003), 1007.

White, Sheri N., et al. "Ambient Light Emission from Hydrothermal Vents on the Mid-Atlantic Ridge." *Geophysical Research Letters* (August 2002).

Whitworth, Thomas, III. "The Antarctic Circumpolar Current." *Oceanus* (Summer 1988), 53-58.

Worm, Boris, et al. "Impacts of Biodiversity Loss on Ocean Ecosystem Services." *Science* (November 3, 2006), 787-790.

Yoerger, Dana R., et al. "Autonomous and Remotely Operated Vehicle Technology for Hydrothermal Vent Discovery, Exploration, Sampling." *Oceanography* (March 2007), 152-161.

Zalasiewicz, Jan, et al. "Are We Now Living in the Anthropocene?" *GSA Today* (February 2008), 4-8.

Online Reports

Intergovernmental Panel for Climate Change (IPPC). "Summary for Policymakers." In *Climate Change 2007: Synthesis Report.* Available online at www.ipcc.ch/pdf/assessment-report/ar4/syr/ar4_syr_spm.pdf.

Pickerell, John. 2004. "Two New Dinosaurs Discovered in Antarctica." National Geographic News (March 9, 2004). Available online at http://news.nationalgeographic.com/news/2004/03/0309_040309_polardinos.html

Other

Boyer, Peter, and Elizabeth Haywood. *Islands of the Southern Ocean.* Information for Delegates to the International Forum on the Sub-Antarctic. Hobart, Tasmania, July 2006.

Dodd, Andrew. *Antarctica: Something Rich and Strange.* Living Planet 1. 2000.

United Nations Law of the Sea Convention. Signed at Montego Bay, Jamaica, December 10, 1982. U.N. Doc. A/Conf.62/122, reproduced in 21 I.L.M. 1261 (1982).

United Nations Environmental Program. *Ecosystems and Biodiversity in Deep Waters and High Seas.* UNEP Regional Seas and Studies No. 178. 2006. UNEP/IUCN, Switzerland.

Web Links

The following Web links appear in the margins of the main text throughout the atlas. These links are by no means exhaustive, but they do provide some of the best ocean content available online. You will find a wide range of articles, videos, satellite images, and real-time data that will supplement the information contained in this book.

Chapter 1: Ocean Basics

page 26, Earth's water

U.S. Geological Survey, global water
http://ga.water.usgs.gov/edu/earthwherewater.html
U.S. Geological Survey, U.S. water
http://water.usgs.gov
U.S. Geological Survey, water science
http://ga.water.usgs.gov/edu/

page 29, plate tectonics

"This Dynamic Earth: The Story of Plate Tectonics"
http://pubs.usgs.gov/gip/dynamic

page 30, GRACE Mission

http://www.csr.utexas.edu/grace/

page 40, tides and tidal predictions

http://www.oceanservice.noaa.gov/education/kits/tides/welcome.html
http://tidesandcurrents.noaa.gov/tide_pred.html

page 46, Tsunami research

NOAA Pacific Tsunami Warning Center
http://nctr.pmel.noaa.gov/
NOAA Center for Tsunami Research
http://www.prh.noaa.gov/ptwc/

Chapter 2: Ocean Life

page 64, marine microbes

International Census of Marine Microbes
http://www.coml.org/descrip/icomm.htm

page 67, Large Marine Ecosystems

http://www.lme.noaa.gov/Portal/

page 68, Tree of Life Web Project

http://www.tolweb.org/tree/

page 69, marine species databases

Census of Marine Life
http://www.coml.org/
World Registry of Marine Species (WoRMS)
http://www.marinespecies.org/

page 71, animal facts

www.nationalgeographic.com/animals

Chapter 3: Ocean Past

page 92, alternate plate reconstructions

Paleomap Project
http://www.scotese.com/

page 96, prehistoric animals

http://animals.nationalgeographic.com/animals/prehistoric.html

Chapter 4: The Atlantic Ocean

page 112, Alfred Wegener

"This Dynamic Earth: The Story of Plate Tectonics"
http://pubs.usgs.gov/gip/dynamic/
Alfred Wegener
http://earthobservatory.nasa.gov/Library/Giants/Wegener/

page 116, National Geographic archives

http://ngm.nationalgeographic.com/archives

page 119, Lost City Expedition

University of Washington
http://www.lostcity.washington.edu/

page 120, Bermuda Atlantic Time-Series Study

http://bats.bios.edu/

page 124, the Gulf Stream

Cooperative Institute for Marine and Atmospheric Sciences
http://oceancurrents.rsmas.miami.edu/atlantic/gulf-stream.html

page 125, Monaco Museum

http://www.oceano.mc/

page 125, Christopher Columbus

"Age of Exploration" online exhibit, Mariners' Museum
http://www.mariner.org/educationalad/ageofex/columbus.php

page 126, **Atlantic storms**
"27 Storms: Arlene to Zeta"
NASA Goddard Space Flight Center
http://svs.gsfc.nasa.gov/goto?3354
Hurricane Katrina Sea-Surface Temperature
http://svs.gsfc.nasa.gov/goto?3240

page 128, **J. Craig Venter Institute**
http://www.tigr.org/

page 130, **biosphere animation**
SeaWiFS Biosphere Data over the North Pacific
http://svs.gsfc.nasa.gov/goto?3471

Chapter 5: The Pacific Ocean

page 155, **Ring of Fire**
http://pubs.usgs.gov/gip/dynamic/fire.html
http://oceanexplorer.noaa.gov/explorations/07fire/welcome.html

page 158, **hydrothermal vents**
Pacific Marine Environmental Laboratory
http://www.pmel.noaa.gov/vents/

page 160, **Woods Hole Oceanographic Institution**
http://www.whoi.edu/

page 162, **seamount biology**
http://seamounts.sdsc.edu/

page 162, **virtual fly-throughs of the Mariana Arc**
http://oceanexplorer.noaa.gov/explorations/04fire/background/marianaarc/marianaarc.html

page 169, **Monterey Bay**
Monterey Bay Aquarium Research Institute
http://www.mbari.org/
Monterey Bay National Marine Sanctuary
http://montereybay.noaa.gov/

page 171, **Pacific currents**
NOAA's Cooperative Institute for Marine and Atmospheric Sciences
http://oceancurrents.rsmas.miami.edu/atlantic/

page 171, **El Niño**
http://www.elnino.noaa.gov/

page 174, **Tropical Atmosphere Ocean array**
http://www.pmel.noaa.gov/tao/

page 176, **SeaWiFS Biosphere Data over the North Atlantic**
http://svs.gsfc.nasa.gov/goto?3468

page 179, **Charles Darwin Foundation**
http://www.darwinfoundation.org/

page 179, **World Conservation Union**
http://cms.iucn.org/

Chapter 6: The Indian Ocean

page 196, **tsunamis**
http://www.tsunami.noaa.gov/
http://tsunami.gov/
http://www.prh.noaa.gov/ptwc/

page 198, **Indian Ocean coral reefs**
National Institute of Oceanography (Goa, India)
http://www.reefindia.org/index.htm

page 199, **Indian Ocean currents**
http://oceancurrents.rsmas.miami.edu/

page 200, **ocean wind**
http://winds.jpl.nasa.gov/

page 204, **whaling**
International Whaling Commission
http://www.iwcoffice.org/
Indian Ocean as whale sanctuary
http://www.iwcoffice.org/conservation/sanctuaries.htm

page 205, **coral reefs**
http://www.coralreef.noaa.gov
http://www.coralreefalliance.org
http://www.nature.org/reef

page 211, **natural resources of the Persian Gulf**
http://www.eia.doe.gov/emeu/cabs/Persian_Gulf/Background.html

Chapter 7: The Arctic Ocean

page 224, **Arctic animations**
"A Tour of the Cryosphere"
http://svs.gsfc.nasa.gov/goto?3181

Comparison of Minimum Sea Ice between 2005 and 2007
http://svs.gsfc.nasa.gov/goto?3469
Global Rotation showing Seasonal Landcover and Arctic Sea Ice
http://svs.gsfc.nasa.gov/goto?3404

page 226, **Arctic mapping and imaging**
Center for Coastal and Ocean Mapping
http://ccom.unh.edu/
International Bathymetric Chart of the Arctic Ocean
http://www.iode.org/
http://www.ngdc.noaa.gov/mgg/bathymetry/arctic/arctic.html

page 227, **vents and seep communities on the Arctic seafloor**
http://www.arctic.noaa.gov/essay_vogt.html

page 229, **Seamounts Online database**
http://seamounts.sdsc.edu/

page 235, **Fram Museum (Oslo, Norway)**
http://www.fram.museum.no/en/

page 236, **Arctic research buoys**
International Arctic Buoy Programme
http://iabp.apl.washington.edu

page 236, **Beaufort Gyre**
Beaufort Gyre Expedition Project
http://www.whoi.edu/beaufortgyre/index.html

page 239, **Arctic weather**
National Snow and Ice Data Center
http://nsidc.org/data/parca/
Arctic Research Center
http://www.iarc.uaf.edu/

page 241, **Northwest Passage**
NOVA's "Arctic Passage" program Web site
http://www.pbs.org/wgbh/nova/arctic/

page 244, **Arctic sea ice**
NASA's Earth Observing System
http://eospso.gsfc.nasa.gov/
Canadian Cryospheric Information Network
http://www.ccin.ca/

Chapter 8: The Southern Ocean

page 256, **International Hydrographic Organization (IHO)**
http://www.iho.shom.fr/

page 256, **Antarctica animation**
"Antarctica: A Flying Tour of the Frozen Continent"
http://svs.gsfc.nasa.gov/goto?2175
AMSR-E Antarctic Sea Ice
http://svs.gsfc.nasa.gov/goto?3497

page 259, **Mosaic of Antarctica**
http://earthobservatory.nasa.gov/Study/MOA/index.html

page 259, **United Nations Antarctic Treaty of 1959**
http://www.state.gov/t/ac/trt/4700.htm

page 262, **International Polar Year 2007-2008**
http://www.ipy.org/

page 263, **U.S. McMurdo Station**
http://www.nsf.gov/od/opp/support/mcmurdo.jsp

page 267, **Commonwealth Scientific and Industrial Research Organization**
http://www.cmar.csiro.au/

page 271, **Larsen Ice Shelf**
NASA's Earth Observatory
http://earthobservatory.nasa.gov/Study/LarsenIceShelf/

page 274, **Census of Antarctic Marine Life**
http://www.caml.aq/

Chapter 9: Ocean Exploration

page 282, **history of ocean exploration**
NOAA timeline
http://oceanexplorer.noaa.gov/history/history.html

page 284, **H.M.S. *Challenger* expedition**
http://oceanexplorer.noaa.gov/explorations/03mountains/background/challenger/challenger.html

page 290, **research submarines**
Shirshov Institute of Oceanology
http://www.ocean.ru/eng/
French Research Institute for Exploitation of the Sea
http://www.ifremer.fr/anglais/institut/index.htm
Japan Agency for Marine-Earth Science and Technology
http://www.jamstec.go.jp/e/

page 292, **international ocean research**
Japanese Oceanograph Research Institution (JAMSTEC)
http://www.jamstec.go.jp/e/
French Research Institute for Exploitation of the Sea (IFREMER)
http://www.ifremer.fr/anglais/

page 293, **Introduction to GIS**
http://www.gis.com/

Chapter 10: Ocean Future

page 304, **Law of the Sea**
http://www.un.org/Depts/los/index.htm
http://www.itlos.org/

page 305, **Exclusive Economic Zones**
http://www.eoearth.org/article/Exclusive_economic_zone_(EEZ)
http://nauticalcharts.noaa.gov/csdl/eez.htm

page 306, **Integrated Ocean Observing System (IOOS)**
http://www.ocean.us

page 236, **population figures**
U.S. and World Population Clocks, U.S. Census Bureau
http://www.census.gov/main/www/popclock.html

page 308, **Oil Pollution Act**
http://www.fws.gov/laws/lawsdigest/oilpoll.html
http://www.epa.gov/region09/waste/sfund/oilpp/
http://uscg.mil/ccs/npfc/

page 313, **Sea Around Us Project**
http://www.seaaroundus.org/default.htm

page 319, **Marine Protected Areas**
http://sanctuaries.noaa.gov/
http://mpa.gov/

Other Ocean Links of Interest

Aquarius, NOAA's undersea research laboratory
http://www.uncw.edu/aquarius/

BYU Center for Remote Sensing
http://www.scp.byu.edu/

CITES Convention on International of Trade in Endangered Species
http://www.cites.org/

Digital Earth
http://svs.gsfc.nasa.gov/goto?663

Google Earth
http://earth.google.com

Marine Biology Web
http://life.bio.sunysb.edu/marine bio

National Geographic MapMachine
www.nationalgeographic.com/maps

National Oceanographic Data Center
http://www.nodc.noaa.gov

NCBI Taxonomy homepage
http://www.ncbi.nlm.nih.gov/taxonomyhome.html

Ocean Color
http://oceancolor.gsfc.nasa.gov/

Ocean Motion and Surface Currents
http://oceanmotion.org/

Oceans Alive
http://www.oceanslive.org/portal/

Ocean Surface Topography from Space
http://sealevel.jpl.nasa.gov/

Sea Surface Temperature, 2005
http://svs.gsfc.nasa.gov/goto?3191

SeaWiFS Biosphere Global Rotation from 1997 to 2006
http://svs.gsfc.nasa.gov/goto?3420

Tagging of Pacific Pelagics program
www.topp.org

Underwater Photography
www.nationalgeographic.com/underwaterphotos

Visible Earth
http://visibleearth.nasa.gov/

Woods Hole Oceanographic Institute
http://www.whoi.edu/

Subject Index

Boldface indicates illustrations.

Map Place-Name Index

THE FOLLOWING SYSTEM is used to locate a place on a map in this atlas. The boldface type after an entry refers to the page on which the map is found; the letter-number combination refers to the grid square in which the particular place name is located. The edge of each map is marked horizontally with numbers and vertically with letters. In between, at equally spaced intervals, are small triangles. If these small triangles were connected with lines, each page would be divided into a grid. Take Santa Clara Island, for example. The index entry reads "**Santa Clara Island,** *Juan Fernández Is., Chile, S. Pac. Oc.* **147** K15." On page 147, Santa Clara Island is located within the grid square where row K and column 15 intersect (see diagram, right).

A place name may appear on several maps, but the index lists only the best presentation. Usually, this means that a feature is indexed to the largest-scale map on which it appears in its entirety. The name of the ocean, sea, country, and/or island chain in which a feature lies is shown in italic type and is sometimes abbreviated.

The index lists more than proper names. Some entries include a feature description in colored type, as in "**Bawean,** island, *Indonesia, Java Sea* **181** P7." When a feature or place can be referred to by more than one name, both may appear in the index with cross-references. For example, the entry for Isla de Pascua reads "**Pascua, Isla de** *see* **Easter Island,** *Chile, S. Pac. Oc.* **147** J13." That entry is "**Easter Island (Isla de Pascua),** *Chile, S. Pac. Oc.* **147** J13."

Examples:

Argentine Basin, *S. Atl. Oc.* **105** N5
— feature name / grid square / page number / ocean / page number

Forcados, port, *Nigeria* **106** J9
— feature name / feature description / country / ocean / grid square / page number

Great Nicobar, island, *Nicobar Is., India, Ind. Oc.* **187** E7
— feature name / island chain / grid square / page number

Abbreviations:

Arch.	*Archipelago, -piélago*	Medit.	*Mediterranean*
Atl.	*Atlantic*	N.	*North*
B.	*Bahía, Baie, Bay*	Oc.	*Ocean*
Ch.	*Channel*	Pac.	*Pacific*
E.	*East*	Pass.	*Passage*
G.	*Golfe, Golfo, Gulf*	S.	*South*
Ind.	*Indian*	Str.	*Strait, Stretto*

Abaco Island, *Bahamas, N. Atl. Oc.* **106** G2
Abaco Islands, *Bahamas, N. Atl. Oc.* **140** A7
Ābādān, *Iran* **212** A2
Ābādān, Jazīreh-ye, *Iran, Persian G.* **212** B3
Ābādān, Ra's-e, *Iran, Persian G.* **212** B3
Abaiang, atoll, *Gilbert Is., Kiribati, S. Pac. Oc.* **164** D8
'Abd al Kuri, island, *Yemen, Arabian Sea* **186** C5
Abemama, atoll, *Gilbert Is., Kiribati, S. Pac. Oc.* **164** D8
Abiadh, Ras el, *Tun.* **132** G2
Abidjan, *Côte d'Ivoire* **107** J8
Abrolhos Bank, *S. Atl. Oc.* **105** L5
Abrolhos Seamounts, *S. Atl. Oc.* **105** L6
Abū al Abyaḍ, island, *U.A.E., Persian G.* **213** L10
Abū 'Alī, island, *Saudi Arabia, Persian G.* **212** F4
Abū Ath Thāmah, Ḥayr, *Persian G.* **212** G6
Abubacer Ridge, *Medit. Sea* **131** H5
Abu Dhabi *see* Abū Ẓaby, *U.A.E.* **213** K10
Abū 'Uwayd, Rās, *Egypt, Red Sea* **210** D3
Abū Madd, Ra's, *Saudi Arabia, Red Sea* **210** D4
Abū Maḥārah, Ra's, *Saudi Arabia, G. of Bahrain* **212** J5
Abū Mūsá, island, *Iran, U.A.E., Persian G.* **213** H11
Abū Sa'fah, Fasht, *Persian G.* **212** F5
Abū Sharjah, Ra's, *Sudan, Red Sea* **210** F4
Abū Shawk Reefs, *Red Sea* **210** F5

Abu Sôma, Râs, *Egypt, Red Sea* **210** C3
Abū Ẓaby, cape, *U.A.E., Persian G.* **213** K10
Abū Ẓaby (Abu Dhabi), *U.A.E.* **213** K10
Acklins Island, *Bahamas, N. Atl. Oc.* **141** C9
Actéon, Groupe, *Tuamotu Arch., Fr. Polynesia, Fr., S. Pac. Oc.* **165** G14
Ad Dammām, *Saudi Arabia* **212** G5
Ad Dawḥah (Doha), *Qatar* **212** J7
Adak Island, *Andreanof Is., U.S., N. Pac. Oc.* **146** C8
Adare, Cape, *Antarctica* **251** F11
Addu Atoll, *Maldives, Ind. Oc.* **186** E7
Adelaide, *Austral.* **164** J3
Adelaide Island, *Antarctica, S. Pac. Oc.* **250** J8
Aden, *Yemen* **186** C4
Aden, Gulf of, *Ind. Oc.* **186** C4
Adham, Fasht, *Persian G.* **212** H6
Adi, island, *Indonesia* **187** E14
Admiralty Island, *Alexander Arch., U.S., N. Pac. Oc.* **147** B11
Admiralty Islands, *Bismarck Arch., P.N.G., N. Pac. Oc.* **164** D4
Adriatic Sea, *Medit. Sea* **132** C4
Adventure Bank, *Str. of Sicily* **132** G3
Aegean Sea, *Medit. Sea* **132** F8
Aegir Ridge, *Norwegian Sea* **104** D8
Afognak Island, *U.S., G. of Alas.* **147** B10
Agalega Islands, *Mauritius, Ind. Oc.* **186** F5
Agassiz Fracture Zone, *S. Pac. Oc.* **145** K11
Agassiz Valleys, *G. of Mex.* **139** G13
Agattu Island, *Near Is., U.S., N. Pac. Oc.* **146** C7
Agrihan, island, *N. Mariana Is., U.S., N. Pac. Oc.* **164** A4
Agulhas, Cape, *S. Af.* **184** J1
Agulhas Bank, *Ind. Oc.* **184** J1
Agulhas Basin, *Ind. Oc.* **184** K1
Agulhas Plateau, *Ind. Oc.* **184** K2
Ahunui, atoll, *Tuamotu Arch., Fr. Polynesia, Fr., S. Pac. Oc.* **165** G14
Ailinglapalap Atoll, *Ralik Chain, Marshall Is., N. Pac. Oc.* **164** C7

Ailuk Atoll, *Ratak Chain, Marshall Is., N. Pac. Oc.* **164** C7
Ain Sukhna, *Egypt* **186** A2
Airabu, island, *Kep. Anambas, Indonesia, S. China Sea* **181** L4
Aitutaki Atoll, *Cook Is., N.Z., S. Pac. Oc.* **165** G11
Ajaccio, *Fr.* **132** D1
Akimiski Island, *Can., Hudson B.* **106** E2
Akpatok Island, *Can., Hudson Str.* **106** D3
Akrítas, Akrotírio, *Gr.* **132** G7
Akutan Island, *Aleutian Is., U.S., N. Pac. Oc.* **147** B9
Alacrán, Arrecife, *G. of Mex.* **138** H8
Alamagan, island, *N. Mariana Is., U.S., N. Pac. Oc.* **164** A4
Alaminos Bank, *G. of Mex.* **138** C7
Alaminos Canyon, *G. of Mex.* **138** D5
Åland Islands, *Fin., Baltic Sea* **106** D10
Alanya, *Turk.* **133** H12
Al 'Aqabah, *Jordan* **210** B3
Al 'Arabīyah, island, *Saudi Arabia, Persian G.* **212** E5
Alaska, region, *U.S.* **216** J3
Alaska Peninsula, *N. Am.* **145** B9
Alaska, Gulf of, *N. Pac. Oc.* **147** B10
Al Bahrain, Durrat, *Bahrain, Persian G.* **212** H5
Al Baṣrah, *Iraq* **212** A2
Al Bāṭinah, island, *Saudi Arabia, Persian G.* **212** F4
Albatross Bank, *Caribbean Sea* **140** F8
Albatross Plateau, *N. Pac. Oc.* **147** F13
Al Bazm al Gharbī, island, *U.A.E., Persian G.* **213** K9
Alborán, Isla de, *Sp., Alboran Sea* **131** H4
Alboran Sea, *Medit. Sea* **131** H4
Albuquerque, Cayos de, *Col., Caribbean Sea* **140** J5
Aldabra Islands, *Seychelles, Ind. Oc.* **186** F4
Alderdice Bank, *G. of Mex.* **138** C6
Alejandro Selkirk Island, *Juan Fernández Is., Chile, S. Pac. Oc.* **147** K15

Aleutian Basin, *Bering Sea* **144** B7
Aleutian Islands, *U.S., N. Pac. Oc.* **146** B7
Aleutian Trench, *N. Pac. Oc.* **144** C7
Alexander Archipelago, *U.S., N. Pac. Oc.* **147** B11
Alexander Island, *Antarctica, Bellingshausen Sea* **250** H8
Alexandra Land, *Franz Josef Land, Russ., Arctic Oc.* **219** D10
Alexandretta *see* İskenderun, *Turk.* **133** H13
Alexandria *see* El Iskandarîya, *Egypt* **133** L11
Alexandria Canyon, *Medit. Sea* **133** K11
Al Fāw, *Iraq* **212** B3
Al Fuḥayḥil, *Kuwait* **212** C2
Al Fujayrah, *U.A.E.* **213** J13
Al Fuwayriṭ, *Qatar* **212** H6
Algeciras, *Sp.* **106** G8
Alger (Algiers), *Alg.* **131** G7
Algerian Basin, *Medit. Sea* **131** G6
Algerian-Tyrrhenian Trough, *Medit. Sea* **132** G1
Algiers *see* Alger, *Alg.* **131** G7
Algodones, Bahía, *Mex., G. of Mex.* **138** F2
Al Ḥamrīyah, *U.A.E.* **213** J12
Al Ḥasānī, island, *Saudi Arabia, Red Sea* **210** D4
Alhucemas, Peñón de, *Sp., Alboran Sea* **131** H4
Al Ḥudaydah, *Yemen* **210** J7
Al Ḥurqūṣ, island, *Saudi Arabia, Persian G.* **212** E4
Alicante, *Sp.* **131** G5
Alicante Canyon, *Medit. Sea* **131** G6
Alice Shoal, *Caribbean Sea* **140** G6
Alida Reef, *S. China Sea* **181** M5
Alijos Rocks, *Mex., N. Pac. Oc.* **147** E12
Al Jahrā', *Kuwait* **212** C2
Al Janāḥ, island, *Saudi Arabia, Persian G.* **212** F5
Al Jinnah, island, *Saudi Arabia, Persian G.* **212** F4
Al Jubayl, *Saudi Arabia* **212** F4
Al Jurayd, island, *Saudi Arabia, Persian G.* **212** F5
Al Khawr, *Qatar* **212** H7
Al Khīrān, *Kuwait* **212** D3
Al Khubar, *Saudi Arabia* **212** G5
Al Kuwayt (Kuwait), *Kuwait* **212** C2

Al Lādhiqīyah (Latakia), Syr. 133 H13
'Allak, Ra's al, Qatar, Persian G. 212 J7
Al Manāmah (Manama), Bahrain 212 H5
Almería, Sp. 131 G4
Almina, Punta, Sp. 131 H3
Al Mubarraz, island, U.A.E., Persian G. 213 K9
Al Mughayrā', U.A.E. 213 L9
Alob, Ras, Eritrea, Red Sea 210 K6
Alor, island, Indonesia 187 F13
Alpha Cordillera, Arctic Oc. 216 G8
Alphonse Island, Seychelles, Ind. Oc. 186 F5
Al Qaffāy, island, U.A.E., Persian G. 212 K7
Al Qamar Bay, Yemen, Arabian Sea 186 C5
Al Qaṭif, Saudi Arabia 212 G5
Al Qirān, island, Saudi Arabia, Persian G. 212 E4
Al Qunfudhah, Saudi Arabia 210 G6
Al Qurayyin, island, Saudi Arabia, Persian G. 212 E4
Al 'Uqayr, Saudi Arabia 212 H5
Al 'Uwaynidhīyah, island, Saudi Arabia, Red Sea 210 C4
Al Wajh, Saudi Arabia 210 D4
Al Wakrah, Qatar 212 J7
Al Yāsāt, island, U.A.E., Persian G. 212 L7
Amami Islands, Ryukyu Is., Japan, E. China Sea 146 E4
Amanu, atoll, Tuamotu Arch., Fr. Polynesia, Fr., S. Pac. Oc. 165 F14
Amatique, Bahía de, G. of Hond. 140 G1
Amazon Fan, N. Atl. Oc. 105 J5
Ambarli, Turk. 106 F11
Ambergris Cay, Belize, Caribbean Sea 140 E2
Ambergris Cays, Turks & Caicos Is., U.K., N. Atl. Oc. 141 D10
Ambrym, island, Vanuatu, S. Pac. Oc. 164 F7
Amchitka Island, Rat Is., U.S., N. Pac. Oc. 146 C8
America-Antarctic Ridge, S. Atl. Oc. 248 F5
Amery Basin, Ind. Oc. 248 C8
Amery Ice Shelf, Ind. Oc. 248 D8
Amindivi Islands, Lakshadweep, India, Arabian Sea 186 C7
Amiot Islands, Antarctica, Bellingshausen Sea 107 R3
Amirante Isles, Seychelles, Ind. Oc. 186 E5
Amirante Trench, Ind. Oc. 186 F5
Amlia Island, Andreanof Is., U.S., N. Pac. Oc. 146 C8
Amorgós, island, Kikládes, Gr., Aegean Sea 133 G9
Amoy see Xiamen, China 180 A9
Ampere Seamount, N. Atl. Oc. 104 G8
Amphitrite Group, Xisha Qundao, China, S. China Sea 180 E7
Amsterdam, Neth. 106 E9
Amsterdam, Île, Fr., Ind. Oc. 186 K8
Amund Ringnes Island, Can. 106 B1
Amundsen Gulf, Can., Arctic Oc. 218 K6
Amundsen Plain, S. Pac. Oc. 249 J10
Amundsen Sea, S. Pac. Oc. 251 H9
Amvrakikós Kólpos, Gr., Ionian Sea 132 F7
Anáfi, island, Kikládes, Gr., Aegean Sea 133 H9
Anaa, atoll, Tuamotu Arch., Fr. Polynesia, Fr., S. Pac. Oc. 165 F13
Anacortes, U.S. 147 C12
Anadyr, Gulf of, Bering Sea 146 A8
Ana María, Golfo de, Cuba, Caribbean Sea 140 D6
Anambas Islands, Indonesia, S. China Sea 187 D11
Anambas, Kepulauan, Indonesia, S. China Sea 181 L4
Anatahan, island, N. Mariana Is., U.S. 187 C16
Anatolia, region, 104 F11
Anatolian Trough, Aegean Sea 132 F8
Anatom, island, Vanuatu, S. Pac. Oc. 164 G7
Anaximander Ridge, Medit. Sea 133 H11
Anclitas, Cayo, Jardines de la Reina, Cuba, Caribbean Sea 140 D6
Anclote Keys, U.S., G. of Mex. 139 C13
Ancona, It. 132 C3
Andaman Basin, Andaman Sea 185 C10
Andaman Islands, India, B. of Bengal 187 C9
Andaman Sea, Ind. Oc. 187 D10
Andreanof Islands, Aleutian Is., U.S., N. Pac. Oc. 146 C8
Ándros, island, Kikládes, Gr., Aegean Sea 132 G8
Andros Island, Bahamas, N. Atl. Oc. 140 B7
Anegada, island, Virgin Is., U.K., N. Atl. Oc. 141 E14
Anegada Passage, Virgin Is., Caribbean Sea 141 E14
Angola Basin, S. Atl. Oc. 105 L9
Angola Plain, S. Atl. Oc. 105 L9
Anguilla, island, Virgin Is., U.K., N. Atl. Oc. 141 E14
Anguilla Cays, Bahamas, N. Atl. Oc. 140 B6
Anjou Islands, New Siberian Is., Russ., Arctic Oc. 218 D5
Ann, Cape, Antarctica 250 D7
Annaba (Bône), Alg. 132 G1
Annobón, island, Eq. Guinea, S. Atl. Oc. 107 K9
An Nu'mān, island, Saudi Arabia, Red Sea 210 C3
Antalya (Attalia), Turk. 133 G11
Antalya Basin, Medit. Sea 133 H11
Antalya Körfezi, Turk., Medit. Sea 133 H11
Antalya Trough, Medit. Sea 133 H12
Antarctic Peninsula, Antarctica 248 J7
Antibes, Fr. 132 C1
Anticosti Island, Can., G. of St. Lawrence 106 E3
Antigua, island, Leeward Is., Antigua & Barbuda, N. Atl. Oc. 141 F15
Antipodes Fracture Zone, S. Pac. Oc. 249 G11
Antipodes Islands, N.Z., S. Pac. Oc. 146 L8
Anton Dohrn Seamount, N. Atl. Oc. 106 E8
Antón Lizardo, Punta, Mex. 138 K4
Antūfīsh, Jazīrat, Yemen, Red Sea 210 J6
Antwerp, Belg. 106 E9
Anuta (Cherry Island), Sta. Cruz Is., Solomon Is., S. Pac. Oc. 164 F7
Anvers Island, Palmer Arch., Antarctica, S. Pac. Oc. 107 R3
Apôtres, Îles des, Crozet Is., Fr., Ind. Oc. 186 L4
Apalachee Bay, U.S., G. of Mex. 139 A12
Apalachicola Bay, U.S., G. of Mex. 139 B11
Apapa-Lagos, Nigeria 107 J9
Apia, Samoa 165 F10
Aqaba, Jordan 186 A3
Aqaba, Gulf of, Red Sea 210 C3
'Arab, Khalīg el, Egypt, Medit. Sea 133 L10
Arabian Basin, Arabian Sea 184 C6
Arabian Peninsula, Asia 184 B4
Arabian Sea, Ind. Oc. 186 C6
Arafura Sea, Ind. Oc. 187 F14
Arcas, Cayos, Mex., G. of Mex. 138 J6
Archimedes Seamount, Medit. Sea 132 J5
Arctic Institute Islands, Russ., Kara Sea 219 B9
Arḑ, Ra's al, Kuwait, Persian G. 212 C2
Ardasier Reefs, S. China Sea 181 J8
Arecibo, P.R., U.S. 141 E12
Arenas, Cayo, Mex., G. of Mex. 138 H7
Argentine Basin, S. Atl. Oc. 105 N5
Argentine Plain, S. Atl. Oc. 105 P4
Argentine Rise, S. Atl. Oc. 107 N4
Argolikós Kólpos, Gr., Sea of Crete 132 G8
Ari Atoll, Maldives, Ind. Oc. 186 D7
Arno Atoll, Ratak Chain, Marshall Is., N. Pac. Oc. 164 C8
Arorae, island, Gilbert Is., Kiribati, S. Pac. Oc. 164 D8
Arrowsmith Bank, Caribbean Sea 140 D2
Aru Islands, Indonesia 187 E14
Aruba, island, Lesser Antil., Neth., Caribbean Sea 141 J11
Aruba Gap, Caribbean Sea 141 H9
Arzanah, island, U.A.E., Persian G. 212 K8
Arzew, Alg. 106 G9
As Salāmah, island, Oman, Persian G. 213 G13
Ascension, island, U.K., S. Atl. Oc. 107 K7
Ascensión, Bahía de la, Mex., Caribbean Sea 140 E2
Ascension Fracture Zone, S. Atl. Oc. 105 K7
Ashāţ, Jazīrat al, Qatar, Persian G. 212 K7
Ashmore Island, Austral., Timor Sea 164 F1
Ash Sha'm, U.A.E. 213 H12
Ash Shāriqah see Sharjah, U.A.E. 213 J12
Asia Islands, Indonesia, N. Pac. Oc. 164 D2
Asinara, Isola, It., Medit. Sea 132 E1
'Asīs, Ra's, Sudan, Red Sea 210 H5
'Askar, Ra's al, Saudi Arabia, Red Sea 210 G6
Assab, Eritrea 210 K7
Assumption Island, Seychelles, Ind. Oc. 186 F4
Astipálea, island, Kikládes, Gr., Aegean Sea 133 H9
Astove Island, Seychelles, Ind. Oc. 186 F4
Astrid Ridge, S. Atl. Oc. 248 E6
Asuncion, island, N. Mariana Is., U.S., N. Pac. Oc. 164 A4
Aswad, Ar Ra's al, Saudi Arabia, Red Sea 210 F5
Ata, island, Tonga, S. Pac. Oc. 165 G9
Atafu, island, Tokelau, N.Z., S. Pac. Oc. 165 E10
Atchafalaya Bay, U.S., G. of Mex. 138 B7
Athens see Athína, Gr. 132 G8
Athína (Athens), Gr. 132 G8
Atiu, island, Cook Is., N.Z., S. Pac. Oc. 165 G11
Atka Island, Andreanof Is., U.S., N. Pac. Oc. 146 C8
Atlantic-Indian Basin, S. Atl. Oc. 248 E5
Atlantic-Indian Ridge, S. Atl. Oc. 248 E4
Atlantis Fracture Zone, N. Atl. Oc. 104 G5
Atlantis II Deep, Red Sea 210 F5
Atlantis II Fracture Zone, Ind. Oc. 184 J5
Attalia see Antalya, Turk. 133 G11
Attu Island, Near Is., U.S., N. Pac. Oc. 146 C7
Atwater Valley, G. of Mex. 139 C9
Atwood see Samana Cay, island, Bahamas, N. Atl. Oc. 141 C9
Aubarede Point, Philippines 180 E11
Auckland, N.Z. 164 J8
Auckland Islands, N.Z., S. Pac. Oc. 146 L7
Augusta, It. 106 G10
Aur, island, Malaysia, S. China Sea 181 L3
Austral Islands (Tubuai Islands), Polynesia, Fr. Polynesia, Fr., S. Pac. Oc. 165 G12
Aves (Bird Island), Venez., Caribbean Sea 141 G14
Aves, Islas de, Lesser Antil., Venez., Caribbean Sea 141 J12
Aves Ridge, Caribbean Sea 141 H14
'Awhah, island, Kuwait, Persian G. 212 C3
Axel Heiberg Island, Sverdrup Is., Can., Arctic Oc. 218 H8
Ayon Island, Russ., E. Siberian Sea 218 E4
Ayu Islands, Indonesia 187 E14
Azores, islands, Port., N. Atl. Oc. 106 G6
Azores Plateau, N. Atl. Oc. 104 F6
Azov, Sea of, Black Sea 133 B14
Az Zawr, Kuwait 212 D3

Bāb al Mandab, strait, Djibouti, Yemen, Red Sea 186 C4
Babar, island, Indonesia 187 F14
Babelthuap, island, Caroline Is., Palau, N. Pac. Oc. 164 C3
Babuyan, island, Babuyan Is., Philippines, Luzon Str. 180 D11
Babuyan Channel, Philippines, Luzon Str. 180 D11
Babuyan Islands, Philippines, Luzon Str. 180 D11
Bac Lieu, Vietnam 180 H4
Bacan, island, Indonesia, Molucca Sea 187 E13
Badu Island, Austral., Torres Str. 187 F15
Baffin Basin, Bafflin B. 104 C3
Baffin Bay, U.S., G. of Mex. 138 D2
Baffin Bay, N. Atl. Oc. 106 B3
Baffin Island, Can. 219 L9
Baguio Point, Philippines 180 D11
Bahdūr, island, Sudan, Red Sea 210 H5
Bahía Blanca, Arg. 107 N3
Bahía, Islas de la, Hond., Caribbean Sea 140 F2
Bahrain, island, Bahrain, Persian G. 212 H5
Bahrain, Gulf of, Persian G. 212 H5
Baḩrgān, Damāgheh-ye, Iran, Persian G. 212 B4
Bai Bung, Mui, Vietnam 180 H3
Bairiki, island, Kiribati, S. Pac. Oc. 146 G7
Bairiki see Tarawa, Kiribati 164 D8
Baja California, N. Am. 145 E12
Bajo Nuevo, Cayo, Caribbean Sea 140 G6
Baker Island, Polynesia, U.S., N. Pac. Oc. 165 D9
Balabac, island, Philippines 181 J9
Balabac Strait, Malaysia, Philippines 181 J9
Balboa, Pan. 147 F15
Balearic Islands, Sp., Medit. Sea 131 F7
Balearic Sea, Medit. Sea 131 F6
Balembangan, island, Malaysia 181 J9
Bali, island, Lesser Sunda Is., Indonesia 181 Q8
Bali, Selat, Indonesia, Ind. Oc. 181 Q8
Bali Sea, Indonesia 181 Q8
Balikpapan, Indonesia 146 G3
Balintang Channel, Philippines, Luzon Str. 180 D11
Balkan Peninsula, 104 F10
Ballantyne Strait, Can., Arctic Oc. 218 J7
Balleny Fracture Zone, Antarctica, S. Pac. Oc. 249 E11
Balleny Islands, Antarctica, S. Pac. Oc. 251 E11
Balleny Trough, S. Pac. Oc. 249 E11
Ball's Pyramid, island, Austral., Tasman Sea 164 J6
Baltic Sea, 106 E10
Baltimore, U.S. 106 F2
Banâ , Râs, Egypt, Red Sea 210 E3
Banaba (Ocean Island), Micronesia, Kiribati, S. Pac. Oc. 164 D7
Banda Sea, S. Pac. Oc. 187 E13
Bandar-e 'Abbās, Iran 213 F13
Bandar-e Būshehr, Iran 212 C6
Bandar-e Chārak, Iran 213 G10
Bandar-e Deylam, Iran 212 B5
Bandar-e Khoemir, Iran 213 F12
Bandar-e Khomeynī, Iran 212 A3
Bandar-e Lengeh, Iran 213 G11
Bandar-e Maqām, Iran 213 F9
Bandar-e Rīg, Iran 212 C5
Bandar-e Sūzā, Iran 213 G12
Bandar-e Ţāherī, Iran 212 E8
Bandar Seri Begawan, Brunei 181 K8
Banggi, island, Malaysia 181 J9
Banghāzī (Benghazi), Lib. 132 K6
Bangka, island, Indonesia 181 N4
Bangkok see Krung Thep, Thailand 180 F2
Banī Forūr, island, Iran, Persian G. 213 H10
Banks Island, Can., Arctic Oc. 218 K6
Banks Islands, Vanuatu, S. Pac. Oc. 164 F7
Banyak Islands, Indonesia, Ind. Oc. 187 D10
Banzare Seamounts, Ind. Oc. 248 B8
Barahona, Dom. Rep. 141 E10
Baram, Tanjong, Malaysia 181 K7
Baranof Island, Alexander Arch., U.S., N. Pac. Oc. 147 B11
Barataria Bay, U.S., G. of Mex. 138 B8
Barbacoas, Bahía de, Col., Caribbean Sea 140 K8
Barbados, island, N. Atl. Oc. 141 H16
Barbados Ridge, N. Atl. Oc. 141 J16
Barbareta, Isla, Is. de la Bahia, Hond., Caribbean Sea 140 F2
Barbuda, island, Leeward Is., Antigua & Barbuda, N. Atl. Oc. 141 F15
Barcelona, Sp. 131 E7
Barcelona, Venez. 141 K13
Bard Ḩalq, Ra's, Saudi Arabia, Persian G. 212 D3
Bardawîl, Sabkhet el, Egypt, Medit. Sea 133 L12
Barents Plain, Arctic Oc. 217 E10
Barents Sea, Arctic Oc. 219 C10
Barentsøya, island, Svalbard, Nor. 106 B10
Bari, It. 132 E5
Barīdī, Ra's, Saudi Arabia, Red Sea 210 E4
Barīm (Perim), island, Yemen, Red Sea 210 K7
Barque Canada Reef, S. China Sea 180 H7
Barr, Ra's al, Bahrain, Persian G. 212 H5
Barracuda Plain, N. Atl. Oc. 104 H4
Barranquilla, Col. 140 J8
Barren, Nosy, Madagascar, Mozambique Ch. 186 G4
Barrow Canyon, Arctic Oc. 216 H5
Barrow Island, Austral., Ind. Oc. 187 G12
Barrow, Point, U.S. 218 H4
Barshah, Ra's al, Kuwait, Persian G. 212 B2
Barú, Isla, Col., Caribbean Sea 140 K8
Bāsa 'īdū, Iran 213 G11
Basilan, island, Sulu Arch., Philippines 181 J11
Basra, Iraq 186 A4
Bass Strait, Austral. 164 K4
Bass, Îlots de see Marotiri, Austral Is., Fr. Polynesia, Fr., S. Pac. Oc. 165 H13
Bassas da India, islands, Fr., Mozambique Ch. 186 G3
Basse-Terre, peninsula, Guadeloupe, Fr. 141 F15
Basse-Terre, Guadeloupe, Fr. 141 G15
Basseterre, St. Kitts & Nevis 141 F14
Bastia, Fr. 132 D2
Basu, island, Indonesia 181 M3
Bataan Peninsula, Philippines 180 F10
Batabanó, Golfo de, Cuba, Caribbean Sea 140 C4
Batan, island, Batan Is., Philippines, Luzon Str. 180 C11
Batan Islands, Philippines, Luzon Str. 180 C11
Batangas, Philippines 180 F10
Bathurst Island, Austral., Timor Sea 187 F14
Bathurst Island, Parry Is., Can., Arctic Oc. 218 J8
Bathymetrists Seamounts, N. Atl. Oc. 105 J7
Baţīn, Khawr al, Persian G. 213 K10
Batu Islands, Indonesia, Ind. Oc. 187 E10
Bawal, island, Indonesia 181 N6
Bawean, island, Indonesia, Java Sea 181 P7
Bay'ah, Oman 213 H13
Baydarata Bay, Russ., Kara Sea 219 A11
Bazm, Khawr al, Persian G. 213 L9
Be, Nosy, Madagascar, Mozambique Ch. 186 F4
Beagle Gulf, Austral., Timor Sea 187 F14
Bear Islands, Russ., E. Siberian Sea 218 D4
Beata, Isla, Dom. Rep., Caribbean Sea 141 F10
Beata Escarpment, Caribbean Sea 141 F9
Beata Plain, Caribbean Sea 141 G10
Beata Ridge, Caribbean Sea 141 G9
Beaufort Sea, Arctic Oc. 218 J5
Beaufort Shelf, Beaufort Sea 218 J5
Beaufort Slope, Beaufort Sea 216 H5
Becerro, Cayos, Hond., Caribbean Sea 140 G4
Begur, Cap de, Sp. 131 D7
Beirut see Beyrouth, Leb. 133 J13
Beirut Escarpment, Medit. Sea 133 K13
Bejaïa (Bougie), Alg. 131 G8
Bejaïa, Golfe de, Alg., Medit. Sea 131 G8
Belcher Channel, Can. 218 J8
Belcher Islands, Can., Hudson B. 106 E2
Bélep, Îles, New Caledonia, Fr., S. Pac. Oc. 164 G6
Belgica Bank, Greenland Sea 217 G11
Belitung (Billiton), island, Indonesia 181 N5
Belize City, Belize 140 F1
Belize Fan, Caribbean Sea 140 E2
Bellingshausen Plain, S. Pac. Oc. 248 J7
Bellingshausen Sea, S. Pac. Oc. 250 H8
Belyy Island, Russ., Kara Sea 219 B10
Bengal, Bay of, Ind. Oc. 187 C9
Benghazi see Banghāzī, Lib. 132 K6
Bengkalis, island, Indonesia, Str. of Malacca 181 L2
Benham Seamount, Philippine Sea 164 B1
Benidorm, Sp. 131 F6
Benidorm Canyon, Medit. Sea 131 G6
Bennett Island, New Siberian Is., Russ., Arctic Oc. 218 D6
Bequia, island, Windward Is., St. Vincent & the Grenadines, N. Atl. Oc. 141 H15
Berau, Gulf of, Indonesia, Ceram Sea 187 E14
Berhala, Selat, Indonesia, S. China Sea 181 M3
Bering Island, Russ., Bering Sea 146 B7

AL LĀDHIQĪYAH – BERING ISLAND | MAP PLACE-NAME INDEX 339

Bering Sea, N. Pac. Oc. 146 B8
Bering Strait, Russ., U.S. 218 G2
Berkner Island, Antarctica, Weddell Sea 250 G8
Bermuda Rise, N. Atl. Oc. 104 G3
Bernier Island, Austral., Ind. Oc. 187 H12
Berry Islands, Bahamas, N. Atl. Oc. 140 A7
Beru, island, Gilbert Is., Kiribati, S. Pac. Oc. 164 D8
Beyrouth (Beirut), Leb. 133 J13
Biak, island, Indonesia, N. Pac. Oc. 187 E15
Bight Fracture Zone, N. Atl. Oc. 104 E5
Bikar Atoll, Ratak Chain, Marshall Is., N. Pac. Oc. 164 B7
Bikini Atoll, Marshall Is., N. Pac. Oc. 164 B7
Bila, Tanjung, Indonesia 181 L5
Bilbao, Sp. 106 F8
Bill Baileys Bank, N. Atl. Oc. 104 D7
Billiton see Belitung, island, Indonesia 181 N5
Biloxi, Miss., U.S. 139 A9
Bilugyun Island, Myanmar 187 C10
Bimini Islands, Bahamas, N. Atl. Oc. 140 A6
Bintan, island, Kep. Riau, Indonesia 181 M3
Bioko, island, Eq. Guinea, G. of Guinea 107 J9
Bird Island see Aves, Venez., Caribbean Sea 141 G14
Birnie Island, Phoenix Is., Kiribati, S. Pac. Oc. 165 D10
Birsa Bank, Str. of Sicily 132 H3
Biscay Plain, N. Atl. Oc. 104 F8
Biscay, Bay of, N. Atl. Oc. 106 F8
Biscayne, Key, U.S., N. Atl. Oc. 140 A5
Biscayne Bay, U.S. 140 A5
Biscoe Islands, Antarctica, Bellingshausen Sea 107 R3
Bīshah, Ra's al, Iraq, Persian G. 212 B3
Bismarck Archipelago, Melanesia, P.N.G., S. Pac. Oc. 164 D5
Bismarck Sea, P.N.G., S. Pac. Oc. 164 E5
Bismuna, Laguna, Nicar., Caribbean Sea 140 H4
Bizerte, Tun. 132 G2
Bjornøya, island, Nor., Barents Sea 106 B10
Black Rock, S. Georgia, U.K., Scotia Sea 107 P5
Black Sea, 133 C12
Blake Plateau, N. Atl. Oc. 104 G2
Blake-Bahama Ridge, N. Atl. Oc. 104 G2
Blanc, Cap, 106 H7
Blanquilla, Isla, Lesser Antil., Venez., Caribbean Sea 141 J13
Bluefields, Nicar. 140 J4
Bluefields, Bahía de, Nicar., Caribbean Sea 140 J4
Boa Vista, island, C. Verde Is., C. Verde, N. Atl. Oc. 106 H7
Boca Chica Key, Fla. Keys, U.S., G. of Mex. 139 F14
Bocas del Toro, Archipiélago de, Pan., Caribbean Sea 140 K4
Bo Hai, bay, Yellow Sea 146 D3
Bohol, island, Philippines 187 C13
Bohol Sea, Philippines 187 D13
Bojeador, Cape, Philippines 180 D10
Bolinao, Cape, Philippines 180 E10
Bolivar Peninsula, U.S. 138 B4
Bollons Tablemount, S. Pac. Oc. 249 F13
Bol'shevik Island, N. Land, Russ., Arctic Oc. 218 C8
Bol'shoy Begichev Island, Russ., Laptev Sea 218 B7
Bombay see Mumbai, India 186 B7
Bombay Reef, S. China Sea 180 E7
Bombay Shoal, S. China Sea 180 H9
Bonaire, island, Lesser Antil., Neth., Caribbean Sea 141 J12
Bonaire Basin, Caribbean Sea 141 J12
Bonaparte Archipelago, Austral., Timor Sea 187 G13
Bône see Annaba, Alg. 132 G1
Bone, Teluk, Indonesia 181 N10
Bonerate, island, Indonesia, Flores Sea 181 Q10
Bonifacio, Bocche di, Medit. Sea 132 E2
Bonin Islands, Japan, Philippine Sea 144 E5
Bonin Trench, N. Pac. Oc. 144 E5
Bonny, Nigeria 107 J9
Boothia, Gulf of, Can. 218 L8
Boothia Peninsula, Can. 216 L8
Bora-Bora, island, Society Is., Fr. Polynesia, Fr., S. Pac. Oc. 165 F12
Borden Island, Queen Elizabeth Is., Can., Arctic Oc. 218 H7
Boreas Plain, Greenland Sea 217 F12
Borgne, Lake, U.S. 138 A8
Borneo (Kalimantan), island, Greater Sunda Is., Asia 181 M7
Bornholm, island, Den., Baltic Sea 106 E10
Boronga Islands, Myanmar, B. of Bengal 187 B9
Bosporus see İstanbul Boğazı, Turk. 133 E10
Bostāneh, Khorān-e, Persian G. 213 F12
Botany Bay, Austral. 146 K6
Bothnia, Gulf of, Baltic Sea 106 D10
Bougainville, island, Solomon Is., P.N.G., S. Pac. Oc. 164 E5
Bougie see Bejaïa, Alg. 131 G8
Bouma Bank, G. of Mex. 138 C6
Bounty Islands, N.Z., S. Pac. Oc. 164 L8
Bounty Trough, S. Pac. Oc. 144 L7
Bouvet, island, Nor., S. Atl. Oc. 250 F4
Bowers Ridge, Bering Sea 144 B8
Bowie Seamount, N. Pac. Oc. 145 C11
Boxall Reef, S. China Sea 180 H8
Boynes, Îles de, Kerguelen Is., Fr., Ind. Oc. 186 L7
Bozorg, Tonb-e, Iran, Persian G. 213 H12
Brabant Island, Palmer Arch., Antarctica, S. Pac. Oc. 107 R3
Brač, island, Croatia, Adriatic Sea 132 C5
Bradenton, Fla., U.S. 139 D13
Brava, Costa, Sp. 131 E7
Brazil Basin, S. Atl. Oc. 105 L6
Brazza Seamounts, S. Atl. Oc. 105 K9
Bremerhaven, Ger. 106 E9
Bretón, Cayo, Jardines de la Reina, Cuba, Caribbean Sea 140 D6
Breton Island, U.S., G. of Mex. 138 B8
Breton Sound, U.S., G. of Mex. 138 B8
Brindisi, It. 132 E5
Brisbane, Austral. 164 H5
Bristol Bay, Bering Sea 147 B9
Bristol Island, S. Sandwich Is., U.K., Scotia Sea 107 Q6
Brixham, U.K. 106 E8
Broa, Ensenada de la, Cuba, G. de Batabanó 140 C4
Brodeur Peninsula, Can. 217 K9
Broken Ridge, Ind. Oc. 185 J9
Bromley Plateau, S. Atl. Oc. 105 M6
Broom Sound, Austral., Coral Sea 187 G16
Brown Bank, N. Atl. Oc. 140 D8
Brown Reef, S. China Sea 180 H9
Bruce Ridge, Scotia Sea 105 Q6
Bruce Rise, Ind. Oc. 249 C9
Brunei Bay, Brunei, Malaysia, S. China Sea 181 K8
Brunsbüttel, Ger. 106 E9
Brus, Laguna de, Hond., Caribbean Sea 140 G2
Būbiyān, island, Kuwait, Persian G. 212 B2
Buccaneer Bank, Caribbean Sea 140 D5
Buck Reef, S. China Sea 181 K7
Buenaventura, Col. 147 G15
Buenos Aires, Arg. 107 N4
Bugsuk, island, Philippines 180 H9
Bū Kuskayshah, Ra's, U.A.E., Persian G. 213 K10
Buldānī, Fasht, Persian G. 212 E4
Bullard Fracture Zone, S. Atl. Oc. 248 G5
Bumbah, Khalīj al, Lib., Medit. Sea 132 K8
Bunguran Selatan see Natuna Selatan, Kepulauan, Indonesia, S. China Sea 181 L5
Bunguran Utara see Natuna Besar, Kepulauan, Indonesia, S. China Sea 181 K5
Bunyu, island, Indonesia, Celebes Sea 181 K9
Buor-Khaya Bay, Russ., Laptev Sea 218 B5
Burdwood Bank, S. Atl. Oc. 105 P4
Burgana Bank, Caribbean Sea 141 J13
Burias, island, Philippines, Sibuyan Sea 180 F11
Bûr Saʻîd (Port Said), Egypt 210 A2
Buru, island, Moluccas, Indonesia 164 D2
Busan, S. Korea 146 D4
Busuanga, island, Calamian Group, Philippines 180 G10
Butaritari, atoll, Gilbert Is., Kiribati, S. Pac. Oc. 164 D8
Buton, island, Indonesia 164 E1
Bylot Island, Can., Baffin B. 219 K9

Ca Na, Mui, Vietnam 180 G5
Caballones, Cayo, Jardines de la Reina, Cuba, Caribbean Sea 140 D6
Cable Bank, Persian G. 212 G8
Cabo Falso, Bancos del, Caribbean Sea 140 G4
Cabrera, island, Balearic Is., Sp., Medit. Sea 131 F7
Cagayan Islands, Philippines, Sulu Sea 180 H11
Cagayan Sulu Island, Philippines, Sulu Sea 181 J9
Cagliari, It. 132 F1
Cagliari, Golfo di, It., Medit. Sea 132 F2
Caicos Bank, N. Atl. Oc. 141 D10
Caicos Islands, Turks & Caicos Is., U.K., N. Atl. Oc. 141 C10
Caicos Passage, N. Atl. Oc. 141 C9
Caillou Bay, U.S., G. of Mex. 138 B7
Cairns, Austral. 164 F4
Calabrian Rise, Ionian Sea 132 G5
Calamian Group, Philippines 180 G10
Calayan, island, Babuyan Is., Philippines, Luzon Str. 180 D11
Calcanhar, Point, 107 K6
Calcasieu Lake, U.S. 138 A5
California Seamount, N. Pac. Oc. 147 F12
California, Gulf of, N. Pac. Oc. 147 E13
Callao, Peru 147 H15
Callou Bank, S. China Sea 180 H5
Cam Pha, Vietnam 180 C4
Cam Ranh, Vietnam 180 G5
Camagüey, Archipiélago de, Cuba, N. Atl. Oc. 140 C6
Camiguin, island, Babuyan Is., Philippines, Luzon Str. 180 D11
Campbell Island, N.Z., S. Pac. Oc. 146 L7
Campbell Plateau, S. Pac. Oc. 144 L7
Campbell Seamount, N. Pac. Oc. 147 C10
Campeche, Mex. 138 K7
Campeche Bank, G. of Mex. 139 G9
Campeche Bay, Mex., G. of Mex. 138 J5
Campeche Escarpment, G. of Mex. 138 G7
Can Tho, Vietnam 180 H4
Canada Basin, Arctic Oc. 216 H5
Canada Plain, Arctic Oc. 216 H5
Canarreos, Archipiélago de los, Cuba, Caribbean Sea 140 C4
Canary Basin, N. Atl. Oc. 104 G7
Canary Islands, Sp., N. Atl. Oc. 106 G7
Canberra, Austral. 164 J5
Cancún, Mex. 140 D2
Çandarlı Körfezi, Turk., Aegean Sea 133 F9
Candia see Iráklio, Gr. 133 H9
Çankkale Boğazı (Dardanelles, Hellespont), Turk. 133 F9
Cannes, Fr. 132 C1
Canouan, island, Windward Is., St. Vincent & the Grenadines, N. Atl. Oc. 141 H15
Cantiles, Cayo, Arch. de los Canarreos, Cuba, Caribbean Sea 140 C4
Canton see Guangzhou, China 180 B7
Cape Barren Island, Furneaux Group, Austral. 187 K16
Cape Basin, S. Atl. Oc. 105 N9
Cape Breton Island, Can., G. of St. Lawrence 106 F4
Cape Coral, Fla., U.S. 139 D14
Cape Plain, S. Atl. Oc. 105 N9
Cape Rise, S. Atl. Oc. 105 N10
Cape Town, S. Af. 107 M10
Cape Verde Basin, N. Atl. Oc. 104 H6
Cape Verde Islands, C. Verde, N. Atl. Oc. 106 H7
Cape Verde Plain, N. Atl. Oc. 104 H7
Cape Verde Terrace, N. Atl. Oc. 104 H7
Cap-Haïtien, Haiti 141 E9
Capraia, island, It., Medit. Sea 132 D2
Capri, island, It., Tyrrhenian Sea 132 E4
Captiva Island, U.S., G. of Mex. 139 D13
Caracas, Venez. 141 K12
Caratasca, Cayo, Hond., Caribbean Sea 140 G4
Caratasca, Laguna de, Hond., Caribbean Sea 140 G4
Carbonara, Capo, It. 132 F2
Cargados Carajos Bank, Mauritius, Ind. Oc. 184 G6
Cargados Carajos Shoals (St. Brandon), Mauritius, Ind. Oc. 186 G6
Cariaco Basin, Caribbean Sea 141 K13
Caribbean Sea, N. Atl. Oc. 107 J2
Caribbean Sea's deepest point, 140 E6
Carlsberg Ridge, Ind. Oc. 184 D6
Carmen, Isla del, Mex., G. of Mex. 138 L7
Carmen, Laguna del, Mex., G. of Mex. 138 L5
Carnatic Shoal, S. China Sea 180 H9
Carnegie Ridge, S. Pac. Oc. 145 G14
Carney Island, Antarctica, Amundsen Sea 251 H10
Car Nicobar, island, Nicobar Is., India, B. of Bengal 187 D9
Caroline Island, Line Is., Kiribati, S. Pac. Oc. 165 E12
Caroline Islands, Micronesia, N. Pac. Oc. 164 C3
Carpentaria, Gulf of, Austral., Arafura Sea 164 F3
Carriacou, island, Windward Is., Grenada, N. Atl. Oc. 141 J15
Cartagena, Col. 140 K8
Cartagena, Sp. 131 G5
Cartagena Canyon, Medit. Sea 131 G6
Cartier Island, Austral., Timor Sea 164 F1
Cartier Islands, Austral., Ind. Oc. 187 F13
Carúpano, Venez. 141 J14
Casablanca, Mor. 106 G8
Cascadia Basin, N. Pac. Oc. 145 C12
Castle Island, Bahamas, N. Atl. Oc. 140 C8
Cat Island, Bahamas, N. Atl. Oc. 140 B8
Cat Island, U.S., G. of Mex. 138 A8
Catanduanes, island, Philippines, Philippine Sea 187 C13
Catania, It. 132 G4
Catoche, Cabo, Mex. 139 H10
Catoche Knoll, G. of Mex. 139 F11
Catoche Tongue, G. of Mex. 139 G11
Catwick Islands, Vietnam, S. China Sea 187 C11
Cawston Shoal, S. China Sea 180 E7
Cay Sal Bank, N. Atl. Oc. 140 B6
Cayman Brac, island, Cayman Is., U.K., Caribbean Sea 140 E6
Cayman Islands, U.K., Caribbean Sea 140 E5
Cayman Ridge, Caribbean Sea 140 E3
Cayman Trench, Caribbean Sea 140 F3
Cayman Trough, Caribbean Sea 140 E5
Ceara Plain, S. Atl. Oc. 105 K5
Ceara Ridge, N. Atl. Oc. 105 J5
Cebu, island, Philippines 187 C13
Cedar Key, U.S., G. of Mex. 139 B13
Cedros Island, Mex., N. Pac. Oc. 147 E12
Cedros Trench, Philippine Sea 145 E12
Cefalu Basin, Tyrrhenian Sea 132 G4
Celebes see Sulawesi, island, Indonesia 164 D1
Celebes Basin, Celebes Sea 185 D13
Celebes Sea, 181 K11
Celtic Sea, N. Atl. Oc. 106 E8
Cenderawasih, Teluk, Indonesia, N. Pac. Oc. 164 D3
Central Pacific Basin, N. Pac. Oc. 144 F8
Central Reef, S. China Sea 180 H7
Ceram, island, Moluccas, Indonesia 164 D2
Ceram Sea, 164 D2
Cerf Island, Seychelles, Ind. Oc. 186 F4
Cerigo see Kíthira, island, Gr., Medit. Sea 132 H8
Ceuta, Sp. 131 H3
Ceva-i-Ra, reef, Fiji Is., S. Pac. Oc. 164 G8
Chafarinas, Islas, Sp., Alboran Sea 131 H4
Chagos Archipelago (Oil Islands), U.K., Ind. Oc. 186 E7
Chagos Trench, Ind. Oc. 184 F7
Chagos-Laccadive Plateau, Ind. Oc. 184 C7
Chain Fracture Zone, S. Atl. Oc. 105 K7
Challenger Deep, N. Pac. Oc. 164 B4
Challenger Fracture Zone, S. Pac. Oc. 145 K12
Cham Island, Vietnam, S. China Sea 187 C11
Chandeleur Islands, U.S., G. of Mex. 139 B9
Chandeleur Sound, U.S., G. of Mex. 138 B8
Chang, Ko, Thailand, G. of Thai. 180 G2
Channel Islands, U.K., English Ch. 106 E8
Channel Islands, U.S., N. Pac. Oc. 147 D12
Charcot Island, Antarctica, Bellingshausen Sea 107 R2
Charleston, U.S. 106 G2
Charlie-Gibbs Fracture Zone, N. Atl. Oc. 104 E5
Charlotte Bank, S. China Sea 181 J5
Charlotte Harbor, U.S., G. of Mex. 139 D13
Chatham Island, Chatham Is., N.Z., S. Pac. Oc. 165 K9
Chatham Islands, N.Z., S. Pac. Oc. 165 L9
Chatham Rise, S. Pac. Oc. 144 L7
Chaun Bay, Russ., E. Siberian Sea 218 E3
Cheduba Island, Myanmar, B. of Bengal 187 B9
Chelyuskin, Cape, Russ. 218 C8
Chennai (Madras), India 186 C8
Cherry Island see Anuta, Sta. Cruz Is., Solomon Is., S. Pac. Oc. 164 F7
Chesha Bay, Russ., Barents Sea 219 A12
Chesterfield, Îles, New Caledonia, Fr., Coral Sea 164 G6
Chetumal, Mex. 140 E1
Chetumal, Bahía de, Mex., Caribbean Sea 140 E1
Chiba, Japan 146 D5
Chichagof Island, Alexander Arch., U.S., N. Pac. Oc. 147 B11
Chichi Jima Rettō, Bonin Is., Japan, N. Pac. Oc. 187 A15
Chile Basin, S. Pac. Oc. 145 J15
Chile Rise, S. Pac. Oc. 145 K14
Chilung, Taiwan, China 146 E4
Chinchorro, Banco, Caribbean Sea 140 E2
Chinook Trough, N. Pac. Oc. 144 D8
Chios see Híos, island, Gr., Aegean Sea 133 F9
Chirikof Island, U.S., G. of Alas. 147 B10
Chiriquí, Lago de, Pan., Caribbean Sea 140 K4
Chittagong, Bangladesh 187 B9
Chiwan, China 146 E3
Choctawhatchee Bay, U.S., G. of Mex. 139 A10
Choiseul, island, Solomon Is., S. Pac. Oc. 164 E6
Chon Buri, Thailand 180 F2
Chonos Archipelago, Chile, S. Pac. Oc. 147 L15
Christmas Island, Austral., Ind. Oc. 187 F11
Christmas Island see Kiritimati, Line Is., Kiribati, N. Pac. Oc. 165 D12
Chukchi Peninsula, Russ. 216 F2
Chukchi Plain, Arctic Oc. 216 F5
Chukchi Plateau, Arctic Oc. 216 G6
Chukchi Sea, Arctic Oc. 218 F3
Chuuk (Truk Islands), Caroline Is., F.S.M., N. Pac. Oc. 164 C5
Cilacap, Indonesia 187 F11
Cinco Balas, Cayos, Jardines de la Reina, Cuba, Caribbean Sea 140 D6
Cirebon, Indonesia 181 Q5
Ciudad Madero, Mex. 138 H2
Civitavecchia, It. 132 D3
Clarence Island, S. Shetland Is., Antarctica, Drake Pass. 107 Q4
Clarion Bank, N. Atl. Oc. 141 D9
Clarion Fracture Zone, N. Pac. Oc. 145 F10
Clarión Island, Revillagigedo Is., Mex., N. Pac. Oc. 147 F12
Clark Basin, Caribbean Sea 140 J5
Clavering Island, Greenland, Den. 106 B7
Claypile Bank, G. of Mex. 138 C5
Clearwater, Fla., U.S. 139 C13
Clerke Rocks, Antarctica, S. Atl. Oc. 107 Q6
Clipperton, island, Fr., N. Pac. Oc. 147 F13
Clipperton Fracture Zone, N. Pac. Oc. 145 G10
Coats Island, Can., Hudson B. 106 D2
Coatzacoalcos, Mex. 138 L5

340 MAP PLACE-NAME INDEX | BERING SEA — COATZACOALCOS

Cobb Seamount, N. Pac. Oc. 147 C11
Coburg Island, Can. 106 B2
Coche, Isla, Venez., Caribbean Sea 141 J14
Cochinos, Bahía de (Bay of Pigs), Cuba, Caribbean Sea 140 C5
Cochinos, Cayos, Hond., Caribbean Sea 140 G2
Cochons, Île aux, Crozet Is., Fr., Ind. Oc. 186 L4
Coco, Cayo, Arch. de Camagüey, Cuba, N. Atl. Oc. 140 C6
Coco-de-Mer Seamounts, Ind. Oc. 184 E5
Cocos Island, C.R., N. Pac. Oc. 147 G14
Cocos (Keeling) Islands, Austral., Ind. Oc. 187 F10
Cocos Ridge, N. Pac. Oc. 145 G14
Coetivy Island, Seychelles, Ind. Oc. 186 E5
Coiba Island, Pan., N. Pac. Oc. 147 F15
Colón, Pan. 140 K6
Colmer Knoll, Caribbean Sea 140 D2
Colombian Basin, Caribbean Sea 140 H8
Colombo, Sri Lanka 186 D8
Colon Ridge, N. Pac. Oc. 147 G14
Colorados, Archipiélago de los, Cuba, G. of Mex. 139 G12
Columbia Seamount, S. Atl. Oc. 105 L6
Columbus Bank, N. Atl. Oc. 140 C8
Commander Islands, Russ., Bering Sea 146 B7
Commodore Reef, S. China Sea 180 H8
Comoro Islands, Ind. Oc. 184 F4
Comstock Seamount, N. Pac. Oc. 145 C9
Conception Island, Bahamas, N. Atl. Oc. 140 B8
Con Co, Dao, Vietnam, S. China Sea 180 E5
Congo Canyon, S. Atl. Oc. 105 K10
Congo Fan, S. Atl. Oc. 105 K9
Conrad Fracture Zone, S. Atl. Oc. 105 Q7
Con Son, island, Vietnam, S. China Sea 180 H4
Constanţa, Rom. 106 F11
Constantinople see İstanbul, Turk. 133 E10
Cook Inlet, G. of Alas. 147 B10
Cook Islands, Polynesia, N.Z., S. Pac. Oc. 165 F11
Cook Strait, N.Z. 164 K8
Coote Rock, Persian G. 213 G12
Copano Bay, U.S., G. of Mex. 138 C3
Coral Sea, S. Pac. Oc. 164 F5
Coral Sea Basin, Coral Sea 144 H6
Corfu see Kérkira, island, Ionian Is., Gr., Ionian Sea 132 F6
Cornaglia Seamount, Tyrrhenian Sea 132 F2
Corner Seamounts, N. Atl. Oc. 104 G4
Cornwall Island, Can. 106 B1
Cornwallis Island, Queen Elizabeth Is., Can., Arctic Oc. 218 K8
Cornwallis South Reef, S. China Sea 180 H8
Coro, Golfete de, Venez., G. de Venezuela 141 J11
Coronation Bank, S. China Sea 180 H6
Coronation Island, S. Orkney Is., Antarctica, Scotia Sea 107 Q5
Corpus Christi, Tex., U.S. 138 C3
Corpus Christi Bay, U.S., G. of Mex. 138 C3
Corregidor, island, Philippines, Manila B. 180 F10
Corrientes, Bahía de, Cuba, Caribbean Sea 140 C3
Corse (Corsica), island, Fr., Medit. Sea 132 D1
Corse, Cap, Fr. 132 D2
Corsica see Corse, island, Fr., Medit. Sea 132 D1
Corsica Terrace, Tyrrhenian Sea 132 D2
Corso-Ligurian Basin, Medit. Sea 132 D1
Corvo, island, Azores, Port., N. Atl. Oc. 106 F6
Cosmoledo Group, Seychelles, Ind. Oc. 186 F4
Cosmonaut Sea, Ind. Oc. 250 D6
Cow and Calf Islands, Myanmar, B. of Bengal 187 C10
Cozumel, Isla, Mex., Caribbean Sea 140 D2
Cres, island, Croatia, Adriatic Sea 132 C4
Crescent Group, Xisha Qundao, China, S. China Sea 180 E6
Cretan Trough, Sea of Crete 133 H9
Cretan-Rhodes Ridge, Medit. Sea 133 H9
Crete see Kríti, island, Gr., Medit. Sea 132 H8
Crete, Sea of, Medit. Sea 133 H9
Creus, Cap de, Sp. 131 D7
Croker Island, Austral., Arafura Sea 187 F14
Crooked Island, Bahamas, N. Atl. Oc. 141 C9
Crooked Island, U.S., G. of Mex. 139 A11
Crooked Island Passage, Bahamas, N. Atl. Oc. 140 C8
Crotone, It. 132 F5
Crozet Basin, Ind. Oc. 184 K6
Crozet Islands, Fr., Ind. Oc. 186 L4
Crozet Plateau, Ind. Oc. 184 L4
Cruiser Tablemount, N. Atl. Oc. 104 G6
Cruz del Padre, Cayo, Arch. de Sabana, Cuba, N. Atl. Oc. 140 B5
Cruz, Cabo, Cuba 140 D7
Crystal Bay, U.S., G. of Mex. 139 B13
Cuba, island, Caribbean Sea 140 C5
Cubagua, Isla, Venez., Caribbean Sea 141 J14
Cu Lao Re, island, Vietnam, S. China Sea 180 E5
Cu Lao Thu, island, Vietnam, S. China Sea 180 H5
Culebra, island, P.R., U.S., N. Atl. Oc. 141 E13
Culion, island, Calamian Group, Philippines 180 G10
Cumaná, Venez. 141 K14
Cumberland Islands, Austral., Coral Sea 187 G16
Curaçao, island, Lesser Antil., Neth., Caribbean Sea 141 J11
Curaçao Ridge, Caribbean Sea 141 H11
Curtis Island, Kermadec Is., N.Z., S. Pac. Oc. 165 H9
Cuvier Plateau, Ind. Oc. 185 H11
Cuyo Islands, Philippines, Sulu Sea 180 G10
Cyclades see Kikládes, islands, Gr., Aegean Sea 133 G9
Cyprus Basin, Medit. Sea 133 J12

Dacia Seamount, N. Atl. Oc. 106 G8
Ḑadnā, U.A.E. 213 J13
Daesan, S. Korea 146 D4
Dafī, Dawḩat ad, Persian G. 212 F4
Dagupan, Philippines 180 E10
Dahlak Archipelago, Eritrea, Red Sea 210 J6
Dahlak Kebr, island, Dahlak Arch., Eritrea, Red Sea 210 J5
Dahra Valley, Medit. Sea 131 G7
Daito Islands, Japan, Philippine Sea 146 E4
Dalian, China 146 D4
Dallas Reef, S. China Sea 181 J7
Dalmā, island, U.A.E., Persian G. 212 K8
Dalupiri, island, Babuyan Is., Philippines, Luzon Str. 180 D11
Damar, island, Indonesia, Banda Sea 187 F14
Damas Cays, Bahamas, N. Atl. Oc. 140 B6
Damietta, Egypt 106 G11
Damietta Banks, Medit. Sea 133 K11
Damietta Mouth of the Nile, Egypt 133 K12
Dampier, Austral. 187 G12
Dampier Archipelago, Austral., Ind. Oc. 187 G12
Da Nang, Vietnam 180 E5
Danger Island, Chagos Arch., U.K., Ind. Oc. 186 E7
Danger Islands see Pukapuka Atoll, Cook Is., N.Z., S. Pac. Oc. 165 E10
Dardanelles see Çanakkale Boğazı, Turk. 133 F9
Darién, Golfo de see Uraba, Golfo de, Col., Caribbean Sea 140 L7
Darnley, Cape, Antarctica 250 C8
Darwin Island, Galápagos Is., Ecua., N. Pac. Oc. 147 G14
Dās, island, U.A.E., Persian G. 212 J8
Das Rocas, Atol, Braz., S. Atl. Oc. 107 K6
Datu, Tanjong, Malaysia 181 L5
Datuk, island, Indonesia, S. China Sea 181 M5
Dauphin Island, U.S., G. of Mex. 139 A9
Davao, Philippines 164 C2
Davis Strait, N. Atl. Oc. 106 C4
Dayyīnah, island, U.A.E., Persian G. 212 J8
De Gerlache Seamounts, S. Pac. Oc. 249 J9
De Soto Canyon, G. of Mex. 139 B10
Deadman Bay, U.S., G. of Mex. 139 B12
Delarof Islands, Aleutian Is., U.S., N. Pac. Oc. 146 C8
Delaware Bank, N. Atl. Oc. 141 J15
Delaware Bay, U.S. 106 F2
Demerara Plain, N. Atl. Oc. 105 J5
Demerara Plateau, N. Atl. Oc. 105 J4
Denis, island, Seychelles, Ind. Oc. 186 E5
Denmark Strait, N. Atl. Oc. 106 C7
D'Entrecasteaux Islands, P.N.G., Coral Sea 164 E5
Dernieres, Isles, U.S., G. of Mex. 138 B7
Désappointement, Îles du, Tuamotu Arch., Fr. Polynesia, Fr., S. Pac. Oc. 165 F14
Desecheo, island, P.R., U.S., N. Atl. Oc. 141 E12
Desroches, island, Seychelles, Ind. Oc. 186 E5
Desterrada, Isla, Mex., G. of Mex. 138 H8
Detroit Seamount, N. Pac. Oc. 146 C7
Detroit Tablemount, N. Pac. Oc. 144 C7
Devils Hole, N. Sea 104 E9
Devon Island, Can. 106 B1
Devon Shelf, Bafflin B. 104 B2
Devon Slope, Bafflin B. 104 B3
Deylam, Khalīj-e, Persian G. 212 B5
Deyyer, Iran 212 E7
Dezhneva, Mys (East Cape), Russ. 218 G3
Diamantina Fracture Zone, Ind. Oc. 185 J11
Dibā, Dawḩat, Persian G. 213 H13
Diego Garcia, island, Chagos Arch., U.K., Ind. Oc. 186 F7
Difnein, island, Eritrea, Red Sea 210 H5
Dili, Timor-Leste 164 E2
Dinagat, island, Philippines, Philippine Sea 187 C13
Diomede Islands, Russ., U.S., Bering Sea 147 A9
Dios, Cayos de, Arch. de los Canarreos, Cuba, Caribbean Sea 140 C5
Dirk Hartog Island, Austral., Ind. Oc. 187 H12
Discovery Deep, Red Sea 210 F5
Discovery Great Reef, Spratly Is., S. China Sea 180 H7
Discovery Reef, S. China Sea 180 E6
Discovery Tablemount, S. Atl. Oc. 105 N8
Disko see Qeqertarsuaq, island, Greenland, Den., Baffin B. 219 K11
Dodecanese see Dodekánissa, islands, Gr., Aegean Sea 133 G9
Dodekánissa (Dodecanese), islands, Gr., Aegean Sea 133 G9
Dog Island, U.S., G. of Mex. 139 B12
Dog Rocks, Bahamas, N. Atl. Oc. 140 B6
Doha see Ad Dawḩah, Qatar 212 J7
Dolak, island, Indonesia, Arafura Sea 164 E3
Doldrums Fracture Zone, N. Atl. Oc. 105 J5
Dolly Cays, Bahamas, N. Atl. Oc. 140 B7
Dominica, island, Leeward Is., Caribbean Sea 141 G15
Dominica Passage, N. Atl. Oc. 141 G15
Donghai Dao, China, S. China Sea 180 C6
Dorre Island, Austral., Ind. Oc. 187 H12
Dragon's Mouths, strait, Trinidad & Tobago, Caribbean Sea 141 J15
Drake Passage, 250 J7
Dreyer Bank, S. China Sea 180 F8
Dry Tortugas, islands, U.S., G. of Mex. 139 F13
Dubai (Dubayy), U.A.E. 213 J11
Dubayy see Dubai, U.A.E. 213 J11
Dubrovnik (Ragusa), Croatia 132 D5
Duc de Gloucester, Îles, Tuamotu Arch., Fr., S. Pac. Oc. 147 J10
Du Chaillu Seamounts, S. Atl. Oc. 105 K9
Ducie Island, U.K., S. Pac. Oc. 165 G16
Duff Islands, Sta. Cruz Is., Solomon Is., S. Pac. Oc. 164 E7
Dugi Otok, island, Croatia, Adriatic Sea 132 C4
Dukhān, Qatar 212 J6
Duluth, U.S. 106 F1
Dumaran, island, Philippines, Sulu Sea 180 H10
Dumshaf Plain, Norwegian Sea 217 F13
Dunkerque, Fr. 106 E9
Dunqunāb, Khalīj, 210 F4
Durban, S. Af. 186 H2
Duwayhin, Dawḩat, Persian G. 212 K6

East Antarctica, region, Antarctica 251 D9
East Aves Escarpment, Caribbean Sea 141 H14
East Bay, U.S., G. of Mex. 138 B4
East Bay, G. of Mex. 138 B8
East Breaks, G. of Mex. 138 C4
East Brother, island, Bahamas, N. Atl. Oc. 140 A6
East Caicos, island, Caicos Is., Turks & Caicos Is., U.K., N. Atl. Oc. 141 C10
East Cape see Dezhneva, Mys, Russ. 218 G3
East Caroline Basin, N. Pac. Oc. 144 G5
East Cay, Caribbean Sea 140 G6
East China Sea, N. Pac. Oc. 146 E4
Easter Fracture Zone, S. Pac. Oc. 145 J12
Easter Island (Isla de Pascua), Chile, S. Pac. Oc. 147 J13
East Falkland, island, Falkland Is., U.K., S. Atl. Oc. 107 P4
East Flower Garden Bank, G. of Mex. 138 C5
East Indiaman Ridge, Ind. Oc. 185 H10
East Isaac, island, Bahamas, N. Atl. Oc. 140 A6
East Mariana Basin, N. Pac. Oc. 144 F6
East Novaya Zemlya Trough, Kara Sea 217 B10
East Pacific Rise, S. Pac. Oc. 145 L13
East Scotia Basin, Scotia Sea 105 Q6
East Sea see Japan, Sea of, N. Pac. Oc. 146 D4
East Siberian Sea, Arctic Oc. 218 E4
East Tasman Plateau, Tasman Sea 144 L6
Eauripik Atoll, Caroline Is., F.S.M., N. Pac. Oc. 164 C4
Eauripik Rise, N. Pac. Oc. 144 G5
Ebeling Reef, S. China Sea 181 M4
Ebon Atoll, Ralik Chain, Marshall Is., N. Pac. Oc. 164 C7
Ebro River Delta, Sp. 131 E6
Edgeøya, island, Svalbard, Nor., Arctic Oc. 219 D11
Edinburgh Reef, Caribbean Sea 140 G4
Edoras Bank, N. Atl. Oc. 104 E7
Edremit Körfezi, Turk., Aegean Sea 133 F9
Éfaté, island, Vanuatu, S. Pac. Oc. 164 F7
Egeria Fracture Zone, Ind. Oc. 184 G6
Egmont Islands, Chagos Arch., U.K., Ind. Oc. 186 E7
Eiao, island, Marquesas Is., Fr. Polynesia, Fr., S. Pac. Oc. 165 E14
Eickelberg Seamount, N. Pac. Oc. 145 C11
Eight Degree Channel, Arabian Sea 186 D7
Eirik Ridge, N. Atl. Oc. 104 D5
Eivissa, Sp. 131 F6
El Alamayn, Egypt 133 L10
Elat, Israel 210 B3
Elba, island, It., Medit. Sea 132 D2
Elbow Cays, Bahamas, N. Atl. Oc. 140 B5
Elephant Island, S. Shetland Is., Antarctica, Drake Pass. 107 Q4
Eleuthera Island, Bahamas, N. Atl. Oc. 140 A7
El Iskandarîya (Alexandria), Egypt 133 L11
Ellef Ringnes Island, Sverdrup Is., Can., Arctic Oc. 218 J8
Ellesmere Island, Queen Elizabeth Is., Can., Arctic Oc. 219 J9
Ellsworth Land, Antarctica 250 H8
Elphinstone Reef, Red Sea 210 D3
El Suweis (Suez), Egypt 210 B2
Eltanin Fracture Zone, S. Pac. Oc. 249 J10
Emerald Basin, S. Pac. Oc. 249 E13
Emerald Fracture Zone, S. Pac. Oc. 249 E12
Emperor Seamounts, N. Pac. Oc. 144 C7
Emperor Trough, N. Pac. Oc. 144 C7
Enderbury Island, Phoenix Is., Kiribati, S. Pac. Oc. 165 D10
Enderby Land, Antarctica 250 D7
Enderby Plain, Ind. Oc. 248 D6
Endurance Ridge, Weddell Sea 105 R5
Enewetak Atoll, Marshall Is., N. Pac. Oc. 164 B6
Engano, Cabo, Dom. Rep. 141 E11
Enggano, island, Indonesia, Ind. Oc. 181 P3
English Channel, N. Atl. Oc. 106 E8
Epicharmos Seamount, Medit. Sea 132 J5
Eratosthenes Tablemount, Medit. Sea 133 J12
Erben Tablemount, N. Pac. Oc. 147 D11
Erromango, island, Vanuatu, S. Pac. Oc. 164 G7
Error Tablemount, Arabian Sea 184 C5
Escocesa, Bahía, Dom. Rep., N. Atl. Oc. 141 E11
E.S.E., Cayos del, Col., Caribbean Sea 140 J5
Española Island, Galápagos Is., Ecua., S. Pac. Oc. 147 G14
Espiritu Santo, island, Vanuatu, S. Pac. Oc. 164 F7
Espíritu Santo, Bahía del, Mex., Caribbean Sea 140 E2
Est, Île de l', Crozet Is., Fr., Ind. Oc. 186 L5
Estero Bay, U.S., G. of Mex. 139 D14
'Eua, island, Tonga, S. Pac. Oc. 165 G9
Euboea see Évia, island, Gr., Aegean Sea 132 F8
Europa Island, Fr., Mozambique Ch. 186 G3
Évia (Euboea), island, Gr., Aegean Sea 132 F8
Ewing Bank, G. of Mex. 138 C6
Exmouth Plateau, Ind. Oc. 185 G12
Explora Escarpment, Weddell Sea 248 G6
Explorer Tablemount, Caribbean Sea 140 F4
Exuma Cays, Bahamas, N. Atl. Oc. 140 B7
Exuma Sound, Bahamas, N. Atl. Oc. 140 B7

Fadiffolu Atoll, Maldives, Ind. Oc. 186 D7
Faial, island, Azores, Port., N. Atl. Oc. 106 F6
Fais, island, Caroline Is., F.S.M., N. Pac. Oc. 164 C3
Fakahina, atoll, Tuamotu Arch., Fr. Polynesia, Fr., S. Pac. Oc. 165 F14
Fakaofu, island, Tokelau, N.Z., S. Pac. Oc. 165 E10
Fakarava, atoll, Tuamotu Arch., Fr. Polynesia, Fr., S. Pac. Oc. 165 F13
Falkland Agulhas Fracture Zone, S. Atl. Oc. 105 P6
Falkland Escarpment, S. Atl. Oc. 105 P4
Falkland Islands, U.K., S. Atl. Oc. 107 P4
Falkland Plateau, S. Atl. Oc. 105 P4
Falkland Trough, S. Atl. Oc. 105 P4
Fangatau, atoll, Tuamotu Arch., Fr. Polynesia, Fr., S. Pac. Oc. 165 F14
Fangataufa, atoll, Tuamotu Arch., Fr. Polynesia, Fr., S. Pac. Oc. 165 G14
Fanning Island see Tabuaeran, Line Is., Kiribati, S. Pac. Oc. 165 C11
Farallon de Medinilla, island, N. Mariana Is., U.S., N. Pac. Oc. 187 C16
Farallon de Pajaros, island, N. Mariana Is., U.S., N. Pac. Oc. 164 A4
Farallon Islands, U.S., N. Pac. Oc. 147 D12
Farasān, Jazā'ir, Saudi Arabia, Red Sea 210 H6
Faraulep Atoll, Caroline Is., F.S.M., N. Pac. Oc. 164 C4
Farewell, Cape, Greenland, Den. 219 L14
Farewell, Cape, N.Z. 164 K8
Faris Seamount, N. Pac. Oc. 147 B10
Faroe Bank, N. Atl. Oc. 104 D8
Faroe-Iceland Ridge, N. Atl. Oc. 217 G15
Faroe Islands, Den., Norwegian Sea 106 D8
Faroe-Shetland Trough, N. Atl. Oc. 217 F16
Farquhar Group, Seychelles, Ind. Oc. 186 F4
Fārsī, island, Iran, Persian G. 212 E5
Fataka (Mitre Island), Sta. Cruz Is., Solomon Is., S. Pac. Oc. 164 F7
Fatu Hiva, island, Marquesas Is., Fr. Polynesia, Fr., S. Pac. Oc. 165 E14
Fawley, U.K. 106 E9
Faylakah, island, Kuwait, Persian G. 212 C3
Felixstowe, U.K. 106 E9
Ferguson Seamount, N. Pac. Oc. 146 E7
Fernandina Island, Galápagos Is., Ecua., S. Pac. Oc. 147 G14

COBB SEAMOUNT – FERNANDINA ISLAND | MAP PLACE-NAME INDEX 341

Fernando de Noronha, island, Braz., S. Atl. Oc. 107 K6
Ferraz Ridge, S. Atl. Oc. 105 L6
Fieberling Tablemount, N. Pac. Oc. 145 E11
Fiery Cross Reef, S. China Sea 180 H7
Fiji Islands, Fiji Is., S. Pac. Oc. 144 H8
Fiji Plateau, S. Pac. Oc. 144 H7
Filchner Ice Shelf, Weddell Sea 248 G8
Finike Trough, Medit. Sea 133 H11
Finland, Gulf of, Baltic Sea 106 D11
First Thomas Shoal, S. China Sea 180 H8
Fiume see Rijeka, Croatia 132 B4
Flamingo Cay, Bahamas, N. Atl. Oc. 140 C8
Flat Island, Spratly Is., S. China Sea 180 G8
Flemish Cap, N. Atl. Oc. 104 F5
Flinders Island, Austral., Ind. Oc. 187 J14
Flinders Island, Furneaux Group, Austral. 187 K16
Flint Island, Line Is., Kiribati, S. Pac. Oc. 165 F12
Flores, island, Azores, Port., N. Atl. Oc. 106 F6
Flores, island, Lesser Sunda Is., Indonesia 181 R10
Flores Sea, Indonesia 181 Q10
Florida, peninsula, 104 G2
Florida, Straits of, U.S. 140 B5
Florida Bay, U.S., G. of Mex. 139 F14
Florida Escarpment, G. of Mex. 139 D11
Florida Keys, U.S., G. of Mex. 139 F14
Florida Middle Ground, G. of Mex. 139 C12
Florida Plain, G. of Mex. 139 E11
Fogo, island, C. Verde Is., C. Verde, N. Atl. Oc. 106 H7
Forūr, island, Iran, Persian G. 213 G11
Forūr Shoal, Persian G. 213 G11
Forcados, Nigeria 107 J9
Formentera, island, Balearic Is., Sp., Medit. Sea 131 F6
Formigas Reef, Caribbean Sea 140 E8
Formigas, Ilhéus, Azores, Port., N. Atl. Oc. 106 G7
Fort Myers, Fla., U.S. 139 D14
Fort Walton Beach, Fla., U.S. 139 A10
Fort-de-France, Martinique, Fr. 141 G15
Fortune Bank, Ind. Oc. 186 F5
Fos, Fr. 106 F9
Foul Bay, Red Sea 210 E3
Four Mountains, Islands of the, Aleutian Is., U.S., N. Pac. Oc. 146 C8
Four North Fracture Zone, N. Atl. Oc. 105 J5
Foveaux Strait, N.Z. 164 L7
Foxe Basin, 104 C2
Fram Basin, Arctic Oc. 217 F9
France, Île de, Greenland, Den., Greenland Sea 219 G11
Francis Island, Antarctica, Weddell Sea 107 R3
Franz Josef Land, Russ., Arctic Oc. 219 D10
Fraser Island, Austral., Coral Sea 164 H5
Freeport, U.S. 106 G1
Friendship Shoal, S. China Sea 181 J7
Frigate, island, Seychelles, Ind. Oc. 186 E5
Frio, Cape, 107 M5
Frontera, Punta, Mex. 138 L6
Fuerte, Isla, Col., Caribbean Sea 140 K7
Fuerteventura, island, Canary Is., Sp., N. Atl. Oc. 106 G7
Fuga, island, Babuyan Is., Philippines, Luzon Str. 180 D11
Fujairah, U.A.E. 186 A5
Funafuti, island, Tuvalu, S. Pac. Oc. 146 H8
Funafuti, Tuvalu 164 E8
Furneaux Group, Austral. 164 K5
Futuna, island, Vanuatu, S. Pac. Oc. 164 G7
Fuzhou, China 180 A10

Gabes, Tun. 132 J2
Gabes, Gulf of, Tun., Medit. Sea 132 J2
Gaeta, Golfo di, It., Tyrrhenian Sea 132 E3
Gafatîn, island, Egypt, Red Sea 210 C3
Gaferut, island, Caroline Is., F.S.M., N. Pac. Oc. 164 C4
Gaffney Ridge, S. China Sea 180 F9
Galápagos Fracture Zone, S. Pac. Oc. 145 G10
Galápagos Islands, Ecua., S. Pac. Oc. 147 G14
Galápagos Rift, N. Pac. Oc. 145 G14
Galápagos Rise, S. Pac. Oc. 145 H14
Gallinas, Punta, Col. 141 H10
Galveston, Tex., U.S. 138 B4
Galveston Bay, U.S., G. of Mex. 138 B4
Galveston Peninsula, U.S. 138 B4
Gambia Plain, N. Atl. Oc. 105 J6
Gambier, Îles, Tuamotu Arch., Fr. Polynesia, Fr., S. Pac. Oc. 165 G14
Gambier Fracture Zone, Ind. Oc. 249 D11
Ganāveh, Iran 212 B5
Ganges Fan, B. of Bengal 184 C8
Gardar Ridge, N. Atl. Oc. 104 D6
Gardner Pinnacles, Hawaiian Is., U.S., N. Pac. Oc. 147 E9
Gascoyne Tablemount, Tasman Sea 164 J6
Gasparilla Island, U.S., G. of Mex. 139 D13
Gata, Cabo de, Sp. 131 G5
Gávdos, island, Gr., Medit. Sea 132 J8
Gdańsk, Pol. 106 E10
Gebe, island, Indonesia 187 E14
Gela Basin, Medit. Sea 132 G3
Gelam, island, Indonesia 181 N6
Gelasa, Selat, Indonesia 181 N4
Genoa see Genova, It. 132 C1
Genova (Genoa), It. 132 C1
Genova, Golfo di, It., Ligurian Sea 132 C1
Genovesa Island, Galápagos Is., Ecua., N. Pac. Oc. 147 G14
Geographe Bay, Austral., Ind. Oc. 187 J12
Geographical Society Island, Greenland, Den. 106 C7
George Bligh Bank, N. Atl. Oc. 104 D7
George Land, Franz Josef Land, Russ., Arctic Oc. 219 D10
George Town, Malaysia 187 D10
George V Fracture Zone, Ind. Oc. 249 D11
Gettysburg Seamount, N. Atl. Oc. 106 G8
Ghāghah, island, U.A.E., Persian G. 212 K7
Ghār, Ra's al, Saudi Arabia, Persian G. 212 F4
Ghadīra, Sha'b, Red Sea 210 D3
Ghent, Belg. 106 E9
Ghurāb, Ra's al, U.A.E., Persian G. 213 K10
Gibbs Seamount, Caribbean Sea 141 F14
Gibraltar, U.K. 131 H3
Gibraltar, Strait of, N. Atl. Oc. 131 H3
Giglio, island, It., Tyrrhenian Sea 132 D2
Gijón, Sp. 106 F8
Gilbert Islands, Micronesia, Kiribati, S. Pac. Oc. 164 D8
Gilbert Seamount, N. Pac. Oc. 145 C10
Gilbert Seamounts, N. Pac. Oc. 147 C10
Gioia Tauro, It. 106 F10
Gladstone, Austral. 146 J6
Gloria Ridge, N. Atl. Oc. 104 E5
Glorieuses Islands, Fr., Ind. Oc. 186 F4
Gloucester, Îles Duc de, Tuamotu Arch., Fr. Polynesia, Fr., S. Pac. Oc. 165 G13
Glover Reef, Caribbean Sea 140 F2
Gökçeada, island, Turk., Aegean Sea 133 E9
Gökova Körfezi, Turk., Aegean Sea 133 G10
Gold Coast, Af. 105 J8
Gomera, island, Canary Is., Sp., N. Atl. Oc. 106 G7
Gonaïves, Haiti 141 E9
Gonâve, Golfe de la, Haiti, Caribbean Sea 141 E9
Gonâve, Île de la, Haiti, Caribbean Sea 141 E9
Good Hope, Cape of, Af. 107 N10
Gorda, Banco, Caribbean Sea 140 G4
Gorda, Cayo, Hond., Caribbean Sea 140 G4
Göteborg, Sw. 106 D10
Gotland, island, Sw., Baltic Sea 106 D10
Gough, island, U.K., S. Atl. Oc. 107 N8
Gozo, island, Malta, Medit. Sea 132 H4
Gracias a Dios, Cabo, Nicar. 140 G4
Graciosa, island, Azores, Port., N. Atl. Oc. 106 F6
Graham Bell Island, Franz Josef Land, Russ., Arctic Oc. 219 D9
Graham Island, Queen Charlotte Is., Can., N. Pac. Oc. 147 C11
Grain Coast, 105 J8
Grainger Bank, S. China Sea 181 J6
Gran Canaria, island, Canary Is., Sp., N. Atl. Oc. 106 G7
Grand Bahama Island, Bahamas, N. Atl. Oc. 140 A7
Grand Banks of Newfoundland, N. Atl. Oc. 104 F4
Grand Caicos, island, Caicos Is., Turks & Caicos Is., U.K., N. Atl. Oc. 141 C10
Grand Cayman, island, Cayman Is., U.K., Caribbean Sea 140 E5
Grande Cayemite, island, Haiti, Caribbean Sea 141 E9
Grande de Santa Marta, Ciénaga, Col., Caribbean Sea 140 J8
Grande Terre, island, Kerguelen Is., Fr., Ind. Oc. 186 L7
Grande, Cayo, Jardines de la Reina, Cuba, Caribbean Sea 140 D6
Grande, Cayo, Lesser Antil., Venez., Caribbean Sea 141 J12
Grande-Terre, peninsula, Guadeloupe, Fr. 141 F15
Grand Lake, U.S. 138 B6
Grand Terre Islands, U.S., G. of Mex. 138 B8
Granville, Arrecife, G. of Mex. 138 H8
Grappler Bank, Caribbean Sea 140 E8
Great Australian Bight, Ind. Oc. 187 J14
Great Bahama Bank, N. Atl. Oc. 140 B6
Great Barrier Island, N.Z., S. Pac. Oc. 164 J8
Great Barrier Reef, Coral Sea 164 F4
Great Bitter Lake, Egypt 210 A2
Great Britain, island, U.K., N. Atl. Oc. 104 E8
Great Channel, India, Indonesia, Ind. Oc. 187 D10
Great Coco Island, Myanmar, Ind. Oc. 187 C9
Great Dividing Range, Austral. 164 F4
Greater Antilles, islands, Caribbean Sea 140 D6
Greater Sunda Islands, Asia 185 E11
Great Exuma, island, Exuma Cays, Bahamas, N. Atl. Oc. 140 B8
Great Guana Cay, Exuma Cays, Bahamas, N. Atl. Oc. 140 B7
Great Harbour Cay, Berry Is., Bahamas, N. Atl. Oc. 140 A7
Great Inagua Island, Bahamas, N. Atl. Oc. 41 D9
Great Isaac, island, Bahamas, N. Atl. Oc. 140 A6
Great Koldeway, island, Greenland, Den., Greenland Sea 219 G12
Great Meteor Tablemount, N. Atl. Oc. 104 G6
Great Nicobar, island, Nicobar Is., India, Ind. Oc. 187 D10
Great Pearl Bank, Persian G. 213 J9
Green Cay, Bahamas, N. Atl. Oc. 140 B7
Green Islands, Melanesia, P.N.G., S. Pac. Oc. 164 E5
Green Knob, G. of Mex. 138 D8
Greenland, island, Den. 217 J12
Greenland Fracture Zone, Greenland Sea 217 F12
Greenland Plain, Greenland Sea 217 F12
Greenland Sea, N. Atl. Oc. 106 B8
Grenada, island, Windward Is., Caribbean Sea 141 J15
Grenada Basin, Caribbean Sea 141 H15
Gröll Seamount, S. Atl. Oc. 107 L6
Groote Eylandt, island, Austral., G. of Carpentaria 187 F15
Grosvenor Seamount, N. Pac. Oc. 144 E7
Guacanayabo, Golfo de, Cuba, Caribbean Sea 140 D7
Guadalcanal, island, Solomon Is., S. Pac. Oc. 164 E6
Guadalupe Island, Mex., N. Pac. Oc. 147 E12
Guadeloupe, island, Fr., N. Atl. Oc. 141 G15
Guadeloupe Passage, N. Atl. Oc. 141 F15
Guadeloupe Seamount, N. Pac. Oc. 144 E7
Guadiana, Bahía, Cuba, G. of Mex. 139 H12
Guajaba, Cayo, Arch. de Camagüey, Cuba, N. Atl. Oc. 140 C7
Guajira, Península de la, Col. 141 J10
Guam, island, U.S., N. Pac. Oc. 164 B4
Guana, Cayo, Arch. de los Canarreos, Cuba, Caribbean Sea 140 C5
Guanaja, Isla de, Is. de la Bahía, Hond., Caribbean Sea 140 F3
Guancanayabo Trough, Caribbean Sea 140 E4
Guangzhou (Canton), China 180 B7
Guantánamo, Bahía de, Cuba, Caribbean Sea 140 D8
Guatemala Basin, N. Pac. Oc. 145 F14
Guayaquil, Ecua. 147 G15
Gûbâl, Strait of, Red Sea 210 C3
Guerrero, Cayos, Nicar., Caribbean Sea 140 H4
Guguan, island, N. Mariana Is., U.S., N. Pac. Oc. 187 B16
Guiana Basin, N. Atl. Oc. 105 J4
Guimaras, island, Philippines 187 C13
Guinchos Cay, Bahamas, N. Atl. Oc. 140 C7
Guinea Basin, S. Atl. Oc. 105 K8
Guinea Plain, S. Atl. Oc. 105 K8
Guinea Rise, S. Atl. Oc. 105 K8
Guinea Terrace, N. Atl. Oc. 105 J7
Guinea, Gulf of, N. Atl. Oc. 107 J9
Gulf of Mexico's deepest point, 138 E7
Gulfport, Miss., U.S. 138 A8
Gunnerus Bank, Cosmonaut Sea 248 E6
Gunnerus Ridge, Cosmonaut Sea 248 D6
Gusinaya Bank, Barents Sea 217 B12
Gwangyang, S. Korea 146 D4
Gyda Peninsula, Russ. 217 A10

Ha'apai Group, Tonga, S. Pac. Oc. 165 G9
Habibas Escarpment, Medit. Sea 131 H5
Habomai Islands, Russ., N. Pac. Oc. 146 D5
Ḩadārībah, Ra's al, Egypt, Red Sea 210 F4
Ḩadd, Ra's al, Oman 184 B6
Haddummati Atoll, Maldives, Ind. Oc. 186 D7
Hagemeister Island, U.S., Bering Sea 147 B9
Haha Jima Rettō, Bonin Is., Japan, N. Pac. Oc. 187 A15
Haifa see Ḩefa, Israel 133 K13
Haikou, China 180 C6
Hailing Dao, China, S. China Sea 180 C7
Hailouto, island, Fin., G. of Bothnia 106 D11
Hainan, island, China, S. China Sea 180 D6
Haiphong, Vietnam 180 C4
Haitan Island, China, E. China Sea 187 A13
Ḩālat al Baḩrānī, island, U.A.E., Persian G. 213 K10
Ḩālat al Ḩayl, island, U.A.E., Persian G. 213 K9
Halba Desēt, island, Eritrea, Red Sea 210 K7
Haldia, India 187 B9
Half Moon Reefs, Caribbean Sea 140 G4
Half Moon Shoal, S. China Sea 180 H8
Halifax, Can. 106 F3
Halīleh, Ra's-e, Iran, Persian G. 212 D6
Hall Basin, Can., Greenland, Den. 217 H10
Hall Islands, Caroline Is., F.S.M., N. Pac. Oc. 164 C5
Halmahera, island, Moluccas, Indonesia 164 D2
Halmahera Sea, Indonesia 187 E14
Halten Bank, Norwegian Sea 217 E15
Ḩālūl, island, Qatar, Persian G. 212 H8
Hamamet, Gulf of, Tun., Medit. Sea 132 H2
Hamburg, Ger. 106 E9
Ḩamrā', Jazīrat al, U.A.E., Persian G. 213 H12
Ḩanīsh al Kabīr, Jazīrat al, Yemen, Red Sea 210 K7
Ḩanyūrah, Ra's, U.A.E., Persian G. 213 K11
Hao, atoll, Tuamotu Arch., Fr. Polynesia, Fr., S. Pac. Oc. 165 G14
Hardy Reef, S. China Sea 180 H8
Harmil, island, Eritrea, Red Sea 210 J5
Harris Seamount, N. Pac. Oc. 145 C9
Hartman Abrolhos, islands, Austral., Ind. Oc. 187 H12
Ḩasan, Ra's al, Saudi Arabia, Red Sea 210 G6
Ḩaşyān, Ra's, U.A.E., Persian G. 213 J11
Ḩāţibah, Ra's, Saudi Arabia, Red Sea 210 F5
Hatteras, Cape, 106 G2
Hatteras Plain, N. Atl. Oc. 104 G3
Hatutu, island, Marquesas Is., Fr. Polynesia, Fr., S. Pac. Oc. 165 E14
Havana, Cuba 140 C4
Ḩawār, Jazīrat, Bahrain, Persian G. 212 H6
Hawai'i, island, Hawaiian Is., U.S., N. Pac. Oc. 165 A12
Hawaiian Islands, U.S., N. Pac. Oc. 144 E8
Hawaiian Ridge, N. Pac. Oc. 145 E9
Hay Point, Austral. 146 J6
Hayes Fracture Zone, N. Atl. Oc. 104 G5
Hayes Reef, S. China Sea 181 K7
Hazen Strait, Can. 218 J7
Heard Island, Austral., Ind. Oc. 250 B7
Hearst Island, Antarctica, Weddell Sea 107 R3
Hecataeus Knoll, Medit. Sea 133 J12
Hecate Strait, N. Pac. Oc. 147 C11
Ḩefa (Haifa), Israel 133 K13
Heimaey, island, Ice., N. Atl. Oc. 219 H15
Hellenic Trench, Medit. Sea 132 H7
Hellenic Trough, Medit. Sea 132 H7
Helen Island, Palau, N. Pac. Oc. 164 D2
Helen Shoal, S. China Sea 180 D7
Hellespont see Çanakkale Boğazı, Turk. 133 F9
Henderson Island, U.K., S. Pac. Oc. 165 G15
Henderson Ridge, G. of Mex. 139 E10
Henderson Seamount, N. Pac. Oc. 145 E12
Hendorābi, island, Iran, Persian G. 213 G9
Hengām, island, Iran, Persian G. 213 G12
Henrietta Island, New Siberian Is., Russ., Arctic Oc. 218 D6
Herald Bank, S. China Sea 180 E7
Herald Cays, Austral., Coral Sea 187 G16
Herald Reef, S. China Sea 181 K7
Herbert Island, Greenland, Den. 106 B3
Herdman Seamount, S. Atl. Oc. 105 P9
Hereheretue, atoll, Tuamotu Arch., Fr. Polynesia, Fr., S. Pac. Oc. 165 G13
Herodotus Abyssal Plain, Medit. Sea 132 K8
Herodotus Seamount, Medit. Sea 132 J6
Herodotus Trough, Medit. Sea 132 J7
Heron Valley, Medit. Sea 132 H5
Hervey Islands, Cook Is., N.Z., S. Pac. Oc. 165 G11
Hess Escarpment, Caribbean Sea 140 G7
Hess Rise, N. Pac. Oc. 144 D7
Hess Tablemount, N. Pac. Oc. 165 A10
Hick's Cays, Belize, Caribbean Sea 140 F1
Hierro, island, Canary Is., Sp., N. Atl. Oc. 106 G7
Hikueru, atoll, Tuamotu Arch., Fr. Polynesia, Fr., S. Pac. Oc. 165 F13
Hilāl, Ra's al, Lib. 132 K7
Hinchinbrook Island, Austral., Coral Sea 187 G16
Hindī Gider, island, Sudan, Red Sea 210 G4
Hinlopen Trough, Arctic Oc. 104 A10
Híos (Chios), island, Gr., Aegean Sea 133 F9
Hispaniola, island, Greater Antil., Caribbean Sea 141 E10
Hispaniola Basin, N. Atl. Oc. 141 D9
Hiva Oa, island, Marquesas Is., Fr. Polynesia, Fr., S. Pac. Oc. 165 E14
Hjort Trench, S. Pac. Oc. 249 E12
Ho Chi Minh City (Saigon), Vietnam 180 G4
Hoàng Sa see Xisha Qundao, S. China Sea 180 E6
Hobart, Austral. 164 K4
Hoffman's Cay, Berry Is., Bahamas, N. Atl. Oc. 140 A7
Hog Island, U.S., G. of Mex. 139 B13
Hogsty Reef, Bahamas, N. Atl. Oc. 141 C9
Hokkaido, island, Japan 146 D5
Holbox, Isla, Mex., G. of Mex. 139 H10
Homosassa Islands, U.S., G. of Mex. 139 B13
Honda, Bahía, Col., Caribbean Sea 141 J10
Honduras, Gulf of, Caribbean Sea 140 F2
Hong Gai, Vietnam 180 C4
Hong Kong (Xianggan), China 180 B8
Honiara, Solomon Is. 164 E6
Hon Khoai, island, Vietnam, S. China Sea 180 H3
Hon Lon, island, Vietnam, S. China Sea 180 G5
Hon Me, island, Vietnam, G. of Tonkin 180 D4
Honolulu, Hawaii, U.S. 165 A11
Honshu, island, Japan 146 D5

342 MAP PLACE-NAME INDEX | FERNANDO DE NORONHA – HONSHU

Hope, Point, *U.S.* **218** G3
Hopen, island, *Svalbard, Nor., Arctic Oc.* **219** D12
Hormoz, island, *Iran, Persian G.* **213** F13
Hormuz, Strait of, *Persian G.* **213** G13
Horn, Cape, *S. Am.* **107** Q3
Horne, Îles de, *Wallis Is., Fr., S. Pac. Oc.* **165** F9
Horn Island, *U.S., G. of Mex.* **139** A9
Horseshoe Cove, *U.S., G. of Mex.* **139** B13
Hotspur Seamount, *S. Atl. Oc.* **105** L6
Hound Point, *U.K.* **106** E8
Houston, *U.S.* **106** G1
Howell Hook, *G. of Mex.* **139** E12
Howland Island, *Polynesia, U.S., N. Pac. Oc.* **165** D9
Huahine, island, *Society Is., Fr. Polynesia, Fr., S. Pac. Oc.* **165** F12
Huangpu, *China* **146** E3
Hudson Bay, **106** D1
Hudson Canyon, *N. Atl. Oc.* **104** F3
Hudson Strait, **106** D3
Hue, *Vietnam* **180** E5
Hugo Island, *Palmer Arch., Antarctica, S. Pac. Oc.* **107** R3
Humboldt Plain, *S. Pac. Oc.* **145** L15
Hunter, island, *Vanuatu, S. Pac. Oc.* **164** G8
Hunter Islands, *Austral.* **187** K16
Huon, Île, *New Caledonia, Fr., S. Pac. Oc.* **164** F6
Huon Gulf, *P.N.G., Solomon Sea* **164** E4
Hurghada, *Egypt* **210** C3
Hvar, island, *Croatia, Adriatic Sea* **132** D5
Hyères, Îles d', *Fr., Medit. Sea* **131** D8

Iberian Basin, *N. Atl. Oc.* **104** F7
Iberian Peninsula, **104** F8
Ibiza, island, *Balearic Is., Sp., Medit. Sea* **131** F6
İçel *see* Mersin, *Turk.* **133** G13
Iceland, island, *N. Atl. Oc.* **104** D7
Iceland Basin, *N. Atl. Oc.* **104** D7
Iceland Plateau, *N. Atl. Oc.* **104** C7
Ifalik Atoll, *Caroline Is., F.S.M., N. Pac. Oc.* **164** C4
Ihavandiffulu Atoll, *Maldives, Ind. Oc.* **186** D7
IJmuiden, *Neth.* **106** E9
Ikaría, island, *Gr., Aegean Sea* **133** G9
Iligan Point, *Philippines* **180** D11
Iltis Bank, *S. China Sea* **180** E7
Imarssuak Seachannel, *N. Atl. Oc.* **104** E5
Immingham, *U.K.* **106** E9
Imperia, *It.* **132** C1
Inaccessible Island, *U.K., S. Atl. Oc.* **107** N8
Inaccessible Islands, *Antarctica, S. Atl. Oc.* **107** Q5
Incheon, *S. Korea* **146** D4
Indochina Peninsula, *Asia* **144** F2
Indomed Fracture Zone, *Ind. Oc.* **184** K4
Indus Fan, *Arabian Sea* **184** B6
Ingleses, Bancos, *G. of Mex.* **138** H6
Inner Hebrides, islands, *U.K., N. Atl. Oc.* **106** E8
Investigator Ridge, *Ind. Oc.* **185** F10
Investigator Shoal, *S. China Sea* **181** J8
Iolkós *see* Vólos, *Gr.* **132** F8
Ionian Abyssal Plain, *Ionian Sea* **132** H6
Ionian Gap, *Medit. Sea* **132** J6
Ionian Islands, *Gr., Ionian Sea* **132** G6
Ionian Sea, *Medit. Sea* **132** G5
Iráklio (Candia), *Gr.* **133** H9
Ireland, island, *N. Atl. Oc.* **104** E8
Iriomote, island, *Ryukyu Is., Japan, N. Pac. Oc.* **187** B13
Irving Reef, *S. China Sea* **180** G8
Irving Seamount, *Medit. Sea* **133** K10
Isabela, Cabo, *Dom. Rep.* **141** D10
Isabela Island, *Galápagos Is., Ecua., S. Pac. Oc.* **147** G14
Isachenko Island, *Russ., Kara Sea* **219** B9
Isakov Seamount, *N. Pac. Oc.* **144** E6
Ischia, island, *It., Tyrrhenian Sea* **132** E4
Iselin Bank, *S. Pac. Oc.* **249** F11
Ishigaki, island, *Ryukyu Is., Japan, N. Pac. Oc.* **187** B13
İskenderun (Alexandretta), *Turk.* **133** H13
İskenderun Körfezi, *Turk., Medit. Sea* **133** H13
Islas Orcadas Rise, *S. Atl. Oc.* **105** P6
Isra-tu, island, *Eritrea, Red Sea* **210** J5
İstanbul (Constantinople), *Turk.* **133** E10
İstanbul Boğazı (Bosporus), *Turk.* **133** E10
Itajaí, *Braz.* **107** M5
Itbayat, island, *Batan Is., Philippines, Luzon Str.* **180** C11
Itu Aba Island, *Spratly Is., S. China Sea* **180** H8
Iturup, island, *Kuril Is., Russ., N. Pac. Oc.* **146** C5
Iviza, island, *Balearic Is., Sp., Medit. Sea* **106** F9
Ivory Coast, **105** J8
Iwo Jima *see* Iwo To, island, *Japan, N. Pac. Oc.* **164** A4
Iwo To (Iwo Jima), island, *Japan, N. Pac. Oc.* **164** A4
Izabal, Lago de, *Guatemala* **140** G1
İzmir (Smyrna), *Turk.* **133** F9
İzmir Körfezi, *Turk., Aegean Sea* **133** F9
Izu Trench, *N. Pac. Oc.* **144** E5

Jabal Şabāyā, Jazīrat, *Saudi Arabia, Red Sea* **210** G6
Jabal Zuqar, Jazīrat, *Yemen, Red Sea* **210** K7
Jabrīn, island, *Iran, Persian G.* **212** E6
Jabuka Shoal, *Adriatic Sea* **132** D4
Jackson Atoll, *Spratly Is., S. China Sea* **180** H8
Jacksonville, *U.S.* **106** G2
Jaime Seamount, *Medit. Sea* **131** F7
Jakarta, *Indonesia* **181** P4
Jalitah Island, *Tun., Medit. Sea* **132** G1
Jaluit Atoll, *Ralik Chain, Marshall Is., N. Pac. Oc.* **164** C7
Jamaica, island, *Greater Antil., Caribbean Sea* **140** E7
Jamaica Cay, *Bahamas, N. Atl. Oc.* **140** C8
Jamaican Plain, *Caribbean Sea* **140** G6
James Ross Island, *Antarctica, Weddell Sea* **107** R4
Jan Mayen, island, *Nor., Norwegian Sea* **106** C8
Jan Mayen Fracture Zone, *Norwegian Sea* **104** C8
Jan Mayen Ridge, *Norwegian Sea* **104** C8
Japan, Sea of (East Sea), *N. Pac. Oc.* **146** D4
Japan Trench, *N. Pac. Oc.* **144** D5
Jardines de la Reina, islands, *Cuba, Caribbean Sea* **140** D6
Jārīm, Fasht al, *Persian G.* **212** G5
Jarvis Island, *U.S., N. Pac. Oc.* **165** D11
Jāsk, *Iran* **213** H15
Jason Peninsula, *Antarctica* **105** R4
Jasper Seamount, *N. Pac. Oc.* **147** E12
Java (Jawa), island, *Greater Sunda Is., Indonesia* **181** Q5
Java Ridge, *Ind. Oc.* **185** F11
Java Sea, *Indonesia* **181** P5
Java Trench, *Ind. Oc.* **185** F11
Jawa *see* Java, island, *Greater Sunda Is., Indonesia* **181** Q5
Jawaharlal Nehru, *India* **186** B7
Jayapura, *Indonesia* **164** D3
Jeannette Island, *New Siberian Is., Russ., Arctic Oc.* **218** D5
Jebel Ali, *U.A.E.* **186** A5
Jebel Dhanna, *U.A.E.* **186** B5
Jeddah, *Saudi Arabia* **210** F5
Jehangire Reefs, *S. China Sea* **180** E7
Jeju Island, *S. Korea, E. China Sea* **146** D4
Jemaja, island, *Kep. Anambas, Indonesia, S. China Sea* **181** L4
Jembongan, island, *Malaysia, Sulu Sea* **181** J9
Jens Munk Island, *Greenland, Den.* **106** D5
Jerba Island, *Tun., Medit. Sea* **132** J2
Jérémie, *Haiti* **141** E9
Jerez, Punta, *Mex.* **138** G2
Jiguey, Bahía de, *Cuba* **140** C6
Jimmu Seamount, *N. Pac. Oc.* **146** C7
Jingū Seamount, *N. Pac. Oc.* **146** D7
Jiulong, *China* **180** B8
Jiuzhou Yang, bay, *China, S. China Sea* **180** B7
Jīzān, *Saudi Arabia* **210** H7
Johnston Atoll, *U.S., N. Pac. Oc.* **165** B10
Johor Baharu, *Malaysia* **181** L3
Joinville Island, *Antarctica, Weddell Sea* **107** R4
Jolo, island, *Sulu Arch., Philippines* **181** K11
Jones Sound, *Can., Baffin B.* **219** J9
Jordan Knoll, *G. of Mex.* **139** G12
Joseph Bonaparte Gulf, *Austral., Timor Sea* **164** F2
Josephine Seamount, *N. Atl. Oc.* **104** G7
Joulter Cays, *Bahamas, N. Atl. Oc.* **140** A6
Juan de Fuca Ridge, *N. Pac. Oc.* **145** C11
Juan de Nova Island, *Fr., Mozambique Ch.* **186** G3
Juan Fernández Islands, *Chile, S. Pac. Oc.* **147** K15
Juaymah, *Saudi Arabia* **186** A4
Jubail, *Saudi Arabia* **186** A4
Judge Seamount, *N. Pac. Oc.* **146** E7
Julia Shoal, *S. China Sea* **180** H5
Juventud, Isla de la (Isle of Youth), *Cuba, Caribbean Sea* **140** D4

Kabaena, island, *Indonesia* **181** P11
Kadavu, island, *Fiji Is., S. Pac. Oc.* **164** G8
Kaho'olawe, island, *Hawaiian Is., U.S., N. Pac. Oc.* **165** A12
Kai Islands, *Indonesia* **164** E3
Kalao, island, *Indonesia, Flores Sea* **181** Q10
Kalaotoa, island, *Indonesia, Flores Sea* **181** Q11
Kalbā, *U.A.E.* **213** J13
Kalimantan, region, *Indonesia* **181** M7
Kamarān, island, *Yemen, Red Sea* **210** J7
Kamchatka Peninsula, *Asia* **144** B6
Kammu Seamount, *N. Pac. Oc.* **146** D7
Kanaga Island, *Andreanof Is., U.S., N. Pac. Oc.* **146** C8
Kandla, *India* **186** B7
Kane Basin, *Can., Greenland, Den.* **217** H9
Kane Fracture Zone, *N. Atl. Oc.* **104** H4
Kangaroo Island, *Austral., Ind. Oc.* **164** J3
Kangean, Kepulauan, *Indonesia* **181** Q8
Kanton, island, *Phoenix Is., Kiribati, S. Pac. Oc.* **146** G8
Kaohsiung, *Taiwan, China* **180** B10
Kapingamarangi Atoll, *Caroline Is., F.S.M., N. Pac. Oc.* **146** G6
Kara Sea, *Arctic Oc.* **219** C9
Karachi, *Pak.* **186** A6
Karaginskiy Island, *Russ., Bering Sea* **146** B7
Karakaralong Islands, *Indonesia* **187** D13
Karakelong, island, *Indonesia* **187** D13
Karamian, island, *Indonesia, Java Sea* **181** P8
Karimata, island, *Kep. Karimata, Indonesia* **181** N5
Karimata, Kepulauan, *Indonesia* **181** N5
Karimata, Selat, *Indonesia* **181** N5
Karimunjawa, Kepulauan, *Indonesia, Java Sea* **181** P6
Karkar, island, *P.N.G., Bismarck Sea* **187** E16
Karompa, island, *Indonesia, Flores Sea* **181** Q11
Kárpathos, island, *Gr., Medit. Sea* **133** H9
Kárpathos Stenón, *Gr., Medit. Sea* **133** H9
Kashima, *Japan* **146** D5
Kasr, Ra's, *Sudan, Red Sea* **210** H5
Kássos, island, *Gr., Medit. Sea* **133** H9
Kássos Stenón, *Gr., Medit. Sea* **133** H9
Katīb, Ra's al, *Yemen, Red Sea* **210** J7
Kattegat, strait, **106** E10
Kaua'i, island, *Hawaiian Is., U.S., N. Pac. Oc.* **165** A11
Ka'ula, island, *Hawaiian Is., U.S., N. Pac. Oc.* **165** A11
Kavála (Neapolis), *Gr.* **132** E8
Kavaratti, island, *Lakshadweep, India, Arabian Sea* **186** C7
Kawasaki, *Japan* **146** D5
Kayak Island, *U.S., G. of Alas.* **147** B10
Kayangel Islands, *Palau, N. Pac. Oc.* **187** D14
Kazan Rettō *see* Volcano Islands, *Japan, N. Pac. Oc.* **164** A4
Kéa, island, *Kiklådes, Gr., Aegean Sea* **132** G8
Keathley Canyon, *G. of Mex.* **138** D5
Kebrit Deep, *Red Sea* **210** E4
Keeling Islands *see* Cocos Islands, *Austral., Ind. Oc.* **187** F10
Kefaloniá, island, *Ionian Is., Gr., Ionian Sea* **132** G6
Kelvin Seamount, *N. Atl. Oc.* **104** F3
Kenai Peninsula, *U.S.* **216** K2
Kennedy Channel, *Can., Greenland, Den.* **219** H9
Kerguelen Islands, *Fr., Ind. Oc.* **186** L7
Kerguelen Plateau, *Ind. Oc.* **184** L7
Kérkira (Corfu), island, *Ionian Is., Gr., Ionian Sea* **132** F6
Kermadec Islands, *N.Z., S. Pac. Oc.* **165** H9
Kermadec Trench, *S. Pac. Oc.* **144** K8
Kern Seamount, *N. Pac. Oc.* **147** D9
Ketoy, island, *Kuril Is., Russ., N. Pac. Oc.* **146** C6
Key West, *Fla., U.S.* **140** B5
Khafji, Ra's al, *Saudi Arabia, Persian G.* **212** D3
Khambhat, Gulf of, *India, Arabian Sea* **186** B7
Khān, Ra's-e, *Iran, Persian G.* **212** E6
Khark, island, *Iran, Persian G.* **212** C5
Khārkū, island, *Iran, Persian G.* **212** C5
Kharrār, Shi'b, *Red Sea* **210** E5
Khaşab, *Oman* **213** H13
Khayseh, Ra's, *Oman, Persian G.* **213** H13
Khor Fakkan, *U.A.E.* **186** A5
Kidurong, Tanjong, *Malaysia* **181** L7
Kikaiga, island, *Ryukyu Is., Japan, N. Pac. Oc.* **187** A14
Kikládes (Cyclades), islands, *Gr., Aegean Sea* **133** G9
Kili Island, *Ralik Chain, Marshall Is., N. Pac. Oc.* **164** C7
King, Cayo, *Nicar., Caribbean Sea* **140** H4
King George Island, *S. Shetland Is., Antarctica, Drake Pass.* **107** Q4
King Island, *Austral., Bass Str.* **164** K4
King Island, *U.S., Bering Sea* **147** A9
Kingman Reef, *U.S., N. Pac. Oc.* **165** C11
King Sound, *Austral., Ind. Oc.* **187** G13
Kingston, *Jam.* **140** E7
Kingston Shoal, *S. China Sea* **181** J6
Kingstown, *St. Vincent & the Grenadines* **141** H15
King William Island, *Can., Arctic Oc.* **218** L8
Kiritimati (Christmas Island), *Line Is., Austral., N. Pac. Oc.* **165** D12
Kirkwood Islands, *Antarctica, Bellingshausen Sea* **107** R3
Kīsh, island, *Iran, Persian G.* **213** G10
Kiska Island, *Rat Is., U.S., N. Pac. Oc.* **146** C8
Kita Daitō Island, *Daito Is., Japan, Philippine Sea* **146** E4
Kita Iwo To, *Volcano Is., Japan, N. Pac. Oc.* **187** A15
Kíthira (Cerigo), island, *Gr., Medit. Sea* **132** H8
Kíthnos, island, *Kiklådes, Gr., Aegean Sea* **132** G8
Kitty Hawk Seamount, *S. China Sea* **180** H6
Klaipėda, *Lith.* **106** E10
Klein Curaçao, island, *Lesser Antil., Neth., Caribbean Sea* **141** J11
Knipovich Ridge, *Greenland Sea* **104** B9
Kobe, *Japan* **146** D5
Kodiak Island, *U.S., G. of Alas.* **147** B10
Kodiak Seamount, *N. Pac. Oc.* **145** B10
Kola Peninsula, *Russ.* **217** B13
Kolbeinsey Ridge, *N. Atl. Oc.* **104** C7
Kolguyev Island, *Russ., Barents Sea* **219** B12
Kolumadulu Atoll, *Maldives, Ind. Oc.* **186** D7
Komodo, island, *Indonesia* **181** Q10
Komsomolets Island, *N. Land, Russ., Arctic Oc.* **218** C8
Kong, Koh, *Cambodia, G. of Thai.* **180** G3
Kong Karls Basin, *Barents Sea* **104** A11
Kong Karls Land, *Svalbard, Nor.* **106** B11
Korčula, island, *Croatia, Adriatic Sea* **132** D5
Korean Peninsula, *Asia* **144** D4
Korinthiakós Kólpos, *Gr., Ionian Sea* **132** G7
Kórinthos Canal, *Gr.* **132** G8
Kornat, island, *Croatia, Adriatic Sea* **132** C4
Kos, island, *Dodekánissa, Gr., Aegean Sea* **133** G9
Kosrae (Kusaie), island, *Caroline Is., F.S.M., N. Pac. Oc.* **164** C6
Kota Baharu, *Malaysia* **181** J2
Kota Kinabalu, *Malaysia* **181** J8
Kotzebue Sound, *U.S., Chukchi Sea* **218** H3
Kra, Isthmus of, *Thailand* **180** H1
Kríti (Crete), island, *Gr., Medit. Sea* **132** H8
Krk, island, *Croatia, Adriatic Sea* **132** B4
Krung Thep (Bangkok), *Thailand* **180** F2
Krylov Seamount, *N. Atl. Oc.* **104** H6
Kuala Terengganu, *Malaysia* **181** K3
Kuantan, *Malaysia* **181** K3
Kubbar, island, *Kuwait, Persian G.* **212** C3
Kūchek, Tonb-e, *Iran, Persian G.* **213** H11
Kūh, Ra's al, *Iran, Persian G.* **213** H14
Kumzār, *Oman* **213** G13
Kunashir, island, *Kuril Is., Russ., N. Pac. Oc.* **146** C5
Kunié *see* Pins, Île des, *New Caledonia, Fr., S. Pac. Oc.* **164** G7
Kupreanof Island, *Alexander Arch., U.S., N. Pac. Oc.* **147** B11
Kure Atoll, *Hawaiian Is., U.S., N. Pac. Oc.* **146** E8
Kuria Muria Islands, *Oman, Arabian Sea* **186** B5
Kuril Basin, *Sea of Okhotsk* **144** C5
Kuril Islands, *Russ., N. Pac. Oc.* **146** C6
Kuril Trench, *N. Pac. Oc.* **144** D5
Kuşadası Körfezi, *Turk., Aegean Sea* **133** G9
Kusaie *see* Kosrae, island, *Caroline Is., F.S.M., N. Pac. Oc.* **164** C6
Kut, Ko, *Thailand, G. of Thai.* **180** G2
Kutch, Gulf of, *India, Arabian Sea* **186** B7
Kuwait *see* Al Kuwayt, *Kuwait* **212** C2
Kuwayt, Jūn al, *Persian G.* **212** C2
Kvarner, bay, *Croatia, Adriatic Sea* **132** C4
Kvarnerić, bay, *Croatia, Adriatic Sea* **132** C4
Kvitøya, island, *Svalbard, Nor., Arctic Oc.* **219** D11
Kwajalein Atoll, *Ralik Chain, Marshall Is., N. Pac. Oc.* **164** C7
Kyushu, island, *Japan* **146** D4
Kyushu-Palau Ridge, *Philippine Sea* **144** F5

Labrador, region, **104** D3
Labrador Sea, *N. Atl. Oc.* **106** D4
Labrador Basin, *N. Atl. Oc.* **104** E5
Labuan, island, *Malaysia, S. China Sea* **181** K8
Laccadive Sea, *Arabian Sea* **186** C7
La Costa Islands, *U.S., G. of Mex.* **139** D13
La Désirade, island, *Guadeloupe, Fr., N. Atl. Oc.* **141** F15
Laem Chabang, *Thailand* **146** F2
Laem Pho, island, *Thailand, G. of Thai.* **181** J2
Laffān, Ra's, *Qatar, Persian G.* **212** H7
Lake Charles, *U.S.* **106** G1
Lakonikós Kólpos, *Gr., Medit. Sea* **132** H7
Lakshadweep, islands, *India, Arabian Sea* **186** C7
Lampedusa, island, *Is. Pelagie, It., Medit. Sea* **132** H3
Lāna'i, island, *Hawaiian Is., U.S., N. Pac. Oc.* **165** A12
La Nao, Cabo de, *Sp.* **131** F6
Lan Island, *Taiwan, China, Philippine Sea* **187** B13
Lan Yü, island, *Taiwan, China, Philippine Sea* **180** C11
Lancaster Sound, *Can., Baffin B.* **219** K9
Langkawi, island, *Malaysia, Str. of Malacca* **181** J1
Lankiam Cay, *Spratly Is., S. China Sea* **180** G8
Lanzarote, island, *Canary Is., Sp., N. Atl. Oc.* **106** G7
La Orchila Basin, *Caribbean Sea* **141** J13
La Palma, island, *Canary Is., Sp., N. Atl. Oc.* **106** G7
La Perouse Pinnacle, *Hawaiian Is., U.S., N. Pac. Oc.* **165** A10

HOPE — LA PEROUSE PINNACLE | MAP PLACE-NAME INDEX 343

Laptev Sea, Arctic Oc. 218 C7
Lārak, island, Iran, Persian G. 213 G13
Largo, Cayo, Arch. de los Canarreos, Cuba, Caribbean Sea 140 C5
Largo, Key, Fla. Keys, U.S., G. of Mex. 139 F15
Larsen Ice Shelf, Weddell Sea 248 H7
La Sola, island, Venez., Caribbean Sea 141 J14
Las Palmas, Canary Is., Sp. 106 G7
La Spezia, It. 132 C2
Latakia see Al Lādhiqīyah, Syr. 133 H13
Latakia Basin, Medit. Sea 133 H13
La Tortuga, Isla, Venez., Caribbean Sea 141 J13
Lau Basin, S. Pac. Oc. 144 J8
Lau Group, Fiji Is., S. Pac. Oc. 165 F9
Laurentian Fan, N. Atl. Oc. 104 F4
Lau Ridge, S. Pac. Oc. 144 J8
Laurie Island, S. Orkney Is., Antarctica, Scotia Sea 107 Q5
Laurot Islands see Laut Kecil, Kepulauan, Indonesia, Java Sea 181 P9
Laut, island, Indonesia, S. China Sea 181 K5
Laut, island, Indonesia 181 P8
Laut Kecil, Kepulauan (Laurot Islands), Indonesia, Java Sea 181 P8
Lavacaa Bay, U.S., G. of Mex. 138 B3
Lāvān, island, Iran, Persian G. 213 G9
Lavoisier Island, Palmer Arch., Antarctica, S. Pac. Oc. 107 R3
Laysan Island, Hawaiian Is., U.S., N. Pac. Oc. 146 E8
Leclaire Rise, Ind. Oc. 248 B6
Leeward Islands, Lesser Antil., Caribbean Sea 141 F14
Lefkáda, island, Ionian Is., Gr., Ionian Sea 132 F7
Leghorn see Livorno, It. 132 C2
Le Havre, Fr. 106 E9
Leizhou Bandao, China 180 C6
Lemesos (Limassol), Cyprus 133 J12
Lena Tablemount, Ind. Oc. 248 C6
Lena Trough, Arctic Oc. 104 A8
Lesbos see Lésvos, island, Gr., Aegean Sea 133 F9
Lesbos Basin, Aegean Sea 133 F9
L'Esperance Rock, Kermadec Is., N.Z., S. Pac. Oc. 165 J9
Les Saintes, islands, Guadeloupe, Fr., Caribbean Sea 141 G15
Lesser Antilles, islands, Caribbean Sea 141 F14
Lesser Sunda Islands, Indonesia, Ind. Oc. 164 E1
Lésvos (Lesbos), island, Gr., Aegean Sea 133 F9
Levantine Basin, Medit. Sea 133 J10
Lexington Seamount, S. China Sea 180 F6
Leyte, island, Philippines 164 C1
Lianyungang, China 146 D3
Licosa, Punta, It. 132 E4
Lifou, island, Loyalty Is., New Caledonia, Fr., S. Pac. Oc. 164 G7
Ligeti Ridge, Weddell Sea 105 Q6
Lighthouse Point, U.S. 139 B12
Lighthouse Reef, Caribbean Sea 140 F2
Ligurian Sea, Medit. Sea 132 C1
Līmā, Oman 213 H13
Līmā', Ra's, Oman, Persian G. 213 H13
Limassol see Lemesos, Cyprus 133 J12
Límnos, island, Gr., Aegean Sea 133 F9
Linapacan, island, Calamian Group, Philippines 180 G10
Lincoln Island, Xisha Qundao, China, S. China Sea 180 E7
Lincoln Sea, Arctic Oc. 219 G9
Line Islands, Kiribati, S. Pac. Oc. 165 C11
Lingga, island, Kep. Lingga, Indonesia 181 M3
Lingga, Kepulauan, Indonesia 181 M3
Linosa, island, Is. Pelagie, It., Medit. Sea 132 H3
Linosa Trough, Medit. Sea 132 H3
Lion, Golfe du, Fr., Medit. Sea 131 D7
Lipari, Isole, It., Tyrrhenian Sea 132 F4
Lisbon, Port. 106 F8
Lisburne, Cape, U.S. 218 G3
Lisianski Island, Hawaiian Is., U.S., N. Pac. Oc. 146 E8
Litke Trough, Arctic Oc. 104 A10
Little Andaman, island, Andaman Is., India, B. of Bengal 187 C9
Little Bahama Bank, N. Atl. Oc. 140 A7
Little Cayman, island, Cayman Is., U.K., Caribbean Sea 140 E5
Little Exuma, island, Exuma Cays, Bahamas, N. Atl. Oc. 140 B7
Little Inagua Island, Bahamas, N. Atl. Oc. 141 D9
Little San Salvador, island, Bahamas, N. Atl. Oc. 140 B8
Liuch'iu Yü, island, Taiwan, China, S. China Sea 180 B10
Liverpool, U.K. 106 E8
Livingston Island, S. Shetland Is., Antarctica, Drake Pass. 107 Q4
Livorno (Leghorn), It. 132 C2
Lloyd Ridge, G. of Mex. 139 D10
Loaita Island, Spratly Is., S. China Sea 180 G8
Lobos, Cayo, Mex., Caribbean Sea 140 E2
Lobos, Isla de, Mex., G. of Mex. 138 H3
Lofoten, island, Nor. 106 C10
Loks Land, Can. 106 D3
Lomblen, island, Indonesia 164 E1
Lombok, island, Lesser Sunda Is., Indonesia 181 Q9
Lombok, Selat, Indonesia 181 Q8
Lomonosov Ridge, Arctic Oc. 216 E7
London Reef, Caribbean Sea 140 H4
London Reefs, S. China Sea 180 H7
Long Beach, U.S. 147 D12
Longboat Key, U.S., G. of Mex. 139 D13
Long Cay, Bahamas, N. Atl. Oc. 140 C8
Long Island, Bahamas, N. Atl. Oc. 140 B8
Long Island, P.N.G., Bismarck Sea 187 E16
Long Key, Fla. Keys, U.S., G. of Mex. 139 F14
Lord Auckland Shoal, S. China Sea 180 H9
Lord Howe Island, Austral., Tasman Sea 164 H6
Lord Howe Rise, S. Pac. Oc. 144 J6
Lorien Bank, N. Atl. Oc. 104 E7
Los Angeles, U.S. 147 D12
Losap Atoll, Caroline Is., F.S.M., N. Pac. Oc. 164 C5
Los Frailes, islands, Venez., Caribbean Sea 141 J14
Los Hermanos, islands, Lesser Antil., Venez., Caribbean Sea 141 J13
Los Monjes, Islas, Lesser Antil., Venez., Caribbean Sea 141 H10
Los Roques, Islas, Lesser Antil., Venez., Caribbean Sea 141 J12
Los Roques Basin, Caribbean Sea 141 H12
Los Testigos, islands, Venez., Caribbean Sea 141 J14
Louisa Reef, S. China Sea 181 J7
Louisiade Archipelago, P.N.G., Coral Sea 164 F5
Louisiana Offshore Oil Port, U.S. 106 G1
Louisville Ridge, S. Pac. Oc. 144 J8
Low Cay, Caribbean Sea 140 G6
Loyalty Islands, New Caledonia, Fr., S. Pac. Oc. 164 G7
Lubang Island, Philippines, S. China Sea 180 F10
Lü Island, Taiwan, China, Philippine Sea 187 B13
Lund Valley, G. of Mex. 139 D9
Luodou Sha, island, China, S. China Sea 180 C6
Lü Tao, island, Taiwan, China, Philippine Sea 180 B11
Luzon, island, Philippines 164 B1
Luzon Strait, Philippines, China 180 C10
Lyakhov Islands, New Siberian Is., Russ., Arctic Oc. 218 C5
Lys Shoal, S. China Sea 180 G8

Macauley Island, Kermadec Is., N.Z., S. Pac. Oc. 146 J8
Macclesfield Bank, S. China Sea 180 E7
Machona, Laguna, Mex., G. of Mex. 138 L5
Mackenzie King Island, Queen Elizabeth Is., Can., Arctic Oc. 218 J7
Mackenzie Trough, Beaufort Sea 216 J5
Macquarie Island, Austral., S. Pac. Oc. 251 D12
Macquarie Ridge, S. Pac. Oc. 144 L6
Madagascar, island, Ind. Oc. 184 H4
Madagascar Basin, Ind. Oc. 184 H5
Madagascar Plateau, Ind. Oc. 184 H4
Maddalena, Isola, It., Medit. Sea 132 E2
Madeira, island, Madeira Is., Port., N. Atl. Oc. 106 G7
Madeira Islands, Port., N. Atl. Oc. 106 G7
Madras see Chennai, India 186 C8
Madre, Laguna, Mex., U.S., G. of Mex. 138 D2
Madre de Deus, Braz. 107 L5
Madura, island, Indonesia 181 Q7
Madura, Selat, Indonesia, Bali Sea 181 Q7
Maéwo, island, Vanuatu, S. Pac. Oc. 146 H7
Mafia Island, Tanzania, Ind. Oc. 186 F3
Magallanes Bank, N. Atl. Oc. 140 C7
Magdalena Fan, Caribbean Sea 140 J7
Magellan Rise, N. Pac. Oc. 144 G8
Magellan Seamounts, N. Pac. Oc. 144 F6
Magerøya, island, Nor. 106 C11
Mahé Island, Seychelles, Ind. Oc. 186 E5
Maiana, atoll, Gilbert Is., Kiribati, S. Pac. Oc. 164 D8
Mai-Liao, Taiwan, China 146 E3
Maine, Gulf of, N. Atl. Oc. 106 F3
Mainland, island, Shetland Is., U.K., N. Atl. Oc. 106 D8
Maio, island, C. Verde Is., C. Verde, N. Atl. Oc. 106 H7
Maisí, Cabo, Cuba 141 D9
Maíz Grande, Isla del, Nicar., Caribbean Sea 140 J4
Maíz Pequeña, Isla del, Nicar., Caribbean Sea 140 J4
Majorca, island, Balearic Is., Sp., Medit. Sea 106 F9
Majores del Cabo Falso, Cayos, Hond., Caribbean Sea 140 G4
Majuro, Marshall Is. 164 C8
Majuro Atoll, Marshall Is., N. Pac. Oc. 144 F7
Makarov Basin, Arctic Oc. 216 E6
Makarov Seamount, N. Pac. Oc. 144 E6
Makassar see Ujungpandang, Indonesia 181 P10
Makassar Strait, Indonesia 181 N9
Makatea, island, Tuamotu Arch., Fr. Polynesia, Fr., S. Pac. Oc. 165 F13
Makemo, atoll, Tuamotu Arch., Fr. Polynesia, Fr., S. Pac. Oc. 165 F13
Maléas, Akrotírio, Gr. 132 H8
Malacca, Strait of, Indonesia, Malaysia 181 K1
Málaga, Sp. 131 G4
Malaita, island, Solomon Is., S. Pac. Oc. 164 E6
Malakula, island, Vanuatu, S. Pac. Oc. 164 F7
Malay Peninsula, Asia 185 D10
Malden Island, Line Is., Kiribati, S. Pac. Oc. 165 E12
Maldive Islands, Ind. Oc. 184 D7
Male Atoll, Maldives, Ind. Oc. 186 D7
Mallawli, island, Malaysia, Sulu Sea 181 J9
Mallorca, island, Balearic Is., Sp., Medit. Sea 131 F7
Maloelap Atoll, Ratak Chain, Marshall Is., N. Pac. Oc. 164 C7
Malpelo Island, Col., N. Pac. Oc. 147 G15
Malta, island, Malta, Medit. Sea 132 H4
Malta Channel, Medit. Sea 132 H4
Malta Rise, Medit. Sea 132 H4
Malta Trough, Medit. Sea 132 H3
Malvinas, Islas see Falkland Islands, U.K., S. Pac. Oc. 147 L16
Man Island, Bahamas, N. Atl. Oc. 140 A7
Manam, island, P.N.G., Bismarck Sea 187 E16
Manama see Al Manāmah, Bahrain 212 H5
Mandab, Bāb al, Red Sea 210 K7
Manfredonia, It. 132 E4
Manfredonia, Golfo di, It., Adriatic Sea 132 E5
Mangaia, island, Cook Is., N.Z., S. Pac. Oc. 165 G11
Mangalore, India 186 C7
Mangareva, island, Is. Gambier, Fr. Polynesia, Fr., S. Pac. Oc. 165 G14
Mangole, island, Indonesia 187 E13
Manihi, atoll, Tuamotu Arch., Fr. Polynesia, Fr., S. Pac. Oc. 165 F13
Manihiki Atoll, Cook Is., N.Z., S. Pac. Oc. 165 E11
Manihiki Plateau, S. Pac. Oc. 145 H9
Manila, Philippines 180 F10
Manila Bay, Philippines, S. China Sea 180 F10
Manila Trench, S. China Sea 180 F10
Mannar, Gulf of, India, Sri Lanka, Ind. Oc. 186 D8
Man-of-War Cay, Bahamas, N. Atl. Oc. 140 C8
Manra, island, Phoenix Is., Kiribati, S. Pac. Oc. 165 E10
Manrec, Ras, Eritrea, Red Sea 210 J6
Mansel Island, Can., Hudson B. 106 D2
Mantanani Islands, Malaysia, S. China Sea 181 J8
Manua Islands, Amer. Samoa, U.S., S. Pac. Oc. 165 F10
Manuae, island, Society Is., Fr. Polynesia, Fr., S. Pac. Oc. 165 F12
Manui, island, Indonesia 181 N11
Manus, island, Admiralty Is., P.N.G., N. Pac. Oc. 164 D4
Manzala, Buheirat el, Egypt, Medit. Sea 133 K12
Manzanilla Bank, N. Atl. Oc. 141 K15
Manzanillo, Cuba 140 D7
Manzanillo, Mex. 147 F13
Map Ta Phut, Thailand 146 F2
Mapia Islands, Indonesia, N. Pac. Oc. 164 D3
Mapmaker Seamounts, N. Pac. Oc. 144 E6
Maqdam, Ra's, Sudan, Red Sea 210 G4
Maracaibo, Venez. 141 J10
Maracaibo, Lago de, Venez., G. de Venezuela 141 K10
Marakei, atoll, Gilbert Is., Kiribati, S. Pac. Oc. 164 D8
Maralie Reef, S. China Sea 180 H7
Marawwaḩ, island, U.A.E., Persian G. 213 K9
Marcus see Minami Tori Shima, Japan, N. Pac. Oc. 164 A5
Marcus Hook, U.S. 106 F2
Maré, island, Loyalty Is., New Caledonia, Fr., S. Pac. Oc. 164 G7
Margarita, Isla de, Venez., Caribbean Sea 141 J14
Margetts Seamount, S. China Sea 180 F7
Maria van Diemen, Cape, N.Z. 164 J8
Maria, Îles, Austral Is., Fr. Polynesia, Fr., S. Pac. Oc. 165 G12
Mariana Islands, N. Pac. Oc. 144 F5
Mariana Trench, N. Pac. Oc. 144 F5
Mariana Trough, Philippine Sea 144 F5
Marías Islands, Mex., N. Pac. Oc. 147 E13
Marie Byrd Land, Antarctica 251 H9
Marie-Galante, island, Guadeloupe, Fr., Caribbean Sea 141 G15
Marie Louise Bank, S. China Sea 180 G9
Marinduque, island, Philippines 180 F11
Mariner Shoal, Persian G. 213 G11
Marino, Cay, Spratly Is., S. China Sea 180 H8
Marion Island, Prince Edward Is., S. Af., Ind. Oc. 186 L3
Mariveles Reef, S. China Sea 181 J7
Marlim Field, Braz. 107 M5
Marmagao, India 186 C7
Marmara Denizi, sea, Turk. 133 E10
Maro Reef, Hawaiian Is., U.S., N. Pac. Oc. 146 E8
Marotiri (Îlots de Bass), Austral Is., Fr. Polynesia, Fr., S. Pac. Oc. 165 H13
Marquesas Fracture Zone, S. Pac. Oc. 145 H10
Marquesas Islands, Fr. Polynesia, Fr., S. Pac. Oc. 165 E14
Marquesas Keys, Fla. Keys, U.S., G. of Mex. 139 F13
Marrāk, island, Saudi Arabia, Red Sea 210 J6
Marsaxlokk, Malta 106 G10
Marseille, Fr. 131 C8
Marsh Island, U.S., G. of Mex. 138 B6
Marsh Reef, S. China Sea 180 H3
Marshall Islands, N. Pac. Oc. 144 F7
Marsili Seamount, Tyrrhenian Sea 132 F4
Martaban, Gulf of, Myanmar, Andaman Sea 187 C10
Martin Vaz Islands, Braz., S. Atl. Oc. 107 L6
Martinez, U.S. 147 D12
Martinique, island, Windward Is., Fr., Caribbean Sea 141 G15
Martinique Passage, N. Atl. Oc. 141 G15
Marutea, atoll, Groupe Actéon, Fr. Polynesia, Fr., S. Pac. Oc. 165 G14
Marvin Spur, Arctic Oc. 216 G8
Masāwik, Shi'b, Red Sea 210 C3
Masalumbu, Kepulauan, Indonesia, Java Sea 181 P8
Masbate, island, Philippines 187 C13
Mascarene Basin, Ind. Oc. 184 F5
Mascarene Plain, Ind. Oc. 184 G4
Mascarene Plateau, Ind. Oc. 184 E5
Mashābih, island, Saudi Arabia, Red Sea 210 D4
Māsheh, Khwor-e, Persian G. 213 G10
Masira, island, Oman, Arabian Sea 186 B5
Masira, Gulf of, Oman, Arabian Sea 186 B5
Massawa, Eritrea 210 J5
Massawa Channel, Red Sea 210 J5
Mastūrah, Ra's, Saudi Arabia, Red Sea 210 E5
Matagorda Bay, U.S., G. of Mex. 138 C3
Matagorda Island, U.S., G. of Mex. 138 C3
Matagorda Peninsula, U.S. 138 C3
Mataiva, atoll, Tuamotu Arch., Fr. Polynesia, Fr., S. Pac. Oc. 165 F13
Matak, island, Kep. Anambas, Indonesia, S. China Sea 181 L4
Matasiri, island, Kep. Laut Kecil, Indonesia, Java Sea 181 P8
Maţbakh, Ra's al, Qatar, Persian G. 212 H7
Mathematicians Seamounts, N. Pac. Oc. 145 F13
Matthew, island, Vanuatu, S. Pac. Oc. 164 G8
Matua, island, Kuril Is., Russ., N. Pac. Oc. 146 C6
Maud Rise, S. Atl. Oc. 248 F6
Maug Islands, N. Mariana Is., U.S., N. Pac. Oc. 187 B16
Maui, island, Hawaiian Is., U.S., N. Pac. Oc. 165 A12
Mauke, island, Cook Is., N.Z., S. Pac. Oc. 165 G12
Maupihaa, island, Society Is., Fr. Polynesia, Fr., S. Pac. Oc. 165 F12
Maupiti, island, Society Is., Fr. Polynesia, Fr., S. Pac. Oc. 165 F12
Maures Escarpment, Medit. Sea 131 D8
Maurice Ewing Bank, S. Atl. Oc. 105 P5
Mauritius Trench, Ind. Oc. 184 H5
Maury Seachannel, N. Atl. Oc. 104 E6
Maxwell Fracture Zone, N. Atl. Oc. 104 F6
Maya, island, Indonesia 187 E11
Mayaguana Island, Bahamas, N. Atl. Oc. 141 C9
Mayaguana Passage, Bahamas, N. Atl. Oc. 141 C9
Mayagüez, P.R., U.S. 141 E12
Mayotte, island, Fr., Ind. Oc. 186 F4
Mayraira Point, Philippines 180 D10
Mayreau, island, Windward Is., St. Vincent & the Grenadines, Caribbean Sea 141 H14
Mazarron Escarpment, Medit. Sea 131 G5
McKean Island, Phoenix Is., Kiribati, N. Pac. Oc. 165 D9
M'Clintock Channel, Can. 218 K8
M'Clure Strait, Can., Arctic Oc. 218 J7
Mecoacán, Laguna, Mex., G. of Mex. 138 L6
Medina Bank, Medit. Sea 132 J4
Medina Escarpment, Medit. Sea 132 J4
Mediterranean Ridge, Medit. Sea 132 J7
Mediterranean Sea, N. Atl. Oc. 106 G9
Mediterranean Sea's deepest point, 132 G7
Mednyy Island, Russ., Bering Sea 146 B7
Mega, island, Indonesia, Ind. Oc. 187 E10
Megísti, island, Gr., Medit. Sea 133 H11
Mehetia, island, Society Is., Fr. Polynesia, Fr., S. Pac. Oc. 165 F13
Mekong River Delta, Vietnam 180 H4
Melanesia, islands, Pac. Oc. 164 D4

344 MAP PLACE-NAME INDEX | LAPTEV SEA – MELANESIA

Melbourne, Austral. 164 J4
Melekeok, Palau 164 C3
Melilla, Sp. 131 H4
Melita Bank, Medit. Sea 132 J4
Melita Valley, Medit. Sea 132 J4
Mellish Seamount, N. Pac. Oc. 146 D8
Melville Island, Austral., Timor Sea 164 E2
Melville Island, Parry Is., Can., Arctic Oc. 218 J7
Melville Peninsula, Can. 217 L9
Menard Fracture Zone, S. Pac. Oc. 145 L12
Mendeleyev Plain, Arctic Oc. 216 F6
Mendeleyev Ridge, Arctic Oc. 216 F6
Mendelssohn Seamount, N. Pac. Oc. 145 E9
Mendocino Fracture Zone, N. Pac. Oc. 145 D9
Mengalum, island, Malaysia, S. China Sea 181 J8
Menorca, island, Balearic Is., Sp., Medit. Sea 131 F8
Mentawai, Kepulauan, Indonesia, Ind. Oc. 181 N1
Mergui Archipelago, Myanmar, Andaman Sea 187 C10
Merir, island, Palau, N. Pac. Oc. 164 C2
Mersin (İçel), Turk. 133 G13
Merz Seamount, S. Atl. Oc. 105 P9
Messina, It. 132 G4
Messina, Stretto di, It., Medit. Sea 132 G4
Messiniakós Kólpos, Gr., Medit. Sea 132 G7
Meteor Rise, S. Atl. Oc. 105 P9
Meteor Seamount, S. Atl. Oc. 105 P9
Mexico, Gulf of, N. Atl. Oc. 106 H1
Mexico Basin, G. of Mex. 138 F7
Miami, Fla., U.S. 140 A5
Miangas, island, Indonesia 187 D13
Micronesia, islands, N. Pac. Oc. 164 C4
Mid-Adriatic Basin, Adriatic Sea 132 D4
Midai, island, Indonesia, S. China Sea 181 L5
Mid-Atlantic Ridge, S. Atl. Oc. 248 H2
Middle America Trench, N. Pac. Oc. 145 F13
Middle Andaman, island, Andaman Is., India, B. of Bengal 187 C9
Middleton Basin, Coral Sea 146 J6
Middleton Island, U.S., G. of Alas. 147 B10
Middleton Reef, Tasman Sea 164 H6
Mid-Indian Basin, Ind. Oc. 184 F8
Mid-Indian Ridge, Ind. Oc. 184 E6
Mid-Pacific Mountains, N. Pac. Oc. 144 E6
Midway Islands, Hawaiian Is., U.S., N. Pac. Oc. 146 E8
Míkonos, island, Kikládes, Gr., Aegean Sea 133 G9
Miladummadulu Atoll, Maldives, Ind. Oc. 186 D7
Milford Haven, U.K. 106 E8
Mili Atoll, Ratak Chain, Marshall Is., N. Pac. Oc. 164 C8
Miller Seamount, N. Pac. Oc. 147 C10
Milne Seamounts, N. Atl. Oc. 104 F5
Mílos, island, Kikládes, Gr., Aegean Sea 132 G8
Mina Al Ahmadi, Kuwait 186 A4
Mīnā' al Faḩl, Oman 186 B5
Minami Iwo To, island, Japan, N. Pac. Oc. 164 A4
Minami Tori Shima (Marcus), Japan, N. Pac. Oc. 164 A5
Mindanao, island, Philippines 164 C1
Mindoro, island, Philippines 164 B1
Mindoro Strait, Philippines 180 G10
Minicoy, atoll, Lakshadweep, India, Arabian Sea 186 D7
Minorca, island, Balearic Is., Sp., Medit. Sea 106 F9
Minto Reef, Caroline Is., F.S.M., N. Pac. Oc. 164 C5
Mira Por Vos, island, Bahamas, N. Atl. Oc. 140 C8
Miri, Malaysia 181 K7
Mirtoon Basin, Sea of Crete 132 G8
Mish'āb, Bandar al, Persian G. 212 E3
Mish'āb, Ra's al, Saudi Arabia, Persian G. 212 E3
Miskān, island, Kuwait, Persian G. 212 C2
Miskitos, Cayos, Nicar., Caribbean Sea 140 G4
Misool, island, Indonesia 187 E14
Mişrātah, Lib. 132 K4
Mississippi Canyon, G. of Mex. 138 C8
Mississippi Fan, G. of Mex. 139 D9
Mississippi River Delta, U.S. 139 B9
Mississippi Sound, U.S., G. of Mex. 138 A8
Misteriosa Bank, Caribbean Sea 140 E4
Misurata Valley, Medit. Sea 132 J4
Mitchell Escarpment, G. of Mex. 139 F14
Mitiaro, island, Cook Is., N.Z., S. Pac. Oc. 165 G12
Mitre Island see Fataka, Sta. Cruz Is., Solomon Is., S. Pac. Oc. 164 F7
Mitsio, Nosy, Madagascar, Mozambique Ch. 186 F4
Miyako, island, Ryukyu Is., Japan, N. Pac. Oc. 187 B13
Mizushima, Japan 146 D4
Mljet, island, Croatia, Adriatic Sea 132 D5
Moa, island, Indonesia 164 E2
Moa Island, Austral., Torres Str. 187 F15
Mobile, Ala., U.S. 139 A9
Mobile Bay, U.S., G. of Mex. 139 A9
Mobile Point, U.S. 139 A9
Mohns Ridge, N. Atl. Oc. 217 E13
Mohotani (Motane), island, Marquesas Is., Fr. Polynesia, Fr., S. Pac. Oc. 165 E14
Moín, Bahía de, C.R., Caribbean Sea 140 K4
Molloy Deep, Arctic Oc. 219 F11
Moloka'i, island, Hawaiian Is., U.S., N. Pac. Oc. 165 A12
Molokai Fracture Zone, N. Pac. Oc. 145 E10
Molucca Sea, 164 D2
Moluccas, island, Indonesia 164 D2
Mona, Isla, P.R., U.S., Caribbean Sea 141 E12
Mona Passage, N. Atl. Oc. 141 E12
Mongstad, Nor. 106 D9
Mono, Punta, Nicar. 140 J4
Mono Rise, Caribbean Sea 140 J6
Montagu Island, S. Sandwich Is., U.K., Scotia Sea 107 Q6
Montecristo, island, It., Medit. Sea 132 D2
Montego Bay, bay, Jam., Caribbean Sea 140 E6
Montego Bay, Jam. 140 E7
Montevideo, Uru. 107 N4
Montréal, Can. 106 F2
Montserrat, island, Leeward Is., U.K., Caribbean Sea 141 F15
Moonless Mountains, N. Pac. Oc. 145 E11
Moorea, island, Society Is., Fr. Polynesia, Fr., S. Pac. Oc. 165 F12
Morales, Laguna de, Mex., G. of Mex. 138 G2
Morane, island, Is. Gambier, Fr. Polynesia, Fr., S. Pac. Oc. 165 G14
Morant Cays, Jam., Caribbean Sea 140 F8
Morant Point, Jam. 140 F7
Morant Trough, Caribbean Sea 140 E8
Moresby Island, Queen Charlotte Is., Can., N. Pac. Oc. 147 C11
Morotai, island, Moluccas, Indonesia 164 D2
Morris Jesup Rise, Arctic Oc. 217 F10
Morro, Punta del, Mex. 138 K3
Morrosquillo, Golfo de, Col., Caribbean Sea 140 K8
Mortlock Islands, Caroline Is., F.S.M., N. Pac. Oc. 164 C5
Moruroa, atoll, Tuamotu Arch., Fr. Polynesia, Fr., S. Pac. Oc. 165 G14
Mosquitos, Golfo de los, Pan., Caribbean Sea 140 K5
Mostaganem, Alg. 131 H6
Motagua Fan, Caribbean Sea 140 F3
Motane see Mohotani, island, Marquesas Is., Fr. Polynesia, Fr., S. Pac. Oc. 165 E14
Motu One, island, Society Is., Fr. Polynesia, Fr., S. Pac. Oc. 165 F12
Mouchoir Bank, N. Atl. Oc. 141 D10
Mouchoir Passage, Turks & Caicos Is., U.K., N. Atl. Oc. 141 D10
Mozambique Channel, Ind. Oc. 186 G3
Mozambique Escarpment, Ind. Oc. 184 K2
Mozambique Plateau, Ind. Oc. 184 J3
Mudayrah, Kasr, Persian G. 212 C3
Muerto Cay, Cayos Miskitos, Nicar., Caribbean Sea 140 G4
Muertos Cays, Bahamas, N. Atl. Oc. 140 B5
Muertos Trough, Caribbean Sea 141 F12
Muḩarraq, Jazīrat al, Bahrain, Persian G. 212 G6
Muhayyimāt, island, U.A.E., Persian G. 212 K7
Mujeres, Isla, Mex., Yucatan Ch. 139 J10
Mukawwar, island, Sudan, Red Sea 210 F4
Muko Jima Rettō, Bonin Is., Japan, N. Pac. Oc. 187 A15
Mulaku Atoll, Maldives, Ind. Oc. 186 D7
Mullet Key, U.S., G. of Mex. 139 C13
Mumbai (Bombay), India 186 B7
Muna, island, Indonesia 181 P11
Munifāh, Saudi Arabia 212 E3
Munīfah, Dawḩat, Persian G. 212 E3
Muḩammad, Râs, Egypt, Red Sea 210 C3
Murayr, island, Egypt, Red Sea 210 E3
Murmansk, Russ. 219 C13
Murmansk Rise, Barents Sea 217 C12
Murray Fracture Zone, N. Pac. Oc. 145 E9
Mūsá, Khowr-e, Persian G. 212 B3
Musallamīyah, Dawḩat al, Persian G. 212 F3
Musandam, Ra's, Oman, Persian G. 213 G13
Mushţ Rimnī, bank, Persian G. 212 F6
Musicians Seamounts, N. Pac. Oc. 145 E9
Mussau Islands, Bismarck Arch., P.N.G., N. Pac. Oc. 164 D5
Mustang Island, U.S., G. of Mex. 138 C3
Mustique, island, Windward Is., St. Vincent & the Grenadines, Caribbean Sea 141 H15
Muuga, Est. 106 D11
Mwali, island, Comoros, Ind. Oc. 186 F4
My Tho, Vietnam 180 H4

N

Nagoya, Japan 146 D5
Nakhon Si Thammarat, Thailand 180 H1
Namaqua Seamount, S. Atl. Oc. 107 M9
Namonuito Atoll, Caroline Is., F.S.M., N. Pac. Oc. 164 C5
Namorik Atoll, Ralik Chain, Marshall Is., N. Pac. Oc. 164 C7
Nampō Shotō, Japan, N. Pac. Oc. 187 A15
Namyit Island, Spratly Is., S. China Sea 180 H8
Nansen Basin, Arctic Oc. 216 D8
Nansen Ridge, Arctic Oc. 216 D8
Nanshan Island, Spratly Is., S. China Sea 180 G8
Nanumanga, island, Tuvalu, S. Pac. Oc. 164 E8
Nanumea, atoll, Tuvalu, S. Pac. Oc. 164 E8
Naples, Fla., U.S. 139 E14
Naples see Napoli, It. 132 E4
Napoli (Naples), It. 132 E4
Napoli, Golfo di, It., Tyrrhenian Sea 132 E4
Napuka, atoll, Is. du Désappointement, Fr. Polynesia, Fr., S. Pac. Oc. 165 F14
Nares Bank, S. China Sea 180 G8
Nares Plain, N. Atl. Oc. 104 H3
Nasca Ridge, S. Pac. Oc. 145 J15
Nassau, Bahamas 140 A7
Nassau, island, Cook Is., N.Z., S. Pac. Oc. 165 F11
Natal Basin, Ind. Oc. 184 H3
Natuna Besar, island, Kep. Natuna Besar, Indonesia, S. China Sea 181 K5
Natuna Besar, Kepulauan (Bunguran Utara), Indonesia, S. China Sea 181 K5
Natuna Selatan, Kepulauan (Bunguran Selatan), Indonesia, S. China Sea 181 L5
Naturaliste Plateau, Ind. Oc. 185 J12
Nauru, island, Nauru, S. Pac. Oc. 144 G7
Navassa Island, U.S., Caribbean Sea 140 E8
Navidad Bank, N. Atl. Oc. 141 D11
Náxos, island, Kikládes, Gr., Aegean Sea 133 G9
Nay, Mui, Vietnam 180 G5
Nāy Band, Damāgheh-ye, Iran, Persian G. 212 F8
Nāybandī, Iran 212 F8
Nazar, Shi'b, Red Sea 210 E5
Nazareth Bank, Ind. Oc. 184 F6
Ndeni see Nendo, island, Sta. Cruz Is., Solomon Is., S. Pac. Oc. 164 E7
Neapolis see Kavála, Gr. 132 E8
Near Islands, Aleutian Is., U.S., N. Pac. Oc. 146 C7
Necker Island, Hawaiian Is., U.S., N. Pac. Oc. 165 A11
Necker Ridge, N. Pac. Oc. 145 E9
Negonego, atoll, Tuamotu Arch., Fr. Polynesia, Fr., S. Pac. Oc. 165 G14
Negros, island, Philippines 164 C1
Neiba Valley, Caribbean Sea 141 F10
Neilson Reef, S. Pac. Oc. 165 H13
Nelsons Island, Chagos Arch., U.K., Ind. Oc. 186 E7
Nendo (Ndeni), island, Sta. Cruz Is., Solomon Is., S. Pac. Oc. 164 E7
Neptuna Banks, S. China Sea 180 E7
Nevis, island, Leeward Is., St. Kitts & Nevis, Caribbean Sea 141 F14
New Britain, island, Bismarck Arch., P.N.G., S. Pac. Oc. 164 E5
New Caledonia, island, Fr., S. Pac. Oc. 164 G7
New Caledonia Basin, S. Pac. Oc. 144 J7
Newcastle, Austral. 146 K6
New England Seamounts, N. Atl. Oc. 104 F3
Newfoundland Basin, N. Atl. Oc. 104 F5
Newfoundland Plain, N. Atl. Oc. 104 F5
Newfoundland Ridge, N. Atl. Oc. 104 F5
Newfoundland, Island of, Can., G. of St. Lawrence 106 E4
New Georgia, island, Solomon Is., S. Pac. Oc. 164 E6
New Guinea, island, Indonesia, P.N.G. 164 E3
New Hanover, island, Bismarck Arch., P.N.G., N. Pac. Oc. 164 D5
New Hebrides Trench, S. Pac. Oc. 144 J7
New Ireland, island, Bismarck Arch., P.N.G., N. Pac. Oc. 164 D5
New Orleans, La., U.S. 138 B8
New Providence Island, Bahamas, N. Atl. Oc. 140 B7
New Siberian Islands, Russ., Arctic Oc. 218 D6
New York, U.S. 106 F2
New Zealand, S. Pac. Oc. 144 K7
Ngatik Atoll, Caroline Is., F.S.M., N. Pac. Oc. 164 C6
Ngulu Atoll, Caroline Is., F.S.M., N. Pac. Oc. 164 C3
Nha Trang, Vietnam 180 G5
Nias, island, Indonesia, Ind. Oc. 187 E10
Nice, Fr. 132 C1
Nicholas Channel, N. Atl. Oc. 140 B5
Nicobar Islands, India, B. of Bengal 187 D9
Niger Fan, G. of Guinea 105 J9
Nightingale Island, U.K., S. Atl. Oc. 107 N8
Nihoa, island, Hawaiian Is., U.S., N. Pac. Oc. 165 A11
Ni'ihau, island, Hawaiian Is., U.S., N. Pac. Oc. 165 A11
Nikitin Seamount, Ind. Oc. 184 E8
Nikumaroro, island, Phoenix Is., Kiribati, S. Pac. Oc. 165 E9
Nile Fan, Medit. Sea 133 K11
Nine Degree Channel, India, Arabian Sea 186 C7
Ninetyeast Ridge, Ind. Oc. 185 H9
Ningbo, China 146 E4
Nintoku Seamount, N. Pac. Oc. 146 D7
Niobe Seamount, Caribbean Sea 140 F3
Nipe, Bahía de, Cuba 140 D8
Niuafo'ou, island, Tonga, S. Pac. Oc. 165 F9
Niuatoputapu, island, Tonga, S. Pac. Oc. 165 F9
Niue, island, N.Z., S. Pac. Oc. 165 G10
Niulakita, island, Tuvalu, S. Pac. Oc. 165 E9
Niutao, island, Tuvalu, S. Pac. Oc. 164 E8
Njazidja, island, Comoros, Ind. Oc. 186 F4
Nonouti, atoll, Gilbert Is., Kiribati, S. Pac. Oc. 164 D8
Nora, island, Dahlak Arch., Eritrea, Red Sea 210 J5
Nordaustlandet, island, Svalbard, Nor. 106 A11
Nordoyar, islands, Faroe Is., Den., Norwegian Sea 106 D8
Norfolk, U.S. 106 G2
Norfolk Island, Austral., S. Pac. Oc. 164 H7
Norfolk Ridge, S. Pac. Oc. 144 J7
Norske Bank, Arctic Oc. 104 A10
Norske Islands, Greenland, Den. 106 A7
Norte, Cayo, Mex., Caribbean Sea 140 E2
North American Basin, N. Atl. Oc. 104 G4
North Andaman, island, Andaman Is., India, B. of Bengal 187 C9
North Australian Basin, Ind. Oc. 185 F12
North Caicos, island, Caicos Is., Turks & Caicos Is., U.K., N. Atl. Oc. 141 C10
North Cape, N.Z. 164 J8
North Cape, Nor. 219 D13
North Cay, Col., Caribbean Sea 140 G5
North Danger Reef, S. China Sea 180 G8
Northeast Hawaiian Ridge, N. Pac. Oc. 144 D8
North East Land, Svalbard, Nor., Arctic Oc. 219 E11
Northeast Pacific Basin, N. Pac. Oc. 145 D9
Northeast Providence Channel, Bahamas, N. Atl. Oc. 140 A7
Northeast Shea, bank, S. China Sea 180 H8
Northern Cay, Belize, Caribbean Sea 140 F2
Northern Mariana Islands, U.S., N. Pac. Oc. 187 B16
North Fiji Basin, S. Pac. Oc. 144 H7
North Island, N.Z., S. Pac. Oc. 164 K8
North Land, Russ., Arctic Oc. 218 C8
North Luconia Shoals, S. China Sea 181 K7
North Malosmadulu Atoll, Maldives, Ind. Oc. 186 D7
North New Hebrides Trench, S. Pac. Oc. 144 H7
North Pole, 219 F9
North Sea, N. Atl. Oc. 106 E9
Northumberland Islands, Austral., Coral Sea 187 G16
North Vereker Bank, S. China Sea 180 C8
North Viper Shoal, S. China Sea 181 J8
Northwest Atlantic Mid-Ocean Canyon, N. Atl. Oc. 104 D4
Northwest Georgia Rise, S. Atl. Oc. 105 P5
Northwest Pacific Basin, N. Pac. Oc. 144 D6
Northwest Providence Channel, Bahamas, N. Atl. Oc. 140 A6
North West Rocks, Col., Caribbean Sea 140 G5
Northwind Escarpment, Arctic Oc. 216 G5
Northwind Plain, Arctic Oc. 216 G5
Northwind Ridge, Arctic Oc. 216 G5
Norton Sound, Bering Sea 147 A9
Norvegia, Cape, Antarctica 250 F6
Norwegian Basin, Norwegian Sea 104 D8
Norwegian Sea, N. Atl. Oc. 106 C9
Nottingham Island, Can., Hudson Str. 106 D2
Nouméa, New Caledonia, Fr. 164 G7
Nova Scotia, region, 104 F3
Novaya Zemlya, Russ., Arctic Oc. 219 B10
Nuageuses, Îles, Kerguelen Is., Fr., Ind. Oc. 186 L7
Nuevo, Baja, G. of Mex. 138 H6
Nuevo, Bajo, Caribbean Sea 140 G6
Nuevo, Banco, G. of Mex. 138 J6
Nui, atoll, Tuvalu, S. Pac. Oc. 164 E8
Nuku'alofa, Tonga 165 G9
Nukufetau, atoll, Tuvalu, S. Pac. Oc. 164 E8
Nuku Hiva, island, Marquesas Is., Fr. Polynesia, Fr., S. Pac. Oc. 165 E14
Nukulaelae, atoll, Tuvalu, S. Pac. Oc. 165 E9
Nukumanu Islands, Melanesia, P.N.G., S. Pac. Oc. 164 E6
Nukunonu, island, Tokelau, N.Z., S. Pac. Oc. 165 E10
Nukuoro Atoll, Caroline Is., F.S.M., N. Pac. Oc. 164 C5
Numfoor, island, Indonesia 187 E14
Nunivak Island, U.S., Bering Sea 147 B9
Nupani, island, Sta. Cruz Is., Solomon Is., S. Pac. Oc. 164 E7
Nurra Escarpment, Medit. Sea 132 E1
Nurse Cay, Bahamas, N. Atl. Oc. 140 C8

MELBOURNE — NURSE CAY | MAP PLACE-NAME INDEX 345

Nusabarung, island, Indonesia, Ind. Oc. 181 Q7
Nzwani, island, Comoros, Ind. Oc. 186 F4

O'ahu, island, Hawaiian Is., U.S., N. Pac. Oc. 165 A12
Oakland, U.S. 147 D12
Ob' Bank, Greenland Sea 217 F11
Ob, Gulf of, Russ., Kara Sea 219 A10
Ob' Tablemount, Ind. Oc. 248 C5
Obi, island, Indonesia 187 E14
Ocean Cay, Bahamas, N. Atl. Oc. 140 A6
Ocean Island see Banaba, Micronesia, Kiribati, S. Pac. Oc. 164 D7
Oceanographer Fracture Zone, N. Atl. Oc. 104 G5
October Revolution Island, N. Land, Russ., Arctic Oc. 218 C8
Odesa, Ukr. 106 F11
Oeno Island, U.K., S. Pac. Oc. 165 G15
Oil Islands see Chagos Archipelago, U.K., Ind. Oc. 186 E7
Oita, Japan 146 D4
Ojin Seamount, N. Pac. Oc. 146 D7
Okhotsk, Sea of, N. Pac. Oc. 146 B6
Okinawa, island, Ryukyu Is., Japan, E. China Sea 146 E4
Okino Daitō Jima, Japan, Philippine Sea 164 A2
Öland, island, Sw., Baltic Sea 106 E10
Old Bahama Channel, N. Atl. Oc. 140 C6
Oleniy Island, Russ., Kara Sea 219 A9
Olga Basin, Barents Sea 217 D11
Oliva Bank, Medit. Sea 131 F7
Olongapo, Philippines 180 F10
Oman, Gulf of, Ind. Oc. 186 B5
Ona Basin, Scotia Sea 105 Q4
Onekotan, island, Kuril Is., Russ., N. Pac. Oc. 146 C6
Ono-i-Lau, island, Lau Group, Fiji Is., S. Pac. Oc. 165 G9
Oporto, Port. 106 F8
Oran, Alg. 131 H5
Oranjestad, Aruba, Neth. 141 H11
Orca Basin, G. of Mex. 138 D7
Orchila, Isla, Lesser Antil., Venez., Caribbean Sea 141 J13
Orfanoú, Kólpos, Gr., Aegean Sea 132 E8
Orkney Islands, U.K., N. Atl. Oc. 106 D8
Oroluk Atoll, Caroline Is., F.S.M., N. Pac. Oc. 164 C5
Orona, island, Phoenix Is., Kiribati, S. Pac. Oc. 165 E10
Orphan Knoll, N. Atl. Oc. 104 E5
Osaka, Japan 146 D5
Osborn Plateau, Ind. Oc. 185 G9
Otranto, Strait of, Medit. Sea 132 E6
Ottawa Islands, Can., Hudson B. 106 D2
Ouest, Île de l', Kerguelen Is., Fr., Ind. Oc. 186 L7
Outer Bailey, N. Atl. Oc. 104 D7
Outer Hebrides, islands, U.K., N. Atl. Oc. 106 D8
Ouvéa, island, Loyalty Is., New Caledonia, Fr., S. Pac. Oc. 164 G7
Owen Fracture Zone, Ind. Oc. 184 D5

Pacific-Antarctic Ridge, S. Pac. Oc. 249 F11
Padang, island, Indonesia, Str. of Malacca 181 L2
Padangtikar, island, Indonesia 187 E11
Padangtikar Maya, island, Indonesia 181 M5
Padre Island, U.S., G. of Mex. 138 D3
Pag, island, Croatia, Adriatic Sea 132 C4
Pagai Selatan, island, Kep. Mentawai, Indonesia, Ind. Oc. 181 N1
Pagai Utara, island, Kep. Mentawai, Indonesia, Ind. Oc. 181 N1
Pagan, island, N. Mariana Is., U.S., N. Pac. Oc. 164 B4
Pago Pago, Amer. Samoa, U.S. 165 F10
Paisley Seamount, Ind. Oc. 186 F3
Palau, island, Palau, Philippine Sea 144 F4
Palau Trench, N. Pac. Oc. 144 F5
Palawan, island, Philippines 180 H9
Palawan Passage, Philippines, S. China Sea 180 H9
Palawan Trough, S. China Sea 181 J7
Palermo, It. 132 G3
Palikir, F.S.M. 164 C6
Palk Strait, India, Sri Lanka, Ind. Oc. 186 C8
Palma, Sp. 131 F7
Palmas, Cape, 107 J8
Palm Deira, site, U.A.E., Persian G. 213 J11
Palmer Archipelago, Antarctica, S. Pac. Oc. 107 R3
Palmerston Atoll, Cook Is., N.Z., S. Pac. Oc. 165 F11
Palm Jebel Ali, site, U.A.E., Persian G. 213 J11
Palm Jumeirah, site, U.A.E., Persian G. 213 J11
Palmyra Atoll, U.S., N. Pac. Oc. 165 C11
Palos, Cabo de, Sp. 131 G5
Panaitan, island, Indonesia, Selat Sunda 181 Q4
Panama, Pan. 147 F15
Panama Basin, N. Pac. Oc. 145 G15
Panama Canal, Pan. 140 K6
Panama City, Fla., U.S. 139 A11
Panama Plain, Caribbean Sea 140 J6
Panay, island, Philippines 180 G11
Pangkalpinang, Indonesia 181 N4
Pangutaran Group, Sulu Arch., Philippines 181 J10
Panjang, island, Kep. Natuna Selatan, Indonesia, S. China Sea 181 L5
Pantelleria, island, It., Str. of Sicily 132 G3
Papeete, Fr. Polynesia, Fr. 165 F13
Papua, Gulf of, P.N.G., Coral Sea 187 F16
Paracel Islands see Xisha Qundao, China, S. China Sea 180 E6
Paradwip, India 187 B9
Paraguaná, Península de, Venez. 141 J11
Paramushir, island, Kuril Is., Russ., N. Pac. Oc. 146 C6
Paranaguá, Braz. 107 M5
Parece Vela, island, Japan, Philippine Sea 164 A3
Paria, Gulf of, Trinidad & Tobago, Caribbean Sea 141 K15
Parker Bank, G. of Mex. 138 C6
Parker Seamount, N. Pac. Oc. 147 C10
Parry Bank, Arctic Oc. 104 A10
Parry Channel, Arctic Oc. 218 K7
Parry Islands, Queen Elizabeth Is., Can., Arctic Oc. 218 J7
Pascagoula, Miss., U.S. 139 A9
Pascua, Isla de see Easter Island, Chile, S. Pac. Oc. 147 J13
Pasir Gudang, Malaysia 187 D11
Passero, Capo, It. 132 H4
Passu Keah, island, Xisha Qundao, China, S. China Sea 180 E6
Patagonia, region, S. Am. 105 P3
Pate Island, Kenya, Ind. Oc. 186 E3
Pátra (Patrae), Gr. 132 G7
Patrae see Pátra, Gr. 132 G7
Patrick Stewart Bank, Persian G. 213 G13
Patton Escarpment, N. Pac. Oc. 145 D12
Patton Seamounts, N. Pac. Oc. 147 B10
Payong, Tanjong, Malaysia 181 K7
Paz Bank, Caribbean Sea 140 D6
Pearl and Hermes Atoll, Hawaiian Is., U.S., N. Pac. Oc. 146 E8
Pearson Reef, S. China Sea 180 H7
Peary Channel, Can., Arctic Oc. 218 H8
Pechora Bay, Russ., Barents Sea 219 A12
Pedro Bank, Caribbean Sea 140 F6
Pedro Cays, Jam., Caribbean Sea 140 F6
Pejantan, island, Indonesia, S. China Sea 181 M4
Pekalongan, Indonesia 181 Q5
Pelabuhanratu, Teluk, Indonesia, Ind. Oc. 181 Q4
Pelagie, Isole, It., Medit. Sea 132 H3
Peleng, island, Indonesia 164 D1
Peloponnisos, peninsula, Gr. 132 G7
Pemanggil, island, Malaysia, S. China Sea 181 L3
Pemba Island, Tanzania, Ind. Oc. 186 E3
P'enghu Ch'üntao (Pescadores), islands, Taiwan, China, Taiwan Str. 180 B10
Pengiki, island, Indonesia, S. China Sea 181 M5
Penguin Reef, S. China Sea 180 E7
Penrhyn Atoll (Tongareva), Cook Is., N.Z., S. Pac. Oc. 165 E11
Pensacola, Fla., U.S. 139 A10
Pensacola Bay, U.S., G. of Mex. 139 A10
Pentecost, island, Vanuatu, S. Pac. Oc. 164 F7
Pérez, Isla, Mex., G. of Mex. 138 H8
Perhentian Besar, island, Malaysia, S. China Sea 181 J3
Perim see Barīm, island, Yemen, Red Sea 210 K7
Perlas, Cayos, Nicar., Caribbean Sea 140 H4
Perlas, Laguna de, Nicar., Caribbean Sea 140 H4
Pernambuco Plain, S. Atl. Oc. 105 K6
Peros Banhos, atoll, Chagos Arch., U.K., Ind. Oc. 186 E7
Persian Gulf, Ind. Oc. 186 A4
Persian Gulf's deepest point, 213 G9
Perth, Austral. 187 J12
Perth Basin, Ind. Oc. 185 H11
Peru Basin, S. Pac. Oc. 145 H14
Peru-Chile Trench, S. Pac. Oc. 145 H15
Pescadores see P'enghu Ch'üntao, islands, Taiwan, China, Taiwan Str. 180 B10
Pescara, It. 132 D4
Peter I Island, Antarctica, S. Pac. Oc. 251 J9
Petersen Bank, Ind. Oc. 249 C9
Petit Bois Island, U.S., G. of Mex. 139 A9
Petley Reef, S. China Sea 180 H8
Phangan, Ko, Thailand, G. of Thai. 180 H1
Philadelphia, U.S. 106 F2
Philippine Basin, Philippine Sea 146 F4
Philippine Islands, N. Pac. Oc. 185 C13
Philippine Sea, N. Pac. Oc. 146 F4
Philippine Trench, Philippine Sea 164 B1
Phillip Island, Austral., S. Pac. Oc. 164 H7
Phleger Bank, G. of Mex. 138 C6
Phoenix Islands, Polynesia, Kiribati, S. Pac. Oc. 165 E9
Phu Quoc, Dao, Vietnam, G. of Thai. 180 H3
Phuket, island, Thailand, Andaman Sea 187 D10
Pianosa, island, It., Medit. Sea 132 D2
Pichones, Cayos, Hond., Caribbean Sea 140 G4
Pickle Reef, Caribbean Sea 140 D5
Pickle Seamount, Caribbean Sea 140 D5
Pico, island, Azores, Port., N. Atl. Oc. 106 F6
Pico Fracture Zone, N. Atl. Oc. 104 F5
Pigailoe, island, Caroline Is., F.S.M., N. Pac. Oc. 187 D16
Pigs, Bay of see Cochinos, Bahía de, Cuba, Caribbean Sea 140 C5
Pikelot, island, Caroline Is., F.S.M., N. Pac. Oc. 164 C4
Pimlico Island, Bahamas, N. Atl. Oc. 140 A7
Pinang, island, Malaysia, Str. of Malacca 181 K1
Pine Islands, Fla. Keys, U.S., G. of Mex. 139 F14
Pine Islands, U.S., G. of Mex. 139 D13
Pingelap Atoll, Caroline Is., F.S.M., N. Pac. Oc. 164 C6
Pingouins, Îles des, Crozet Is., Fr., Ind. Oc. 186 L4
Pini, island, Indonesia, Ind. Oc. 181 M1
Pins, Île des (Kunié), New Caledonia, Fr., S. Pac. Oc. 164 G7
Piombino, It. 132 D2
Pioneer Fracture Zone, N. Pac. Oc. 145 D10
Piraeus, Gr. 106 G11
Pitcairn Island, U.K., S. Pac. Oc. 165 G15
Pitt Island, Chatham Is., N.Z., S. Pac. Oc. 165 L9
Plana Cays, Bahamas, N. Atl. Oc. 141 C9
Platte Island, Seychelles, Ind. Oc. 186 E5
Plenty, Bay of, N.Z., S. Pac. Oc. 164 J8
Pliny Trench, Medit. Sea 133 J9
Pohang, S. Korea 146 D4
Pohnpei (Ponape), island, Caroline Is., F.S.M., N. Pac. Oc. 164 C6
Poinsett, Cape, Antarctica 251 C10
Point au Fer Island, U.S., G. of Mex. 138 B7
Pole Plain, Arctic Oc. 216 D7
Policastro, Golfo di, It., Tyrrhenian Sea 132 F4
Polillo Islands, Philippines, Philippine Sea 180 F11
Polynesia, islands, N. Pac. Oc. 165 B10
Ponape see Pohnpei, island, Caroline Is., F.S.M., N. Pac. Oc. 164 C6
Ponce, P.R., U.S. 141 E12
Ponta da Madeira, Braz. 107 K5
Pontchartrain, Lake, U.S. 138 A8
Pontianak, Indonesia 181 M5
Ponza, island, It., Tyrrhenian Sea 132 E3
Porcupine Bank, N. Atl. Oc. 104 E7
Porcupine Plain, N. Atl. Oc. 104 E7
Po River Delta, It. 132 B3
Porlamar, Venez. 141 J14
Port Angeles, U.S. 147 C12
Port Arthur, U.S. 106 G1
Port-au-Prince, Haiti 141 E9
Port-de-Bouc, Fr. 106 F9
Port Elizabeth, S. Af. 186 J1
Portete, Bahía de, Col., Caribbean Sea 141 J10
Port Hedland, Austral. 187 G12
Port Kelang, Malaysia 187 D10
Port Kembla, Austral. 146 K6
Portland, Me., U.S. 106 F3
Portland, Oreg., U.S. 147 C12
Portland Bight, Jam., Caribbean Sea 140 F7
Portland Point, Jam. 140 F7
Port Moresby, P.N.G. 164 E4
Port of Spain, Trinidad & Tobago 141 J15
Porto Santo, island, Madeira Is., Port., N. Atl. Oc. 106 G7
Port Said see Bûr Sa'îd, Egypt 210 A2
Portsmouth, U.S. 106 G2
Port Sudan, Sudan 210 G4
Port-Vila, Vanuatu 164 F7
Port Walcott, Austral. 187 G12
Possession, Île de la, Crozet Is., Fr., Ind. Oc. 186 L5
Pourtales Escarpment, G. of Mex. 139 F14
Pourtales Terrace, G. of Mex. 139 F14
Powell Basin, Scotia Sea 105 Q4
Praslin, island, Seychelles, Ind. Oc. 186 E5
Pratas Island, Taiwan, China, S. China Sea 180 C9
Pratas Reef, S. China Sea 180 C9
Pratt Seamount, N. Pac. Oc. 145 B10
President Thiers Bank, S. Pac. Oc. 145 J10
Pribilof Islands, U.S., Bering Sea 146 B8
Prickly Pear Cays, Anguilla, U.K., Caribbean Sea 141 E14
Primorsk, Russ. 106 D11
Prince Charles Island, Can., Hudson B. 219 L10
Prince Consort Bank, S. China Sea 181 J6
Prince Edward Fracture Zone, Ind. Oc. 184 L2
Prince Edward Island, Can., G. of St. Lawrence 106 F3
Prince Edward Island, Prince Edward Is., S. Af., Ind. Oc. 186 L3
Prince Edward Islands, S. Af., Ind. Oc. 186 L3
Princess Charlotte Bay, Austral., Coral Sea 187 F15
Prince Gustaf Adolf Sea, Can., Arctic Oc. 218 J8
Prince of Wales, Cape, U.S. 218 G3
Prince of Wales Bank, S. China Sea 181 J6
Prince of Wales Island, Can., Arctic Oc. 218 K8
Prince of Wales Island, Alexander Arch., U.S., N. Pac. Oc. 147 B11
Prince of Wales Island, Austral., Torres Str. 187 F15
Prince Patrick Island, Queen Elizabeth Is., Can., Arctic Oc. 218 J7
Prince Regent Inlet, Can. 218 K8
Príncipe, island, Sao Tome & Principe, G. of Guinea 107 K9
Prins Karls Forland, island, Svalbard, Nor. 106 B9
Protector Basin, Scotia Sea 105 Q4
Providence Island, Seychelles, Ind. Oc. 186 F4
Providencia, Isla de, Col., Caribbean Sea 140 H5
Providenciales, island, Caicos Is., Turks & Caicos Is., U.K., N. Atl. Oc. 141 C9
Prunes Seamount, Medit. Sea 131 G6
Ptolemy Trench, Medit. Sea 132 J8
Pueblo Viejo, Laguna de, Mex., G. of Mex. 138 H2
Puerto Barrios, Guatemala 140 G1
Puerto Cabello, Venez. 141 K12
Puerto Cortés, Hond. 140 G2
Puerto Limón, C.R. 140 K4
Puerto Plata, Dom. Rep. 141 D10
Puerto Quetzal, Guatemala 147 F14
Puerto Rico, island, U.S., Caribbean Sea 141 E12
Puerto Rico Trench, N. Atl. Oc. 141 D12
Pukapuka, atoll, Tuamotu Arch., Fr. Polynesia, Fr., S. Pac. Oc. 165 F14
Pukapuka Atoll (Danger Islands), Cook Is., N.Z., S. Pac. Oc. 165 E10
Pukarua, atoll, Tuamotu Arch., Fr. Polynesia, Fr., S. Pac. Oc. 165 F14
Pula, Croatia 132 B4
Pulap Atoll, Caroline Is., F.S.M., N. Pac. Oc. 164 C5
Pulau Bukom, Singapore 187 E11
Pulley Ridge, G. of Mex. 139 E12
Pulo Anna, island, Palau, N. Pac. Oc. 164 C2
Pulusuk, island, Caroline Is., F.S.M., N. Pac. Oc. 164 C5
Puluwat Atoll, Caroline Is., F.S.M., N. Pac. Oc. 164 C4
Punta Gorda, Bahía de, Nicar., Caribbean Sea 140 J4
Punto Fijo, Venez. 141 J10
Puysegur Point, N.Z. 164 L7
Pygmy Shoal, S. China Sea 180 E8
Pyramid Rock, Xisha Qundao, China, S. China Sea 180 E7

Qarnayn, island, U.A.E., Persian G. 212 J8
Qārūh, island, Kuwait, Persian G. 212 D3
Qeqertarsuaq (Disko), island, Greenland, Den., Baffin B. 219 K11
Qerqenah Islands, Tun., Medit. Sea 132 J2
Qeshm, Iran 213 F13
Qeshm, island, Iran, Persian G. 213 G12
Qimusseriarsuaq, bay, Greenland, Den., Baffin B. 219 J10
Qingdao, China 146 D3
Qinhuangdao, China 146 D3
Qiongzhou Haixia, strait, China, S. China Sea 180 C6
Qishrān, island, Saudi Arabia, Red Sea 210 G5
Qizhou Liedao, China, S. China Sea 180 D6
Québec, Can. 106 F3
Quan Dao Nam Du, island, Vietnam, G. of Thai. 180 H3
Queen Charlotte Islands, Can., N. Pac. Oc. 147 C11
Queen Elizabeth Islands, Can., Arctic Oc. 218 J7
Queen Maud Land, Antarctica 248 F7
Qui Nhon, Vietnam 180 F5
Quintero, Chile 147 K16
Quita Sueño Bank, Caribbean Sea 140 H5
Qulay'ah, Ra's al, Kuwait, Persian G. 212 D2
Qulay'ah, Ra's al, Saudi Arabia, Persian G. 212 G5
Quo Iboe, Nigeria 107 J9
Quraynayn, Ruqq, Persian G. 212 J7
Qutū', island, Saudi Arabia, Red Sea 210 H6
Quway', Sha'b, Red Sea 210 C3

Raas, island, Indonesia 181 Q8
Rabaul, P.N.G. 164 E5
Raccoon Cay, Bahamas, N. Atl. Oc. 140 C8
Rach Gia, Vietnam 180 H4

346 MAP PLACE-NAME INDEX | NUSABARUNG — RACH GIA

Ragged Island, Bahamas, N. Atl. Oc. 140 C8
Ragusa see Dubrovnik, Croatia 132 D5
Raiatea, island, Society Is., Fr. Polynesia, Fr., S. Pac. Oc. 165 F12
Raijua, island, Indonesia 181 R11
Raivavae (Vavitu), island, Austral Is., Fr. Polynesia, Fr., S. Pac. Oc. 165 G13
Rakahanga Atoll, Cook Is., N.Z., S. Pac. Oc. 165 E11
Rakan, Ra's, Qatar, Persian G. 212 H6
Rakiura see Stewart Island, N.Z., S. Pac. Oc. 164 L7
Ralik Chain, Micronesia, Marshall Is., N. Pac. Oc. 164 C7
Ramree Island, Myanmar, B. of Bengal 187 B9
Rancheria Basin, Caribbean Sea 141 J9
Rangiroa, atoll, Tuamotu Arch., Fr. Polynesia, Fr., S. Pac. Oc. 165 F13
Rangsang, island, Kep. Riau, Indonesia 181 M3
Ranguana Cay, Belize, Caribbean Sea 140 F1
Raoul Island (Sunday), Kermadec Is., N.Z., S. Pac. Oc. 165 H9
Rapa, island, Austral Is., Fr. Polynesia, Fr., S. Pac. Oc. 165 H13
Raraka, atoll, Tuamotu Arch., Fr. Polynesia, Fr., S. Pac. Oc. 165 F13
Raroia, atoll, Tuamotu Arch., Fr. Polynesia, Fr., S. Pac. Oc. 165 F13
Rarotonga, island, Cook Is., N.Z., S. Pac. Oc. 165 G11
Ra's al-Khaimah, U.A.E. 213 H12
Rasshua, island, Kuril Is., Russ., N. Pac. Oc. 146 C6
Ra's Tannūrah, Saudi Arabia 212 G5
Rat Islands, Aleutian Is., U.S., N. Pac. Oc. 146 C8
Ratak Chain, Micronesia, Marshall Is., N. Pac. Oc. 164 C7
Ravahere, atoll, Tuamotu Arch., Fr. Polynesia, Fr., S. Pac. Oc. 165 G13
Ravenna, It. 106 F10
Rawaki, island, Phoenix Is., Kiribati, S. Pac. Oc. 165 E10
Rayong, Thailand 180 G2
Reao, atoll, Tuamotu Arch., Fr. Polynesia, Fr., S. Pac. Oc. 165 G14
Recherche, Archipelago of the, Austral., Ind. Oc. 187 J13
Redang, island, Malaysia, S. China Sea 181 K3
Red River Delta, Vietnam 180 C4
Red Sea, Ind. Oc. 210 D3
Red Sea's deepest point, 210 G5
Redonda, island, Leeward Is., Antigua & Barbuda, Caribbean Sea 141 F15
Reed Bank, S. China Sea 180 G9
Reggio di Calabria, It. 132 G4
Renauld Island, Palmer Arch., Antarctica, S. Pac. Oc. 107 R3
Rennell, island, Solomon Is., S. Pac. Oc. 164 F6
Researcher Ridge, N. Atl. Oc. 104 J4
Resolution Island, Can. 106 D3
Réunion, island, Fr., Ind. Oc. 186 G5
Revillagigedo Island, Alexander Arch., U.S., N. Pac. Oc. 147 B11
Revillagigedo Islands, Mex., N. Pac. Oc. 147 F13
Reykjanes Ridge, N. Atl. Oc. 104 E6
Rhodes see Ródos, island, Gr., Medit. Sea 133 H10
Rhodes Basin, Medit. Sea 133 H10
Rhône Fan, Medit. Sea 131 D7
Rhône River Delta, Fr. 131 C8
Riau, Kepulauan, Indonesia 181 M3
Richards Bay, S. Af. 186 H2
Richmond, U.S. 147 D12
Rifleman Bank, S. China Sea 181 J6
Riga, Latv. 106 E11
Riiser-Larsen Peninsula, Antarctica 248 E7
Rijeka (Fiume), Croatia 132 B4
Rimatara, island, Austral Is., Fr. Polynesia, Fr., S. Pac. Oc. 165 G12
Rimini, It. 132 C3
Ringvassøy, island, Nor. 106 C10
Rio de Janeiro, Braz. 107 M5
Rio Grande, Braz. 107 M4
Rio Grande Rise, S. Atl. Oc. 105 M6
Ríohacha, Col. 141 J9
Rīshahr, Iran 212 D6
Rizhao, China 146 D3
Roatán, Isla de, Is. de la Bahía, Hond., Caribbean Sea 140 F2
Robertson Island, Antarctica, Weddell Sea 107 R4
Robesen Channel, Can., Greenland, Den., Lincoln Sea 219 H9
Robinson Crusoe Island, Juan Fernández Is., Chile, S. Pac. Oc. 147 K15
Roca Partida Island, Revillagigedo Is., Mex., N. Pac. Oc. 147 F13
Roca Partida, Punta, Mex. 138 L4
Rockall, island, U.K., N. Atl. Oc. 106 E7
Ródos (Rhodes), island, Gr., Medit. Sea 133 H10
Rodrigues, island, Mauritius, Ind. Oc. 186 G6
Rodrigues Fracture Zone, Ind. Oc. 184 G6
Rojo, Cabo, Mex. 138 H3
Roma (Rome), It. 132 D3
Romanche Fracture Zone, N. Atl. Oc. 105 K7
Romanche Gap, S. Atl. Oc. 105 K7
Romang, island, Indonesia 187 F14
Romano, Cape, U.S. 139 E14
Romano, Cayo, Arch. de Camagüey, Cuba, N. Atl. Oc. 140 C7
Rome see Roma, It. 132 D3
Ron, Mui, Vietnam 180 D4
Roncador Bank, Caribbean Sea 140 H6
Roncador, Cayo de, Col., Caribbean Sea 140 H5
Ronde Island, Windward Is., Grenada, Caribbean Sea 141 J15
Rong, Koh, Cambodia, G. of Thai. 180 G3
Rongelap Atoll, Marshall Is., N. Pac. Oc. 164 B7
Ronne Ice Shelf, Weddell Sea 248 G8
Roosevelt Island, Antarctica, Ross Sea 251 F10
Rosalind Bank, Caribbean Sea 140 F5
Rosario, Cayo del, Arch. de los Canarreos, Cuba, Caribbean Sea 140 C5
Rosario, Islas del, Col., Caribbean Sea 140 K8
Rosario Bank, Caribbean Sea 140 E4
Rose Atoll, Amer. Samoa, U.S., S. Pac. Oc. 165 F10
Roseau, Dominica 141 G15
Rose Island, Bahamas, N. Atl. Oc. 140 A7
Rosetta Mouth of the Nile, Egypt 133 K11
Ross Bank, Ross Sea 249 F10
Ross Ice Shelf, Ross Sea 249 F9
Ross Island, Antarctica, Ross Sea 251 F10
Ross Sea, S. Pac. Oc. 251 F10
Røst Bank, Norwegian Sea 217 E14
Rota, island, N. Mariana Is., U.S., N. Pac. Oc. 164 B4
Rothschild Island, Antarctica, Bellingshausen Sea 107 R3
Roti, island, Lesser Sunda Is., Indonesia 164 E1
Rotterdam, Neth. 106 E9
Rotuma, island, Fiji Is., S. Pac. Oc. 164 F8
Royal Bishop Banks, S. China Sea 180 H5
Royal Charlotte Reef, S. China Sea 181 J7
Royal Island, Bahamas, N. Atl. Oc. 140 A7
Royalist Bank, S. China Sea 181 J4
Rum Cay, Bahamas, N. Atl. Oc. 140 B8
Rūmī, Shi'b, Red Sea 210 G4
Rupat, island, Indonesia, Str. of Malacca 181 L2
Rurutu, island, Austral Is., Fr. Polynesia, Fr., S. Pac. Oc. 165 G12
Russkiy Island, Russ., Kara Sea 218 B8
Ruwais, U.A.E. 186 B5
Ryukyu Islands, Japan, E. China Sea 146 E4
Ryukyu Trench, N. Pac. Oc. 144 E4
Saaremaa, island, Est., Baltic Sea 106 D11
Saba, island, Leeward Is., Neth., Caribbean Sea 141 F14
Saba Bank, Caribbean Sea 141 F14
Sabah, region, Malaysia 181 K9
Sab'ah, Shi'b as, Red Sea 210 E4
Sabana, Archipiélago de, Cuba, N. Atl. Oc. 140 C5
Sabina Shoal, S. China Sea 180 H9
Sabinal, Cayo, Arch. de Camagüey, Cuba, N. Atl. Oc. 140 C7
Sabine Lake, U.S. 138 B5
Sable, Cape, U.S. 139 E14
Sable Island, Can., N. Atl. Oc. 106 F4
Sabtang, island, Batan Is., Philippines, Luzon Str. 180 C11
Sackett Bank, G. of Mex. 138 C8
Saffānīyah, Ra's as, Saudi Arabia, Persian G. 212 E3
Saigon see Ho Chi Minh City, Vietnam 180 G4
St. Andrews Bay, U.S., G. of Mex. 139 A11
St.-Barthélemy, island, Leeward Is., Fr., Caribbean Sea 141 F14
St. Brandon see Cargados Carajos Shoals, Mauritius, Ind. Oc. 186 G6
St. Croix, island, Virgin Is., U.S., Caribbean Sea 141 F13
St. Esprit Shoal, S. China Sea 180 D7
St. Eustatius, island, Leeward Is., Neth., Caribbean Sea 141 F14
St. George Island, U.S., Bering Sea 147 B9
St. George Island, U.S., G. of Mex. 139 B12
St. George, Cape, U.S. 139 B11
St. Helena, island, U.K., S. Atl. Oc. 107 L8
St. John, island, Virgin Is., U.S., Caribbean Sea 141 E12
St. John, Can. 106 F3
St. John Island, Russ., Sea of Okhotsk 146 B5
St. John's, Antigua & Barbuda 141 F15
St. Joseph Bay, U.S., G. of Mex. 139 B11
St. Joseph Island, U.S., G. of Mex. 138 C3
St. Kitts, island, Leeward Is., St. Kitts & Nevis, Caribbean Sea 141 F14
St. Lawrence, Gulf of, 106 E3
St. Lawrence Island, U.S., Bering Sea 146 B8
St. Lucia, island, Windward Is., Caribbean Sea 141 H15
St. Lucia Channel, N. Atl. Oc. 141 H15
St.-Marc, Canal de, Haiti, Caribbean Sea 141 E9
St. Martin, island, Leeward Is., Fr., Neth., Caribbean Sea 141 E14
St. Matthew Island, U.S., Bering Sea 146 B8
St.-Paul, Île, Fr., Ind. Oc. 186 K8
St. Paul Island, U.S., Bering Sea 146 B8
St. Peter and St. Paul Rocks, Braz., S. Atl. Oc. 107 K6
St. Petersburg, Fla., U.S. 139 C13
St. Peterburg, Russ. 106 D11
St. Pierre and Miquelon, Fr., G. of St. Lawrence 106 F4
St. Pierre Island, Seychelles, Ind. Oc. 186 F4
St. Thomas, island, Virgin Is., U.S., Caribbean Sea 141 E13
St. Vincent, island, Windward Is., St. Vincent & the Grenadines, Caribbean Sea 141 H15
St. Vincent, Gulf, Austral., Ind. Oc. 187 J15
St. Vincent Island, U.S., G. of Mex. 139 B11
St. Vincent Passage, N. Atl. Oc. 141 H15
Saipan, island, N. Mariana Is., U.S., N. Pac. Oc. 164 B4
Sakhalin Island, Russ., Sea of Okhotsk 146 C5
Sakishima Islands, Japan, S. China Sea 146 E4
Sal, island, C. Verde Is., C. Verde, N. Atl. Oc. 106 H7
Sal, Cay, Bahamas, N. Atl. Oc. 140 B5
Sal, Cayo de, Lesser Antil., Venez., Caribbean Sea 141 J12
Salālah, Oman 186 C5
Salamanca, Roches, Kerguelen Is., Fr., Ind. Oc. 186 L7
Sala-y-Gómez, island, Chile, S. Pac. Oc. 147 J13
Sala y Gómez Ridge, S. Pac. Oc. 145 J14
Saldanha Bay, S. Af. 107 M10
Salerno, It. 132 E4
Salerno, Golfo di, It., Tyrrhenian Sea 132 E4
Salisbury Island, Can., Hudson Str. 106 D2
Salmon Bank, N. Pac. Oc. 146 E8
Salomon Islands, Chagos Arch., U.K., Ind. Oc. 186 E7
Salonica see Thessaloníki, Gr. 132 E8
Salûm, Khalîg el, Egypt, Medit. Sea 133 K9
Salvador, Braz. 107 L5
Salvage Islands, Port., N. Atl. Oc. 106 G7
Salwá, Saudi Arabia 212 K6
Salwá, Dawḩat, Persian G. 212 J5
Samaná, Bahía de, Dom. Rep., N. Atl. Oc. 141 E11
Samana Cay (Atwood), Bahamas, N. Atl. Oc. 141 C9
Samar, island, Philippines 164 B1
Sambarūn Bank, Persian G. 213 G9
Samoa Islands, Polynesia, S. Pac. Oc. 165 F10
Sámos, island, Gr., Aegean Sea 133 G9
Samothráki, island, Gr., Aegean Sea 133 E9
Samui, island, Thailand, G. of Thai. 187 C10
Samui, Ko, Thailand, G. of Thai. 180 H1
Samut Prakhan, Thailand 180 F2
Şanāfīr, island, Saudi Arabia, Red Sea 210 C3
Sanak Islands, Aleutian Is., U.S., N. Pac. Oc. 147 B9
San Ambrosio Island, Chile, S. Pac. Oc. 147 J15
Sanana, island, Indonesia 187 E13
San Andrés, Isla de, Col., Caribbean Sea 140 H5
San Andrés, Laguna de, Mex., G. of Mex. 138 H2
San Antonio, Chile 147 K16
San Antonio Bay, U.S., G. of Mex. 138 C3
San Antonio Reef, G. of Mex. 139 H11
San Antonio, Cabo, Cuba 139 H11
San Benedicto Island, Revillagigedo Is., Mex., N. Pac. Oc. 147 F13
San Bernardo, Islas de, Col., Caribbean Sea 140 K8
San Blas, Archipiélago de, Pan., Caribbean Sea 140 K6
San Blas, Cape, U.S 139 B11
San Blas, Golfo de, Pan., Caribbean Sea 140 K6
San Clemente, island, Channel Is., U.S., N. Pac. Oc. 147 D12
San Cristóbal Island, Galápagos Is., Ecua., S. Pac. Oc. 147 G14
San Cristobal, island, Solomon Is., S. Pac. Oc. 164 F6
Sand Cay, Spratly Is., S. China Sea 180 H8
Sandoval, Boca de, Mex., G. of Mex. 138 F2
San Félix Island, Chile, S. Pac. Oc. 147 J15
San Felipe, Cayos de, Cuba, Caribbean Sea 140 C4
San Francisco, U.S. 147 D12
Sangeang, island, Indonesia, Flores Sea 181 Q10
Sangihe, island, Indonesia 187 D13
Sangihe Islands, Indonesia 164 C1
Sanibel Island, U.S., G. of Mex. 139 D13
San Ildefonso, Cape, Philippines 180 E11
San Jorge, Gulf of, S. Atl. Oc. 107 P3
San Juan, P.R., U.S 141 E13
San Juan, Punta, Mex. 138 L5
San Lorenzo, Braz. 107 M4
San Matías Gulf, S. Atl. Oc. 107 N3
San Miguel Islands, Philippines, Sulu Sea 187 D12
San Nicolas, island, Channel Is., U.S., N. Pac. Oc. 147 D12
San Pedro de Macorís, Dom. Rep. 141 E11
San Pietro, Isola di, It., Medit. Sea 132 F1
San Remo, It. 132 C1
San Salvador (Watling), island, Bahamas, N. Atl. Oc. 140 B8
San Salvador Island, Galápagos Is., Ecua., S. Pac. Oc. 147 G14
Santa Catalina, island, Channel Is., U.S., N. Pac. Oc. 147 D12
Santa Clara Island, Juan Fernández Is., Chile, S. Pac. Oc. 147 K15
Santa Cruz de Tenerife, Canary Is., Sp. 106 G7
Santa Cruz Island, Galápagos Is., Ecua., S. Pac. Oc. 147 G14
Santa Cruz Islands, Melanesia, Solomon Is., S. Pac. Oc. 164 E7
Santa Isabel, island, Solomon Is., S. Pac. Oc. 164 E6
Santa Maria, island, Azores, Port., N. Atl. Oc. 106 G7
Santa Maria di Leuca, Capo, It. 132 F6
Santa María Island, Galápagos Is., Ecua., S. Pac. Oc. 147 G14
Santa María, Cayo, Cuba, N. Atl. Oc. 140 C6
Santa Marta, Col. 140 J8
Santanilla, Islas (Swan Islands), Hond., Caribbean Sea 140 F4
Sant' Antioco, Isola di, It., Medit. Sea 132 F1
Santa Panagia, It. 106 G10
Santaren Channel, Bahamas, N. Atl. Oc. 140 B6
Santa Rosa Island, U.S., G. of Mex. 139 A10
Santiago de Cuba, Cuba 140 D8
Santo Antão, island, C. Verde Is., C. Verde, N. Atl. Oc. 106 H6
Santo Domingo, Dom. Rep. 141 E11
Santo Domingo Basin, Caribbean Sea 141 E11
Santoríni see Thíra, island, Kikládes, Gr., Aegean Sea 133 H9
Santos, Braz. 107 M5
Santos Plateau, S. Atl. Oc. 105 M5
San Vicente, Chile 147 K15
Sanya, China 180 D5
São Jorge, island, Azores, Port., N. Atl. Oc. 106 F6
São Miguel, island, Azores, Port., N. Atl. Oc. 106 G6
Saona, Isla, Dom. Rep., Caribbean Sea 141 E11
São Nicolau, island, C. Verde Is., C. Verde, N. Atl. Oc. 106 H7
São Sebastião, Braz. 107 M5
São Tiago, island, C. Verde Is., C. Verde, N. Atl. Oc. 106 H7
São Tomé, island, Sao Tome & Principe, G. of Guinea 107 K9
Sapanjang, island, Indonesia 181 Q8
Sapudi, island, Indonesia 181 Q8
Sarasota, Fla., U.S 139 D13
Sarasota Bay, U.S., G. of Mex. 139 D13
Sarawak, region, Malaysia 181 L7
Sardegna (Sardinia), island, It., Medit. Sea 132 E1
Sardinia see Sardegna, island, It., Medit. Sea 132 E1
Sardino-Balearic Abyssal Plain, Medit. Sea 131 E8
Sargo Plateau, Arctic Oc. 216 F6
Sarigan, island, N. Mariana Is., U.S., N. Pac. Oc. 164 B4
Sarkān, Ra's, Oman, Persian G. 213 H13
Saronikós Kólpos, Gr., Sea of Crete 132 G8
Saros Körfezi, Turk., Aegean Sea 133 E9
Satawal, island, Caroline Is., F.S.M., N. Pac. Oc. 164 C4
Saunders Island, S. Sandwich Is., U.K., Scotia Sea 107 Q6
Saunders Reef, Red Sea 210 H5
Savai'i, island, Samoa, S. Pac. Oc. 165 F9
Savannah, U.S. 106 G2
Savanna-la-Mar, Jam. 140 E6
Savona, It. 132 C1
Savu Sea, Indonesia 164 E1
Sawqirah Bay, Oman, Arabian Sea 186 B5
Sawu, island, Indonesia 181 R11
Saya de Malha Bank, Ind. Oc. 184 F6
Şayyaḩ, Ra's, Saudi Arabia, G. of Bahrain 212 H5
Scandinavia, region, 104 D10
Scarborough Reef, S. China Sea 180 F9
Scawfell Shoal, S. China Sea 181 J4
Schmidt-Ott Seamount, S. Atl. Oc. 107 N10
Scotia Ridge, Scotia Sea 107 Q4
Scotia Sea, S. Atl. Oc. 107 Q5
Scott Island, Antarctica, S. Pac. Oc. 251 F11
Seahorse Shoal, S. China Sea 180 G9
Seal Cay, Bahamas, N. Atl. Oc. 140 C8
Seal Cays, Caicos Is., Turks & Caicos Is., U.K., N. Atl. Oc. 141 D10
Seattle, U.S. 147 C12
Sebaou Canyon, Medit. Sea 131 G7
Sebatik, island, Indonesia, Malaysia, Celebes Sea 181 K9

RAGGED ISLAND – SEBATIK | MAP PLACE-NAME INDEX 347

Seguam Island, Andreanof Is., U.S., N. Pac. Oc. 146 C8
Seine Seamount, N. Atl. Oc. 106 G7
Selaru, island, Indonesia 187 F14
Selayar, island, Indonesia 181 P10
Semarang, Indonesia 181 Q6
Sembuni Reefs, S. China Sea 181 L5
Senja, island, Nor. 106 C10
Senkaku Islands, Japan, E. China Sea 187 A13
Sentinelle Bank, Medit. Sea 132 G2
Senyavin Islands, Caroline Is., F.S.M., N. Pac. Oc. 164 C6
Sepetiba, Braz. 107 M5
Sept-Îles, Can. 106 E3
Serasan, island, Kep. Natuna Selatan, Indonesia, S. China Sea 181 L5
Sérifos, island, Kikládes, Gr., Aegean Sea 132 G8
Serpent's Mouth, strait, Trinidad & Tobago, N. Atl. Oc. 141 K15
Serrana Bank, Caribbean Sea 140 G5
Serranilla Bank, Caribbean Sea 140 G6
Sète, Fr. 131 C7
Seward Peninsula, U.S. 216 G3
Seychelles, islands, Ind. Oc. 184 E5
Sfax, Tun. 132 J2
Shâkir, island, Egypt, Red Sea 210 C3
Shaban Deep, Red Sea 210 D3
Shag Rocks, U.K., Scotia Sea 107 P5
Shah Allum Shoal, Persian G. 212 G8
Shangchuan Dao, China, S. China Sea 180 C7
Shanghai, China 146 E4
Shannon, island, Greenland, Den., Greenland Sea 219 G12
Shantar Islands, Russ., Sea of Okhotsk 146 B5
Shantou (Swatow), China 180 B9
Sharā'iwah, island, Qatar, Persian G. 212 J7
Sharjah (Ash Shāriqah), U.A.E. 213 J12
Shark Bay, Austral., Ind. Oc. 187 H12
Sharm el Sheikh, Egypt 210 C3
Shatskiy Rise, N. Pac. Oc. 144 E6
Shaṭṭ, Ra's osh, Iran, Persian G. 212 C5
Shaybārā, island, Saudi Arabia, Red Sea 210 D4
Shaykh Mas'ūd, Ra's, Oman, Persian G. 213 G13
Shelikhov Gulf, Sea of Okhotsk 146 B6
Shenzhen, China 180 B7
Shepherd Islands, Vanuatu, S. Pac. Oc. 164 F7
Shetland Islands, U.K., N. Atl. Oc. 106 D9
Sheyū, Iran 213 F9
Shiashkotan, island, Kuril Is., Russ., N. Pac. Oc. 146 C6
Shikoku, island, Japan 146 D4
Ship Island, U.S., G. of Mex. 139 A9
Shiqitah, Ḥayr, Persian G. 212 G5
Shīr, Ra's osh, Iran, Persian G. 213 H14
Shirshov Ridge, Bering Sea 144 B7
Shroud Cay, Exuma Cays, Bahamas, N. Atl. Oc. 140 B7
Shumagin Islands, U.S., N. Pac. Oc. 147 B9
Siargao, island, Philippines 187 C13
Siau, island, Indonesia 187 D13
Siberia, region, Asia 216 D3
Siberut, island, Kep. Mentawai, Indonesia, Ind. Oc. 181 N1
Sibiryakova Island, Russ., Yenisey G. 219 A9
Sibu, island, Malaysia, S. China Sea 181 L3
Sibuyan, island, Philippines, Sibuyan Sea 180 G11
Sibuyan Sea, Philippines 180 G11
Sicilia (Sicily), island, It., Medit. Sea 132 G4
Sicilian Basin, Ionian Sea 132 H5
Sicily see Sicilia, island, It., Medit. Sea 132 G4
Sicily, Strait of, Medit. Sea 132 G3
Sicily-Malta Escarpment, Ionian Sea 132 G4
Sidra see Surt, Lib. 132 L5
Sidra, Gulf of see Surt, Khalīj, Lib., Medit. Sea 132 K5
Sierra Leone Basin, N. Atl. Oc. 105 J7
Sierra Leone Fracture Zone, N. Atl. Oc. 105 J5
Sierra Leone Rise, N. Atl. Oc. 105 J7
Siesta Key, U.S., G. of Mex. 139 D13
Sigsbee Escarpment, G. of Mex. 138 E6
Sigsbee Plain, G. of Mex. 138 G6
Sikka, India 186 B7
Silhouette, island, Seychelles, Ind. Oc. 186 E5
Silver Bank, N. Atl. Oc. 141 D11
Silver Bank Passage, N. Atl. Oc. 141 D10
Silver Plain, N. Atl. Oc. 104 H3
Silvertown Bank, Caribbean Sea 140 D5
Simeulue, island, Indonesia, Ind. Oc. 187 D10
Simushir, island, Kuril Is., Russ., N. Pac. Oc. 146 C6
Sin Cowe Island, Spratly Is., S. China Sea 180 H8
Sines, Port. 106 F8
Singapore, Singapore 181 L3
Singapore Strait, S. China Sea 181 L3
Singkep, island, Kep. Lingga, Indonesia 181 M3
Sipang, Tanjong, Malaysia 181 L6
Siple Island, Antarctica, Amundsen Sea 251 H10
Sipura, island, Kep. Mentawai, Indonesia, Ind. Oc. 181 N1
Siracusa, It. 132 G4
Şīr Banī Yās, island, U.A.E., Persian G. 212 K8
Şīr Bū Nu'ayr, island, U.A.E., Persian G. 213 J10
Sir Edward Pellew Group, Austral., G. of Carpentaria 187 G15
Sirik, Tanjong, Malaysia 181 L6
Sírna, island, Dodekánissa, Gr., Aegean Sea 133 H9
Sīrrī, island, Iran, Persian G. 213 H11
Sirte Plain, Medit. Sea 132 J6
Sirte Rise, Medit. Sea 132 J5
Siyāl, Jazā'ir, Egypt, Red Sea 210 E4
Sjaeland, island, Den., Kattegat 106 E10
Sjubre Bank, Greenland Sea 104 A9
Skagerrak, strait, 106 D9
Skeleton Coast, Af. 105 L10
Skíros, island, Vóries Sporádes, Gr., Aegean Sea 132 F8
Slave Coast, 105 J9
Smith Island, S. Shetland Is., Antarctica, Drake Pass. 107 Q3
Smith Sound, Can., Greenland, Den., Baffin B. 219 J9
Smyrna see İzmir, Turk. 133 F9
Snipe Keys, Fla. Keys, U.S., G. of Mex. 139 F14
Snow Hill Island, Antarctica, Weddell Sea 107 R4
Society Islands, Polynesia, Fr. Polynesia, Fr., S. Pac. Oc. 165 F12
Socorro Island, Revillagigedo Is., Mex., N. Pac. Oc. 147 F13
Socotra, island, Yemen, Arabian Sea 186 C5
Sohm Plain, N. Atl. Oc. 104 G4
Sol, Costa del, Sp. 131 H4
Solomon Islands, S. Pac. Oc. 144 G6
Solomon Sea, S. Pac. Oc. 164 E5
Solor, island, Indonesia 181 R11
Šolta, island, Croatia, Adriatic Sea 132 C5
Soltānī, Khowr-e, Persian G. 212 C6
Somali Basin, Ind. Oc. 184 E4
Somali Peninsula, Af. 184 D4
Sombrero, island, Anguilla, U.K., N. Atl. Oc. 141 E14
Somerset Island, Can., Arctic Oc. 218 K8
Songkhla, Thailand 181 J2
Sonmiani Bay, Pak., Arabian Sea 186 A6
Sonsorol Islands, Palau, N. Pac. Oc. 164 C2
Sōfu Gan, island, Nampō Shotō, Japan, N. Pac. Oc. 187 A15
Sorol Atoll, Caroline Is., F.S.M., N. Pac. Oc. 164 C3
Sorøya, island, Nor. 106 C10
Soudan Bank, Ind. Oc. 186 G5
Sousse, Tun. 132 H2
South Adriatic Basin, Adriatic Sea 132 D5
Southampton, U.K. 106 E8
Southampton Island, Can., Hudson B. 106 D2
South Andaman, island, Andaman Is., India, B. of Bengal 187 C9
South Australian Basin, Ind. Oc. 185 K14
South Australian Plain, Ind. Oc. 251 B12
South China Basin, S. China Sea 180 F8
South China Sea, N. Pac. Oc. 187 D11
South China Sea's deepest point, 180 G7
South East Cape, Austral. 164 L4
Southeast Indian Ridge, Ind. Oc. 185 K9
Southeast Pacific Basin, S. Pac. Oc. 145 L14
Southern Long Cay, Belize, Caribbean Sea 140 F1
Southern Thule, island, S. Sandwich Is., U.K., Scotia Sea 107 Q6
South Fiji Basin, S. Pac. Oc. 144 J7
South Georgia, island, S. Georgia, U.K., Scotia Sea 107 P6
South Georgia Ridge, S. Atl. Oc. 105 P4
South Georgia Rise, S. Atl. Oc. 105 P6
South Indian Basin, Ind. Oc. 249 B9
South Island, N.Z., S. Pac. Oc. 164 K7
South Luconia Shoals, S. China Sea 181 K7
South Male Atoll, Maldives, Ind. Oc. 186 D7
South Orkney Islands, Antarctica, S. Atl. Oc. 250 H6
South Pole, Antarctica 250 F8
South Sandwich Islands, U.K., S. Atl. Oc. 250 H5
South Sandwich Trench, S. Pac. Oc. 248 H5
South Shetland Islands, Antarctica, Drake Pass. 250 J7
South Shetland Trough, S. Atl. Oc. 107 Q3
South Tasman Rise, Tasman Sea 144 L5
South Vereker Bank, S. China Sea 180 C8
Southwest Aukland Rise, S. Pac. Oc. 249 E12
Southwest Cay, Col., Caribbean Sea 140 H5
Southwest Indian Ridge, Ind. Oc. 184 L2
Southwest Pacific Basin, S. Pac. Oc. 145 J9
Spartel, Cap, Mor. 131 H3
Spencer Gulf, Austral., Ind. Oc. 164 J3
Spiess Seamount, S. Atl. Oc. 105 P9
Spitsbergen, island, Svalbard, Nor., Arctic Oc. 219 E11
Spitsbergen Bank, Barents Sea 217 D12
Spitsbergen Fracture Zone, Arctic Oc. 217 F11
Split, Croatia 132 C5
Spratly Island, Spratly Is., S. China Sea 180 H6
Spratly Islands, S. China Sea 181 J7
Squillace, Golfo di, It., Ionian Sea 132 F5
Starbuck Island, Line Is., Kiribati, S. Pac. Oc. 165 E12
Staten Island, Arg., Drake Pass. 107 Q3
Ste. Marie, Cape, Madagascar 186 H4
Ste. Marie, Nosy, Madagascar, Ind. Oc. 186 G4
Stewart Island see Rakiura, N.Z., S. Pac. Oc. 164 L7
Stewart Seamount, S. China Sea 180 E10
Stiffe Bank, Persian G. 213 G9
Stocks Seamount, S. Atl. Oc. 105 L6
Store Koldewey, island, Greenland, Den. 106 B7
Storøya, island, Svalbard, Nor. 106 A11
Strabo Trench, Medit. Sea 133 J9
Stuart Island, U.S., Bering Sea 147 A9
Sture, Nor. 106 D9
Su'ādī, Shi'b, Red Sea 210 G4
Suakin Archipelago, Sudan, Red Sea 210 G5
Subi, island, Kep. Natuna Selatan, Indonesia, S. China Sea 181 L5
Subi Reef, S. China Sea 180 G8
Sud, Canal du, Haiti, Caribbean Sea 141 E9
Suðuroy, island, Faroe Is., Den., Norwegian Sea 106 D8
Suez see El Suweis, Egypt 210 B2
Suez, Gulf of, Red Sea 210 B2
Suez Canal, Egypt 210 A2
Suflānī, Shi'b as, Red Sea 210 E5
Sugarloaf Key, Fla. Keys, U.S., G. of Mex. 139 F14
Suiko Seamount, N. Pac. Oc. 146 C7
Sukadana, Teluk, Indonesia, S. China Sea 181 N5
Sula Islands, Indonesia 164 D1
Sulawesi (Celebes), island, Indonesia 164 D1
Sullom Voe, Shetland Is., U.K. 106 D9
Sulu Archipelago, Philippines 181 K10
Sulu Basin, Sulu Sea 185 D13
Sulu Sea, Malaysia, Philippines 181 J10
Sumatra, island, Indonesia 187 D10
Sumba, island, Lesser Sunda Is., Indonesia 181 R10
Sumbawa, island, Lesser Sunda Is., Indonesia 181 R9
Sumisu, island, Nampō Shotō, Japan, N. Pac. Oc. 187 A15
Sunda, Selat, Indonesia 181 Q4
Sunda Shelf, S. China Sea 181 K5
Sunday see Raoul Island, Kermadec Is., N.Z., S. Pac. Oc. 165 H9
Supiori, island, Indonesia, S. Pac. Oc. 187 E14
Surabaya, Indonesia 181 Q7
Surat Thani, Thailand 180 H1
Surt (Sidra), Lib. 132 L5
Surt, Khalīj (Gulf of Sidra), Lib., Medit. Sea 132 K5
Surtsey, island, Ice., N. Atl. Oc. 219 H15
Suva, Fiji Is. 164 F8
Suvadiva Atoll, Maldives, Ind. Oc. 186 E7
Suwannee Sound, U.S., G. of Mex. 139 B13
Suwarrow Atoll, Cook Is., N.Z., S. Pac. Oc. 165 F11
Svalbard, islands, Nor., Arctic Oc. 219 E11
Sverdrup Islands, Queen Elizabeth Is., Can., Arctic Oc. 218 J8
Svyataya Anna Fan, Arctic Oc. 217 D9
Svyataya Anna Trough, Kara Sea 219 C9
Swains Island, Amer. Samoa, U.S., S. Pac. Oc. 165 E10
Swallow Reef, S. China Sea 181 J7
Swan Islands see Santanilla, Islas, Hond., Caribbean Sea 140 F4
Swan Trough, Caribbean Sea 140 F4
Swatow see Shantou, China 180 B9
Sweet Bank, G. of Mex. 138 C7
Sydney, Austral. 164 J5

Tabiteuea, atoll, Gilbert Is., Kiribati, S. Pac. Oc. 164 D8
Tablas, island, Philippines 180 G11
Tabuaeran (Fanning Island), Line Is., Kiribati, S. Pac. Oc. 165 C11
Tacoma, U.S. 147 C12
Tafahi, island, Tonga, S. Pac. Oc. 165 F9
Tahiti, island, Society Is., Fr. Polynesia, Fr., S. Pac. Oc. 165 F12
Ţāhrū'ī, Iran 213 G14
Tahuata, island, Marquesas Is., Fr. Polynesia, Fr., S. Pac. Oc. 165 E14
Taibei see Taipei, Taiwan, China 180 A11
T'aichung, Taiwan, China 146 E4
Taipei (Taibei), Taiwan, China 180 A11
Taiwan, island, Taiwan, China 164 A1
Taiwan Banks, S. China Sea 180 B9
Taiwan Strait, China, N. Pac. Oc. 180 B9
Takaroa, atoll, Tuamotu Arch., Fr. Polynesia, Fr., S. Pac. Oc. 165 F13
Takutea, island, Cook Is., N.Z., S. Pac. Oc. 147 J9
Talaud Islands, Indonesia, S. Pac. Oc. 164 C2
Taliabu, island, Indonesia 187 E13
Tamana, island, Gilbert Is., Kiribati, S. Pac. Oc. 164 D8
Tambelan, Kepulauan, Indonesia, S. China Sea 181 L5
Tamiahua, Laguna de, Mex., G. of Mex. 138 H2
Tampa, Fla., U.S. 139 C13
Tampa Bay, U.S., G. of Mex. 139 C13
Tampico, Mex. 138 H2
Tanāqīb, Ra's at, Saudi Arabia, Persian G. 212 E3
Tanaga Island, Andreanof Is., U.S., N. Pac. Oc. 146 C8
Tanahbala, island, Indonesia, Ind. Oc. 181 M1
Tanahjampea, island, Indonesia, Flores Sea 181 Q10
Tanahmasa, island, Indonesia, Ind. Oc. 181 M1
Tanega, island, Japan, N. Pac. Oc. 187 A14
Tang, Koh, Cambodia, G. of Thai. 180 H3
Tanger (Tangier), Mor. 131 H3
Tangier see Tanger, Mor. 131 H3
Tanimbar Islands, Indonesia 164 E2
Tanjung Pelepas, Malaysia 187 D11
Tanjungkarang-Telukbetung, Indonesia 181 P4
Tanna, island, Vanuatu, S. Pac. Oc. 164 G7
Tao, Ko, Thailand, G. of Thai. 180 H1
Taongi Atoll, Ratak Chain, Marshall Is., N. Pac. Oc. 164 B7
Tapul Group, Sulu Arch., Philippines 181 K10
Tarabulus, Leb. 133 J13
Ţarābulus (Tripoli), Lib. 132 K3
Tarakan, island, Indonesia, Celebes Sea 181 L9
Taranto, It. 132 E5
Taranto, Golfo di, It., Ionian Sea 132 E5
Taranto Valley, G. di Taranto 132 F5
Tarawa, island, Gilbert Is., Kiribati, S. Pac. Oc. 144 G7
Tarawa (Bairiki), Kiribati 164 D8
Ţarfā', Ra's aţ, Saudi Arabia, Red Sea 210 H6
Ţarīf, U.A.E. 213 L10
Tarifa, Punta de, Sp. 131 H3
Tarragona, Sp. 131 E6
Tārūt, island, Saudi Arabia, Persian G. 212 G5
Tasman Escarpment, Ind. Oc. 249 C13
Tasman Fracture Zone, Ind. Oc. 249 E12
Tasmania, island, Austral. 164 K5
Tasman Plain, Tasman Sea 144 K6
Tasman Sea, S. Pac. Oc. 146 K6
Tatakoto, atoll, Tuamotu Arch., Fr. Polynesia, Fr., S. Pac. Oc. 165 F14
Tatar Strait, Sea of Okhotsk 146 C5
Taupo Tablemount, Tasman Sea 164 J6
Tauranga, N.Z. 146 K8
Taveuni, island, Lau Group, Fiji Is., S. Pac. Oc. 165 F9
Tawi Tawi, island, Sulu Arch., Philippines 181 K10
Taymyr Peninsula, Russ. 216 B8
Tebingtinggi, island, Indonesia, Str. of Malacca 181 M3
Teesport, U.K. 106 E9
Tegal, Indonesia 181 Q5
Tehuelche Fracture Zone, Scotia Sea 105 Q5
Tel Aviv-Yafo, Israel 133 K13
Tela, Hond. 140 G2
Tema, Ghana 107 J9
Tematagi, island, Tuamotu Arch., Fr. Polynesia, Fr., S. Pac. Oc. 165 G14
Temoe, atoll, Is. Gambier, Fr. Polynesia, Fr., S. Pac. Oc. 165 G15
Templer Bank, S. China Sea 180 G9
Ténaro, Akrotírio, Gr. 132 H7
Ten Degree Channel, India, B. of Bengal 187 C9
Tenerife, island, Canary Is., Sp., N. Atl. Oc. 106 G7
Tenggol, island, Malaysia, S. China Sea 181 K3
Tenji Seamount, N. Pac. Oc. 146 C7
Ten Thousand Islands, U.S., G. of Mex. 139 E14
Teraina (Washington Island), Line Is., Kiribati, S. Pac. Oc. 165 C11
Terceira, island, Azores, Port., N. Atl. Oc. 106 F6
Términos, Laguna de, Mex., G. of Mex. 138 L7
Terrebonne Bay, U.S., G. of Mex. 138 B7
Texas City, U.S. 106 G1
Thássos, island, Gr., Aegean Sea 132 E8
Thailand, Gulf of, S. China Sea 180 G2
Thamesport, U.K. 106 E9
The Brothers, islands, Bahamas, N. Atl. Oc. 140 C8
The Brothers, islands, Egypt, Red Sea 210 D3
The Brothers, islands, Yemen, Arabian Sea 186 C5
The Elbow, bank, G. of Mex. 139 C12
The Flat, bank, Persian G. 213 G12
The Pearl-Qatar, site, Qatar, Persian G. 212 J7
Thermaïkós Kólpos, Gr., Aegean Sea 132 E8
The Snares, islands, N.Z., S. Pac. Oc. 164 L7
Thessaloníki (Salonica), Gr. 132 E8
The Witties, islands, Cayos Miskitos, Nicar., Caribbean Sea 140 H4
The World, site, U.A.E., Persian G. 213 J11
Thíra (Santoríni), island, Kikládes, Gr., Aegean Sea 133 H9
Thitu Island, Spratly Is., S. China Sea 180 G8
Tho Chu, Dao, Vietnam, G. of Thai. 180 H3

348 MAP PLACE-NAME INDEX | SEGUAM ISLAND – THO CHU

Three Brothers, islands, *Chagos Arch., U.K., Ind. Oc.* **186** E7
Three Kings Islands, *N.Z., S. Pac. Oc.* **164** J8
Thu Island, *Vietnam, S. China Sea* **187** C11
Thunder Knoll, *Caribbean Sea* **140** F5
Thursday Island, *Austral.* **146** H5
Thurston Island, *Antarctica, S. Pac. Oc.* **251** H9
Tib, Ras el, *Tun.* **132** G2
Tierra del Fuego, island, *Arg., S. Atl. Oc.* **107** P3
Tikei, atoll, *Tuamotu Arch., Fr. Polynesia, Fr., S. Pac. Oc.* **165** F13
Tikopia, island, *Sta. Cruz Is., Solomon Is., S. Pac. Oc.* **164** F7
Tiladummati Atoll, *Maldives, Ind. Oc.* **186** D7
Tilbury, *U.K.* **106** E9
Tílos, island, *Dodekánissa, Gr., Aegean Sea* **133** H10
Timbalier Island, *U.S., G. of Mex.* **138** B7
Timbun Mata, island, *Malaysia, Celebes Sea* **181** K10
Timor, island, *Lesser Sunda Is., Indonesia, Timor-Leste* **164** E1
Timor Sea, *Ind. Oc.* **164** F2
Tinggi, island, *Malaysia, S. China Sea* **181** L3
Tinian, island, *N. Mariana Is., U.S., N. Pac. Oc.* **164** B4
Tínos, island, *Kikládes, Gr., Aegean Sea* **133** G9
Tioman, island, *Malaysia, S. China Sea* **181** L3
Tīrān, island, *Saudi Arabia, Red Sea* **210** C3
Tobago, island, *Trinidad & Tobago, N. Atl. Oc.* **141** J15
Tobago Basin, *N. Atl. Oc.* **141** H16
Tobi, island, *Palau, N. Pac. Oc.* **164** D2
Togian, Kepulauan, *Indonesia, Teluk Tomini* **181** M11
Tokara Islands, *Ryukyu Is., Japan, N. Pac. Oc.* **187** A14
Tokelau, island, *Polynesia, N.Z., S. Pac. Oc.* **165** E10
Tokuno, island, *Ryukyu Is., Japan, N. Pac. Oc.* **187** A14
Tokyo, *Japan* **146** D5
Tolo, Teluk, *Indonesia* **181** N11
Tomini, Teluk, *Indonesia* **181** M10
Tonb, Ra's-e, *Iran, Persian G.* **212** B5
Tonga Islands, *Polynesia, S. Pac. Oc.* **165** G9
Tongareva *see* Penrhyn Atoll, *Cook Is., N.Z., S. Pac. Oc.* **165** E11
Tongatapu Group, *Tonga, S. Pac. Oc.* **165** G9
Tonga Trench, *S. Pac. Oc.* **144** J8
Tongue of the Ocean, *Bahamas, N. Atl. Oc.* **140** B7
Tonkin, Gulf of, *China, Vietnam, S. China Sea* **180** C5
Torremolinos, *Sp.* **131** H4
Torres Islands, *Vanuatu, S. Pac. Oc.* **164** F7
Torres Strait, *Austral., P.N.G.* **164** E4
Tortola, island, *Virgin Is., U.K., Caribbean Sea* **141** E13
Tortue, Île de la, *Haiti, N. Atl. Oc.* **141** D9
Tortugas Terrace, *G. of Mex.* **139** F13
Tortugas Valley, *G. of Mex.* **139** G13
Toulon, *Fr.* **131** D8
Traill Island, *Greenland, Den.* **106** C7
Traversay Islands, *S. Sandwich Is., U.K., Scotia Sea* **107** Q6
Tregrosse Islets, *Austral., Coral Sea* **164** F5
Tressler Bank, *Ind. Oc.* **249** C9
Triángulo Oeste, island, *Mex., G. of Mex.* **138** J6
Triángulo Sur, island, *Mex., G. of Mex.* **138** J6
Trieste, *It.* **132** B4
Trieste, Golfo di, *It., Adriatic Sea* **132** B3
Trindade, island, *Braz., S. Atl. Oc.* **107** L6
Trindade Seachannel, *S. Atl. Oc.* **105** L6
Trinidad, island, *Trinidad & Tobago, N. Atl. Oc.* **141** K15
Trinity Bay, *U.S., G. of Mex.* **138** B4
Trinity Islands, *U.S., G. of Alas.* **147** B10
Tripoli *see* Ţarābulus, *Lib.* **132** K3
Tripolitanian Valley, *Medit. Sea* **132** J4
Tristan Da Cunha Group, *U.K., S. Atl. Oc.* **107** N8
Tristan Da Cunha Island, *U.K., S. Atl. Oc.* **107** N8
Triton Island, *Xisha Qundao, China, S. China Sea* **180** E6
Trobriand Islands, *P.N.G., Solomon Sea* **164** E5
Tromelin, island, *Fr., Ind. Oc.* **186** G5
Truk Islands *see* Chuuk, *Caroline Is., F.S.M., N. Pac. Oc.* **164** C5
Truro Shoal, *S. China Sea* **180** E9
Tuamotu Archipelago, *Polynesia, Fr. Polynesia, Fr., S. Pac. Oc.* **165** F13
Tubarão, *Braz.* **107** L5
Ţubruq, *Lib.* **132** K8
Tubuai, island, *Austral Is., Fr. Polynesia, Fr., S. Pac. Oc.* **165** G13
Tubuai Islands *see* Austral Islands, *Polynesia, Fr. Polynesia, Fr., S. Pac. Oc.* **165** G12
Tufts Plain, *N. Pac. Oc.* **145** C10
Tunis, *Tun.* **132** G2
Tunis, Gulf of, *Tun., Medit. Sea* **132** G2
Tunisian Plateau, *Medit. Sea* **132** H3
Tureia, atoll, *Tuamotu Arch., Fr. Polynesia, Fr., S. Pac. Oc.* **165** G14
Turks Islands, *Turks & Caicos Is., U.K., N. Atl. Oc.* **141** D10
Turneffe Islands, *Belize, Caribbean Sea* **140** F2
Tuticorin, *India* **186** D8
Tutuila, island, *Amer. Samoa, U.S., S. Pac. Oc.* **165** F10
Tuvalu, islands, *Tuvalu, S. Pac. Oc.* **144** H7
Tyab, *Iran* **213** F14
Tyara, Cayo, *Nicar., Caribbean Sea* **140** H4
Tyrrhenian Basin, *Tyrrhenian Sea* **132** F4
Tyrrhenian Sea, *Medit. Sea* **132** F3

Ua Huka, island, *Marquesas Is., Fr. Polynesia, Fr., S. Pac. Oc.* **165** E14
Ua Pou, island, *Marquesas Is., Fr., S. Pac. Oc.* **147** H11
Ua Pu, island, *Marquesas Is., Fr. Polynesia, Fr., S. Pac. Oc.* **165** E14
'Udayd, Fasht al, *Persian G.* **212** K7
Udintsev Fracture Zone, *S. Pac. Oc.* **249** J11
Ujelang Atoll, *Ralik Chain, Marshall Is., N. Pac. Oc.* **164** C6
Ujungpandang (Makassar), *Indonesia* **181** P10
Ulithi Atoll, *Caroline Is., F.S.M., N. Pac. Oc.* **164** C3
Ulsan, *S. Korea* **146** D4
Umboi, island, *P.N.G., Bismarck Sea* **187** E16
Umm Al Anbar, Ruqq, *Persian G.* **212** K7
Umm al Fayyārīn, island, *Oman, Persian G.* **213** H13
Umm al Ghanam, island, *Oman, Persian G.* **213** G13
Umm al Marādim, island, *Kuwait, Persian G.* **212** D3
Umm al Qaywayn, *U.A.E.* **213** J12
Umm Ḩaşāh, Ra's, *Qatar, Persian G.* **212** H6
Umm Ḩish, Ra's, *Qatar, Persian G.* **212** H6
Umm Na'sān, island, *Bahrain, Persian G.* **212** H5
Umm Qaşr, *Iraq* **212** B2
Umm Sa'īd, *Qatar* **186** A5
Umm Urūmah, island, *Saudi Arabia, Red Sea* **210** D4
Umnak Island, *Aleutian Is., U.S., N. Pac. Oc.* **147** C9
Unalaska Island, *Aleutian Is., U.S., N. Pac. Oc.* **147** C9
Ungava Peninsula, **104** D2
Unimak Island, *Aleutian Is., U.S., N. Pac. Oc.* **147** B9
Union, island, *Windward Is., St. Vincent & the Grenadines, Caribbean Sea* **141** H14
Union Reefs, *S. China Sea* **180** H8
Upolu, island, *Samoa, S. Pac. Oc.* **165** F10
Uraba, Golfo de (Golfo de Darién), *Col., Caribbean Sea* **140** L7
Urup, island, *Kuril Is., Russ., N. Pac. Oc.* **146** C6
Ushakova Island, *Russ., Arctic Oc.* **219** C9
'Ushayriq, Ra's, *Qatar, Persian G.* **212** H6
'Ushsh, island, *U.A.E., Persian G.* **212** K8
Utila, Isla de, *Is. de la Bahia, Hond., Caribbean Sea* **140** F2
Utirik Atoll, *Ratak Chain, Marshall Is., N. Pac. Oc.* **164** B7
Utupua, island, *Sta. Cruz Is., Solomon Is., S. Pac. Oc.* **164** F7
Uvea, island, *Wallis Is., Fr., S. Pac. Oc.* **165** F9

Vache, Île à, *Haiti, Caribbean Sea* **141** E9
Vaitupu, atoll, *Tuvalu, S. Pac. Oc.* **164** E8
Valdez, *U.S.* **147** B10
Valdivia Fracture Zone, *S. Pac. Oc.* **145** K14
Valdivia Seamount, *S. Atl. Oc.* **107** M9
Valencia, *Sp.* **131** F5
Valencia, Golfo de, *Sp., Medit. Sea* **131** F6
Valencia Trough, *Balearic Sea* **131** F6
Valletta, *Malta* **132** H4
Valley Head, *Philippines* **180** D11
Valparaíso, *Chile* **147** K16
Vancouver, *Can.* **147** C12
Vancouver Island, *Can., N. Pac. Oc.* **147** C12
Van Diemen Gulf, *Austral., Arafura Sea* **187** F14
Vanguard Bank, *S. China Sea* **181** J6
Vanikolo Islands, *Sta. Cruz Is., Solomon Is., S. Pac. Oc.* **164** F7
Vanua Levu, island, *Fiji Is., S. Pac. Oc.* **164** F8
Vanuatu, islands, *Vanuatu, S. Pac. Oc.* **144** H7
Vao, Nosy, *Madagascar, Mozambique Ch.* **186** G4
Vaticano, Capo, *It.* **132** F4
Vatoa, island, *Lau Group, Fiji Is., S. Pac. Oc.* **165** G9
Vava'u Group, *Tonga, S. Pac. Oc.* **165** G9
Vavitu *see* Raivavae, island, *Austral Is., Fr. Polynesia, Fr., S. Pac. Oc.* **165** G13
Vaygach Island, *Russ., Arctic Oc.* **219** A11
Vélez de la Gomera, Peñón de, *Sp., Alboran Sea* **131** H4
Vema Fracture Zone, *Ind. Oc.* **184** F6
Vema Fracture Zone, *N. Atl. Oc.* **105** J4
Vema Seamount, *S. Atl. Oc.* **105** M9
Veneta, Laguna, *It., G. di Venezia* **132** B3
Venezia (Venice), *It.* **132** B3
Venezia, Golfo di, *It., Adriatic Sea* **132** B3
Venezuela, Golfo de, *Venez., Caribbean Sea* **141** J10
Venezuelan Basin, *Caribbean Sea* **141** G11
Venezuelan Plain, *Caribbean Sea* **141** H12
Venice *see* Venezia, *It.* **132** B3
Ventspils, *Latv.* **106** E10
Veracruz, *Mex.* **138** K3
Verde, Cape, **106** H7
Verde, Cay, *Bahamas, N. Atl. Oc.* **140** C8
Vereker Banks, *S. China Sea* **180** C8
Vermilion Bay, *U.S., G. of Mex.* **138** B6
Vernadskiy Fracture Zone, *N. Atl. Oc.* **105** J5
Vernon Basin, *G. of Mex.* **139** D11
Vesterålen, island, *Nor.* **106** C10
Vestfjorden, bay, *Nor.* **106** C10
Viareggio, *It.* **132** C2
Victoria Island, *Can., Arctic Oc.* **218** K7
Victoria Land, *Antarctica* **251** E10
Vidal Plain, *N. Atl. Oc.* **105** J4
Vieques, island, *P.R., U.S., Caribbean Sea* **141** E13
Vinh, *Vietnam* **180** D4
Viper Shoal, *S. China Sea* **181** J8
Virgin Gorda, island, *Virgin Is., U.K., Caribbean Sea* **141** E13
Virgin Islands, *U.S., U.K., Caribbean Sea* **141** E13
Vis, island, *Croatia, Adriatic Sea* **132** D5
Visayan Sea, *Philippines* **187** C13
Viscount Melville Sound, *Can.* **216** K7
Vishakhapatnam, *India* **186** B8
Vitória Seamount, *S. Atl. Oc.* **105** L6
Viti Levu, island, *Fiji Is., S. Pac. Oc.* **164** G8
Vityaz Trench, *S. Pac. Oc.* **144** H7
Vivorillo, Cayos, *Hond., Caribbean Sea* **140** G4
Vize Island, *Russ., Kara Sea* **219** C9
Volcano Islands (Kazan Rettō), *Japan, N. Pac. Oc.* **164** A4
Vólos (Iolkós), *Gr.* **132** F8
Vóries Sporádes, islands, *Gr., Aegean Sea* **132** F8
Voring Plateau, *Norwegian Sea* **217** E14
Voronin Trough, *Kara Sea* **217** C9
Vostok Island, *Line Is., Kiribati, S. Pac. Oc.* **165** E12

Wüst Seamount, *S. Atl. Oc.* **105** M8
Waar, island, *Indonesia, G. of Cenderawasih* **187** E14
Waccasassa Bay, *U.S., G. of Mex.* **139** B13
Wai, Koh, *Cambodia, G. of Thai.* **180** H3
Waigeo, island, *Indonesia, N. Pac. Oc.* **164** D2
Wake Island, *U.S., N. Pac. Oc.* **164** A7
Wales Island, *Can.* **106** C1
Walker Ridge, *G. of Mex.* **138** E7
Wallaby Plateau, *Ind. Oc.* **185** G11
Wallace Bank, *S. China Sea* **180** H5
Wallis Islands, *Fr., S. Pac. Oc.* **165** F9
Walters Shoal, *Ind. Oc.* **184** J4
Walton Bank, *Caribbean Sea* **140** F6
Walvis Ridge, *S. Atl. Oc.* **105** M9
Warbab, island, *Kuwait, Persian G.* **212** B2
Washington Island *see* Teraina, *Line Is., Kiribati, S. Pac. Oc.* **165** C11
Water Cay, *Bahamas, N. Atl. Oc.* **140** C8
Water Cays, *Bahamas, N. Atl. Oc.* **140** B7
Watling *see* San Salvador, island, *Bahamas, N. Atl. Oc.* **140** B8
Weber Basin, *S. Pac. Oc.* **144** G4
Weddell Plain, *S. Atl. Oc.* **248** F5
Weddell Sea, *S. Atl. Oc.* **248** G7
Weizhou Dao, *China, G. of Tonkin* **180** C5
Welker Seamount, *N. Pac. Oc.* **145** B11
Wellesley Islands, *Austral., G. of Carpentaria* **187** G15
Wellington, *N.Z.* **164** K8
Wessel Islands, *Austral.* **187** F15
West Antarctica, region, *Antarctica* **249** G9
West Bay, *U.S., G. of Mex.* **138** B4
West Breaker, island, *Caribbean Sea* **140** G6
West Caicos, island, *Caicos Is., Turks & Caicos Is., U.K., N. Atl. Oc.* **141** C9
West Caroline Basin, *N. Pac. Oc.* **144** G5
Western Reef, *S. China Sea* **180** H7
West European Basin, *N. Atl. Oc.* **104** F7
West Falkland, island, *Falkland Is., U.K., S. Atl. Oc.* **107** P4
West Flower Garden Bank, *G. of Mex.* **138** C5
Westman Islands, *Ice., N. Atl. Oc.* **106** D7
West Mariana Basin, *Philippine Sea* **144** F5
West Scotia Basin, *Scotia Sea* **105** Q4
West York Island, *Spratly Is., S. China Sea* **180** G8
Wetar, island, *Indonesia* **164** E2
Whale Cay, *Berry Is., Bahamas, N. Atl. Oc.* **140** A7
Wharton Basin, *Ind. Oc.* **185** G10
White Lake, *U.S.* **138** B6
White Sea, *Arctic Oc.* **219** B13
Whitewater Bay, *U.S., G. of Mex.* **139** E14
Wilhelmshaven, *Ger.* **106** E9
Wilkes Land, *Antarctica* **251** D9
Willemstad, *Curaçao, Neth.* **141** J11
Williams Island, *Bahamas, N. Atl. Oc.* **140** B6
Willis Islets, *Austral., Coral Sea* **164** F5
Wilsons Promontory, *Austral.* **164** K4
Windward Islands, *Lesser Antil., Caribbean Sea* **141** J15
Windward Passage, *N. Atl. Oc.* **141** D9
Witu Islands, *P.N.G., Bismarck Sea* **187** E16
Woleai Atoll, *Caroline Is., F.S.M., N. Pac. Oc.* **164** C4
Wolf Island, *Galápagos Is., Ecua., N. Pac. Oc.* **147** G14
Woodlark Islands, *P.N.G., Solomon Sea* **164** E5
Wotje Atoll, *Ratak Chain, Marshall Is., N. Pac. Oc.* **164** C7
Wounta, Laguna de, *Nicar., Caribbean Sea* **140** H4
Wowoni, island, *Indonesia, Banda Sea* **187** E13
Wrangel Island, *Russ., Arctic Oc.* **218** F4
Wrangel Plain, *Arctic Oc.* **216** E7
Wuvulu Island, *P.N.G., S. Pac. Oc.* **187** E15
Wyandot Seamount, *S. Atl. Oc.* **105** N9
Wyville Thomson Ridge, *N. Atl. Oc.* **104** D8

Xaafuun, Cape, *Somalia* **186** C5
Xauen Bank, *Alboran Sea* **131** H4
Xiamen (Amoy), *China* **180** A9
Xianggan *see* Hong Kong, *China* **180** B8
Xingang, *China* **146** D3
Xisha Qundao (Paracel Islands, Hoàng Sa), *China, S. China Sea* **180** E6

Yaghan Basin, *Scotia Sea* **105** Q3
Yaku, island, *Ryukyu Is., Japan, N. Pac. Oc.* **187** A14
Yaku Islands, *Japan, E. China Sea* **146** E4
Yalahán, Laguna de, *Mex., G. of Mex.* **139** H10
Yalkubul, Punta, *Mex.* **139** H9
Yamal Peninsula, *Russ.* **217** A10
Yamdena, island, *Indonesia* **187** F14
Yana, Gulf of, *Russ., Laptev Sea* **218** C5
Yanbu, *Saudi Arabia* **186** B3
Yanbu'al Baḩr, *Saudi Arabia* **210** E5
Yap Islands, *Caroline Is., F.S .M., N. Pac. Oc.* **164** C3
Yap Trench, *N. Pac. Oc.* **144** F5
Yapen, island, *Indonesia, Teluk Cenderawasih* **164** D3
Yasawa Group, *Fiji Is., S. Pac. Oc.* **164** F8
Yellow Sea, *N. Pac. Oc.* **146** D4
Yenisey Gulf, *Russ., Kara Sea* **219** A9
Yeosu, *S. Korea* **146** D4
Yermak Plateau, *Arctic Oc.* **217** F11
Yokohama, *Japan* **146** D5
York, Cape, *Austral.* **164** E4
Youth, Isle of *see* Juventud, Isla de la, *Cuba, Caribbean Sea* **140** D4
Yucatan Basin, *G. of Mex.* **104** H2
Yucatan Channel, *Cuba, Mex.* **140** C3
Yucatan Escarpment, *Caribbean Sea* **140** E2
Yucatán Peninsula, *Mex.* **139** J9
Yucatan Plain, *Caribbean Sea* **140** E2
Yuryaku Seamount, *N. Pac. Oc.* **146** D7
Yusuf Ridge, *Alboran Sea* **131** H5
Yuzhnyy, *Ukr.* **106** F11

Zabargad, Geziret, *Egypt, Red Sea* **210** E4
Zabīd, Ra's, *Yemen, Red Sea* **210** K7
Zadar (Zara), *Croatia* **132** C4
Zákinthos, island, *Ionian Is., Gr., Ionian Sea* **132** G7
Zakūm, Ruqq az, *Persian G.* **213** K9
Zanzibar, island, *Tanzania, Ind. Oc.* **186** E3
Zapiola Ridge, *S. Atl. Oc.* **105** P5
Zapotitlán, Punta, *Mex.* **138** L4
Zara *see* Zadar, *Croatia* **132** C4
Zawr, Ra's az, *Kuwait, Persian G.* **212** D3
Zeebrugge, *Belg.* **106** E9
Zenker Seamount, *S. Atl. Oc.* **107** N8
Zhanjiang, *China* **180** C6
Zhokhova, island, *New Siberian Is., Russ., Arctic Oc.* **218** D5
Zhoushan Qundao, *China, E. China Sea* **187** A13
Zirkūh, island, *U.A.E., Persian G.* **213** K9
Zirkūh Island, *U.A.E.* **186** B5
Zubayr, Jazā'ir az, *Yemen, Red Sea* **210** J6
Zubayr, Khawr az, *Persian G.* **212** B3
Ẕulūm, Dawḩat aẕ, *Persian G.* **212** H5
Zuqāq, island, *Saudi Arabia, Red Sea* **210** H6
Zwar, Ra's az, *Saudi Arabia, Persian G.* **212** F4

Authors and Acknowledgments

About the Authors

Called "Her Deepness" by the *New Yorker* and the *New York Times,* a "Living Legend" by the Library of Congress, and *Time* magazine's first "Hero for the Planet," **Sylvia Earle** has led more than 60 expeditions as an oceanographer and explorer, authored 170 publications, and lectured in 70 countries. She is an Explorer in Residence at the National Geographic Society, the leader of the Sustainable Seas Expeditions, the chairman of Deep Ocean Exploration and Research, the council chair for the Harte Research Institute, the president of Deep Search, and formerly the chief scientist of NOAA. She has founded three companies and serves on various corporate and nonprofit boards. A graduate of St. Petersburg College and Florida State University with an M.A. and Ph.D. from Duke University, Earle holds 17 honorary doctorates and many more accolades, including the Order of the Golden Ark by the Netherlands, the Department of Interior's Conservation Service Award, the National Women's Hall of Fame, the American Academy of Achievement, and medals from the Explorers Club, the Society of Women Geographers, National Wildlife Federation, the National Parks Conservation Association, the Lindbergh Foundation, Barnard College, the Philadelphia Academy of Sciences, and the New England Aquarium.

Linda K. Glover has been a leader in ocean science, policy, and public outreach for decades. Her research work includes shipboard science in the North Atlantic, Caribbean, and Indian Ocean, with reports supporting navy operations and publications presenting basic research in marine geology and ancient climates. Glover has served as an oceanographer for the U.S. Navy and as a senior ocean policy analyst for a presidential commission, Vice President Al Gore's Environmental Task Force, and the National Ocean Conference of 1998. As head of GloverWorks Consulting, she works across government, commercial, and nonprofit entities, and she serves on the board and executive committee for the Bermuda Institute of Ocean Sciences. She is widely known for translating complex scientific concepts and jargon into language accessible to the general public and has published books on ocean conservation and space science.

About the Foreword Writers

Eric Lindstrom is Physical Oceanography Program Scientist in the Earth Science Division at NASA Headquarters in Washington, D.C. He holds degrees in Earth and planetary sciences from Massachusetts Institute of Technology and in physical oceanography from the University of Washington. In 2001 Lindstrom was awarded NASA's Exceptional Service Medal for developing a unified oceanography program at NASA integrated with those of other agencies.

Dr. Richard W. Spinrad, the NOAA Assistant Administrator for Research, is a professional certified oceanographer with over thirty years' experience in public service, academic research, private industry, and nongovernmental organizations. He is an internationally sought speaker and subject matter expert on a range of critical oceanographic programs, issues, and interests.

Author Acknowledgments

A number of individuals not only made this ocean opus possible but also combined talent, dedication, scholarship, and good humor to make the many months of preparation pure pleasure.

First among those to be recognized is Garrett Brown, whose equanimity and personal commitment kept the project on an even keel throughout. Thanks, too, to Nina Hoffman, Barbara Brownell Grogan, and Kevin Mulroy, who consistently supported what proved to be an unexpectedly ambitious project; researcher and education specialist Andrea McCurdy; Carl Mehler and Tibor G. Tóth for their cartographic and artistic genius in connection with the volume's exceptional maps and charts; Cinda Rose, Cliff Owen, Kevin Eans, and Gary Hincks for their fine sense of artistry and style; Eric Lindstrom and Richard Spinrad for their opening essays and steady endorsement and for the support of their agencies, NASA and NOAA, especially for help in developing a significant collateral education program. We are grateful to Dan Laffoley, Josh Willis, and Daniel Fornari for reviewing sections of this book, to Tim Keeney for his consistent support, and to the distinguished scientific experts who enhanced this volume by sharing essays on topics of special interest.

Personal thanks are due from Sylvia Earle to colleagues, friends, and family for their unwavering cheer throughout. From Linda Glover, thanks are enthusiastically offered to Sylvia Earle for this wonderful learning and relearning experience; to Peter Furze, Jenifer Clark, William Ruddiman, and Ellen Prager for particular information supporting the fact boxes in the margins of this book; and personal thanks to Jeni, Rod and Teri, Muv, and especially to Randolph, for their interest, patience, and support over the past year.

Publisher Acknowledgments

The National Geographic Book Division staff would like to thank the passionate and talented individuals who helped shape the contents of this book: Edward Vanden Berghe, Institute of Marine and Coastal Sciences, Rutgers University; Ben Best, Duke University; Norma Brinkley, University of Maryland; Darlene Trew Crist, Census of Marine Life; Jeanne Fink, National Geographic Society; Patrick Halpin, Duke University; Sara Hickox, Census of Marine Life; Kristen Hickman, National Geographic Society; Melissa R. Jordan, National Geographic Society; Larry Mayer, Center for Coastal and Ocean Mapping / Joint Hydrographic Center, University of New Hampshire; Jean Moyer, National Geographic Society; Sandra Squires, Ocean Futures Society; Dirk Steinke, Biodiversity Institute of Ontario, University of Guelph; Ariel Thigpen, enterACKed, LLC; Boris Worm, Dalhousie University; and Dirk Zeller, Sea Around Us Project (www.seaaroundus.org), Fisheries Centre, University of British Columbia.

The NGS staff also acknowledge the many people at NASA and NOAA who contributed many of this book's fine maps, satellite imagery, and data: Nicolo E. DiGirolamo, NASA Goddard Space Flight Center; Chelle Gentemann, Remote Sensing Systems; Gustavo Jorge Goni, USDC/NOAA/AOML/PHOD; Norman Kuring, NASA Goddard Space Flight Center; David Long, BYU Center for Remote Sensing; Ricardo Matano, COAS Oregon State University; Susan Merle, NOAA Vents Program; Claire Parkinson, NASA Goddard Space Flight Center; Beth Russell, NOAA's Science on a Sphere; Dan Metzger, NOAA's National Geophysical Data Center; Dudley Shelton, COAS Oregon State University; and Michael Watkins and Josh Willis, NASA Jet Propulsion Laboratory.

The editor would personally like to thank his father, Ronald W. Brown, for inspiring in him a love and respect for what the Psalmist describes as "the sea, great and wide, which teems with things innumerable, living things both small and great."

Illustration Credits

Artwork by Gary Hincks pages 28-29, 35, 37 (UP RT), 38 (ALL), 41 (UP), 46, 56 (BOTH), 63 (UP), 66, 68-69 (LO), 90, 91 (ALL), 115, 155, 156 (INSET), 158 (CT), 160, 231, 244, 266, 311.

INTRODUCTION 2-3, Fred Bavendam/Minden Pictures; 4-5, Ron & Valerie Taylor/ARDEA; 6, Georgette Douwma/npl/Minden Pictures; 8, David Doubilet; 12-13, Chris Newbert/Minden Pictures; 14-15, Hiroya Minakuchi/Minden Pictures.

OCEAN BASICS 16-17, NASA Goddard Space Flight Center Image by Reto Stöckli (land surface, shallow water, clouds). Enhancements by Robert Simmon (ocean color, compositing, 3D globes, animation). Data and technical support: MODIS Land Group; MODIS Science Data Support Team; MODIS Atmosphere Group; MODIS Ocean Group Additional data: USGS EROS Data Center (topography); USGS Terrestrial Remote Sensing Flagstaff Field Center (Antarctica); Defense Meteorological Satellite Program (city lights); 24-25, Bob Barbour/Minden Pictures; 27, Paul Sutherland/NationalGeographicStock.com; 30 (ALL), Michael Watkins, NASA GRACE Satellite Mission and the University of Texas; 31, Reinhard Dirscherl/Visuals Unlimited; 32-33, World Ocean Floor Panorama, Bruce C. Heezen and Marie Tharp, 1977, Copyright by Marie Tharp 1977/2003. Reproduced by permission of Marie Tharp Maps, LLC, 8 Edward Street, Sparkill, New York 10976; 34, Photo mosaic compiled by M. Elend in collaboration with D.S. Kelley and J.R. Delaney of the University of Washington and D.R. Yoerger, Woods Hole Oceanographic Institution. Reprinted with permission from SCIENCE, Vol. 281, July 10, 1998. Copyright 1998 American Association for the Advancement of Science; 36, Tim Laman; 39, Ira Block/NationalGeographicStock.com; 42 (BOTH), Josh Willis, NASA Jet Propulsion Laboratory; 43 (UP), Josh Willis, NASA Jet Propulsion Laboratory; 43 (LO), Dudley Chelton, The College of Oceanic and Atmospheric Sciences at Oregon State University and NASA; 45, NASA and CNES TOPEX/POSEIDON satellite mission; 47, Fred Bavendam/Minden Pictures.

OCEAN LIFE 48-49, David Doubilet; 52-53, Bill Curtsinger; 55, David Doubilet; 57, David Doubilet; 58, Caroline Trewhitt; 59, Norbert Wu/Minden Pictures; 60, Fred Bavendam/Minden Pictures; 61 (UP), Wolcott Henry; 61 (LO), Chris Newbert/Minden Pictures; 64, Wolcott Henry; 65 (UP LE), Kevin Raskoff/MBARI; 65 (UP RT), Steven Haddock/MBARI; 65 (LO), Bruce Robison/MBARI; 67, Flip Nicklin/Minden Pictures; 69, David Doubilet; 70, David Doubilet; 73 (UP LE), Peter Parks/iq-3d/SeaPics.com; 73 (UP RT), Diego Barucco/Dreamstime.com; 73 (UP CT LE), Eric V. Grave/Photo Researchers, Inc.; 73 (UP CT RT), Steve Gschmeissner/Photo Researchers, Inc.; 73 (LO CT LE), Sylvia Earle; 73 (LO CT RT), Sylvia Earle; 73 (LO LE), Sylvia Earle; 73 (LO RT), Sylvia Earle; 74 (UP LE), Marc Chamberlain/SeaPics.com; 74 (UP RT), Sylvia Earle; 74 (UP CT LE), Sylvia Earle; 74 (UP CT RT), Sylvia Earle; 74 (LO CT LE), Sylvia Earle; 74 (LO CT RT), Sylvia Earle; 74 (LE LE), Sylvia Earle; 74 (LO RT), Paul Nicklen/NationalGeographicStock.com; 77 (UP LE), George Grall; 77 (UP RT), Wolcott Henry; 77 (UP CT LE), Sinclair Stammers/Photo Researchers, Inc.; 77 (UP CT RT), Darlyne A. Murawski; 77 (LE CT LE), L. Newman & A. Flowers/Photo Researchers, Inc.; 77 (LO CT RT), Darlyne A. Murawski; 77 (LO LE), Sylvia Earle; 77 (LO RT), Jonathan Blair; 78 (UP LE), Andrew J. Martinez/Photo Researchers, Inc.; 78 (UP RT), Sylvia Earle; 78 (UP CT LE), Sylvia Earle; 78 (UP CT RT), Paul Nicklen; 78 (LO CT LE), Andrew Syred/Photo Researchers, Inc.; 78 (LO CT RT), Bill Curtsinger; 78 (LO LE), Peter Parks/iq-3d/SeaPics.com; 78 (LO RT), Sylvia Earle; 81 (UP LE), Sylvia Earle; 81 (UP RT), Doug Perrine/SeaPics.com; 81 (UP CT LE), Sylvia Earle; 81 (UP CT RT), Marc Chamberlain/SeaPics.com; 81 (LO CT LE), Darlyne A. Murawski; 81 (LO CT RT), Sylvia Earle; 81 (LO LE), Bates Littlehales; 81 (LO RT), Sylvia Earle.

OCEAN PAST 86-87, Albert J. Copley/Visuals Unlimited; 89, Pandromeda/DAMN FX; 91, NASA-GSFC SVS; 94 (UP), Townsend P. Dickinson; 94 (LO), Jurgen Freund/npl/Minden Pictures; 95 (UP), Wayne Lynch; 95 (LO), Kam Mak; 96, Gary Staab/Lair Group Inc./NGM Art/DAMN FX; 98, Image created at Columbia University using the Marine Geoscience Data System's GeoMapAppVG application; 99, Carsten Peter; 100, Darlyne A. Murawski/NationalGeographicStock.com; 101, Dr. Carl N. Shuster.

ATLANTIC OCEAN 102-103, Image created using NASA Aqua satellite mission, MODIS Sensor data, provided by NASA Goddard Space Flight Center, NASA Ocean Biology Processing Group; 108-109, Image created using Sea Surface Temperature data provided by Remote Sensing Systems; 110-111, Frans Lanting; 113, Brian Skerry; 114, Emma Hickerson/NOAA; 116, Sólarfilma; 117, Emory Kristof/NationalGeographicStock.com; 118, Deborah S. Kelley, School of Oceanography, University of Washington; 119 (UP), Emory Kristof/NationalGeographicStock.com; 119 (LO), David Shale/npl/Minden Pictures; 120 (UP), Raul Touzon/NationalGeographicStock.com; 120 (LO), Flip Nicklin/Minden Pictures; 121, NASA; 122, AQUA satellite mission MODIS sensor data provided by NASA's Ocean Biology Production Group, images provided by Ricardo Matano, COAS, Oregon State University; 123 (UP), Heidi M. Cullen, Lamont-Doherty Earth Observatory; 123 (LO), James P. Blair; 124, Provided by the University of Miami/Rosenstiel School of Marine and Atmospheric Science; 125, Courtesy BIOS; 127 (UP), NASA Goddard Space Flight Center Image generated by Hal Pierce, Earth Sciences Division Laboratory for Atmospheres in the Mesoscale Atmospheric Processes Branch; 127 (LO LE), Image provided by Gustavo Goni (NOAA), Pedro DiNezio (University of Miami) and Joaquin Trinanes (University of Santiago, Spain); 127 (LO CTR), NASA TRMM satellite; 127 (LO RT), NASA GOES-12 satellite; 128 (UP), Doug Allan/npl/Minden Pictures; 128 (LO), Tim Watts; 129, Jonathan Blair; 130, Jonathan Blair; 135, Bill Curtsinger/NationalGeographicStock.com; 136, National Geographic Photographer William Albert Allard; 137, David Doubilet.

PACIFIC OCEAN 142-143, Image created using NASA Aqua satellite mission, MODIS Sensor data, provided by NASA Goddard Space Flight Center, NASA Ocean Biology Processing Group; 148-149, Image created using Sea Surface Temperature data provided by Remote Sensing Systems; 150-151, Norbert Wu/Minden Pictures; 153, Doug Perrine/SeaPics.com; 157 (LE), John B. Corliss; 157 (RT), Susan Merle, NOAA's Vents Program, Oregon State University; 158, NOAA; 159 (ALL), Woods Hole Oceanographic Institution; 161, Woods Hole Oceanographic Institution; 162, Susan Merle, NOAA's Vents Program, Oregon State University; 163, Norbert Wu/Minden

Pictures; 168, Wolcott Henry/NationalGeographicStock.com; 169, National Geographic Maps/Bathymetry data by Monterey Bay Aquarium Research Institute, Land topographic data by USGS, Satellite image by Space Imaging; 170, Tim Laman/NationalGeographicStock.com; 172-173 (ALL), Globe imagery created from NASA and CNES TOPEX/Poseidon satellite data. Cutaway images created from NOAA moored ocean buoys; 175 (UP), Norbert Wu/Minden Pictures; 175 (LO), Steven Haddock/MBARI; 176, D. Parer and E. Parer-Cook/npl/Minden Pictures; 177, David Doubilet; 178, Norman Kuring, NASA, Goddard Space Flight Center, using AQUA satellite mission MODIS sensor data provided by NASA's Ocean Biology Production Group; 179 (UP), Tui De Roy/Minden Pictures; 179 (LO), Sylvia Earle.

INDIAN OCEAN 182-183, Image created using NASA Aqua satellite mission, MODIS Sensor data, provided by NASA Goddard Space Flight Center, NASA Ocean Biology Processing Group; 188-189, Image created using Sea Surface Temperature data provided by Remote Sensing Systems; 190-191, Ralph Lee Hopkins/NationalGeographicStock.com; 193, Chris Newbert/Minden Pictures; 194-195, Cousteau Society/Getty Images; 196, Norbert Wu/Minden Pictures; 197, NASA ASTER image from Terra satellite; 198, Solvin Zankl/npl/Minden Pictures; 199, David Doubilet; 200, Dudley Chelton, COAS, Oregon State University, NOAA National Environmental Satellite, Data and Information Service blending microwave measurements from AMSR and infrared measurements from the AVHRR; 202 (BOTH), DigitalGlobe via Getty Images; 202-203, National Geographic Maps/Source-Vasily V. Titov, Tsunami Research Program, NOAA. Tsunami simulation by Eric L. Geist, USGS; 204 (UP), Flip Nicklin; 204 (LO), Mike Parry/Minden Pictures; 205, Reinhard Dirscherl/Visuals Unlimited; 206 (BOTH), Dr. Hans W. Fricke; 207, Georgette Douwma/npl/Minden Pictures; 208-209, Christoph Hormann; 211, Norman Kuring, NASA, Goddard Space Flight Center, using AQUA satellite mission MODIS sensor data provided by NASA's Ocean Biology Production Group.

ARCTIC OCEAN 214-215, Image created using NASA Aqua satellite mission, MODIS Sensor data, provided by NASA Goddard Space Flight Center, NASA Ocean Biology Processing Group; 220-221, Image created using Sea Surface Temperature data provided by Remote Sensing Systems; 222-223, Norbert Rosing/NationalGeographicStock.com; 225, Paul Nicklen; 227, Flip Nicklin/Minden Pictures; 228, IBCAO data compilation, Jakobsson, M., Macnab, R., Mayer, M., Anderson, R., Edwards, M., Hatzky, J., Schenke, H-W., and Johnson, P., 2008, An improved bathymetric portrayal of the Arctic Ocean: Implications for ocean modeling and geological, geophysical and oceanographic analyses, v. 35, L07602, Geophysical Research Letters, doi:10.1029/2008GL033520. Courtesy Larry Mayer, Center for Coastal and Ocean Mapping, University of New Hampshire; 229, Gale Mead; 230, Paul Nicklen/NationalGeographicStock.com; 232-233 (ALL), Images courtesy of Claire Parkinson and Nick DiGirolamo, NASA Goddard Space Flight Center; 234, David Long, BYU Center for Remote Sensing, Image created from NASA's SeaWinds scatterometer data; 235, Jim Brandenburg/Minden Pictures; 236, Flip Nicklin/Minden Pictures; 237, Flip Nicklin/Minden Pictures; 238, Norman Kuring, NASA, Goddard Space Flight Center, using AQUA satellite mission MODIS sensor data provided by NASA's Ocean Biology Production Group; 239, Jeff Schmaltz/NASA MODIS satellite; 240 (UP), Paul Nicklen/NationalGeographic Stock.com; 240 (LO), Martha Holmes/npl/Minden Pictures; 241, Paul Nicken/NationalGeo graphicStock.com; 242, Mark Peterson/CORBIS; 244, Data courtesy of Claire Parkinson and Nick DiGirolamo, NASA Goddard Space Flight Center.

SOUTHERN OCEAN 246-247, Image created using NASA Aqua satellite mission, MODIS Sensor data, provided by NASA Goddard Space Flight Center, NASA Ocean Biology Processing Group; 252-253, Image created using Sea Surface Temperature data provided by Remote Sensing Systems; 254-255, Maria Stenzel; 257, Norbert Wu/Minden Pictures; 259, Robert A. Rohde; 261, Norbert Wu/Minden Pictures; 262, Maria Stenzel; 263, Norman Kuring, NASA, Goddard Space Flight Center, using AQUA satellite mission MODIS sensor data provided by NASA's Ocean Biology Production Group; 264-265 (ALL), Images courtesy of Claire Parkinson and Nick DiGirolamo, NASA Goddard Space Flight Center; 268, NASA/JPL/University of Arizona; 269 (UP LE), NASA, J. Bell (Cornell U.) and M. Wolff (SSI); 269 (UP RT), NASA/JPL/Space Science Institute; 269 (LO LE), Maria Stenzel; 269 (LO RT), NASA; 270 (ALL), NASA; 271, David Long, BYU Center for Remote Sensing, Image created from NASA's SeaWinds scatterometer data; 272-273, Norbert Wu/Minden Pictures; 273, Norbert Wu/Minden Pictures; 274, Flip Nicklin/Minden Pictures; 275, Norbert Wu/Minden Pictures.

OCEAN EXPLORATION 276-277, Emory Kristof; 280-281, David Doubilet; 283, Cary Wolinsky; 285 (UP), Geoff Dann/Dorling Kindersley © The Wallace Collection, London; 285 (LO), National Maritime Museum, Greenwich, London, MoD Art Collection; 286, Al Giddings; 287, Emory Kristof; 288, Brian Skerry; 289, Courtesy Webb Research Corporation; 290 (UP), Chief Photographer's Mate Charles Lee Wright, Sr., USN, Courtesy Alfred S. McLaren Captain, USN (Ret.); 290 (LO), Randy Olson; 291, NASA, STS-77 shuttle mission; 292-293, Courtesy NOS/NOAA; 294, Courtesy NOAA National Data Buoy Center; 295, Kip Evans.

OCEAN FUTURE 296-297, Created by NOAA's Science on a Sphere® Project with data provided by John C. Kostelnick at the College of Mathematics and Natural Sciences, Haskell Indian Nations University; 298-299, B. Halpern, K. Selkoe, C. Kappel, and F. Micheli, National Center for Ecological Analysis and Synthesis, University of California, Santa Barbara; 300-301, Richard Herrmann/SeaPics.com; 303, Steve McCurry; 307, Gary Gaugler/Visuals Unlimited; 308, Norbert Wu/Minden Pictures; 309 (BOTH), Greenpeace/Alex Hofford; 310 (BOTH), Susan Middleton; 312, Kim Westerskov/DeepSeaPhotography.com; 314, Sylvia Earle; 316, Gale Mead; 318, R. Steven Nerem, Colorado Center for Astrodynamics Research, University of Colorado, Boulder, Colorado; 319, Sylvia Earle; 320, Wood, L. J. (2008). MPA Global: A database of the world's marine protected areas. Sea Around Us Project, UNEP-WCMC, WWF, and IUCN-WCPA. www.mpaglobal.org; 322, Brian Skerry; 323, Amos Nachoum/SeaPics.com.

THE LAST WORD 325, Brian Skerry.

OCEAN
An Illustrated Atlas
SYLVIA A. EARLE AND LINDA K. GLOVER

Published by the National Geographic Society

John M. Fahey, Jr., *President and Chief Executive Officer*

Gilbert M. Grosvenor, *Chairman of the Board*

Tim T. Kelly, *President, Global Media Group*

John Q. Griffin, *President, Publishing*

Nina D. Hoffman, *Executive Vice President;
    President, Book Publishing Group*

Prepared by the Book Division

Kevin Mulroy, *Senior Vice President and Publisher*

Leah Bendavid-Val, *Director of Photography Publishing
    and Illustrations*

Marianne R. Koszorus, *Director of Design*

Barbara Brownell Grogan, *Executive Editor*

Elizabeth Newhouse, *Director of Travel Publishing*

Carl Mehler, *Director of Maps*

Staff for This Book

Garrett Brown, *Editor*

Cinda Rose, *Art Director*

Al Morrow, *Design Assistant*

Cliff Owen, *Lead Illustrations Editor*

Andrea McCurdy, *Project Coordinator*

Judith Klein, *Text Editor*

Sven M. Dolling, Steven D. Gardner, Thomas L. Gray, Lee McAuliffe,
    Michael McNey, Nicholas P. Rosenbach, Gregory Ugiansky,
    and XNR Productions, *Map Editing, Research, and Production*

Meredith Wilcox, *Illustrations Specialist*

Kevin Eans, *Illustrations Editor*

Christine Tanigawa, *Proofreader*

Christina Solazzo, *Editorial Assistant*

William Christmas and Amber Laughlin, *Geography Interns*

Jennifer A. Thornton, *Managing Editor*

Rick Wain, *Production Manager*

R. Gary Colbert, *Production Director*

Manufacturing and Quality Management

Christopher A. Liedel, *Chief Financial Officer*

Phillip L. Schlosser, *Vice President*

Chris Brown, *Technical Director*

Nicole Elliott, *Manager*

Monika D. Lynde, *Manager*

Rachel Faulise, *Manager*

Founded in 1888, the National Geographic Society is one of the largest nonprofit scientific and educational organizations in the world. It reaches more than 285 million people worldwide each month through its official journal, NATIONAL GEOGRAPHIC, and its four other magazines; the National Geographic Channel; television documentaries; radio programs; films; books; videos and DVDs; maps; and interactive media. National Geographic has funded more than 8,000 scientific research projects and supports an education program combating geographic illiteracy.

For more information, please call
1-800-NGS LINE (647-5463)
or write to the following address:
National Geographic Society
1145 17th Street N.W.
Washington, D.C. 20036-4688 U.S.A.

Visit us online at www.nationalgeographic.com/books

For information about special discounts for bulk purchases, please contact National Geographic Books Special Sales: ngspecsales@ngs.org

For rights or permissions inquiries, please contact National Geographic Books Subsidiary Rights: ngbookrights@ngs.org

ISBN 978-1-4262-0319-0

Library of Congress Cataloging-in-Publication Data

Earle, Sylvia A., 1935
    Ocean: an illustrated atlas / by Sylvia A. Earle and Linda K. Glover.
        p. cm.
    Includes index.
    ISBN 978-1-4262-0319-0 (hardcover : alk. paper)
    1. Ocean--Maps. 2. Oceanography--Charts, diagrams, etc. 3. Submarine geology--Maps. 4. Marine biology--Maps. 5. Marine resources--Maps. 6. Marine resources conservation--Maps. I. Glover, Linda K. II. National Geographic Society (U.S.) III. Title.
    G2800.E24 2008
    912'.1962--dc22

                                2008020861

Printed in Italy

This book was published by the National Geographic Society with support from the National Aeronautics and Space Administration Grant No. NNX07AM33G and from the National Oceanographic and Atmospheric Administration, U.S. Department of Commerce Grant No. NA08OAR4600741.

Any opinions, findings, and conclusions or recommendations expressed in this material are those of the authors and do not necessarily reflect the views of the National Aeronautics and Space Administration, the National Oceanographic and Atmospheric Administration or the U.S. Department of Commerce.

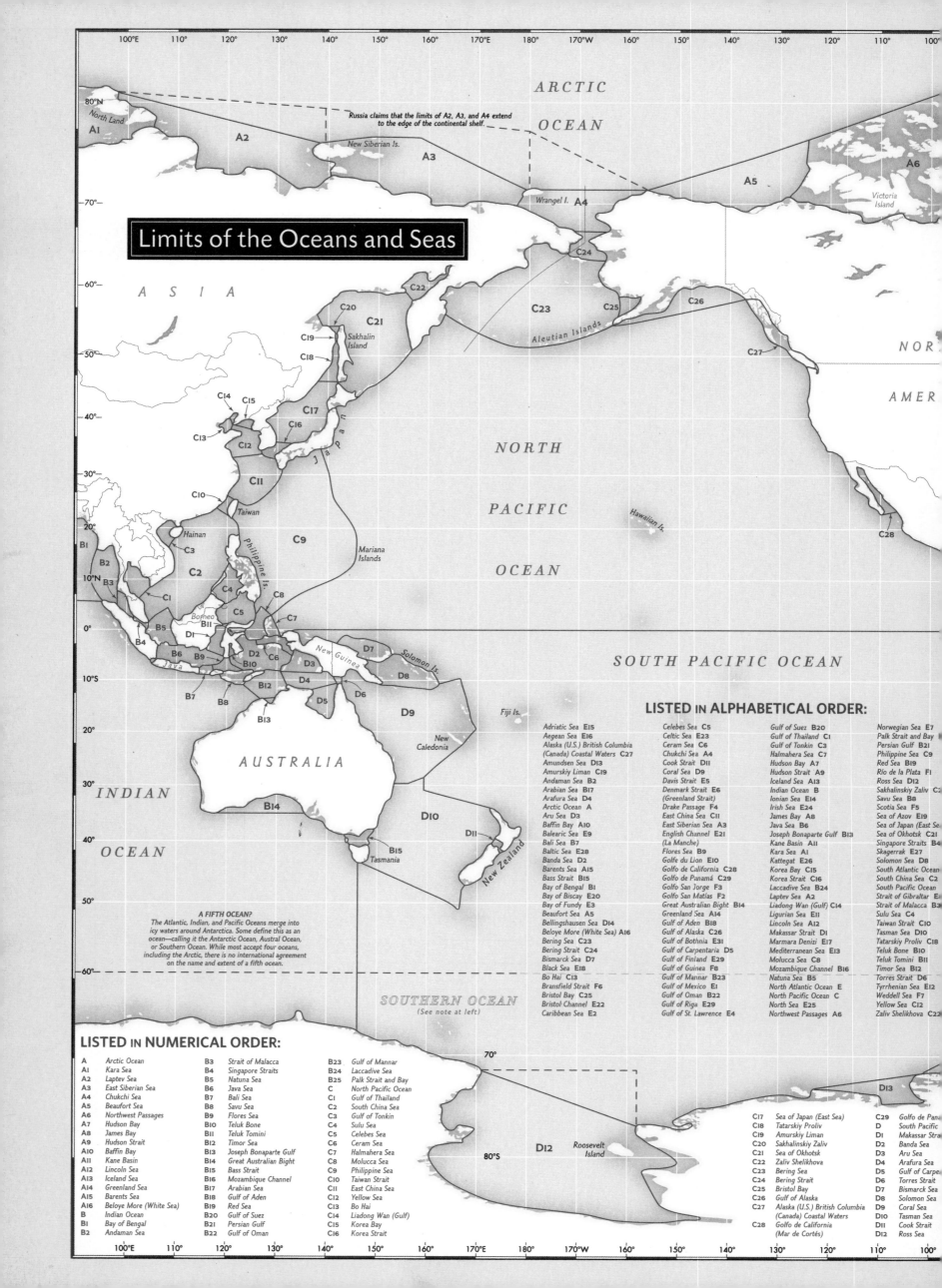

Limits of the Oceans and Seas

ARCTIC OCEAN

Russia claims that the limits of A2, A3, and A4 extend to the edge of the continental shelf.

ASIA

NORTH PACIFIC OCEAN

SOUTH PACIFIC OCEAN

INDIAN OCEAN

AUSTRALIA

SOUTHERN OCEAN
(See note at left)

AMER

NOR

A FIFTH OCEAN?
The Atlantic, Indian, and Pacific Oceans merge into icy waters around Antarctica. Some define this as an ocean—calling it the Antarctic Ocean, Austral Ocean, or Southern Ocean. While most accept four oceans, including the Arctic, there is no international agreement on the name and extent of a fifth ocean.

LISTED IN ALPHABETICAL ORDER:

Adriatic Sea E15	Celebes Sea C5	Gulf of Suez B20	Norwegian Sea E7
Aegean Sea E16	Celtic Sea E23	Gulf of Thailand C1	Palk Strait and Bay
Alaska (U.S.) British Columbia	Ceram Sea C6	Gulf of Tonkin C3	Persian Gulf B21
(Canada) Coastal Waters C27	Chukchi Sea A4	Halmahera Sea C7	Philippine Sea C9
Amundsen Sea D13	Cook Strait D11	Hudson Bay A7	Red Sea B19
Amurskiy Liman C19	Coral Sea D9	Hudson Strait A9	Río de la Plata F1
Andaman Sea B2	Davis Strait E5	Iceland Sea A13	Ross Sea D12
Arabian Sea B17	Denmark Strait E6	Indian Ocean B	Sakhalinskiy Zaliv C2
Arafura Sea D4	(Greenland Strait)	Ionian Sea E14	Savu Sea B8
Arctic Ocean A	Drake Passage F4	Irish Sea E24	Scotia Sea F5
Aru Sea D3	East China Sea C11	James Bay A8	Sea of Azov E19
Baffin Bay A10	East Siberian Sea A3	Java Sea B6	Sea of Japan (East Sea)
Balearic Sea E9	English Channel E21	Joseph Bonaparte Gulf B13	Sea of Okhotsk C21
Bali Sea B7	(La Manche)	Kane Basin A11	Singapore Straits B4
Baltic Sea E28	Flores Sea B9	Kara Sea A1	Skagerrak E27
Banda Sea D2	Golfe du Lion E10	Kattegat E26	Solomon Sea D8
Barents Sea A15	Golfo de California C28	Korea Bay C15	South Atlantic Ocean
Bass Strait B15	Golfo de Panamá C29	Korea Strait C16	South China Sea C2
Bay of Bengal B1	Golfo San Jorge F3	Laccadive Sea B24	South Pacific Ocean
Bay of Biscay E20	Golfo San Matías F2	Laptev Sea A2	Strait of Gibraltar E
Bay of Fundy E3	Great Australian Bight B14	Liadong Wan (Gulf) C14	Strait of Malacca B3
Beaufort Sea A5	Greenland Sea A14	Ligurian Sea E11	Sulu Sea C4
Bellingshausen Sea D14	Gulf of Aden B18	Lincoln Sea A12	Taiwan Strait C10
Beloye More (White Sea) A16	Gulf of Alaska C26	Makassar Strait D1	Tasman Sea D10
Bering Sea C23	Gulf of Bothnia E31	Marmara Denizi E17	Tatarskiy Proliv C18
Bering Strait C24	Gulf of Carpentaria D5	Mediterranean Sea E13	Teluk Bone B10
Bismarck Sea D7	Gulf of Finland E29	Molucca Sea C8	Teluk Tomini B11
Black Sea E18	Gulf of Guinea F8	Mozambique Channel B16	Timor Sea B12
Bo Hai C13	Gulf of Mannar B23	Natuna Sea B5	Torres Strait D6
Bransfield Strait F6	Gulf of Mexico E1	North Atlantic Ocean E	Tyrrhenian Sea E12
Bristol Bay C25	Gulf of Oman B22	North Pacific Ocean C	Weddell Sea F7
Bristol Channel E22	Gulf of Riga E29	North Sea E25	Yellow Sea C12
Caribbean Sea E2	Gulf of St. Lawrence E4	Northwest Passages A6	Zaliv Shelikhova C22

LISTED IN NUMERICAL ORDER:

A	Arctic Ocean	B3	Strait of Malacca	B23	Gulf of Mannar		
A1	Kara Sea	B4	Singapore Straits	B24	Laccadive Sea		
A2	Laptev Sea	B5	Natuna Sea	B25	Palk Strait and Bay		
A3	East Siberian Sea	B6	Java Sea	C	North Pacific Ocean		
A4	Chukchi Sea	B7	Bali Sea	C1	Gulf of Thailand	C17	Sea of Japan (East Sea)
A5	Beaufort Sea	B8	Savu Sea	C2	South China Sea	C18	Tatarskiy Proliv
A6	Northwest Passages	B9	Flores Sea	C3	Gulf of Tonkin	C19	Amurskiy Liman
A7	Hudson Bay	B10	Teluk Bone	C4	Sulu Sea	C20	Sakhalinskiy Zaliv
A8	James Bay	B11	Teluk Tomini	C5	Celebes Sea	C21	Sea of Okhotsk
A9	Hudson Strait	B12	Timor Sea	C6	Ceram Sea	C22	Zaliv Shelikhova
A10	Baffin Bay	B13	Joseph Bonaparte Gulf	C7	Halmahera Sea	C23	Bering Sea
A11	Kane Basin	B14	Great Australian Bight	C8	Molucca Sea	C24	Bering Strait
A12	Lincoln Sea	B15	Bass Strait	C9	Philippine Sea	C25	Bristol Bay
A13	Iceland Sea	B16	Mozambique Channel	C10	Taiwan Strait	C26	Gulf of Alaska
A14	Greenland Sea	B17	Arabian Sea	C11	East China Sea	C27	Alaska (U.S.) British Columbia
A15	Barents Sea	B18	Gulf of Aden	C12	Yellow Sea		(Canada) Coastal Waters
A16	Beloye More (White Sea)	B19	Red Sea	C13	Bo Hai	C28	Golfo de California
B	Indian Ocean	B20	Gulf of Suez	C14	Liadong Wan (Gulf)		(Mar de Cortés)
B1	Bay of Bengal	B21	Persian Gulf	C15	Korea Bay	C29	Golfo de Pana
B2	Andaman Sea	B22	Gulf of Oman	C16	Korea Strait	D	South Pacific
						D1	Makassar Stra
						D2	Banda Sea
						D3	Aru Sea
						D4	Arafura Sea
						D5	Gulf of Carpe
						D6	Torres Strait
						D7	Bismarck Sea
						D8	Solomon Sea
						D9	Coral Sea
						D10	Tasman Sea
						D11	Cook Strait
						D12	Ross Sea